RMS MAURETANIA (1907)

RMS MAURETANIA (1907)
QUEEN OF THE OCEAN

DAVID F. HUTCHINGS

The History Press

Dedicated to Katherine and Elizabeth Pritchard
(Kitty and Betty of Southsea, Hampshire), the
late daughters of the first captain of the first
Mauretania

…and not forgetting Lilia, Ruby and Jude

Illustration Credits
Front Cover: C.E. Turner's truly evocative portrait of the *Mauretania* at
speed. This image was used widely for advertising. (Author's collection)
Back Cover: A pristinely painted *Mauretania* sits serenely on a sparkling sea
during one of her Caribbean cruises (Author's collection)
Page 4: The ship's plans, taken from a contemporary issue of *Engineering*,
8 November 1907.
Page 6: Workmen paint the ship's hull, taken on a No. 2 Brownie by
E.E. Cox

First published 2019

The History Press
The Mill, Brimscombe Port
Stroud, Gloucestershire, GL5 2QG
www.thehistorypress.co.uk

British Library Cataloguing in Publication Data.
A catalogue record for this book is available from the British Library.

ISBN 978 0 7509 8584 0

Typesetting and origination by The History Press
Printed in Turkey by Imak

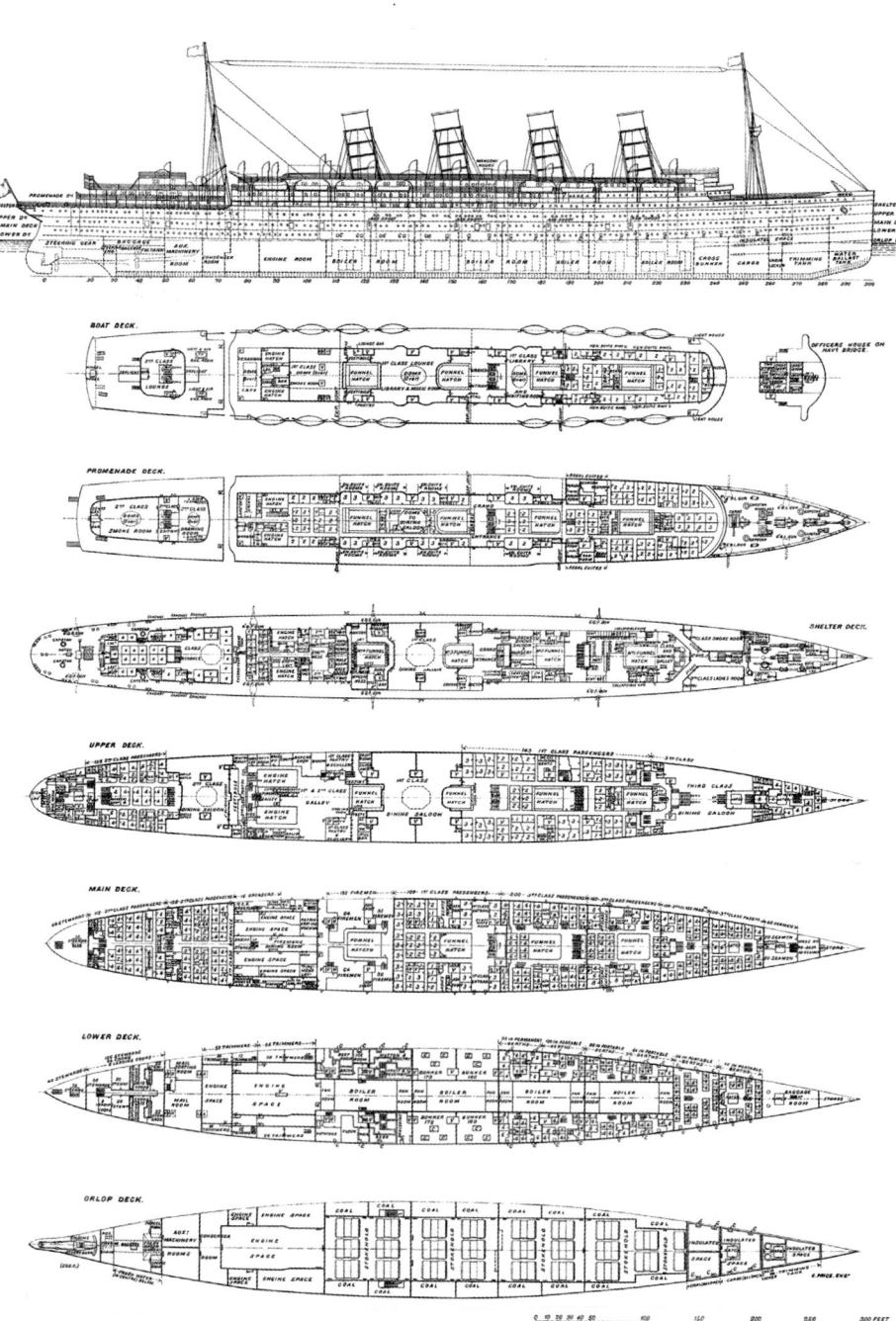

CONTENTS

INTRODUCTION

During the course of my lifelong love of ocean liners, one ship always stood at the vanguard in the histories that I read, setting the gold standard for the others. This one ship was the Cunard liner *Mauretania*, undoubtedly in many minds – even in spite of the reputation of the beloved *QE2* – the most famous (rather than infamous) ship in the world.

Dwarfed as she would have been by today's cruising and ocean-going behemoths, the *Mauretania* – latterly given the epithet of 'The Grand Old Lady of the Atlantic' – was nevertheless impressive. With her four huge funnels, she and her sister, the ill-fated *Lusitania*, were the first ships to sport four propellers, were the first major liners to be driven by the then recently introduced and innovative Parsons turbines, were the fastest ships in the world (the *Mauretania* held the fabled Blue Ribband for an incredible undefeated twenty-two years!), and were the first to exceed the gross tonnage of the previous largest contemporary ship in the world by an amazing 50 per cent.

Even the fictional heroine Rose in James Cameron's multi-Oscar-winning blockbuster *Titanic* was impressed. On emerging from her limousine at the dockside she looks up from beneath her fashionably large picture hat, gazes rather indifferently at the *Titanic* and says: 'I don't see what all the fuss is about. It doesn't look any bigger than the *Mauretania!*'

Even part of the yard where the *Mauretania* had been built has been remembered in ballad: 'The Neptune was the last to go …' as Jimmy Nail sang evocatively in 'Big River', even though the Wallsend Shipyard was the last to close, not the Neptune.

This current volume was started many years ago, then I retired and paused in my writing. During the interim other publications on the subject appeared, most notably those by Peter Newall and J. Kent Layton, all of us following in the footsteps of Humfrey Jordan, whose now eagerly sought-after classic Mauretania: *Landfalls and Departures of Twenty Five Years* appeared in 1936 shortly after the great ship had been sent to the breakers.

I hope that this volume will differ from those that have come before in as much as I was most fortunate in discovering fresh sources of information, some sources found by happenchance, others by 'being in the right place at the right time'. If the first few chapters prove to be too technically orientated, please feel free to fast forward! Firstly, I started my post-shipwright apprenticeship working life as a draughtsman at the Admiralty Experiment Works (AEW, now QinetiQ) at Haslar where models of the New Cunarders had been tested thoroughly and relevant Books of Letters still exist that cover the model tests on the great ship and her sister. Then, in a much later position as Technical Librarian at shipbuilders Vosper Thornycroft, a gentleman introduced himself as having worked at Swan Hunter and Wigham Richardson, the *Mauretania*'s builders, and showed me a treasure that he had saved from wilful destruction when the yard had closed – the collated manuscripts of the builder's and official trials. Consequently, it is hoped that the casual reader will not be deterred by the necessarily semi-technical tone (hopefully not overly so) of the first few chapters and that a little perseverance will prevail.

I was again very fortunate that, at the end of one of my lectures given in Portsmouth, a delightful lady introduced herself as one of the two daughters born to the liner's first captain, Captain Pritchard, and his new wife after his retirement from the sea. From the two sisters (to whom this book is partly dedicated) I gleaned much of value.

Therefore a special thanks to these two delightful sisters, Elizabeth and Katherine Pritchard, who so very generously passed on to me their father's gilt-inscribed, red-leatherette-bound presentation copy of the

November 1907 Special Number of *The Shipbuilder*, a copy that must have given the Captain much pleasurable and informative reading, as it surely has done so to me. Four superb shipyard photographs of the ship that used to hang in the hall of the Captain's house on The Wirral originated from the same generous source, as did the opportunity to photograph the Captain's presentation silver (the coffee and tea service that the author sent to auction on behalf of the sisters ended up one hundred years later in the Commodore's cabin on board the mighty *Queen Mary 2* – from one commodore to another with a century in between!)

Multiple visits to the National Archives (formerly the Public Record Office) at Kew over many years yielded much fascinating and original information about the crew, which I believe is now recounted for the first time.

Amongst the pile of published material that I consulted (*see* Bibliography) were technical publications, learned society papers, the ship's Crew Agreements (logs), and the online archives of several newspapers, to all of whom I owe a great debt; the British Newspaper Archive especially is a treasure. Recovered stories from the newspapers include the one about the ship, a man, and a gun; another about a Christmas race during which the *Mauretania* carried her own Phileas Fogg.

I have not attempted to make lists of voyages or captains as these have been adequately and so ably documented in other works. Nor have I made use of footnotes that can make a tedious interruption to any narrative. But I do hope that this book will provide something of a fresh insight into the conception and career of a magnificent icon of our great British maritime and engineering heritage. As speeds and times of passages are especially contentious, with different newspapers often reporting different records for the same voyage, I have generally called on Humfrey Jordan's book as my general guide, although in places I have preferred to quote noon-to-noon distances run; durations of voyages quoted are either marker-to-marker (lightships, etc.) or from undocking to docking. Corrections, please, for future editions.

In the Foreword to his ship-biography of 1934 *RMS* Mauretania – *The Ship and Her Record*, Gerald Aylmer wrote presciently: 'Future generations will undoubtedly regard the grand old Mauretania as the Cutty Sark of the steam age'. Considering the ship's innovations, history and records, perhaps he was right.

The sirens are sounding. Let the voyage begin!

David F. Hutchings
Lee-on-The Solent,
Hampshire
March 2019

The magnificent *Mauretania* passes a big yacht during Cowes Week. (Cunard Christmas Number, 1929)

ACKNOWLEDGEMENTS

Many of the photographs used to illustrate this book were sourced on the inescapable but invaluable online auction house eBay – and any of these that may have been bought without my being aware of any existing copyright I can only apologise to the copyright owner and hope to make amends in future editions of this book. The remainder of the photographs I hope I have credited correctly and my sincerest thanks go to those who allowed me to use their images.

My thanks go especially to the late sisters Elizabeth and Katherine Pritchard for allowing me to use the portrait of their father, Captain John Pritchard, his illuminated retirement address, presentation silver and other items, all of which were personal and unique. My deepest appreciation to Katherine (Kitty) for granting me permission to pass on both the portrait and the illuminated address to Merseyside Maritime Museum as her gift.

I would also thank for their time, advice and expertise Ernest Andrews (Secretary of the Manchester Association of Engineers) for Max Wilkinson's Papper on the demolition of the *Mauretania*; Nigel Allan; Mark A. Baber; Ralph Bonfield; Colin Boyd (part-time Tyne & Wear Museum and Archives and full-time *Mauretania* expert); Robert Bracken of *Titanic* International; Mark Chirnside; Anthony Cooke of Carmania Press; Des and Ulla Cox (Maritime Memories and producers of the fabulous Snowbow 'Great Liners' DVD series); Patric Dickson; Tony and Mike Dixon for using extracts from Uffa Fox's book; Jack Eaton; Charles Haas; Brian Hawley of Luxury Liner Row; Robert Hunter; the late Captain Peter Jackson; Captain Derrick Kemp; my old friend Richard de Kerbrech; the late John Maxtone-Graham; Bill Miller; Simon Mills; the late Peter Newall; Paul Perry; Mike Poirier; Ian Rae (Drawing Office colleague and valued guide to the shipyards on the River Tyne); Eric Sauder; Ken Smith; another good friend, David L. Williams; the Estate of Patric Dickinson and the late Captain Robin Woodall.

The following organisations and those helpful people within them should also be mentioned with gratitude:

Atlantic Mutual Insurance Company, Madison, New Jersey; Amgueddfa Ceredigion (Ceredigion Museum), Aberystwyth (Michael Freeman); British Newspaper Archive; Charles Miller Ltd., (Auctioneers); The National Archives, Kew (previously the Public Record Office); The Parliamentary Archives, House of Lords Record Office (Simon Gough); Southampton SeaCity Museum; Southampton Reference Library (David Hollingsworth); Tyne & Wear Archives Service (Carolyn Ball, L. Edwards); Institute of Mechanical Engineers (Mike Claxton). QinetiQ, Haslar (formerly AEW), the Admiralty Experiment Works (Nick Ireland); and David Swan.

Special thanks to Colin M. Baxter for his wonderful watercolour; Professor Ian Buxton for permission to quote from his article in *Mariners' Mirror* (*see* Bibliography); Eric Longo, my deepest thanks and gratitude for so generously and expertly sharing his in-depth knowledge of the ship and providing resolutions and answers to many of my questions; and to Hamish Bryson, who rescued the Builders' and Owner's Trials record manuscripts from certain destruction. And, not least, my thanks to Amy Rigg and Jezz Palmer at The History Press for their patience, forbearance and enthusiasm!

Thank you all so very, very much!

PROLOGUE

'THE SEA ... HAS MOODS TO FILL THE STOREHOUSE OF THE MIND ...'

(Hilaire Belloc)

And once as the great yachts passed Fort Gilkicker
Out at Spithead, there passed them hurrying inward
The *Mauretania*, the truly most beautiful
Of steamships ever built –
Perfection fabulous, never again to be known,
Never never again,
And I saw these thoroughbred creatures of seaman-kind
Race on the English-summer-coloured-water ...

In his poem 'Lament for the Great Yachts', Patric Dickinson describes with great eloquence an idyllic sun-sparkled 1920s August day during Cowes Week, that annual regatta of yachting on the multi-layered calcite green waters of Spithead and The Solent, both busy stretches of water that lay to the north of the verdant shores of the Isle of Wight. With a brisk sou'westerly breeze blowing up from the English Channel that spurred galloping white horses to generously fleck the lively water's surface, patchily darkened by broad, narrow-banded lines of shadow cast by high-drifting cumulus set against a perfect blue sky, the whole panorama gave animated background colour to an equally animated, ever-changing marine spectacular.

To see a big liner in these conditions was always thrilling, but when that ship was the superb *Mauretania* (still the fastest liner in the world at that time) steaming inwards, her voyage done as she headed towards Southampton, smoke tumbling from her four huge black and orangey-red funnels, the effect was one of completeness and perfection.

After passing between the sea-bound forts known as 'Palmerston's Follies', with Portsmouth and Fort Gilkicker way over to starboard and Seaview, Ryde, and then the little town of Cowes nestling beneath wooded hills close by to port on the Isle of Wight, the great liner contrasted dramatically with, but merged with in a shared beauty of line and form, the great yachts that sped alongside her.

Gliding imperiously through the billowing craft that raced in sporting earnest in these beautiful waters, she made a slight turn to port at the Prince Consort buoy taking her past the exclusive Royal Yacht Squadron quartered in Cowes Castle before coming abreast of the Prince's Green on the town's seafront. At this point she made a sweep to starboard into the Thorn Channel between Stanswood Bay and Calshot Spit to port and the tide-hidden Bramble Bank and Thorn Knolls to starboard.

The *Calshot Spit* lightvessel marked another turn, this time to port, that took her into Southampton Water with Calshot Castle on the peninsula guarding the Water's entrance off on her port side, backdropped by the expanse of the New Forest. Off to starboard the quarter-mile, Royal Military Hospital at Netley stretched its million-bricked bulk along the shore as she headed towards her destination that laid directly ahead – her bustling home port of Southampton where the London express awaited.

This, then, is the story of a fabled ship – greatly lauded in her day and deeply mourned in her passing

FROM COOK TO 'KITCHENER'

Sixty feet above the cold waters of the North Sea, Commodore John Pritchard stood on the pristine teak gratings that protectively covered the Bridge decking of the new Cunard liner *Mauretania*. She was on a course that would take her north-about round the British Isles. The Captain must have felt justifiably proud, even if only inwardly, as his new charge made her way steadily past the eastern coast of Britain that lay way over to port. Of the two sister ships that had just been completed for the Cunard Steamship Company the *Mauretania* was the newest by a few weeks and the company had faith that the partnership of ship and captain would make the new liner into a breathtaking record-breaker.

She had recently passed her builder's Sea Trials and would soon be running Cunard's own Acceptance Trials as soon as a dry-docking had been completed to remove any remaining launching fitments and to clean and paint her hull after her maiden arrival in Liverpool, her current destination and her future home port.

As the Captain gazed over the Bridge wing's forward bulwark (or dodger) towards the grey, calm waters that came towards him and at the misty, distant horizon ahead, the wind in his face must have felt keen as the speed of the ship overrode and exceeded the light breeze that blew that mid-autumnal afternoon of Tuesday, 22 October 1907. In another vessel powered with reciprocating engines a steady, incessant vibration would have been expected, but practically nothing could be sensed on this new wonder-ship beneath his feet.

With a displacement of almost 38,000 tons, a gross tonnage of 31,938 and an overall length of 790ft, the new, sleek *Mauretania* was the largest and the most eagerly awaited liner in the world just as her sister

ship *Lusitania* had been and, as soon as her forthcoming trials were completed, she also had the potential of becoming the fastest. With a beauty that reflected the regal Edwardian poise of the 'Gilded Age', the new ship had caught the imagination of the 'Empire on which the Sun never set', an empire based upon British and Irish yards that had built half the world's tonnage of ships as well as a great percentage of the railways and bridges that served a quarter of the globe. An elegant sheer graced the liner's perfectly proportioned black hull that was, in turn, surmounted by a multi-tiered, brilliant white superstructure dramatically crowned with four huge funnels painted in the famed orange-red, black-banded and black-topped livery of her owners, the Cunard Steamship Company, and by ranks of large cowled ventilators. Within her elegant form she exemplified all that was best in British maritime engineering.

Having just sailed, freshly painted, a few hours before from her birthplace on the River Tyne in Northumberland, *Mauretania* would, after her official Sea Trials, provide a worthy running mate to the *Lusitania*, which had already entered service to great acclaim – there had been two months between their keel layings and three-and-a-half months between their launchings. The sisters would soon be competing for the North Atlantic speed record (the Blue Riband) in an *almost* friendly – but, in actual fact, deadly earnest – over-the-border rivalry as soon as they started their three-weekly service to New York on the most famous sea passage of them all – the transatlantic crossing.

Together these two ships would provide a serious challenge to the German express liners that – at the envious inclination of the British King's nephew, Kaiser Wilhelm II – had come to dominate, in both size and speed, the prestigious North Atlantic passenger route, taking away cherished records long held by great British (and a few American) liners almost as a matter of national right.

The Captain

Captain Pritchard had every reason to be proud of his achievements – not that it was in his nature to express such a feeling. The second child and only boy in a brood of four siblings, he had been born in the Welsh port of Caernarfon in 1846 (according to an estimate in the 1911 Census) but was orphaned at around the age of 10. In spare moments away from the local National School in Caernarfon he busied himself on the Welsh coastal schooner *Gleen*, while fulfilling a last wish of his mother by taking lessons in navigation from a retired Master Mariner, a tradition in that part of the country for a boy who wanted to make a life at sea.

At 13, after finally deciding to make the sea his career ('the best of all schools' as he would later say) he signed ship's articles and his first taste of professional life at sea – at 12 shillings (60p) a month – was as a ship's cook 'peeling potatoes for the captain' on a coal-carrying schooner, the *William* (according to the 'Journal of Commerce'). [Note: Other reports make mention of the *Eleanor Thomas*.] He eventually achieved the lowly post of seaman and, at 21 years of age, obtained his Second Mate's certificate through, as he said, 'the hard school of navigation' and two years later went to Liverpool to join a vessel trading to India and the Far East. While in Japan he bought a finely painted pair of tall Satsuma flask vases, their necks adorned with moulded dragons, a fine souvenir of his first trip of 'going foreign'. He spent about six years on this run and by the age of 27 he had earned his First Mate's certificate, two years later qualifying as a Master. Being a thrifty Welshman, he had saved enough of his hard-earned wages and became part-owner and captain of a ship by purchasing one share of a brig, the *Sybil Wynne,* capable of carrying 800 tons of cargo (usually good Welsh slate) to South America.

Leaving sail to gain experience in steam, he went to Wallsend-on-Tyne to take delivery of the *Princess of Wales,* one of the smallest steamers to have been built to date. He later joined Edward Bates and Sons

Standing on the port wing of the Bridge, Captain John Pritchard gazes ahead over the ship's bow. (Estate of Captain Pritchard/Author's collection)

of Liverpool (a descendant, Percy Bates, would become Chairman of Cunard), staying with them for four-and-a-half years. Then, in 1880, aged 35 and armed with his 'ticket', John Pritchard joined the prestigious Cunard line of steamships as a Junior Deck Officer, his Master's certificate being the required minimum qualification.

On 15 January 1881, a few months after Junior Officer Pritchard had joined the *Samaria* (2,574gt; 1868), the ship's captain put him in charge of a lifeboat that was launched in the most appalling weather in order to rescue the crew of a Welsh schooner, the *Mary* of Aberystwyth – his familiarity with the Welsh language undoubtedly helping to allay the fears of the survivors. For this act he was later awarded the Silver Medal of the Royal Humane Society. On his return to Liverpool he was promoted to Third Officer and transferred to the *Atlas* (2,393gt; 1873).

After fourteen years in Cunard's service, promotion to Captain finally came his way. So, from being Chief Mate on the *Cephalonia* (5,517gt; 1882), he received his first command, sailing on the small *British Queen* (772gt; 1862), by then reduced to plodding on the company's service between Liverpool and Le Havre. His next command was somewhat larger, the freighter *Sylvania* (5,598gt; 1895). Rejoining the *Samaria* as

Captain he took an active part in another rescue, this time going to the assistance of the distressed, 80-ton coastal schooner *Lucy Wentworth* out of New England that had been blown out to sea. Because of the rescue and prevailing atrocious weather, the *Samaria* arrived in Liverpool five days late.

Captain Pritchard then took delivery of the *Saxonia* from her builders (14,280gt; 1900 – the largest, if not the fastest or longest ship in the Cunard fleet) and took her on her maiden voyage on 22 May 1900. It was in October of that year – and again in very rough conditions – that the Captain led the rescue of two men hanging onto a capsized pilot's boat from the American pilot vessel *Louise*, 200-miles east of the Boston lightship. The Captain was again in command of the *Sylvania* when she was commissioned to transport mules to South Africa's Cape in 1901 during the Second Boer War. By now he had held command of all the Atlantic Cunarders except the *Umbria*.

His demeanour and approach resulted in Captain Pritchard becoming a firm favourite with his various ships' crews and an asset to the company by being popular with all classes of passenger, many purposely travelling with him. A contemporary report described Captain Pritchard as 'a man of middle height, with a thick-set, sturdy frame, an iron constitution, and a face that would be a fortune to a diplomatist – shrewd, wise, tactful, patient, good-humoured, vigilant, and, above all, strong'. It was said that his facial expression never changed, whether he was facing a gale at sea after thirty-six hours on the Bridge or returning to his peaceful home of The Anchorage in Bertram Drive at Meols, near Hoylake on The Wirral, Cheshire, where he relished speaking in his native Welsh. Having the reputation of being a kindly man, he was once asked how he would enforce Cunard's regulation of having the upper decks cleared of passengers by midnight. He replied that, should a recalcitrant passenger still be on deck at that late hour, he would merely order the bosun to 'Clean decks!' with a persuasive seawater hose! Because of the Captain's 'genius of organisation', he had been nicknamed The Sea Kitchener (after General Horatio Kitchener).

In 1904 Captain Pritchard made a further claim on maritime history when Guglielmo Marconi, the 'Father of Wireless' (even if he was not exactly the inventor of it), travelled with him as a passenger on board Cunard's then crack liner, the *Campania* (12,950gt; 1893), a former Blue Ribband holder. Her equally prestigious sister, *Lucania,* had been the very first liner on which the novelty of wireless telegraphy had been fitted commercially, *Campania* being similarly fitted in 1901. Marconi's plans to set up an operation in Britain had met with hostile resistance from the Post Office (its own system and monopoly of inland telegraphy would be threatened), so he concentrated his efforts on spanning the airwaves of the Atlantic and the first liner to be fitted with the new device, even with its limited range, had been the crack *Kaiser Wilhelm der Grosse* (14,349gt), which had appeared in 1897, the year of Queen Victoria's Diamond Jubilee. Losing that innovative technical lead, as well as public accolade, to the Germans was not all that the British had to contend with that year as the new, fast German liner had immediately captured the Blue Ribband and, at one stroke, not only taken the edge off Britannia's globally important Imperial celebrations but also affirmed the Kaiser's ambitions for Teutonic ascendancy.

By now Captain Pritchard and Marconi had developed a personal friendship. After travelling 'out' with the Captain, the wireless entrepreneur relished a return voyage with him while conducting on-board experiments with a more powerful transmitter. Marconi wrote a note:

Marconi Station
Glace Bay
Cape Breton
Canada

24th May 1905

Dear Captain Pritchard

We have been in Canada and the [*sic*] N.S. [Nova Scotia] much longer than I expected, but hope to have the pleasure of returning with you on your next homeward trip.

The new long distance Wireless Station is almost completed and I am looking forward to being able to carry out some very interesting and important tests with it from the '*Campania*'.

My wife is so glad we are going to cross on the 'Campania' and asks me to remember her kindly to you.

We would be so glad if we could again be granted the honour and pleasure of being at your table during the voyage.

With best regards
Believe me
Very sincerely yours

G. Marconi.

During the course of this keenly anticipated return voyage the Captain was encouraged to send a signal to his wife from mid-Atlantic, his scepticism evaporating when he received a rapid reply from Poldhu in Cornwall. The following year the *Campania* became the first ship to have continuous wireless contact with both sides of the Atlantic. From then on, a ship would comfortingly not be alone on the ocean. As a sign of his esteem, Signor Marconi presented Captain Pritchard with a photograph of himself signed: 'Yours very sincerely – G. Marconi – RMS Campania – 10th June, 1904'.

Captain Pritchard's subsequent commands included the fine new *Caronia* (19,690gt; 1905) – she and her sister ship *Carmania* became known as the 'Pretty Sisters'. This pair had been ordered from the Clydebank shipyard of John Brown & Company and were designed to be identical and driven by 'up-and-down' reciprocating engines. However, a drastic change in the design of the *Carmania* occurred when building was halted to allow her after end to be redesigned to house three propeller shafts driven by recently introduced revolutionary turbines.

While on an off-season Mediterranean cruise, Captain Pritchard took the *Caronia* into the inner harbour at Alexandria in Egypt, a feat that even the port authorities had considered an impossible task for a vessel of her size. It was from the same ship that, on 27 August 1907, the Captain took soundings of the recently deepened 'New' Ambrose Channel. At 7 miles long and dredged initially to a width of 800ft and a depth of 35ft, the Channel, named after John Wolfe Ambrose, bisected a huge sandbank,

Sandy Hook, which had hitherto hindered the New York approaches, obviating a hazardous sharp bend around the Southwest Spit (and saving fuel in the process). By her passage through the Channel the *Caronia*, with pilot Hank Cramer on the Bridge, officially opened the improved waterway, proving that the Channel was safe for the imminent maiden arrival of the huge *Lusitania* on 13 September 1907. Unfortunately, the improved Channel did not prevent the *Carmania* from grounding for twelve hours four months later!

The Rise of the German Challenge

The development of the two new big Cunarders, the *Lusitania* and *Mauretania*, had been influenced by many considerations and events, mostly connected with the protection and prestige of Great Britain and its extensive Empire.

It all started at the 1889 Naval Review, one of those ceremonial occasions that the British did so well, held in the waters of The Solent between the English mainland and the Isle of Wight. The Royal Navy's fleet was assembled to honour Kaiser Wilhelm II, crowned the previous year as German Emperor of a recently unified country formed from several small independent Teutonic states.

To create a good impression of both himself and Germany, the Kaiser arrived spectacularly in The Solent on 2 August (during the grand high-society yachting event of Cowes Week) by making a Prussian-style entrance aboard the royal steam yacht, the *Hohenzollern*, escorted by no fewer than twelve warships – not an immodest showing for a country whose major naval ambitions were still a decade away. The British (still under the imperial yet distant rule of the Kaiser's still-bereaved grandmother, Queen Victoria, to whom he was absolutely devoted) made him an Honorary Admiral of the Royal Navy, which delighted the still-anglophile but erratically autocratic monarch – 'Fancy wearing the same uniform as St. Vincent or Nelson, it is enough to make me quite giddy.' Additionally his uncle, Edward, Prince of Wales, enabled him to become a member of the ultra-exclusive Royal Yacht Squadron, but the membership never fully regarded him as a 'gentleman'.

Also making a maiden appearance at the Naval Review following her recent delivery from Belfast shipbuilders Harland and Wolff was the epoch-making White Star liner *Teutonic* (9,685gt), named in German honour. After calling into Liverpool to embark Thomas Ismay (the Chairman of the White Star Line) and his guests, the liner sailed south to join the huge gathering of immaculately turned out warships and merchantmen in readiness for Imperial inspection. Luxuriously appointed, the *Teutonic* was not only White Star's first twin-screwed steamer (and built without cross-yards on her masts in case of mechanical malfunction), she had also been constructed with a unique feature. In eight locations around the liner's upper decks thickened, reinforced steel pads had been built into her structure. Normally concealed beneath removable deck covers, each pad could house a 4.7in quick-firing gun, thus speedily converting the ship into an Armed Merchant Cruiser (AMC), a generous annual Admiralty subsidy being made available for the purpose. To achieve her status as an AMC the *Teutonic* had also been built for speed and within a year she would gain and hold the coveted Blue Ribband for a short while. The arming of merchant vessels was not new (many an English monarch from Saxon times onwards had adopted this ploy), but to specifically build a merchant ship with that dual role built into her was innovative.

The *Teutonic* caused quite a considerable amount of interest when she arrived in The Solent and the Kaiser, accompanied by his brother, Prince Henry of Prussia; his Uncle Bertie, the Prince of Wales; and Admiral von Tirpitz inspected her on 4 August, ironically a date that anticipated by exactly twenty-five years the eruption of a dreadful conflict that would become known as The Great War. As well as observing the ship's luxuriousness of her passenger appointments Wilhelm was not slow in recognising the ship's potential as an effective naval unit: 'We must have some of these,' he was heard to remark to an aide. The Kaiser's maritime ambitions developed from this state visit and he intended to stimulate in his so-far indifferent fellow countrymen an interest for the sea that might, eventually, lead to the development of an Imperial German Navy (and empire). His growing thirst for glory included an attitude of 'winning for winning's sake' in yachting, an attitude that the British abhorred as unsportsmanlike. Within a decade

Wilhelm's wish would be fulfilled with his shipowners producing over a dozen *hilfskreuzen* (auxiliary cruisers), some of which were the fastest ships in the world , taking from the British the coveted Blue Ribband.

But by 1895 the Kaiser had become suspicious of Britain's ambitions and motives, and while on board the *Hohenzollern* during that year's Cowes Week he gave an audience to the British Prime Minister, Lord Salisbury, which became known as 'The Cowes Interview'. The Prime Minister declined a second meeting, which infuriated the Kaiser and, within a year, the Kaiser had become *persona non grata*. An attempted later reconciliation failed and led to his eventual abandonment of Cowes and him setting up his own 'Kiel Week'.

British suspicion was exacerbated by German support of the Transvaal Boers' opposition to British South Africans, who had populated the independent Boer state with gold miners. After the repulsion of a small 'invasion' by a group of irregular British 'militants' in what became known as 'The Jameson Raid' undertaken as an excuse to 'protect' British miners' interests and to overthrow President Kruger's government, the Kaiser had unadvisedly sent the President a message of support, the so-called 'Kruger Telegram'. Anglo-German relations predictably went down a further notch.

As a consequence, the Kaiser's aspirations were becoming widely known: he ambitiously wanted his developing nation to be on an equal standing with Great Britain and this could only be attained by creating overseas colonies and becoming a world power in both naval and merchant shipping. Although his 'Prussianised' armies were rapidly becoming the most powerful on the European continent, the Kaiser wanted most of all 'to seize the trident' from the British. Until now Britain had felt safe as long as the German armies were contained within Europe, but a strong German naval force was the cause of much concern.

Another mighty Review took place on 26 June 1897, with the greatest-ever gathering of warships in one anchorage. This was the Diamond Jubilee Review, celebrating Queen Victoria's achievement in becoming the longest-ever reigning British monarch, and brought together a staggering 165 warships of the Royal Navy, the greatest fleet that the world had ever seen, including fifty battleships, lined up in four rows each 5 miles long, and the *Teutonic* made a second appearance as a naval auxiliary. By now the concept of using a fast liner as an AMC had become part of naval policy, one that the Germans were eagerly following.

Kaiser Wilhelm was determined to emulate, if not exceed, the British in building for size, speed and luxury, and imperiously enjoined the owners of his nation's two most prominent shipping lines, Hamburg America (HAPAG) and North German Lloyd (*Norddeutscher Lloyd* – NDL) to develop their own resources and not to depend, as they had done, on British naval architects, drawing offices and shipyards (especially Fairfield's) for their vessels, however splendid. As a consequence Germany, in this very year of Wilhelm's grandmother's Jubilee, introduced a magnificent liner in an audacious coup when the first four-funnelled 'super-ship' (a British idea, a potent symbol that became synonymous with size, speed and later – by association – safety), was launched on 4 May 1897 by AG Vulcan, Stettin, for the NDL. Named after Wilhelm's grandfather, the *Kaiser Wilhelm der Grosse*, the ship was a sensation, Johannes Poppe's richly carved decor lavishly assaulting the eye with Baroque splendour. Her reciprocating engines, driving two propellers, developed 31,000 horsepower, giving her a speed of 22.5 knots that made Cunard's old *Campania* seem slow by comparison. Other than for Brunel's *Great Eastern*, currently languishing in her final days, the *Kaiser* was the largest and the longest liner in the world and the standard was set for the next seventeen years, the first decade of which was dominated by the Germans. The power plant of the *Deutschland* (16,502grt; 1900) pushed the size of reciprocating engines to their economic and practical limits and future fast ships would have to use larger, more numerous power plants. This and the greater fuel capacity required would sacrifice revenue-earning space and make speedy sea transport prohibitively expensive.

In November of that Jubilee year the *Kaiser Wilhelm der Gross,* with her low, sleek profile, took the Blue Ribband from an affronted Britain and, with the *Kaiser Wilhelm II* (named after the Kaiser himself) and the later *Deutschland* of Albert Ballin's Hamburg America Line (HAPAG), kept the Ribband for the following six years while creaming off a large share of the Atlantic passenger trade. While the *Deutschland* was plagued with vibration – she was not known as the 'Cocktail Shaker' for nothing – the high speeds of these German vessels that exceeded anything that Britain had worried the Admiralty.

New Technology

But there was something waiting in the wings at this latest Jubilee Review that made the Royal Navy – and all the representatives of the visiting navies – take notice. Something entirely novel and revolutionary. Making her debut in The Solent at the Review was a small steam yacht, the *Turbinia*. After obtaining permission to steam through the assembled warships, this sleek vessel proceeded to upset the naval applecart by actually dashing through the lines at a greater speed than had been authorised – 34 knots, the fastest warship at that time barely making 27!

Launched on 2 August 1894, for the Marine Steam Turbine Company Limited, this small craft had a displacement of 44.5 tons, a length of 103ft 9in, a beam of 9ft and a 3ft draught. Her unique propulsion consisted of a three-stage axial-flow steam turbine developed by her owner, the Hon. Sir Charles Algernon Parsons. Driven by steam from a 2,000 shaft horsepower (SHP) three-drum, water-tube, coal-fired boiler, her top speed was an incredible 34.5 knots through two 12ft 6in-long outer shafts and one inner shaft each fitted with three 18in-diameter propellers. This set-up was an attempt to reduce propeller blade erosion induced by high speeds. Later known as 'cavitation' erosion, this phenomenon created voids filled with gas that emanated from the low-pressure flow of seawater around a propeller, the resultant bubble expanding before collapsing, creating noise and causing pitting of the propeller blade's surface.

Hitherto eliciting little attention, Parsons' Wallsend-built craft was now dramatically wresting the interest of the assembled naval might of the British Empire and its guests as it powered through the water in a rush of steam, flame, smoke and spray, her turbulent wake piling up astern in a foaming mass. The display gave 'the Lords of the Admiralty and its officers and men on board their ships the greatest shock that the British Navy had received since the death of Nelson'. Guests, including Members of Parliament, sheltering from the sun under canvas awnings on board Cunard's liner, *Campania*, looked on in amazement, many not realising the importance of what they were witnessing as naval picket boats made vain attempts to catch up with the errant intruder. *Turbinia*'s manoeuvrability was also proven as she increased speed to avoid collision with a French yacht.

Traditional naval thinking was astounded by the little vessel's sensational performance, as were marine professionals and observers, all greatly impressed by the technological revolution being enacted before them. Prince Henry of Prussia sent her engineer-owner his congratulations before any disciplinary action could be taken – and asked for a repeat performance! The *Turbinia* drew up alongside the *Teutonic* and Thomas Ismay, the Chairman of the White Star Line, boarded her for an exhilarating and enlightening trip around the bay. Parsons had achieved his aim: he had once said: 'If you believe in a principle, never damage it with a poor impression.' He had certainly proved his point. The Germans may not have realised it but the reciprocating machinery that would drive their *Kaiser Wilhelm der Grosse*, currently being completed at Stettin and due to make her debut in September, was already technically outmoded.

After further high-speed trials attended by the British Admiralty, Parsons soon set up the Turbinia Works at Wallsend. Two turbine-driven torpedo boats were built and these were purchased from their respective builders in 1899; a larger warship, a turbine-driven cruiser, HMS *Amethyst* (3,000 tons displacement) followed in 1903. Her three sisters were powered by conventional reciprocating engines and the comparative results favoured the turbine. As a result, an important major warship would make her appearance in 1905 rendering all other warships practically obsolete overnight through her superior power, both in speed and arrangement of armament, as will later be seen.

Since that startling demonstration of the turbine's power several shipping companies in the competitive commercial world of merchant shipping had also taken heed of the major advance in marine engineering. Consequently, various vessels were built with small, compact turbines as their prime movers, the first being a Clyde steamer, the *King Edward* (551grt; 1901; 3,500shp) built for the Turbine Steamer Syndicate by Wm. Denny and Bros. at Dumbarton. Having three direct-drive turbines constructed by the Parsons Marine Steam Turbine Co. of Newcastle, both she and the later, slightly larger, *Queen Alexandra*, made deep impressions on the shipping companies, as did the cross-Channel railway steamers *Brighton* of the London, Brighton & South Coast Railway Company and the South Eastern & Chatham Railway Company's *The Queen*.

In the private sector, two turbine steam yachts were also built – *Tarantula* and *Emerald*. The honour of being the first turbine steamer to cross the Atlantic fell to the latter, built for Sir Christopher Furness (owner of iron works and collieries, Chairman of Palmers Shipbuilding and Iron Company Limited, and founder of the Furness steamship line). Subsequently, two large turbine-driven transatlantic passenger vessels were built for the Allan Line, who brought out the *Victorian* and the *Virginian* in 1905 (10,635/10,734gt; 15,000shp).

Parsons' approach to the Cunard Steamship Line in December received a rebuttal when they replied ten months later: '[T]he Board does not see its way to adopt turbine machinery.' But, after observing the success of the turbine-driven destroyer HMS *Amethyst* there was a change of corporate heart and, on 20 August 1903, Cunard formed a Turbine Committee, which instructed that the construction of the *Carmania* (19,525gt; 1904) at John Brown's Clydebank shipyard be delayed while her after end was redesigned to house turbine engines. A direct comparison could then be made between the performances of the *Carmania* and the conventionally engined *Caronia*; a 'bold experiment' as Cunard's Naval Architect Leonard Peskett described the decision. Fitted with three shafts (*Caronia* had two) *Carmania* would prove to be the slightly faster of the two as well as the more comfortable ship, but she was the more expensive ship to run in terms of coal consumption. The naval architecture of the ships was also an advance on previous Cunard vessels with high superstructures that encompassed more enclosed decks than before; they also incorporated enclosed Bridges – a luxury for their Navigating Officers.

The results of comparing these two ships with equal dimensions, displacements and boiler power gave Cunard the necessary information on which to base a decision for the motive power for their next major project, a pair of already proposed superliners that would combine both size and great speed and would result in the two most powerful merchant ships the world had ever seen.

By 1901 any aspirations for an Anglo-German alliance were at an end and 'after 1902 events seem[ed] to move towards … débâcle with the inevitability of a Greek tragedy; the lines were drawn, the time and place of the break alone remained to be determined' as it was realised that it would be the Germans, rather than the French, who would be Britain's next adversary should a conflict arise. To underline this recognition and to shake off Britain's previous policy of Splendid Isolation, the Prince of Wales, now crowned King Edward VII after the death of his mother, Queen Victoria, on 22 January 1901, aged 81, travelled to Portugal, Italy and France, forging an Entente Cordiale on his own initiative. The entente with the French was a personal diplomatic triumph for the King and to seal it the French fleet arrived off Cowes in 1905 on an official state visit.

Gradually the already strained relationship between Edward, his German nephew and their respective governments deteriorated further and alarm bells rang loud in Berlin and Potsdam as the idea of 'encirclement' by Great Britain and her recently acquired European allies took hold.

The Culmination

Back on the Atlantic route, the peace of the Edwardian summer – that carefree *belle époque*, the decade of the 'Gilded Age' – continued. Various centres of unrest and dissatisfaction in parts of Europe meant that record numbers of emigrants were uprooting and transferring their lives and those of their families to the United States – the land of promise and opportunity. The international steamship lines vied with each other to carry this very lucrative trade and, at the beginning of the twentieth century, a tariff war broke out among the liner companies. It would take an American financier to attempt to control – and profit from – the mayhem, a situation that would force the British Government to take action.

Two years after Captain Pritchard had proved the worth of the *Carmania*, he stood on the Bridge of the *Mauretania* – a testament to Cunard's faith in Sir Charles Parsons' radical engine. Beneath the Captain's feet steamed not only the largest moving object to have been wrought so far by Man but the culmination of much sophisticated thought, design expertise, skill of construction and naval planning, all driven by the political and military requirements of the day.

The coming of the *Mauretania* had been five years in the planning – and she was about to prove her worth just as the good Captain – 'The Sea Kitchener' – was, yet again, to prove his.

2

'A HEROIC EFFORT OF WILL ...'

(Jeremy Paxman)

The existence of this trade [to North America] as a profitable one is mainly due to the ever-increasing prosperity of the great nations of North America, and their close and enduring connection in race and sympathy with the countries of Europe ...

So wrote Leonard Peskett, Cunard's Naval Architect, in his 1914 paper 'The Design of Steamships from the Owner's Point of View', read to the Institution of Naval Architects. He continued:

There are two prime motives that stimulate the owner to build ships – the desire to open new routes and the desire to amplify or improve existing services ... he probably finds it desirable to repeat former successes, or to court new ones with improved types.

Within Peskett's 'Mission Statement' lay the history of North Atlantic steam navigation. A steamship line that could offer a regular, fast and efficient service to deliver the Royal Mails across the Atlantic had long been sought, and it was realised that it could only be achieved by using a company with a fleet with evenly matched ships.

An early mail service by sailing vessels had been provided across the North Atlantic to New York via British-governed Caribbean islands and, later, with direct sailings by packet ships (a 'packet' being a leather Post Office satchel) between Falmouth in Cornwall and Halifax, Nova Scotia. Established in 1754, this service took fifty days for a crossing and it was not until 1818 that the American Black Ball Line began a regular service maintained by hard-driven vessels with crossings taking about thirty days. Seventeen months later a ship with a steam engine, the *Savannah*, left its namesake port to cross the Atlantic. Although she only spent three-and-a-half days under steam she proved a point by taking twenty-three days to reach Ireland.

The gauntlet had been thrown down to provide an efficient steam service and Brunel's pioneering wooden paddle steamer *Great Western* (1,340gt; 1837) proved the point by having coal to spare after crossing from Bristol to New York in 1838 after her competition with the *Sirius*, which did not. The later iron-built *Great Britain* (1,930gt; 1843) showed promise with the *Great Western* as providers of a speedy service but – as fast as this duality of mismatched vessels was – they were unable to maintain an efficient, regular passage, especially if one ship was out of service. It took Haligonian (N.S.) Samuel Cunard to propose to Her Britannic Majesty's Government that with four identical paddle steamers a *regular* mail service could be provided. The contract was signed on 4 May 1830, and the service began thirteen months later as the British and North American Royal Mail Steam-Packet Company. Four small sail-assisted wooden steamers (1,154 tons; 203.7ft long and 31.8ft beam) – *Britannia, Acadia, Caledonia* and *Columbia* – started to plod their steady, often stormed-tossed, ways across the North Atlantic to meet the stipulations laid down by the Lords of the Admiralty on behalf of the British Government.

As increasing numbers of well-heeled passengers were attracted to the service the more demanding and critical they became. Two years after *Britannia* had left Liverpool on 4 July 1840 on her maiden voyage, the great British author Charles Dickens embarked at the outset of his American tour. There were eighty-six passengers on this January crossing to Halifax and Dickens later included an account of his passage in his *American Notes*. Having been given fairly high hopes of his cabin from illustrations, his first impressions were not complimentary:

I shall never forget the one-fourth serious and three-fourths comical astonishment, with which ... I opened the door of, and put my head into , a 'state room'... utterly impracticable, thoroughly hopeless, and profoundly preposterous box ... engaged for 'Charles Dickens Esquire and Lady' ... a very flat quilt, covering a very thin mattress, spread like a surgical plaster on a most inaccessible shelf.

He continued to describe the Dining Room as 'long narrow apartment, not unlike a gigantic hearse' in which a few sorrowful-looking stewards warmed their hands over a stove.

While emigrants continued to be transported cheaply by sailing vessels, passenger travel in relatively fast and regular early steamships was still for the elite. Speed was of the essence for the transport of mails and for passengers who wanted to spend as little time as possible on the notorious Atlantic. This led to increasing expectations of comfort and speed, and the ship that held the requisite standards was sure to attract the cream of the trade. An early luxury was a cabin with its own light as cabins had previously shared an oil lamp perched on top of a dividing bulkhead. Oil lamps were replaced by electric light (Cunard pioneered this innovation); benches gave way to swivel chairs in dining rooms and these later surrendered to chairs of the four-legged type, although still firmly chained to the deck.

As other steamship lines entered the fray, the desire to own the fastest ship became commercially paramount, assuring its owners of custom – and profit, and to achieve this ambition technical innovations in naval architecture and marine engineering, improvements in the aesthetics of outward appearance and internal luxuriousness of decor and appointments became essential. Comfort was often a victim of vibration from more powerful engines that were necessary to achieve a precious fraction-of-a-knot advantage.

Even before the Germans joined in the commercial and naval races, improvements in marine engineering had been swift to appear. Paddlewheels gave way to single propellers, but screw-driven ships required masts, spars and sails in case of machinery breakdown (Cunard's *Etruria*, which left New York in late February 1902, broke her propeller shaft and was not heard of for two weeks). Oscillating engines were superseded by compound; single shafts gave way to twin (Inman's elegant *City of New York* of 1888 being the first); then reciprocating engines gave way to turbines driving triple screws in 1904 with the appearance of the Allan liners *Victorian* and *Virginian*. Standards of accommodation gradually caught up with the changes: First Class had been sited aft in the early paddle steamers (engines were amidships), as it had been during the days of sailing ships. But as screw propulsion took over, engines were sited further aft until First Class in its old position became untenable and was moved to amidships where there was less noise and propeller vibration and less motion in a seaway.

Shipbuilding also improved: hulls that were once constructed of wood on iron frames (composite) were later built entirely of iron. This met with resistance and a ban being imposed by the Admiralty, as noted Naval Architect David K. Brown observed:

... numerous splinters would be generated and ... the hole made in the hull would have jagged edges ... impossible to plug.
... the Admiralty decided not to build any more iron hulled ... The use of iron for merchant vessels increased rapidly despite an attempt by the Admiralty to stop mail subsidies of iron steamers since it was said that such ships were unsuitable to act as auxiliary cruisers in the event of war.

Vulnerable iron was then superseded by tougher wrought iron and this in turn by steel – a lighter, stronger material. As naval architecture became more of a science, construction methods advanced with improvements in design, framing and the positioning of watertight bulkheads. Professional societies and committees were formed to revise technical recommendations; theories were propounded and lessons learnt from sometimes hard experience.

William Pearce, a shrewd shipbuilder and businessman who ran the Fairfield Shipbuilding and Engineering Company at Govan, reasoned that if competition could be stimulated between major shipowners such as Guion, Cunard and other prominent lines, and if these could be persuaded to commission fast steamships, then much of the potential work would be directed towards his yard. To attract custom, Pearce designed a fast '5-Day Steamship' in 1888, the first vessel to be envisaged with four funnels – this number needed to exhaust the gases from an increased number of boilers.

Pearce also developed the idea of the fast 'Ocean Greyhound' and devised the concept of the Blue Ribband (a 'ribband' being a slender timber batten used in various forms and applications in shipbuilding) – an accolade awarded to the fastest ship crossing the North Atlantic. Winning this award would mean that a company could profitably gain an advantage. Pearce's yard built 'flyers' such as the *Alaska*, *Umbria* and *Etruria*, each of which easily won the precious accolade, and his yard even built the entire North German Lloyd fleet, which included several fast ships.

The yard's 12,950grt *Campania* and *Lucania* built for Cunard in 1893 were magnificent record-breakers, taking the laurels from White Star's *Majestic* and *Teutonic*. As a consequence, White Star gave up the expensive and often uncomfortable quest for speed, opting instead for greater size and comfort. These two Cunarders were powered by two huge five-cylinder triple-expansion reciprocating engines developed by the yard and the largest of their type ever built. With their simple lines, straight stems instead of clipper bows, gigantic raked funnels and lack of fussy detail so beloved of their rivals they rendered all other liners obsolete. It would be fair to say that the Cunard brand emanated from these two superb ships – powerful, modern and luxurious. With speeds of 22 knots, the two ships held the Blue Ribband for three years.

That desirable but expensive maritime trinity of luxury, speed and size would lead to many a failure – and not a few tragedies. Lessons were learnt along the way, rules were made to regulate ship design and construction, and the public eagerly looked forward to improvements as each big new vessel entered the race, their captains becoming national heroes. Passenger lists were scoured by newspaper editors to see which aristocrat or millionaire was arriving or departing and on which notable liner – the resultant column inches of newsworthy copy providing free publicity for both ship and company.

The Kaiser's expansionist ambitions were unintentionally exposed when, on 10 September 1901, Germany's new liner, the *Kronprinz Wilhelm*, sailed on a gala trial trip from Bremen to Leith in Scotland. At a well-attended reception in Edinburgh, Prince A. de Arenberg, President of the Suez Canal Company, proposed a toast to the 'North German Lloyd Company' and promised – perhaps forgetting it was under British control – that the Suez Canal 'would be steadily deepened and widened' to make it navigable for ships of the new liner's size. His statement must have sent shivers down Whitehall's political spine that Britain's extensive Eastern Empire might be threatened – where merchant ships sailed then protective warships would follow, provided German coaling stations be established along the route.

In May 1901, an ambitious proposal was presented to the Cunard Board by Lord Inverclyde to commission two fast, gigantic liners, half as big again as anything that had previously put to sea. This audacious proposal was prompted by many factors – political, commercial and strategical – that combined to regain the advantage lost to the fast German liners and to the four-ship class 20,000 ton that White Star were building. With this in mind, Cunard began to seriously consider and develop a design for two vessels, preliminary proposals being prepared by the company's Technical Department in June 1901 under the leadership of the General Superintendent, James Bain, and Chief Naval Architect, Leonard Peskett.

In 1902 an additional challenge to Cunard and to British security suddenly entered the equation. The White Star Line (Cunard's archrival) was persuaded to sell a controlling interest to a giant American combine – the International Mercantile Marine Company (IMMCo.), a combination of the American Line, the Atlantic Transport Company and the British-owned Leyland and Dominion Lines). The combine was masterminded by wealthy American financier J. Pierpont Morgan, who had previously united the American railroads (as he did with those of the iron, steel and electricity industries) to obviate destructive rate wars. His scheme now extended to the North Atlantic to transport American-made goods across the North Atlantic on American-owned ships.

IMMCo. assessed the White Star Line as being ripe for takeover shortly after the line's founder and chairman, Thomas Henry Ismay, died on 23 November 1899, and his son and successor, J. Bruce Ismay, entered into negotiations. The last liner launched for White Star under Ismay senior's leadership had been the sumptuous, hugely funnelled *Oceanic* in 1899 (the Kaiser, a guest at her launch, described her as 'the crowning glory of the Nineteenth Century'). In spite of her gold-plated light fittings, she had been built as an AMC with a government subsidy; an intended sister ship (to have been named *Olympic* – a name that would re-emerge seven years later) never reached fruition. Before the deal was negotiated, White Star had ordered the construction of four liners of large size and comfort but of medium speed. The first of the quartet, the *Celtic*, was the first liner to exceed 20,000 tons, becoming the then largest in the world. To complete the 'Big Four' between 1901 and 1906 the progressively larger *Cedric*, *Baltic* and *Adriatic* were of between 21,904 and 24,541gt The deal between White Star and the IMMCo. was signed on 4 February 1902 (for some reason, Cunard's new Chairman, William Watson, was not informed until 8 March) and, with an influx of new capital, two even larger ships were planned.

Although two major British and French lines, Cunard and the *Compagnie Générale Transatlantique* (C.G.T. – The French Line) had so far managed to escape Morgan's embrace, the main German transatlantic lines, HAPAG (*Hamburg-Amerikanische Packetfarhrt Aktien-Gesellschaft*, more conveniently known as the *Hamburg-Amerika Linie* or Hamburg-American Line) and NDL (*Norddeutscher Lloyd* or North German Lloyd) had, by late 1901, entered into a close alliance with the American combine to share routes and profits.

With the financial threat posed by Morgan and the developing military and commercial concerns that were emerging from across the North Sea ('The German Ocean'), the British Government became increasingly pressured and was on the brink of allowing the IMMCo. to make a bid for Cunard, now under the chairmanship of George Arbuthnot Burns (the second Lord Inverclyde), the proposal only needing the concurrence of the company's shareholders. However, it was brought to His Majesty's Government's attention that if the company's liners were absorbed into Morgan's empire, they might – because of America's increasing isolationism – be denied them in times of conflict as AMCs. These fears proved unfounded as it was agreed on 1 August 1903, (eighteen months after IMMCo's acquisition of White

Star, which was considered a sad blow to British pride) that only the shares of White Star and *not* the ships themselves would be transferred to the Americans. So the British Government, with a sigh of relief, still retained its military claim to the line's vessels – the company's ships would still sail under the British flag and be manned by British crews, with the Admiralty either hiring or purchasing the vessels. In fact, Britain retained the right to purchase or hire any *British* ship within, or built for, the IMMCo. and these could not be transferred to a foreign company without governmental permission. In addition, any future fast vessels 'of uncommercial speed' built for White Star as AMCs were included in the agreement.

Meanwhile, the Cunard Line progressed its plans for two fast, large ships for its Atlantic service. A five-man committee under the Chairmanship of Lord Camperdown was formed of representatives from the Admiralty, the Treasury, the Post Office and the Institute of Naval architects to consider the many aspects of the design, including the subsidy that the vessels should attract according to power and speed. The Committee reported its recommendations for the ships:

Average Ocean Speed	First Cost Building	Engine Power	Annual Subsidy
Knots	£	IHP	Annual Subsidy
20	350,000	19,000	9,000
21	400,000	22,000	19,500
22	470,000	25,500	40,500
23	575,000	30,000	67,5000
24	850,000	40,000	110,500
25	1,000,000	52,000	149,000
26	1,250,000	68,000	204,000

An initial governmental suggestion that the company concur with a revision of the Admiralty and Post Office mail contract whereby the company would not transfer ships to foreign ownership was rejected by Cunard as being against shareholders' interests. A series of negotiations ground to a halt and, shortly afterwards, an offer for the company's shares was received, through an agent, from 'foreign interests'. In a mood of purely financial defiance, Cunard rejected the offer and cannily waited for an improved one. Alarm bells again rang seriously loud in Whitehall's marbled corridors of power.

Losing patience with governmental inaction, Lord Inverclyde wrote in candid terms to the First Lord of the Admiralty, Lord Selborne, telling the Government to stop procrastinating or he would recommend that Cunard's shareholders accept the generous 180 per cent offer from Morgan:

I think the time has come when you should say what you intend to do with regard to the Cunard Company and not continue on the present indefinite course. If you do not intend to make any arrangement with us but prefer to work with somebody else I would much rather that you would say so and let us know where we are …

In any case, a time is coming when I must let my shareholders know what has been going on, so that they may judge for themselves whether their interests have been properly looked after and, moreover, the Directors of the Company cannot put off certain arrangements which they have in view, but which have latterly have been held in abeyance, to give you time to make up your mind whether to do anything or not.

Another card that Inverclyde played to his Company's advantage stemmed from Sir Christopher Furness's (noted shipowner and Cunard shareholder) intention to revive his plan to form a large British consortium as a direct challenge to the IMMCo. into which he hoped to draw Cunard, who were initially, along with the Government, in favour of the scheme. But by June 1902, the Government had declined to underwrite the plan and it petered out.

Pressed by his shareholders after the lost opportunity with the Americans and the collapse of the Furness scheme, Lord Inverclyde continued to harangue the Government until a frank meeting was held on 30 July 1902, between Cunard, the Government (represented by Sir Ernest Cassel – friend, banker and Privy Counsellor to King Edward VII) and the recently appointed Postmaster General, Joseph Austen Chamberlain, an able and experienced politician. Two months later, Inverclyde felt confident enough to write to his shareholders on 30 September:

Sir or Madam,

With reference to my circular of 31 May last, I have now the honour to inform you that I have concluded negotiations with His Majesty's Government on behalf of the Cunard Company. The following are the principal terms of the agreement.

1. The Cunard Company to build two large steamers for the Atlantic trade of high speed.

2. The agreement is to remain in force for 20 years from the completion of the second of these vessels.

3. The Cunard Company pledges itself until the expiry of the agreement to remain a purely British undertaking, and that under no circumstances shall the management of the Company be in the hands of, or the shares or the vessels of the Company, be held by other than British subjects.

4. During the currency of the agreement the Cunard Company is to hold at the disposal of the Government the whole of its fleet including the two new vessels, and all other vessels built, the Government being at liberty to charter or purchase all or any such vessels at agree rates.

5. The Cunard Company also undertakes not to unduly raise freights or to give any preferential rates to foreigners.

6. The Government are to lend the money for the construction of the two new vessels, charging interest at two and three quarters per cent per annum. The security for the loan is to be a first charge on the two new vessels, the present fleet and the general assets of the Cunard Company.

7. The Cunard Company is to repay the loan by annual payments extending over 20 years.

8. From the time the new vessels commence to run, the Government are to pay the Cunard Company at the rate of £150,000 per annum instead of the present Admiralty subvention.

A meeting of the shareholders will be convened as soon as practicable for the purpose of obtaining their approval to such alterations in the Articles of Association as will be required to enable the directors to enter into a formal agreement embodying these terms.

I am,
Etc

The stage was being set for a quantum leap in shipbuilding that would astound the world. So much so that, by December 1902, outline specifications for a 'Steel Triple Screw Steam Ship' were put forward for a vessel (of as yet, apparently, undetermined dimensions) that, when 'final arrangements have been made with the Admiralty, Board of Trade, and Lloyd's' a ship capable of 24¾ knots ('starting the voyage at a mean draught of 33' 6"') and built 'under special survey to meet the requirements of the British Admiralty as a transport or armed cruiser', would render all other merchant ships obsolete.

The Chairman's well-considered proposals were accepted practically *in toto* by the Government on 24 October, with an added proviso that the entire Cunard fleet be held as a guarantee in an agreement, published as *Cd. (Command) 1703* on 30 July 1903, 'between The Admiralty, the Board of Trade, and the Postmaster General and the Cunard Steamship Company, Limited' and signed by Lord Walter Talbot Kerr and Admiral William May (both for the Commissioners for executing the Office of Lord High Admiral of the United Kingdom); G.W. Balfour for the Board of Trade and Austen Chamberlain, Postmaster General and, for Cunard, Directors Lord Inverclyde, William Watson and William Forwood.

The basic outlines of the document are often mentioned, but seldom are relevant passages quoted, even in part, so it may be of interest to do so, even in the governmental prose that excluded punctuation:

… and whereas the Company has in contemplation the building of two steamships of large size and having a speed of from 24 to 25 knots per hour [*sic*]

And whereas His Majesty's government is desirous that the Company's lines should be maintained under the British flag …

… the Company shall forthwith cause to be built for it in the United Kingdom with all due dispatch two steamships of large size capable of maintaining a minimum average ocean speed of from 24 to 25 knots an hour [*sic*] in moderate weather …

…the master officers and engineers in charge of a watch shall always be British subjects and that three-fourths of the crew shall be British subjects …

… all certificated officers other than engineers and not less than half the crew … shall belong to the Royal Naval Reserve or the Royal Naval Fleet Reserve …

To permit the Admiralty … reasonable provision … for the fitting of such pillars and supports … as to enable guns to be carried on any vessel …

To sell no vessel of the speed of 17 knots or upwards …

His Majesty's Government shall advance to the Company a sum … not exceeding … two million six hundred thousand pounds … at the rate of 2¾ per cent per annum …

… to be repaid in twenty years.

The stipulation that the 'Mail-ships shall be in all cases good substantial and efficient steam-vessels of adequate capacity power and speed and shall be provided and kept by the Company seaworthy and in adequate repair and readiness to the satisfaction of the Postmaster General' would be kept to the letter. From the recommendations an annual (subvention) of £150,000 for the two ships (or, per vessel, 'seventy-five thousand pounds … as from the date upon which the first of the two steamships … shall sail on her first voyage …') had been granted under the Navy Estimates in addition to the £68,000 per vessel in mail subsidies. The latter sum would be increased by 26/3d (twenty-six shillings and three-pence) for every extra ton of mail carried over a base of 100 tons. Penalties would be imposed for speeds below those stipulated. Additional to the subvention, an extra 30/- (thirty shillings [£1.50p]) per ton would be paid for Cunard to provide officers and crew, or 25/- per ton should the Admiralty make provision in lieu. The loan would be secured by the two new ships along with the general assets of the company, including the entire Cunard fleet.

From the Post Office's point of view, mails would be delivered to the ships both at Liverpool and during their calls into Queenstown (Cobh), with mails to the latter being rushed across St George's Channel from London via Dublin. Express trains and steam packets would service the mails on each Saturday in order to catch one of the liners during its call into that delightful Southern Irish port. However, Cunard did not favour the Irish call as it would seriously interrupt an outward express sailing but *Cd. 1703* required that the steamers:

> … proceed direct to Queenstown, or
> … remain at Queenstown until the Mails, to be there embarked have been received on board, or
> Immediately upon receipt of such Mails to proceed direct to New York.

Cunard's concern was understandable. Should the mails be delayed then the liners' schedules would be jeopardised and attract a Post Office penalty – in modern parlance, a catch-22 situation.

After the threat posed by the IMMCo, safety clauses were built into *Cd. 1703* that precluded any financial involvement by foreign interests:

> It is to be regarded as a cardinal principle of the Company that it is to be and remain under British control, and accordingly –
> A) No foreigner [Americans, take note!] shall be qualified to hold office as a Director of the Company or to be employed as one of the principal officers of the Company.
> (B) No share in the Company shall be held by or in trust for or be in any way under the control of any foreigner or foreign corporation or any corporation under foreign control.

'Principal officers of the Company' meant all those from the masters and officers of the ships; superintendents; company secretaries; the General Manager; and, of course, the Directors. The door was now firmly closed to Pierpont Morgan's plans or any other 'Johnny Foreigner' who might dare to presume upon what was becoming a national asset!

There were seventeen fast transatlantic liners on the North Atlantic by the time Cunard concluded its deliberations and the principal particulars of the five fastest were tabulated in a paper ('On Some Points of Interest in Connection With the Design, Building, and Launching of the "Lusitania"' by W.J. Luke) read to the Institution of Naval Architects on 21 March 1907:

	Campania 1892		Kaiser Wilhelm der Grosse 1897		Deutschland 1900	Kron Prinz [sic] Wilhelm 1901	Kaiser Wilhelm II (der Zweit) 1902	
	ft.	in.	ft	in.	ft.	ft.	ft.	in.
Length overall	622	0	648	6	684	663	706	6
Length B. P.	600	0	625		663	- - - - - [664]	678	0
Breadth	65	3	66		67	66	72	0
Moulded Depth	42	6	43		44	43	44	2
Ordinary draught	25	0	28		29	29	29	6
Displacement, tons	18,000		20,880		23,620	21,300	26,500	
Reputed speed, knots	22		22.8		23.5	23.5	23.5	
I.H.P.	30,000		32,000		36,000	36,000	39,000	
Grate surface, sq.ft	2,630		2,618		2,188	2,702	3,121	
Heating surface, sq.ft	82,000		84,285		85,468	93,865	107,643	
Type of draught	Open Stokehold		Open Stokehold		Howden's Forced	Open Stokehold	Open Stokehold	

Earlier proposals submitted by Swan and Hunter's shipyard for a large, fast vessel were dusted off and after a study was made of similar liners built between 1880 and 1904 – including details of speed-trial results – principal dimensions of the intended new Cunarders evolved. A length-to-breadth ratio of 8.6 was determined (a length of 10 beams was originally considered) with final dimensions estimated as 760ft length and 88ft breadth. Yet another consideration was the number of passengers that were to be carried above the Upper Deck. The fast German ships had not been restricted in this respect but British ships such as the *Campania* carried about half the number of their German counterparts.

Machinery anticipated for this wonder steamer would follow the old pattern but on a massive scale:

> Triple screw engines to be of the inverted direct-acting quadruple expansion type, balanced on the Yarrow-Schlick-Tweedy system,

having cranks to each set. The engines and boilers to be made to the requirements of the Board of Trade for a passenger certificate, to be cleared at Lloyd's and to pass American survey.

The engines and boilers to develop, at a speed of piston not exceeding 1,000 ft. per minute, the power necessary to drive the ship continuously at 24¾ knots per hour [sic], when loaded at sea.

The cylinders for each set to be five or six in number, as may hereafter be decided, namely – H.P [High Pressure], 1 first M.P. [Medium Pressure], 1 second M.P., and 2 L.P. [Low Pressure] cylinders.

In later correspondence the dimensions for Yard Number 367 at John Brown's Clydebank shipyard were specified more accurately:

In Dec. 1902 the Cunard proposals were for a ship 750' x 76' x 52'.

In April 1903, the size of a model experimented on at Haslar, and on our own part tried at Dumbarton was 760' x 85'.

In March 1904 the dimensions had advanced to 760' x 87'-6" x 60'. And a note was given (by Mr. Bain [Cunard's General Superintendent]) to Sir P. Watts [the Admiralty's Chief of Naval Construction] at the Admiralty of this size, in order that a final model might be run.

Names were being suggested for the two ships as early as November 1904, and varied in their appeal: *Stampalia* and *Octonia* (two Greek islands); *Britannia* and *Hesperia*; *Albania* and *Moravia* – names still being considered by the Board a year later.

3

AN EXPERIMENT IN WAX AND WOOD: THE PERFECT FUSION OF ART AND SCIENCE

(Semi-technical)

The desire to achieve the accolade and enormous prestige of owning the fastest ship on the North Atlantic run – and *fast* meant *large* as a hull had to be big and strong enough to house extra boilers as well as the huge amounts of coal needed to provide steam for the bigger engines and increased horsepower involved – resulted in quantum leaps in ship design. Even the aim of achieving a small increase in speed led to tonnage increases, in some instances of 50 per cent, a phenomenon not uncommon as the nineteenth century turned into the twentieth.

From its founding the vessels of the Cunard Steamship Company tended to follow, rather than innovate, contemporary trends in shipbuilding and engineering. Although reduced to being a floating advertisement for a department store, Brunel's *Great Eastern* remained the largest ship built to date in both length and tonnage, but Cunard's *Servia* (7,392grt, 1881) was the next largest and most powerful ship of her time. She was also Cunard's first ship to be built of lighter-than-iron steel, the first to have electric lighting, and the first to have remote-controlled watertight doors. Cunard had also been late (1860) in entering the emigrant trade, previously relying on their reputation of catering for the upper end of the passenger market. A proud boast of Cunard was that they had never lost a life in peacetime but this claim was not quite accurate as, in October 1905, a huge wave hit the *Campania*, staving in side shell doors before washing through that section of the ship and taking five lives as a dreadful tribute.

By the end of the nineteenth century the Cunard Steamship Company's by now two ageing racers, the *Campania* and *Lucania*, the first ocean liners to sport twin screws, had long since relinquished their speed honours to German competition and the company was building larger but slower liners such as its largest vessel at that time, the *Ivernia* (14,058gt; 1899; Swan Hunter, Wallsend-on-Tyne). *Ivernia* was quickly followed by the *Saxonia* (14,281gt; 1900; John Brown, Clydebank). The towering funnels of these two vessels were, at 106ft, reputed to be the tallest ever placed on liners, giving the duo the epithet of 'Ships on Sticks'! The slightly smaller *Carpathia* (13,555gt; 1902) had also been entrusted to Swan & Hunters' yard whose first building for Cunard had been the *Ultonia* (8,845gt) in 1898.

Swan Hunter's shipyard had submitted a speculative design in 1901 for a slightly larger vessel with a speed of 24-plus knots obtained on three screws powered by the usual, but considerably higher-powered, five-cylindered reciprocating engines, while John Brown of Clydebank had come forward with a design for a 725ft vessel with an 80ft beam. Initial Cunard proposals for two vessels were of 750ft in length with a breadth of 76ft and a depth of 49ft, with a speed of 25 knots provided by three sets of enormous quadruple-expansion reciprocating engines producing 59,000hp. An early 1902 breakdown of Cunard's general particulars were:

Weights	Tons
Hull	17,500
Machinery	9,300
Coal	5,000
Passengers & Stores	1,000
Total	32,800
IHP	55,000

Three huge funnels of the *Campania/Lucania* type would sit atop the whole structure to exhaust boiler gases, a design very similar to a 1900 proposal by the Hon. Charles Parsons – but his ship would have been powered by his own turbines that, together with the boilers, would have been strategically sited below the waterline.

Four favoured shipbuilders were sent revised preliminary General Arrangements and specifications for consideration, comments and estimates of costs and delivery times. John Brown and Company of Clydebank; the prestigious Fairfield Company of Govan, which had built several fast Cunarders; C.S. Swan and Hunter on Northumberland's River Tyne in England; and Vickers, Sons and Maxim of Barrow in Cumberland (now Cumbria), primarily manufacturers of armour plate and ordnance but latterly of warships, were invited to tender. Harland & Wolff at Belfast had been omitted from the list of invitees because of their perhaps *too* close involvement with Cunard's major competitors, the White Star Line and other companies under the IMMCo. umbrella.

The engines proposed to power the new express liners had evolved from the triple-expansion engines first fitted to the 15-knot iron steamer *Aberdeen* (3,684gt, 1882), an Australian emigrant carrier of the Aberdeen Line. This type of engine had made its debut on the North Atlantic on the Inman Line's twin-screw Blue Ribband holders, the beautiful *City of New York* and *City of Paris* (10,499gt; 1888 and 1889). Further advances in this type of engine were made in 1894 before being superseded by quadruple-expansion engines, the optimum size for the latter being reached with the big German liners, *Kaiser Wilhelm II* that steamed at 23.5 knots on 700 tons of coal per day, and the much slower *Deutschland*, 17.5 knots.

The Evolving Design

For centuries the building of ships had been an art, generally being constructed using the 'rule of thumb' by Master Shipwrights, which sometimes caused mistakes in the ship's form resulting in heavy, slow vessels with poor seakeeping qualities, poor resistance to the sea, increased power requirements and poor stability. But by the late eighteenth and early nineteenth centuries the science of naval architecture was being taken seriously and by the mid-nineteenth century the profession was attracting a following of brilliant academics. They investigated the seakeeping problem and reported their findings to learned societies such as the Institution of Naval Architects (INA), later to be given a Royal charter to become the Royal Institution of Naval Architects (RINA).

After studying mathematics and classics at Oxford, William Froude found employment as a favoured assistant to that most eminent of Victorian engineers, Isambard Kingdom Brunel, working with this tireless genius on the technical development of the Great Western Railway. Later, advising with calculations for the legendary *Great Eastern*, Froude came to realise the importance of mathematically and methodically conducting experiments with accurately scaled ship models to prove the worth and efficiency of new theories and designs, and he conducted some early experiments in the fields of resistance and seakeeping by using his own recording instrumentation with the intent of scientifically and accurately forecasting a ship's behaviour at sea, primarily for vessels of the Royal Navy.

Froude's early work on the River Dart used wooden models of two differing hull forms (prosaically named *Raven* and *Swan*), which led to the establishment of Froude's Law that stated:

> … for similar models the resistance diagrams should be similar at velocities directly proportional to the square root of the dimensions and that at such velocities the resistance should be as the cube of the dimensions.

Amazingly, this formula would still be in use decades after its conception. The Admiralty was so impressed with Froude's work that, in 1870, it granted him £2,000 to construct a pioneering towing tank, 275 x 36 x 10ft deep, at Chelston Cross in Devon for his hydrodynamic experiments and he undertook to operate it for two years to prove the soundness of his theories. His pioneering work with precision measuring and model-making machinery, investigations into the stability, wave-making resistance, seakeeping and propulsion of new ship designs began earnestly in 1872 and put Britain in the vanguard of the science of naval design, ultimately producing naval vessels that were faster and more seaworthy than any previously built. Other nations soon sought to emulate Froude's achievements in the hope of improving the quality of their own naval architecture. Seven years later Robert Edmund Froude continued this important work following his father's death in Cape Town.

By now hollow models were being produced from hard paraffin wax, an initially expensive material that could be cast into rough shape in a clay mould and then shaped with templates, machinery and scrapers. This method had an advantage over wooden models in that the wax was waterproof; had a consistent, smooth surface; was easily and quickly formed or altered; and the scrapings and, later, the models themselves could be recycled in the melting pot.

With the expiry of the lease of the Chelston Cross site the important work was transferred in 1886 to a new site – with land available for expansion – next to Brunel senior's Gunboat Yard opposite the Georgian Royal Naval Hospital at Haslar, an outlying district of Gosport in Hampshire. Chosen because of its isolated location, a mile or so from the great Royal Dockyard of Portsmouth that lay just across the busy harbour, a new facility was built incorporating a covered towing tank 400 x 20 x 9ft deep, containing half a million gallons of fresh water that was, in those pre-chlorine days, kept clean by eels scavenging algae blooms. To conduct an experiment a model was suspended and floated beneath a travelling wooden, hollow-box-framed carriage pulled along tank-side rails at predetermined velocities to emulate in scaled form the proposed speed of the full-sized ship. This pull was exerted via a rope wound round a Beauchamp Tower steam engine, a unique cylindrical type of engine that gave an essential constant pull.

Designated the Admiralty Experiment Works (AEW), this new tank eventually became known as the 'No. 1 Towing Tank'. As it was mainly concerned with the model testing of future warship designs, it was a rare occurrence indeed to see it used for the testing of a merchant hull, albeit a hull that would be of auxiliary use to the Admiralty, and such a model would be one worthy of great study.

A new establishment, the Admiralty Fuel Experimental Station, joined AEW on the Haslar site in 1902. AFES's remit was to study the use of still scarce oil as a future fuel for the Royal Navy. The United States of America and the Russian Empire were the main sources of oil so, at the beginning of the twentieth century, coal was still king, with coaling stations established all over the world to supply British warships and merchant ships that protected and traded to all parts of the British Empire, and would remain dominant as the prime fuel for another twenty years until an abundant supply of oil could be assured. It was proposed that the coal-fired 'New Express Liners' would eventually be converted to burn oil fuel once this commodity became more readily available.

The original specifications for the new Cunarders required that scaled model tests be carried out to determine the dimensions and parameters of the proposed vessels and to test alternative models in the Experiment Tank at Haslar to give data for the Indicated Horsepower (IHP) required. So, on the instruction of Sir Phillip Watts, the Director of Naval Construction (DNC) in November 1902, AEW – under the superintendency of Robert Froude – began construction of the first of a series of scale models of hulls from 'Tables of Offsets' submitted by the contractors and Cunard. Each perfectly scaled wax model of each variant of the new design – about 10ft long (depending on the variant) – was hollow with side thicknesses of about 2in and ballasted with bags of lead shot to replicate any desired draught. Every model was identified by a two-lettered ascending designation and the ensuing reports of experiments referred to Cunard models from *OI* to *RI*. The handwritten reports (filed in letter books) were each headed, in perfect copperplate 'Atlantic Liner Model Experiments', the first being submitted in mid-December 1902. Because of Admiralty involvement the reports came under the 1889 Official Secrets Act and were securely, classified as 'Strictly Confidential'.

AEW thus commenced a complex series of experiments over several weeks, initially on three forms of model. The first model (*OI*) represented

An early concept for the two New Cunarders showed them with three huge funnels, six massive reciprocating engines and, uniquely, four propellers with an aperture in the deadwood between the after pair as if it had been originally intended to fit a third propeller. (*Scientific American*)

the 523ft [*sic*] *City of Paris*, enlarged to 710ft, and the other two were based on Cunard's 600ft [*sic*] *Campania*, the first model being designated *OJ*. The second version of the same ship, *OK*, had its dimensions extrapolated ('pulled out') to 750ft. Both of these fine ships had been contemporary record-breakers and were considered as excellent bases for the new vessels. By the time of the experiments the *City of Paris* was then known, after changes of owner and name, as the *Philadelphia*.

The AEW model results accurately predicted the resistance that a full-sized hull under various sea states experienced when a layer of water around the wetted surface of the hull moved forward with the ship whilst the ocean around remained relatively static. The resultant friction between these two layers of water created a resistance that lost some of the horsepower (Indicated Horsepower – IHP) generated by the engines. The power remaining after producing certain other phenomena (such as the waves created by the vessel's movement) is known as the Effective Horse Power (EHP). From the results it was calculated how much additional fuel was needed to overcome resistance and to compensate for EHP losses.

By December 1902 some preliminary test results had been obtained from the trio of models *OI*, *OJ* and *OK*, all of which had been run 'naked', that is without rudders, distinctive rudder bossings (or 'swellings') and shaft bossings (enclosed shaft tubes). These appendages were later added when further information as to their possible locations was received, the same models being used but given sub-numerals, e.g. for the *Campania*-form model based on *OJ* (a 'naked' model, 1/38 full size, no appendages) the follow-ups were designated *OJ2* (as *per OJ* but with shaft tubes and associated webs, and rudder swelling added, but no rudder); *OJ3* (as for *OJ2* but with stern post cut back for screw experiments); and *OJ4* (without tubes and webs – as *per OJ* – but with stern post as in *OJ3*). As the *Campania* model proved to be inefficient at speeds of more than 24½ knots, 12in was added to the proposed draught. From late 1902 to March 1903 a steady string of Haslar reports on dozens of model experiments were sent to the DNC's office. A comparison was made with seakeeping results from the German liner *Kaiser Wilhelm der Grosse*, apparently obtained surreptitiously by Robert Froude travelling incognito on the German record-breaker!

Froude was assisted in his complex tasks by teams of skilled tradesmen, who made the models from drawings prepared by technical draughtsmen and the latter also plotted graphs from experiment results. Members of the very professional Royal Corps of Naval Constructors (RCNC) mathematically calculated the forms of hulls and analysed the model results. Amongst the RCNC group was one Edward Wilding, who remained at Haslar for only a few short years before submitting his resignation in January 1904. Wilding then went to Harland & Wolff's shipyard in Belfast, where his invaluable experience involved him in the design of the future huge Olympic–class liners for White Star.

By comparing the results from the various model forms against AEW's standard brass datum model (*Iris*) it was anticipated that the experiments would result in the best possible form being selected with a length, beam and depth sufficient to carry enough fuel, power plant and revenue-earning capacity to drive the ships forward at the highest, most economically viable speed. Stability was also considered essential to ensure the safety of the ship as well as the comfort of the passengers. Cunard's specifications and Admiralty requirements insisted on port and starboard longitudinal bulkheads enclosing the Engine and Boiler Rooms that, with the twelve transverse bulkheads and intermediate wing bulkheads, would divide the ship into 175 watertight compartments. The space between the wing bulkheads and the ship's side were to be coal bunkers that would aid in protecting engines and boilers from horizontal incoming shellfire; if more than two of these spaces were breached by a hostile attack then the ship's metacentric height (GM) could be compromised, an excessive list would create a negative GM and cause capsize.

The principal dimensions of a ship were used in several vital calculations such as in determining the fineness of the underwater form of hull. Each vessel has a block coefficient, which is basically a comparison derived from its underwater volume contained within a cuboid (rectangular block), with its volume comprising the ship's length between perpendiculars, extreme breadth, and a height of the mean draught. Simply, a brick would have a block coefficient (Cb) of 1.0, a bluff-formed, slow cargo ship might have a Cb of 0.9, whilst a fast destroyer with very fine forward and aft forms would have a Cb in the range of 0.55. However, the fine forward form of a fast ship might mean a very lively and wet ship. The new Cunarders' block coefficients were originally planned to be in the region of between 0.631 and 0.648; the final value appears to have been kept an Admiralty secret and was not published but may have been 0.58, indicating that the underwater hull would be very fine indeed.

Fuel consumption could be estimated as part of the displacement calculations and that depended on what type of coal was going to be used. 'Best Welsh' had a high calorific value with more steam being raised from a pound of coal compared to a cheaper fuel of lesser value to achieve the same amount of heat; in addition it would take up more bunker space, which meant less space for revenue-earners such as passengers and cargo.

By 9 January 1903, a modified model of OI had been tested, but this version incorporated an innovative swelling (rudder bossing) built into the stern casting above the rudder head that looked rather like a wasp's abdomen. Edmund Froude considered that 'at the higher speeds particularly, the rudder swelling may sensibly diminish the resistance'.

Eight weeks later paraffin wax models based on the various Lines' plans submitted by the tendering shipbuilders – Vickers Maxim (OI [?]); Swan Hunter (ON) and John Brown (OQ) – had been made, tested, and the results evaluated and reported. Experiments on Swan's form, model ON, were then repeated but in a finer form that represented 1,000 tons less in displacement. Brown's model, OQ, also represented a similar reduction and was tested at both departure and arrival draughts. Even so, the latter's results gave a poor showing and did not produce good results for fuel economy, falling 'a good deal short of the [reduction of] 5,500 [EHP] specified in the DNC's letter.'

Following model tests between January and February 1903, an increase of 1ft in the required draught was proposed by Cunard's Technical Department with the proviso:

that the official trials should be such that the mean speed on six consecutive runs between Cumbrae and Pladda Lighthouses, loaded down to a mean draught of 29 ft. 6 ins. even keel, should not be less than 25½ knots; and that an average speed of 25 knots should be maintained for at least 1,000 miles …

This change in specification had partly been prompted by the New York Harbor authority's decision to deepen the new Ambrose Channel to a width of 2,000ft and a depth of 45ft. As a result, increased beams of 80ft and 88ft were considered for the new design.

Subsequently, models *OR* and *OS* were tested in March, the latter results – after comparing with the results obtained from the methodical tests from the other experiments – gave an idea of the:

limit, for these ships, of advantageous fining, with given extreme dimensions, the diminished weight available for machinery and coal, in consequence of the diminished displacement, sufficing nevertheless for an equal or higher speed, in consequence of the diminished scale of resistance.

The results from OR and OS were, as Froude frankly reported:

suggestive, considering that in this investigation, every additional ton of displacement which does not conduce to additional speed, is so much *dead waste.* [author's emphasis]

In April 1903, after several other model variants (*OM; ON; OO; OQ;* etc.) had been made and tested, AEW's own derived model was recommended for acceptance and Swan's must have been quietly satisfied that the results were not too far removed from their own proposals. At this point, because of breadth restrictions at their yard, Vickers dropped out of the tendering process. In spite of initial optimism, Brown's declared that they were not able to build to the evolved draught because of the depth limitations of the River Clyde and reluctantly withdrew from the tendering process, only to triumphantly re-enter the competition when the Clyde Trustees pledged to deepen the river to enable the launch and delivery of deep-draughted vessels.

In October 1903, Swan's built a large, manually operated, 1/16-scale wooden model (wood would allow an ease of modification of form) of the hull 47ft 6in in length to confirm – and extend – in open water the results from AEW's excellent towing tank. Constructed of two thicknesses (probably double diagonal) of Yellow Pine, the model (launch) was driven by four battery-powered electric motors, each

with its own shaft and propeller and carried technicians and apparatus to record torques and thrusts on the shafts. (John Brown's shipyard conducted its own tests in Scotland for the *Lusitania* with the result that the two ships would differ in many details, both externally and internally but mainly in efficiency and performance.) To evaluate the effects of wind resistance on hull and superstructure at various speeds, the erection of rudimentary superstructure and funnels – the latter being initially placed in two sets of two in the 'German style' (even as late as the winter of 1905/06 the shipbuilders' magazine, *The Mid-Tyne Link* showed four funnels spaced in pairs) – gave some excellent results. In an 18-knot wind, for example, it was found that an increase of 20 per cent in power was required to maintain the same speed over that obtained in calm weather.

By using this large model, manoeuvred up and down the segmentally shaped 100ft wide, 24ft deep and quarter-mile long Northumberland Dock (2 miles downstream from Wallsend), the shipyard would be able to confirm Cunard's and the Admiralty's hull design and make absolutely certain that, with the inclusion of propellers, shafts and supporting A brackets, bossings and rudder forms, their model would achieve the most efficient hull arrangement possible. Propeller designs (twelve sets, precision-made by the Wallsend Slipway & Engineering Company, were tested during 500 runs) were tested on the model as their numbers, sizes and positions still had to be ascertained. The launch, being made of wood, enabled changes in configuration to be easily undertaken, one of which was the elimination of the 'deadwood' (the aft end form of the keelson) between the after set of propellers. This basic modification enabled the ship model to achieve turning circles in 25 per cent less space than previously required. Towing tests were also undertaken to verify Haslar's experiments that had been carried out in still, calm water conditions. Under the superintendence of Swan's Naval Architect, E.W. DeRusett and over a period of two years, nearly 5,000 experiments were run and, on completion of the experiments, the launch was retained, particularly for proving modified propeller designs.

The Northumberland Dock trials resulted in the adoption of four three-bladed propellers of diameter 17ft, pitch 15ft 9in and developed area 92sq.ft (as was the practice, each bronze blade would be bolted onto a cast steel hub). Swan's investigations were subsequently verified by AEW and, on 18 January 1904, Froude was able to report that the inclusion of four propellers (the first of this number to be fitted to *any* ship) showed promise as 'the results are interesting and … incidentally suggest the conclusion that the best efficiency would be obtained by having the outer [the forward propellers driven by the high pressure turbines] screws in-turning and the inner screws [after, low pressure] out-turning'. This technically innovative recommendation was readily approved by Cunard and the Admiralty.

In March, after much thorough technical experimentation and analysis based on a methodical, scientific approach, AEW came up with a hull form (details of which were initially sent to Sir Phillip Watts at the Admiralty in order that a final model, *PN*, might be made) of 760ft b.p. (between perpendiculars), 790ft overall; a moulded beam (width of ship to outside of frames, i.e. inside of hull plates) of 87ft 6in; and a moulded depth (keel to Shelter Deck) of 60ft 6in. The draught of 33ft 6in took into consideration revised facilities in New York's harbour approaches.

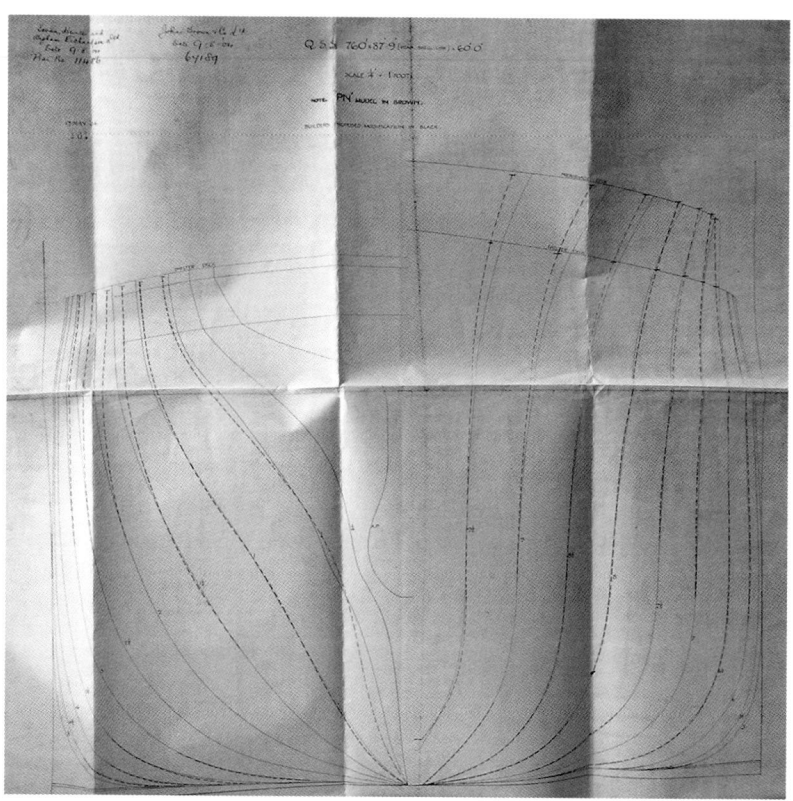

A drawing that shows 'Work in Progress' as a Body Lines drawing suggested by AEW has been returned by a potential contractor with suggested modifications shown in dotted lines. The after-lines in this set of drawings still showed a substantial deadwood with an aperture in it and a rudder of a 'pintle' type. (QinetiQ, Haslar)

The wooden towing carriage at the Admiralty Experimental Works at Haslar under which models of the New Cunarders were towed and tested. (QinetiQ, Haslar)

A displacement of 32,700 tons had been determined from model OS and the initial power requirement of 59,000ihp for the required speed was increased by the results of the resistance experiments to 60,000.

Haslar sent sets of revised Lines to both Swan's and Brown's shipyards for comment, both yards returning these plans to AEW on 9 May marked with their proposed modifications. Swan Hunter numbered its copies of the Body Plan 'No. 11486' and John Brown & Co. theirs '67189', and the Lines 'Plan 11487' and '67188' respectively. AEW received these on the 17th and made its final model experiments.

The naval architecture of the new Cunard Express Liners was now at a stage where detailed design and draughting work (using drawing boards and benches, splines, weights, pencils, set squares, tee squares, rulers, Fuller's, slide-rules and other drawing and calculating instruments along with sheets and rolls of paper, linen, etc.) could be progressed in the design and drawing offices of the two chosen yards with completed drawings being submitted to Cunard and the Admiralty for approval.

What was once a waxen dream was on its way to becoming a steel-hard reality as art and science were expertly combined. The new North Atlantic liners would be technological spearheads!

'The Will to Do, the Soul to Dare ...'

(Sir Walter Scott)

Messrs C.S. Swan and Hunter at Wallsend had come into being on 1 January 1880, when the widow of Charles Sheriton Swan (who had been killed by a paddlewheel after falling overboard from a cross-Channel ferry) joined forces with a young Wearside shipbuilder, George Burton Hunter, who assumed the chairmanship of a new company, C.S. Swan and Hunter, building vessels of all types for international as well as British customers. By the late nineteenth century Wallsend had developed into a small town of around 6,000 persons and was – prior to the development of shipbuilding in 1852 – famous for its coalmining, saltpans and glassworks. With the establishment of shipbuilding as a major employer the population had quadrupled by the beginning of the twentieth century. C.S. Swan and Hunter notably built three major ships for the Cunard Steamship Company – the first, *Ultonia* (8,845gt; 1898), had been laid down as Yard Number 252 for the New Zealand SNC Ltd, before Cunard took over the contract and renamed the ship. *Ivernia* (14,058gt) followed in 1900. After the acquisition and clearance of a nearby chemical works the shipyard increased the size of the ships that it could build to over 600ft, and it was while making alterations to the yard and the laying down of a slip ('C-Berth') that the easternmost end of a wall built by the legions of the Roman Emperor Hadrian was unearthed – hence the name of the town, 'Wallsend'. The company

now laid down a third Cunarder, *Carpathia* (13,555gt; 1903) which had heroism in her future.

A month before the signing of the momentous agreement between Cunard and the Government on 30 July 1903, a report in *The Scotsman* expressed its doubt that Scotland would be offered one of the ships, suggesting that both might be built in England, but George Hunter knew that this would not be possible because of space restraints. To increase his acreage of land and length of waterfront he entered into negotiations with his near neighbour, Wigham Richardson and Company Limited, whose yard, the Neptune Works, was at Low Walker, up river to the west. As a result the two yards were amalgamated on 28 May 1903, to form Swan, Hunter and Wigham Richardson Limited in anticipation of building the largest ship that the world had yet seen. The new company was registered on 15 June 1903.

Between the two yards lay another establishment, the Tyne Pontoons and Dry Docks Company: this was now absorbed to create a first-division shipyard with a waterfrontage of 4,000ft. Unlike Brown's at Clydebank, the new company did not have its own engine-building works so, concurrent with its formation, it acquired a controlling interest in the marine engine, ship-repair and boiler-making business, the Wallsend Slipway and Engineering Company Limited, sited downriver. Under the guidance of a brilliant engineer, Andrew Laing (it was said he never took a holiday), the engine-building company was reluctant to lose its independence, so instead chose to form a close association with the shipbuilders previously having built engines for many of their vessels, including the *Ivernia* and *Carpathia*. Laing and his Chief Draughtsman, Thomas McPherson, took on the new Cunarders.

Two large slipways were laid out at the western end of Swan Hunter's old Wallsend Yard on the site of the old Schlesinger & Davies yard, which had closed in 1893 (C.S. Swan, Hunter Co. bought the land in 1897 to build large floating docks), over which an enormous, double, steel and glass-roofed structure, based on those covering the East Yard, was erected by SH&WR's own workforce, enabling work to be carried out in all weathers. Officially known as A- and B-Berths these structures, locally known as the 'Wallsend Sheds', were 682ft long (728ft including roof overhangs) and 144ft in height (the supporting columns were 133ft high), the westernmost shed (built over Slip No. 1

on which the new Cunarder would be built) had a width of 95ft, while No. 2 was wider by 8ft.

Each shed was provided with seven electric overhead cranes mounted on trackways in the roofs, and arc lights would allow work to continue at night – a stark and modern contrast to the gas or oil lighting that the majority of the workforce experienced at home. Four of the travelling cranes had a lifting capacity of 3 tons, the others 5 tons. Working together the cranes could, if required, lift 40 tons and tandem lifts could handle 10-ton loads.

Adjoining the new berths new workshops were erected housing punching and countersinking machines; bending and straightening rolls; and 70ft long gas-heated furnaces to heat frames which, once heated, would be bent into shape, not by men wielding sledgehammers as before, but by portable frame-bending machines (developed by George Hunter), which could be slotted into perforations in the thick steel before being transported by trains of the North Eastern Railway Company (who had obligingly extended their lines) to the building berth.

Confidential technical specifications of the two new ships gave minimum heights between decks at the mid-length:

	Feet	Inches
Boat Deck to Promenade Deck..	8	6
Promenade to Shelter Deck...	9	0
Shelter to Upper Deck...	10	0
Upper to Main Deck...	9	0
Main to Lower Deck...	8	0
Lower to Orlop Deck..	8	6
Upper Orlop to Lower Orlop Deck...................................	8	3

(Orlops are 'part' decks, usually placed fore and aft of larger, deeper compartments).

The new ships were to be classed 100A1 at Lloyd's (their highest specification) and the turbines built under special survey. The Design and Drawing Offices were cautioned that:

> As the weight of all material to be worked into the hull, fittings and machinery is of vital importance, it is essential in getting out the designs of the various parts that the greatest care should be taken to avoid unnecessary weight, every part to be as light as possible, consistent with the necessary strength. With this object in view, all arrangements are to be simplified. Efficiency to be aimed at by sound design and by the use of the best materials.

Mr DeRussett, SH&WR's Chief Naval Architect, suggested reducing weight by using high-tensile steel (HTS) for all the hull plating and bulkheads. Although initially expensive, this would, he calculated, save between 10 and 20 per cent in hull weight, the savings being used for extra revenue space. Although he was generally overruled, some HTS would be used in specified areas. While the Drawing Office (under Chief Draughtsman J.J. Pescod) progressed with plans the British public was fed with enough information to encourage their national pride; namely, that the two ships were primarily being built – or so the newspapers would have them believe – to regain the Blue Ribband for Britain. Even the shipbuilding fraternity was fed the public line and an article in *The Mid-Tyne Link* asked, in its very first edition, the question of the day:

> Since the blue ribbon [*sic*] of the Atlantic, so long held by British-owned vessels, has been won from us by the German lines, the question has often been asked, how and when will it be regained? The problem will no doubt be satisfactorily solved by the two express passenger steamships now being built to the order of the Cunard Steamship Company … [which] … had entered into an agreement with the Government whereby the Company would build two new Atlantic greyhounds to wrest the blue ribbon [*sic*] of the Atlantic from the Germans …

That the ships were primarily being built for a more serious purpose was not mentioned; the Blue Ribband, the resurgence of national pride and the British *status quo* were quite sufficient to collectively elicit British popular support.

Even in America, the land of superlatives, the press nurtured an air of excitement. Periodicals and newspapers were full of expectation although, in May 1904, the *New York Times* reported that the displacements of the ships were still not being made available. In the same edition Rear Admiral Melville, a 'great American expert', expressed 'grave doubts' that the ships would be successful, and claimed that his views were supported by other (unidentified) authorities in England and Europe.

Published impressions of the new ships did not reflect the advances in design that were being achieved until quite late in the process. A July 1904 profile in *The Mid-Tyne Link* illustrated the earlier three-funnelled, three-boiler-roomed design but the article proudly stated 'the new Cunarder will be the largest and most important craft ever to put into the water from a Tyneside yard and indeed from any shipyard'. A later edition showed the correct number of funnels but still configured in the German fashion.

On 10 September *Scientific American* carried illustrations of a model of the 25-knot 'New Cunard Turbine Steamer' being displayed at the magnificent St Louis World's Fair in Missouri that coincided with the rather shambolic Third Olympiad Games. This handsome model depicted a powerful-looking vessel of an enlarged, three-funnelled *Campania*–type. It had four *four*-bladed propellers but still with the redundant deadwood in between, although with an aperture in it between the aftermost, almost overlapping, screws. A balanced rudder was also in evidence, protected from shellfire by its total submersion. The splendid award-winning model repeated other features (besides the three funnels) that had, by that time, been designed out, including a slightly raked bow; a stepped Bridge front; and eleven lifeboats on each side – the latter feature presciently well in excess of the current British Board of Trade's regulations.

Although Cunard had not publicised the ship's dimensions *Scientific American* astutely observed that:

> their length will be found to run close to 800 feet, their beam to about 88 feet, their draught to 35 feet, and the displacement will not be short of 40,000 tons …

Public expectancy grew:

> … the new Cunarder will be the largest and most important craft ever put into the water from a Tyneside yard, and indeed from any shipyard; and the reputation of the River Tyne as a shipbuilding centre will be greatly enhanced by the building of such a liner.

And so indeed it would.

Turbines and Talks

> Build me straight, O worthy Master!
> Staunch and strong, a goodly vessel,
> That shall laugh at all disaster,
> And with wave and whirlwind wrestle!
> (H.W. Longfellow)

In a heavy seaway, vessels tend to flex longitudinally: this two-directional bending is known as 'hogging' when the ship's midships section is supported by a wave, leaving the extremities relatively unsupported, and 'sagging' when, conversely, the bow and stern are supported. As these conditions particularly stress plating sited high in the former case, and plating along the ship's bottom in the latter, special consideration has to be given to the structure in these areas.

The tendering firms questioned the strength of the original Cunard hull design and, after much calculation, decided that the location of the strength deck should be the Shelter Deck rather than the Upper – or Bulkhead Deck (the uppermost level of the bulkheads). Amongst his other work, Professor J. Meuwissen of Swan's was tasked to investigate both the problem of strength and the all-important question of riveting. To alleviate stresses along the strength deck it was decided to employ high-tensile steel (HTS) from the Main Deck upwards to the Shelter Deck. Not only was this material capable of withstanding higher stresses than mild steel but it was also stronger, which meant that thinner plates could be used with a consequent substantial saving of weight. The use of HTS had been proven on smaller Clyde-built vessels such as the *America*, built by Thomson's in 1883, and the torpedo boat destroyer *Sokol*, built by Yarrow's to Russian order in 1894. In 1887 the steel had been used in the construction of the magnificent Forth Rail Bridge in areas subject to severe compression.

The Turbine Committee

As a speculative venture Tyneside shipbuilders Hawthorne Leslie at Hebburn and Armstrong Whitworth of Elswick, in conjunction with Parsons, had built two turbine-driven torpedo boats HMS *Viper* and *Cobra*, (344/375 tons light displacement, both 1899) and then sold to the Admiralty under a guarantee that the ships would achieve 37 knots. Subsequently the Admiralty ordered HMS *Amethyst* from Armstrong's (1905; 3,000 tons displacement; three shafts; 12,000shp; 22.5 knots) which, compared to her three conventionally powered sisters, suitably impressed the Lords of the Admiralty enough to convene their own Turbine Committee, formed under the chairmanship of that redoubtable naval thinker and reformer, Admiral Sir John 'Jackie' Fisher, Commander-in-Chief and Port Admiral, Portsmouth. Spurred on by German Naval Laws that were expanding her navy, Fisher would presciently forecast in 1908 that a conflict with Germany *would* occur – probably starting after the harvest in 1914 – and recalled British naval units stationed abroad. He also recognised the Navy's engineering department as a profession in its own right, an occupation not previously considered suitable for gentlemen.

With Admiralty interest in their new project, Cunard was now well advised to reconsider the use of turbines so shortly after their blank refusal of Parsons' offer in 1903. As originally conceived the new Cunarders were to be powered by three sets of tandem quadruple-expansion five–cylinder reciprocating engines with a total of over 60,000ihp, but it is said that George Hunter suggested that turbines of unprecedented power should be considered as the required reciprocating machinery would be massive, spatially extravagant, enormously heavy, and expensive to run. After considering the arguments Lord Inverclyde proved to be the turbine's champion when his lordship convened a high-level committee to investigate the claims for turbines and, within three weeks of *Cd. 1703* being published authorising the two new steamers, appointed many eminently qualified men to serve in its ranks. As Lloyd's Register would be undertaking special surveys of the ships when under construction and afterwards, the registration society requested that their Chief Engineer Surveyor, James Milton, be allowed to sit on the committee, the chair of which was taken by James Bain (Cunard's Superintendent Engineer in charge of the Technical Department, and Engineering Lieutenant W.H. Wood R.N. was appointed as the committee's secretary. Other committee members were: Engineer Rear Admiral H.J. Oram C.B. (Deputy Engineer-in-Chief to the Royal Navy); Andrew Laing (Wallsend Slipway Company); Sir William H. White K.C.B. (Messrs. C.S. Swan & Hunter Limited, Newcastle-Upon-Tyne and late Director of Naval Construction); Sir Thomas Bell (Engineering Manager, John Brown & Co. Limited, Clydebank); and William Brock (Denny Brothers, Dumbarton), while the Honourable Sir Charles Parsons, whose approach to Cunard had met with a blank refusal in 1903, enthusiastically gave advice aided by results of tests on cross-Channel turbine vessels. George Hunter declined an invitation to join as he was 'unable to devote the necessary time to the work'.

Six months later, on 25 February 1904, Cunard's Turbine Committee reported its findings to the Cunard Board that, on 25 March, readily accepted the recommendations to adopt the engine and set about to satisfy itself of the engine's efficiency. The company's two largest vessels, *Caronia* and *Carmania* (20,000grt), were currently under construction at John Brown's shipyard at Clydebank and, as *Caronia* was too far advanced in her build, it was decided to delay the completion of *Carmania* in order to radically modify her afterbody and equip her with turbines and three shafts in lieu of *Caronia*'s reciprocating engines and two shafts. Then, once in service, a direct comparison could be made between the performances of the two otherwise identical ships, just as the Royal Navy had done with HMS *Amethyst* and her sisters. Completing construction of the aft ends of the huge ships was delayed until results were available from the *Carmania*.

Ship	Keel laid	Launched	Engine
Caronia	29 October 1903	13 July 1904	Reciprocating
Carmania	19 May 1904	21 February 1905	Turbine
Lusitania	16 June 1904	7 June 1906	Turbine
Mauretania	18 August 1904	20 September 1906	Turbine

Once appointed as First Sea Lord of the Board of Admiralty 'Jacky' Fisher formed yet another committee – the Committee on Designs – to consider a '1st Class Battleship', a superior 21-knot battleship that would give her name to a whole generation of 'super-battleships'… *Dreadnought*. This revolutionary, epoch-making, turbine-driven, fast battleship (17,900 tons displacement; 23,000SHP) would be armed with a uniform main battery of 12in guns, rather than previously where battleships had fewer large guns complemented by a range of smaller weapons, the fall of combined shot making it difficult to assess accurate range for each calibre. So from February 1903, while confirmation experiments were being carried out on Swans' large model of the Express Liner on the Tyne, AEW at Haslar busied themselves experimenting with models of the new warship and, two years later, presented a final report for a battleship that would render all other capital ships obsolete – not only those of Germany but also Britain's own! Not only did *Dreadnought*'s propulsive power and the revolutionary arrangement of her armament shake the navies of the world and create a scramble to update now obsolescent fleets but the much-vaunted claim that the Royal Dockyard in Portsmouth had built her in a mere year and a day alarmed foreign governments to the core. In fact, the keel of the *Dreadnought* had been laid down in May, slightly earlier than had been publicised, and by the time of her 'official' keel laying on 2 October 1905, construction had been progressed up to her tank-tops. Through this deception the British achieved a splendid propaganda coup. The revolution that was the *Dreadnought* severely jolted German naval ambitions and signalled the start of 'The Great Naval Race', the consequences of which were unimaginable when her building commenced in Portsmouth's Royal Dockyard.

This important ship was launched by HM King Edward VII on 10 February 1906, and her introduction into service gave Britain a substantial head start in naval modernisation and an advantageous lead in naval supremacy. After her commissioning, the quadruple-screwed *Dreadnought* crossed the North Atlantic at a comfortable, vibration-free, economical cruising speed of 17 knots. The Germans were slower in adopting the turbine, the name ship of the 24.8-knot von der Tann-class not being completed until 1909.

Tragically, during this exciting period the Chairman of the Cunard Steamship Company, Lord Inverclyde, died at Wemyss Castle on 8 October at the very early age of 44 after undergoing a series of unsuccessful surgical procedures. Succeeded as chairman by 65-year-old American-born William Watson, Inverclyde's legacy was about to astonish the world.

4

FROM THE WAYS TO THE WATERS

Poet John Masefield immortalised the building of the mighty *Queen Mary* in 1934 by describing the mining of the metal ores that ultimately became her plates, frames, boilers, engines and a thousand other metallic items. Earlier in the century prolific Edwardian author Rudyard Kipling penned his paean to industry in 'The Secret of the Machines':

We were taken from the ore-bed and the mine,
  We were melted in the furnace and the pit—
We were cast and wrought and hammered to design,
  We were cut and filed and tooled and gauged to fit.
Some water, coal, and oil is all we ask,
  And a thousandth of an inch to give us play:
And now, if you will set us to our task,
  We will serve you four and twenty hours a day! …

… You can start this very evening if you choose,
And take the Western Ocean in the stride
  Of seventy thousand horses and some screws!

    The boat-express is waiting your command!
    You will find the *Mauretania* at the quay,
    Till her captain turns the lever 'neath his hand,
    And the monstrous nine-decked city goes to sea …

… Though our smoke may hide the Heavens from your eyes,
It will vanish and the stars will shine again,
Because, for all our power and weight and size,
We are nothing more than children of your brain!

The first turbine vessel to be completed at Swan Hunter and Wigham Richardson's Neptune Yard had been the 270ft-long, triple-screw, luxury steam yacht *Albion* (Yard number 718). Of 1,260 tons (Thames Measurement), the yacht had been designed by Sir William White for Sir George Newnes, owner of *Strand Magazine*, publishers of Arthur Conan Doyle's famous Sherlock Holmes stories, and launched on 24 November 1905.

The SH&WR contract number 601 (the first after the shipyards' amalgamation) was finally signed on 18 May 1905, and the new Cunarder was given the shipyard (build) number 735. After much experimentation the vessel's dimensions were finalised with a length between perpendiculars of 760ft; her overall length of 790ft exceeded by 5ft that of her Clyde-built sister, which gave the Tyneside vessel the distinction of being the longest ship afloat – this was due to a radial plan of stern being adopted rather than the Scottish elliptical plan. A moulded breadth of 87ft 6in, moulded depth of 60ft 6in (6in more than her Clyde-built sister) and a draught of 36ft 2½in (2½in more than her sister) completed her vital statistics. In profile her sheer's lowest point – roughly two-thirds of her length from forward - rose 8ft forward to her bow and 3ft 4in aft to lift her stern, giving her a racy appearance as well as assisting to drain her upper decks. She had a summer freeboard of 25ft 1½in.

After the final Specifications were released on 14 April 1904, the completion of the Lines, Body-Plans and General Arrangements (these drawings being the 'bible' to which the ship's final layout would be arranged) were completed, followed by detailed drawings of structure, plate positions, riveting schemes, engines, piping, cabling, etc. being prepared by the shipbuilder's Drawing Office. Once sufficient drawings had been produced, checked and approved, a start was made on the ship.

As expected, the shipbuilders were presented with a list of conditions, some salient points being:

- The ship had to be ready to run her trials on 18 November 1907.

- Cunard technical staff to be given access to inspect both materials and work.

- A shipbuilders' guarantee on all materials and work to be in place for twelve months after delivery of vessel.

- The ship to run at least six builder's Sea Trials in a progressively increasing series of runs at 12, 15, 18, 21, 23 and 25 knots.

- After the ship's arrival in Liverpool a dry-docking to be undertaken to clean and paint hull and remove any remains of launching gear. The ship to be coaled and Official Trials to be run taking the mean of three double runs of not less than 25¼ knots between Holy Island (Arran) and Ailsa Craig.

- A similar speed then to be achieved between Corsewall [or Corswall] and Chicken Lights (Loch Ryan and the Isle of Man respectively). A forty-eight-hour endurance trial of 1,200 miles [two 'voyages', each leg being of 300 miles] to be run at 24¾ knots between lights.

- If, over the ensuing twelve months, the ship's average speeds should fall below 24½ knots then a penalty would be liable for each 0.1 knot of £10,000.

- The cost to Cunard for their new ship to include the cost of all materials, fittings, and wages; 15 per cent of the former for 'Establishment' charges [specified overheads]; building insurance; expenses incurred in delivering ship to Liverpool; costs of dry-docking, coals for trials; 5 per cent profit on total costs for profit margin.

Names were needed for the two liners and a flurry of correspondence was exchanged between Cunard's Board and Andrew Mearns, the company's Secretary. The company was also inundated with over 460 suggestions from an enthusiastic public, the inspiration for many ranged from the bizarre to the intellectually challenging; offerings included *Albania, Alpis Julia, Arcarnania, Cymuria, Karavi Nisia, Moravia, Hesperia, Oxia, Makaronia, Manfredonia, Xenthis,* and *Zenobia.* The more readily identifiable appellations included *Hibernia, Britannia* (there were already twenty-three of these plying the seas) and *Olympia; Aquitania* was a contender and would re-emerge for a future building. The final names were chosen at a Board meeting held on 8 October 1905: Brown's Yard Number 367 would be called *Lusitania* (the current Portugal) and Swan Hunter's Yard Number 735 *Mauritania;* the latter changing three months later more famously to *Mauretania* following 'expert advice' (the modern country was Mauritania whereas the Roman province after which the ship was being named was Mauretania). The numbers now had names.

The building of the *Mauretania* was comprehensively covered in several contemporary technical journals, not the least being technically informative editions of *The Shipbuilder* (November 1907, with one of a limited run of gold-embossed editions being presented to Captain Pritchard [now in the possession of the current author]) and *Engineering* also of November 1907. It is not the current writer's intention to attempt to emulate these excellent and thorough publications but to briefly touch on some points of the heavy industrial construction processes that were involved as a celebration of the contemporary might of British industry.

The Lines Plans were sent to the shipyard's Mould Loft to be transferred full-scale to the Loft's wooden floor, where any imperfections could be ironed out and faired and then used for many purposes such as arranging plate positions and making moulds for frames. Moulds were taken to the thick, perforated bending slabs and steel dogs (clips) inserted in the slab's holes around the shape of the mould. Heated steel section was then pulled out of the furnace and bent around the form of the mould made by the dogs.

The Steel Structure

Steel plate and sections were delivered to the shipyard by rail and stored in stockyards until required. The first plate for the *Mauretania* was cut to size after being marked out by two men holding a taut length of fine, strong string, liberally rubbed with chalk, and held against the plate between two measured points while a third pinged it between thumb and forefinger to deposit a white line to delineate a cutting mark. The line was centre-punched to prevent erasure. The plate was then transferred to the Plate Shears in the new Plate Shop and trimmed to the marked line. Other chalk lines marked rows of rivets, the centres of which were centre-punched prior to drilling. Between that first ping of a chalked line and the crack of a champagne bottle much effort would be expended.

Hull plates (the position of each one inked on a wooden Half Block model of the hull in the Drawing Office) underwent several processes, especially where curvature was required, and were prepared by electrically driven flanging machines, plate shears, hole-punchers, edge-planers, mangle rollers, bending rollers, angle bar cutting and bevelling machines. After much preparation of steel and ways the first keel plate, part of the outer keel from which the vessel would grow outwardly, was laid down on 18 August under the westernmost of the two great glass-covered canopies of Swan Hunter and Wigham Richardson's West Yard at Wallsend. This keel would be made up of three layers, the outer plates of which were 50in wide, the middle 30½ and the inner 58, with a total thickness in places of over 3in. On its centre line and at right angles to the outer keel the vertical keel was erected, and on top of this was laid a second series of horizontal fore and aft plates to form the inner keel. Together inner, outer and vertical keels formed a very strong girder that would support the entire ship. Plates were strongly connected by riveted butt-straps and angle bars.

At each frame position on both sides of the keelson, floors (deep, vertical webs that supported the plating of outer and inner bottoms) extended hornlike outwards, port and starboard, to the turn of bilge. Vertical longitudinals, equal in depth to the floors and spaced every few feet apart athwartships and parallel to the centre girder ran fore and aft, thus further dividing the inner bottom into cellular spaces. Five of these longitudinals (including the keelson) were continuous, whilst the others were 'intercostal' – that is, erected between each set of floors. The floors in way of watertight bulkheads were kept solid (as were the five continuous longitudinals in way of tanks) but elsewhere they were punctured by lightening holes, the latter openings reducing weight and serving as manholes, piping throughways, and controlled-flooding apertures.

From the keel twelve strakes (lines) of hull plating (the first next to the outer keel being called the garboard strake) extended outwards on either side to the turn of bilge with edges lapping its neighbour. From there up to the Shelter Deck the plates were erected in the 'in-and-out' fashion. At the turn of bilge a margin plate capped the outer extremities of the 'horns' of the cellular double bottom formed by the floors, longitudinals and inner and outer plating – creating a very substantial platform on which to construct the body of the ship and providing an enormously strong 'egg box' structure – 5ft deep under the Boiler Rooms and holds and 6ft deep under the Engine Rooms. The double-bottom spaces would initially be used to carry water ballast to maintain the ship's stability but, as the ship was designed to be eventually fuelled by oil, the pitch of rivets in these cellular areas were probably spaced to provide oil-tight rather than watertight seams.

Tall, elegantly curved J-shaped 10in channel bar frames, the ribs of the vessel, were then firmly secured with flanged brackets at their bases to the margin plates, their spacings varying according to location: frames spaced 32in apart spanned the long midships section; 25in spacing towards the stern; and 26in forward. Wider frames (prefabricated from plate and angle bar) were incorporated at every fourth frame space in the Boiler Rooms, and at every second frame within the Engine Room. This substantial framing extended up to the Strength Deck where lighter framing – 5½in to 6 or 7in bulb angle bar of varying thicknesses – supported the thinner plating of the superstructure, thus keeping the critical centre of gravity as low as possible.

The vertical flanges of the 10in deep channel bar transverse deck beams, split at each end to form weight-saving Y-shaped knees, connected port and starboard frames up to the Shelter Deck (the designated Strength Deck), and, above that, beams were formed from bulb angle bar that reduced in scantlings (sizes) as the superstructure heightened. Beams of adjacent decks within the main hull were connected at eight-foot intervals by four rows of vertical 'Mannesmann' tubular pillars later to be richly encased in polished woods. The camber (athwartship curvature to allow drainage of exposed decks) of the beams would likely have been to the Admiralty formula of a 9in rise for every 16ft of beam.

Above left: Like a titanic jigsaw the construction of the double bottom progresses to the tank-tops. The claw-like hydraulic riveting machine rests (bottom middle) above the growing structure with its access manholes. 26 November 1904. (Author's Collection)

Below left: Typical of contemporary British heavy engineering, the mild-steel stern-frame castings temporarily assembled at the Darlington Forge Company's foundry showing the after 'A'-shaft brackets and rudder pintle. (*Engineering* 14 September 1906/Author's collection)

Above: Almost disappearing into the autumnal mist of late October. The upper strakes of plating are yet to be riveted to the mighty hull. A plethora of scaffolding, platforms, and shoring create a misconception of confusion. (Author's Collection)

Additional 'tween-deck support was provided by large tubular ventilation shafts extending down from the Sun Deck to the Boiler Room. These shafts led up to swan-necked ventilation cowls that provided a distinguishing feature between the *Mauretania* and her sister with her shallow canister ventilators topped with hinged dustbin-lid-type covers.

Decks above machinery spaces would be left open (but strengthened) after the launch to allow for the shipping hatches for boilers and turbines. To assist in the lifting of the upper casing of each turbine for inspection of the rotors, box girders at Main Deck level straddled the longitudinal bulkheads in way of the inner and outer Engine Rooms.

Eight large bow and stern castings, manufactured by the Darlington Forge Company, were brought to the yard by rail: the stern frame arrived as two castings (one of 48 tons, the other of 6); two after shaft brackets each of 23½ tons; two forward shaft brackets totalled 48 tons; a heel ('elephant's foot') casting (9 tons); and the three-part balanced rudder (to be bolted together), along with its stock and pintle, weighed 64 tons.

Inboard of the frames that flanked the Boiler and Engine Rooms, other substantial frames were fabricated from 12in channel bar for the lower two-thirds and 7in channel for the upper. Extending from the Tank Top to the Main Deck, these frames supported the inner longitudinal watertight bulkheads constructed from high-tensile silicon steel (HTS), the space between the bulkheads and ship's sides creating coal bunkers, the coal acting as protection against horizontal shell fire.

Typically, plating of less than ¾in was of carbon steel (mild steel); above that thickness HTS steel was used and where extra strength was required to overcome concentrated stresses and where weight had to be reduced high in the structure. HTS strengthened the 'corner' connection between the hull sides and the Main and Shelter Decks – the top edges of the 'ship-girder' – while the lower corners of the girder strength was provided by the cellular bottom. The upper strake of side plating immediately below the Shelter Deck amidships consisted of HTS plating laid over 12/20ths thick mild steel (shipbuilders worked in plate thicknesses in multiples of twentieths of an inch) which thinned as it extended downwards and fore and aft, the upper four strakes being 22/20ths, the lowest 20/20ths. The extent of the side high-tensile plating from amidships ranged from 130 to 92ft aft, and 230 to 129ft forward, reducing as the strakes descended.

Bottom and side plating was laid clinker (or clincher) fashion from the outer keel to the turn of the bilge and lapped from the turn of bilge upwards as the hull rose and angled slightly inwards, this inward slope known as 'tumblehome'. Shell plates and some deck plates were generally 5ft wide, 35ft long and 2½ to 3 tons in weight while others were a record 48ft in length, weighing 4 to 5 tons. As the ship did not have a well deck forward to dissipate heavy seas taken over the bow the Bridge front was heavily constructed from 1in plate.

Templates made from 4 by 3/8in wooden battens, made to size at the ship at a plate's position, with rivet locations in frames and in adjacent plates already in place, were taken to the Plate Shop where a plate was cut to size and rivet holes punched or drilled 1/32in greater than the rivet diameter. Diameters of rivets was generally determined by the thinner of the two plates being connected plus ¼in, but in the case of HTS doubling the thickness of the doubler warranted larger diameters of rivets being used, their material governed by the lower of the two qualities of steel being connected. Rivet holes in the HTS plates were drilled as punching embrittled the steel and created a burr around the holes' edges. Thicker plates were drilled and holes were slightly tapered to enable a tighter joint to be achieved as rivets cooled and contracted. Punching was used for mild-steel plates of less than ½in thick with the rims of the holes being de-burred to ensure a good faying (contact) surface. These pre-drilled plates, with lace-like perimeters, appearing as if they would tear as they were hoisted to the ship, were offered to the space that they would occupy. Bolts, spaced every few holes apart, temporarily but securely held the plate in position prior to riveting and, if any were slightly displaced ('drifted'), a drifting tool would be inserted and manipulated until the holes aligned or, if the drift was excessive, a reamer (a tapered, fluted 'drill') was used although its use was considered the result of poor preparation.

With each plate temporarily bolted into place the riveting teams set to work. Mild steel rivets were used throughout the hull (a suitable HTS rivet had not been developed), the arrangements and spacings of rivets having been specified by the ship's designers. Eight hydraulically operated riveting machines, suspended from travelling trolleys located beneath the roof of the construction hall or from guyed derricks extending from half-height of the building hall's framework, were used to rivet sections that had little or no curvature. The more complex hull sections that had a degree of curvature were riveted by the hard, noisome slog of two men wielding heavy, long-shafted hammers alternately striking the glowing rivet in quick succession.

Rivets were heated to a cherry-red malleability in specially designed oil-fired braziers attended by a Rivet – or Furnace – Boy who, using long tongs, picked a rivet out of the furnace and threw it to the riveting team where a Catcher caught the rivet in a bucket and fed the glowing steel into a rivet hole from the inside of the ship. The Catcher would then firmly press a 'dolly' (a lump of steel) against the internal head of the rivet while, outside, skilled Riveters would commence their work in a steady, practised, staccato cacophony that could be heard over much of Wallsend, as they hammered the point of the red-hot rivet into shape: points of countersunk rivets were hammered into a slightly raised, almost flat, head above the angled countersunk hole; domed or snap-headed rivets would be hammered into a dome against the flat surface of the plate – prominently visible along the Strength Deck. The rivets contracted as they cooled, pulling the two steels together in a tight bond, Rivet spacings varied depending on location: where watertightness was essential (i.e. in the lower deck areas) the rivets would be pitched five diameters apart, and six diameters pitch for non-watertight applications. Where an oil-tight seal would be required in any future conversion a pitch of four diameters was probably employed. A good team could fasten 800–900 rivets in a day.

Where two plates overlapped or butted (edge-to-edge) together with a strap behind the butt the faying part of the overlapping plate or butt strap had to be made completely watertight by caulking, a very noisy operation whereby the exposed edge was slightly split along its length using a pneumatically driven chisel. The 'inner' split edge was then driven against the surface of the adjacent plate. Again, Wallsend would have been audibly aware of this process … and all this before the advent of Health and Safety!

Above the Shelter Deck 'houses' were constructed, set back from the side of the ship, the space between ship's side and deckhouse being the basis of the Promenade Deck. The roofs of the houses on the Shelter Deck were also extended outwards to create the Boat Deck above. Plating for these houses was of necessarily lighter scantlings

and, as stressing would occur in the houses and decks that formed the superstructure due to the flexing of the hull in a heavy seaway, three transverse expansion joints were included to take up any longitudinal movement. These joints were sited: No. 1 just aft of No. 4 Boiler (Room) hatch, No. 2 just forward of No. 3 Boiler (Room) hatch, No. 3 just forward of No. 2 Boiler (Room) hatch.

To increase the width of the Promenade Deck and the Boat Deck above it, an additional 20in was added to overhang the hull but not beyond the width of the tumblehome (inward slope of the ship's side). The *Lusitania* did not have this widening feature.

Bilge keels, intended to reduce the ship's double roll to twenty seconds, were placed along the turn of hull, 226ft long and 3ft deep, constructed in a V-shape from ½in steel and packed with wood.

Watertight bulkheads of stiffened HTS divided the vessel into watertight compartments. There were twelve complete transverse bulkheads; two longitudinal bulkheads in Engine and Boiler spaces; and five partial bulkheads on each side of Boiler and Engine Rooms. The majority extended up to the Main Deck, the remainder only up as far as the Orlop Decks fore and aft. Those bulkheads in way of the Boiler Rooms forward (including the collision bulkhead) and aft of the Engine Room extended up to the Upper Deck and, in satisfying the Admiralty's specifications, exceeded the 1891 Bulkhead Committee's recommendations. With decks dividing the ship horizontally, *The Scotsman* reassuringly announced that: 'The total number of separate watertight divisions in the *Mauretania* is 175, rendering the ship practically unsinkable'. Five years later when the *Olympic* and *Titanic* were being built the press would omit the qualifying adjective 'practically'.

To assist in the eventual shipping of boilers, turbines and other heavy machinery, once the ship was afloat, SH&WR took delivery of a powerful new floating crane. Aptly named *Titan*, it had been built at a cost of £22,500 by the *Duisburger-Maschinenbau-Actien-Gessellschaft* of Duisburg in Germany. Capable of lifting 140 tons (exceeding any other lift on the north-east coast) the jib had a maximum outreach of 44ft. Self-propelled (6 knots; four steam engines; two rudders), the crane was fitted with two sliding platforms to carry the machinery to be fitted.

The driving force of the ship. In the days before propellers were cast in one piece, each screw was made up of blades bolted onto a steel hub (shown here). (Author's Collection)

The *Mauretania* was fully plated by 7 September 1906 and, by the time she was ready for launching, both ship and wooden supporting poppets fore and aft together weighed 16,800 tons. A total of 7,620sq.ft of bearing surface put a pressure on the launching ways of 2.2 tons per square foot. To ease the movement of the hull during the launch 17,150sq.ft of the ground and sliding ways was greased with 290½cwt (20 hundredweight [cwt] = 1 ton) of tallow, 12½cwt of train oil and 22cwt of soft soap.

Launching – and Called to Account

The day of 20 September 1906 was a gala day on Tyneside. The launching of the world's biggest liner was to be celebrated with a naming by Lady Anne Emily Innes-Ker, Dowager Duchess of Roxburghe (widow of the 7th Duke), and a former Mistress of the Robes to Queen Victoria. The Dowager also happened to be the sister-in-law of Lord Tweedmouth, the First Lord of the Admiralty, and aunt to Winston Churchill, then Member of Parliament for Manchester North West. It had originally been hoped that the ship would have been launched by Queen Alexandra accompanied by the King during a summer royal visit to the area, but the ship was not finished in time.

After a pre-launch reception in a pavilion, a party of ladies and gentlemen from the official party, each of whom bore a large ivory-coloured and beautifully embossed gilt-edged invitation card, was driven to the Wallsend Engineering Company's premises where inspections were made of the liner's machinery and other equipment. A photographer was on hand to record the intrepid adventurers – including the Duchess of Roxburghe, the ladies in their large, expensive picture hats and the men in their starched collars – as their motorcade, watched by other worthies in their Sunday best lining the motorcade's route, drove through a novelty tunnel created by the ship's funnels laid end-to-end and large enough in diameter 'to allow two locomotives … to pass each other inside' – large whitewashed arrows painted on a temporary wooden highway indicating the route. The motorcade then drove through workshops where turbines, boilers and massive multi-bladed rotors had been arranged on parade for a hurried

(and probably disinterested) inspection. At the end of the grand tour the chauffeurs drove their charges back to the shipyard where a band was playing cheerful airs, including an especially composed piece 'The *Mauretania* March' by Hebburn composer Robert Saint.

The shores supporting the hull were meanwhile being knocked away by gangs of Shipwrights (*THE* Shipbuilders), lowering the hull onto the slipway and leaving the ship restrained by eight iron triggers ready to be released from the launching platform. The River Tyne had been dredged and the cross-Tyne ferry landing stages on both banks had been dismantled to avoid risk of collision. The ship, painted grey for the great day (this would show her to best advantage for the photographers) lay in readiness with her stern pointing proudly out of the building shed and her four huge three-bladed propellers painted white. She presented a spectacular sight.

On returning to the building berth the guests strode towards the launching platform before the Dowager Duchess was decorously escorted up the approach ramp by a top-hatted and very proud George Hunter. Mr Wigham Richardson was already on the large stand constructed at the stem of the vessel that towered above. Thousands of invitations had been issued for entry to the shipyard for its workers and their families; neighbouring shipyards, such as R. & W. Hawthorn and Leslie & Co. Ltd, had also issued tickets to view the launch from their own premises.

Awaiting the Duchess on the VIP platform were the Duchess's sister-in-law, Lady Evelyn Innes-Ker; Mr Francis and Lady Anne Bowes-Lyon; the First Lord of the Admiralty (Lord Tweedmouth); William Watson, Chairman of Cunard; the company's Vice-chairman, William Forwood; Secretary and directors A.D. Mearns, Alfred Booth and Ernest Cunard. The company's technical and seagoing departments representatives included A.P. Moorhouse (General Manager); Mr Thompson (Superintending Engineer); James Bain (General Superintendent); and Leonard Peskett (Chief Naval Architect). Lord Inverclyde's widow, Mary, represented her late husband's deep commitment, while Charles Parsons must have been deeply gratified to see before him the heights that his turbine engine had achieved in the few short years since its invention. Other shipbuilders and owners rubbed shoulders with representatives of the Church, Government and the Admiralty.

Mid September 1906, nearing the day of launching. The ways were extended into the river to allow a safe passage for the ship during the most dangerous journey that she would make and would be covered by a high tide on the day of the launching. Mounted on the after deck is a temporary boiler needed to supply steam during the launch and fitting-out. (Collection of Eric Longo)

In the build-up to the excitement *The Scotsman* had commented:

> The launch of the Cunard liner Mauretania … marks an epoch in the development of the steamship. It is no exaggeration to say that the construction of the Mauretania, and the sister steamer the Lusitania, represents by far the most stupendous task ever entrusted to shipbuilders … the largest, fastest, and most luxuriously appointed steamships afloat … In the architectural treatment of the public rooms and cabins the owners and builders have aimed at surpassing everything at present attempted in the way of ship decoration and comfort …

On the north and south banks of the Tyne and on quays to the east and west of the building slip thousands of people had gathered. On the Durham side's Ballast Hill (an artificial hill made from colliers' discharged ballast) Novocastrians and visitors occupied every vacant space so that the mound – 'black with spectators … seemed to be built of humanity' – looked like a human pyramid. In spite of an overcast sky and an occasional shower the river, too, was busy with craft of all kinds and kept clear of the slipway for safety, their decks laden with sightseers. The *Newcastle Daily Chronicle* noted that the Shields ferry was 'laden like a Norwegian timber boat with a good paying deck cargo … passengers seemed to be hanging onto her funnel and to the sides of the wheelhouse'.

Launchings from other British shipyards competed for the headlines that day, including the 729ft *Adriatic* built to the order of the White Star Line and launched, as usual for that company, without formal ceremony from Harland and Wolff's Belfast yard. When she entered the water, the *Adriatic* took the accolade of being for five short hours – after the *Lusitania* – the second largest ship in the world. Edwardian confidence in its engineering was at its zenith. *Adriatic's* first captain – White Star's Senior Captain and Commodore of the Line, E.J. Smith (later to take the even larger *Olympic* and then *Titanic* on their maiden voyages) – confidently said on her maiden arrival in New York: 'I cannot imagine any condition which would cause a ship to founder. I cannot conceive of any vital disaster happening to this vessel. Modern shipbuilding has gone beyond that.' Also taking to the water that day was the cruiser, HMS *Shannon*, launched by Countess Carrington from Number 7 Slip in Chatham Dockyard.

Inspired by the imminent launch, 'Professor' William Browning, perhaps playing on the antecedence of his literary surname but certainly affected by the majesty of the new ship, bullishly penned a piece of doggerel, seemingly knowing even less about poetry than he did about ships:

MAURETANIA

You talk about a Liner,
An ocean wave deviner,
   The smartest ever launched upon the Tyne.
The pink of all perfection,
Demanding glad reflection
   Of all who have to track across the brine.

Built by the British Nation,
The lickers of Creation;
   Northumbranites and Durhamites, ye ken,
The Sage who drew and planned her,
And the men who launched and manned her,
   Have the praise of poet, press and pen.

To tell about her cables,
Would seem like Aesop's fables,
   And her anchors are all up-to date-and fashion.
They would hold her in a twister,
When the gale is blizzard blister,
   And the storm king mad with anger, rage and passion.

See her engines all in motion,
As she leaps across the ocean,
   And her engineers and greasers in her glory,
And her four huge brass propellers,
Graphic fortune tellers,
   Which night and day, shall tell a running story.

Her boilers in their wonder,
Can make a noise like thunder,

When they blow off steam and set the whistles roaring.
Whilst her trimmers and her stokers,
Are no half-hearted jokers,
   Indeed, they are the boys to set her boring.

Her grand saloon and splendour,
And ladies sweet and tender,
   And millionaires who love to spend their gold,
And her crew of sturdy tars, Neptune's sons and Mars
   Protecting her and all that's in her hold.

The captain's tact and art, shall help him play his part,
   Whilst every voyage shall have its pleasing tale,
This liner's got to go, let tide be ebb or flow,
   Or, in the calm, or through the heavy gale.

Be proud you smart Wallsenders, to be sea king defenders,
   Your fame shall fly around the mighty world,
Set all the bells a ringing, and lads and lassies singing,
   Let flags of every nation be unfurled.

And let us repeat, that the lady brave and sweet,
   Who calls her 'Mauretania' ahoy,
Shall be right glad at heart, to play a noble part,
   To break the bottle with the wine of joy.

Arue! Hurray! Hurrah! To see her slide away,
   And set the Tyne a welling, swelling, foaming,
And to listen to the cheers, of sturdy men and dears,
   Who wish her God's good luck in all her roaming.

At 4.15 p.m. in a warm, light north-easterly wind that ruffled the feathers, flowers and veils of the ladies' large picture hats, the ship was named in a necessarily brief speech so as not to miss the fullness of the 7ft 7in tide. The Duchess then pulled a trigger that released a bottle of Champagne to break against the towering bow. As the retaining triggers were released simultaneously the great hull slowly began to move:

And see! She stirs!
She starts, – she moves – she seems to feel
The thrill of life along her keel!

(H.W. Longfellow)

With gathering momentum, and to the accompaniment of a 'great and sustained cheering' the *Mauretania* slid gracefully down the ways. Proudly watching her was the team of Shipwrights under their Foreman in charge of launching arrangements, Andrew Gray, who had prepared the liner for this very moment.

Once the ship was moving (she reached a speed of 14 knots as she entered her element) her acceleration had to be checked until she came to a standstill at a calculated point in the river by employing six bundles of drag chains (five large bundles of 81 tons and one larger bundle comprising five smaller 20.4-ton bundles placed forward) on each side of the hull, each attached by a cable to an eye-plate connected to the hull along the waterline under the fo'c'sle and Bridge areas. As each bundle was jerked into action the sudden strain imposed on the cable was relieved by restraints progressively breaking. When the hull still had 33ft of her length on the ways the aftermost bundle was the first to be shocked into action, clanking and rumbling its way down the slip in a low cloud of rust dust and grease vapour. The last bundle jerked into action when the bow was 87ft out into the river, adding resistance to the accelerating hull until braking it into stillness precisely at its appointed resting place.

As she left the ways that extended 30ft into the 45ft-deep river, the liner gave a graceful curtsey as her bow dropped from the end of the ways. Baulks of timber, disengaging from the fore poppet, careered about her bow, shooting to the surface with their new-found buoyancy.

To increase the safe width for movement the ship entered the river diagonally, the distance from the quay line at Wallsend to the opposite quay wall at Hebburn being 1,130ft. An anchor, attached by cable to the liner's port side, had previously been buried in the mud over 300ft to the west of the shipyard, intended to slew her stern around should the need arise; it was dragged 120ft into the river during the launch

Prior to the launching, official guests were taken on a motorcade tour of the shipyard and engine works. Here the motorcade has reached the turbine shop where the mighty engines were lined up on parade for inspection. The ship's sponsor, the Duchess of Roxburghe, is in the first car nearest to the camera, which has created more interest than the revolutionary machinery! (*The Shipbuilder*, Estate of Captain Pritchard/Author's collection)

and a second restraining anchor, attached by a cable to the Bridge front, was dropped at a designated point. Her first, perilous journey had taken many months of complex and minute calculation that left nothing to chance but took a mere seventy seconds to achieve. Restrained by the now-still drag chains, the hull came to a halt after travelling 951ft, her bow coming to rest 93ft from the edge of the ways, her stern 222ft from the Hebburn quay.

As the ship was carefully ushered to her fitting-out berth, a post-launch luncheon for the principal guests was held in the yard's Mould Loft. Sir William White, proposing the toast of 'The *Mauretania* of the Cunard Company', gave a brief summary of the problems that had been overcome. William Watson responded on behalf of the company and paid fulsome tribute to his late predecessor's great vision and achievement.

Lord Tweedmouth, First Lord of the Admiralty since 1905, then spoke on behalf of the Admiralty and of his sister-in-law, who had just launched the great ship. Regarding the vessel's possible use in time of conflict, he hoped that the Admiralty, in spite of its involvement, might only be 'sleeping partners' and trusted that the magnificent ship and her sister might be spared from 'ever having ... to serve the King in war', adding, amidst general approbation, that they 'added a great strength to this great nation.' ('Hear, hear!')

With the ship safely afloat a breakdown of the weights of the ship showed that her hull of 19,898 tons and her yet-to-be-installed machinery totalled 29,300 tons. Other tonnage measurements were 25,138 under (Shelter) deck; gross 31,938 (this was based on 100cu.ft to the ton measured in designated areas such as revenue-earning spaces); and a net tonnage of 8,986. In calculating the ship's displacement it was estimated that the 567 First-, 464 Second- and 1,138 Third-Class fare-paying passengers would weigh in at 1,000 tons. With Tons per Inch (TPI – a figure calculated to submerge the hull by one inch) of 111.4 tons, a full load of passengers would increase the ship's draught by 9in! Conversely, a full load of coal would increase the draught by 55in.

A proud George Hunter escorts the ship's sponsor, the Duchess of Roxburgh, up to the specially built launch platform. (Author's Collection)

On return to the slipway the official guests trudge their way to the launch platform as the band plays jaunty tunes, the ship towering above. (Photo by permission of Richard Smye)

Official guests wait expectantly for the moment of launching. (Author's Collection)

Above left: Workmen and visitors watch as the ship's increasing momentum is checked as the first cable holding a bundle of drag chains tautens, creating a cloud of rust dust from the now moving clattering bundle. Note the film crew on the raised platform to the right. (Author's Collection)

Above right: With the *Mauretania* finally afloat, great baulks of timber that had held her securely break away and broach the surface in a powerful display of force and foam. (Estate of Captain Pritchard/ Author's collection)

Left: The liner is soon surrounded by craft carrying jubilant sightseers. (Collection of Charles A. Haas)

Mauretania's hull had been constructed using 12,066 tons of steel plate, and labour charges to erect this cost £6 9s 4d (six pounds, nine shillings and four pence, or £6.47p) per ton totalling £78,021. The 4,239 tons of steel-bar sections used for frames, beams, stiffening, etc. at £6 0s 1d per ton cost another £25,450 in labour. Four million rivets at £2,907 were hammered home to hold the whole structure together and the two types used weighed a total of 1,044 tons (31 tons and 1,013 tons costing £244 and £7,699 respectively). Labour for erecting this material cost £128,798, which represented £7 5s 3d per ton. One hundred and seven tons of iron plate (£707) had also been used. Packing and mouldings accounted for 288 tons, and 1,163 tons of off-cut steel went for scrap, earning a rebate of £2,907, while 1,439 tons of other items of material cost £5,647.

The final cost to Cunard was £1,827,666, well in excess of the contracted price of £1,301,000. The *Lusitania* had cost £1,625,463 (after rebates) with engines being built in-house, and her builders kept their overheads down as they also owned the steel mills that produced the plate. Wages on the Clyde were also lower than those on the Tyne by 11 per cent, the latter having received a pay rise. With a fifty-three-hour working week on the Tyne (an hour less than on the Clyde), the *Mauretania* had taken an estimated 13 million man-hours to build. The *Lusitania* had taken 5 per cent more!

SH&WR's Directors' Note Book discreetly recorded the yard's costs:

Iron and Steel	£239,771
General Work	£605,569
Electric Light	£30,861
Winches, etc.	£5,897
Charges★	£110,638
Hull	£992,736
plus:	
Machinery	£834,930
Total Net Cost	£1,827,666

★ 'Charges' were Establishment Charges ('overheads' in modern parlance) that covered expenses incurred in, but not directly associated with, the build of the ship, e.g. maintenance, cleaning, clerical staff, Drawing Office staff, yard and depreciation, etc. A complex system of payments was paid by Cunard to SH&WR at landmark stages of the ship's build, the last of these being made on 27 May 1907.

Moored at her fitting-out berth, the *Mauretania* ships one of her boilers brought to the berth on the deck of *Titan*, the floating crane. (Tyne and Wear Archives L4673)

With two-and-a-half funnels in place, a large fitting is lowered into the ship by the floating crane, *Titan*. (A. Clark)

A month after the euphoria of the launch, George Hunter was called before the Cunard Board to explain the cost of the ship, the most expensive to have been built to date, in what must have been an uncomfortable interview. William Watson later wrote to GBH in frank terms:

On the facts and figures now before us, we are forced to the conclusion that either

1. If the expenditure can be justified, your original estimate was grossly underestimated to induce us to build the ship, or

2. If your original estimate was a fair and reasonable one, your expenditure since you secured the contract has been utterly reckless.

The result to us is the same in either case. You must clearly understand that a ship costing upwards of £1,700,000 is not the ship we ordered, and is not the ship you contracted to build, and that we will pay no such sum …

Indeed the vessel was not the ship originally contracted for as Hunter's estimate was based on the *original* specifications (excluding interior decor). Exasperated, he replied two days later, a week before Christmas:

While we deeply regret any disappointment you feel at the cost of this Steamship, we have received your letter of the 15th inst with surprise.

We think you are aware that any estimates we make are always made in good faith, and to the best of our ability, on the particulars we have before us.

There has been no reckless expenditure on our part, and you are aware the cost of building the Steamship has been and is being incurred under the control and supervision of your Board and of your technical Staff and we are not responsible for it. If the control and responsibility had been left in our hands the cost would have been greatly reduced and we believe would have been approximately in accordance with the first estimates.

We note your desire to reduce the expenditure on the Vessel and we shall be glad to carry out any instructions we receive from you in any way that is possible and consistent with the obligations imposed upon us by the contract. The Ship is being built under your directions. Please give us your definite instructions as to what reductions in cost if any we

are able to make. We have made some suggestions to Mr. Bain today and hope to write further on this question tomorrow.

Cunard could not accept the 12 per cent difference in the price of the two ships but, although they eventually realised that the increases in costs were down to changes in specification that were being supervised by their own representatives, they still decided to demand a rebate.

Eighteen months later, after reviewing all building costs their solicitors, Hill Dickinson, concluded that SH&WR should rebate the difference between their ship and that of John Brown's:

If these figures can be substantiated then in our opinion, it follows that Messrs. Swan & Hunter have not used reasonable care to prevent unnecessary cost, and further that they have incurred more cost than was reasonably necessary for the carrying out of the general work, and that they should be held liable to you in damages for this sum of £203,000.

That massive claim was whittled down through lengthy negotiations between the two principals until £1,812,252 was agreed on as a price for the *Mauretania*. By the time that all these negotiations were concluded Cunard realised that they had two very fine and superbly crafted ships of which they − and the nation − could justly be proud and that these two new tools of their trade would bring honour to those who ran them and social prestige to those who sailed in them.

George Hunter must have been doubly pleased: his bill been paid and his yard was well and truly now in the top league of British shipbuilders.

Tours and Tunnels

The Tyne!
The Tyne!
The coaly Tyne!
It's mighty mucky
But it's mighty fine!
…The Queen of all the rivers.
(Traditional)

The machinery that had been inspected during the pre-launch motorcade on 20 September was impressive: twenty-three 100-ton double-ended boilers (22ft in length x 17ft 3in in diameter); two single-ended boilers of the same diameter but 11ft 4½in in length, the boilers having four furnaces on each end with a total fire grate area of 4,060sq.ft, and 159,000sq.ft of heating surface (working pressure 195psi); two high-pressure, two low-pressure and two astern turbines (turbines with a reversing capability had not yet been developed) made up the Engine Room.

These turbines (details of which were not released at the time) were masterpieces of heavy industrial and precision engineering, a tribute to the energies and determination of Andrew Laing. In the high-pressure (HP) ahead turbine the thousands of blades measured, depending at which 'stage' they were sited, from 12in to 30in in length and were mounted on a hollow shaft (the rotor) 3ft in diameter. The casing measuring 45ft 8in in length and the whole assembly weighed 72 tons. The series (stages) of blades for the low-pressure (LP) turbines, also driving ahead, had shafts 4ft 4in in diameter that carried blades ranging from 8 to 22in in length, the drums being 11ft 8in in diameter, 48ft 2in in length and each weighing 126 tons. The astern turbines were 30ft 1¼in in length.

The *Mauretania*'s bunker capacity allowed for 6,075 tons of the all-important best Welsh steaming coal at 45cu.ft per ton (coal of a lesser calorific value would have taken up more space). The holds had capacity for 98,340cu.ft of cargo.

The fitting-out of the liner was undertaken while the ship was moored against two brickwork dolphins placed a few yards away from the wharf. Workmen accessed the ship via wide gangways that rose and fell with the tides.

Again, the reader's attention is drawn to the reprints of contemporary publications for a detailed account of the liner's decor, but one of the least-accounted tasks amongst the thousands to be undertaken was the laying of decking and flooring, both of which provided noise and thermal insulation as well as covering up the underlying steel plating.

Beautiful Yellow Pine lined the decks in many passenger areas. Acid-free to prevent corrosion, the wood was light yellow when freshly cut and although becoming brownish with age, regular washing and scrubbing would keep it looking fresh. Clean, straight-grained and free from knots,

The First-Class Dining Saloon extended through two decks. (Author's Collection)

A rare view of a corridor in First Class. (SH&WR photo)

it did not warp or twist during seasoning and was easily worked. Once laid and caulked, this lovely wood presented a most pleasing appearance. Where it was used it was generally 4in wide with thicknesses varying from 2 to 3in (up forward the deck around the anchor and warping gear deck planking was increased to 6in thick because of the extra wear in that area). The deck was lined out so that planks ran fore-and-aft in straight lines and parallel to the ship's centre line. Bordering the Promenade (320ft long and 16ft wide) and Boat Decks, a 6in margin of water-resistant teak gave a very smart finish and where curved boundaries occurred skilfully notched margins took the ends of the straight planks. Hard-wearing teak was also laid under capstans, etc.

A glance at the underside of an unlined deck would indicate how deck planking had been secured as evenly spaced nuts lined the horizontal beam flanges, the deck having been drilled with 5/8in-diameter holes spaced a plank width apart. As each plank was temporarily laid it was drilled upwards from the deck head below with a hole of the same diameter. A counter-bored hole of a larger diameter to suit the head of the fixing bolt was then drilled downwards into the plank to a depth sufficient to take the head of the securing bolt, its grommet (a washer of, perhaps, leather) and closing (sealing) dowel.

The steel deck and underside of each plank were liberally coated with white lead paint before the planks were laid. Galvanised 5/8in, square-necked (to avoid turning) bolts were then gently hammered downwards into the hole with a grommet (felt washer) under its head until the bolt was firmly in place. Another grommet was placed on the shaft from under the deck head and secured by a galvanised nut, the projecting bolt shaft being neatly trimmed off – a labour-intensive operation in the quest to achieve perfection. Once bolted down, the remaining hole in the plank was filled with a round wood dowel driven in with its grain in line with that of the planking to prevent the ingress of water and trimmed to deck level.

Prior to laying, the edges of each planking were slightly bevelled and once in position with its neighbour the resultant V groove was caulked with one thread of cotton and three threads of oakum (old Stockholm-tarred rope that had been teased out), the filling being tightly packed by Shipwrights wielding an elegant caulking mallet and one of several types of caulking iron that bore such names as a 'beetle' or 'horse iron'. Once the filling was tightly packed the remaining depression was filled with hot pitch, allowed to cool and harden, and then raked out and the process repeated. Butting ends of planks were also caulked with butts being placed to keep at least five or six planks between each butt. Nearer to the ship's completion the entire deck was planed to a smooth surface and kept in pristine condition by regular hosing and scrubbing (see Captain Pritchard's remarks in Chapter 1!).

Inside the Second-Class house aft 5/16in-thick corticene flooring (a buff-coloured linoleum made from a mix of powdered cork and linseed oil with a canvas backing) was laid in cabins and alleyways after plate edges had been levelled with bitumen; sound-proofing rubber tiling floored the Second-Class entrance. Other floorings were specified, some of which are selected below. The simplified descriptions of the locations in which they were used also give a quick tour of the ship:

Tiling – Vitreous tiling by the Porcelain Tile Co. of Manley in 4¼ x 3" octagons with 1" black (and blue) dots in the following 3rd C [Class] places:-

Shelter Deck:- Mens, womens lavatories, hospitals, baths &c [etc], Service closets, petty officers, Seamens & Stewards lavatories.

Upper Deck:- mens & womens lavatories, service closets, stewards & cooks bathroom & hospital bathroom.

Main Deck:- Service closets, greasers & trimmers lavatories &c & all service closets on Boat, Promenade & Lower decks.

Total quantity laid:- 440 [square] yds [yards]. The above firm also supplied & fixed about 800 of white enamelled channelling in lavatories &c.

Vitreous tiling by Doulton & Co. Ld in the following first class places:- B&W [black and white] in Officers & Engineers Bathrooms &c, 2nd C Ladies & Gents baths & lavatories on Upper & Main Decks (240 [square] yds).

Mosaic by Doulton in 2nd C Smokeroom Lavatory on Promenade Dk, Childrens WC & bath, ladies & gents baths & lavatories on Shelter dk (70 yds). Gutter channelling for above places by Porcelain Tile Co. ...

... Indiarubber Tiling – by Silvertown Co. ['India Rubber, Gutta Percha and Telegraph Works Co. Ltd., of Silvertown'] laid in 1st Class Main Entrances on Boat, Promenade, Shelter, Upper & Main Decks & consists of 18" white octagons with 3" black square & black & white strips for border. All 3/8" thick. Area 670 [square] yds. Also 18" white octagon & 3" black square in 2nd C Main Entrances on P, S, U & M Decks, lavatories & WCs at aft end of Prom'de dk & corridors at fore end of library on Boat Deck. 8" white octagon & 2" black squares on ½ landings of 2nd C Stairways & vestibules to Smoke room on Boat Deck. Similar tiling to above but pneumatic in vestibule between smoke room & lounge on Boat deck. Area 5634 [square] yds.

Green & white tiling in 1st C Lavatories, baths &c on B.P.U. & Main decks also in Captain's bath room. Area 331 [square] yds.

Parquetry – The whole of the floor of the 1st C Dining Saloon on Upper Deck, & Smoke Room on Boat deck laid with 1" thick parquetry on wood deck & the 2nd C Saloon (dining) on Upper deck laid with 7/8" parquetry on wood deck. Area 1" [thick] – 8080 [square feet]. 7/8" [thick] – 3600 [square feet] ...

For the *Lusitania*'s interiors (presumably her sister would be similar) Cunard stipulated:

Everything in connection with the designing and decorating of the First Class accommodation is to be of the best character, workmanship and material, but the Directors do not desire anything of an extravagant nature. The simpler the work, so long as it is good, the better, and the more the cost can be kept down, the more satisfactory it will be to the Cunard Company, provided the general effect is tasteful and pleasing.

The contract for the interior decoration in First Class was awarded to Harold Peto of Bradford-on-Avon. A son of Sir Samuel Morton Peto (whose portfolio included Nelson's Column and the Houses of Parliament) the younger Peto was an architect who loved the Italian Renaissance, and the Arts and Crafts movement. His proposals, submitted on 13 April 1905, were accepted on 21 September, his fee being 5 per cent of the cost of the work with all associated work being approved by him. The final bill for the interior decoration (including sub-contractors' work) came to £132,072. First Class occupied five decks (Main, Upper, Shelter, Promenade and Boat Decks) with access between each being via the Grand and other staircases or by the lifts that ran from the Main to Boat Decks. Panelled in finely figured French Walnut the lifts' grilles were of an unusual material, aluminium, and given the form of finely wrought iron. Floors to the entrances to each deck were laid with India rubber while a 'delightful shade' of green carpet adorned the stairs.

A special edition of *The Shipbuilder* admirably described the interiors of a few of the First-Class areas:

Dining Saloons – First in importance in regard to size are the two first-class dining saloons – the upper and the lower – situated on the upper and shelter decks. Between the two rooms is a large open space surmounted by a dome, the whole producing a lofty and airy effect. The dining rooms are panelled in straw-coloured [weathered] oak, in the style of Francis I [Mellier and Company of London were sub-contractors]. One of the charms of this style is that no piece of carving is an exact reproduction of its neighbour [adding to the cost of the ship] … Some of the most delicate work is shown upon the arched bulkheads which run at right angles to the sides of the ship. All the carving in these rooms has been cut back from the face of the solid wood [expensive!] … The aim of the designer [Peto] has been to keep the larger and lower room richer in carving, leading up to a simpler treatment of the upper dining saloon, and terminating with the crowning feature of the dome … a groined one, in cream and gold … small circles [plaques] … introducing the signs of the Zodiac.

The rooms are upholstered in deep pink, and a fine sixteenth century tapestry at one end of the lower apartment gives an admirable effect … floor of lower … parquetry … carpet… in pleasing tone of cerise red. Small tables … accommodate from 5 to 14 passengers … upper saloon … 2 to 6 persons can be seated at each table. … lower room … 87 feet long, extends the full width of the ship … 328 passengers. The upper … is 62 feet long by 66 feet wide, and seats 152 persons. The height from the floor of the lower dining saloon to the top of the dome is about 28 feet.

Lounge and Music Room [First Class] … is situated on the boat deck … 80 ft. long, 56 ft. wide, and 11 ft. 9 in. high. … It is difficult at first to realise that one is afloat when in this beautifully shaped room, with its rows of stately columns and its graceful semi-circular bays … Panelling, columns and pilasters are of [scarce South African – and soon to be extinct] mahogany … panels cross-veneered … dull polished a rich golden brown … mouldings and all … carvings … fully gilt.

Sixteen pilasters of Fleur de Pêche marble with ormolu capitols and bases, a chimney-piece of the same materials, soft creamy curtains with coloured borders, and three fine panels of French [Aubusson] tapestry … Oval dome [said to have cost £17,000] of wrought iron [glazed with ground glass] with gilt ornaments, and the plainly panelled white ceiling from which are suspended crystal electroliers, complete a room unequalled in any steamship …

The carpet and furniture … of the same cream tone as the curtains with a trellis-work of laurel and roses, recalling … the colours of the tapestry … chairs and sofas, of polished beech covered in various coloured brocades …

Library and Writing Room – [work again undertaken by Mellier & Co.] … a somewhat smaller room than the lounge, is situated on the same deck and is decorated in the same style [Louis XVI], although the colour scheme is entirely different. The room will probably be regarded by many passengers as the most beautiful in colour in the ship … The wall panelling is of sycamore stained a silver grey. The veneering has been so selected as to bring out the fine grain … the carved mouldings are gilt, but the gold used has a slightly greenish tint to harmonise with the panelling … A bookcase forms the panelling of one side of the central portion of the room, the delicate carving and gilt trellis of the doors greatly enhancing the appearance of the wall. On the opposite side … is a carved chimney-piece of white statuary marble, surmounted by a mirror similar in design to the central doors of the bookcase, which it faces and reflects.

The carpets and curtains are of deep rose colour, the latter relieved by borders of coloured brocade. This colour also predominates in the covering of the seats [the latter framed in] mahogany … with large tapestry panels flanked by duplicate pillars of grained marble.

The Nursery on the Shelter Deck was 21ft x 30ft and could seat thirty-six children (plus one on the large rocking horse). Sub-contracted to Robson & Sons of Newcastle upon Tyne, the room was panelled in white enamelled mahogany and hung with Edgar Mitchell's painted panels illustrating the nursery rhyme 'Four-and-Twenty Blackbirds'.

For the gentlemen's after-dinner retreat the ubiquitous Smoking Room – 52ft long, 50ft wide and 11ft 9in high to its wagon-headed ceiling – was panelled in richly carved quartered French Walnut with an inlaid border of sycamore. Recesses were furnished with divans and card tables, but two recesses at one end contained writing tables. A beautifully carved chimneypiece with a curved hood was sited at the fore end; described as one of many 'notable achievements of British craftsmanship'. Carved out of solid walnut, its frieze above was modelled on a fine example by Della Robbia held in South Kensington Museum. On its hearth lay a striking basket grate and handsome fire-dogs – too heavy for one man to lift – based on those in the Palazzo Varesi. Semicircular paintings depicting 'Old New York' and 'Old Liverpool' adorned the frieze of vellum-coloured plasterwork at each end of the room.

The following descriptions come from the few pages of the hand-printed Specification that were available at the time of writing and demonstrate the differences in the accommodations of the three classes (the reader is again referred to reprints of contemporary technical journals). The *Mauretania* was adorned with beautifully polished woods, many of which had been well seasoned; the corresponding areas of the *Lusitania* were white enamelled with gold highlights. It was calculated that the two sisters offered 50 per cent more light and promenade deck space per passenger than any other liner afloat.

The *Mauretania*'s accommodation included:

1st Class Accommodation – 54 of the best rooms panelled & decorated by TL&Co. [Turner, Lord & Co], 4 'Sheraton', 4 'Adams' & 6 'white' rooms by Robson of N.C [of Newcastle upon Tyne]. All supplied with Wilton Carpets, panelled ceilings &c. Remaining 1st C Rooms by S.H&W.R. in best style. Corridors polished mahogany on Promenade Deck, remainder painted with white 'Satinette' enamel –

Total No. of Passengers	1st Class	567 in 253 rooms
	2nd Class.	464 in 266 rooms
	3rd Class	1138 in 278 rooms
		2169 in 797 rooms.
	Crew & c.	849
	Total	3018

Sixty-two other rooms were created by constructing 'skeleton' frames of the spaces which were then shipped to Edinburgh upholsterers, Morison and Company. The rooms' ceilings, panelling and furniture were made to the templates, dismantled and returned to the shipyard for re-erection on board. The more luxurious rooms created were:

… Regal & En-Suite rooms (1st Class) – on Promenade & Boat Decks – by Turner, Lord & Co. – consisting of 2 regal suites on Promenade Dk containing Dining, Drawing & 2 bedrooms each with bath &c, & 12 en-suites containing parlour & bedrooms & baths &c. Upholstered in various coloured silks with silk panelling. Regal suite dining room seats 6 [people], & parlour has 3 easy chairs & table.

Verandah Café – On After end of Boat Deck aft of Smoke room & connected thereto by vestibule. Lined out in teak & supplied with teak tables & chairs (rustic design) by J.P. White of Bedford. Lattice work seats all round, & 12 tables with 30 chairs, square topped, ventilating skylight over. After end completely open to weather. Room 21' x 50' …

Second Class was well catered for but with a lesser opulence:

Dining Saloon (2nd Class) – 61 foot long x full width of Ship on Upper deck aft of main galley & pantries. In light oak Georgian style with carved cornice. Floor 7/8 [inch] oak parquetry with Brussels Carpet runners of bottle green colour & similar coloured frieze Velvet on upholstered chairs.

19 [?] oak-topped tables to seat 250. Piano in light oak by Broadwood at fore end. Side board at aft end.

Drawing Room (2nd Class) – 30' x 40' – on Promen'de deck aft in maple & gold Louis XVIth period. Dome over centre – Piano by Broadwood at aft end. Sofas & chairs upholstered in Crimson frieze velvet & Crimson Brussels carpet on wood deck. 10 occasional tables, 2 double x 2 single writing tables, 2 book cases & 16 small & 4 arm chairs.

Smoke Room (2nd Class) – 51' 6" x 40' – on Promenade Deck aft in late Georgian Style. Mahogany panels & seats inlaid with Box wood & Burr mahogany. Upholstered in dark blue velvet pile moquette. Linoleum on floor over wood deck & dark blue carpet runners, Dome over centre as in Drawing room. 21 occasional tables, 4 double writing tables, 50 chairs. Vestibule, lavatory & bar at after end.

Lounge (2nd Class) – 44' x 42' – on Boat deck aft & forms house round Entrance (2nd C). Panelled in mahogany & upholstered in dark blue moquette & blue carpet-runners on wood deck. 17 occasional tables, & 14 chairs. Buffet at After end.

A new feature for Second Class was a large deck. For those travelling in the more populous Third Class the conditions were simpler but still, with electric lighting and regular meals, perhaps more comfortable than the homes left behind:

Dining Saloon (3rd Class) – 84' long x full width of ship on Upper deck forward. 23 tables & 314 revolving birch chairs. Room panelled with polished ash & teak mouldings. Sliding shutters to sidelights. Floor covered with 5/16 [inch] corticene. Piano by Broadwood at end.

Smoke Room (3rd Class) – on port side of Shelter dk to seat 80 people at 6 tables – (74 revolving chairs).

The safety of the ship depended on thirty-nine electrically operated watertight doors manufactured by Stone and Co. Fitted on the Stone-Lloyd system, they included eight bunker doors fitted in No. 2 Boiler Room and two in the fore end of No. 1 Boiler Room. All, fitted with alarm bells, were in accordance with Board of Trade regulations. An automatic electric indicator in the Wheelhouse showed whether doors were open or shut. There were also forty hinged watertight doors (made by Mechan and Sons of Glasgow), varying in size from 5ft 3in high x 2ft wide to 6ft by 4½ft, fitted on the outside of the ship at each coaling chute, and made watertight by lengths of wick soaked in white lead (replaced at each coaling session). Twenty-two vertically sliding doors (4ft 10in x 2ft 8in clear opening) were installed as internal accesses to the bunkers. By this date the US Navy had developed bunker doors that could crush any coal hindering the closing of doors but it is not known whether the Mechan and Sons' doors had this capability.

Skilfully and surely the ship was being brought to completion.

5

LIVERPOOL, NORTH ABOUT

The keel of the *Mauretania*'s slightly older sister had been laid down on 16 June 1904, at John Brown & Company's Clydebank shipyard as Yard Number 367 and, after nearly two years of construction, was launched as the *Lusitania* by Mary, Lady Inverclyde, by then the widow of the late chairman, at 12.30 p.m. on the warm, late spring day of Thursday, 7 June 1906. As the new Cunarder entered the baptismal waters of the River Clyde she had the distinction of being, at 31,000 gross tons, the largest as well as, at 787ft in overall length, the longest vessel in the world. The *Lusitania* would soon accede that honour to her younger sister still growing on the slipways of the Tyne.

Full of national pride, an eager 200,000 people had watched the beautiful new *Lusitania* sail on her maiden voyage from Liverpool on Saturday, 7 September 1907, under the command of Commodore James Watt, with the expectation that she would wrest the Blue Ribband from the Germans. Steaming via Queenstown, she arrived at New York five days and fifty-four minutes later with the hopes of a record passage shattered after encountering fog over Newfoundland's Grand Banks. She missed defeating Hamburg America Line's (*Hamburg-American Packetfahrt-Actien-Gesselschaft* – 'HAPAG') *Deutschland* record by a paltry thirty minutes, arriving in New York on, suitably, Friday the 13th. The *Lusitania*'s next sailing from Liverpool on Saturday, 5 October proved to be an epoch-making journey. On her second arrival she passed Sandy Hook at 12.17 a.m. on 11 October, easily taking the westward record with a time of four days, nineteen hours and fifty-three minutes at an average speed of an incredible 23.99 knots, becoming the first ship ever to make the passage in under five days. Germany's ten-year – and admittedly magnificent – dominance of the North Atlantic came to a

formal closure when HAPAG's General Manager in New York, Gustav Schwabe, metaphorically handed over the Blue Ribband to Cunard's Vernon Brown, along with generous congratulations. Leaving New York on her eastward crossing on 19 October, the triumphant 'Lucy' returned at an average of 23.61 knots in four days, twenty-two hours and thirty minutes, beating *Norddeutscher Lloyd*'s (North German Lloyd – NDL) *Kaiser Wilhelm II*'s eastbound record held since June 1904. She now had the record for both westward and eastward passages and on her third crossing to New York she bettered herself by arriving at Sandy Hook after four days, eighteen hours and forty minutes, on four of the days exceeding 600 miles a day. The gauntlet was down, daring her English sister to do better!

As the *Lusitania* was grabbing the headlines, the *Mauretania*, her black-topped crimson funnels proclaiming her presence like four great beacons above her light-grey hull and white superstructure, was preparing to make her debut from the Tyne on 17 September, a date that should have celebrated the 46th birthday of Lord Inverclyde, had he lived to witness this crowning glory of his endeavours.

Mauretania had been afloat for just under a year and, without the advantage of a dry-docking (the nearest one large enough to take her was in Liverpool), her bottom plates had grown foul with marine growth that would create resistance to the flow of the ocean around her; data sheets for her imminent Builder's Sea Trials would be annotated 'Vessel lying in river 12 months before trial'. Boilers had been fired well in advance of her departure in order to test them, her engines run without engaging the propellers, and the wisps of smoke that had curled upwards from her funnels now increased in their choking intensity as the excitement – and professional concern – of sailing time approached, a creditable month before the contracted time!

Cunard would not have control of the ship until Builder's Sea Trials had been completed to the shipyard's satisfaction and, until then, the liner belonged to them. From the Bridge down to the boiler rooms temporary staff had been taken on for the duration of the next few days, although Cunard would have observers on board. The shipyard was represented by a small army of naval architects, draughtsmen, tradesmen, etc., detailed to note any deficiencies in the ship's structure and to observe and record the operation of a myriad of machines and equipment from the great turbines to coal consumption, measuring, calibrating and noting readings and observations in notebooks collated daily into one master record.

At 9.30 a.m. – about an hour before high tide that allowed for a sufficient depth of water beneath her keel for the duration of her passage to the open sea – and attended by the tugs *Snowdon*, *Washington*, *Gauntlet* and *President* (from South Shields), and two powerful Dutch tugs, the *Poolzee* and *Oceaan* – that had arrived the day before, the mighty *Mauretania*, under her own steam, edged away from her berth against the dolphins that had been her home since her launching almost a year previously. Under the guidance of South Shields pilot Thomas Young she progressed slowly down the river at a cautious 3 knots, belching thick, black clouds of coal smoke from her impressive funnels. A second, North Sea pilot, also from South Shields, (John Burn?) whose ward she would be when at sea was also on board, both pilots ensuring the safe navigation of the ship by using their specialised local knowledge of river, channels, tides, currents and landmarks. Cunard's Captain John Pritchard was on board at SH&WR's request.

Before she left it was noted that at draughts of 31ft 1in forward and a trim by the stern of 1ft, almost on an even keel, her displacement was 34,750 tons. Her first sailing was made an occasion of rejoicing in the town and thousands lined the river's banks and every vantage point to watch her as she processed slowly downstream. Thousands more would later read of the great event, undoubtedly wishing that they had been there. *The Times* commented:

The enthusiasm was extraordinary; the entire population seemed to have turned out to welcome the huge vessel. In the boroughs of North and South Shields the school children were given a holiday for the occasion. The Tyne was gay with bunting on every side, and when the Mauretania came in sight all the steamers lying in the harbour mingled the sounds of their whistles in an indescribable din, and the Mauretania responded with her hoarse diapasons …

In a carnival atmosphere that was brimming to overspill with local pride, a little girl was told: 'Now remember this, it's very important!' Excited, she was sick on her bonnet strings!

With 'Slow Ahead' indicated on her glistening brass Bridge-to-Engine Room telegraphs, the *Mauretania* steamed north-eastwards down the river at around 3 knots in regal procession attended by her tugs and a flotilla of sightseeing craft including the River Tyne Commissioners' steam yacht, whose occupants must have been most gratified that such a deep-draughted vessel was able to sail on a neap tide down the river. Had they not insisted on dredging the river to a depth of 30ft over the preceding twelve months (against the wishes of the Tynemouth Corporation) the liner's entry into service would have been delayed until the spring tide at the end of the month. Accompanied all the while by steam whistles and cheering, the liner followed the course of the river and, as she headed due east, she passed Jarrow to starboard where, in the eighth century, the Venerable Bede had written his epoch-making *The Ecclesiastical History of the English People*.

Leaving the towers of the Low and High Light beacons behind to port, she steamed on with the Fish Quay on the Northumberland side of the river, where a score of trawlers created a raucous cacophony of steam whistles like fish wives cackling their greetings to a giant sister. The *Mauretania* then passed through The Narrows with its wooden-legged jetties: the Pilots' landing stage to starboard in Durham and Lloyd's Hailing Station on her port side. The Station, as was its wont, signalled its customary challenge: 'What ship and where bound?' The great vessel responded accordingly with: 'Mauretania. Bound for trials.' (It might just be apocryphal that the ship retorted on her return into the river with: 'Mauretania. What town?')

Having passed the Signal Station, the *Mauretania* is still surrounded by accompanying tugs and many pleasure craft. Thousands of spectators lined both banks of the Tyne. (Author's Collection)

Then on the starboard side lay the Herd Groyne that ran almost parallel to the river, its bouldered mole and walkway another vantage point from which to view the ship as she passed to the outer harbour. Trails of steam again issued from the whistles on her two forward funnels in salute to the excited throng and His Majesty's Ships *Satellite* and *Furious* saluted the similarly grey-hulled *Mauretania* before she turned slightly to port to pass an old ex-Third Rate, seventy-four-gun, Man o' War, the *Wellesley,* moored in the river just beneath Clifford's Fort over to port. This old once-distinguished

'wooden wall', built originally as HMS *Boscawen*, was now in aged retirement as a Royal Naval and merchant service training ship whose complement of 13- to 16-year-old trainees (placed on board after local assessment as being socially at risk) manned the rigging of the Nelsonic warship, where they lustily sang 'Rule Britannia' and 'A Life on the Ocean Wave'; they wound up their performance with the National Anthem. The passing liner must have inspired many of those young hearts with a longing to one day join the mighty vessel and leave their impoverishment behind them.

Before the *Mauretania* left Tyneside the diminutive *Turbinia* moored alongside her to demonstrate the great advances the turbine had made in a few short years. (Author's Collection)

The children's penny *St George's Magazine* later wrote: 'The Tyne is proud of the Mauretania, and with reason, for she is surely, as the Americans say, "the limit"', but on the hill beyond the training ship and concealed beneath the smoking chimney pots of a town fiercely proud of its shipbuilding achievements, poverty dwelt in houses that co-existed with disease and squalor, their occupants looking down at a spectacle that represented the huge divide between their own circumstances and the wealth and dreams that were beyond their ken and aspirations. Undoubtedly, the great liner's first departure would be the cause of discussion at Saturday's Bigg Market, remaining in local lore for years to come.

After an extraordinary passage, the wider part of the river was reached and the attending tugs released their charge, her whistles still acknowledging her send-off. From the crowds on either bank, and on the watching and accompanying craft, a great cheer went up as, at 10.45 a.m., the *Mauretania* passed The Black Middens, a rocky outcrop that had, in 1864, claimed three ships on one notorious night. Above the river to starboard in South Shield's Marine Park people halted their perambulations to watch the ship approach the North Sea as the now independent liner, still accompanied by a celebratory flotilla, passed over what remained of a sandbar and steamed on between the iconic pincer-like projections of the North and South Piers. Formed by two great granite breakwaters, these piers, each with its guardian lighthouse, guarded the Tyne's entrance like the horns of a giant stag beetle. The North Pier – the masonry of a ruined, ancient abbey at its landward end – still sported an extra lighthouse standing on the remains of an earlier pier demolished in a great storm ten years previously. A tall crane, *Goliath*, brooded over the rebuilding work as the *Mauretania*, picking up speed, entered the open expanse of the North Sea, where she came to a stop in order to adjust her compasses.

Ahead lay four days of intensive trials – 'conducted in secret' according to *The Times*. These designated 'Preliminary Speed Trials' would test her hull and machinery to the limit. Her manoeuvrability would be under scrutiny and her speed, over a Measured Mile, would indicate the power generated by her engines and the quantity of coal required for a particular distance of travel. Both speed and manoeuvrability would be professionally compared against her exhaustive model tests at Haslar. After completion of these trials her Contractor's Acceptance Trials would be run to ascertain that the specifications and stipulations laid down in the 1903 Agreement had been met.

Trials were to be conducted off St Abbs Head over a measured mile determined by lining up two landmarks at each end of the mile, the ship being run up to full power by the time that the first set of markers was met. A mean of the speeds over each pair of runs was taken and, following Admiralty practice, six runs (three with the tide and three against with wind speed and direction taken into consideration) were made over a period of four hours on each day with a 'mean of means' being calculated to give a true speed. Runs at a series of slower speeds were then made so that a curve of Indicated Horsepower (IHP, taken at the engines) could be constructed to represent their values from the lowest to the highest speeds. Another phenomenon affecting a ship's speed – and one that required careful measurement – was propeller 'slip'; as water is not an unyielding medium, the slip is a percentage of the efficiency of a propeller's thrust lost in pushing a quantity of water away from the direction of a ship's motion – a maritime version of skidding – and the power required to push that water is taken from that available to drive the ship. The horsepower transmitted to the shaft (Shaft Horsepower – SHP) less the loss created by slip gave the IHP. Recorded slip for the *Mauretania* over the first day's runs at 22.245 knots was 9.49 per cent of the propeller's efficiency. At the conclusion of each run the radius of her turning circle was carefully noted.

The public awaited any snippets of news about these 'secret' trials and all reports, however ill-informed, helped to swell the nation's collective chest.

The Shipbuilder's Sea Trials

The *Mauretania's* first set of trials were run from Wednesday, 18 September to Saturday, 21 September 1907, between the Tyne and the beautiful St Abb's Head just over the Scottish border. It was almost throwing down a challenge to the land that had produced her sister ship, the very successful *Lusitania*.

One of a series of dramatic photographs by famed local photographer Gladstone Adams as the liner approaches the mouth of the River Tyne. (Author's Collection)

Large sheets of neatly pencilled results recorded details of wind and sea states over the duration of each day's trials as well as the ship's displacement tonnage based on her fore and aft draughts that indicated, by calculating her 'Tons per Inch' (TPI – the weight required to increase or decrease her draught by 1in), how much fuel and water had been consumed. This made her ride progressively and slightly higher in the water, resulting in marginally higher speeds.

These sheets recorded other readings, including a mass of data taken in the Boiler Rooms from steam-pressure gauges; readings of shaft revolutions and torsionmeters of both high-pressure and low-pressure turbines. and condenser pressures. Air pressures of the Howden Fans that created a forced draught to the boilers were duly noted and dozens more. Throughout the trials two double-ended (DE) and two single-ended (SE) boilers were dedicated to work auxiliary machinery only. Two tables of results were obtained on each of the first three of the four days of trials: the first set made from readings taken while under way, generally between 10.30 a.m. when she left the Tyne for St Abb's Head (some 80 miles to the north) and 7 p.m., and the second (overlapping) set was recorded during the measured mile runs that began at 2.30 p.m., generally completing by 4.30. On the last day of trials she ran on the Hartley Mile off Whitley Bay.

Brief summaries of the results are as follows:

Shipbuilder's Trials:
Day 1 – Wednesday, 18 September

With 1,000 men on board, this first full day of trials was run off St Abb's Head on the dramatically beautiful rocky coastline of Berwickshire, where there was particularly deep water and sea space for turning. On the 300ft-high cliffs of the Head stood a lighthouse, reached by a flight of steps leading down from the Lightkeeper's house above, that acted as a marker. The ship's draught forward was about 29ft 3in; aft 32ft 3in with a recorded mean of 30ft 9in. A reduction of 350 tons in coal and water since leaving the Tyne currently gave her a displacement of 34,400 tons.

Builder's trials now commenced in earnest and the first measurements of port and starboard machinery and other equipment were taken at 10.30 a.m., the first of many half-hourly readings. In boiler rooms and machinery spaces temperatures, revolutions, etc. were recorded by qualified staff, whose notes were later collated in larger-format books. As this vital recording commenced the liner was readied for her first run over the measured mile, the prevailing light nor'-westerly wind making the sea choppy. Her engines were by now warmed up, fed by a constant pressure of steam (which varied between 155 and 193psi [pounds per square inch]) over the course of the day. Revolutions on her high-pressure and low-pressure turbines were gradually increased as the time came for the first of her half-hourly speed trials. Increasing averages of 88.8, 91.8, 104.2, 111.9, 120.2, 138.2 and 141.7 revolutions per minute (rpm) acted as a build-up to the first speed trial, which started after lunch.

The first of six runs began at 2.10 p.m. when the *Mauretania* began a timed run northwards over the mile. The return run began at 2.25 p.m. Two other double runs were made that day: 2.55 p.m. north and 3.18 p.m. south, and then 3.40 p.m. north and '4.3' [*sic* 4.30] south. Those manning the lighthouse at St Abb's had a ringside seat of these historic trials, although on one occasion they were more interested in having their photograph taken than watching the great ship as she steamed speedily by in all her impressive beauty!

During the trials the speed of each set of two runs was progressively increased. Revolutions per minute (here given as a 'mean of means', i.e. an average of averages) for the three sets were 155.81; 158.18 and 164.495rpm respectively. The ship's speed for the first run north was 21.62 knots but, for some unspecified reason, the southwards result was simply recorded as 'Lost'. However, the mean speeds for the last two runs were a very creditable 22.245 and 23.028 knots. Times on the nine passes over the mile were 3m 1s; 3m 13.5s; 2m 37s; 2m 53.5s; 2m 28s; 2m 35s; 2m 20s; 2m 29s; and 2m 33.4s. At the end of each mile she was steered to the eastwards in a great turning circle in order to regain both the mile and to safely clear the land. It was noted that when her helm was put over to 15° she heeled 'over to about 6°'.

The result at the end of the first day produced a 'Mean of Means' speed of 22.361 knots. This form of calculation, preferred by the Admiralty, gave the best figure of a ship's speed in still water, although owners still preferred an average speed of a day's runs that, in this case, would have been 22.46 knots. Even though the ship had, as mentioned, been noted as having been 'lying in river 12 months before trial' she was already showing her paces.

Day 2 – Thursday, 19 September

Trials started at 9.00 a.m. in a light north-westerly wind with the sea state being described as 'smooth' with draughts of 27ft 8½in forward and 32ft 10½in aft with a mean draught of 30ft 3½in. Her displacement was 33,890 tons (510 tons less than the previous day). Readings were again taken at half-hourly intervals based on a similar format to the previous day's. After her warm-ups her nine progressive speed runs (i.e. a single northwards run and four pairs of return runs) were made over the mile between 11.47 a.m. and 3.18 p.m. The runs took advantage of a high tide – steaming south she sailed with the tide and against it as she headed north. The following table from Henry Booker's notebook recorded her measured mile speeds for the day:

Time	Direction	Duration	Speed Over Mile (knots)	Average Speed (knots)
12.00 noon	South	3 mins. 1 sec.	19.88	
12.40 p.m.	North	3 mins. 13.5 secs.	18.60	19.24
1.17 p.m.	South	2 mins. 37 secs.	22.95	
1.42 p.m.	North	2 mins. 53.5 secs.	20.72	21.83
2.05 p.m.	South	2 mins. 28 secs.	24.35	
2.32 p.m.	North	2 mins. 35 secs.	23.22	23.78
3.00 p.m.	South	2 mins. 20 secs.	25.73	
3.18 p.m.	North	2 mins. 29 secs.	24.18	24.95
4.23 p.m.	South	2 mins. 33.4 secs.	23.46	[*return to anchorage*]

As she passed over the course she parted the smooth sea much as a horse-drawn plough cut its rustic furrows. The foaming water elegantly curled away from her sharp bow's lean lines in a smooth, shallow arc of a long, white wave, which reached its trough just below the first funnel before cresting just aft of the second, the sign of a thoroughbred, the wave seemingly static against her as she surged forward at high speed. The waves took a few minutes to reach land, where they crashed in high plumes against the rocks or else thundered onto level beaches, taking the unwary observer by surprise as they foamed in rollers up the strand.

Her run north began at 11.47 a.m. but, as her speed was not noted, the first run of the first recorded set began at 12.12 p.m. when she ran south. Her mean speed for this pair was 19.246 knots with a slip of 5.52 per cent. The second set realised 21.82 knots (6.11 per cent); the third 23.77 (8.01 per cent) and on the fourth – starting at 2.58 p.m. – she attained a magnificent 25.71 knots, taking two minutes twenty seconds as she headed south with the tide. The return leg to the north at 3.18 gave 24.93 knots at 177.1rpm with 9.38 per cent propeller slip, and a final run south at 4.23 indicated 23.46 knots – taking two minutes thirty-three and two-fifth seconds but, being a single run, this was not officially counted. 'Admiralty (mean) speed' for the day was calculated at 22.67 knots. Fan Room temperatures showed that Number 1 Fan Room became the hottest with readings of up to 112°F – but these temperatures were up to 20° greater than the Boiler Rooms that they were cooling. The last readings of the day were taken, as usual, at 7.00 in the evening, the vessel returning to her night anchorage off Tynemouth where the men enjoyed a dinner and compared results and experiences.

As the use of wireless might have given away too many confidential details, during the course of the trials messages were sent ashore using the age-old medium of carrier pigeons released from the ship when she was off the Farne Islands!

Day 3 – Friday, 20 September

Trials were again run between St Abb's Head and the Tyne (2–6 p.m.); weather conditions had reduced to a light wind and a smooth sea; forward draught was 28ft 1in; aft 32ft 2in; and a mean of 30ft 1½in indicated a displacement of 33,650 tons.

A group photograph, taken on the North-About voyage, including many who had taken part in the creation of the liner. Seated in the front centre is George Hunter and, behind him (standing), is Captain John Pritchard. (*The Shipbuilder*/Estate of Captain Pritchard/Author's Collection)

An Admiralty mean of a commendable 25.945 knots was calculated from the six runs off St Abb's with finishing and starting speeds being the same, her stride apparently not being affected by the current. The second run (south) of the first pair and the first run (north) of the second pair were recorded at an astonishing 26.27 knots (30.23 miles per hour). This achievement celebrated in grand style the first anniversary of her launch and must have led to many mutual congratulations being exchanged in the dining rooms and crew messes that evening!

Day 4 – Saturday, 21 September

A draught of 27ft 7in forward and 32ft 1in aft gave a mean of 29ft 10in. Displacement at the start of the day's trials was 33,250 tons, a total of 1,500 tons less than when she had first sailed from the Tyne due to the use of coal and feed water. This was to be the day of her speed trials over the Hartley Measured Mile off the sandy beaches of Whitley. A northerly breeze gave the sea a chop. Enough data had been obtained from measuring the machinery outputs over the previous four days to satisfy the builders' representatives as to its satisfactory performance so, after a later start of 11 a.m., only two pairs of slow-speed runs were made and these gave means of 12.66 knots (3.72 per cent slip) and 17.15 knots (4.5 per cent slip). An Admiralty mean of 14.84 knots was calculated.

The last trial of the day – a one-off event – was the Astern Trial. For this she went full ahead at 25 knots at 153.25rpm before switching to the Astern Turbines, which took a very short forty-five seconds to effect. With the two inner propellers thrashing astern as they opposed a still forward moving ship, it took a further three minutes fifty-eight seconds for the ship to come to a stop in a distance of about three-quarters of a mile after attaining her fullest speed astern of 118rpm. Going astern at high speed increased the likelihood of cavitation, which occurs, as described in Chapter 1, when bubbles collapse against the propeller blades, causing vibration and erosion. This, combined with the engines reaching a critical speed (where the speed of rotation approaches a natural frequency resulting in a resonance) creates vibrations in both engines and shafts, which are felt throughout the ship. It may have

been at this point that the Captain is said to have told the Engine Room in no uncertain terms that he was being shaken off the Bridge! The *Lusitania* had suffered from vibration aft during her trials, even in an ahead mode, and was returned to the Clyde to be stiffened in the areas affected; the additional tubular pillars between deck and overhead beams altered her after accommodation configuration as a result.

From the following table it can be seen that with 3-knot increases up to full speed massive increases in Shaft Horsepower were required with a resultant huge cost in coal and in the efforts of the Firemen, along with increasingly higher losses in efficiency due to propeller slip:

Speed (Knots)	Revolutions per Minute	Shaft Horsepower	Steam Pressure at HP Turbine	Average Slip for 4 Propellers %
12	86	7,700	X	X
15	102	14,200	X	X
18	121	22,500	X	(5.5)
21	144	32,100	75	5.7
24	171	54,000	113	9.9
26	191	80,000	168	13.5

X = Not recorded

At the conclusion of her trials an estimated 50,000 people turned out to see the *Mauretania*'s return to the Tyne attended once again by six tugs. Once at the builders she was swung in the river to face downstream to ease her next departure – for Liverpool.

A day after the ship's return to the Tyne a report in *The Thunderer* (*The Times*) stated that the White Star Line was planning a new class of liner of 840ft in length and propelled by a combination of reciprocating and turbine engines; the Germans would follow with a ship larger than the White Star giants but slower than the new Cunarders. Respectively, these proposals were for the Olympic-class and the even bigger Vaterland-class.

After structural modifications to reduce vibration and with the liner freshly painted in Cunard colours (her hull changed from trials grey to black) she was prepared for her departure for Liverpool, taking on stores and 1,000 tons of coal. On 17 October she was opened for public inspection with visitors paying half a crown (2s 6d, 12½p.) for the privilege. Queues formed at the gangways and the estimated 23,000 people who trooped aboard 'expressed intense delight at the magnificence of the vessel'.

The Leaving for Liverpool – North-About

Tuesday, 22 October 1907 was another gala day on Tyneside as the great liner, the pride of the river, was leaving for her registered home port of Liverpool. Four hundred privileged guests, invited to witness the official handing over, then boarded her to sail on the special delivery cruise to Lancashire. Distinguished guests included Lord Brassey (the publisher of *Brassey's Naval Annual* that listed the two sisters as Armed Merchant Cruisers); Mary, Lady Inverclyde; and the Lord Mayor and Lady Mayoress of Newcastle. Other passengers would be actively interested in her technical progress and performance: her Naval Architect, Leonard Peskett, and his wife; James Burns, the new Lord Inverclyde and a director of the Cunard Line; Sir William White from the Admiralty; Mr A.F. Yarrow; Swan Hunter's Mr J. Meuwissen; and engine builder Andrew Laing. The crew signed 'Coastal Articles' for the short trip.

As a tribute, Sir Charles Parsons' plucky little pioneering steam yacht *Turbinia* would be called upon, like a steel bridesmaid to her huge sister, to lead the great liner on the latter's departure for her official trials, and the steam yacht had been taken to sea for a few test runs to ensure that she was fit for the occasion. On her return she moored diminutively under the shelter of the *Mauretania's* starboard bow, dramatically demonstrating how far Parsons' system of marine propulsion had progressed in ten short years. But Fate shook her fickle finger and, just when the *Mauretania* was about to move off from her berth, the yacht's temperamental air pump failed. The *Mauretania* moved into the stream alone without her tiny mentor. A short while

after missing this second greatest moment in her proud life the little craft was almost cut in two by a ship launched from the south side of the river. The badly buckled *Turbinia* was hoisted ashore, where she remained for some time as a curiosity.

With her large cowl ventilators smartly and carefully aligned and facing forward, the *Mauretania* pulled away from her mooring dolphins at two o'clock. As on her maiden journey down the Tyne, she was surrounded by a myriad of small, jubilant craft. For her careful, regal progress down the Tyne she was preceded by the tugs *Challenger* (skipper Robert 'Punch' Stewart) and *Snowdon*.

Men, women – many with babes in arms – and children in their thousands, 'Geordies' of Newcastle on the northern shore of the Tyne and 'Posh Geordies' or 'Pit Yakkers' of Durham on its southern, watched as 'The Pride of the Tyne' slipped slowly away, ostensibly never to return. Once more *The Times* was on hand to report the occasion for an eager readership:

All Tyneside seemed to take a holiday on the occasion, for all Tynesiders are proud of the greatest ship which has ever been borne by the waters of the historic river, or by any other waters for that matter. Indeed, one might have thought that the greater part of the population of Northumberland and of Durham had gathered on both banks to bid … farewell to the ship as she left her birthplace. Every point from which any view could be obtained was crowded by dense masses of spectators. The river outside the fairway was covered with craft of all kinds, some of which accompanied the Mauretania as far as the pierheads and beyond, and all of which made jocund but discordant music with a continuous hooting of their steam whistles.

Enthusiastically, 'KH' sent a postcard to her mother in Manchester:

I went to Tynemouth yesterday to see the Mauretania leave the Tyne. It was well worth seeing. I wish you had been there. There were thousands present …

The passage down the Tyne took about eighty minutes and, after passing the two piers, the *Mauretania* lay offshore for a while to

With a shortage of ladies, to enjoy the short trip, gentlemen play deck golf. (Author's Collection)

adjust compasses. Then, at 6.10 p.m., Lord Inverclyde's widow, Mary, visited the Navigating Bridge, where she was invited to ring the Engine Room telegraphs for the ship to go 'Slow Ahead'. To mark the occasion, Thomas Bell, chairman of the ship's engine builders, presented her ladyship with a gold bracelet in the form of tiny gold turbine blades surrounding a rotor ring of diamonds. Captain Pritchard had not been forgotten in the celebrations as the shipyard presented him with an elegant silver tea and coffee set, the tray bearing an engraved inscription of appreciation and the pots, creamer and sugar bowl an initial 'P' in copperplate script. Beneath their feet the enormous vessel was now in almost imperceptible motion en route for the River Mersey and the great maritime city of Liverpool, whose name she proudly bore in brass letters across her elegant counter stern, set beneath her own. However, it would not be a pleasure cruise for all on board; it was reported by the press that no records were taken on this voyage but, from seven o'clock that evening of departure shortly after getting under way, the first of many machinery readings were taken hourly until five o'clock on the morning of arrival, Thursday the 24th.

At five o'clock the next morning, the 23rd, the *Mauretania*'s engines were stopped, perhaps for safety, for a couple of hours; it might have been the narrow reaches of the oft-treacherous Pentland Firth, heralded by sighting the Pentland Skerries, that caused her Navigators 'to wait for daylight'. Under way again just before 7 a.m. (the weather was excellent, with a barometric pressure of 30.01in and a light wind blowing over a smooth sea), the *Mauretania* was worked up to 18.9 knots; five of the double-ended boilers and two of the single-ended were unused during this 'cruise'. Speed, taken from the 'curve constructed from preliminary trial data, corresponding to revolutions', showed a gradual increase to 21.9 knots by midday, then slowly decreasing to 20.6 knots by seven. The Engine Room reached a temperature of 94°F during this time but there was an increase of 3° two hours later at a speed of 0.1 knot less. Temperatures in the Fan Rooms, sited fore and aft of the Boiler Rooms, fell from 91 to 85°F during the course of the day's steaming. Draughts – and thus displacements – were not noted during the course of the trip, as these observations were impossible to make while the ship was under way.

Working passenger Dr Schlick stood by his 'Pallograph', a 'beautiful instrument' described as 'a simple seismic device' that recorded horizontal and vertical pulses caused by impingement of propeller forces against the hull. Vibration from the turbines was virtually absent as, being rotary, these did not involve the massive mechanical movements that distinguished the superseded reciprocating engines. Another traveller, a photographer, made a record of the voyage, photographing passengers as they strolled the decks and, from the Crow's Nest, photographed Captain Pritchard, arm raised in a cheery wave.

A log of the North About voyage was not readily available at the time of writing so one report, that of the Cunarder liner *Carpathia* – from the same yard and with some of the same guests and officials that were now aboard the *Mauretania* – has been extemporised. The *Carpathia* had sailed from Newcastle on Wednesday, 22 April 1904, taking four days to make her leisurely Caledonian circumnavigation, sometimes slowing to allow her passengers to appreciate the scenic beauties of the coastline. Although the *Mauretania*'s route may have differed from that of the *Carpathia*, the following account from *The Mid-Tyne Link* gives an impression of the journey, even though some views were obscured by late-autumn mist:

Soon the vessel [Carpathia] was making progress down the river [Tyne], the object of an admiring crowd on both sides of the river. Ere long she had crossed the bar and was riding proudly in her native element …

'Liverpool North about' was the next order … the big liner turned … and we soon lost sight of the cliffs of old Tynemouth as we forged ahead … up the Northumbrian coast …

The following morning we found ourselves off the fine red granite city of Peterhead … and a few fishing boats quite near, making a very fine sea and landscape combined. Losing sight of Peterhead and passing Rattray Head, we had an open sea run of from 70 to 80 knots [*sic* – miles], with nothing in view save the blue sea, and here and there a passing coaster, fishing trawler, collier or occasional sailing vessel …

Admiral Lord Charles Beresford, who had been present at the launching, had informed Lord Inverclyde that his Royal Navy squadron would be manoeuvring in the North Sea and would keep a look out for the *Mauretania*. But no such sighting was made except for a small torpedo boat destroyer on routine duty, sighted off Cape Wrath on Wednesday. *The Mid-Tyne Link* continued:

The coast of Caithness was next in view, with a glimpse of Wick in the distance; and then … Duncansby Head, where we signalled. All on board not directly occupied in the navigation of the steamship were lost in contemplation of the beautiful coast scenery. Passing the Pentland Skerries, with the weather gloriously fine [*Mauretania* was experiencing equally ideal weather conditions with light winds and a smooth sea], the numerous islets, creeks and headlands, the bold outline of the Orkneys with a few white specks which we knew to be cottages, and the equally fine coast of the mainland, completed a picture at once so solemn and so full of rugged grandeur that it could not readily be effaced from the memory …

Making headway through the Pentland Firth, and passing Dunnet Head [where the Lloyd's Station reported the *Mauretania* as having safely passed], brought us into the Atlantic swell. The evening saw us off Cape Wrath …

Next morning we entered the Little Minch. We had lain to in the Minch for about four hours in the night … prudent to do so on account of the difficult navigation … that morning a general survey of the ship was made by … press representatives … The afternoon was spent in gazing at the magnificent scenery of the Hebrides and the coast of the mainland. Rugged, bleak and bare it certainly appeared, with its wind-swept hills, its wave-beaten cliffs, and its treeless moorland … The whole scene from the Pentland Skerries to the Island of Barra, is one of surpassing grandeur, some of the passengers who had visited the Norwegian fjords declaring this coast to be equally imposing.

Between eulogising about the passing Scottish landscapes deck games were organised by those on board and simple fun was had in gymkhanas, potato races, deck golf, egg-and-spoon races and the traditionally over-strenuous all-male tug of war. Many a bracing walk was taken along her lengthy promenades; blanketed teak deckchairs and beef tea providing a warm respite.

The *Mauretania* arrived off the Bar that fouled the entrance to the River Mersey at 5 a.m. on Thursday, 24 October (just a few short weeks after the 'Lucy's' maiden departure) and anchored. Breakfast was taken, during which Alderman Richardson of Newcastle proposed, on behalf of the guests, a well-received 'hearty vote of thanks and appreciation for the very splendid and withal extremely kindly and considerate hospitality with which they had been entertained by their hosts'. Lord Brassey seconded the vote and 'warmly congratulated the builders on the success of the Mauretania' and paid 'a justly-earned tribute … to the officers, crew and servants of the ship'.

Four hours later the 'Maury' (as she was becoming affectionately known) crossed the Bar on a full tide and anchored off New Brighton on the Mersey's southern shore. Here the 'North About' passengers disembarked onto tenders and landed via the Prince's Landing Stage just before noon. The people of Liverpool, denied a good view of the new liner, were compensated by the arrival of the *Lusitania*.

The next day, *Mauretania* headed for the Canada Graving Dock as an essential prerequisite to ensure that her underwater hull was completely cleaned and to remove any vestige of her launching gear. After completion of the work the dock was flooded on 30 October and the freshly painted *Mauretania* floated out. After mooring in mid-stream against the specially built Cunard Buoy on The Sloyne she was coaled in readiness for the official trials that would prove her capable of meeting the challenges and demands for which she had been designed. Just lying in the stream the liner consumed nearly 5 tons of coal an hour keeping her auxiliary machinery running. Another ton per furnace (132) would be required to raise steam.

'The Way of the Ship in the Midst of the Sea …'

(David K. Brown)

Before starting her all-important Contractor's Sea Trials (i.e. Cunard's) a precise amount of coal was taken on to ensure that her fore and aft draughts were at those calculated to reflect her expected displacement when two days out of Queenstown and halfway across the Atlantic.

Steaming northwards from Liverpool into Scottish waters, the *Mauretania* anchored overnight in Wemyss Bay, overlooked by Castle Wemyss (formerly Wemyss House) with its terraced gardens cascading down to the sea at the end of Undercliff Road. Until recently the castle had been the home of the late George Arbuthnot Burns, Second Baron Inverclyde of Castle Wemyss, once Chairman of the Cunard Line and reputedly the richest man in Scotland. Before his lordship's death two years previously this prominent white sandstone edifice had been the scene of many a house party for an elite Edwardian social set: long, languid weekends and summer yachting regattas and cruises, and parties that occasionally ran the risk of scandalising local Calvinistic sensibilities by gaining the reputation of being rather risqué: 'The Castle was always a source of gossip; apparently Inverclyde was a bit of a ladies man and enjoyed the wild entertainment of the day … drunken skinny dipping off the castle pier was often seen at his parties!'

The now-widowed Lady Inverclyde must have harboured mixed emotions as this proud reminder of her late husband's vision lay beneath the castle, a silent salute of engineering perfection gleaming in freshly painted Cunard livery. At night, in sight of the large house, the splendid *Mauretania* sparkled, bejewelled with gleaming ropes of brightly lit windows and portholes that reflected towards the castle on the rippled, darkened waters of the Firth, dimly illuminating the pale grey smoke that curled upwards from her great funnels before disappearing into the starlit sky above.

It had been thought that the *Mauretania* would emulate the trials programme of her elder sister and, on the conclusion of her important forty-eight-hour endurance steaming trial, anchor at the Tail o' The Bank on the Clyde. But this was not to be. Of the two sets of official trials planned to start the following day, the first would test her endurance over forty-eight hours of continuous steaming to prove a vital stipulation in Section 10 of the 1903 Agreement, which specified that the *Mauretania* (and her sister) be 'capable of maintaining a minimum average ocean speed of 24½ knots'. This would take the ship through four 304-mile transits of the North Channel, the Irish Sea and St George's Channel, each transit of twelve hours being arranged so that tides on each leg could be averaged over the whole trial. The second set of trials would test her speed capabilities over a measured mile.

A famously spectacular photograph of the *Mauretania* as she steams towards the Skelmorlie Measured Mile, paint eroded by speed at her bow. The Cloch Point Lighthouse can be seen on the distant shoreline. (Collection of Ambrose Greenway)

On this double north-south-north course the ship would steam from Corswall (or Corsewall) Point on the northern tip of the Rhinns of Galloway, Wigtownshire (now restyled Dumfries and Galloway), to the Longships Lighthouse sited on Carn Bras in the Atlantic (about 1 mile west from Sennen on the Cornish cliffs at Land's End) and back. She proudly passed Corswall Point at 8.01 p.m. on Sunday, 3 November. Her draughts, 32ft 5in forward and 32ft 6in aft, gave her a displacement of 36,634 tons, making her ride slightly high in the water, showing the top of the upper edge of her red-painted boot topping.

The *Mauretania* looked magnificent as she forged ahead on a choppy sea that carried a slight swell created by a strong Force 7 that blew from about four points (45°) on the port bow for the first two hours and then from right ahead. Passing Wexford on the starboard beam, the ship soon made the Tuskar Rock Light as she passed from the Irish Sea into St George's Channel. Here she met the Atlantic swell and, as a well-designed steamer should, proved her worth. Her roll, timed at between ten to twelve seconds for a single swing, and her pitch – four seconds – were assessed to be long enough 'not be disturbing to passengers'.

This first part of the trial ended when the liner arrived off the Longships light at 7.35 the following morning. She turned in a white-waked arc in readiness for the return leg (her turning circle being achieved within a diameter of three-and-three-quarters of her length), passing the southerly lighthouse at 7.57 a.m. By now the sea had smoothed with hardly a trace of wind save that generated by her forward surge.

Those on board must have fervently urged the ship to make the *exact* twelve hours as she approached her northern marker, but it took just two minutes over that to complete this first northward run, making Corswall at 7.59 that evening! Turning without pause, the liner quickly regained Corswall at 8.12 p.m., forging ahead on her second run to the south. A calm-to-light easterly wind created a slight swell that animated an otherwise smooth sea coming from ahead, bearing within it a late autumnal chill. A sharp lookout was kept but the rain that made visibility difficult cleared as the morning progressed.

Arrival off the Longships on 5 November was recorded at a very precise '7.18½ a.m.'. The ultimate run left Cornish waters almost eighteen minutes later at 7.36, by which time the weather had deteriorated with a strong head wind that generated a choppy sea. From seaward the *Mauretania* must have created an impressive sight as she charged headlong into an opposing tide on this last run that took precisely the same time as the first, finishing at 7.38 p.m. Draughts were now 28ft 4in forward and 30ft 2in aft. Speeds for the forty-eight-hours continuous run calculated against tides and currents, had been 26.283, 25.263, 27.367 and 25.263 knots, giving a mean speed over the period of 26.044 knots, a magnificent effort that was a good knot-and-a-half above the contracted speed.

The ship was now readied for her speed trials on the following day, 6 November. The first part of these trials was to be run over the Skelmorlie Measured Mile, adjacent to Wemyss Bay, in six double runs; the second part, the sixth set, between Holy Island and Ailsa Craig.

Departing Wemyss Bay, the *Mauretania*, drawing 29ft 6in forward and 31ft 6in aft, began her passes over the exact nautical mile of the Skelmorlie Measured Mile, each extremity being marked ashore by two sighting pylons that, when aligned, marked the beginning or end of the run. At the northern end of the mile the posts were accentuated by a church spire on the slopes behind Skelmorlie and those at the southern end were distinguished by Skelmorlie Castle at Meigle. The ship was worked up to speed by the time the start of the mile was reached and at the end of each run the ship veered either to port or starboard (as before, a helm of 15° caused the ship to heel 6°) to ensure that the ship was taken safely away from the coast. After each pass the wave patterns created by the ship took a few minutes to reach the shore and often took observers and strollers along the strand by surprise. In later years the speed of ships using the Skelmorlie Measured Mile would be restricted to a mere 18 knots in order to avoid these mini-tsunamis!

Of the six planned double runs on the Skelmorlie Mile only five doubles were completed, the first of which commenced at 9.35 a.m., return run at 9.58; the others being made at 10.15 and 10.38; 10.55 and 11.15. The seventh pass at 11.43 a.m. (the first of the fourth pair of runs) was 'spoiled owing to governor stopping engines'. These safety devices were Aspinall's Patent 'Marine' Engine Governors – a safety steam cut-out device that had been fitted to the main stop valves to 'prevent racing and broken shafts' should the turbines exceed 230rpm. In this instance the engines had inexplicably shut down at a lower rate of 190rpm, depriving the turbines of steam. The ship glided to rest within a few lengths. Two more doubles were then run at 1.08 and 1.27 p.m.; and 1.47 and 2.05 p.m.

Mean speeds for the pairs of Progressive Trials were 18.32, 20.93, 22.83, 25.64, and 26.03 knots, although the latter speed (with a propeller slip of 11.66 per cent) was noted as having been made on a 'Bad course and boilers priming' – perhaps it was thought that the ship could have done better as the second run of this particular set realised a speed of 26.54 knots. Mean horsepower for these speeds was 21,209, 31,714, 44,744, 67,019 for the void run and 66,457.5, with 78,080 being the final horsepower recorded for the day.

A note contained within the Trials Records emphasises, most oddly in view of the vital importance of the trials, that the ship was not given a sufficient 'run-up' after each turn in order to come up to speed before entering the mile. As the course was also run at a slightly askew angle, a professional assumption was made to compensate for these unplanned deviations:

Note – In all these runs the ship was turned about and had not a sufficient length of run before entering the mile to have accelerated to full speed, or to be steady on her true course. Actual observation proved also that her course on the mile diverged greatly from the true course; representing an error in true speed of 1 to 3%. At maximum speed this represented about three quarters of a knot.

This adjusted speed gave a very satisfactory result that must have greatly pleased all of those on board, from those who stood imperiously on the Bridge gratings to the labouring Firemen on the Stokehold floors. Down in the heart of the ship's main Engine Room, temperatures during the day had been in the high eighties. By comparison, the Boiler Rooms that provided the engines with steam remained relatively comfortable at between 67 and 69°F; Fan Room temperatures were again a little higher.

For the final trial on 6 November the ship was taken further out to sea in order to obtain a speed over a greater set distance:

Runs on a --- [defaced entry, but other entries state '16 knots' (sic – miles)] course, 'Ailsa Craig' to Holy Island.

The northern starting point of these trials was Holy Island, 2 miles due east of the Isle of Arran, while, at the southern extremity of the run, Ailsa Craig (colloquially known as 'Paddy's Milestone' to the thousands of Irish emigrants and other travellers who passed the outcrop) was about 10 miles to the west of South Ayrshire and the first of three passes over this course started at five in the afternoon; ship's displacement 33,640 tons on draughts 29ft 6in forward and 31ft 6in aft, the final two runs following at half-hourly intervals. With tides affecting speeds, the first leg of the high-speed trial was accomplished in thirty-seven minutes thirty-five seconds, realising a speed of 25.6 knots. The return journey was achieved in just under two minutes less – thirty-five minutes fifty-four-seconds – at an amazing 26.75 knots!

Comparisons were made with the Lusitania's results and a blueprint – 'Results of Progressive and Official Trials After Ships Bottom Had Been Painted' – for the earlier ship was consulted. These similar trials had been carried out between 27 July and 1 August in fine summer weather, except for a 'stiff breeze to a moderate gale' that had been encountered on 30 July. The Lusitania's draughts had been slightly deeper, indicating a larger displacement of 37,078 tons at the trials' outset. Her best mean speed had been 26.46 knots on a run between Chicken Rock lighthouse, standing off the south-west coast of the Isle of Man, and Corswall Point and, later that same day, a good mean speed 25.99 knots between Holy Isle and Ailsa Craig. Indications were that the Mauretania would be more fuel-hungry than her Scottish-built sister: at 12 knots the Lusitania consumed an estimated 16.1 tons per hour, her boilers requiring 161 tons of water during that period. In comparison, the Mauretania burnt 16.5 tons of coal and used 165 tons of water. At the higher speed of 25.5 knots, 44.7 tons of coal and 447 tons of water were used by the 'Lucy', and 46.4 tons of coal and 494 tons of water by her sister. After her trials the

Looking magnificent at speed with paint worn away at her entry, this photo seems to have been retouched after her trials for publicity purposes to show the Stars and Stripes at her fore-truck as a flag of destination. (Author's Collection)

Lusitania was again repainted with the white sheer line that marked the lower edge of her superstructure being heightened, obviating the white-painted strake forward that would have otherwise have shown the ravages of the sea.

As records are not available for the auxiliary machinery in use on board the *Mauretania* it may be assumed that it was similar to that used on the *Lusitania* up to a speed of 23.3 knots:

4 feed pumps; 4 Hotwell pumps; 1 auxiliary circulating pump; 1 auxiliary air pump; 3 bilge pumps; 2 water service pumps; 1 sanitary pump; 4 oil pumps; 3 Turbo Generators; exhausting to auxiliary condenser; 2 sets of main circulating pumps; 4 twin wet air pumps; 1 stern tube pump; and 2 evaporators for washing water, etc.

… and during the 'Lucy's' forty-eight-hour full-power trial additional auxiliary machinery was brought into play: four main feed pumps; one auxiliary circulating pump; one auxiliary air pump; two evaporators for feed make-up for nine-hours; and two ballast pumps for three hours.

The average speed for the *Mauretania's* late afternoon runs off Ailsa were excellent – a very satisfying 26.17 knots, or slightly over 30 land miles per hour. With revolutions per minute averaging 190.8, the low-pressure turbine had, at its outer diameter, rotated at over 9,000 feet per minute with a clearance of 8/100ths of an inch (2mm) between the revolving mass of turbine blades and the casing! After a day's fast steaming the Boiler Room temperatures were still only between 66 and 70°F, which handsomely demonstrated the Fan Rooms' efficaciousness. Mean horsepower had been 77,990 and the mean propeller slip 11.13 per cent (the equivalent slip on her Builder's Trials with a fouled bottom had been 13.5 per cent).

The *Mauretania* presented a splendid sight that late autumn afternoon. With no wind to ruffle its placid surface, the pond-like sea curled easily away from the *Mauretania's* stem in an elegant, white-frothing wave as her great turbines whirred in their smooth, high-speed rotations. At the base of her stem a thin fan of water indicated her high speed and a white tumult issued from her stern as her four screws brazenly bored their way through the churning ocean, relentlessly pushing the liner forward.

Leaving Ailsa at 8 p.m., the *Mauretania* steamed south towards Liverpool. Even during this two-hour journey (for which an allowance of coal had been made) notes were made of the feed-water consumption of her main machinery:

Main Feed Pumps	841,000	[pounds weight]
Hotwell Pumps	839,000	
Auxiliaries	112,100	
Turbines and Feed Make Up	726,900	
Turbo Generators, etc	2,000	[?]

The arrival of the *Mauretania* back into the Mersey (draughts 28ft 8in forward and 30ft 2in aft; displacement 33,420 tons) made a spectacular finale for a maritime city that had been celebrating its seventh century. A great pageant, described both as a 'Memorable Celebration' and an 'Unqualified Success', had been held in August, and the euphoria continued with Cunard's introduction of their two new liners. Both anniversary and the *Mauretania* were commemorated on a special medallion commissioned by Cunard.

Cheered by huge crowds in late autumn, the Kaiser made a state visit to London before attempting to reconcile the differences between London and Berlin (much of it of his own making). The German Imperial Chancellor, Prinz von Bülow, applauded the reception given to the Kaiser, proclaiming that the mistrust between the two nations over the past ten years had been a 'huge misunderstanding'. But this heady atmosphere was soon blown away. During the following year's Cowes Week the Kaiser gave an interview to the *Daily Telegraph* on board the German Imperial Yacht *Hohenzollern* and expressed some autocratic opinions that were not in line with those of his government. In giving the so-called 'Cowes Interview' he succeeded in criticising the British on their colonial failings ('You English are mad, mad, mad as March hares') while protesting the innocence of Germany's military expansion and colonial ambitions; he then criticised the Franco-Russo Alliance as well as the Japanese. German and British governments were aghast, the latter's assessment that Germany was 'out to dominate Europe' seemingly accurate.

Already strained relations took another downward turn.

6

'BEHOLD A CITY ON TH' INCONSTANT BILLOWS ...'

Henry V, Act 3 (William Shakespeare)

Thousands of sightseers, enthused with a heady mix of patriotism, pride and curiosity, crowded Liverpool's Prince's Landing Stage and other vantage points on the wet early evening of Saturday, 16 November 1907, their sodden umbrellas glistening in what little light remained after the earlier sunset. The port was saying bon voyage to the second of the great new liners on her maiden voyage after almost losing them to Southampton as there had been rumours that Cunard might leave the Mersey for the Test. Other steamship lines used the southern port, a convenient gateway to continental traffic. At Cunard's April AGM, William Watson had said that such an arrangement would be left in 'abeyance for the present'. The imperative grew with White Star's experiment when their new *Adriatic* led an express mail and passenger service from Southampton on 5 June. There were further rumours that Cunard would take over White Star's Liverpool–America mail contract to encourage Cunard to remain at Liverpool, and the Mersey Docks and Harbour Board voted to provide 'a mechanical baggage conveyor to facilitate the disembarkation of passengers' luggage from the giant new steamships *Lusitania* and *Mauretania*'. In another move, Cunard opened new, larger offices at 29–30 Cockspur Street in London, the prestigious shipping capital of the world.

Now that the long-anticipated day had arrived, Captain John Pritchard stood proudly in command of the largest – and potentially the fastest – ship in the world. In his cabin were a few personal items, including a red leather-bound copy of the recently published 'Special Number' of the renowned technical periodical *The Shipbuilder*, his gilt-embossed personalised copy given to him by the shipbuilders. His copy would become well-thumbed.

Under the Captain's command were several hundred crew in deck, engine, hotel and catering departments. His second in command was Chief Officer William Crathorne, others on the Bridge were D. Newton, First Officer; C. Cay, Second; F. Storey, Third; A. Grey, Extra Third; and B. Dunphis (*sic*), Fourth; all the Navigating Officers held Master Mariner certificates (colloquially known as 'tickets') – some even held Extra Master's certificates – having trained under sail and held command in another company. As the government contract under which the new Cunarders had been built required that the officers and half of the crew should be British and reservists in either His Majesty's Royal Naval Reserve or Royal Naval Fleet Reserve, the *Mauretania* flew the Blue Ensign rather than the Red from her jackstaff. All crew members were required to sign the ship's Articles (the Crew Agreement that, according to Section 253 of the Merchant Shipping Act of 1894, listed 'The names ages and places of birth of all the crew … their ratings [positions] on board, their last ships' etc.) and this they did, according to department, on designated days between 11 and the 13 November. Captain Pritchard, the first to sign on, then signed the completed Articles, dated the day before the voyage began, on this occasion 15 November. By signing the Articles the crew contracted themselves to stay on the ship from the day of departure from Liverpool to the day that she returned – a whole round voyage – and at the end of each voyage the documents had to be delivered to the Board of Trade, under the threat of a hefty fine, 'by the master within forty-eight hours after the arrival of the ship at her final port of destination in the United Kingdom'.

Among those signing on were Telegraphists William Davies and J.R. Robinson, who were occupying posts regarded as almost being in the realms of science fiction as their Marconi wireless apparatus miraculously connected the ship with the shore when hundreds of miles from land. Ships to date usually had just one operator, so the *Mauretania* was at the forefront in the developing field of this new technology by having a two-man twenty-four-hour radio watch. Five Bandsmen comprised the small orchestra that would serenade the First-Class passengers, while forty-two Able Bodied Seamen ensured that the ship was correctly docked and generally looked after in a seamanlike fashion.

In the Engine Department, Chief Engineer John Currie (transferred from the *Carmania* after gaining much valuable experience with that ship's turbines) presided over seventy-six Engineers and Engine Room staff from one Senior Second and two Second Engineers (these three providing one officer to a watch of eight hours); a Senior Third and two Junior Thirds; three Fourths, Fifths, Sixths and Sevenths, two Eighth Engineers, two Ninths and – at the bottom of the hierarchy – Eleventh, Twelfth, Thirteenth and Fourteenth Engineers, the latter position being held by 22-year-old Alex Allan, who was joining his first ship. To assist in working the engines, forty-eight Greasers signed on the ship's Articles on 13 November at a wage of £5 10s (£5.50) per month, whilst the Chief Engineer received £35 per month. Two Storemen looked after the Engine Departments' tooling requirements.

Forward in the Boiler Rooms was the 'Black Gang', which consisted of 121 Trimmers (£4 10s per month) who shovelled coal from the bunkers into wheelbarrows before taking it to the floorplates in front of the boilers. There Firemen began their incessant back-breaking labour of feeding the precious fuel into the voracious boilers. The 201 Firemen and Leading Firemen, mostly Liverpool–Irish (Murphys, McGuinnesses, Smiths and Brannigans were well represented), were

The *Mauretania* sailed at night on her maiden voyage but this photo shows a later departure at 5 p.m. on Saturday, 30 July 1910. (Author's Collection)

A rare view of the *Mauretania* alongside a misty and as yet uncompleted Pier 54 after her maiden arrival in New York. 30 November 1907. (Collection of Eric K. Longo)

mostly young, aged between 20 and 30, although, at 59, Bernard Surely from Newry was by far the oldest. Many of the Black Gang had transferred either from other of the company ships (*Caronia*, *Etruria*, *Lusitania* and *Campania*) or from vessels of other lines – *Empress of Britain*, *Oceanic*, etc.; these tough men joined the ship at 7 a.m. on the morning of the 15th in order to raise steam. It was evident that many were uneducated, making their mark with an 'X' against their name. Undoubtedly, after signing Articles, most of this tough bunch went ashore and celebrated in traditional liquid style by spending the next few hours in a dockland pub, imbibing hefty amounts of ale as they were not allowed alcohol on board. Fines were levied on those who contravened the company's orders.

As seven Firemen and two Trimmers failed to join ('FTJ') the ship after signing on (perhaps because of the pre-voyage celebrations), eight others were hurriedly recruited as replacements, along with one Assistant Engineer. Trimmer John Barrow was incorrectly listed as a deserter prior to the voyage beginning and a letter written on a sheet of the ship's heavily embossed notepaper had to be sent to Head Office stating that this was not the case.

In the Chief Steward's (catering) Department, William Boyden (£15 per month) had 239 staff under him, including two Head Waiters (Head Waiter William Barton was on £8 per month). Seven Bakers, two Confectioners, six Butchers, one 'Jewish Cook' (to prepare Kosher meals), twenty-four Waiters, fourteen Stewardesses, two Matrons, one Interpreter, twenty-one Stewards, Lift Attendants, various Mess Stewards (to look after the crew), Stewards' Boys, Plumbers, Storekeepers, Linenkeepers, Printers, Barkeepers, a Barber (at 11*s* a month [55p] he made his money from tips!) plus two assistants, and – to wait at table – there were 209 Waiters (seven failed to join) – many from the *Caronia*.

David Bland (31) from Suffolk, was Chef, an important position that paid £20 per month. Beneath him was the Cook's Department, which had to be on board by 8 a.m. on the 15th having signed the ship's Articles three days before.

At 9 a.m. on sailing day a general muster of the crew preceded exercises in fire and boat station drills. At 12.30 a Board of Trade inspector witnessed the crew at boat drill before inspecting life-saving appliances, bilge pumps and watertight doors. There were great expectations of the new ship, but she had already been beaten in the speed race by a new turbine-driven warship – the torpedo-boat destroyer HMS *Mohawk*. Built at J. Samuel White's shipyard at East Cowes on the Isle of Wight, the warship had reached an amazing 34½ knots over the measured mile the day before. The great Royal Navy really did rule the waves!

At noon on the day of sailing, Third-Class passengers were tendered out to the vessel as she lay moored against the Cunard buoy on The Sloyne (this would save congestion on the Landing Stage and avoid, perhaps cynically, exposing the First-Class ['Saloon'] passengers to the 'lower orders'). Between 3 and 4 in the afternoon the liner transferred to her berth alongside the Prince's Landing Stage where excited Saloon and Second-Class passengers would board, giving them and a few privileged visitors about three hours to familiarise themselves with the ship and their accommodations before the ship sailed.

Princess de Poix, Prince André Pornheowski and jockey Lucian Lyne were among the 2,000 passengers boarding the liner for her first crossing of the North Atlantic. After sailing over on the record-breaking *Lusitania*, two young American passengers were returning to America on this inaugural crossing. Both 21-year-old William Francis Gibbs and his younger brother Frederic had an abiding interest in ships and William had already produced some innovative designs for large, fast Atlantic liners as an accomplished amateur exercise. Greatly impressed by White Star's *Oceanic*, her huge funnels particularly catching his imagination, he would in later years design the super-liner *United States* that became the fastest passenger liner ever to sail the North Atlantic.

Although 200,000 people had turned out on a lovely warm evening back in September to see her sister off on her maiden departure, the estimated 50,000 spectators who braved the cold, wet November evening were rewarded for their stoicism at 7.36 p.m. by the sight of the *Mauretania* pulling away from her berth – 'Stand by Engines' having been rung on the gleaming brass telegraph on the Bridge. The liner was an hour late in sailing due to the 'tardy arrival of the [two] boat train[s]'. Confusion had also reigned with the newly arrived baggage, some mislaid and some mislabelled, exacerbated by the darkness, weather and stewards as yet unaccustomed to the new ship. Nearly £3 million of specie (gold bullion) was loaded to 'further relieve the prevailing financial crisis' in the United States.

Left: A typical publicity drawing demonstrates the coal required for just one crossing of the Atlantic – plus a day's reserve: twenty-two trains of thirty wagons each holding 10 tons to bring the fuel from a dedicated pit! (Author's Collection)

Below left: The coal would be manually loaded into hoppers and hoisted to the coaling ports along both sides of the ship. (Author's Collection)

Below right: Each hopper would be emptied down the chutes into the coal bunkers. (Author's Collection)

The *Mauretania*'s stokehold's a wonderful sight
Sixty-four fires a-burning bright
But you'll shovel coal from morning to night
A-firing the Mauretania

(from 'Firing the *Mauretania*' – traditional)

By the time that the bugle blew for dinner, everything seemed to have been sorted out while, on the Bridge, Cunard's choice Pilot, Commodore Gore, was ready to take her out under the sharp surveillance of Captain Pritchard.

Drawing 34ft 2in forward and aft, a freeboard amidships of 27.2ft and under the supervision of several tugs, the *Mauretania* moved slowly away from the landing stage and into the stream. A heavy downpour did not dampen the spirit of the occasion as fireworks lit up the evening sky and steam whistles from both the great ship and other craft cut through the falling murk. Cheers rising from the still enthusiastic shoreside crowd as they huddled against the strong southerly breeze that drove the drizzle in from the other side of the Mersey were returned from hardy passengers braving the elements.

The *Mauretania* slowly steamed down the river and, as she passed the New Brighton Tower to port at New Holland on The Wirral, a salute of twenty-five guns was fired. At the busy entrance to the Mersey a sailing ship tacked across her bows 'at close quarters' and nearby another ship lay at anchor. The *Mauretania* – by then at half-speed – was skilfully manoeuvred between the two vessels to avoid a collision in a feat of steering and seamanship that elicited much admiration, although the majority of those on board were at dinner blissfully unaware of the near drama.

The Bar lightship was abeam at 9.16 p.m. Fourteen minutes later the Pilot was dropped and the Captain rang for full ahead as the ship headed westwards out into the North Channel. While not being noticeable to the novice, the surge in power and virtual lack of vibration surprised even the most seasoned of travellers. By 10.30 p.m. the ship was abreast Great Orme's Head, a prominent limestone headland jutting out from the North Welsh coast.

Mauretania was 'perfectly steady' according to the headlines copied by the on-board reporter to the *New York Herald*, adding, as she headed southwards towards the Irish Sea at 20 knots through a rough chop in a stiff south-westerly breeze, that she 'skims over the water and is steady as a big hotel'. A misty drizzle promised a thick night. Off Holyhead on the northern tip of Anglesey the wind veered to the north-west as the liner confidently steamed towards St George's Channel and the Celtic Sea. By dawn the weather had much improved, the wind having decreased in strength to give a moderate sea that promised a brighter day.

On the following morning at 8.22 and 236 miles from the Mersey, the Irish pilot boarded the *Mauretania* before she reached Roche's Point at the entrance to Queenstown (Cobh) Harbour. This call was indelibly written into the original Agreement of 1902 to collect mails that had been sent from London via express train and fast mail packet; any delays in the schedule of either would seriously affect the two sisters' sailings, an increasing concern to Cunard. As the *Mauretania* anchored in the Roads, one of the port's paddle steamer tenders came out from the Cunard wharf, heavily laden with bags of mail, additional passengers and baggage. Vendors of fine but expensive Irish lace, purveyors of other crafts, and a group of privileged visitors also came out on the tender to briefly board the ship as a record amount of mail went ashore.

In warm sunshine with little or no wind to worry the surface of the Channel, the *Mauretania* steamed away at 10.45. *Daunt Rock* lightship was soon abeam. Distances steamed for each twenty-four-hour period were ascertained daily at noon using sextant sightings of the Sun at its zenith (weather permitting), thus accurately establishing the ship's position and the mileage covered since the previous sighting. The ship's first noon position was taken just over an hour after leaving Queenstown and showed 30 miles of travel since passing the Rock, indicating that good speed was being made. The eyes of the world were on the liner.

With a promising weather forecast, her next destination was New York and a message received by Cunard that evening said: '*Mauretania* 207 miles west of Fastnet at 10 p.m. Sunday: all well.' Given good weather, it was optimistically anticipated that she would, with a 2½ per cent advantage over the *Lusitania*'s speed, due to improved boilers and slightly more powerful turbines, break the record on this, her first westbound crossing, and better her sister by three hours. Expert opinion was more pessimistic opining that a winter Atlantic record should not be expected: conditions could be considerably different to those experienced on trials and, if they were, a sustained strain on staff in stokeholds and Engine Room would be greater.

Any hope of a record soon dissipated as Mother Nature exerted her unpredictable pressure when, a short eight hours out from Queenstown, it became apparent that the anticipated fine weather would soon became a hope of the past as 'a long, high swell … indicated high winds ahead'. The joys of a winter on the North Atlantic were about to make an impression – not for nothing was 'WNA' added to a ship's Plimsoll markings, devised to ensure safe loading. The ship was heading into the aftermath of a tropical storm and during the night the sea 'got up'. The wind, previously blowing a breeze from the north-west, veered round to become a moderate gale of 40 knots from the south-west and, as Sunday grew into Monday, the sea state made deck excursions decidedly perilous as the ship pitched into huge waves that broke over her foredeck and washed aft to dash against the Bridge front. Although her pitching was described as being more of a 'plunge', it was remarked that she did not roll in these conditions as much as was expected.

Because of the gloom, Monday's noon position could not be fixed by sextant so the ship's position was estimated from propeller revolutions. This dead reckoning gave a day's advance of 571 miles. That same night the ventilation system malfunctioned, with unregulated hot air blowing into the cabins. As it was a cold evening, this did not overly concern the passengers but, conversely, the system was not exhausting the foul air and the problem took several hours to rectify. The aluminium-grilled elevators also became inoperative, remaining intermittently so throughout the voyage.

The gale worsened during Monday afternoon and a vibration accompanied by a fan-like whirring noise began to make itself felt, probably due to the propellers racing as the ship pitched headlong into the sea, thereby setting up a rotational pounding against the ship's afterbody. Some mistook this for vibration from the turbines. As the *Mauretania*'s bow pitched heavily – perhaps 60ft at a time – into the oncoming storm, several windows forward and fo'c'sle railings were damaged. Around three o'clock the massive 10-ton spare anchor, stowed and secured by 2in-thick link chains on the fo'c'sle, broke loose from its fastenings and started a ponderous, dangerous slide around the foredeck. To reduce the anchor's rampage, Captain Pritchard turned the *Mauretania*'s head about to steam in the opposite direction to direct the prevailing south-westerly 60-knot gale behind on the starboard aft quarter. Speed was reduced to about 4 knots – just enough to maintain steerage way.

Believing that the best way to lead is from the front, the Captain donned oilskins over his well-worn, gold-braided uniform and, with a resourcefulness gained from serving in sail, led a party out into the appalling weather to secure the wayward anchor. After an hour-and-a-half's struggle the battle was won by the Captain, who got a line around the anchor and this led to its final capture just after 4.40. By the time the *Mauretania* turned about to resume her course she had steamed 17 miles out of her way. The few observers who had watched the titanic struggle below them had to duck as shipped seas wildly hurled foam towards their higher position. Their fellow passengers, mostly unaware of the drama on the foredeck, comfortably braved the storm in the cocooned luxury of the panelled, brightly lit opulence of the ship's warm interior.

Somehow a quantity of water seeped into No. 2 cargo hold, causing damage to a consignment of laces and trimmings to the value of $5,000; the Mutual Insurance Company paid out. In the Specie Room a consignment of $1,785,000 of gold bars (destined for the banking firm of Heidelbach, Ikelheimer and Co.) remained safe. Shipbuilder George Hunter said that he had not heard of any structural damage happening to either the *Lusitania* or *Mauretania* that would have allowed such ingress of water. He added: 'if there had been any damage done to the hull I should have known of it … I was informed before she sailed for Liverpool that there were no signs of strains in the superstructure. From what I hear the water came from the ballast tanks.'

That same appalling night found the *Lusitania* arriving at Queenstown from New York and, unable to disembark either passengers or mails, she continued to Liverpool. *Mauretania*'s Tuesday noon position, not unsurprisingly, gave a distance travelled of only 464 miles in twenty-five hours. As the prospect of a record voyage evaporated, the disappointed passengers expressed amazement that such a big vessel could be treated as Nature's plaything and succumb to the influence of the waves. Gradually the weather improved, the previous pitching giving way to a long, slow roll in a nor'-easterly wind with a following sea on the starboard quarter. Noon sightings on Wednesday showed that the day's run had increased to 563 miles.

With the bad weather abating, the usual tote on the next noon-to-noon run was taken with bids taken for distances between 561 and 580 miles, although a Mr Maughan, who had superintended the building of the ship, presciently predicted 622 miles; his estimate was almost spot on with a run of 624 miles bettering the record-breaking *Lusitania*'s best daily distance by 6 miles. When the announcement was made just after noon, those in the Smoking Room spontaneously broke into applause with a few hearty cheers for the ship, her Captain, the Engineers, her crew and the on-board observers from the builders – including George Hunter, a 'quiet and unassuming' man who acknowledged the lunchtime compliments with gracious smiles and nods. Although pleased with the reception that his ship was receiving, he firmly declined to accede to calls for a speech.

After lunch, passengers prepared their cabin baggage for collection at 8 a.m. the next day in readiness for disembarkation, while dinner that evening turned into a gala occasion. It was followed by a concert in the Lounge, which included several comic songs being sung by a professional entertainer, Dennis O'Sullivan. On this occasion George Hunter submitted to a call for a speech and he took the opportunity to pay tribute to Cunard for having the 'energy and courage that had made the Mauretania possible'. A customary collection was made for seamen's charities. The high-spirited revellers dispersed at a late hour, not realising the change that would face them in the morning when they awoke to the mournful wailing of the ship's fog siren. A dense mist had descended over the waters during the night and it was difficult to see a distance of more than half the ship's length – at times no more than 50ft. Questions as to the ship's actual location brought forth a variety of 'diplomatic and evasive' replies from the stewards. After the euphoria of the previous day's gala of self-congratulation a gloom settled over the slowed ship as she was carefully conned through the mood-dampening murk. After passing Sandy Hook, the *Mauretania* anchored just after 11 a.m. to wait for visibility to improve over those dangerously busy waters. With the safety of his ship uppermost in his mind, Captain Pritchard issued an announcement that it would remain at anchor, possibly until the following morning:

Owing to delay by fog and insufficient water to cross the bar the captain regrets that he will be unable to land the passengers until to-morrow (Saturday) morning.

The notice had an immediate effect on a group of American businessmen who, as a result of the current financial crisis in the States, had urgent matters that required their attention. The previous evening's votes of confidence evaporated in the ensuing uproar and a deputation approached the Captain and *demanded*, no less, that he make efforts to get the ship into port on time. Captain Pritchard, who could not have slept much over the last seventy-two hours, was a model of patience and explained that he would not endanger his ship, however insistent the demands. The thought of an accident occurring to his brand new charge on her maiden voyage was more than he could tolerate.

During the course of these exchanges the fog lifted effortlessly, and a thankful Captain returned to his Bridge to ease the ship into New York Harbor, even though there was only half a tide. White Star's *Baltic*, which had been passed on Thursday night, came into view astern just as the ship got under way. During the interim, the crew made a regulation search for contraband with a negative result.

The ship was then navigated through the new, deep, 7-mile concourse of the Ambrose Channel that had been tested by Captain Pritchard in the *Caronia* on 27 August; the *Lusitania* had used it, the first ship to officially do so, on her maiden arrival on September's lucky Friday 13th! Passengers crowded the rails as the ship passed the exciting spectacle that never ceased to thrill – the recently come-of-age Statue of Liberty on Bedlow's Island overlooking the entrance to New York's Lower Bay. The liner anchored off Quarantine while her emigrants were transhipped by tenders to the federal immigration station on Ellis Island, run by the US Bureau of Immigration (Immigration and Naturalization Service), to be 'processed' for physical and mental fitness. *Mauretania*'s first delivery of potential new American citizens occurred during a record year for immigration with a staggering 1,004,756 immigrants being screened. It was later assessed that 5 million of these had arrived on Cunard ships over the years. Travelling mostly in Steerage and Third Class, these passengers were the bread and butter of the transatlantic business.

The *Mauretania* slowly continued on her *concours d'élégance* to her berth at Pier 54 (one of the new Chelsea Piers designed by Warren & Wetmore and sited at the foot of West 13th Street) with clouds of steamy breath exuding from her loud siren in response to a cacophony of whistles from other craft on the Hudson River as they greeted the newcomer. Cheers drifted over the water from a considerable crowd lining the Battery. New Yorkers had been excitedly awaiting the arrival of the new wonder ship and such had been the demand for visitor tickets that Cunard posted a notice in the *New York Times* on 24 November:

> The Cunard Steamship Company find it impossible to acknowledge receipt of the thousands of requests and to issue the requisite permits to visit the Steamship Mauretania.
>
> In order to meet the public demand, this steamer will be open for inspection of the public on WEDNESDAY, NOVEMBER 27th, from 9 A.M. to Noon and 2 P.M. to 5 P.M. A limited number of tickets for admission on that date will be on sale at the gate, Pier 54 North River, foot of 13th Street, November 26th and 27th.
>
> ADMISSION 5c. Tickets of admission can only be purchased at Pier 54, PROCEEDS WILL BE DONATED TO SEAMEN'S CHARITIES.

With a slight mist still prevailing, the liner docked at 6.15 that evening as 'Finished with Engines' was rung on the Bridge telegraph, her starboard side against the unfinished pier and her bow pointing towards West 13th Street. She had made the passage from Liverpool in five days, eighteen hours and seventeen minutes at an average speed of 22.21 knots. Her new home in America, the Chelsea Piers, was still under construction and piles of rubble littered the pier. These obstacles did not deter curious sightseers nor the horse-drawn cabs that queued for fares from the newly arrived liner. The 'immense scale' of the new superliner dominated the scene like an arrival from another world. A shoreside inspection of the liner showed the effects of the seas endured on the way over: a large area of black paint on her flared bow plating above the waterline had been stripped down to the grey paint that she had worn on her builder's trials – some reports said even down to the bare metal!

Even though she had not managed to better the *Lusitania*'s westward record, the *Mauretania* would soon show her capabilities.

Homeward Bound

The *Mauretania* remained alongside in New York for fourteen days to coal, clean the ship of coal dust, re-provision and send linen to Cunard's laundry contractor in Manhattan. The public waited excitedly to see what the 'Maury' would do on her return crossing. The day after her maiden arrival crew member Fred Grosvenor was sent ashore to the St Vincent Hospital with an unspecified illness, his balance of wages being sent ashore to the ship's agents.

Unloading cargo was undertaken by Longshoremen hired along New York's West Street, where men assembled outside the piers to await the 'Hiring Man'. The system was open to corruption, and disputes between those chosen and those not would ominously often be settled after dark. On the morning of Wednesday, 27 November a group of 250 Italians, many of them recent immigrants, were waiting for selection and, after a hundred had been picked, one of the remaining men made a remark that was considered offensive. Soon the whole assembly was embroiled in a mass altercation.

Just before officers from four New York Police Department stations arrived, pistol shots punctuated the fracas, a mass stampede ensuing as men ran to avoid injury or arrest. Weapons were hurriedly thrown into the harbour's murky waters, some guns actually bouncing off and marking the side of the *Mauretania*. One excited Longshoreman, apparently forgetting that he could not swim, dived into the water. His brother, seeing his plight, went hand-over-hand along one of the *Mauretania*'s steel mooring hawsers until his sibling could reach his dangling legs. They remained there, suspended over the water locked in an embrace of survival until rescued and arrested by the police. Work on the *Mauretania* ceased until a fresh gang of Longshoremen could be mustered. Some Trimmers became involved in the incident but it was not ascertained whether these were from the *Mauretania*.

It might have been a tragic coincidence that, two days later, two Firemen disappeared from the ship due to 'supposed drowning' after falling into the harbour. The alarm was raised when three crew members, Leading Fireman Lawrence Kelly and Firemen Patrick McGuinness and William Pedley, were walking down the pier as they returned to the ship just after one o'clock in the morning when someone called out for help, shouting that there was a man (perhaps two) in the dock. Kelly thought that he saw one man's head and jumped in but could find no trace. Pedley threw a rope into the water but of the men nothing more was seen. At the 9 a.m. muster it was found that Firemen David McNab and Isaac Goscombe were missing and it was assumed it was they who had been in distress and lost in the cold, murky waters. Had they, as a result of the earlier disturbances, fallen victim to the sinister undercurrent of Longshoremen's vengeful justice of 'after dark etiquette' that so often violently settled many a dispute along the waterfront, or had one fallen in and pulled the other with him after losing his footing after too many Thanksgiving toasts? Two other crewmen failed to return to the ship and were listed as deserters, perhaps enticed ashore by the bright lights and glittering promise of New York. To replace the men lost to the ship through death, desertion or hospitalisation, six others were signed on as substitutes.

On the fine afternoon of Saturday, 30 November a freshening southerly breeze was blowing as the 'Maury' backed out of her berth at 12.15 p.m. at the outset of her first eastward homeward-bound crossing. When Sandy Hook was passed at 2.20 the question was would the *Mauretania* beat her sister's fine achievement?

On Sunday morning the Captain held Divine Service for all passengers and those crew whose duties allowed them to attend, following which the passengers were temporally reassured as the Captain and Purser Graham led their daily examination of the life-saving appliances, seeing 'that they were fit and ready for use'. The noon day sightings showed that the run for the first day had been 490 nautical miles, giving the ship a promising average speed of 23.7 knots. At 8 o'clock that evening three stowaways, the ship's first, were discovered in the Firemen's berths, perhaps having found sympathetic or financially rewarded allies. Stowaways Codliss (aged 50) and 18-year old Kelly, both Liverpudlians, and Meade (43) of County Cork, were detained until they could be handed over to the Liverpool police.

While over the Grand Banks off Newfoundland the breeze fell away and an intermittent fog caused the liner's speed to be reduced by half. In spite of the fog maintaining an irksome presence for thirty hours, 548 miles were logged for Monday and 535 for Tuesday. The fogs were left behind as Tuesday progressed, only to be replaced by a wind that increased into a southerly gale that brought with it a high sea. By Wednesday the gale veered round to the west, reaching 50 knots. With the following sea, in which the liner 'behaved splendidly', the *Mauretania* made 556 miles at over 24 knots. After the initial publicity surrounding the liner's entry into service, many of the passengers expressed surprise at the liner's propensity to adopt a long, steady roll in such conditions. The *Lusitania* wirelessed that she was facing the worst of the weather and was reportedly thirty hours behind schedule. The wind fell away on Thursday, enabling the *Mauretania* to increase speed to 24.08 knots and to make 554 miles, although daily mileages were still behind the *Lusitania's* record daily best of 570. Just after the midday sightings had been made, the ship overtook White Star's *Baltic*, making heavy weather having left New York before the Cunarder.

Daunt's Rock was abeam at 5.49 p.m. (124 miles having been made since noon) on Thursday, 5 December after a passage of 2,507 miles in four days, twenty-two hours and twenty-nine minutes from the Ambrose at an average speed of 23.69 knots. Euphoria reigned when it was realised that the *Lusitania's* record had actually been beaten by twenty-one minutes! An ebullient Chief Engineer expressed an opinion that, once winter was over the ship would have no trouble in making 25 knots.

Having tendered early Thursday evening at Queenstown, the *Mauretania* arrived at the Bar lightvessel at 6 a.m. on Friday and moored for two hours a mile to the south, awaiting sufficient depth of tide before proceeding into the Mersey to the Princes Landing Stage after a run of five days, ten hours and fifty minutes. It then discharged her passengers, which included C.J. Swan of the shipbuilders and his colleague, Mr Vaughan. During the trip these gentlemen had been lauded during a private dinner party for the quality of the ship and for setting a new record. Also on board was Consuelo, the American-born Duchess of Marlborough, who had been studying how the dreadful conditions of the poor in New York were being alleviated with the intention of undertaking similar work in England.

'Right Through!'

A ship does not achieve a record passage without hard work at several levels but it was the efforts of the Stokehold, the Trimmers and Firemen feeding the voracious boilers, though their sheer hard, unremitting back-breaking work, that produced steam in vast quantities that pushed the ship forward. Mostly Liverpool–Irish, this group of men was known as the 'Black Gang' and the big Cunarders – along with White Star's 'Big Four' – were known as the 'Big Scouse Boats'. The men lived a hard life ruled by Watches and the shrill bells that demanded the furnaces be fed in pre-arranged sequences shown by indicators flashing the number of the furnace requiring attention. The men had a code of conduct that relied on mutual trust. Doors and lockers were kept unlocked as anything otherwise implied distrust and woe betide any who broke this trust; heavy leather belts that provided back support and protection were better dispensers of justice than an Engineer's tongue!

The Marine Engineer published an article in July 1889 about the Black Gang on the *City of New York* (the largest and fastest ship of her day) but its relevance seventeen years later still summed up the great divide between deck and engine departments on an ocean-going liner:

A remarkably fast passage has been made by the City of New York which has now reduced the record below the six days between Queenstown and Sandy Hook. Great enthusiasm has been raised in America by this feat, since the American people never fail to applaud a successfully carried out undertaking, whether by foreign people or their own. Much interviewing has been done on the other side, and compliments made; and it is a curious fact that these have all been rendered to the captain of the City of Paris rather than the engineering department.

We do not in any way [desire] to detract from the credit due to a captain and his officers for their skilful navigation of a vessel from port to port, but it is obvious on the face of it that the captain and his officers would be quite helpless in the production of a fast passage were it not for the co-operation and skill of his engineering staff. The extraordinary rapidity of the passages now effected across the Atlantic are due, in the first place, to the excellent design of the vessels and engines, but chiefly, as a matter of fact, to the untiring energy and watchfulness on the part of the engineers in charge of the engines in watching that everything is going right.

Every 10lbs increased pressure carried on the boilers above the average with engines running at high speed, simply means extra forcing of the draught and more laborious exertions on the part of the stokers [Firemen] in keeping up the supply of fuel, and in stoking and placing it on the fires to the best advantage; and every revolution of the engines above their general average means more minute and watching of every journal to prevent it running hot, and the anticipation throughout the engine of any indication of approaching failure or want of strength or soundness. If the details were more carefully gone into, we have no doubt that it would result in finding a record of extra toil and exertion on the part of the stokers and double or treble hours worked by the engineers in charge in amending and adjusting parts threatened by weakness owing to the continuous strain upon them.

There is evidently some considerable injustice still existing in the relative position of the engineering and seafaring staffs respectively, on board our large commercial steamers as in the Navy. It is reported that Capt Watkins has said that he will, in a short time, reduce the record to five days and 12h. Now, not wishing to detract from the evident energy and force of will which the captain may be desirous of applying to all those under him for succeeding in such an effort, we cannot see that he personally can conduce any of the necessary skill or labour that will be required to effect such a purpose.

It is evidently not the captain, but the engine and screws that drive the ship and it is only the engineers that have the technical skill and knowledge to enable them to get more or less out of the engines and boilers in a certain time. We think that, in whatever praise may be conferred for that which has been effected, or in any statements with regards to what may be hoped to be effected in the future, the name of the Chief Engineer, Mr Ernest Gearing [what a splendidly appropriate name for an engineer!], should at least be referred to as a main spring in any such efforts together with that of the captain. Our generation will probably see a considerable change in the direction we indicate in the relative estimate of the seafaring officers of a steamship.

As in the Royal Navy, engineers on a merchant vessel were not accorded status as officers – they were rated as being uneducated non-sailors and were not awarded the executive curl on their uniform braid until 1915. The article concluded:

> … but of late years there has been a great influx of well-educated and well-trained young men who have joined the [merchant] service, and are making their presence felt to the advantage of the profession, and necessarily so, as the boilers and machinery are now of the type that require the highest order of intelligence.

At the bottom of the Engineers' scale on the *Mauretania* were two Tenths, and one Eleventh and Twelfth. The Thirteenth and Fourteenth Engineers were very young, usually from Oxbridge, whose task it was to watch, assist and learn.

Engines, bearings, shafts, etc., were oiled by automatic lubricators attended by twenty Greasers. In the boiler rooms were eleven Leading Firemen supervising 192 Firemen divided into three Watches (4 to 8; 8 to 12; and 12 to 4 a.m. and p.m.). Two Boilermakers maintained the boilers, replacing everything from water tubes to firebricks, and one Plumber, two Electrical Attendants, two Storemen and one Donkeyman made up the remainder of the Chief's staff.

It was an abundant supply of coal in Great Britain that had enabled the nation to prosecute its Industrial Revolution with such vigour and then to maintain a pre-eminent position in the world while developing an empire. That 'Coal was King' (as a cartoon in *Punch* boasted: 'Aha! Peace or war, they can't get on without me!') came at a deadly price. From hundreds of feet below the surface to its burning, coal was accompanied through its brief, consumable life by misery, dirt and dust – and always by poorly paid, dangerous hard work. Accidents took their toll and recent strikes in American mines had been particularly violent and bloody.

Coal was indeed king and oil, because of supply difficulties, had not yet made inroads as a major fuel; *Mauretania*'s boilers were designed to convert to burn the more efficient, less labour-intensive liquid fuel once adequate and constant supplies were assured. The best coal when fired by the best men gave the best results, and the best coal was

After an exceptionally good passage the Stokehold's 'Black Gang' would bang anything bang-able and even formed their own fancy dress band. (Author's Collection)

The Chief Engineer and his team grouped on deck. (Collection of Eric Sauder)

generally accepted as 'Welsh Steaming Coal' (or 'Best Welsh'); with a high carbon content, it could heat more water and produce more horsepower per pound and produce less ash than coal of a lesser quality. Exported worldwide to fuel the Royal Navy and British merchant vessels, Best Welsh sustained an empire that made Britain supremely powerful and influential. Coal from the mines around the Newcastle shipyards was also of a good quality (especially from Haswell, near Sunderland), so the *Mauretania* probably had a local supply of this for her Builder's Trials and delivery voyage.

When at Liverpool the ship was coaled either at the Cunard Buoy at neap tides or in dock, as in New York, the ship being warped away from her berth. In the former instance she was supplied by lighters (these would be towed away if too much of a chop developed to avoid damaging the ship), and in the latter by cranes and barges. Coal was loaded into large baskets, passed up to Loaders on the staging who tipped the fuel into one of twenty coaling ports port and starboard that lead down to the bunkers. The coal ports, 2ft 6in square, had bolted covering plates hinged along their lower edges enabling the covers to swing 45° outboard. Segmented side plates contained the flow of coal, the whole acting as a chute down which the coal cascaded. On completion of coaling the hinged plates were relocated and securely bolted after a double wick soaked in white lead had been wound around the bolts to make a vital watertight seal (grommet) between plate and hull.

At Liverpool 6,770 tons of Best Welsh had been hauled on board the *Mauretania* for her maiden voyage. A margin of perhaps 1,350 tons remained in the bunkers on her arrival in New York so 5,000 tons of American coal (American semi-Anthracite coal was about equal to Best Welsh in carbon content; American hard, dry Anthracite had a slightly higher ash content) was loaded using canvas bags for her return journey lifted from open barges that lay alongside the liner. The labour-intensive, dirty, back-breaking and almost soul-destroying work of coaling could take up to three days. To prevent tarry (talc-like black dust) from seeping through every tiny opening to permeate the ship's pristine interiors, side scuttles and windows were tightly closed and canvas covers rigged along open promenades. But, despite these measures, the Stewards still had a hard job and, even after a thorough cleaning, fine coal dust persisting in vent trunks found its way into the ship.

The eventual superiority of the *Mauretania* over her sister was attributed to several factors, not least a better design of boiler and more efficient forced-draught fans, but, as seen, her coal consumption was slightly higher than that of the *Lusitania* – a meagre 0.4 tons per hour at 12 knots but almost 5 tons more at 25 knots. On the New York run 1,090 tons were required daily to maintain 25 knots. Each boiler room required a team of sixty-four skilled Firemen divided into three, four-hour watches to tend the twenty-three double-ended and two single-ended boilers. With six boilers in each room, three forward and three aft, sporting four furnaces (each of which consumed 1 ton of coal *per* watch) there were 192 hungry furnaces requiring 50 tons of coal *per* hour or almost 23 tons of coal *per* boiler *per* day (including an allowance for auxiliary machinery and domestic feed). The grates, on which the coals were laid, were made up of evenly spaced firebars covering an area of 4,060sq.ft, while the heating area of the water tubes that carried the water to be boiled had a total surface area of 159,000sq.ft. In an Atlantic gale a shovel of coal would weigh several times its actual weight as a Fireman sought to overcome gravity as the ship's bow rose 30-40-50-60 feet, but as the bow pitched into a trough that same shovelful, 'putting on a pitch', would be lighter and easier to handle. Firemen's tools included shovels, rakes (to spread the coals evenly and to prevent soft clinkers from jamming the firebars), and slice bars (a large poker) that, when skilfully run through under the fire and twisted with a slight sideways movement, aerated the fire.

The ship's propellers rotated at 177rpm powered by 66,000shp for 25 knots in service, although 76,000shp had been achieved on trials and this had given 192rpm for a speed of 26 knots. High speed meant additional back-breaking toil for the Black Gang, with Firemen and Trimmers taking great pride in maintaining a good head of steam to keep the reputation of their beloved 'Maury' (aka 'Maurie' or 'Mary'). It was hot, dusty, thirsty work – and as the men were denied alcoholic beverages while on board (tea was consumed by the gallon!) it was no surprise that the Black Gang had a reputation for being hard drinkers. (When ashore and, when comparing their ship's achievements with their opposite numbers from the *Lusitania*, the Gang's reputation as a bunch of hard cases sometimes led to fisticuffs!)

For the double-ended boilers the stoking times of the furnaces had to be staggered as, if furnaces at both ends of a double-ended boiler were opened at the same time, a blow-back could occur resulting in serious consequences for the man feeding the opposing furnaces. The 'Kilroy's Stoking Regulators' prevented any such mishap, their bells set to ring at set periods of time (varying between eight and thirty minutes) depending on how much steam was required. A bell to stoke, a brief respite, then another bell set the Firemen raking and slicing the burning coals, ridding the glowing inferno of ash and broken clinkers (solidified molten ash) using long clinker shovels. A report from a new, turbine-driven battlecruiser of the Royal Navy observed:

> The engine- and boiler-rooms are hell, at sea; one cannot realise the life of the stokers [naval term for Firemen] and other 'saints who toil below' until one actually experiences it. These men's work can vie with any … their whole life … is a vivid succession of discomforts and hardships, unparalleled in severity and monotony.

Furnaces had to be frequently cleaned (fed with fresh coal and ash removed) and 'The Efficient Use of Fuel' noted:

> Cleaning takes several minutes, and before cleaning, the dampers should be checked as much as possible to avoid an inrush of cold air when the doors are open. Fires should not be burned down too low before cleaning, but sufficient fire must be left on the grate to start up rapidly after cleaning.
>
> The water level should be so manipulated as to avoid the need for feeding water to the boiler while cleaning the fires, as otherwise the steam will be rapidly reduced ['Keeping the arrow in the blood' – the red segment of an indicator gauge's face]. Times of cleaning should be arranged to fit with periods of low load. Where there is a bank of boilers [as in the *Mauretania*], boilers should be cleaned in rotation.
>
> For cleaning the fires the slice bar and hoe [rake] are used. The fires should be cleaned out thoroughly, one fire at a time, all ash and clinker being removed so that they will not fuse to the bars or bridge.

About 150 tons of ash was produced daily and fell through the fire-bar gratings into the ash pit. Using 12ft-long ash shovels, it was removed at the end of each watch and drawn into steel wheelbarrows. The Firemen were cautioned that on no account was ash or clinkers to be drawn onto the Stokehold floor for slaking (quenching with water) prior to being barrowed to the 'See's Ash Ejectors' (its workings similar to a flush toilet) or the 'Crompton's Ash Hoists' for overboard discharge as this would lead to corrosion in the floor plates. Unburnt coals were returned to the furnaces.

In firing a furnace the 'spreading' or 'sprinkling' method or the 'side' or 'wing' firing methods were used; if a mis-aimed coal-loaded shovel hit the boiler and spilt its contents, it would have been regarded as a sin (not only did it waste effort but it jarred already sore wrists):

> There are two methods of cleaning hand fired furnaces, namely, the side method and the front-to-back method. In the side method good coal is pushed from one side to the other, and the clinker and ash scraped out by the hoe after being loosened, if necessary, by the slice bar. The burning coal from the other side is then removed to the clean side. A few shovelfuls of fresh coal are added in order to have enough burning coal to cover the entire grate when the cleaning is done. The clinkers are then removed from the second half of the grate, after which the fire is spread evenly over the grate and built up gradually with fresh coal. [The depth of coal – about four inches – on the grates was critical and had to be judged to a nicety as an even distribution of fuel over the fire helped to eliminate smoke].
>
> When starting to clean a thin fire it may be necessary to put fresh coal on the side to be cleaned last in order to have enough burning coal left to start a hot fire quickly …

Incongruously, in spite of their grimy, dusty work, the Firemen often appeared to have clean faces; this was due to constant wiping of sweat with flannel neckerchiefs or 'tail rags', so called as they were tucked behind in wide leather belts. The men could not slack in their tasks as any sign of stalling would be admonished by their peers. Each man had to maintain a set pace while taking care of the tools of his trade; a slice left in the furnace for too long would almost melt and be lost. Once retrieved the end had to be quenched before being hammered back into shape after achieving a certain yellowish hue. A tip for comfort was to wear belt buckles behind as this kept the metal from becoming unbearably hot. Singlets that protected a man's torso from the heat were periodically wrung out!

Trimmers who supplied the Firemen with coal had two functions. One was to shovel coal from the bunker towards the door while ensuring that the extracted coal did not undermine the remaining pile by 'trimming' it to prevent a collapse. A second Trimmer then filled his wheelbarrow from the door before taking the load to the floorplates in front of the furnaces. As with the Firemen with their shovels, Trimmers fought against gravity in a seaway as they pushed their wheelbarrows uphill and then downhill. But it was still back-breaking, exhausting work during the four hours of each of two watches a day. Fireman George Garrett recalled that as Trimmers ran through the boiler rooms with their loaded barrows they would repeatedly shout 'RIGHT THROUGH!' warning others of their approach. At the end of their watch Trimmers stockpiled coal on the Stokehold floor in readiness for the next before it entered the vacated Boiler Room, as Garrett wrote, like 'a subterranean theatre letting in'. Should an individual Fireman create discord with the Trimmers he would find himself surrounded by untidy, impeding piles of the largest, heaviest coals.

Side bunkers were cleaned when their contents had been exhausted and new supplies brought from the large bunker forward of No. 1 Boiler Room. To navigate a heavily loaded wheelbarrow of coal quickly from this bunker to the Stokehold decks in the aftermost No. 4 Boiler Room involved a run of 130 yards and necessitated ducking under low watertight doorframes, dodging between scorching boilers and avoiding searing steam pipes. The ship's speed depended on the speed of these deliveries – a good reason why the Trimmers regarded themselves above their reputation as the lowest of the low.

A Trimmer might have ambition and aspire to become a Fireman who, in turn, might be promoted to Greaser, a cleaner job in the cooler Engine Room. A further promotion would find a Greaser back in the Boiler Room as a Leading Fireman in charge of a squad with a Leading Hand (known as a 'Pusher') to encourage or cajole (in one way or another) or even assist a slower Fireman in keeping his furnaces fed and clean, sometimes by doubling up on the slice bar to break up clinkers jamming the firebars, a sledgehammer sometimes providing an added force on the bar.

A young yacht helmsman and designer, Uffa Fox, worked his way back from a successful sailing tour of North America by signing on as a Trimmer on a ship sailing from New York to Antwerp (probably a Red Star liner). He described the work of a Trimmer as being 'a stoker's [sic] handmaiden' as he wheel-barrowed coals to the furnaces before taking red-hot clinkers and ash away for disposal. He also experienced being buried up to his neck when a mountain of badly trimmed coal collapsed. As did all Trimmers, the impecunious young Vectensian coveted a job as a Fireman and, when an opportunity offered, Uffa took great delight and satisfaction in mastering the skill, considering that the timing and resultant pleasure involved exceeded the delights of golf, the latter not comparing to 'the art and thrill of aiming coal into the exact spot of your choice in the blazing furnace'.

The waste gases (the amount of smoke exuding from the ship's funnels was an indication of good or bad stoking) was drawn off the boilers by one huge uptake in each boiler room. Like monstrous geometric spiders with each pair of legs exhausting a boiler, the uptakes garnered smoke from the furnaces before directing the gases into the shafts that led into the imposing red and black funnels until it spilled into the clean air above the ship in black, billowing clouds, especially when at speed.

The Stokehold men were proud of their work and when a record passage was involved the place erupted with anything bang-able being banged. An improvised fancy-dressed band of Stokehold crew armed with brass instruments, banjos, etc., played ashore to accentuate their pride in a hard job well done. Celebration on board was restricted and those caught under the influence of alcohol received fines imposed by law: 5s (25p) for the first offence and 10s for the next that, for men receiving between £5 and £6 10s (£6.50) per month, was a sizeable chunk out of their hard-earned wages. Lapses of discipline incurred similar fines.

The voracious furnaces required a prodigious and continuous supply of air and this was supplied by fans, parodying in steel the shape of a nautilus shell, which pulled air down through the large, prominent cowl-headed ventilators that stood sentinel along the Sun Deck and forcing it into the oxygen-hungry boilers. The eight Fan Rooms (one fore and aft and above each Boiler Room) contained four W.H. Allen electrically driven fans and operated under the Howden forced-draught system. The Fan Rooms that provided the relatively low temperatures in the *Mauretania*'s Boiler Rooms (recorded at between 68° and 80°F during her forty-eight-hour trials, this afforded the Black Gang a degree of comparative, but still hot, comfort) had also to be kept cool and, although these rooms were usually between 3° and 10° hotter than the Boiler Rooms, they seldom reached temperatures above 88°F (low 80s were average). The lot of the Stokehold's crew was not as bad as that of their predecessors – one hundred firemen and trimmers had committed suicide between 1893 and 1894 by throwing themselves overboard after being driven mad by the heat.

After a strenuous non-stop four-hour stint on each watch, the men were only too glad to queue for a wash, grab some food and crash into tightly packed two-tiered bunks, sixty-four men in each dormitory, for some much-needed sleep before their next watch eight hours later. Sets of bunks were divided into 'cracks' in which men were segregated according to their shore addresses with the names of streets chalked by each crack – Gerard Street, Marsh Lane, Athol Street, etc.; this had the good effect of creating friendly squads and built efficient teamwork.

Food for the Black Gang tended to be monotonous with hash, or 'scouse', being a frequent dish and delivered in containers called 'dixies' by the Watch Caller. But the food was often thrown away, especially by the 12-to-4 watch that was on duty after each dinnertime (it did not do to work on a full stomach). Similarly, breakfast was not eaten by this watch as they were abed; the men felt bad about the waste, especially just after the war that had seen their oft-hungry families ashore subsisting on horsemeat and poor bread. To make up for lost meals a bucket of 'oodle' was always available, the cook's work being covered by the rest of the gang. Diced meat obtained from the stores was kneaded with carrots, onions and potatoes and topped up with three parts water (similar components to the scouse stew) then placed in four buckets, one per Boiler Room. Firmly pressed into a pile of hot coals to prevent movement in a seaway, it was left to simmer until, after frequent tasting, it was declared as being 'the gear'. At 1 a.m., with all fires cleaned and ashes overboard, the buckets were taken up to the watch's dormitory and fairly shared. The men had a ditty for this delicious concoction:

It's not the meat that make us grin,
But the dirty water they boil it in.

Another Boiler Room snack was made from passengers' leftovers: chicken carcasses, chops, remains of joints – anything – all put into blackened rectangular trays and cooked. This pot-mess was called 'the gubbins' and was eagerly devoured from 'the Black Pan'! Gubbins and oodle were often exchanged with the following watch. Pudding (duff) was available twice a week. In the hot atmosphere of the Boiler Rooms copious amounts of tea ('Irish') was essential and, with more than the Board of Trade's stipulated 2oz weekly *per* man available, great quantities were brewed in 7lb jam tins. The *Mauretania* relied as much on 'oodles and Irish' to get her across the Atlantic as much as she did on coal!

There were snacks ('tab-nabs') in the Engine Room, too. Baked potatoes were a favourite and (on the later *Queen Mary* at least) a chief engineer might work himself up as he failed to source the delicious aroma of a 'Baked Idaho á la Main Stop'!

The tough, rough work in the Stokehold went generally unnoticed by those carried in the cosseted comfort of the passenger decks. A preconceived idea of Firemen as a 'grimy, wiry, dishevelled, hard looking lot' was made by young Jack Thayer as he stood atop an upturned lifeboat, sharing it with several of the Black Gang, as the *Titanic* slid below the waves. After mutually fighting for their lives he reassessed his earlier opinion:

… under the surface, they were brave human beings, with generous and charitable hearts.

7

'LONG HAVE I SIGHED FOR A CALM ...'

from 'Maud' by Alfred Lord Tennyson

Articles for the *Mauretania*'s second voyage were opened on 13 December 1907, with departure from Liverpool the following day. As usual the Articles noted the details of the *Mauretania*'s Official Number (124093), her registered tonnages of 31,937 gross and 8,947 net; that she was of 70,000 horsepower; nominal horsepower of engines – 17,955; length 762.2/10ft; beam 88.0/10ft; depth of hold 57.1/10; number of seamen for whom accommodation is certified – 800. Her manager was noted as Andrew D. Mearns at Cunard S.S. Co. Ltd, 8 Water Street, Liverpool. The ship's identification signal *HLTQ*.

Waiting to berth at the Landing Stage on the 14th to embark passengers, she had remained anchored in midstream as the weather was too windy for her anchors to be unshackled and her cables attached to the Cunard Buoy. Around the British coast vessels had been dismasted, blown ashore or severely delayed, and a schooner had disappeared without trace off Dorset's Durleston Point. Ashore the hurricane caused widespread flooding.

It was not unusual for a ship to drag her anchors in strong winds, it often being necessary to weigh anchor, regain the mooring ground and re-anchor. But, on this occasion (Friday 13th!), an extremely strong wind of up to 64mph was blowing, which, in combination with the tide, caught the *Mauretania*. Swinging round, she dragged her anchor and, driven to the windward shore, grounded off the Egremont Ferry on a submerged shelf of compacted sand, a 'hard edge' to the main deep channel and walkable at low tide, that extended from Seacombe to New Brighton. It was not until the early hours of sailing

day that the liner was released, fortunately without damage, aided by the wind, her own power, the Cunard tug *Skirmisher* and the *Alfred* of the Alexandra Towing Co. Ltd. She sailed that evening on schedule.

Leaving Queenstown on Sunday the 15th at 10.40, she achieved an easy 24 knots in now smooth seas until a good blow came in from the south that lasted for two hours before being succeeded by fog. By Monday morning this murk had cleared to be replaced by a sou'-westerly gale; it was hoped that this would not interfere with a good passage. But worse was in store. On Tuesday (17 December) a dropping barometer indicated an approaching hurricane. Seas generated by the previous blow remained as a heavy swell but, as the wind veered round 180°, a 60mph gale arrived accompanied by rain that could be heard approaching a mile away. In difficult and uncomfortable conditions she pitched over westwards (following the old Cunard adage of 'Pitch over and roll home'). Within ten minutes the gale increased to 100mph, literally flattening the sea with its force. Throughout the onslaught the *Mauretania* maintained 15 to 20 knots and the Captain ordered everything be secured, including the deadlights over portholes to prevent flooded cabins. As the hurricane reduced to a gale, heavy seas were still breaking against the ship's exposed side and violently dislodged three lifeboats from their chocks, one boat suffering splintered planking. When the tremendous gale eventually subdued the passengers considered that she had put up a splendid performance, proving herself to be a good sea boat. By Wednesday the sea had moderated with light winds from the north-west.

Towards the end of this storm-ridden crossing the passengers had sufficiently recovered their spirits to organise the usual end-of-voyage concert of piano recitals, songs and recitations in the grand style of Victorian drawing room entertainment, the event chaired by Mr Whitelaw Reid, the American Ambassador to the Court of St James. The Thursday evening concert undoubtedly contained acts of both varying talent on the part of the performers and stamina on the part of the audience. It was a tradition for the Captain to attend these functions, even though Captain Pritchard must have been heartily sated with them after so many years at sea! A customary collection raised the goodly sum of £65 for seamen's charities. Also travelling in First Class were the Canadian Minister for the Interior, the Hon. C. Sefton; the white-bearded Canadian High Commissioner to the United Kingdom and philanthropist, Donald Smith, 1st Baron Strathcona and Mount Royal; and Lucy, Lady Duff-Gordon, also known as 'Lucile' of London and Paris, *haute-couturier* to the wealthy and en route to New York to investigate the possibilities of opening a new branch. Both she and her husband would gain notoriety during a maiden voyage on a White Star liner five years later. In the Mail Room were 3,017 bags (or 'pouches') of Christmas mail.

The *Mauretania* arrived in New York on Saturday, 21 December for the second and last time for 1907 after a crossing of five days and fifty-five minutes at an average speed of 23 knots, the voyage having been described as one being 'so stormy that any attempt [at] record breaking was out of the question'. It may have been after this crossing that 'Edith' – returning to her home in Websterville, Vermont – wrote that she got home safely but 'I have been awful sick, it was a rough voyage … it will be a few years before I go on it again … I was very weak.'

Even at Christmas adventure was not far away. Two days after her arrival, a combination of tide and high wind hit the liner's 45ft-high side, barely sheltered by the temporary single-storeyed shed standing sentinel on the still-incomplete pier at West 13th Street. Captain Pritchard was alerted by cannon-like reports as several 300lb mooring bitts on the pier fractured, the broken head of the first being jerked 20ft into the dock by the released tension of the 6in steel hawser. Pushed by the prevailing weather, the liner's bow swung slowly outwards towards the neighbouring pier.

The presence of coaling barges momentarily arrested the ship's escape, preventing her stern from swinging out and breaking her after hawsers.

Two gangways aft were dragged from the pier and hung suspended from the ship's side, their landward ends dipping into the freezing water. A coal barge, M.P. Smith & Co.'s *Alice P. Rogers* (chartered by the Berwind-White Coalmining Company), was crushed and almost buckled in half between ship and pier. As the barge sank (for the loss of their vessel the barge's owners were later awarded a meagre $106.70) its quick-thinking skipper, Captain Hans Olsen, jumped onto the next barge astern. Pier 54's Superintendent, Captain Roberts, quickly responded to the desperate situation and organised his men to get lines aboard the *Mauretania* with their shoreside loops being warped to mooring bitts on the south side of the pier. The liner was coaxed back to her berth with her donkey engines powering her foredeck winches.

Within twenty minutes a large crowd, attracted by the sharp reports of parting hawsers, had gathered to witness the unfolding Christmas drama and police reservists from Charles Street Station were rushed to control the shoreside 'rubber-neckers'. The high wind subsided as the morning progressed and, almost as if taking advantage of the ensuing calm, a thick fog descended impishly over the port, making navigation on the rivers and harbour extremely hazardous.

Mauretania sailed on schedule on 28 December. Fortunately, there was no record of any of the crew, having spent Christmas away from home and families, being logged for misdemeanours during this time. Perhaps the Captain had been lenient in respect of the festive season! Worryingly, as the ship backed out of her dock, the Chief Engineer reported hearing an untoward noise emanating from the starboard astern turbine casing. The noise abated as the ship surged forward and a record crossing of 23.58 knots was made. But the noise reoccurred when the engines were put astern during manoeuvres during the approach to Queenstown. The liner arrived at Liverpool, after an excellent passage of four days, twenty-three hours and two minutes, on 3 January 1908, having spent New Year at sea. Many of her 1,394 passengers were full of praise for the ship, especially when considering the mid-winter Atlantic. One passenger commented: 'To cross the Atlantic within five days in winter is as much as can be hoped for … and certainly more than was ever dreamt of a few years back.'

A 'rate war' was starting on the Atlantic route. IMM reduced fares by $3.75 following Cunard's refusal to increase Second- and

Third-Class fares by that amount. Cunard eventually fell in line but the IMM reduced its rates by a similar amount again and other lines started to reduce their rates. Before an anticipated conference could be convened, Cunard informed their agents:

> We have to notify you of a further reduction in third class rates to the United States and Canada, which rates are now as follows:- From Liverpool or Queenstown to New York, Boston, Philadelphia, or Baltimore, by the Mauretania, Lusitania, Lucania, Campania, Caronia, and Carmania, £5, 5s (5-pounds, five-shillings); by the Ivernia and Saxonia, £5; and by the Umbria and Etruria, £4, 15s.

Company fares to the Dominion of Canada would be 10s less and fares were proportionately less on the older, slower ships. Following White Star's third round of cuts, Cunard readjusted their new rates to a more reasonable level: rates for the two express giants should remain at £7 15s for Second Class and £5 5s for Third, having been £10 and £9 respectively. It was hoped that the short rate war would see the end of the fare-cutting and a Second-Class rate of £6 5s (which still meant that the passengers in this class travelled in the equivalent of a first-class hotel ashore at a rate of ½d [one halfpenny] a mile!) was finally agreed, although the cuts meant weekly losses of thousands of pounds. To save money Cunard planned to reduce the time spent in New York by the two sisters by introducing Wednesday sailings from that port. A similar Wednesday sailing from Liverpool also countered White Star's Wednesday sailings from Southampton. Cruises to Naples were offered on the *Carpathia* and to Alexandria on the *Caronia*.

For *Mauretania*'s third sailing from Liverpool on Friday, 11 January 1908, Articles were opened on the 10th and it was on this day that a letter of great concern was sent by Board of Trade (BoT) Surveyor, Albert Haslett, from his Canning Dock office following a turbine inspection:

> I beg to report that when on board this vessel on the 6th inst I was informed that some damage had been done to the Starboard Astern turbine, during the voyage just completed.
>
> On examination, I found that 8 rows of blades in the lowest expansion (the whole) and 3 rows in the next expansion had been either carried away entirely, or bent or broken.

The eleven rows have [now] been cut away, and as the turbine is, otherwise, undamaged, it has been arranged that the vessel shall make the voyage to New York without any further repairs. The astern going power will, of course, be slightly reduced, but not to such an extent as to affect the handling of the vessel appreciably. On Wednesday last [8th] she was taken out of Dock, into the river, under her own steam, when the turbine was used, as usual, and I was informed by the Owner's Superintendent performed its work satisfactorily. I was unable to be on board myself owing to other duties occupying my attention [it would have taken Mr Haslett three hours to get ashore, thus missing his next appointment].

The cause of the damage to these blades is not clear. The Chief Engineer has reported that a slight noise was heard, apparently in the starboard astern turbine casing, when leaving New York last voyage, and a louder noise was again heard when the engines were put astern, approaching Queenstown, after running ahead for nearly five days.

The end clearance in these blades is intended to be .135 inch, and appears to be so, when the turbine is cold. This seems to be a large amount, but is most probably insufficient for the conditions under which this turbine works. For when the vessel is running ahead, a vacuum exists in the astern casing, or so [sic] that the whole machine is cooled down to the corresponding temperature say 120° F, or even lower. When the order to go astern is given, and steam is admitted, the blades and rotor will heat up much quicker than the casing, which is also probably distorted by unequal expansion. The clearance will be thus reduced, until the tips of the blades touch, and the blades are disarranged. This condition of things applies specially to the long blades in the lowest expansion.

The Owners have decided to lift the Starboard astern casing, on the vessel's return to this port, in three weeks time, and the question of repairs will then be dealt with, a lay up of three weeks being in contemplation.

Under the circumstances I have not considered it necessary to endorse the Passenger certificate.

I am sir
Your Obedient Servant,

Albert E. Haslett.

Haslett's Principal Officer, Peter Samson, asked whether the Surveyor had been informed by Cunard of the noise before the inspection or whether he had found out about the incident in a casual manner merely by going aboard when he did. Samson was not happy about the way that the survey had been undertaken and hauled Haslett over the coals for not being on board when the ship was taken out into the river:

> Having regard to the great number of passengers this vessel carries and to the extent of the damage to the turbine, it is thought that a Surveyor accompanied by the Senior Engineer Surveyor should have been present when the vessel was using the turbines to go out of dock into the river preparatory to starting on her last voyage. Omissions of this character are alike detrimental to the interests of the public and the Board's staff.

It was not the end of the matter.

Back at sea the *Mauretania*'s next eastbound left New York on 25 January. But she was five men short as, on the previous day, Messrs. Paton, Jones, Cowley, Roche and Black were in prison for 'larceny felony' One DBS (Distressed British Seaman), stranded in New York without a ship, was on board for repatriation and unexpected excitement as, shortly after leaving America, the *Mauretania* was called upon to act in the best traditions of the Brotherhood of the Sea.

Along with two other barges, the *Fall River* of the H. Staples Coal Company had been under tow with 1,500 tons of coal on board when a snow-laden gale blew up. The tow-line broke and soon, in the most appalling conditions, almost 90 miles east of Sandy Hook, all three barges became separated. In a sinking condition and flying her ensign upside down as a signal of distress, the *Fall River* was spotted by the *Mauretania*. Mercifully, the barge's captain, engineer and deckhand took to a boat just before the barge sank and it was from this that they were picked up by the liner, which Captain Pritchard skilfully manoeuvred to create a lee between the small boat and the oncoming waves. The Captain's skill in effecting the rescue would later be recognised by President Roosevelt. Despite the delay, the *Mauretania* broke the record for a single day's steaming when she covered 575 nautical miles between noon on Wednesday and Thursday in the twenty-three-hour eastbound day, arriving at Queenstown on 30 January after a passage of five days, two hours and forty-one minutes (average speed 23.9 knots). The three shipwrecked men were landed in Liverpool the following day.

After the severe weather of winter and the turbine trouble, the *Mauretania* missed one sailing to be thoroughly inspected. She was found to be structurally sound as many minor damages such as crushed railings had been repaired in New York, with broken lifeboats and bent bulwarks being repaired or replaced in Britain. At least it was thought she was sound.

In order to rectify the localised vibrations considered to be emanating from the engine spaces (pulsations from her propellers were the most likely cause) additional bulkheads were constructed amidships around the pantries and storerooms above and below the open areas of the Firemen's Main Deck quarters thereby creating smaller dormitories for the men – which were probably not welcomed.

After her dry-docking, the ship's next sailing was on Saturday, 22 February 1908, arriving in New York on the 28th. Among her First-Class passengers was, quite exotically, an Indian prince – Prince Victor Narayan of Cooch Behar (en route to study agriculture at Cornell University) – and J. Bruce Ismay, Chairman of the rival White Star Line and president of the International Mercantile Marine Company (IMM). Ismay liked to travel on the Cunarders for his annual visit, perhaps using their superior speed over his own ships' in order to reach his destination more speedily. It was said that when he had seen the flag-bedecked *Mauretania* in New York he had changed his mind about not incorporating masts on his planned Olympic-class vessels.

Mauretania departed New York on 7 March, carrying DBS for repatriation, and passed the *Sandy Hook* lightvessel at 11.09 p.m. She arrived at the *Daunt Rock* lightvessel at 4.14 p.m. five days and five minutes later. Quite splendidly she had beaten her own eastward record by two hours and thirty-six minutes. Seasonal improvements in the weather had undoubtedly helped over the 'Long Route' (the northern) – a distance of 2,932 miles. At an average of 24.42 knots, the highest speed ever attained by a steamer on the North Atlantic, she bettered her previous best by 0.48 of a knot and *Lusitania*'s best by 0.8. Unhappily, fog delayed the liner's triumphant entry into the River Mersey, causing her to be anchored for seven hours, not weighing anchor until 12.30 to make her way to the Landing Stage. Not to be outdone, *Lusitania* exceeded her contract speed over a twenty-four-hour period when, during the noon-to-noon period of 9–10 March, she steamed 627 miles at a speed of 25.14 knots. The English-Scottish 'war' at sea was hotting up!

On 4 March, nearly a month after Haslett's original BoT letter, Samson wrote again, reporting in a quieter tone that his junior's earlier technical assessment, if not his methods, had been right:

It was afterwards found that the casing or cylinder was ⅛ inch oval transversely, due, it is believed, to over-heating caused by the friction of the tips of the blades. If this is the correct explanation of the cause of the deformation of the casing, **a serious breakdown of this turbine has only just been averted**. [Author's emphasis].

Keeping his head down, Haslett responded that same day with:

This vessel has been laid up for 3 weeks [following her arrival on 30 January] for general overhaul and dry-docking.

Both astern turbines have been opened up and rotors lifted. The port turbine was found to be in a satisfactory condition …

… and stated that the blades' clearances were from 1/8in to 3/16in and had been filed down. It was an unpleasant revelation to the Wallsend Engineering Co., to Cunard and to the BoT that contortion of the turbine casing had occurred at all. As far back as July 1905, it had been lauded that the turbines' 'drum casing[s] [were] to be made of Whitworth fluid pressed steel' produced by 'squeezing' gases out of the liquid steel during production, an expensive process normally reserved for the manufacture of military ordnance, and 'carefully annealed after being rough machined'. Following tests in February 1907, just as the turbines were being built, recommendations had been made that the steel of the inlet ends of the high-pressure turbine casings along with their ribs, circumferential ribs and circulating jointing flanges should be increased in thickness to provide additional strength.

Perhaps stories of the hard-driving and physically stressful demands of the Stokehold were making the rounds in Liverpool as, of those who signed on for the next voyage, fifteen failed to join and of those boarding a further five deserted. Twenty-one substitutes were taken on and, for an unspecified reason, a Fourth Engineer was transferred to another of the company's ships. Among the new men was a young Jack Phillips, one of the Marconi men – the Wireless Operators – employed not by the shipping line but by the Marconi Company. He would stay with the ship for only a few voyages until he reluctantly transferred to Marconi's transatlantic transmitting station at Clifden, where he remained until 1911. After another short spell at sea with White Star he was sent as Chief Radio Officer to Belfast to supervise the installation of powerful wireless equipment into the new White Star liner *Titanic*, then fitting out at Harland and Wolff's shipyard. Phillips would stay with this liner when she made her maiden voyage in April 1912.

Captain Pritchard lost his dedicated Chief Engineer on arrival at Queenstown at 9 a.m. on 22 March. At some time during the trip from Liverpool, John Currie, who was not one to shirk a hands-on approach, had somehow sustained injuries to those very hands and left his beloved ship after being seen by the ship's physician. Senior Second Engineer John Kendall was installed as his deputy who, along with his men, would be sorely pushed on this crossing as, shortly after leaving Queenstown, the ship encountered a severe westerly gale (the tail end of a hurricane, the 1908 season having started unusually early in the Caribbean) that lasted several days.

During the storm the ship pitched heavily as her fine bow sliced and chopped its way through the steep seas. Eighty-foot waves were encountered that smashed six thick glass windows in the Wheelhouse, injuring Fourth Officer Wingate, causing cuts to his face, and 'sheathing under the Bridge was smashed into kindling wood'. A lifeboat was torn from its davits, several seamen suffered minor injuries while others avoided being washed overboard into the boiling surf by hanging onto railings. Twelve feet of Boat Deck railing was carried away and steel stanchions cracked at their bases. Her Navigators reduced speed as 'combers … curled over the forward part of the superstructure'. So severe was the weather that salt-laden foam reached and stained her funnels!

On her day late arrival in New York on Saturday, 28 March the liner, scarred by her battle with the elements, was docked in a record time for a ship of her size, taking a mere sixteen minutes from putting the first line across to her to the first brow being placed in position. Undergoing basic repairs locally, the ship was sore pressed on this reduced turnaround as she had been rescheduled to depart from the port on a Wednesday, changed under the conditions of her new United States Government Mail contract taken over from the slower White Star Line ships. To exacerbate matters, thirteen men deserted while in New York, perhaps deterred by working in rough weather conditions. An equal number of men were signed on as substitutes. To the credit of all concerned, the liner sailed on time on Wednesday, 1 April. The two Cunard sisters – along with the old flyer, the *Lucania* – were now sailing to a much tighter schedule, their capabilities and potential being pushed to new limits. A day after sailing the first reported on-board death occurred when Third-Class passenger Moses Krunenthal 'departed this life' at Latitude 40.23° north, Longitude 64.01° west; cause of death was logged as 'Apoplexy'. He was buried at sea at six the following morning with 'the usual ceremonies' at Latitude 40.42° north, Longitude 55.15° west.

For eastbound passengers in First Class a thick book awaited them, the *Cunard Souvenir Guide to Europe*, which suggested possible destination hotels in which to stay and, for the wealthy, which cars were available for motor-touring (motor cars were still extremely expensive to purchase, ranging from a few hundred to over a thousand pounds).

Liverpool Saturday sailings by the sisters had not been not changed as these were still required by the British contract, although the Queenstown call was becoming a controversial issue with Cunard. On this particular trip, departing Saturday, 11 April, it was hoped that the *Mauretania* would overhaul the German liner *Deutschland* that had sailed from Southampton the previous day. Chief Engineer John Currie returned to duty after missing one voyage determined, no doubt, that his ship should not sail without him, although he seemed not fully recovered as his trembled, spidery signature blotted as he signed the ship's Articles. There was much pride in the ship that often went unnoticed, the ship's Writer even carefully ruling faint pencil guidelines in the crew logs before neatly writing each crew member's name in copperplate prior to that particular crewman penning his signature or mark.

On this crossing the Chief made his presence felt as the *Mauretania* covered the 2,889 miles in four days, twenty-three hours and fifty-nine minutes, beating the *Lusitania*'s exact five-day crossing by one tiny – although publicity important – minute out of the 7,199 minutes of the crossing. It must have really irked the *Lusitania* lobby by its apparent pretentiousness! The return trip departing New York on 22 April took five days, one hour and fourteen minutes. Thick fog was encountered off the southern coast of Ireland and, as a consequence, the mail was offloaded at Queenstown on Monday, 27 April. The latter part of the trip had been blanketed by sadness as news was received of the loss of HMS *Gladiator* in the western approaches of The Solent on 25 April between the Isle of Wight and Hurst Point on the mainland, after being rammed by the American liner *St Paul* (15,150 tons; 1895).

By the *Mauretania*'s next departure from Liverpool on Saturday, 2 May Mr Currie's signature was almost back to normal and he was well served by his engineering officers as with him were three men (Sutcliffe, Allan and Swanson) who would eventually rise to become chiefs themselves. She also had a new Chief Officer, E.G. Diggle who would also eventually rise to become a captain of the line. Prior to the ship sailing, twenty of the Black Gang failed to join and a further nine deserted. Again, this could have been due to the tough reputation of the ship or to the prevailing dissatisfaction with Stokehold wages. However, by July a Leading Fireman would be receiving £6 10s (£6.50) per month while an Ordinary Fireman would get just £5.

At 11 o'clock on the morning of sailing – and in concurrence with the legal requirements as specified by the Merchant Shipping Act, 1894 – the regulation 'Board of Trade Sports' took place with a general muster of the crew and Numbers 15 and 16 lifeboats (the aft-most) were swung out. A certificate of seaworthiness was then issued enabling the ship to sail. After passing the Fastnet light on 3 May, the ship picked up to full speed. Shortly afterwards a tremendous shock was felt throughout the ship, followed by excessive vibration at the stern. The liner was slowed to enable an assessment to be made and it appeared that a blade had been lost from her port outer propeller. The imbalance in the screw transmitted itself to the shaft, which in turn caused stresses in the latter's bearings that created the great vibration. Witnessing the unsettling incident was Cunard director Sir W.C. Forwood who, in spite of the unwanted excitement, must have been impressed by the deck and engineering officers' fast reactions to the emergency. (Also travelling was the line's Victualling Superintendent, Mr Harry Brown).

It was conjectured that the huge liner had collided with a partly submerged wreck, perhaps ironically so as the United States Revenue Service was currently trialling a specially built 204ft cutter, the *Seneca*. Completed in June, her task would be to seek out and destroy such derelicts that threatened the sea lanes (timber cargoes especially refused to allow a ship to sink peacefully). *Seneca* would not be commissioned until later in November, even then too late to prevent yet another incident befalling the Cunarder.

Using only three propellers, the ship carried on, still crossing in a very creditable five days, six hours and seventeen minutes even after a further delay by fog off Sandy Hook at midday, Friday. The liner, stopped in her tracks, prudently waited for the murk to lift before continuing to dock late on Saturday evening. After the accident it was anticipated that the liner would be dry-docked for repairs on her return to England. Remarkably, it was also thought that this repair would only take a day out from her advertised schedule. Not unsurprisingly, this plan proved to be over-ambitious.

Determination to travel on the world's fastest and most glamorous express boat was not just confined to passengers and crew. At 4.30 on the first afternoon out, no fewer than five stowaways were discovered in a boiler room. Perhaps alarmed by the day's collision, they had made themselves known and in need of rescue! Four days later, as the liner approached New York, two more stowaways were unearthed in the engine department. All seven men were returned to Britain on the *Campania* to face prosecution. While in New York, not all crew were determined to remain with the ship as seven deserted on 13 May, sailing day. It was permissible for a crew member to receive half of his wages as an advance while in New York so the men had not left the ship entirely empty-handed.

It was decided that the damaged propeller would not be repaired until the end of the season and so, after undergoing a thorough inspection, the ship sailed from Liverpool, four days late, on Wednesday, 27 May. It was just as well that on this crossing Cunard had decided to experiment by omitting the Queenstown call and an earlier arrival at New York was anticipated as a result. Even as handicapped as she was, the *Mauretania* remarkably set up two new records on this westbound passage in making the fastest crossing and achieving the best day's run. Passing Daunt('s) Rock at 4.35 on the morning of 28 May, she steamed noon-to-noon distances of over 600 miles, the best being an incredible 635 miles on 31 May. This beat the *Lusitania*'s best by just 3 miles! To the Sandy Hook lightship her passage of four days, twenty hours and fifteen minutes again beat the 'Lucy' by seven minutes with 24.86 knots. The Chief Engineer opined that had a propeller not been left behind in England a saving of six hours would have been a possibility. In spite of the *Mauretania*'s engines having been built under the supervision of a Scot (Andrew Laing) the English/Scottish shipbuilding rivalry was literally speeding up – and what would the *Mauretania* be capable of when once she again had the use of all four propellers?

There was a double milestone in June: the British Government stated that the two sisters had 'satisfied the conditions made by the Government under the agreement for their construction', and that a 'Penny Post' would be introduced to the United States, making the postal rate the same as it was in Great Britain and its Empire. On the next few voyages she would take a few hours over five days on each crossing, not the best that could be expected of her but, under the circumstances, they were still excellent performances.

Missing a hurricane that had bypassed New York, the *Mauretania* arrived off Sandy Hook in darkness on the evening of 1 June. Although expected by Cunard to dock that evening, the Captain wirelessed that he would anchor the ship overnight so as not to jeopardise his ship in the Ambrose Channel. He would safely wait until the next morning's light before entering the harbour at 8 a.m. The liner made an extremely quick turnaround during this call, sailing again on Thursday, 4 June, a day late on her American contract time. On board, as if shaping the future, was returning English balloonist Patrick Alexander.

Throughout the summer season before her anticipated dry-docking, the ship carried on crossing the Atlantic on just three propellers. She was so successful that one London newspaper reported, rather naively, she would continue doing so as this proved that 'the turbine engines run better with three than with four propellers'! Taking advantage of her sister's temporary disability, the *Lusitania* retook the record by bettering her best day's run by 9 miles and her passage time by seven minutes, achieving a crossing in four days, twenty hours and eight minutes. She had covered a superb 641 miles on 7 June. An enthusiastic Scottish journalist did his sums and cannily calculated that the *Lusitania's* 'average rate is better than the *Mauretania's* by 40½ yards per hour'. Towards the end of July Cunard announced that the *Mauretania* was going to be withdrawn from service between November and January to 'make necessary repairs to her propeller'.

Meanwhile, further south in the sunlit waters of The Solent, the great annual royal yachting spectacle of Cowes Week took on an additional lustre in August. The Royal Yacht Squadron had as its flag the White Ensign of the Royal Navy so when HMS *Indomitable*, a new revolutionary lightly armoured, turbine-driven and extremely fast battlecruiser, arrived in Cowes Roads with George, Prince of Wales (like his father, a keen yachtsman) on board as an officer there were opportunities for additional celebrations. The cruiser's transatlantic dash from Canada to Cowes had, at 21.3 knots, beaten the previous best by a large warship by over 2 knots. During the passage a brief, four-hour spurt had achieved 26.4 knots and claimed to better the Cunard sisters' records for a short period. During the crossing HRH had even joined the men and other officers in taking a turn at stoking the boilers! Not to be outshone, Cunard later said that the *Mauretania* had made 27.3-knots over a 300-mile distance during a recent crossing.

Arriving in New York on 6 August amidst storms that were sweeping the Eastern Seaboard, *Mauretania* was eight hours behind her previous record time. On board for this crossing was Sir George and Lady Newnes; Newnes' publishing house counted amongst its titles *The Strand Magazine* that had introduced the extremely popular Sherlock Holmes stories by Sir Arthur Conan Doyle to its readership. On arrival in New York the US Postmaster, George Von L. Meyer, boarded the vessel to meet his family, who were returning to the States. The Postmaster, it seemed, not only wanted his mails to travel speedily but also his family!

Sailing from New York on 12 August, the liner returned to Liverpool with her next departure scheduled ten days later, before which, and for reasons known only to himself, 31-year-old Liverpudlian Fireman James Murphy jumped overboard. Efforts to save him from the Mersey proved futile. During the course of the passage Chief Trimmer Joseph Winker was fined the sum of five shillings (25p) – the equivalent of one-and-a-half day's pay – for threatening to strike the Senior Second Engineer, Mr Kendall. One can only imagine the tensions in the Boiler Room that had caused that near-altercation. *Lusitania* beat her own record on the eastward crossing when she reached Sandy Hook after steaming for four days and fifteen hours – three hours and forty minutes faster than her previous best. Captain Watts opined that his ship could do better still. Captain Pritchard undoubtedly had other ideas even as arrangements were being made for her to go into dry dock for propeller repairs.

Comments in the press that the two sisters were not living up to expectations encouraged Cunard to raise its earlier objection of having to call into Queenstown, which took up several hours of the liners' voyages. If the call into the Irish port was obviated then an early evening arrival in New York could be effected instead of as present when passengers had to remain expensively on board overnight. At least the passengers were happy as W. McCallum wrote home on 29 August that: 'We had a lovely trip across on this splendid vessel.' A suggestion arose of using Holyhead on the island of Anglesey as a terminus for embarking and disembarking passengers, cargo and mails, which would do away with delays at the Bar and enable unhurried arrivals and departures from the Mersey with its tortuous, busy channels and restricting tides. With the looming possibility of the Queenstown call being dropped, the 'All Ireland' group met in Dublin to express its dissatisfaction and sent a deputation to meet with the US Postmaster General in Washington. To this effect the deputation (which included the Lord Mayor of Dublin) sailed to New York, deliberately not on a Cunarder but on the superb *Oceanic* of the Queenstown-faithful White Star Line in September.

Leaving Queenstown at the outset of her thirteenth transatlantic voyage on 12 September, the *Mauretania* ran into foul weather just after passing Daunt Rock. Four days later and 360 miles from Sandy

Hook she met the tail end of a major hurricane that made going particularly onerous. The apparent bad luck of this thirteenth trip had started early for Captain Pritchard. In order to dutifully take his ship out on time he had left his late wife's wake on The Wirral a few hours earlier. To compound the run of ill fortune on the ill-augured voyage, on Wednesday, 16 September a second blade broke, this time from her starboard forward propeller. The effects on the ship were strangely disproportionate, the *New York Times* describing the event as being accompanied by a 'crashing sound. The middle of the vessel seemed to give a lift, and she bobbed up and down almost as if in two parts.'

Dishes and glassware crashed in a cacophony of destruction as passengers were thrown to the decks in a bruised, albeit uninjured, melee. The *New York Times* continued:

> For a second after the accident there was an interval of quiet, and then cries began to resound on all sides; the stateroom doors opened, and many of the passengers ran out to learn what had happened … Following the breaking of the propeller, there was a rush on the part of many in the saloon to get out. Fortunately no one was hurt.

Stewards shouted out for the passengers to remain calm in what was described as 'a short-lived panic'. Bereaved Captain Pritchard reassured anxious and frightened passengers. Women fainted.

The ship was stopped and, as the way was taken off, she turned dangerously broadside to the wind and for half-an-hour she was pounded by seas that broke over her Bridge and superstructure. The stern tube seals must have sprung a leak (some thought that her hull had been punctured) but this was quickly brought under control with pumps.

Fourteen Trimmers were hurt as coal collapsed. Stokers also suffered from the sudden shock and one suffered a broken arm, another a broken leg and a badly lacerated scalp. Strangely, in spite of these occurrences, no mention was made in the log and Cunard went to the later pains of producing 'voluntary' witnesses to counter newspaper reports, calling the claims an exaggeration. In a damage-limitation exercise, a release stated that 'there was no panic amongst the passengers … there was no injury whatever to the ship (other than for the broken blade) …

nothing was displaced or broken and no one was injured.' Threatening newspapers with libel, the Cunard spokesman reiterated: 'I desire to repeat that the ship has met with no damage whatever beyond the loss of [a] blade of [a] propeller … There was no damage to the ship, and the passengers aboard were not aware of the occurrence.'

The voyage was not to be all doom and gloom as on 17 September [*sic* – as the ship was later described as being 'two days outbound from Liverpool' this would have been the 14th] Dr B. Sydney Jones invited, as was usual with the ship's more senior officers, a select group of passengers to be his table companions at dinner. The group, including actress Constance Collier, turned out to be a convivial one and it was decided to form a 'Secret Society', the qualifying members having to be good conversationalists spiced with a degree of high-spiritedness. This faux society that reflected the newfound freedom and morals of the gilded Edwardian Age would eventually boast 169 members, each with a membership number. Calling itself the Ancient and Select Order and Society of Heathens, meetings were held when members were on board. Other suitable candidates – 'novitiates' – included actors, industrialists, aristocrats, politicians, etc. and all 'Heathens' were given high-sounding but humorous titles ('Big Chief', 'Big Benn', etc.).

A certain amount of fine dining to a special menu and imbibing was involved in a new member's rite of passage and, true to his calling, the Doctor insisted that copious amounts of laughter should be involved as being 'the best medicine'. Even the *Mauretania*'s designer, Leonard Peskett, and the Hon. Alexander M. Carlisle (Naval Architect at the Harland and Wolff shipyard in Belfast who had been heavily involved in the design of the *Olympic* and *Titanic*), were brought into this select fold. Others included American composer Jerome Kern and cartoonist-cum-actor Leo Carrillo. During the recent scare a founder–member of the 'Heathens' with the pseudonym 'Little Mother', actress Alice Lloyd (shortly to become the highest-paid vaudeville performer), began to sing 'Over the Hills and Far Away' and other popular songs. This had a calming effect on the troubled passengers and, in appreciation of her efforts, Captain Pritchard invited her to dine at his table before the journey's end, a rare accolade indeed.

The reported effects of what was thought to have been a lost blade, especially felt in the coal bunkers sited well forward of the propellers, seemed rather extreme. More than likely the ship had again been in a collision with an unidentified object – possibly another submerged wreck. The liner was now being navigated using only two propellers, which created navigational problems especially when negotiating the channels into New York, where matters were made worse by fog that delayed her arrival until noon on Saturday: the crossing had taken five days, five hours and fifty-two minutes. Divers examined the liner's bottom and reported: 'ship's hull is undamaged, and … there is no leakage'. Her 23 September departure from New York was delayed for two days, again because of fog. On the Tuesday she met with such abominably heavy weather that several thick-glassed portholes were smashed. Much damage occurred on deck and her Marconi aerial was swept away, rendering communications impossible. Dogged with danger, her return to Liverpool was, quite understandably, the longest so far, taking six days, eighteen hours and eight minutes. After discharging passengers she was immediately dry-docked to enable the damaged three-bladed, starboard propeller to be replaced (strangely, reports indicate only the one). A survey, however, still found her hull to be sound, which was perhaps the last good news that the company would hear.

The westbound sailing that departed Liverpool on 10 October met with strong nor'-nor'-easterly winds, with howling gales later blowing from the south-west. High, heavy rough seas were encountered but remarks were made about her steadiness.

Her last eastbound crossing for 1908 left New York on 21 October (Trafalgar Day, the annual commemoration of Nelson's great victory), taking on board twenty-two shipwrecked officers and men from another Newcastle-built steamship, the *Hesleyside* (1900; Official Number 110353). Their repatriation as Distressed British Seamen (DBS) was on a 'C16' form under which the Captain was obliged (under the Act of 1894) to take them all or risk a fine of £100 per man; they were not legally obliged to work their passage home as they were not signed on the ship's Articles. Three other DBS were also being repatriated and during the passage one required medical attention. Most of her British and European-bound mails were transferred to the *Oceanic*.

The day prior to sailing Captain Pritchard was appointed Commodore of the Cunard Line following the retirement of Commodore Watt of the *Lusitania*. Now, not only could the *Mauretania* fly a swallow-tailed flag embellished with the golden lion of the Cunard Line but Captain Pritchard's annual salary was increased to £1,000 (he would never admit to how much he actually earned) and it was thought that he would take over the command of the 'senior' *Lusitania* when the *Mauretania* went into dry dock, with Captain Dow of the *Carmania* taking over command of 'his' *Mauretania*.

Towards the end of the crossing a seasoned correspondent wrote to her friend: '2½ days of fine weather – now plunging through [a] heavy storm. Beautiful sight.' On arrival at Liverpool on 27 October (five days, five hours and forty-two minutes) the *Mauretania* was taken out of service after her experiences as a veritable battering ram against the worst that the North Atlantic could throw at her, and she was readied for dry-docking. It was planned to dock her in Cammell Laird's dock at Tranmere but these plans fell through due to 'difficulties' and she was laid up pending further arrangements. Members of her crew who were not required found themselves without a berth for the next three months.

'The Damage is Not Serious'

The next day, 28 October 1908, the *Mauretania* was manoeuvred towards the Canada dry dock, where keel blocks had been carefully prepared to support her weight and breast shores lay along the dock's surrounds, waiting to be wedged between the ship and the graving dock's walls. As the ship was slowly approaching the dock sill, even though under the care of ten tugs, she was reportedly caught by the current and collided with the quay wall, indenting her bow and exacerbating an allegedly previously sustained injury. A Cunard spokesman said, again in limitation, that 'the damage was not serious'. She returned to her moorings to await a favourable tide before again attempting the docking procedure.

Perhaps because of its secretive nature, the Admiralty did not deem it necessary to inform the general public that the mighty *Mauretania* had suffered anything more than superficial injuries during the first few months of her career, the Official Secrets Act, 1899 protecting the illusion of the invulnerability and invincibility of the Government-backed 'Wonder Ship'. That the great ship, built to withstand the might of the ocean on which she plied her business, was fallible (and, by inference, the Empire) would be too much for the public. The information released to the press centred on the replacement of the well-publicised broken propeller, which had wonderfully not affected the in-service operation of the liner. But those with any technical knowledge knew that three months in dry dock for the standard procedure of a propeller replacement (normally taking a few days) seemed to be an inordinate length of time. Once the dock had been pumped dry, the ship safely docked down, her keel safely sued on the dock blocks, and her sides supported by a forest of timber breast shores, she was ready for several weeks of intensive activity.

Use had been made of the time since the accident in September for Swan Hunters' on the Tyne (using their large-scale launch for experiments) and the Admiralty Experiment Works at Haslar to develop and design new forward high-pressure turbine-driven propellers that would better meet the high-speed demands of the ship's engines. The three-bladed propellers that had been fitted the previous September were also to be replaced by a new, solid design. Due to high revolutions the original propeller material had proved to be totally inadequate and an enormous amount of erosion had occurred at around 2ft from the propellers' roots (propeller-to-boss connection). The resultant sponge-like pitting (cavitation) had eroded the metal to depths of up to 2½in, and it was likely that this had caused the subsequently weakened blade to fracture and break. The propellers' leading edges were badly chipped from months of hard-pushed, high-speed service; it was estimated that the outer extremities of the propellers had, at 174 revolutions per minute, achieved speeds of 105 miles per hour! (Her highest average revolutions per minute on her trials had been recorded at 196.1). The two new four-bladed propellers, at 19ft 6in in diameter the largest manufactured to date, were cast in one solid piece from 19½ tons of a specially developed material, 'Parsons Special Turbine Alloy', named after the alloy's co-inventor. Expected to have a life of up to four times that of their failed standard high-tension bronze predecessors, the new screws were manufactured by the Manganese Bronze and Brass Company at a cost of £2,000 apiece. The two old 22-ton low-pressure-driven after propellers – including the broken starboard screw – were replaced and this three-bladed pair would

remain in service for the next few months. Because of the various mishaps to the ship, much vital structural repair work – some of it unreported – had to be undertaken and this would require the bulk of the extended docking period with a skilled workforce of 1,000 men being employed. To avoid accidental damage to their blades, the new propellers would be fitted on completion of this other work.

As the underwater hull emerged from the receding waters of the dock it could be seen what had happened during the September event. After ramming a probable derelict, the wreckage had swept aft, collided with the ship's side and damaged hull plating (this caused the avalanche of coal). The first of the unpublicised work was to replace the wing bracket that might have been cracked during the collision or even during the sheering of the local propeller blade back in May, which could have caused a whipping of the shaft before the engine governor had a chance to activate and stop the machinery. As with the new solid propellers, a replacement bracket had to be ordered, moulded, cast, carefully machined and delivered, and it was these procedures that contributed to both the lengthy delay prior to the essential docking and considerably extending the time that the liner would be out of service had only a propeller required replacing. The new casting was delivered to the dockside and manoeuvred on its trolley by a Wallis & Steevens traction engine that steamed, purred, hissed and clanked its mechanical way along the quayside.

Another major repair job was to the liner's stem. The buckling and rippling of the steel at the waterline, indicative of a heavy contact, may or may not have been due to contact with a jetty wall – even her grounding in the Mersey in December could have damaged the bow and buckled and sprung some plates. But, more than likely, collision with a derelict was the cause as the buckling was worse at the waterline, extending only 3 or 4ft above. To facilitate repairs, rivets in way of the damage were drilled out and the plating and bent stem casting removed to several feet above and below the point of impact. Over the previous several weeks a new section had been moulded, cast and predrilled in readiness for fitting. Damaged surrounding plating was also removed. Unreported, a quantity of damaged plates above the turn of bilge between Frames 219 and 190 also required replacement – about five strakes deep extending up from two strakes below the waterline just where the curve of the bow turned into the fullness of the hull in way of the coal bunkers. The damaged plating had to be drilled out (a messy operation considering the immediate vicinity of the bunkers) and new plates moulded, drilled, reamed and riveted into the repair. During the time taken to complete the repairs her standby crew occupied their off-duty hours and a group of Engineers formed an enthusiastic football team that managed to win a splendid silver cup. (Two years later the ship's cricket team won a gold medal, donated by Sir Thomas Lipton, the grocery store and tea magnate.)

On 4 January, after nine long weeks, the once-battered ship was floated out of the Canada Graving Dock. There had been a suggestion that Captain Dow might take command of the ship as Commodore Pritchard might take the *Lusitania*. But, retirement deferred by eighteen months, he was to stay with his old command, expressing a wish that he wanted to show what she could *really* do. The Articles for the first post-dry-docking voyage were opened on 23 January 1909, and the ship sailed on the 24th with a record crossing in the offing. The liner was given a great send-off that was reportedly almost 'akin to the interest displayed in connection with the maiden voyage'. On leaving her home port she steamed 'upwards of 25½ knots per hour [*sic*] ... to Queenstown'.

Twenty-six-year-old Third Engineer N.H. Gibson of Regent Road in Crosby – taken on as a Fourth during the lay-up, playing in the Engineers' football team – was so impressed with the ship's speed that he leant out of fore and aft ports to take snapshots of bow wave and wake as the liner surged through the sea. Cunard's General Superintendent, James Bain, was sailing to judge her performance. He would not be disappointed and considered the new propellers to be a great success. Also on board for the anticipated gala voyage were distinguished passengers from the world of arts, and the aristocratic, political and military sections of society, including Lady Bache Cunard; Mme Toscanini (the wife of the leader of the Metropolitan Opera) and the family of the Chairman of the rival White Star Line – Mrs J. Bruce Ismay and her daughter. A breath of scandal descended on this trip. Card sharps had been active on various Atlantic liners and one, hoping to take advantage of gullible passengers, had been active in the *Mauretania*'s Smoke Room. The man was confronted and, in the undignified fracas that followed, glasses were thrown!

Cunard explained the buckle in the ship's stem as having been caused by contact with a jetty wall. The twisting seems rather too low for this. (Author's Collection)

Safely placed within the Canada Graving Dock in December 1908, the liner begins a lengthy period of repair. Note the canvas covers over the lower stem. (Author's Collection)

Above: The repairs to the stem are dramatically shown with stem casting and plating cut away in way of the buckle. (Author's Collection)

Above right: Plating on the ship's side by the bunkerspace has here been cut away in readiness for renewal. Coal chutes are open and the timber shoring can be clearly seen. (Author's Collection)

Below right: The badly damaged starboard forward (low pressure) propeller is removed. It will be replaced by a four-bladed screw cast in one solid piece. (Author's Collection)

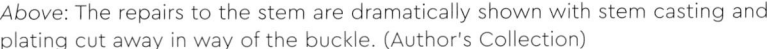

Above left: The third blade of the same propeller showing the erosion caused by high speed. This erosion would later be identified and called cavitation. (Author's Collection)

Above right: The damaged forward port shaft bracket is being removed while its replacement is slung ready for lifting. (Author's Collection)

Left: The Engineers' football team proudly pose on deck with their winners' cup. (Author's Collection)

The new solid, four-bladed starboard forward propeller (made from Parsons Special Turbine Alloy) about to be hoisted up the shaft. (Author's Collection)

A rare view of the balanced rudder with the rudder bossing above. (Author's Collection)

With work completed and the liner freshly painted, her new, sharp bow is seen from the dock head. (Author's Collection)

A group of officials (including Chief Engineer) inspect the new propellers after six months of wear. (Author's Collection)

Cunard felt that the *Mauretania*'s and her sister's contracted calls into Queenstown (Cobh) frustratingly interrupted their journeys and fought to obviate the port from their schedules. This photograph of the *Mauretania* is only a few miles from where her sister would meet her demise. (Courtesy of Senan Maloney)

As soon as the ship left Queenstown, between Daunt Rock and Fastnet, an incredible speed of 27 knots was achieved, which further raised hopes of a record passage. Then Winter North Atlantic made its presence felt as *Mauretania* ran into a succession of gales that remained with her all the way over. But, in spite of the dreadful weather, she still managed to average a very respectable 25 knots and, for five hours on the Monday, she averaged 26.55 knots. She also totalled a record 636 miles on one day, beating her own previous best by a very accurately recorded 2 miles. One can only imagine the Stokehold's opinion of the Captain's insistence on making such speeds in the prevailing weather, but their subsequent elation must have been very noisome!

On Wednesday the barometer fell and the ship found herself sailing through an eerily dead calm that lasted for several strangely dramatic minutes. The sky overhead was bright, although the ship was surrounded by theatrically lowering curtains of steel-grey cloud, which then lifted as if a new act was opening. A fierce north-west squall suddenly erupted, accompanied by 'snow, hail, lightning, and rain in quick succession' enveloping the ship in a scene almost taken from a Shakespearian drama. The *Mauretania*'s speed was reduced to 14 knots for twelve hours as she headed into an almost hurricane-force gale that drove enormous head seas of unimaginable malevolence into her path, but the plucky liner still managed to achieve a creditable day's run of 482 miles. After a trip of five days, two hours and two minutes at an average speed of 23.71 knots, the Captain and others expressed satisfaction with the ship's performance and praised the vibration-free performance of the new propellers.

'A Matter of Great Scientific Interest'

Prior to her long lay-up, the *Mauretania* and her sister, *Lusitania*, had been vying for the honours of the fastest day's run both east and west. Returning to Liverpool on 9 February 1909, on concluding that first post-repair voyage, the *Mauretania* had excelled herself, even though she had steamed through the most appalling weather that the North Atlantic could throw at her (the *Lusitania* had arrived in New York on the 8th, twelve hours late having lost an anchor and several fathoms of cable). Much to the delight of the *Mauretania* lobby, she had taken three records on that remarkable crossing on the 'Long Route' (the southern) of 2,934 nautical miles, taking four days, twenty hours and twenty-seven minutes – thereby beating her own previous best by three hours and forty-five minutes. Her best speed averaged 25.2 knots, exceeding her own record of 24.42 knots, while her third record for that crossing happened between noon Thursday and noon Friday, when the *Mauretania* covered 605 miles at an average speed of 26.17 knots. The passengers, thrilled at the news, arranged a collection, passed on through the Captain, for the Stokehold crew in appreciation of the efforts of the 'Black Gang'. Recognition at last! At Queenstown it had been too rough for the tender to get alongside, so fifty passengers and the mails due for disembarkation continued on to Liverpool. To make up time in the 198 miles between the Tuskar Light in St George's Channel and Point Lynas, she showed her mettle when she worked up to an incredible 27.4 knots. The Pilot boarded with great difficulty.

Her next westward passage scored another victory for armchair patriots as, after departure from Queenstown, she made a record daily run of 671 nautical miles at 26.34 knots, beating Scotland's pride, the *Lusitania,* by 21 miles. Not only was the best daily distance achieved but the 'Maury' also took the record for the whole crossing, clocking up an average of 25.38 knots over the course. With smoke billowing from her four impressive funnels, the sleek *Mauretania* looked magnificent as she beat her way through fine weather with a chop on the water as she passed the *Nantucket* lightvessel at speed just before 2.45 p.m. on the 18th. In a buoyant mood, her passengers lined the railings; the ship's orchestra enthusiastically played 'The Star Spangled Banner'; and ensigns dipped on both speeding giantess and tethered guardian in mutual salute. She had made the crossing on the long course in four days, seventeen hours and fifty minutes, beating the *Lusitania*'s best by one hour and forty-six minutes. Albert Ballin, Chairman of the Hamburg America Line, presented her Captain with a Tiffany silver cigar case inscribed 'Captain John Pritchard from Albert Ballin, February 1909'.

During Voyage 16 a passenger, seemingly suffering from some sort of paranoia, wrote on 30 February telling his correspondent that the rough crossing was the least of his worries as, although he was feeling quite well 'considering we had an unusually rough voyage', he confided: 'The old nervousness returned the first night out … thought I saw the man who attacked me going over and could not sleep …'

The liner's return to Liverpool marked another record by breaking the eastbound crossing at an average of 25.28 knots, beating her previous best by twenty-five minutes. However, these records came at a price as, at very high speeds, the liner burned 1,200 tons of coal per day, at a cost of £1,750. The hard work of the boiler rooms still seemed to deter many Stokehold crew as, before the first voyage of March, nineteen men failed to join the ship and two others deserted.

In the early afternoon of 9 March a stowaway was discovered in the Firemen's quarters. George Howard, a 21-year-old from Liverpool, was placed in detention pending his return to Liverpool and the custody of the local police force. That same day a Third-Class passenger, Thomas Jones, shed his mortal coil in the late afternoon from an unfortunate combination of 'acute alcoholism, pneumonia and epilepsy'. He was buried at sea the following day with the 'customary ceremony'. The ship arrived at Sandy Hook on 11 March just nine minutes behind her record, having crossed from Daunt Rock in four days, seventeen hours and thirteen minutes. However, she could not dock until the following day as the Pilot, Captain Alfred, declined to take the *Mauretania* through the Ambrose Channel during darkness, despite advice from the US War Department that it was safe to do so, recommending that the ship be anchored overnight.

The return trip achieved another record. Over one twenty-four-hour period she made 609 miles at an average speed of 26.33 knots and bettered her record by one hour and twenty-seven minutes. But the trip was not without human problem or tragedy. Firstly, four men deserted in New York and, during the crossing, a Henry Bonner was admitted to the ship's hospital with pneumonia, where he received the 'usual treatment'. By midnight of the 22nd his worsening condition was described as 'very serious' and four hours later he was dead. His body was landed at Liverpool.

After arrival in Liverpool on 22 June the liner was again placed in the Canada Graving Dock, where a surveyor inspected the Parsons Special Turbine Alloy propellers that had been fitted six months before. During this time Captain Pritchard attended a meeting of the Liverpool Local Marine Board on Thursday, 25 March, where he was presented with a pair of binoculars by J.L. Griffiths, the American Consul in Liverpool, on behalf of the President of the United States in recognition of the rescue of the crew of the barge *Fall River* the previous January. The Captain modestly said that he had only done 'what every other British captain would do'. The Consul replied that the Captain was 'as big hearted as he was clear-hearted [*sic*: headed], and he knew how to get the best out of a good ship, and yet he never sacrificed safety for speed'.

Lloyds List, the reputable maritime broadsheet, wrote in May 1909:

The Cunard Company have published figures showing the comparative speeds of the Lusitania and the Mauretania, and of the best performances by runners, oarsmen and horses.

Both liners have crossed the Atlantic at a speed of over 25 nautical miles, or 29.5 land miles per hour. This is equivalent to covering 100 yards in 6.9 seconds. The shortest time on record in which a man has run 100 yards is 9.6 sec. The vessels cover in 8 min 38 sec a distance equivalent to the University boat race course (4.25 miles). The fastest boat race time is 18 min 47 sec.

The fastest Derby winner, however, would beat the Cunard boats over a distance the length of the Derby course (1 mile 4 furlongs 29 yards), the time being: horse, 2 min 36.8 sec, ship, 3 min 5 sec.

The Lusitania and Mauretania, however, maintain their high speed for the whole voyage of about 3,000 miles.

The Captain was determined yet to get even more out of the *Mauretania*.

After inspecting the new four-bladed high pressure-driven screws Surveyor William Norris enthusiastically wrote to the propellers' manufacturers:

To the Manganese Bronze and Brass Co. Limited,
116, Fenchurch Street, E.C.
1st July, 1909.

Dear Sirs, – In accordance with your request, I proceeded to the RMS Mauretania in the Canada Dry Dock, Liverpool, on Tuesday last [29 June], to inspect the new wing propellers lately supplied by you of your special 'Parsons Turbine Alloy' …

This alloy was a manganese bronze alloy containing 50 per cent copper; 44 per cent zinc; 2 per cent nickel; 1.75 per cent manganese; 1 per cent iron; and 0.5 per cent tin. Later referred to as 'Turbadium' in a copy of the letter reprinted in January 1912, it was reassessed as being up to six times more effective than some high-tensile bronzes and was subsequently used for the centre propellers of *Olympic* and *Titanic*, then building at Belfast.

Mr Norris continued:

I understand that these propellers were specially made by you to take the place of other propellers of the ordinary standard high-tension bronze, as used for the propellers of the principal Atlantic liners, which proved subject to erosion [cavitation], apparently resulting from the high revolutions of the engines, combined with the action of broken water under high pressure upon the surface of the blades.

I learnt from the Cunard Steamship Company, that the new wing propellers referred to were fitted in January last and have, therefore, been running for nearly six months. After a thorough examination of these propellers, I found them in perfect condition, there being no sign of wasting or erosion, the surface in fact appeared to be as good in every way as when the castings were first made.

While in Liverpool I also examined the blades of the built-up [original three-bladed] propellers previously fitted to this vessel, and noted with great interest the very extensive erosion which had taken place over a great part of the surface of the same.

These blades, I was informed, had only made three round trips, so that it was obvious such a severe and rapid erosion would very soon have worn out these blades.

I consider it, therefore, a matter of great scientific interest, and one upon which you can be congratulated, in having been successful in producing an alloy which, from the inspection carried out by me, appears to withstand the erosion so satisfactorily.

Yours faithfully,
Wm. J. Norris,
Surveyor for Germanischer Lloyd.

As a consequence of the survey it was decided to replace the remaining two three-bladed propellers with solid-cast Turbadium four-bladers at the ship's next dry-docking. From the alterations made to these unseen, largely unsung but vital organs, the *Mauretania* was in a position to prove the faith of those who sailed in her and of those who followed her progress with such pride, as well as those who travelled upon her by paying a premium to have the advantage of her high speed at their disposal. It was not only her gorgeous panelling that attracted passengers but the reliability of her timetable for which she was rightly renowned and famed. By the end of 1911 the British Admiralty had decided to adopt Turbadium propellers for their high-speed, turbine-driven 'Men o' War' – a decision not entirely of their Lordships' making as propellers of the new material were already, perhaps worryingly, being supplied to 'leading foreign navies'.

Whatever the competition, the *Mauretania* was ready for all that could be expected of her.

8

FISHGUARD

A few days after the presentation of his prized binoculars, Captain Pritchard was in the capital on 29 March 1909, as a guest of honour at the Welsh Club of London. Fellow Welshman and Chancellor of the Exchequer, David Lloyd George, was to have presided over the gathering but was detained by parliamentary business. After speeches and toasts of appreciation (some of which must have been in Welsh, the Captain's native tongue) Captain Pritchard responded:

> … believe me, I would much prefer to be in mid-Atlantic, listening to the singing of a winter gale than I would be here tonight. (Laughter). I should not be afraid of the gale, but I am very nervous indeed when I am called upon to face such a distinguished company as confronts me this evening. (Laughter and applause). I appreciate your kindness to me very much, and I am sorry that the school I went to was the hard school of navigation, and not a school where such eloquence as I have heard here was taught … You have said many kind things not only about me, but also about my ship. Well, she is a beauty; and though she was not built in Wales, it is some consolation to you to realise that she is at least commanded by a Welshman who, years ago, served the early days of his half a century at sea in that best of all schools – the Welsh coasting schooner. (Loud applause)

Back on his beloved ship, the Captain arrived in New York on 9 April with the *Mauretania* bearing signs of the rough seas and strong winds encountered all the way over, which had been particularly atrocious on the Sunday, Monday and Wednesday. The ship had still managed to average just over 25 knots, which pleased her passengers, especially the Hon. Charles Parsons. Also on board was Admiral Baron Sakamoto of the Imperial Japanese Navy, who had been attending the International Naval Conference in London. Rather presciently, he told reporters: 'there is not the slightest doubt as to the friendliness of the United States and Japan'.

Heavy weather prevented a record passage at the end of Voyage 18 on 20 April, although the ship did make an average of 25.42 knots during the crossing. To make up time the liner ran at speed between Queenstown and the Skerries on the north-west corner of Anglesey, albeit with the tide, at an amazing 29 knots!

On 24 April the *Mauretania* left the Prince's Landing Stage at 5.00 in the afternoon but, because of the state of the tide, was not able to cross the Bar until 11.30. This problem was raised at the Thirty-Second Annual Meeting of the Cunard Steamship Company (Limited) when Chairman William Watson stated that, along with the fact that immigrant numbers carried on the company's ships was down by 70 per cent because of an economic crisis in the United States, extra costs were being incurred by the sisters being 'frequently unable to enter the docks at Liverpool owing to want of water (or when having entered to leave when loaded), and in consequence having to remain in the river from the time of sailing, and there carry out the usual work of discharging, loading, coaling, &c., in preparation for a new voyage.' These delays caused expense as well as inconveniencing passengers. Cunard was seriously considering changing its British terminus to Plymouth to take advantage of the lucrative continental traffic. On the positive side, overnight delays while waiting to enter New York had now been obviated as construction of the Ambrose

Channel was almost complete. The question of the *Mauretania's* and *Lusitania's* requirement under the original Agreement of 1903 to call into Queenstown to await delivery of mails from London was also raised in mid-April when the Liverpool Chamber of Commerce wrote to the Postmaster General and pointed out that this contractual call constituted 'a very serious obstacle to the fullest advantage being taken of the capabilities as mail ships of the two vessels'. The Chamber argued 'in the interests of the commercial community of Great Britain' that if the American-bound mails were closed in London on a Friday instead of a Saturday then the mails could be delivered to Liverpool for an earlier sailing on a Saturday instead of being taken to Queenstown for a Sunday loading via the rail-sea-rail links, each subject to delays. The omission of Queenstown would also save ten hours on the entire voyage and enable an earlier arrival in New York and subsequent speedier deliveries. The fear of delays was amply demonstrated when the *Mauretania* arrived at Queenstown at 3.00 in the morning of 25 April because of the delay in Liverpool but, because of the lateness of the mails from London, she did not sail until *seven* hours later at 10.20. Authorities in Queenstown responded that after a fifteen-and-a-half-hour passage from Liverpool the delay at Queenstown was only for an average of three hours twenty-five minutes and that wait could be further reduced if the London mails could be sent by express train, which would get them to the port two hours earlier at 5 a.m. The liner was consequently late arriving at Sandy Hook, spending a night there in the anchorage, and was almost a day late in berthing at Pier 54 even though she had metaphorically arrived earlier than scheduled. Meanwhile, a model of the ship, the largest of a steamer ever made, had been brought over on the *Caronia* for display in a New York store window.

Another record was overturned when, on completion of the following voyage on the morning of 10 May, the liner arrived off Daunt Rock at 10.54 having beaten her previous best eastwards crossing by twenty-four minutes, in spite of being briefly delayed by fog off Fastnet. She had crossed in four days, eighteen hours and eleven minutes, her average speed of 25.7 knots bettering her previous best by a slender but publicity-important 0.09 of a knot. From noon Thursday to noon Sunday she sped along at a wonderful 26.31 knots. She had

also bettered her previous best day's run of 609 miles on Friday noon to Saturday noon by a tenuous single mile.

As June 1909 approached the *Mauretania* was establishing herself as the jewel of the North Atlantic as records disappeared in her wake. The *Lusitania* made occasional attempts to emulate her sister but to no avail. On her arrival at Quarantine at 11.10 on Thursday evening, 20 May, the *Mauretania* had established a new westward record by reaching the *Ambrose* lightship at 9.33 p.m., four days, sixteen hours and five minutes after passing Daunt Rock at 9.42 a.m. on the 16th, beating her previous best of 18 February by one hour and one minute. Her average speed had been 25.62 knots as against her previous best of 25.55.

This May passage was also the first time that the *Mauretania* had arrived at Quarantine on a Thursday night, thus strengthening Cunard's case of dropping Queenstown where, it is remembered, she had been delayed for seven hours waiting for late mails. To add to the excitement of the record passage, both mails and passengers were disembarked in double-quick time. The 1,700 bags of mails were offloaded at Quarantine and reached the New York Post Office by 3.30 on Friday morning for onward transmission, well before the liner had reached her berth. She left Quarantine at 6.30 a.m. and, on reaching her pier ninety minutes later, discharged her passengers including 272 in First Class (Saloon), among them steel, tobacco and rail magnate, philanthropist and art collector P.A.B. Widener. Because of this extraordinary performance, it was hoped that the ship might in future arrive at her berth on a Thursday night instead of a Friday morning. To add to the celebrations of this crossing, the financial crisis in the United States was showing signs of recovery with a 'restoration of confidence and signs of an encouraging outlook' – thanks to financial assistance being given to the US Treasury by J.P. Morgan.

The eastbound return also established a new record. Leaving New York on Wednesday 26 May, her daily runs of 602, 605, 600 and 542 nautical miles took her four days, eighteen hours and twenty-eight minutes, beating her previous best by seventeen minutes in spite of reducing speed because of fog between Brow Head – the most southerly point of Ireland – and Daunt Rock. It was hoped to be alongside in Liverpool by 9.30 that evening but fog again thwarted the Captain's wishes so his ship had to anchor off the Bar. Some 1,100 bags of mails and passengers with urgent business were landed by tender and the ship did not berth until 11.00 the next morning, when the remainder of the 1,092 passengers disembarked.

Sailing from New York on 16 June, *Mauretania* reached Daunt Rock after four days, seventeen hours and twenty-one minutes, and another record of 25.88 knots. The westward record was broken yet again on the next voyage when, in almost perfect weather, the *Mauretania* shortened her passage by seventeen minutes at an average of 25.84 knots, at times exceeding 26 knots. Arriving in New York at 8.45 p.m. on 8 July, the Captain said that she was finely tuned enough to make a Thursday arrival a commonplace. But fog delayed her on this particular crossing, during which her noon time distances travelled had been 68 miles from Daunt Rock to noon Sunday; 663 miles to noon Monday; 630 miles to noon Tuesday; 638 miles to noon Wednesday; and 651 miles to noon Thursday; before another 242 miles brought her to Sandy Hook.

Excitement accompanied the liner on this trip. An altercation arose in the Palm Court when a group of men were admonished for singing a provocative song in order to annoy a lady passenger, whose vociferously protesting male companion indulged in fisticuffs. The men ceased their singing – he apologised. On arrival a group of detectives boarded looking for a gang of thieves who were reported, incorrectly as it transpired, to be on board after a recent massive £100,000 jewellery robbery in London. Among those disembarking was the Duke of Sutherland on a short visit to inspect the site of the forthcoming Hudson-Fulton celebrations. He would be returning on the liner as he wanted to be in Britain to board his magnificent steam yacht *Catania* in readiness for Cowes Week. A passenger sent a traditional postcard from Pier 54 as the liner prepared to sail eastwards on 14 July: 'Arrived on board about 8 this morning … it is simply lovely here … such a nice breeze.'

By now Cunard had decided to use the developing harbour of Fishguard in Wales as a homeward port-of-call to expedite the early arrival of mails and those London and Continental passengers eager to reach their destinations a few hours earlier. To everyone's disappointment, the experimental call into Fishguard was missed as the 3 a.m. arrival would have been an inconvenient hour for disembarkations

The mighty *Mauretania* hoves into view after a record passage. Excited spectators wore their Sunday best for the occasion and many Welsh ladies dressed in their traditional *hetiau Cymreig* (tall, black, truncated-cone-shaped Welsh hats) and red, chequered shawls. (*The Graphic*/Author's collection)

The Great Western Railway's tender *Sir John Hawkins* alongside the giant liner. (Author's Collection)

Voyage 23 for *Mauretania* began on 24 July 1909. Captain Pritchard remained in command. E.G. Diggle stood as Chief Officer with W.H. Hossack as First. John Currie was still ensconced as Chief Engineer and in his department of the 143 Coal Trimmers only 142 would arrive in New York as Robert Gibbons was operated on for acute suppurative appendicitis after leaving his symptoms for too long. This surgical procedure – still in its infancy even after King Edward had fashionably undergone such an operation in June 1902, resulting in the postponement of his Coronation – was undertaken by the ship's Surgeon, Dr B. Sydney Jones, assisted by two qualified passengers; the ship, even at speed, was steady enough not to be slowed. Unhappily, the patient died and passengers raised the handsome sum of $500 for the Fireman's widow. During the New York turnaround a hefty sixteen Firemen and Trimmers deserted, taking with them half their pay.

After the initial delay a confirmation that the Fishguard call would finally commence was issued in early August:

The Cunard Line has decided to call at Fishguard with its New York steamers eastbound, weather and other circumstances permitting, commencing with the Mauretania, sailing from New York Aug. 25, for the purpose of landing passengers and mails for London, the Continent and other places which can be served from Fishguard. The Cunard Line trusts that the call at Fishguard, having for its object the shortening of the journey between America, London, the Continent, &c., will prove of great advantage to the travelling public.

The contracted Queenstown homeward call would still be made early on the morning of 30 August before the first call at Fishguard at about 10.30, where the all-important mails and disembarking London-bound passengers would cut six hours from their journey, even arriving in the metropolis one-and-a-half hours before the *Mauretania* docked in Liverpool! Also, passengers bound for Paris would be entrained for Dover (via Reading), arriving in the vibrant French capital just before midnight. The first tentative call by Cunard into Fishguard had been made a few weeks previously by the *Lucania* (1893; 12,952 gross tons and, at 22 knots, a good running mate for her two giant

sisters). But disaster had struck as, on 14 August, that venerable old liner was severely damaged by fire in Liverpool and, declared a total constructive loss, was sentenced to be broken up. Three days later Cunard announced that they were planning to build a 25,000-ton, 21-knot passenger vessel to replace either of the larger sisters when laid up. This plan had been first mooted eighteen months earlier but, because of the faster turnarounds that were now extant, only one of the two proposed vessels was required. The plans gradually developed to become the magnificent *Aquitania*.

The *Mauretania* continued to astound. On Monday, 9 August she reached Daunt Rock after another record crossing, beating her previous best by a single minute and arriving at the Rock after a passage of four days, seventeen hours and twenty minutes at an average speed of 25.89 knots. During the trip, Dr B. Sydney Jones, aided by surgeon passenger Louis McArthur, operated on a boy for appendicitis, the success of which countered the previous tragedy. In good health, the young lad left the vessel at Liverpool.

Persistent fog and then a gale accompanied by a heavy ahead sea slowed the ship to such an extent on Tuesday, 17 August that the Captain announced that the liner would not dock in New York until Friday. Among the delayed passengers were Lord Strathcona, and politician and wealthy newspaper owner William Randolph Hearst. In contrast to Hearst's anti-Britishness was regular traveller, the American Ambassador to the Court of St James, Whitelaw Reid who, on the evening of the 18th, reprised his role as chairman of the passengers' concert and aimed a barb at Hearst: 'Never was there a time when the relations between England and America were more agreeable and harmonious.'

The ship had crossed in the record time of four days, fourteen hours and thirty-eight minutes, clipping twenty minutes off the *Lusitania*'s best westward run of the previous August. The ships in New York gave the liner a noisy greeting on their sirens after her exciting crossing, but Captain Pritchard did not respond with the ship's whistles, perhaps because one of his passengers was Mrs Isaac Rice, President of the Anti-Noise Society! Captain Pritchard told waiting newsmen that he had slowed his ship in a gale on the Tuesday having narrowly avoided collision with a fishing schooner over

Newfoundland's Grand Banks; disappearances of schooners or their dories were not unknown in this storm-tossed and fog-prone region after encounters with fast express ships.

Fishguard

After much consideration and planning Cunard had chosen the small Welsh town (previously famed as the site of a failed Napoleonic invasion in 1797) as a new port of call because of its easy approach, deep water, and being relatively fog free. The *Mauretania* was scheduled to arrive at Fishguard at the end of her twenty-fourth voyage on Monday, 30 August 1909, where she would inaugurate the recent redevelopments by the Great Western Railway (GWR). Passengers waiting to disembark were given a handsome souvenir book, *Historic Sites and Scenes of England*, made up of 152 gilt-edged pages, hard-bound in maroon leather and embossed with gilt lettering topped by the GWR crest.

The Cunarder's crossing on this inaugural trip almost equalled her westward, being completed in four days, fourteen hours and twenty-seven minutes, beating her previous best by two hours and fifty-four minutes, the 2,807 miles being covered at an average 25.41 knots. Although Germany's ex-record holder, the *Kaiser Wilhelm der Grosse*, had left New York twenty-four hours beforehand, the *Mauretania* had overtaken the German liner; passengers on the 'Maury' bound for Germany even expected to reach their destination before the 'Kaiser' even reached her home port!

If the coming of the railway was the icing on Fishguard's cake then the arrival of the *Mauretania* was the cherry. To celebrate the great liner's appearance a carnival atmosphere permeated the town's streets, quays and railway station, all bedecked with bunting 'distributed with reckless prodigality'. The jubilant procession that wound its way through the streets included the Pembrokeshire Territorials (headed by their military band), tradesmen with emblems of their professions, and excited schoolchildren. Mayors of various towns were in attendance, as were Cunard's senior officials and representatives of the Great Western Railway including its chairman, Lord Churchill. Girls traditionally dressed in *hetiau Cymreig* (tall, black, truncated-cone-shaped Welsh

hats) and red, chequered shawls readied themselves with bunches of flowers and sprigs of local heather to present to the arriving passengers. *En fête*, a great crowd of locals and a mass of sightseers who had arrived by special excursion trains from afar gathered, donned in traditional costumes and Sunday best suits and dresses for the gala, on the bright sunlit hills surrounding the harbour to await the historic arrival of the fastest and greatest liner in the world whose building and record-breaking exploits they had followed with enthusiasm.

Even before the liner made her appearance, three tenders had moved into the roads to receive mails and passengers. Cannon roared to herald the liner's appearance 'cleaving rapidly through the clear, blue waters, a splendid picture of majesty and force' as she passed Strumble Head on the Pen-Caer peninsula (topped by the Iron Age hill fort of Garn Fawr) to starboard and the beautiful peninsula of Dinas Head over to port, just after midday. The great liner anchored, gaily dressed with flags cascading from both mastheads, just after 1.15 p.m. on the seaward side of the yet incomplete breakwater. Had the weather not been so windless the ship would have anchored further into the harbour to avoid difficulties with the tenders; it was hoped, in the future, that large ships might berth against the mole once sufficient dredging had been completed.

The mail tender was the first vessel to move alongside the now-anchored ship, the disembarkation of over 3,000 bags of mail being the first priority. The small vessel rolled as canvas chutes swallowed the valuable pouches. Within fourteen minutes the tender was away to transfer the bags to a mail train that awaited, its steel muscles steaming with impatience, at the nearby Fishguard Harbour station. By 2.12 p.m. the train was rushing on its way. Luggage, bearing stickers that declared 'FISHGUARD' in large type, was then unloaded. Other stickers declaring 'London via Fishguard' summed up the purpose of the new port in the liner's itinerary. Some 170 out of the 240 First-Class (Cabin) passengers were due to disembark at Fishguard. Amongst them, awaiting the call, were a few gentlemen sitting comfortably and well wrapped against the chill in the wicker chairs of the Veranda cafe, taking a last drink whilst their baggage was offloaded. Within ten short minutes the little ship was away, soon to be followed by a second carrying the baggage. Local man Mr Jenkin Evan became the first passenger to step ashore from the tender *Sir Francis Drake*.

Local man Mr Jenkin Evan is the first man to disembark at Fishguard. A previous emigrant, he was paying a visit to his old home. (*The Bystander/* Author's collection)

Undoubtedly, the arrival of his ship into a Welsh port was very gratifying for Captain Pritchard, who said in response to congratulations that he was very proud to open the port of Fishguard for the Cunard Company, and ardently wished it every success (he must have astounded many of his passengers by conversing in his native tongue to those in the reception party). To mark the momentous occasion he was presented with an inscribed silver tankard; cheaper, earthenware souvenir mugs had been sold ashore.

Shortly after the departure of the tenders, the liner weighed anchor and sped her way to Liverpool. From the care of Cunard the baggage was handed over to the servants of the Great Western Railway for transference to the two gleaming, green-liveried express trains that stood waiting and steam shrouded alongside the platform of the shoreside railway station. Here the luggage was lifted, pushed and shoved into the chocolate-and-cream-painted baggage vans by men in the hope of a 'bob' or a 'tanner' (a shilling or a sixpence) tip that would buy them a couple of pints in the local pubs. The *Cunard Ocean Express*, under the control of Driver Fred Gregory, left the station at 2.53 bound for Paddington Station, the GWR's London terminus. The second express followed thirteen minutes later.

Her triumphant arrival in Liverpool marked another record for the fastest voyage, the *Mauretania* completing the Liverpool to Liverpool round trip in nine days, five hours and five minutes (excluding the New York turnaround). However, she was not to have the laurels all to herself as, on Thursday, 2 September the fully booked *Lusitania* (now with new propellers), under the command of Captain Turner, arrived off the *Ambrose* lightship at 4.42 p.m. She landed her passengers at New York at 7.50 after completing the entire crossing in less than five days from Queenstown to the Cunard Pier in New York, the first time that this had ever been achieved as the 'record' passages had been reckoned from Daunt Rock to Sandy Hook. Although delayed at Queenstown for five hours waiting for the mails, once past Daunt Rock she averaged 25.85 knots; a gale had put her two hours behind on the Wednesday.

Arriving in New York Harbor, she steamed 'majestically up the harbor, the crimson rays of the setting sun lighting up her upper works and giant smokestacks' to a spontaneous welcome. Captain Turner generously highlighted the efforts of the Engine Room and Stokehold crews (who had shovelled 4,725 tons of coal) in achieving her record passage of four days, eleven hours and forty-two minutes, which had beaten the *Mauretania*'s best. Clydebank was ecstatic! She would complete the entire round trip in nine days, five hours and three minutes.

Captain Pritchard did not take the challenge lying down and, on her next crossing, a telegram noted that the Mauretania 'steamed

1,367 miles at an average speed of 26 knots which if maintained to the end of the voyage will beat all previous records'. Stops were pulled on both ships and *Lusitania* made her fastest westbound crossing in late August/early September with an average speed of 25.85 knots, but, in spite of that, she had permanently surrendered the Ribband to '*Mauretania* the Magnificent', which, when arriving at Sandy Hook, had beaten her sister's record by seven minutes while lowering her own by forty-six! The Captain reckoned that she could have improved on that had it not been for 'fog and bad coal which was full of stones'.

The voyage that ended in New York on 30 September 1909 was a triumph, assuring the *Mauretania* of the final victory in the familial contest both ways across the Atlantic after a passage of four days, nineteen hours and fifty-one minutes, averaging 26.06 knots. Glasses were raised in Newcastle in celebration; glasses were drained in Glasgow in sorrow; and probably glasses were thrown in Liverpool between the two factions! Astonishingly this ship would retain the Blue Ribband for an incredible twenty years. The end of the voyage was marred by a freak accident when Arthur Connor, a Steward engaged in assisting in the landing of passengers' baggage, was shot through the knee by a revolver packed in a portmanteau belonging to Second-Cabin passenger, J.S. Reid. The hapless steward was sent to St Vincent Hospital for treatment.

The triumph of the liner's late-September crossing was somewhat tarnished by the unhappy announcement on Monday, 4 October that the Chairman of the Cunard Steamship Company, William Watson, had died at his home at Spital, Cheshire, aged 66. A week later Alfred Booth was voted in as the company's new Chairman.

The *Mauretania*'s return trip was turbulent as the remains of a tropical storm battered New England's coast and a proposed attempt by the new Invincible-class battlecruiser HMS *Inflexible*, the flagship of a British squadron that had been in New York as part of the Hudson-Fulton festival, to wrest the eastward record was abandoned after the warship had left New York.

Prior to the ship's sailing from Liverpool on 23 October, Captain Pritchard announced that, after fifty-three years at sea of which thirty had been in the company's service, he wished to take his long-deferred retirement, normally taken at age 63, having stayed on for an extra eighteen months at the company's request. His decision had been spurred by the Board's decision that masters should retire at 62 – especially those of the *Mauretania* and *Lusitania* – to ensure that promotion for junior captains was not blocked. His retirement date was later set for New Year's Day 1910. At the same time it was revealed that Cunard's plans for a new 23-knot liner to run with the *Lusitania* and *Mauretania* were progressing.

When Captain Pritchard sailed from New York on 3 November 1909, for ostensibly the last time, even hard-bitten Longshoremen 'waved their caps and cheered him', both parties unaware that he would be making one more visit when the Cunard directors asked him to stay on for an additional voyage prior to the ship entering her annual lay-up in December. The Captain's final departure from Liverpool on 20 November developed into a very rough passage, although the *Mauretania* still steamed ahead at an average of 25.6 knots (she had managed to steam 658 miles on the Wednesday). Arriving at Sandy Hook in the late afternoon of the 25th, she had to wait overnight in the bay because of high winds and snow. Thanksgiving was spent on board. It was not until the next day that the *Mauretania*, the largest of a backlog of twenty-seven vessels, led the flotilla into the harbour. During the liner's turnaround Captain Pritchard visited his old terminal of Boston where, in June 1900, he had been presented with a loving cup leaving that port for New York.

During the liner's absence a great hurricane-force gale hit the English coast, resulting in the tragic loss of the Isle of Man Steam Packet Company's steamer *Ellan Vannin*, which foundered on 3 December in Liverpool Bay at the mouth of the Mersey in waters through which the *Mauretania* always traversed. All thirty-five crew and passengers on board were lost.

On Captain Pritchard's absolute final westward crossing a group of passengers presented him with a silver salver with an openwork Arts and Crafts border of cherries and leaves. It was inscribed in elegant copperplate:

Captain John Pritchard
RMS Mauretania
Presented by the passengers
on his last Westward voyage
Dec 11 to 16 – 1909

Captain Pritchard by lifeboat No. 2 from a postcard posted to his family on 28 December 1909, before sailing from New York for the very last time before retirement. (Estate of Captain Pritchard/Author's Collection)

Captain Pritchard's cabin was full of flowers, letters and telegrams as he left on his last crossing, his 534th. Beset by fog and 'violent gales', the ship ploughed on but her struggles with the ocean may have proved too much for one Second-Class passenger as, on Christmas Eve, 54-year-old Mrs Margaret Hodgson was found dead in her cabin after suffering heart failure. She was buried at sea on Christmas Day, 1,000 miles from the Irish coast, the service contrasting sharply with the seasonal celebrations. The *Mauretania* still managed to average 25 knots. By the time the liner docked in Liverpool the highly esteemed Captain had gone ashore during the call at Fishguard at 3 p.m. on the 27th. A group of passengers passed resolutions 'wishing him length of days and happiness' and his retirement even made the front pages, the *Daily Mirror* honouring him with the epithet 'the Best Known Sea Captain in the World'.

Because of Captain Pritchard's status as a widower, his fellow captain, 61-year-old Captain Robert Warr of the *Umbria*, made a tongue-in-cheek comment that widower Captain Pritchard would make someone a prize husband. The latter responded with cutting humour: 'You tell Captain Warr for me, that he says everything but his prayers … the widows might wait.' However, the newly retired Captain harboured a personal secret. He had previously said that, after retirement, he intended to close his house and travel the world. But, on 3 February and within five weeks of his retirement, the good Captain married his housekeeper, Katherine Parry, settling down in his house at Meols on the Wirral that she had so carefully tended for him. The Captain would enjoy his garden, a new family of two daughters, Elizabeth and Katherine, and visits from his Welsh-speaking compatriots until his death in 1922. The Captain certainly retired on a professional high as 1909 proved to be the *Mauretania*'s best ever season, with constant fast passages being made. With new propellers she had completed fifteen voyages (thirty crossings) at an average speed of 25½ knots with, incredibly, only a minute's difference between some arrivals.

There was much speculation as to who would be the next Commodore of the Line, carrying with it an extra £125 a year in salary. Captain Turner (52), rather than Captain James Charles (45) of the *Campania*, was marked as favourite as he was the Senior Captain and his record on the *Lusitania* stood him in good stead. Captain Charles took over Turner's old command and Captain Turner, although given the *Mauretania*, had to wait. In the end it was 61-year old Captain Warr of the *Umbria* who was appointed, but he remained on his ship.

The dangers of submerged wrecks (similar to the one that the *Mauretania* may have hit several months earlier) was amply demonstrated when, on 14 October, the Canadian Pacific liner *Empress of Ireland* collided with one en route for Quebec whilst off Cape Chatte, suffering a hole in her bow. Another derelict plagued the approaches to the English Channel for several weeks, causing both the Cunard and White Star Lines to approach the Royal Navy; two warships were sent to tow the remains of the *Saddartha* into Bantry Bay.

Following the *Mauretania*'s winter overhaul, Captain William Turner took command of the ship. A fine seaman, Captain Turner was known affectionately as 'Bowler Bill' due to his preference for wearing a bowler hat [US: 'Derby'] on the Bridge. He was a very private person, often taking his meals in his cabin. W.M. Hammersley became Chief Officer in place of John Diggle, the latter having been promoted to captain and given command of the company's *Cypria*. W.H. Hossack was First Officer and C.D. Cay was Second. On Captain Turner's first crossing in the liner (sailing on Saturday, 29 January 1910) the ship's new Surgeon, David Morgan, left the ship by 'mutual consent' for some unspecified reason. B. Sydney Jones rejoined as substitute. As she readied for sailing Captain Pritchard paid his old command a visit as she lay alongside the Landing Stage, during which time he was the recipient of a surprise presentation by the Stewards' Department, being given a gold watch, a walking stick and a beautifully hand-illuminated address topped with a picture of his first command, the *Sybil Wynne*, with the *Mauretania* being colourfully represented at the bottom. Roses, thistles, shamrock and the Prince of Wales' feathers composed the border of a citation that read:

1858

To
Captain John Pritchard
Dear Sir,
We the members of the Steward Department of the
"R.M.S. Mauretania" wish you to
Accept this Gold Watch and Stick

As tokens of the respect we have for you,
And we feel that we cannot allow you to
Retire from the Cunard Service with-
Out expressing the pride and pleasure
We have at all times experienced in
Sailing under your command.
Wishing you good health and long life
On behalf of the above department
We beg to remain respectfully yours
(Signed) Ewan Hy Hughes; Wm. M.Intosh; Wm. S. Fletcher; D.C. Handlin; Albert Rudge; B. leNayel; John Sands; P. Biddlecombe; Designed and Executed by Ernest I. Bowden.

1909

Sailing from New York on 9 February, the ship carried a theatrical company, producer Charles Frohman's (who famously staged 'Peter Pan' in London) Floating Theatre Company. During the crossing the company performed 'The Climax' by Edward Locke in the Dining Room, the first play to be performed at sea. The ship's Carpenter assisted the theatre's carpenter with the erection of the scenery and the *Mauretania*'s orchestra provided the music.

The Fishguard call came under strong criticism in mid-February when a disgruntled passenger, after being cosseted on the liner for five days, wrote lengthily to *The Times*:

Sir, – I take the liberty of writing to express … the experiences of the passengers of the Mauretania through being induced to land at Fishguard instead of going on to Liverpool, and I do so more with the idea of cautioning prospective travellers than from any vindictive purpose.

We arrived on the Mauretania at Fishguard at 8 o'clock [p.m. – a late arrival], and it was 9.15 [an hour and a quarter does not seem unreasonable time in which to disembark passengers, mail and luggage and get all into trains] before the train left for London; the arrangements were simply disgraceful. The luggage was thrown out without any precaution to protect it from the driving rain; everybody had to fight and collect their own effects as best they could, and then the trouble only commenced. The Great Western Railway Company received a Marconigram stating that the number of passengers who were landing at Fishguard, and instead of making suitable arrangements for their comfort, many of the passengers had to wait until 10.15 p.m. before sitting down to dinner, and we arrived at Paddington at 2.13 a.m.

Considering the wonderful advertisements and articles that have appeared in various papers advocating the Fishguard route. I think that it is only right, in the interests of the travelling public, that these facts should become known, to avoid the said experience that we all had.

The above facts, I feel sure, will be confirmed by everybody who travelled on the Mauretania, and it is the best advertisement possible for the Liverpool route and the London and North-Western Railway Company.

Perhaps your powerful influence in publishing this letter will stimulate both the Fishguard end of the line and the Great Western Railway Company to make suitable arrangements to add to the comfort of travellers, and it is with this object that I take the liberty of addressing you.

Stowaways were a perennial problem and two were discovered after sailing time on 19 February 1910 and landed at Queenstown. Further into the crossing, an American stowaway was rooted out and put ashore in New York; a Liverpudlian was not as lucky as he ended in the ship's Hospital with suspected scarlet fever. He was landed at Ellis Island for detention in the isolation hospital and repatriation. An unlogged accident occurred when the ship lurched, catching Cook Joseph Gurney unawares just as he was lifting a pan of soup. He was fatally scalded.

On the return leg of that voyage dense fog covered the harbour entrance and, after sailing at 8 a.m. on 3 March, the *Mauretania* had to anchor off Liberty Island for safety until the afternoon. But, during the course of the morning, she received a wireless message to say that the Royal Mail Steam Packet Company's *Tagus* (1899; 5,545grt) with over 100 first-class passengers on board and inward bound from Jamaica, had been in collision with a four-masted American schooner, the *Republic*. An exchange of messages showed that, as the slightly damaged *Tagus* was standing by the sailing vessel, the *Mauretania*'s assistance was not required. The following day, once the Cunarder was under way, the new Chief Steward, Bill Brysden, reported sick to the Hospital with suspected influenza. Sadly, this turned into septicaemia. His body was taken ashore at Liverpool on 8 March. Another disembarkation was accompanied with a hint of adventure and excitement when French fugitive Adrian Maderian was led ashore in irons, having had the audacity to escape three (or even four!) times from the so-called 'toughest penal colony of all time' on French Guiana – Devil's Island, which had the reputation of being 'the worst place on earth'.

After lengthy discussions with the postal authorities, Cunard announced (much to its own relief) that Queenstown would be omitted from the eastward schedules.

Captain Turner was as determined as his predecessor to get the best out of the *Mauretania* and on Voyage 32 managed to break the westward record by making the crossing in four days, fifteen hours and twenty-nine minutes, beating Captain Pritchard's record by twenty-six minutes (she might have done better had she not encountered a snowstorm on the Wednesday). On one day she attained a magnificent record speed of 26.79 knots. Both she and her sister had now made a Thursday arrival in New York. Her return to Liverpool was delayed by twenty minutes by the late arrival of a few passengers – which was just as well as two churns of cream, also late, made the sailing as well, much to the relief of watching passengers!

By the Liverpool 2 April departure, Chief Engineer John Currie had retired and Second Engineer John Kendall was promoted in his place. Second was Alex Dunbar and a namesake, James Dunbar, was listed as Thirteenth Engineer but, for some reason, the latter soon left the ship 'by mutual consent'. Before that same voyage ten men failed to join the ship and, not long after her sailing when the liner was just off the Skerries, an American stowaway was discovered in the Firemen's quarters. Mr O'Rourke was landed at Queenstown after a very short trip. On that return voyage the ship carried a king's ransom valued at over £1,000,000 in her Specie Room with 6½ tons of precious metal in the form of gold sovereigns and 1,100 bright bars of silver that, on arrival at the Prince's Landing Stage, was securely transferred from the liner to Liverpool's Lime Street Station for onward transportation to its consignees in London.

At the April meeting of the Cunard Company in Liverpool the Chairman (A.A. Booth) announced that the company were seriously considering, as has been seen, a large ship that would both run in conjunction with the *Lusitania* and *Mauretania* on the New York mail service and run at a lower speed, 22.5 knots, to match the speeds of two White Star liners (*Olympic* and *Titanic*) being built in Belfast. Future fuel was considered so the ship would be built as a coal-burner with a later conversion to oil once supplies could be maintained. It was estimated that, even after considering the higher price of oil, it would represent a saving of £12,000 on *each* transatlantic voyage as fewer Firemen and Trimmers would be needed. Speed and ease of loading directly and cleanly into the ship would be a great advantage.

At Buckingham Palace in London the cigar-loving and very popular King-Emperor Edward VII, under whose reign many technological advances had been made and many beautiful ships designed and built, passed away on 6 May. Known variously as 'The Peacemaker' and 'The Uncle of Europe' (he had been related to nearly every European monarch), his funeral marked 'the greatest assemblage of royalty and rank ever gathered in one place and, of its kind, the last'. Those words would be prescient indeed.

Mauretania was in New York when the death of the King was announced and the liner's ensign was lowered to half mast as a mark of mourning. For the next crossing modifications were made on E-Deck to accommodate the record number of passengers expected during Voyage 38 en route to the funeral – 486 in First Class, 402 in Second and 851 in Third. Edward's death was genuinely mourned by the people of Great Britain, its Empire and allies as he had been a kindly, affable man who believed in decent manners and social improvement, having an abiding interest in the plight of the poor, deprecating anything that would make their lot in life worse ('Tax motors,' he had said, 'tax the rich; but never the poor. Never tax the poor man's food.') He had also been an excellent diplomat and, for a while, managed to keep his nephew, Kaiser Wilhelm II (whom he did not much like), in check. With his uncle now out of the way, Kaiser Wilhelm's ambitions were re-honed on the whetstone of history.

Until 1907 the Germans had spurned any ideas of building turbine steamers but, after a visit paid by Hamburg-America Line's Managing Director, Albert Ballin, to the *Lusitania* in Liverpool, announcements were made for a 47,000 tonner – later changed to 49,000 tons. Eventually three large liners were planned; the Kaiser's hand could be detected in these deliberations.

For the rest of that fast summer season the *Mauretania* bettered her own records. The crew seemed to be content (a strike that affected the White Star Line over differences in pay between British and American Firemen ended before it could spread) but by August the hard driving of the liner continued to take its toll as for the 20 August sailing *twenty-three* men failed to join the ship, mostly Firemen and Trimmers. As the ship approached New York crew member William O'Brien reported sick with 'suffrative tonsillitis'. He remained hospitalised during the ship's turnaround as his illness developed into pneumonia. O'Brien died on-board en route back to England, his body being committed to the deep a day later on 3 September.

The day before that unhappy event saw the *Mauretania* on another mission of mercy when she received a call that a lifeboat was adrift in deteriorating weather. A Liverpudlian steamer, Simpson, Spencer and Young of London's *West Point* (3,074 net tons; 1899), on passage from the Clyde to Savannah, had caught fire on 22 August 600 miles off Cape Race after the Second Engineer had investigated a leaky tap on a tank holding 127 gallons of paraffin (used for navigation lights and cleaning) in the Engine Room. The tap broke, sending a stream gushing outward. The flame in the oil lamp held by the Second did not help matters and the resultant conflagration blazed out of control. The vessel was abandoned on the 28th, sinking shortly afterwards. One lifeboat containing nineteen survivors was picked up by a passing steamer, the Leyland Line's *Devonian*, but the second boat, containing fifteen of the crew and the *West Point*'s captain, could not be located. That is until the *Mauretania* was alerted.

Captain James Pinkham of the sunken vessel had been injured during the course of the drama but still skilfully kept his lifeboat in the shipping lanes to await rescue. This was effected at 10.30 p.m. on 2 September when, after seeing a rocket, Captain Turner brought his great ship to within a short distance of the *West Point*'s lifeboat to provide a lee. Within an astounding thirty-eight minutes, in spite of atrocious weather with a heavy sea running, Captain Pinkham and his remaining crew ('second officer, two engineers, chief steward, carpenter, and ten seamen') were brought aboard. First Officer Edgar Britten later recalled that a surviving fireman, on seeing the *Mauretania* as she hove into sight reassuringly ablaze with lights, said: 'Blimey! It must be Coney Island!' While Captain Pinkham was being treated in the *Mauretania*'s Hospital, a bedraggled, white Persian kitten, 'Omar', emerged from his jacket! The kitten's care was put up for auction, the proceeds of £30 being added to the £90 collected for the rescued crew. Captain Turner was later awarded an illuminated address and medal (not his first) by the Liverpool Shipwreck and Humane Society for his fine navigation and seamanship.

It was then the Captain's turn for sympathy. Before the next voyage sailing (10 September) he developed a very severe cold and remained ashore in Liverpool. The next day, Captain Daniel Dow hurriedly sailed to Queenstown, where the *Mauretania* was waiting for him. Captain Dow was determined to make a show of his first voyage in command of the crack liner as, with the help of lenient weather, she knocked ten minutes off her previous record crossing on the short route in a record-breaking four days, ten hours and forty-one minutes at an average speed of 26.06 knots. She would never repeat that incredible crossing. One can only imagine Captain Turner's thoughts!

However, on reaching Quarantine the liner was delayed because of an extra-thorough medical examination of the Third-Class passengers as one passenger had been sent ashore with scarlet fever. The Pilot, anxious to bring the ship to her berth, got her as far as the Statue of Liberty before officials realised that their count of the Third Class was two fewer than it should have been and she had left Quarantine without clearance. An unpleasant situation was averted when she was permitted to continue to her berth on condition that all Third-Class passengers remain on board overnight until a recount could be affected, much to the annoyance of 400 Americans who thought that they should have been allowed ashore.

Captain Turner was sufficiently recovered to resume command on the next voyage (departing 1 October), with R. Capper as Chief Officer and E.J. Britten as First. Before sailing, fourteen crew members failed to join the ship and a passenger died during the trip from 'alcoholic mania with heart failure'. The ship sometimes seemed to be a good advert against the 'demon drink'!

All eyes were on Belfast on 20 October as the shipyard of Harland and Wolff was launching the huge *Olympic* for the White Star Line. At 882ft 9in in length and over 45,000 gross tons when completed, the liner would be the largest in the world, beating the *Mauretania*'s tonnage by a good 50 per cent and her length by over 100ft. However, the new liner was being built for comfort and luxury, not for speed.

On 28 October, the day before sailing on Voyage 42, a new Bandmaster, 33-year-old Colne-born Wallace H. Hartley, signed on the *Mauretania* having transferred from the *Lusitania* in October at the rate of one shilling per month – although he was regarded as a member of the crew his actual salary was paid by his agents, C.W. and F.N. Black of Liverpool. He gave his address as 11, West Park Street, Dewesbury [*sic*]. It would be Hartley's destiny to become a true hero of the sea within a few short years, as will be recounted later.

In early November, Captain Turner was eager to beat the record set in September by his temporary replacement. Because of a speedy delivery of mails, the *Mauretania* was able to leave Queenstown two hours early. With favourable seas it was calculated that the ship achieved a fantastic 27.67 knots during a nine-hour period. But her great speeds were not always sustainable as she arrived an hour-and-a-quarter behind the record time of September. After passing Nantucket a vicious storm blew rain into her with the force of hail, the thick, misty conditions greatly reducing visibility. To add to the disappointment she grounded for three-quarters-of-an-hour after gently burying her nose into the bank of the Ambrose Channel. Freed after using a combination of engines and a making tide, she completed her misadventure by colliding with the end of her pier!

On board, amongst the gilded 377 in First Class was mining millionaire Benjamin Guggenheim and his family; Lord Decles; Albert Chevalier, a well-known English Cockney music-hall singer ('My Old Dutch'; 'Knocked 'Em in the Old Kent Road'); Lady Maxwell; actress Constance Collier; Baron Kuroda of Japan; and Countess von Osthelm. The Chairman of the White Star Line, J.B. Ismay, was also on board, again with his family, and on arrival told reporters that his line's two new big ships, *Olympic* and *Titanic*, might have to berth at the South Brooklyn piers (if the channels could be deepened there) as the American War Department was reluctant to add 100ft to the Chelsea piers. He indicated that Captain E.J. Smith would probably command the *Olympic* and Captain H.J. Haddock the *Titanic*.

The voyage that commenced on 19 November was quite an eventful one. Because of the fierce weather when the *Mauretania* made her Queenstown call to embark passengers and mails, she was unable to land the Pilot and carried him on to New York. Baron Hermann von Eckardstein underwent an appendectomy; there were two cases of measles in Third Class (a family was taken ashore to the quarantine station on Hoffman Island); and Second-Class passenger George Chichester died of heart disease, while Third-Class passenger British-born George Millingford was found to be suffering from tuberculosis. Refused entry into the United States, he had to be repatriated at the expense of the line that had brought him to America. George never saw his home country again as he died on the ship on 24 November, the day of Thanksgiving in the land of his lost hopes. However, there was some luck of the Irish on board. John M'Cluskey had been working as a farm labourer and he was now on his way to America to claim his sibling's £50,000 bequest!

At the end of November, Cunard announced a 'Christmas Special' for December 1910: the *Mauretania* would sail to New York and back in eleven days in an epoch-making record-breaking voyage. Ridiculed as being an impossible ambition, the great ship would prove her detractors wrong. It would be done and done in record time with everybody, from company Chairman to Boiler Room Trimmer to every newspaper reader, caught up in a tidal wave of enthusiasm.

9

TRIUMPHS AND TRAGEDIES:
THE END OF AN EDWARDIAN DREAM

On 10 December 1910, the *Mauretania* left Liverpool under the command of Captain William Thomas Turner at the outset of an exciting, well-advertised return crossing, Voyage 44: an eleven-day record-breaking 'Christmas Special' transatlantic dash with each crossing made within her normal four-and-a-half days at an expected speed of 26 knots. However, the most remarkable aspect of the voyage would be the ultra-short two-day turnaround in New York – no mean achievement at the time, it having never been attempted before – let alone in the depths of a winter North Atlantic. A Cunard spokesman told the *New York Times*: 'This trip of the Mauretania will be one of the most remarkable in the history of the world.' The newspaper enquired: 'Will the Mauretania succeed in her Titanic effort to establish an unexampled "record"…?' As so much hard work was expected in speedily feeding the boilers with over 1,000 tons of coal per day, the 350 Firemen signed on almost doubled the normal complement.

Over 1,100 passengers (418 First, 229 Second and 533 Third Class) along with 4,324 bags of Christmas mail were making the westbound crossing on this extra-special festive trip. Among those travelling in First Class for the entire gala return voyage was the Right Hon. Alexander Carlisle, General Manager for Harland and Wolff, accompanied by his wife. Although Carlisle had recently been the principal designer of the *Olympic* and *Titanic* he would shortly be resigning from the shipyard, the reported reason being a nervous breakdown. The real reason was a massive disagreement between him and his brother-in-law, the shipyard's Chairman, Lord Pirrie, over a decision to reduce the number

of lifeboats on the new big ships that he had designed to exceed the current regulations by a factor of 4.5 in anticipation of updates to the Board of Trade's regulations. The argument stemmed from the decision to install just over the *existing* regulation number of boats (sixteen), plus four extra collapsibles; the big ships officially exceeded the current legal requirement.

Also included on the distinguished and powerful passenger list were Prince and Princess Albert Radziwill; the Imperial Russian Military Attaché in Washington, Baron de Bode; Colonel Sam Winslow; Mrs Richard C. Kerens, wife of the American Ambassador to the Hapsburg Empire in Vienna; Mrs James R. Roosevelt (the mother of a future President of the United States); Leslie Denny of renowned Scottish shipbuilders, and Mr and Mrs Arthur Ryerson, prominent Philadelphian socialites and frequent travellers. Three special trains brought passengers from London's Euston Station after being afforded a hearty send-off. One train contained a carriage specially reserved for John R. Hegeman, President of the Metropolitan Life Insurance Company. Although too ill to travel even after several months of convalescing in Europe, his sister and brother-in-law embarked.

Departing Liverpool at the outset of her epic journey in 'moderately fair weather' at 5.43 p.m. on the Saturday (reaching Queenstown at 4.11 on Sunday morning), the liner was hit by strong northerly gales on the second and third days out with 'great rollers and high-tumbling seas' – but, as the liner 'ploughed her way magnificently' through the turbulent ocean, these 'terrific gales' were not expected to delay her arrival in New York. On Monday tremendous seas broke over the *Mauretania*'s forecastle with spray reaching to the height of her funnels and, over the Grand Banks (notorious throughout the year for fog, gales and icebergs), snowstorms assailed the ship. This weather was followed by clear skies accompanied by a long cross-swell, which helped the ship to maintain a good but slightly reduced speed. By now the notorious Atlantic had lived up to its reputation, putting the hoped-for record crossing out of reach. Much to the dismay of those on the Bridge (especially as the eyes of the world were upon them), the rough weather resulted in one of the 'worst crossings she [had ever] made', taking four days, twenty hours and seven minutes, her second slowest westward passage of the year. Her daily mileages had been 63 miles to noon after leaving Queenstown on Sunday; 586 miles to noon on Monday; 516 miles to noon Tuesday; a poor 139 weather-reduced miles to noon Wednesday; a magnificent 635 miles to noon Thursday; and 380 miles to pass the *Ambrose* lightvessel on Friday. She had averaged 24.95 knots over the 2,780-mile course.

To speed up various processes she unusually did not stop at Quarantine – which she reached at midnight – but slowed down enough to allow health officials to scramble aboard from their boat that tossed about in the choppy estuary. Similarly with the mails: two mail tenders came alongside and the mail bags were unloaded as the vessels proceeded slowly. Twelve Riggers boarded from a tug to rig handling gear and prepare hatch covers so that unloading her 1,000 tons of cargo could be progressed expeditiously progressed once alongside Pier 54. Foregoing Immigration controls, Journalist William Holt, with a special mission from the British *Daily Mail*, disembarked well before the *Mauretania* berthed. At three in the morning, secured by a safety rope tied under his arms (he was described as 'a diminutive, slightly rotund man') he climbed down a precarious Jacob's ladder into a waiting tug at Quarantine. He had been hurriedly assigned at the very last minute to make the Christmas trip and on arrival in the States was on a very tight schedule.

With the atrocious weather left behind and the moon glinting beautifully from her ice-speckled hull and rigging, the liner arrived at the Cunard Pier at 4.40 a.m. accompanied by a bevy of eleven tugs, their steam freezing along her already frost-patterned sides.

A sketch showing the dreadful weather that the *Mauretania* endured during the westward crossing of her Christmas dash. (*The Sphere*/Author's Collection)

The extremes of weather that she had experienced during the crossing were evidenced by broken ports and missing railings forward, and a large indentation of the bulwarks below the Bridge, sustained after a particularly heavy sea surged over her foredeck. This gave rise to a rumour that her entire Bridge Front had been pushed back by 4in! As the pier walkway was dangerously icy, the berthing of the ship took an hour before a thousand stevedores busied themselves with cargo, baggage and Christmas mail. Twenty-two coal barges were waiting to be placed alongside as soon as the liner berthed in the dock strewn with river ice, which could have posed a problem. Three hundred specially picked coal porters, divided into twelve gangs, then proceeded to transfer 6,200 tons of coal into the liner's bunkers at the rate of 800 tons an hour. Because baggage inspection had been delayed, the passengers were not allowed ashore until well after 7.30 a.m., allowing them to sleep on until the ship had berthed. Once ashore,

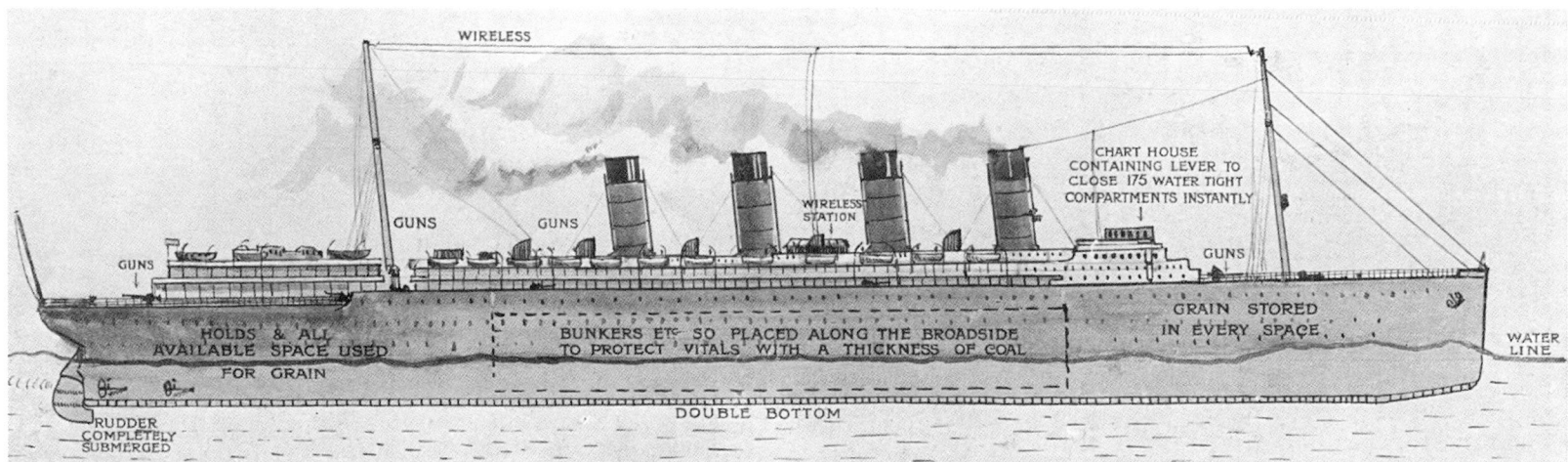

The Christmas dash produced fanciful ideas that the liner and her sister could be converted into grain carriers in time of war. (*The Sphere*, Author's Collection)

the chill wind cancelled any benefit to be had from the steam heaters in the pier shed: it was so cold it was said that the ink in the revenue inspectors' inkwells froze! The ship's staff set to cleaning the ship in readiness for the eastward-bound travellers, who were expected to make her highest passenger list to date with 800 First and Second, and 1,000 Third Class having booked passage. Time was taken to repaint the *Mauretania*'s salt-stained funnels and replace the 8ft length of teak handrail that had been washed away.

Meanwhile, the *Daily Mail* journalist Holt was rushing to Washington in a four hour seven minute record-breaking rail trip from Jersey City undertaken in a terrific destructively freezing gale that even froze the locomotive during necessary halts. In the hectic schedule of his breakneck mission, Holt interviewed politicians (including President Taft) in Washington before returning to New York, with brief twenty-minute interview stops en route in Philadelphia and Baltimore. Back in New York, this latter day 'Phineas Fogg' visited the opera and talked with famed actress Sarah Bernhardt at the Globe theatre, where he related that her dressing room was 'like a hothouse filled with flowers'. Other visits included the Miner's Brewery, the Mayor, New York's Governor, the Ellis Island Immigration Bureau and the Bronx Zoo, before returning, doubtless exhausted, to the *Mauretania* for the return leg of her epoch-making voyage.

Among the 450 First-Class passengers were Lord Decles; Lady Alan Johnstone; Lady Elizabeth Pritchard; Baron Rosen; A.A. Booth, the Chairman of the Cunard Steamship Company; the Marquis de Villavieja; author W.J. Locke: and Australian Dame Nellie Melba, perhaps the most famous singer in the world. As Dame Nellie was indisposed with a cold, she spent much of the crossing in bed on the orders of the ship's Surgeon and declined an invitation to sing in the ship's gala concert held in aid of seamen's charities (and the benefit of the purser's pocket!).

After a remarkably short stay in New York of only thirty-eight hours, the liner was ready to sail but not before she had filled her bunkers with American steaming coal, and water and stores enough for the return trip. Seventy-eight thousand items of linen, sent ashore for laundering, were returned to the ship. Her 1,000 tons of cargo for the return trip, along with 6,824 bags of Christmas mail, included 'apples … for the English Christmas trade'. It was anticipated that the *Mauretania* would

sail just after noon on the 17th, although Captain Turner thought that she would not sail until the advertised time of 6 p.m.; he was proved right because of the late arrival of some mails. The last passenger to board was reporter William Holt who, on returning to New York from his lightning tour, had interviewed more politicians, ridden the subway, inspected the Pennsylvania railroad station, lunched and still found time to buy souvenir presents from six department stores!

Captain Turner was hoping for a record Eastward passage. In a buoyant mood, he happily told a reporter that he anticipated being in Fishguard at a very precise 'five minutes before midnight next Thursday'. After backing into the river, the great liner's turbines whirred into action as she turned downstream while being afforded a raucous, gala farewell. The *Mauretania* looked particularly fine and her rows of newly polished 40lb brass portholes glinted. As she sounded her whistle, it seemed that everything afloat in the harbour responded.

At 25.57 knots she soon passed White Star's *Baltic*, still steaming westwards after leaving Queenstown *before* the big Cunarder the previous Sunday! A 'gentle sea swell … and … beautiful sunshine' provided a welcome respite after the atrocious westward trip, so much so that the passengers felt reassured enough to discard their heavy overcoats when venturing out on deck. The liner met with seas in the latter part of her voyage that caused her to roll considerably and, after a crossing of four days, fifteen hours and fifty-seven minutes, the *Mauretania* arrived at Fishguard at 10.22 p.m. on 23 December, her approach being announced to the spectators by the moving glow of the ship's lights in the sky above Carregwastad Head. Then, under a starlit sky and with lights ablaze that reflected across the water, she emerged from behind the Head and, as she entered the harbour, a gala reception of searchlights, flares and rockets, along with sirens from other vessels, greeted the ship's arrival as crowds ashore cheered. Passengers lined the *Mauretania*'s decks and the sound of the ship's band drifted across the waters. Even before the ship had come to a halt, newsman William Holt had disembarked into a specially chartered tender and train to get his copy to the presses.

The mails were the first ashore at 10.55 before four tenders took 600 passengers in the first disembarkation to be undertaken at the port at night. Passengers and mails were got away by 1.22 a.m. enabling the former to be in London, Paris or Berlin in time for Christmas; five trains headed for London's Paddington Station, with a sixth steaming to Dover with continent-bound travellers. *The London Standard* reported that Alfred Booth, Cunard's Chairman, had travelled to Fishguard to witness the liner's arrival that marked 'the finish of the greatest feat ever recorded in ocean travel', a successful round-voyage described as 'a fine, solid success of organization and efficiency and seaworthiness'. Liverpool greeted *Mauretania*'s arrival on Christmas Eve with a grand welcome similar to Fishguard's, accompanied by a chorus of ships' sirens.

Her average speed for the crossing had been 25.07 knots and her daily noon-to-noon runs had been 387, 582, 532, 578, 580; and 108 nautical miles. Cunard presented a silver salver to Captain Turner as a mark of his achievement; he responded with his usual modesty:

> Sir,
>
> I had not time before leaving Liverpool to write to thank you most sincerely for the handsome salver which you so kindly presented to me in connection with the record voyage of the *Mauretania*. I did not expect to receive any such recognition of my part in the matter. We all on board tried to do our duty as under any ordinary circumstances. It is very gratifying to know that what we did met with the approval of the company, and I shall highly prize this appreciation, and again, sir, thank you most humbly for it.
>
> I remain, sir,
>
> Your grateful and obedient servant,
>
> [Signed]

Cunard's Chairman was equally fulsome in his praise of the Stokehold crew:

> The men who endure the heat and stress of the stoke-hole [*sic*] of the '*Mauretania*' are as willing and cheerful as can found on any liner … They take as much pride in a good day's run as the engineers, and when the '*Mauretania*' breaks a record they parade with a quaint drum-and-fife band, in which any sounding can or kettle is used to add to the 'harmony.'

Her Firemen were justly rewarded with two days extra pay in recognition of their valiant efforts that had ensured the success of the recent extraordinary voyage. A similar Christmas voyage was anticipated for 1911.

The potential significance of the voyage was not lost on the prestigious illustrated British magazine *The Sphere*, which depicted the big Cunarder in war mode, fitted with cannon and full to the gun'les with grain and escorted by a new, fast Invincible-class cruiser. The idea of a transatlantic convoy was quite prescient and in an article, 'The Hidden Lesson of the "Mauretania's" Record', published in its Christmas Eve edition, the magazine enthusiastically commented:

> It is considered possible by many naval experts that the two gigantic Cunard liners would be used as grain carriers in time of war, speeding back and forth across the Atlantic escorted by powerful cruisers, or even trusting to their own guns that give them offensive power almost equal to a cruiser of the 'County' class and their terrific speed. It is believed that one of these boats would arrive from America fully loaded with grain or foodstuff every week. On the outbreak of hostilities [without giving the game away it could be asked with whom?] a matter of four days could convert them into grey-painted monsters with their saloons and staterooms converted into miniature storage holds. The crews of both vessels are all Naval Reserve man, so the manning problem could be quickly overcome and they would instantly be ready to help in conveying the food on which our population depends.

Another illustration was captioned:

> 'Mauretania' in her war paint of grey being convoyed [itself a system that in actuality would take a lot of bitter experience before it was eventually adopted] across the Atlantic by a battleship cruiser [*sic* – battlecruiser] steaming at an average speed of twenty-five knots an hour [*sic*], and in conjunction with the 'Lusitania' keeping up a regular supply of 6,000 tons, or approximately 27,000 quarters, of wheat weekly.

Submarines were at this juncture not considered to present any threat to deep-sea shipping but the speed advantages of the two mighty Cunarders was now under question. The German navy had made great advances since the Kaiser had decided to try to emulate the might of the British Royal Navy. The mercurial build-up of his Imperial Fleet had been brought to a frustratingly temporary obsolescent halt in 1906 when the Royal Navy commissioned HMS *Dreadnought*, the revolutionary turbine-driven battleship. The Germans were not deterred and, by the end of 1910, had produced several of their own fast turbine-driven 'dreadnoughts' in the shape of the Von-der-Tann- and Moltke-classes, each capable of more than 25 knots; the following February would see the keel-laying of the first of the 26½-knot Seydlitz-class, whose speed would pose a serious threat to fast armed merchant cruisers such as the *Lusitania* and *Mauretania*.

Following her heady Christmas dash, the *Mauretania*'s next sailing from Liverpool began on 21 January 1911, with her crew still determined to make a good showing. They and their ship did not disappoint. At noon on the 26th she broke her own record for a day's run by completing 676 miles, 3 miles better than her previous record, at an average speed of 27.04 knots. Unfortunately she was delayed by fog, having to anchor after passing Sandy Hook. Chief Engineer Kendall did not complete the following voyage as he was sent ashore the on 12 February with rheumatic fever when the ship called in at Queenstown. He also missed the subsequent voyage but returned to duty for the 22 April sailing. His place, meanwhile, was taken by Senior Second Engineer, A.T. Howatt, who in turn was replaced by John Heggie. Gales again delayed the ship, giving her a crossing of nearly five days.

Atrocious weather again bedevilled the *Mauretania* on her next crossing, which left Liverpool on Saturday, 4 March. Two days later at sunset the liner met a terrific head-on gale, causing her to plough though tremendously heavy seas that broke over her bow. By midnight the ship was 'staggering along under the repeated shock of a constantly pounding sea' when her bow dipped under one big sea. Before she could recover, another 80ft sea slammed over her port bow and tons of water rushed aft before hitting the Bridge front, where several windows were smashed. The Quartermaster was flung backwards after losing his grip on the wheel, sustaining cuts from flying glass. Twenty-five feet of teak-topped railings were torn from the Boat Deck as the ship was forced to a standstill. This sudden pause in her forward motion, briefly thought to have been caused by a collision, lasted a few seconds, creating a 'short-lived excitement amongst the passengers' before the

ship recovered her composure and regained her way. The liner arrived twelve hours late in New York and, in one of his stoical interviews, Captain Turner said: 'A little spray did come aboard, but there has been worse weather at sea.' Count Leo Tolstoy also gave an interview in the crowded Lounge but talked about his father, the great Russian author.

The celebrated English composer, Sir Edward Elgar, embarked at Liverpool on 25 March and, during the course of the crossing, undoubtedly heard the playing of violinist-Bandmaster Wallace Hartley (perhaps he played the beautifully poignant 'Salut d'Amour' as a tribute to its composer). Elgar returned to England on 3 May. It is also possible that J. Bruce Ismay, the President of IMM and Chairman of the White Star Line, heard Hartley play and persuaded him – or his agents – to move to the *Titanic* for her maiden voyage. An air of adventure was added to the usual excitement of travelling on the *Mauretania* when 39-year-old Sir Ernest Shackleton boarded. This famed polar explorer had, with two companions in their expedition of 1907–09, travelled the furthest south, just falling short of the South Pole by 112 miles. A break from ship-board tradition was effected when the ship's officers were allowed to join passengers in the Dining Room, an improvement over their Messroom situated right forward on the Shelter Deck, a most uncomfortable location during heavy weather!

Saturday, 15 May 1911 was a day of mark as the still-supreme *Mauretania* left Liverpool on her fiftieth voyage, having so far travelled 300,000 miles. Ten days later, Dr G.B. Hunter, the ship's builder, was given the Freedom of Wallsend in recognition of his civic work.

Mauretania's next voyage, departing Liverpool on 3 June 1911, created an administrative and recruiting headache for the Company, as a letter later tried to clarify:

With reference to *Mauretania* having cleared without a Ship's Cook on voyage of 3rd June last … the man who was subsequently signed on board as Ship's Cook was appointed by our Catering Department who believed he was qualified for the position by Sea Service prior to 30/6/08. It has since transpired that the said man had not the necessary qualifications, and we have infringed the law, by placing him upon the agreement … we had no wish or intention of avoiding the regulations, and instructions are being issued to the Department concerned …

The *Mauretania* arrived Stateside just before midnight on 8 June, and many of her passengers elected to stay on board overnight. Among those in First Class was a brilliant German chemist named Otto Hahn who, much later in 1944, would win the coveted Nobel Prize in Chemistry for his discovery of nuclear fission. Six days later thirty men deserted before sailing on 14 June, while on that same day on the other side of 'The Pond', White Star's mighty but supremely elegant 45,000-ton *Olympic* (built for size, luxury and comfort and not for high speed) began her maiden voyage from Southampton and made her maiden westward in five days, sixteen hours and forty-two minutes, at an average speed of 21.17 knots (on the return trip she made the crossing at almost 22.5 knots). The *Mauretania's* title of being the largest ship in the world was no longer hers but her speed record would remain unchallenged. The 'Coronation Special' delivered hopeful *Mauretania* passengers in time for the crowning of King George V at Westminster Abbey on the 22nd.

The summer of 1911 turned out to be particularly hot; people all over the country suffered and many heat-related deaths were reported. The new King and his Queen toured the nation by rail, their carriage cooled by large blocks of ice – and it might have been on account of the unbearable heat in England that, prior to sailing on 24 June, *thirty-one* men failed to join the liner, the stifling weather perhaps exacerbating the Boiler Rooms' temperature. Sailing westwards, the *Mauretania* encountered high seas and then fog over the Grand Banks. On board was a special cargo – the first batch of photographs and newsreels of the recent coronation. The revenue cutter *Hudson*, with a party of American and Canadian newspaper representatives and cinematographic exhibitors on board, headed towards the ship as she lay at Quarantine – at 2 o'clock in the morning – all eager to obtain the 'cargo'. Some hopeful recipients even had fast boats alongside to rush the images ashore in anticipation of a scoop for the early morning editions and evening cinemas. Although it had been promised that once all levied duties had been paid the images could be released and sent ashore, the Customs Service countermanded the collector's assurances and insisted the pictures be returned to the cutter. Customs also wanted to take a passenger ashore so there was a further wait. The cutter did not get to the Battery until 4 o'clock, obviating any newspaper's plans for a scoop.

During the turnaround a further seventeen men deserted and the heat encouraged some men to find a cool sleeping berth on deck, there being no passengers on board until shortly before sailing. On the eve of sailing on 5 July, Donkeyman Edward Hanlow found such a berth. But, during the night, he disappeared. Hanlow had last been seen sleeping on the upper deck at 3.30 a.m., but by morning he had gone, presumed to have fallen overboard. Had he stumbled around during the night or had he celebrated Independence Day the previous day with too much enthusiasm and fallen into the harbour? His counterpane was recovered from the water; his body wasn't.

Celebrations were on board when, on 25 September, a son was delivered to Julia Mottet [*sic*], a Third-Class passenger. A stowaway, Fred Warner of Southampton, was discovered and placed under surveillance until he could be put ashore on Ellis Island prior to repatriation. It appears that on the return leg the Fishguard call was omitted, the port's name being deleted from the log for some unspecified reason.

Meanwhile, 20 September brought what could have been disaster to the still-new White Star liner *Olympic*. After she sailed from Southampton on her fifth voyage she had just completed the reverse 'S' turn between Calshot and Cowes on the Isle of Wight, when HMS *Hawke*, steaming up from the direction of the Needles towards Portsmouth, suddenly veered and rammed into her stern.

Hawke's bow was severely damaged and she limped into Portsmouth for an emergency dry-docking. *Olympic*, her hull deeply penetrated and open to the water, anchored in Osborne Bay. She was later towed back to Southampton for temporary patching before being taken to Belfast for repairs by Harland and Wolff. The accident had been caused by a phenomenon known as 'canal-' or 'shallow-water effect' where the moving water displaced by a large vessel in a shallow or restricted waterway rushes each side of the ship and can draw a smaller vessel into itself. This was later exemplified when *Olympic's* sister ship *Titanic* (both ships under the command of Captain Edward J. Smith) drew the *New York* away from her berth as the latter liner departed Southampton on her maiden voyage in April 1912.

Even after her collision, the lure of the *Olympic* seemed to be irresistible. Waiting to board the *Mauretania* at Liverpool's Princes Landing Stage could be a trial, as one lady wrote in October: 'Will you ever forget the long time we were standing on the upper stage, before we could get aboard?' The lady seemed a little jaded with the Cunarder as she continued: 'I hope to take you through the *Olympic* next year. That is our latest ship,' adding rather derogatorily: 'the *Mauretania* is not to be compared with her. She [*Olympic*] is a beauty.' The large liners continually attracted wealthy and famous passengers who wanted fast as well as publicity-attracting modes of transport: extremely wealthy William Rockefeller, co-founder of Standard Oil, sailed on the return crossing that left New York on 4 October.

Mauretania's 11 November departure from Liverpool proved to be a logistical problem for those manning the vessel as a massive total of forty men failed to join the ship. The following voyage was scheduled to be a repeat of the previous Christmas's hectic but hugely successful Atlantic dash. The liner was due to sail on 9 December but fate took a hand. On that very same evening at 10.30, Cunard's Christmas hopes evaporated when the *Mauretania* broke free from her moorings on The Sloyne. During an unusually strong south-easterly gale and a strong flood tide running, she snapped not only her own cable but two additional 8in hawsers that held her to the Cunard Buoy. Her remaining anchor was let go but this did not hold and the liner drifted, narrowly missing the training ships Conway and Indefatigable; she subsequently grounded on the Pluckington Bank (mud and hard sand) near Dingle. Her siren, blaring in distress, alerted tugs that rushed to her aid. The scheduled voyage was cancelled and, perhaps not coincidentally, seven officers were transferred to other ships and one discharged. A new chef had signed on a few days before (with a name that hopefully did not reflect his culinary skills – David Bland) and it probably did not take him long to regret his choice of ship.

The *Lusitania*, having arrived in port only four days before, was hurriedly readied and made the Christmas voyage in place of her sister, completing the journey in twelve days and seventeen hours. On her return the 'Lucy' went into dry dock for her scheduled overhaul, leaving Cunard without an express liner for its mail service. The old *Campania* did her best to step in until the *Lusitania*'s next sailing in February.

The *Mauretania* was refloated just before noon the next day and, attended by tugs, made her way to a resecured mooring against the Cunard Buoy. Taken into the Canada Graving Dock on the 13th, it

was found that she had badly buckled her keel under the aft Boiler Room, displacing some of the boiler seats. Eighty damaged plates had to be replaced. Between 600 and 700 men worked nearly 700 tons of material into her repairs, which took nine weeks and cost around £50,000. Lost revenue was not included in that figure.

Cunard announced that, because of protests from Irish interests expressed in Parliament, Queenstown would be restored as a port of call on the homeward journey. Earnest consideration was also being given to transferring the express service to Southampton, calling at Plymouth and Cherbourg en route, as the recent grounding of the *Mauretania* in the Mersey and the advent of the *Olympic* and *Titanic* (the latter two being based in Southampton with its double tides and a more direct access to Continental traffic) had given Cunard cause for thought.

The end of February saw the beginning of a nationwide strike by over one million coal miners that lasted until 6 April and many ships were laid up because of the lack of fuel. In the newspapers the coal strike overshadowed the mass actions of Suffragettes who, on 1 March, began militant action in the cause of 'Votes For Women'. In various parts of London plate-glass windows of many prestigious establishments were a favourite target and the new Cunard offices in Cockspur Street were not exempt!

After coming out of her lengthy period in dry dock the *Mauretania*'s first trip of 1912 (2 March) was slow – 20.94 knots, undoubtedly to conserve precious fuel. Appalling weather caused further problems, so much so that when she called into Queenstown the passengers who expected to join the ship (five First, twenty-eight Second and ninety-nine Third) could not board because of heavy seas. Not only did they lose their ship but – according to the *Southampton Times* – they also lost their tempers, giving the local Cunard officials a hard time. The whole crossing was beset by strong westerly winds and very heavy seas, which, as Captain Turner told a reporter, 'Bent a window in the chartroom.' On one day she made only 400 miles – less than two-thirds of her record – 590 at best. During the storm a 24-year-old Steerage passenger, Sophia Beya, died of heart disease and was buried at sea even as the tempest raged about the ship. The protracted journey took five days, seventeen hours and fifty-nine minutes, concluded by a seven-hour delay caused by fog in New York Harbor, which made the liner a day late. Controversial socialite 'Daisy' Greville, Countess of Warwick, made no reference to the crossing in her pre-lecture tour press interviews.

The raison d'être for the *Mauretania* and *Lusitania* had been to serve the country in time of war. The liners' power and speed had been exceeded by recent dreadnought buildings and British seapower was being threatened by the continuing growth and efficiency of the Imperial German Navy in what became known as the 'Great Naval Race' aggravated by various German Naval Acts. On 18 March, in an attempt to justify British naval policy, the First Lord of the Admiralty, Winston Churchill, rose in the House of Commons and impassionedly expressed his concern that Britain's Royal Navy should be able to meet *any* aggression at *any* moment should the need ever arise, and expressed his concern that Great Britain needed its navy more than any other country as: 'the consequences of defeat at sea are so much greater than they would be to Germany or France'. Churchill expanded his argument to Parliament in his imitable style:

> There is no parity of risk. Our position is highly artificial. We are fed from the sea. We are an unarmed people. We possess a very small Army. We are the only power in Europe which does not possess a large Army … We cannot invade any continental state. We do not wish to do so, but even if we had the wish we have not got the power … when we consider our naval strength we are not thinking of our commerce, but of our freedom. We are not thinking of our trade, but of our lives. These are facts which justify British naval supremacy in the face of the world.

With increasing German naval power and improved efficiencies in mind, Churchill then added:

> We must never conduct our affairs so that the Navy of any single Power would be able to engage us at any single moment, even our least favourable, moment, with any reasonable prospects of success.

To this end Britain demanded an enormous fleet that equalled the sum of the next two largest fleets (plus a margin of 10 per cent). Germany had increasingly become *the* threat to the status quo and it grew in stature in May when the German Reichstag passed a Navy Law Amendment Act, the last of five such enactments that enabled the expansion and efficiency of a well-trained German fleet. The British Foreign Secretary, Sir Edward Grey, had said three years previously that, 'Germany was creating a fleet larger than had ever existed before.' For a continental country that should only need to rely on a large army for its security without considering expansionism, it was extremely worrying. To accentuate the Germans' ambitious rise in seapower, the 906ft, 51,680gt *Imperator* was due to be launched in May 1913, for the Hamburg-America Line (HAPAG) just one month after the large and beautifully luxurious *Titanic* (at 46,328 tons briefly the largest ship in the world) was due to make her maiden voyage. A second German ship (for the North German Lloyd), announced on 12 April would, at 54,000 gross tons, then be the world's largest ship.

On the return crossing of the post-refit voyage, ship's Band Leader Wallace Hartley gave a well-received performance – a 'stupendous violin solo' – during the traditional Seamen's Charity Concert 'much to the delight of all those gathered to witness the event'. This would be his swansong for Cunard, subsequently making only one more voyage on his beloved ship (he had made twenty-two voyages on her) before being transferred by his agents to join the brand-new *Titanic,* then completing at Belfast.

In early April there was a rumour that the fugitive campaigner for women's rights, Christabel Pankhurst – daughter of radical socialist Dr Richard Pankhurst and women's suffrage leader Emmeline – was on board under an assumed name after fleeing arrest in Britain. One gentleman who claimed to know Miss Pankhurst said that he recognised her when her veil slipped by her 'aggressive-looking face, with its over-hanging black eyebrows', whereas in actual fact she was 'beautiful, intelligent, graceful, confident, charming, and charismatic'.

During Voyage 61 the 'Maury' called in at Queenstown, as was usual on her second day out, on 14 April 1912. Here 24-year-old Trimmer John Coffey (Discharge Book No. 13665) signed on at £5 10*s* (five pounds, ten shillings – £5.50) per month. Although he came from the Irish port (he had apparently been ashore under the premise of seeing his mother), his address was recorded in the Crew Agreement as '15 Thomas Street, Liverpool' although his mum evidently lived at 12, Sherbourne Terrace in Queenstown. Presumably unable to write, he made his mark in the Crew Agreement with an 'X'. Coffey stated that his previous ship had been the White Star liner *Olympic*, but he must have had second thoughts about his submission as it turned out that he had deserted his last ship on 11 April. A pencilled correction in the Crew Agreement overrode *Olympic*'s name with that of … *Titanic*.

The question that could be asked is why Coffey had left the *Titanic* in such a rush but then joined another liner in the same capacity. Was it because the Stokehold crew were worried about the fire that still burned in the new liner's forward bunker, and was the blaze the reason why over 95 per cent of the Stokehold left the ship in Southampton, not signing on after their short coastal voyage from Belfast? Ships in similar circumstances had not been allowed to sail.

As *Mauretania*'s voyage progressed, tragedy already was in the air as, at 8.25 on the evening of 14 April, an American passenger, 45-year-old wholesale dry goods merchant Stroughton Walker, committed suicide by jumping overboard in position latitude 50°45' north, longitude 16°10' west. The alarm was raised and a lifebuoy fitted with a Holmes light was thrown overboard to mark Walker's approximate last position. An emergency boat was lowered and sent away in charge of the First Officer, F.E. Storey. A search was made to no avail, so the boat returned to the ship at 9.15 to be hoisted back on board. Twenty minutes later the *Mauretania* continued on her way at full speed.

But worse was to follow.

About six hours after the futile search for Mr Walker was terminated, a message was received by *Mauretania*'s wireless telegraphists J. Cornell and J. Boadella (the latter having taken over from L.A. Hancock on this trip) sent from a position of latitude 41°46' N and longitude 50°14' W, about 2,500 miles to the west of the Cunarder, saying that the brand-new *Titanic* had struck an iceberg at 11.40 p.m. (local time) whilst on her maiden voyage and was, unbelievably, sinking.

Two hours and forty minutes later the *Titanic* slid beneath the icy waters of the North Atlantic, breaking in two as she did so, with a great loss of life. Of more than 2,200 people on board, just over 700 survived the ordeal. The *Mauretania* had been helpless to assist but all aboard her keenly felt the loss of the liner. Many of *Titanic*'s passengers – the Ryersons, the Duff Gordons, even Bruce Ismay, the Chairman of the White Star Line – had, at one time or another, sailed on the *Mauretania* and so were known to many of the crew.

Amongst others lost was Band Leader Wallace Hartley, who had left the *Mauretania* to join the new ship. Hartley and his small orchestra had played to calm the passengers as *Titanic*'s bow sank deeper into the ocean, earning themselves a place in the heroic annals of the sea. *Mauretania*'s cellist, Allwand Moody, later recalled a conversation with his late colleague in which he asked Hartley what he would do if he were to be on a sinking ship. Hartley replied, 'I don't think I could do better than play "Oh God, Our Help in Ages Past" or "Nearer My God to Thee".' He chose the latter in the *Titanic*'s final moments and a legend was born.

Trimmer John Coffey must have been mightily relieved at his decision to desert the ship when he did. Waiter Roberts must also have had mixed feelings as he had just transferred to the *Mauretania* from Cunard's smaller *Carpathia* that effected the rescue of the survivors of the disaster, and so missed the excitement, heroism and adventure that had befallen his old ship.

The *Mauretania* arrived at the scene of the tragedy two days after the sinking, coming to a halt in the forlorn hope that missed survivors might be found. Her sailings so far for the year had generally – bar one exception – been at speeds under 25 knots and she was taking over five days to make most trips, but *Mauretania* made that memorable April crossing in exactly five days at an average speed of 24.29 knots. After the sinking of the *Titanic*, postcards, amongst a plethora of commemorative offerings, were issued to a grieving public. As photographs of the lost ship might not have been readily available, cards appeared showing the *Mauretania* but with a *Titanic* caption. In other postcard issues three of her four funnels were blanked out so that the *Mauretania* doubled as the plucky *Carpathia*.

The loss of the White Star liner would have far-reaching effects on the world's shipping, not least that there should be lifeboats for all on board. The *Mauretania* would be greatly affected through the new legislation that subsequently, somewhat belatedly, involved a legal 'catch-up' exercise foreseen by those whose forewarnings of such a disaster had been ignored. Cunard scoured local boatbuilders in New York and, prior to sailing, took on eight new lifeboats and seven life rafts to augment her sixteen now-inadequate boats that had a capacity to hold a mere 976 persons (she could carry 563 First, 464 Second and 1,144 Steerage as well as 812 crew – a total of 2,983). In addition, 3,000 lifebelts and 32 lifebuoys were hastily embarked. Further lifeboats would be fitted in Liverpool and additional davits were later fitted to the Boat Deck, four sets each side of the Grand Staircase and aft by the Second-Class deckhouse.

Other post-*Titanic* changes included the creation of the post of Staff Captain, which relieved Captain Turner of a lot of administrative and mundane work – as well as relieving him of the hated task of socialising with the passengers! Several of the Chief Officer's duties were taken over by the new post, including discipline, inspections, arranging Bridge Watches, cleanliness of every department in the ship, the regular testing of all life-saving and safety appliances, and the supervision of boat and fire drills. Although 'Staffies' were appointed from the company's smaller ships, they would still wear their captain's uniform and have a table in the Dining Saloon. Captain S.G.S. McNeil was appointed to the newly created post at the end of May in readiness for the 1 June departure from Liverpool. Cunard must have thought that there ought to be some recognition that the ship's captain had another captain under him, so the company gave Captain Turner a 20 per cent increase in salary!

At the British Inquiry into the loss of the *Titanic*, Cunard's Naval architect, Leonard Peskett, was summoned to appear as an expert technical witness, as was Captain John Pritchard, called out of retirement to do so on 19 June, and cross-examined by five councils. Subsequent to the inquiry, Leonard Peskett and Harland and Wolff's Naval Architect, Edward Wilding RCNC (he had been involved with the design of the Olympic-class and had travelled with the *Titanic* from Belfast to Southampton), jointly produced a memorandum to show what would happen to the *Mauretania* should she suffer a similar accident to the *Titanic*. Although difficult to make a fair comparison, they calculated that the Cunarder would remain afloat but, due to the ship's side bunkers doubling as watertight compartments, the liner would assume a list of 15 to 20 degrees. To prevent water rising above the top of the local watertight bulkhead, Wilding later said that: 'to avoid severe heel immediately following damage in say two bunkers … cross-flooding must be almost instantaneous to be successful'. Alarm bells should have

The Boat Deck layout of the *Mauretania* was similar to that of the *Titanic*. BoT regulations were adhered to that gave both liners a lifeboat capacity of sixteen (although *Titanic* carried four 'collapsibles'), woefully inadequate for the numbers of passengers carried even though both ships had been initially conceived to carry more. (SH&WR photo)

rung that the longitudinal bulkheads enclosing boiler and engine rooms in the two sisters would present a problem in an emergency.

During his examination, Captain Pritchard told the Inquiry that, in clear weather even at night, it had been his practice to maintain speed unless he saw ice and, should he see an iceberg, he would keep at least 2 miles between it and his ship. On a hazy night he would increase his lookouts and station a man on each bow and two in the Crow's Nest. Asked about lifeboat practice on the *Mauretania*, the Captain said that boat drill was always held for the crew on sailing day and that every qualified man concerned had a badge of competence. It took about six minutes to get the covers off a boat before being swung out and lowered in accordance with Board of Trade regulations and then rowed around the dock before being hoisted back on board. These drills were known as the 'Board of Trade Sports'! The Captain's daily noon inspection of bulkheads and watertight doors was logged.

The Inquiry praised the actions of Captain Rostron and his crew on board the rescue ship *Carpathia*, and subsequently the White Star Line requested that they be allowed to present 100 guineas (£105) to Captain Rostron and 50 guineas each to the ship's Surgeon, Dr Frank McGhee, and to the Chief Steward, Henry Hughes. All other members of the Cunarder's crew received a month's wages and Cunard itself refused any reimbursement in respect of their ship having to return to New York with survivors (described as 'a privilege'), neither would they make any claim 'in respect of salvage, life-saving, or expenses'.

There were extra passengers on the *Mauretania*'s return trip that left New York on 24 April (probably due to many having booked on the first eastward of the *Titanic*), so additional crew was signed on – eleven Waiters, one Stewardess as well as three Seamen and one Sculleryman. However, five Able-bodied Seamen deserted following *Titanic*'s disastrous end. The nerves of many on board must have been further jarred when the *Mauretania*, backing out of Pier 54, swung round on the strong ebb tide and collided with the Pier shed, alarming and scattering many on the quayside. The liner's Bridge rail was bent but, unfazed, Captain Turner continued to back her out before swinging her round to seaward.

She sailed on Voyage 62 on 11 May, having spent twelve days at Liverpool after being hurriedly modified. This trip saw an influx of Firemen and Trimmers transferring to the Cunarder from White Star ships, especially the *Cedric*, perhaps deterred from sailing on ships of that line after the fate that befell many of their compatriots on the *Titanic*. The subsequent trip had several similar transfers from the *Teutonic*.

On 9 June there was a bit of excitement as four of the ship's sixty-person lifeboats manned by different departments raced against each other, perhaps to reassure a worried public about efficiencies, between Castle Point, Hoboken and Cunard's Pier 54. The boat manned by sailors came first as might be expected (their efforts rewarded with a silver cup), Firemen came second, Officers third and Stewards fourth. An ebb tide and a stiff breeze in unseasonably cool conditions were prevalent over the mile course, which was won in six minutes and seven seconds. Subsequently, a challenge was put out to ships of other lines and Cunard undertook to present a cup.

The challenge was taken up on 16 August when one sixty-person boat from each of the *Mauretania* and *Ivernia* of the Cunard Line, and one from the Royal Mail Steam Packet Company's *Orotava* fought it out on a 2½-mile course on New York's North River. The *Mauretania*'s entrant won the race, *Ivernia* came in second but the crew on the Royal Mail Line's boat gave up before the finish.

The 24 June departure from the Princes Landing Stage was fraught as, just after the 'All ashore' bell was sounded for visitors to vacate the ship half-an-hour before sailing at five, a strong wind caught the ship and she began to drift out into the stream. Two aft mooring ropes parted, three overhead gangways were dragged from the Stage (just giving their occupants time to escape), and two baggage-loading belts fell as the distance between ship and pontoon widened. Two forward ropes parted but others held. The ship drifted 20 to 30 yards into the stream before being brought under control and returned to the Stage. With 1,100 passengers on board, the liner was an hour late in sailing.

During the next crossing that left Liverpool on 13 July (for which J. Carruthers had superseded J. Kendall as Chief Engineer) Captain Turner received a wireless message on Wednesday (17th) at 1.30 a.m. from White Star's *Adriatic* informing him that the latter ship had passed an iceberg to within half-a-mile. *Adriatic* was many miles ahead and on a course 5 miles to the north of the Cunarder. Cautiously, Captain Turner took his ship 10 miles further to the south and reduced his speed to 10 knots, which he kept for three hours until the safety of daybreak.

The Captain's caution was supplemented by the 'Frigidometers' that had been fitted to the ship on her last departure from the US. An invention of a Mr A. McNab, one of these 'futuristic' instruments was placed atop the mast and another at keel level, and activated warning bells should the water temperature drop to a level that might indicate the presence of ice. What Mr McNab's reaction was (he was on board to test his invention) when Captain Turner altered course after relying on a mere wireless message is not recorded. The ship's Surgeon may not have been disappointed to see the gadget go ashore with its inventor as previously sea temperatures had been taken by lowering a canvas bucket over the side to obtain a sample, which usually involved a raid on his supply of thermometers!

On the evening following the *Adriatic*'s ice warning the *Mauretania* ran into heavy rains illuminated by spectacular, almost continuous lightning. Even so, the *Mauretania*'s average speed for the voyage was

24.87 knots, completing the course in four days, twenty hours and eleven minutes. During the passage the dangers of the Stokehold were again evidenced when, on the 16th, 29-year-old Trimmer Walter Pemberton died of 'Congestion of both lungs … haemorrhage … chronic meningitis and pleurisy'. The start of the return voyage on the 24th was plagued by thirty-six Firemen and Trimmers failing to join the ship and eight others deserting. Two voyages later twenty-nine Firemen and Trimmers did not turn up for the sailing from Liverpool. Two days into that crossing Trimmer John Higham departed this life after collapsing at 7.30 in the morning of 15th August. His ultimate death, just over three hours later, had been caused by double pneumonia. Eleven hours later Higham was buried at sea. Nine deserted when the ship reached New York. On the voyage commencing 31 August the *Mauretania* left Liverpool at 5.13 p.m. but, before she sailed, a staggering thirty-nine men (mostly Trimmers) failed to join and the ship's Surgeon transferred to another of the company's ships. The liner arrived at Queenstown the next day, from where she sailed at 9.52 a.m. Off Daunt Rock the ship was searched, as usual, for contraband but none was found.

New York was reached on 6 September and, after her usual stop off at Quarantine to offload her emigrant passengers for health inspections at the Immigrant Inspection Station on Ellis Island, she upped anchor and sailed on to Pier 54 to disembark the remaining passengers. Five days later the ship sailed from the Hudson at 1 a.m., the sisters' new time of departure in lieu of the earlier 9 a.m. as this allowed the ships to make a more convenient arrival at Fishguard.

Amongst the First-Class passengers arriving in New York on 28 September was Vincent Astor, now head of that famous family. This handsome 20-year-old had recently inherited an estimated $69 million from his late father, John Jacob Astor, who had died in the *Titanic* tragedy; his pregnant stepmother, 18-year-old Madeline, was saved. After his father's death, Vincent became known as 'The Richest Boy in the World', deserting his college education to manage his family's vast portfolio of interests; Vincent would have his own share of life's tragedies.

An unusually large number of men transferred from the *Lusitania* for the 12 October sailing. A vast fortune in £341,000 ($1,660,000) in gold sovereigns was stowed in the Specie Room for the 7 December departure from Liverpool, which was the last of the year and it turned out to be the *Mauretania's* third-slowest crossing to date, taking five days, thirteen hours and thirteen minutes at an average of 21.28 knots and was the first of a series of slow westward crossings, the following one taking twenty-two minutes over six days. During this turbulent passage the ship averaged a poor 19.64 knots. A blizzard delayed the *Mauretania's* first sailing of 1913 on Sunday, 12 January 1913, by sixteen hours until 9 a.m. and her call into Queenstown was cancelled. Four days out she was hit by 'hurricane weather', slowing the liner down to 14 knots. On the Wednesday, as the liner dipped her plunging bow into heavy seas, a huge wave tore aft, carrying away over 30ft of railings, broke several ports and damaged lifeboat supports – all over 70ft above the waterline! All that day she was judiciously kept to half-speed, only managing to cover 204 miles, progressing to 331 miles the next day with full speed only being achieved for two hours. The severe weather was left behind on Friday when she worked up to full speed 'in spite of strong head winds and [a] rough sea'. The oft-angry Atlantic behaved itself on Saturday as if nothing had happened and the liner forged ahead at full speed in an almost smooth sea. Captain Turner had been on the Bridge for much of the trip, and subsequently received just praise for his exemplary seamanship. It might have been because of the rough weather but 27-year-old James Cudman died ashore in hospital of injuries incurred on board during the crossing. His grieving parents buried him in Liverpool's Anfield Cemetery on 31 January.

On the second day out on the start of Voyage 73, which started on 1 February, a stowaway, James Flynn – a US citizen – was found in the Trimmers' quarters. He was put ashore at Queenstown in charge of the Company's agent. Might a Trimmer have smuggled the stowaway on board to supplement his own meagre income? On a sadder note, two days before reaching New York 3-year, 8-month-old Violet Richardson died of sudden heart failure 'supervening on diphtheria and pulumonia [*sic*]' after being admitted to the ship's Hospital on the day of sailing, her illness causing the ship's surgeon, B. Sydney Jones (now returned from a previous transfer) to perform a tracheostomy. Assisting him was Dr Frank McGee, who had treated the survivors from the *Titanic* while he was the Surgeon on board the rescue ship *Carpathia*. Violet's little body was committed to the deep at four that afternoon.

At 1 a.m. on 5 March the *Mauretania* pulled away from Pier 54 at the start of another eastward crossing, her 400 First-Class passengers including Cunard's own Captain Arthur Rostron (with his wife), late of the *Carpathia*, returning home after being presented with a gold medal by President Taft for his heroic part in rescuing the survivors from the sunken *Titanic*. During the voyage the *Mauretania* used the new 'Long Course', 40 miles south of the old track, adding 150 miles to her journey.

While the *Mauretania* was moored against the Cunard Buoy on the Mersey awaiting her turn at the Landing Stage, a Fireman, aptly named Fell, who had come aboard just after 8 a.m., lost his footing while descending a ladder to the Firemen's Mess. He fractured two ribs but did not report to the ship's Hospital until twelve hours later, his breath still reeking of alcohol. He was sent ashore on *Skirmisher*, the Cunard tender. The Stokehold was under constant strain and on 13 April Fireman James Gaffrey literally dropped dead at his post. The liner was still berthed in New York when, on the day before sailing on 21 May, sixteen Firemen and Trimmers deserted the ship, and a DBS (Distressed British Seaman) was taken on board. James Dean was literally distressed; assessed as being 'of unsound mind', he was placed under the care of the ship's Surgeon throughout the crossing.

Even after the ship had docked in Liverpool, drama was not far away. When Trimmer Thomas Johns of Cardiff jumped overboard, a buoy was thrown into the water and an emergency boat lowered. The buoy was recovered but of the hapless Trimmer there was no sign. He was presumed drowned. By the beginning of the next voyage thirty-four Firemen and Trimmers failed to join and two more deserted on the Landing Stage. But there was good news for Staff Captain Hassock (he had taken over from F.G. Brown): he had been given command of the *Ultonia* and was replaced by Captain M.G. Malin.

The *Mauretania* still retained her popularity with a public that still largely made its own entertainment at home and she featured (along with some pictures of her interiors) on the cover of popular sheet music such as 'He's on the Boat that Sailed Last Wednesday'. Even trams and small excursion boats carried her illustrious name.

On 24 June, King George V conferred the honorary rank of Commander of the Royal Naval Reserve (RNR) on Commodore Turner (he had been made Commodore of the Cunard Line in

March), a singular honour indeed as, not being in the Reserve, it made him instantly senior to his own officers who were lieutenants in the RNR. A few weeks later, on 11 July, a gala was presented on the River Mersey when thousands of spectators crowded the waterfronts of Liverpool and The Wirral to watch Their Majesties King George V and Queen Mary progress down the river on board the Mersey Docks and Harbour Board's Yacht *Galatea* (acting as a Royal Yacht, she flew the King's Standard on her foremast and the White Ensign on her mainmast) en route to open the first phase of the Mersey Docks and Harbour Board's magnificent new Gladstone Dock.

In doing so they passed through an assemblage of thirty-five ships, including two naval guardships, gathered in review – a marine display – to honour the royal couple. The *Mauretania* was Number 15 in the longer of two rows of merchant ships, her line being anchored in mid-stream (the shorter line was moored over towards the New Brighton and Birkenhead shores). Cunard's turbine test bed, the *Carmania*, was further downstream at berth Number 4. Ahead of the *Mauretania* was the *Media* and, astern, the *Politician*. Scores of small spectator craft, tugs and yachts lay moored between the New Brighton and Egremont piers

The 'Marine Display' held on the River Mersey on 11 July 1913. (left to right: *Empress of Ireland* of Canadian Pacific, Harrison's *Media*, and the *Mauretania*). The review attracted a lot of attention from the shore, with the spectators hoping to catch a glimpse of the King and Queen. (Author's Collection)

and off Birkenhead and further upstream the training ships *Conway* and *Indefatigable* were dressed in honour of the occasion.

The *Galatea* came alongside the flag-bedecked *Mauretania* and the King and Queen, ascending the port side accommodation ladder, were formally received by Commander Turner RNVR, wearing full formal naval uniform complete with fore-and-aft cocked hat (a marked change from the bowler that he favoured when on the Bridge). After introductions to the Cunard's Chairman, Alfred Booth, and the ship's officers (Staff Captain W.H. Hossack; Frederick Manley, Chief Officer; and either A. Riddle or J.C. Townley as First Officer as, on that big day, the former transferred to another Cunard ship), the King and Queen inspected a line-up of deckhands smartly turned out in Guernsies with 'Cunard' embroidered in white across their chests. After meeting other crew members, the royal couple took tea before being ushered back onto their temporary Royal Yacht. The rest of the afternoon was occupied with further inspections, bands, and salutes, terminating with the main event, the formal opening of the new dock with the *Galatea* steaming through a ribbon strung across its entrance. On shore a choir sang 'Land of Hope and Glory'. The *Mauretania* sailed for New York the next day.

The ship was briefly haunted in August as, on the 12th at 10.30 in the evening, Trimmer William Murray was taken to the ship's Hospital suffering from 'Alcoholic delirium tremens'. So severe was his case that he died seventy-five minutes later and his body was committed to the deep at eight the following morning with the usual ceremony. At 6 o'clock that same evening a strange apparition appeared when the deceased made a most unexpected appearance – he was alive! The Trimmer had been misidentified whilst under the influence and it was another Trimmer, John Fisher, whose remains had slid so ceremoniously over the side! Under influence of other spirits, five Able-Bodied Seamen (ABS) and a Quartermaster (QM) were hauled before the Captain on 21 August for being either drunk and unfit for duty, or absent from duty. They were each fined the statuary 5 shillings and their names logged.

One of many shipping companies using the port of Liverpool was the Isle of Man Steam Packet that ferried passengers to and from the island. The funnel colours of the company were identical to Cunard's, which led to four passengers boarding the brand-new, 1,877-ton,

313ft-long, single-funnelled ferry *King Orry* on 30 August mistaking her for the *Mauretania*, only to discover their error when far out into the North Channel!

Desertions still plagued the ship. Before the departure of 11 October, twelve men failed to join after signing on and nine ABS and seven Firemen deserted the liner for the bright lights of New York, taking their effects and half their wages with them.

The call into Queenstown for mails again came into question in the latter part of 1913. William Donegan, Secretary to the Cork Harbour Commissioner, protested that the Cunarders could have safely used Queenstown as both the *Mauretania* on 9 November and *Lusitania* on the 23rd bypassed the port due to unfavourable weather; 941 and 705 sacks of mail were missed respectively, loaded later by other ships, although *Mauretania* still delivered 4,250 sacks of mail and 3,210 bags of parcels ('mostly Christmas and New Year's gifts'). Also being delivered was F.W. Woolworth, founder of the famous chain of stores. After a three-year campaign by Cunard (in spite of opposition by the British Postmaster General and Irish representatives) Queenstown was finally dropped from the westbound schedule. So, from Saturday, 28 February 1914, the big Cunard liners stopped calling at the port, saving ten hours on each voyage. It was thought that the big White Star liners would follow suit, and it was said that the real losers would be 'the vendors of Irish lace, blackthorn sticks, green stone ornaments, and shillalahs [sic] and bog oak pipes'!

The liner sailed for Liverpool at 6 p.m. for her annual lay-up on 16 December, being sent off on her final eastward crossing for 1913 by a large crowd. There were 1,100 passengers including Swedes and Norwegians, many of whom sang melodious traditional Christmas songs of their native lands as the ship sailed.

Crossing the Atlantic in 1914 would be little different compared to 1913, with five days being the average time. The weather had a lot to do with it – blizzards raged across Britain and, on 5 January, an oil tanker sank 20 miles off Sandy Hook during a particularly dreadful storm.

But before the *Mauretania* could start her 1914 season she had to complete her annual overhaul in the Canada Dry Dock that included extensive work on her turbines, many of the thousands of blades being replaced by new ones brazed onto the rotor using gas stored in 7ft-high cylinders. The gases used were compressed coal gas and oxygen; coal gas bottles were painted red and had a left-handed thread connector, whereas oxygen bottles were black with a right-handed thread. On 27 January work progressed on the starboard high-pressure turbine and a bottle of coal gas was requested just before 9.30 p.m. Suspicions were not raised when the red-painted bottle was found to have a right-handed thread. When the gas was lit an almighty explosion erupted that could be felt throughout the ship. Three men (Engine Fitters George Coventry and Sam Gidman, and ship's Engineer James Thomas) were blown apart. Seven others were seriously injured, one of whom, John MacGee, died later in hospital.

Dense smoke prevented immediate rescue and the fire that erupted was extinguished using the ship's hoses; the fire brigade that had been summoned stood down as a result. The liner's Master at Arms, George Hennessey, quickly put on a smoke helmet to start a rescue effort until the smoke cleared enough to allow others in. Other than for the injured starboard turbine, there was no other damage caused but the ship's sailing scheduled for 14 February was cancelled until 7 March. By a strange coincidence, a similar explosion occurred on the Canadian Pacific liner *Empress of Ireland* the next day. Fortunately no one was killed and only one man was slightly injured. Although compensation for the *Mauretania*'s victims' families was claimed, it would take until April 1916 for a settlement to be made, at least for Mrs Coventry when she was awarded £300 damages and £100 for each of her two children.

For the rescheduled 7 March sailing the ship had a Relief Captain, the charismatic James S.W. Charles (015759), allowing Will Turner (02168) to take over the brand-new 45,647gt, 901ft *Aquitania* (to which he had been appointed six days previously) in readiness for her maiden voyage on 30 May. A new Staff Captain, J. Marshall, supervised lifeboat practice on the morning of the day of sailing (sailing time being at 2.30 p.m.). Adhering to Board of Trade regulations, the crew was mustered; all boats were swung out under davits (boat gear had been examined the day before) and the after boats were lowered. Crew also mustered at Fire Stations and Bulkhead Doors were examined and 'found correct'. However, before sailing, nine Stewards failed to join the ship, as did *forty-one* Firemen and ten Trimmers. Seven others deserted at the Landing Stage. The weather might have been

a deterrent as the westward trip took five days, seventeen hours and three minutes. As the voyage progressed, some of the substitutes taken on in Liverpool were found to be incompetent at their jobs and were disrated as being unable to 'perform their several duties'. The next crossing to New York (also with Captain Charles in command) was the liner's slowest ever, taking six days, nine hours and seven minutes. The rest of the crossings up to June all took over five days.

The first of April has been celebrated by pranksters since early times and the day did not pass unnoticed in 1914 on board the *Mauretania*. At 4.40 in the morning a Seaman, Patrick McKeown, raised a false alarm and roused many a sleeping passenger. He was apprehended, brought before the Captain and fined the obligatory 5 shillings. Asked if he had anything to say, he responded: 'I have got something to say to it …' but his reply was not logged – was it 'April Fool!'? Two ABS were fined the same amount for disobedience to an officer's order. Despite both denying the charge, they were fined the mandatory 'five bob'.

Prior to the 18 April departure, there was a mass failure to join of thirty-eight Firemen and, unusually, Greasers. Ten Trimmers followed suit. For the return sailing from New York the ship was full and included in the First Class was Sir Bache Cunard, grandson of the founder of the shipping company that bore his name. Sir Bache was returning to his large country house at Nevill Holt Hall, in Leicestershire. The ship was again seen off by an enthusiastic large crowd.

Twenty-five men declined to take up their posts in the Boiler Rooms for the May Day sailing and:

> In consequence of the large number of changes in crew, we were obliged at the last moment to engage a large number of substitutes and as some of the men shipped were not of the Standard we usually get, we engaged three men over the complement; these as before stated were Engaged at the last moment and there was no time to report to BoT [Board of Trade].

On the second day out, Nightwatchman William Taylor died of heart failure and, at 8 a.m. the next morning, was committed to the deep with 'naval religious rites being observed'. The balance of his wages less 'deductions for tobacco (9*d*) [9 pence] and Insurance (8*d*)' came to

£2 17s 1d. At the end of the crossing sixteen deserted in New York, taking their effects with them.

A day out from New York, on 27 May on the return trip, two stowaways were discovered in the Engineers' Department and were kept under surveillance until the ship reached Liverpool, where they faced prosecution. Unusually, they were heading eastwards rather than west. Also on this trip were three Distressed British Seamen; deemed unfit for work, one of them even needed medical attention.

The first voyage of June starting on the 6th obviously did not appeal to many of the Black Gang as thirty-six Firemen and nine Trimmers failed to appear after signing the Crew Agreement and two more deserted at the Landing Stage. Again the log noted:

> On account of the large number of men failing to join, it was necessary for us to engage a large number of substitutes … The BoT were notified through [the] owners on Eng. 2 Form.

Leaving New York on the 16th was no better as there were ten desertions and thirteen failed to join, including one Lift Attendant, Stewards and a Grill Cook. Passengers, too, came aboard with their tragedies. Elisa Spük (Eina Spiik?), a 27-year-old Finnish Second-Class passenger from Helsinfors (Helsinki), boarded on 7 June to escort her 17-year-old brother, Helge, who wanted to work in the States. Elisa was already working in America as a maid but had decided that she did not want to return. After spending two days looking aft over the stern she took Helge by the arms as he came to take her to lunch, kissed him, said 'Goodbye' and jumped overboard. A lifebuoy was thrown into the sea to mark the approximate spot where she had fallen, the ship was put about, and an emergency boat lowered. The search was futile with no trace of the suicide being found. After fifty minutes the boat was recalled and shipped.

Emigrants hoping to find a new life in the United States travelled in their hundreds of thousands from Europe and further afield, finding passage on one of the scores of ships plying the North Atlantic. Sometimes, after health and other inspections on Ellis Island, an occasional hopeful would be refused entry (it was put to the delivering shipping company to return that unfortunate to the port of departure) and the disappointment might prove to be too much to bear. This could have been the case of a returnee who, after becoming insane, was deported on 7 July sailing from New York. Looking after these sad cases must have been an onerous duty for the crew member assigned to the job and this proved to be the case with First-Class Waiter Sydney Smith as he was fined the usual 5 shillings for failing to obey 'the lawful command' of the Chief Steward in standing by the patient. When the charge was read out to him Smith, instead of the usual 'nothing to say', must have regarded himself to have been unfairly treated as he replied that he 'would see the Board of Trade in Liverpool'. On arrival at Fishguard, Mrs J. Clayton, a Stewardess, deserted the ship and must have disembarked on one of the tenders without being spotted. Three DBS were landed at Liverpool on the ship's arrival.

Liverpool's waterfront had begun to change. Since early 1913 George's Dock, the old dock between the Royal Liver Building and the Mersey Docks and Harbour Board's Offices, had been a hive of activity as it was to become the basement of a new block, the Cunard Building. Based on the architecture of the Farnese Palace in Rome, this majestic new structure of Portland stone and marble and fine carvings would be the headquarters of the Cunard Steam Ship Company. Popularly and justifiably called 'The Passengers' Palace', the three buildings together would in time be known as 'The Three Graces'.

Before the building could be finished, changes beyond the control of Cunard, Liverpool, or the Government would occur that would change the world forever.

10

WAR COMES TO THE *MAURETANIA*

The most tragic thing about the [Great] War was not that it made so
many dead, but that it destroyed the tragedy of death …
(John Peale Bishop)

genuine sorrow do I witness the end of a friendship, which Germany
loyally cherished. We draw the sword with a clean conscience and
clean hands.

The day after the *Mauretania*'s sailing on 27 June the heir presumptive
to the Austro-Hungarian throne and Inspector General of the
Army, Archduke Franz Ferdinand, and his wife Sophie, Duchess of
Hohenberg, were assassinated while on an official visit to the Bosnian
capital of Sarajevo.

From this event in the troubled Balkans an almost imperceptible
wave of political crisis gained momentum in Europe that became
a blood-drenched buffer to the Gilded Age. In a tangled web of
alliances, Germany urged Austria-Hungary to declare war on Serbia
on 28 July, promising support if Russia became involved. In the
'Black week' that followed war was declared and Russia, in order
to protect its interests in the Balkans and its alliance with Serbia,
ordered a general mobilisation of its recently strengthened army on
31 July and declared war. As Russia was allied to France, Germany
demanded that Belgium allow it to cross its territory to attack the
French, but Britain and France (as well as Germany ironically) had
promised to protect Belgian neutrality. The British public was as
yet unaware of what lay in store for them as the Kaiser, ignoring
much Franco-German history, proclaimed as Germany prepared to
invade France:

With heavy heart I have been compelled to mobilise my army against
a neighbour at whose side it has fought on many a battlefield. With

With Captain Charles in command, the *Mauretania* had left Liverpool
on a scheduled departure on Saturday, 1 August 1914, after the
now-usual desertions with twenty-three Firemen and nine Trimmers
failing to join. Desertions from other departments were also becoming
commonplace as six deck and catering staff also decided not to appear
in time for the departure as that pivotal and fateful day unveiled in
Europe. The crossing was full of tension for those on board as the
situation in Europe was left behind and the shores of the mother
country disappeared over the horizon. Two days later, in fulfilment of
the obligations of the 1903 Agreement, the *Mauretania* and her sister,
the *Lusitania,* were requisitioned as Armed Merchant Cruisers when
they received the following message:

I beg to inform you that circumstances of grave national import, which
announced by Royal Proclamation, render it necessary to requisition
the S.S.s [steamships] 'Lusitania' and 'Mauretania' from the dates of their
arrival in England for service as AMCs.

Cunard's General Manager made the Admiralty aware that the
company would not allow the two valuable liners to sail unless the
Admiralty indemnified them against war risks on the homeward
voyage, and a 'Confidential' telegram relayed this expression to
Their Lordships:

Your urgent confidential telegram regarding Lusitania Mauretania received. Lusitania is at present in New York. Mauretania is now on way to New York where she is due next Friday [7th]. Whilst anxious to assist by putting these ships at disposal of the Admiralty yet in view of grave conditions now obtaining we are unable to allow the Lusitania to leave New York unless the Admiralty indemnify the company against war risks upon her doing so and the same position will apply to the Mauretania. Kindly reply so that we may give necessary instructions.

After her dramatic change of course after the declaration of war, the *Mauretania* arrives at Halifax on 6 August to discharge her passengers. (Author's Collection)

A rare occasion on which both sisters were in dock together, seen here in the Sandon Dock. (Author's Collection)

The Admiralty agreed and, to prepare the sisters for their new roles, gave instructions for the vessels to be taken to Liverpool. Captain E.G.H. Gamble RN was appointed to superintend the fitting-out of the two ships and, once converted, the AMCs would be under the command of two other Royal Navy captains: Captain Vivian H.C. Bernard would have the *Lusitania* and the *Mauretania* would be under the charge of Captain C. Fowler. Plans had already been made for the conversion of the two ships as they returned to Liverpool and work included:

1. Clearing of linings under gundeck [i.e. four positions on Promenade Deck foredeck, and eight positions on Shelter Deck] in wake [sic: way] of gun positions.

2. Clearing of wood deck on gundeck in wake of gun positions.

3. Clearing of spaces to be appropriated for magazines.

4. Taking down cabin bulkheads and doors not required.

5. Clearing as far as possible Third Class Passenger accommodation on lower deck 'F'. [i.e. Lower Deck that had been fitted with portable berths]

6. Painting letters at gangways and staircases corresponding to each deck. [This was naval practice to assist those embarked in identifying where they were on the ship]

7. Screening of lights [blackout] and painting of weather surfaces. [paint the exterior of the ship in a military colour]

It appears that instruction no. 2 was carried out at some gun positions on the *Lusitania* as a gun mounting was bolted into position, probably while the ship was still at sea, before the eventual cancellation of the requisition order.

In spite of last-minute intense diplomatic activity in the hope of keeping British isolationist status during those few summer weeks, peace in Europe inexorably collapsed like a house of cards. After twelve days of political tension war suddenly rushed in on Britain when, on the night of 3–4 August, the German army invaded Belgium to force a way through to France. As the gas-fuelled street lamps of London were being lit in the falling dusk of that Summer Bank Holiday, the eve of war, British Foreign Secretary Sir Edward Grey famously remarked to a friend as they looked outwards from Grey's office: 'The lamps are going out all over Europe; we shall not see them lit again in our life-time.' At 11 p.m. (midnight in Germany) on 4 August Great Britain declared war on Germany and its allies. Like Grey's lamps, the Edwardian Dream and the years of peace that had been taken for granted was, almost imperceptibly, extinguished.

With tensions running high on the westward-bound *Mauretania*, an urgent message tapped its way into the Wireless Room at 1.30 (GMT) on the morning of 5 August, its receipt and contents being duly logged at a position of 41°44'N 46°33'W (approximately 1,370 nautical miles from New York):

> Received from the Admiralty, via Poldhu Marconi Station, news that war had broken out between England [*sic*] and Germany.

This grave news was followed by another important communication logged the following day at 8.30 (GMT) when at 43°33'N 61°14'W:

> Received instructions by wireless from HMS *Essex* to proceed to Halifax [Nova Scotia] and to remain there pending Admiralty instructions.

(HMS *Essex* had been one of the guardships [along with HMS *Caronia*, an AMC taken up from Cunard service] stationed just outside American territorial waters to prevent the escape of German ships immobilised by the war in New York. The cruiser had been involved in an earlier diplomatic incident on 14 September when an American tug had delivered some newspapers to the *Ambrose* lightvessel along with a letter for the warship. A boat from the *Essex* eventually arrived to pick up the letter and this action was enough for the United States to protest that its neutrality had been compromised).

When the message from HMS *Essex* was received the *Mauretania* was in thick fog off Sable Island, about 660 nautical miles from New York, and her helm was immediately put over 90° to starboard so abruptly that she heeled considerably – much to the consternation and imbalance of many passengers – as she changed course and headed towards Halifax, Nova Scotia, only 160 nautical miles away. She put on all speed, achieving an incredible 27½ knots. There was a fear that German cruisers (the Kaiser's warships were alerted by the code word 'EGIMA' that hostilities should start) might be operating off the American coast and it was rumoured that a German warship – possibly SMS *Dresden* – had been sighted 20 miles away.

The officers did not tell the passengers that war had been declared although rumour was rife and, after that message from *Essex* had been received, an embargo was placed on passengers sending and receiving wireless messages, by which prohibition some correctly assumed that hostilities had commenced. Other warlike precautions were taken: ports were blacked out with canvas ('To keep the rain out' the passengers were told!), exterior lights were extinguished, the Promenade Deck shrouded in canvas and all exterior access doors locked. When the fog cleared it was seen that the liner was being escorted by the hard-working *Essex*. On that same day Cunard's Chairman, Alfred Booth, authorised Richard Webb of the Admiralty to report that, as the ship now stood insured under the new scheme, the company did not intend 'to pursue the question of the indemnity any further'.

High speed, maintained throughout that eventful crossing, ensured a fast passage and the *Mauretania* arrived at Halifax early in the morning of 6 August, much to the surprise of the Canadian port. The Admiralty required that naval officers be embarked on the ship(s) for their return journeys: 'from Halifax or elsewhere … with discretionary powers as to controlling course and conduct of ship in any emergency; and to see that Admiralty interests were properly safeguarded in the circumstance of the voyage'.

Hurried arrangements were made for the 1,670 passengers to continue their journeys; First Class did not disembark until the evening, when special trains took them and the mails to New York. Among the passengers in First Class was P.A.S. Franklin, President of the IMM combine, Cunard's principal rival on the Atlantic. Twenty-three passengers of German or Austrian descent were, pending proof of US citizenship, detained. Some First-Class passengers on the Cunarder were annoyed at the unwanted detour to Canada so hired their own train to New York (a fifteen-hour journey along an initially single track of the Inter-Colonial Railroad), while those awaiting the 'Cunard Specials' (for which extra carriages had to be found) were shown to sleeping cars for First Class, tourist cars for Second and day coaches for Third. Customs and Immigration awaited the passengers at New York's Grand Central Station. The White Star liner *Cedric*, carrying 4,800 passengers, arrived in Halifax a short while after the big Cunarder, putting extra strain on those trying to organise onward transport. By noon on 9 August two Seamen (Brennan and O'Donnell) from the 843 crew had deserted the ship, taking their effects, while another (W. Reynolds) left by 'mutual consent'. Two days later First-Class Waiter Walter O'Malley followed the deserters. Perhaps the three men, all seemingly Irish, did not want to be embroiled in a fight of Britain's making.

Eventually, neither *Lusitania* nor *Mauretania* would be employed in their intended belligerent capacities (as will be seen later). However, it was arranged with Cunard that a payment of one month's hire should be made to enable the *Lusitania* to be kept at the disposal of the Admiralty. As she approached her homeport at the end of Voyage 92 on 11 August, a message was received from an observation station announcing the *Lusitania*'s progress towards the Mersey:

AMC Lusitania bearing South West five miles steering N.E. 15 knots …

Even before her arrival she had been raised to the status of 'AMC'. Cunard was notified on the 16th that the 'Lucy' was to be kept at the disposal of the Admiralty for a period of one month dated from the day after her return on a hire rate of £37,995. It was suggested in the press that the *Lusitania* would transfer to Portsmouth Dockyard for conversion into her cruiser role.

In the Ship's Articles and Agreements for the *Mauretania* an additional clause required that the crew:

… agree to serve on board the said Ship in the several capacities expressed against their respective names on a voyage … of not exceeding one year duration to any ports within the limits of 15 degrees North and 60 degrees South latitude, commencing at Liverpool proceeding hence to O.H.M.S. and/or any other ports within the above limits, trading in any

rotation and to end at such port in the United Kingdom or Continent of Europe (within Home Trade limits) as may be required by the Master …

… and it was stipulated that:

The crew shall consist of 3 Officers; a Carpenter; 1 Boatswain; 24 Able-bodied Seamen; 3 Engineers; 90 Firemen; 60 Trimmers; 20 Stewards; and 2 Cooks.

The two sisters were abruptly released from the requisition order on 11 August with the signal:

Admiralty do not propose to take up Mauretania and Lusitania for the present. They can therefore resume their ordinary sailings.

… received just in time to stop the first bulkheads being ripped out of the *Lusitania*, which had arrived that same day. The great outlay required to requisition the ships for which they had been so expensively designed was also prevented, a decision that would be amply justified five weeks later. It was probably while in Nova Scotia that the liner was painted grey (as the *Lusitania* had been in New York) so as to make it 'as inconspicuous as possible': a white superstructure was a giveaway, especially on a moonlit night! With the initial scare somewhat subdued, the *Mauretania* sailed for Liverpool on 14 August, provisioned but – for the first time in Cunard history – devoid of passengers. Five days later and a day away from Liverpool a vessel was spotted, challenged and one pass made around it. The small, slower ship identified herself as a Dutch passenger liner repatriating Americans.

The Director of Transports wrote to Cunard on 17 August laying down their conditions of hire for the *Mauretania*. They stipulated that, because of the increased danger to life created by the war, the entire ship's crew would be engaged for the duration – or for the period during which the ship would be on Admiralty charter, optimistically adding 'whichever is the shorter'. The ship's senior officers were offered temporary naval commissions and a £10 allowance towards an RNR uniform. It took over three months for the new captain of the ship, Captain Arthur Rostron (of *Titanic* fame), to argue that if the crew were to come under Naval

Discipline then they should reap the benefits of having continuous pay when on leave and be offered the naval practice of limited free rail travel, i.e. two paid warrants a year with a three-month qualification period.

The liner made three further sailings to New York before the effects of war took hold but not before the needs of war were met as Able-bodied Seaman T. Hawney was 'called for mobilization'. On sailing day, 29 August, direct to New York seven men in the Catering and Deck departments failed to join, one deserted at the Landing Stage along with eleven Firemen and Trimmers. Perhaps fleeing the war, a 25-year-old Englishman, Laurence Richardson, was discovered stowing away. In New York ten Waiters and one Sculleryman, perhaps surplus to requirements, were transferred to the *Carpathia*, and another Sculleryman preferred a transfer to the Stokehold as a Fireman. Before returning to Britain, crew member F. Martinez deserted, 'taking effects', and off Fire Island on the first day out on the return trip two stowaways were apprehended: 27-year-old Englishman John Kenshaw was found early in the morning and 39-year-old US citizen Hugh Colter after lunch. These two brought the stowaway numbers on board up to four as two others had been transferred from Cunard's *Laconia*. The second day out of the return eastward saw twenty Firemen and Trimmers being logged for being absent from duty (mostly on the 6 a.m. watch) – including one George Washington! Each man was fined the standard 5 shillings, deducted from their hard-earned monthly wage of just over £5. The ship was taking over five days to cross the Atlantic in both directions at a speed of just over 24 knots. Fishguard was bypassed for safety on the way home.

Even after all the expense involved in their development, the use of large liners as Armed Merchant Cruisers was put firmly in doubt very early on in the War. On 26 August the old British cruiser HMS *Highflyer* caught the *Mauretania*'s old adversary, the German liner *Kaiser Wilhelm der Grosse*, which had had been requisitioned by the German Navy as an AMC. She had already sunk three ships – but not until her captain, Captain Reymann, had ensured the safety of their crews. Two other ships were allowed to go free after it was found that women and children were on board. The AMC was taking on bunkers off Río de Oro on the coast of Spanish North Africa when she was discovered by HMS *Highflyer*, which challenged the German ship to identify herself. The German

AMC replied 'What ship is that?' 'His Britannic Majesty's ship *Highflyer*,' came the reply, 'you are the *Kaiser Wilhelm Der Grosse*. In the King's name we call upon you to surrender.' Then came the *Kaiser*'s brave and defiant reply: 'A German commander never surrenders. We fight for our God and Kaiser.' She was then allowed half-an-hour's grace before an exchange of fire began that lasted from 3.10 p.m. until 4.45 p.m. when the black-and-grey German liner ran out of ammunition and was abandoned by her crew. Whether or not the liner was sunk by the British cruiser or scuttled with dynamite was contested by both sides.

The only action that occurred between two expensively built AMCs was a battle involving a 'doppelganger'. Cunard's first turbine steamer *Carmania* had, like her sister *Caronia*, been requisitioned as an AMC and sent on patrol as part of the North America and West Indies Squadron with her bolted-on cannon from the Royal Naval Dockyard in Bermuda. Meanwhile, the handsome Hamburg-South America's *Cap Trafalgar* (18,700grt) had also been converted into an AMC by the German Imperial Navy whilst she was in Buenos Aires. A futile cruise looking for British shipping ensued, the *Cap Trafalgar* eventually turning up at the island of Trinidad on 13 September to take on coal from two colliers. By this time the German liner had had one of her three funnels removed by her crew and had been repainted to disguise her as … the *Carmania*!

On 14 September the real *Carmania* saw smoke above the island and went to investigate. The surprised *Cap Trafalgar* steamed away to the south before turning to face the *Carmania* and, at 12.10 p.m., fired the first shot. During the action the *Carmania* was hit nearly eighty times, her Bridge destroyed and set on fire. The 'Cap', her Bridge also on fire, managed to slowly pull away but, because of a hit below the waterline, she developed a list, lifeboats were lowered, the list worsened until, finally, she capsized and sank. This action became the only such between two AMCs throughout the war and, as with the previously mentioned engagement, showed that the thin plating and high superstructures of large liners – along with their huge consumption of not easily replaceable coal and use of a large manpower to run them – proved that these vessels were extremely vulnerable and not suited to this form of warfare. Shell hits into the side of a ship might be alleviated by coal bunkers but plunging fire from above was another matter. Smaller liners would, however, find employment in the northern approaches to the North Sea, where they provided valuable assistance with the Tenth Cruiser Squadron in effectively blockading German supply lines and causing a great deal of hardship in Germany. The *Carmania* was salvaged and repaired, surviving to fight another day, but the suitability of using large liners as fast cruisers was, literally, in the firing line.

While the duel was being fought in the South Atlantic, the *Mauretania* had her own battle when berthing at Liverpool on 14 September, as during a gale she was blown against the Princes Landing Stage, a part of which was stove in by 4ft and three of its approach bridges badly damaged. Sailing to New York five days later, the ship's complement was noted as:

29 Stewardesses and Matrons

34 Stewards, Cooks, etc.

35 in Engine Department

42 Greasers

220 Firemen

160 Trimmers

233 Waiters, Night Watchmen, Boots, Bedroom Stewards [majority of Waiters and Bedroom Stewards being in First Class]

120 Stewardess, Matrons [additional to above?], Chefs, Butchers, Bakers, Confectioners, Scullery men, Porters, Cooks (vegetable, sauce, etc.)

59 other Cooks, Waiters (First Class)

Before leaving Liverpool, forty-eight Firemen and ten Trimmers failed to join, and seven Seamen, one Bos'un's Boy, two First-Class Waiters, one Second- and one Third-Class Waiter, one Second Cook and one Scullery Man deserted, their motives open to conjecture.

Many Americans fleeing Europe were on the passenger list, as were the two daughters of a London store owner, Violette and Rosalie Selfridge. Shipboard activities went on as usual, with the passengers'

customary concert being held in the Third-Class Dining Saloon (this saved messing up the First-Class Lounge and also gave a 'village hall' feeling to the proceedings) at 8 p.m. on the Wednesday evening before arrival in New York, 'by permission of Captain J.T.W. Charles, C.B., R.D., R.N.R.'. The usual offerings of songs, musical solos and recitations were presented to the expectant audience, with a collection being made during the interval. The evening concluded with lusty renderings of 'America' and 'God Save the King'.

On arrival in New York, forty-two First-Class Waiters, twenty-nine Second-Class Waiters, two Bedroom Stewards and two Third-Class Waiters were transferred from Cunard's *Franconia* (then lying at Boston) and from the *Andania* berthed in Montreal to replace those who had deserted at the last minute in Liverpool. For the return sailing a consignment of cargo had been shipped with the 'utmost secrecy'. Under the cover of darkness, six crates containing 'machinery' were stowed in the 'afterhold' (Baggage Room). A much larger crate, covered by a tarpaulin, was stowed aft on 'B Deck' (Sun Deck) and securely lashed down; the content of this was a Glenn Curtiss seaplane called *America* (the smaller crates contained the aircraft's two engines) that was capable of carrying ten men, 2,000lb of cargo, or making a transatlantic flight. All were destined for a 'private' consignee in Britain. The potential significance of the secret shipment would not have been lost on any German agent lurking along the waterfront; it would mean that Cunard was in breach of a convention that prohibited the carriage of potential military equipment on civilian vessels and could – and later would – be used as a propaganda weapon. The aircraft was contraband. Six similar craft had been ordered and *America* was later renamed *H4* by its consignee, the Royal Naval Air Service.

Just outside American waters, the *Mauretania* exchanged signals with, and probably stopped to pick up homeward-bound mails from, another Cunarder, the Armed Merchant Cruiser *Caronia*, which had been painted black and was now an 'HMS' stationed in the area around the *Ambrose* lightvessel to prevent any German merchant vessel that might attempt to make a dash for the Fatherland.

On the *Mauretania*'s last voyage, which started on 10 October, she lost more men when forty-four Firemen and Trimmers and twenty-one bedroom and catering staff declined to join the ship after signing on, and eight Firemen and Trimmers deserted the liner at the Landing Stage. As the mails were being brought up from the Mail Room in readiness for offloading in New York, a seconded Fireman, Eugene Fanning, refused to carry some of the bags and was then abusive to the Officer in Charge. He was also absent from duty for three days (17th, 19th and 20th) after leaving New York for the morning and evening 4-to-8 watches. He was fined 15/- (15 shillings) – five shillings for each offence, a large part of his wages. The liner made her last return to Liverpool on 27 October before being re-requisitioned into Government service.

Meanwhile, on the Continent, the British had captured the strategic Belgian town of Ypres from the Germans during the First Battle of Ypres fought between 19 October and 22 November 1914. Among the British troops was probably the young Engineer Gibson who had stood by the *Mauretania* during her major dry-docking in 1908 and who had played football for the Engineers' team during that long lay-up. Gibson had taken his watch to a local repairers but when he went to collect his timepiece the shop was no longer there!

The raison d'être for the liner and her sister ship *Lusitania* had already been called into question in the early days of the war but another event caused the Admiralty to finally doubt their decision to use the two ships for the purposes for which they had so expensively been built. Up to and during the first few months of the Great War submarines had been regarded as purely short-range, shallow-water defensive weapons (Admiral Sir Arthur Wilson had even pronounced them 'damned un-English'), but a decade earlier Admiral 'Jackie' Fisher had presciently warned of their potential for bettering a battleship. The offensive nature of the craft became more apparent as the British suffered one particularly ignominious defeat that suddenly gave the underwater weapon a deadly prominence. The awakener took place on 22 September. Three slow, obsolete cruisers were plodding along at 10 knots in line ahead patrolling the North Sea and supporting warships out of Harwich. HMSs *Aboukir*, *Hogue* and *Cressy* were manned mainly by Reservists and were part of the 7th Cruiser Squadron. As they would not have stood much of a chance against a modern German cruiser, the ships were known as the 'Live Bait Squadron'.

Germany had not had much success with their submarines during the first few weeks of the war but, at 6.20 a.m., submarine *U-9* under the command of *Kapitänleutnant* Otto Weddigen fired one torpedo at the nearest ship, the *Aboukir*, from a range of 550yd. Hit on the starboard side, the cruiser soon capsized and sank. As a submarine had not been sighted it was thought that a mine had been involved, so her two sister ships began rescuing survivors from the water. Weddigen could not believe his luck and, within a short space, all three cruisers were on the bottom. Not only did around 1,450 sailors perish in the ninety-minute debacle but the reputation of the Royal Navy suffered at a time when it badly needed support. Conversely, the reputation of the submarine as an active and fearsome weapon was established and Weddigen and his crew returned home to heroes' welcomes and the award of many Iron Crosses.

Another notable event took place in the North Sea when the first merchant ship fell victim to a U-boat under the command of *Kapitänleutnant* Johannes Feldkirchner when his *U-17* surfaced and challenged a small 866-ton British steamer, the SS *Glitra* owned by Christian Salvesen & Co., of Leith, en route from Grangemouth to Stavanger in Norway carrying a cargo of iron plates, oil, and coke and coal. Like the *Mauretania*, the steamer had been built on the River Tyne by Swan Hunter's for the Saxon Line as their *Saxon Prince*. Acting strictly according to the International Cruiser Rules – the 'Prize Rules' – the German commander stopped the vessel and then sent a search party over to the British steamer. He then gave her crew time to abandon ship before sinking her with explosive charges. *U-17* then towed the survivors' lifeboats a few miles towards neutral Norwegian waters, where torpedo boat HMNoS *Hai*, which had stood by in helpless neutrality as the sinking took place, took over the tow, taking the small boats to nearby Skudeneshavn. With the gentlemanly behaviour of Feldkirchner, perhaps accompanied by an amount of saluting and heel-clicking, it might turn out that the war at sea might not be too bad after all for merchant ships.

On 27 October, another huge blow was dealt to the Admiralty and the Royal Navy. A brand-new super-dreadnought battleship, HMS *Audacious* of the 2nd Battle Squadron, was manoeuvring during an exercise when at 8.45 a.m. she struck a mine that had been laid

With HMTS *Mauretania* at anchor in the distance, a confident group of young midshipmen go ashore on Lemnos for a picnic. (Imperial War Museum Q013406)

In this rare photograph the ship is laid up on the Clyde while it is repainted as a hospital ship. (Private Collection)

off Tory Island by a German AMC, the auxiliary minelayer *Berlin*. The mine blew a hole in the underbelly of the battleship below her thick belt of armoured plating. As the battleship was settling by the stern, the White Star liner *Olympic* arrived on the scene and at 1.30 p.m. took the floundering warship in tow, moving slowly towards Lough Swilly. The tow broke and was taken up by other ships until the casualty was too affected by her injuries to carry on. Because of poor damage control (vital watertight hatches had negligently been left open), the ship heeled over and capsized at 8.45 p.m., remaining visible on the surface for fifteen minutes until one, two and then three massive explosions tore open the hull. Later investigations ascertained that the first explosion had come from B-magazine, possibly caused by high-explosive shells cascading from the ammunition racks, exploding and subsequently igniting the cordite magazine. Amateur photographers on board the *Olympic* had their film confiscated in an effort to keep the incident secret from the Germans, and the warship's crew were told to keep quiet. However, the American press were not so reticent in publishing accounts along with the few photographs that had not been confiscated.

As the bloodiest of wars scythed its way into 1915, the *Mauretania* remained idle at her berth. Although she took up valuable quay space that could have been used for war work, her idyll would not last for long.

Early in May two announcements were published. The first came from the German Embassy in Washington, which took an advertisement in the press 'warning Americans not to travel in British liners'. The second announcement came from Cunard. Perhaps taking heart that German submarines (bar a very few) did not have a long range, it was decided that the *Mauretania* would be placed back on the North Atlantic to support the *Lusitania*, which had carried on with a reduced service since the outbreak of the war, their high speeds being their assurance against the remote possibility of attack. The schedule for the revitalised joint service would see *Lusitania* sailing from Liverpool on 15 May and 12 June, return sailing from New York on 29 May and 26 June with *Mauretania*'s Liverpool departures on 29 May and 26 June, New York departures 12 June and 10 July.

As far as the North Atlantic trade was concerned it would almost be business as usual.

Above left: In her second 'tour' during the Gallipoli Campaign the liner was converted to His Majesty's Hospital Ship *Mauretania* and sailed from Southampton. Painted as such, she is seen here in Southampton Water. (Author's Collection)

Below left: HMHS with a 'Black Carrier' alongside that brought wounded from the tragedy of the Gallipoli Peninsula to Lemnos. (Collection of Ambrose Greenway)

Above: Sick troops, some in khaki some in blue hospital uniform, enjoy the curative benefits of sunshine during their journey home. In three voyages as HMHS she carried a total of 6,298 sick and wounded troops and 2,307 medical staff. (*A Merchant Fleet at War*, Archibald Hurd)

A group of Medical Officers taken with Captain Rostron (second row, fifth from left). (*A Merchant Fleet at War*, Archibald Hurd)

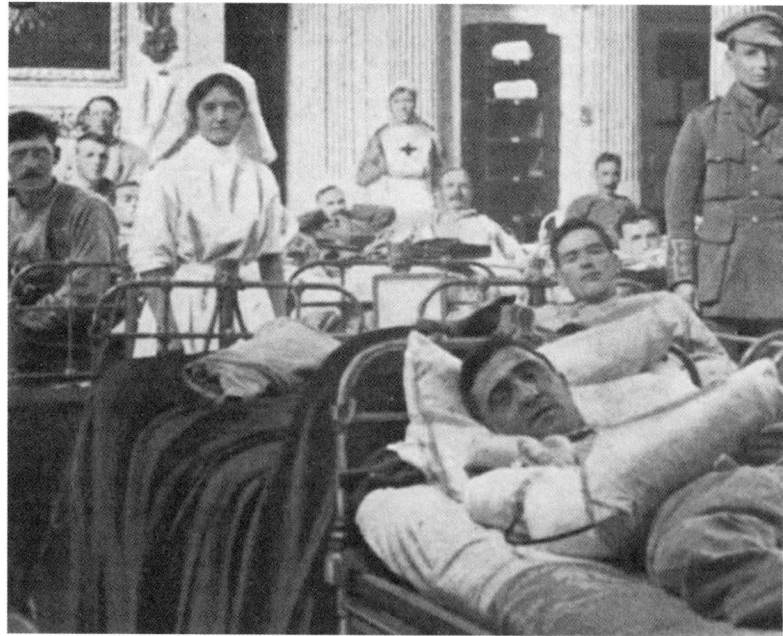

A lounge room converted to a hospital ward on the *Aquitania* showing a Medical Officer, Orderlies, Nurses, and VADs. Upper public rooms were typically converted to take cot cases to enable patients to have access to the open decks, while 'walking wounded' were berthed below in crowded and stuffy conditions. (Author's Collection)

LUSITANIA:
'We Shall Meet on that Beautiful Shore.'

At the outbreak of the Great War, Britain commenced a naval blockade of the northern approaches to the 'German Ocean' (the North Sea) to prevent war materiel, foodstuffs and other sea-borne supplies from reaching Germany. The Tenth Cruiser Squadron was formed of Armed Merchant Cruisers (AMCs – or 'Admiralty Made Coffins' as their crews called them) to assist in this blockade. In November Britain declared the North Sea a 'war zone'. This effective blockade, which caused much suffering among the German population, resulted in a retaliation so, on 4 February 1915, the German Government gave notice that:

(1) The waters around Great Britain and Ireland, including the whole of the English Channel, are hereby declared to be a War Zone. From February 18 onwards every enemy merchant vessel encountered in this zone will be destroyed, nor will it always be possible to avert the danger thereby threatened to the crew and passengers.

(2) Neutral vessels also will run a risk in the War Zone, because in view of the hazards of sea warfare and the British authorization of January 31 of the misuse of neutral flags, it may not always be possible to prevent attacks on enemy ships from harming neutral ships.

The U-boat threat was in the ascendency in early 1915. British anti-submarine measures involved heavy nets and minefields; depth charges were still in a dangerous infancy and would not become sufficiently reliable until March 1916. Ramming was another countermeasure but, although secretly advocated by the Admiralty, this led to problems relating to the rules of warfare as the instruction had the adverse effect of making every British vessel a potential belligerent in the eyes of the Germans. This was exemplified when in March a homeward-bound ferry, the unarmed civilian cross-Channel ferry *Brussels* steaming to Harwich from the Hook of Holland, was ordered to stop by the *U-33*. Captain Charles Fryatt attempted to ram the fragilely built submarine, which crash-dived to avoid destruction.

On 23 April, cross-Channel ferry services were temporarily suspended and the Germans now considered that a ship's bow constituted a weapon. Fourteen months later, Captain Fryatt's ship was surrounded by German destroyers and the Captain taken prisoner, tried for using a non-combatant vessel in an act of war, sentenced to death and shot.

Later designs of German *Unterseebooten* (U-Boats) were able to reach the waters between the west coasts of the British mainland and Ireland, and one submarine, the *U-21*, actually shelled the small island of Walney on Friday, 29 January. This attack followed the shelling of the eastern coastal towns of Scarborough, Hartlepool and Whitby on 16 December by the Imperial German Navy that resulted in scores of civilian casualties. The German Navy did not have it all its own way and were discouraged from sortieing into the North Sea for some time when, on 24 January, the Royal Navy gave them a drubbing at the Battle of Dogger Bank.

An effective anti-submarine defence lay in Room 40, a room of secrets at the Admiralty where enemy signals were deciphered using captured code books enabling regularly reported courses of chatty U-boats to be closely monitored. The signals were passed to the Admiralty, who interpreted them and took care that any action did not make the Germans aware that their signals were being intercepted. Unbeknown to Room 40, the British Directorate of Military Intelligence (MI5) had devised a plan to divert German forces away from the hard-pushed Western Front by sending a false signal that a fleet of troopships and warships would invade the German coast after sailing from British west coast and Irish ports. Even though by early 1915 the British had abandoned this ruse (the Dardanelles campaign had begun, which required large numbers of troopships and warships) the unadvised Germans were still on their guard, and, convinced by the ruse, sent troops to the coast – a move seen by equally uninformed British generals as being preparations to invade England!

Leaving the German naval base at Emden on 30 April 1915 was the submarine *U-20*, under the command of *Kapitänleutnant* Walther Schwieger, described as a popular and pleasant officer and an efficient submariner. After sinking three vessels in the Irish Sea and St George's Channel – firstly a small sailing schooner, the *Earl of Latham*, and then the Harrison cargo sister ships *Candidate* and *Centurion* – the

Kapitänleutnant was ready to return home, retaining three torpedoes for the perilous journey. Because of MI5's machinations, Schwieger was on the lookout for troopships amongst his potential victims, so when the *Lusitania* with her four black funnels hove into view on 7 May he perhaps thought her to be a troop carrier heading towards Germany. The *Lusitania* had been painted in a black/grey livery in November 1914, repainted in Cunard livery three months later, and painted yet again in the black/grey scheme for this current well-advertised voyage, perhaps leading the German coxswain to believe that the 'Lucy' had at last been converted to her naval auxiliary role as detailed in readily available reference books such as *Brassey's Naval Annual*. The ship, being a registered AMC, had earlier been prepared to take on cannon as at least one seating pad had been uncovered for such an event and temporarily disguised with a coil of rope. The German spies would probably have been aware of this. The four-funneller could also have been mistaken for the *Mauretania* that, after leaving Liverpool's Sandon Basin after being laid up since January, might have been sailing north-about around Ireland rather than chance the Irish Sea now known to be patrolled by U-boats.

On 22 April the German Embassy in New York issued a warning informing passengers sailing on the North Atlantic that a War Zone existed around the shores of Great Britain. However, this 'Notice to Travellers' did not appear until the morning of *Lusitania*'s sailing on 1 May and, when it did appear in one New York newspaper, it was printed beneath an advert promoting the *Lusitania*'s next voyage. The location of the notice may have been happenchance, but it was taken to indicate that the Germans intended to sink this particularly prestigious ship (the American vessel *Gulflight* had been torpedoed that same day) and many erstwhile passengers received anonymous warnings not to sail. In spite of the warnings, 198 American citizens chose the *Lusitania* instead of a slower neutral vessel, her speed being proclaimed as her best defence against attack. What was not generally known was that No. 4 Boiler Room had been closed down as a coal economy, with the result that the liner's speed had been reduced to 21 knots (if that). The ship's efficiency was exacerbated by the signing on of inexperienced and unruly Firemen as many of the regular men had been ushered into naval service.

The fabulous *Lusitania* sailed on May Day, Saturday, 1 May for Liverpool, where she would be joined by her sister on a recently announced revived transatlantic service, her next sailing from Liverpool scheduled for 15 May. Among her passengers were Canadian nurses and men travelling to England eager to enlist and join the fight. As the Cunarder headed out towards the open sea she passed several German liners, including previous Blue Ribband holders and the great *Vaterland*, tied up and immobile at their Hoboken piers and unable to leave due to the almost-illegal British blockade. Once outside American waters the liner stopped to take on homeward-bound mails from a blockading guardship, her smaller fleet-mate HMAMC *Caronia*. Although the *Lusitania's* Wireless Room was under strict orders not to send messages, she could receive and at 8:30 on the evening of 6 May as she approached British waters an instruction came in from the Admiralty: 'To all British ships 0005: Take Liverpool pilot at Bar and avoid all headlands, pass harbours at full speed, steer mid-channel course. Submarines off Fastnet.'

As the Cunarder's usual peacetime course took her to within a mile of Ireland's southern coast, Captain Turner, to follow instructions, stayed at least 12 miles out so that headlands could be avoided. Fastnet was by now well astern as was, hopefully, the submarine menace. The next morning the Admiralty sent out a general message at 11.25: 'Submarine active in southern part of Irish Channel, last heard of twenty miles south of Coningbeg light vessel. Make certain Lusitania gets this,' then at 12:40: 'Submarine five miles south of Cape Clear, proceeding west when sighted at 10.00 a.m.' The passengers were now at lunch. The Captain wanted to cross the Bar at the mouth of the Mersey at high tide, as to wait offshore would be taking an unnecessary risk. He already had experience of the war when in command of the Cunarder *Transylvania* earlier that year during a previous submarine scare. The *Lusitania's* contraband cargo had been an American-made 14in naval gun and its mounting, and he had diverted into Queenstown to await destroyer escort. Through the agency of German spies it was known that the now non-combatant ship was carrying war contraband including 4,200 boxes of 0.32in ammunition (1,000 rounds to a box), 1,250 cases of empty shrapnel shells (four shells to the box), and eighteen cases of non-explosive fuses, all supplied by American companies. There was also a quantity of detonators amongst the illicit cargo.

Fog plagued the early morning of the 7th and the *Lusitania's* speed was reduced to 15 knots but, once the mist had cleared, the Captain ordered an increase to 18 knots. Because of the mist, the ship's exact position was not clear so 'Bowler Bill', an experienced old navigator trained in the ways of sail, wanted the reassurance of a four-point bearing (1 point = 11.25°) from prominent landmarks off the port bow. An accurate position would allow the Captain to know when to turn the ship to port to enter the Irish Sea (always a hazardous operation with land to either side) and to calculate his vital time of arrival at the Bar. The lighthouse on the Old Head of Kinsale, a prominent and potentially dangerous headland, suited his purpose admirably and the Captain estimated that, on closing the land, the sighting would take forty minutes while keeping a steady course. It would not have been too long before the ship's Navigators could have taken a noon-day solar fix, taking just a few minutes to do so, but this would have only given latitude and the liner would have by then steamed several miles further east towards the Irish Sea.

Waiting on the cliffs of the Old Head of Kinsale in County Cork was a group of spectators, including 6-year-old G. Henderson who, with his father and brothers, was on holiday and enjoying the sunny weather and hoping to see the famed liner pass by. They saw a big liner (memory recalled with black funnels) arriving from the west, apparently bound for Queenstown. They were not the only ones watching; Schwieger was also observing the incognito *Lusitania* (there were only a quartet of British four-funnelled steamers that he could currently choose for identification purposes) approaching from his port quarter and logged that she was not flying any national flag from her jackstaff. He was surprised when the big steamer changed course from 67° east to a steady one of 87° east, which enabled the liner's Navigators to obtain their captain's requested four-point bearing. The huge ship now presented an unbelievably advantageous starboard broadside to the *U-20*. Schwieger noted in his log:

> 2.25 p.m. [German time] … Steamer alters to starboard and sets course for Queenstown [*sic*] so permitting an approach for a shot. Proceed at high speed until 3 p.m. in order to gain bearing.

Schwieger, still unable to believe his luck at the Cunarder's favourable course, ordered the firing of a single torpedo:

Clear bow shot from 700 metres (G. Torpedo set for 3 metres depth, inclination at 90 degrees, estimated speed 22 knots). Torpedo hits starboard side close abaft the bridge, followed by a very unusually large explosion with a violent emission of smoke (far above the foremost funnel). In addition to the explosion there must have been a second one (boiler or coal or powder). The superstructure above the point of impact and the bridge are torn apart [sic], fire breaks out [sic], a thick cloud of smoke envelopes the upper bridge. The ship stops at once and very quickly takes on a heavy list to starboard, at the same time starting to sink by the bow. She looks as if she will quickly capsize.

Schwieger was astonished at the effect of the solitary torpedo. It had taken *two* of these weapons, each warhead containing 270lb of high explosive, to sink the much smaller cargo liner *Centurion* the day before. The torpedo struck at 2.10 p.m. with a detonation that Captain Turner thought sounded like a door suddenly and loudly banging shut. A plume of water and wreckage rose from behind the fore funnel, reaching a height of several scores of feet, before heavily descending aft on the rapidly advancing liner's upper decks, wrecking two lifeboats as it did so. A pause, then a second deeper detonation, a low rumbling coming from within the ship. Its cause has long since been debated – had it been suspended coal dust created by the first explosion, a second torpedo (a claim countered by Schwieger's log) – or perhaps the ammunition (but this was stowed well away from the torpedo's impact)? Or was it the inrush of cold Atlantic water hitting the boilers' red-hot furnaces that sealed the ship's fate? The *Kapitänleutnant* continued in his log:

Much confusion on board; boats are lowered into the water. Apparently considerable panic; several boats, fully laden, are hurriedly lowered, bow or stern first and at once fill with water. Owing to the list fewer boats can be cleared away on the port side than on the starboard side … the name Lusitania in gold letters is visible…

According to reports the ship's name had been painted over but the angle of heel of the ship may have caused the sun to illuminate the raised lettering. Schwieger expressed surprise at what the periscope was showing him as civilians – women and children as well as men,

and not the troops that he might have been expecting – struggled for desperate survival in the appalling conditions that had suddenly been thrust upon them by his actions. It was either he or a later writer who added a compassionate concern in the logbook for the humanity that fought for life in the cold waters …

I could not fire a second torpedo into the mass of people saving themselves.

With her steering gear now deprived of steam after pipes had ruptured, the *Lusitania* surged uncontrollably forward. Her stern rose as she sank by the head, listing to starboard as she did so as the flooded starboard coal bunkers were countered by the still-buoyant port bunkers. Chaos marked the launching of lifeboats: some upending as they were launched, others swinging outboard away from the list, while portside boats, rendered useless by the list, lurched inboard. A trail of the living, the dead, wreckage and broken boats marked the curving wake of the dying ship, her forward downward motion only being brought to an end as her forefoot hit the sea bed 300ft below. Schwieger's final entry stated:

From the Old Head of Kinsale bears 358 degrees 14 miles. Wreck lies in 90-metres of water. (Distance from Queenstown 27-miles.) Position 51 degrees 22'6 N 8 degrees 31'W. The land and lighthouse very clearly visible.

The holidaying family on the Old Head were aghast as they saw a plume of water rise from the side of the ship away from their view, followed a few seconds later by the sound of an explosion. In a letter to the magazine *Ships Monthly*, Henderson the younger recalled:

there was a sudden explosion and the ship quickly appeared to list to starboard and started to sink by the bows. At the time we did not know the name of the ship but I still remember the horror of seeing her slowly slide beneath the waves, her funnels smoking and her propellers well out of the water.

(Mr Henderson also recalled local fishing boats sailing with food and petrol that, his father believed, were supplies for U-boats).

Between the first detonation and the liner's disappearance, the whole tragic enactment had taken a mere eighteen awful minutes, leaving a legacy of a few wooden boats and a few hundred lives that the liner gave back to the land. Of the 1,265 passengers and 694 crew that had boarded the ship in New York 1,198 did not survive. One hundred and twenty-eight American citizens died that day, both famous and unnoticed, and President Woodrow Wilson's American isolationism came under pressure; a flurry of diplomatic notes between Washington and Berlin ensued. The United States was not yet ready for war either politically, or in the willingness of the population, or in the readiness of its small armed forces. It would take further American losses over the next two years to create a final diplomatic fracture.

With some bellicosity, Berlin released a press statement:

> The Mauretania or any other British liner will be torpedoed, sunk, and meet the same fate of the Lusitania if our submarines can reach them. And that they can has been demonstrated.

Three months after the sinking, Herr Goetz, a German medallist, issued a satirical medal showing on its obverse Death selling tickets from a Cunard kiosk and, on the reverse, the *Lusitania* sinking (a reused image of a ram-bowed warship) with a military aircraft stowed on her foredeck representing Britain-bound contraband, perhaps based on the crated aircraft shipped on the *Mauretania* the previous September. The date on the 2in bronze medallion showed 5 May but was quickly reissued with the correct date (Goetz said that he had taken the incorrect date from a newspaper). For purposes of anti-German propaganda, the medallion was later copied by a British store and widely circulated. Sold for a shilling, the proceeds were given to the British Red Cross and St Dunstan's Blinded Soldiers' and Sailors' Hostel.

Since their introductions into service the two great Cunarders had inspired many a music hall and domestic song ('Take Me Back to Yankee Land' etc.) but, after the torpedoing of the *Lusitania*, the tone of the compositions darkened; children in Great Britain were so affected by the popular reaction to the sinking that they made up their own song to provide a rhythmic chant to accompany one of their time-honoured skipping games. Facts were disingenuously changed by these innocents (inured by many years of British jingoism) to protect the essential rhythm of their rhyme, which they sang to the tune of 'The Big Ship Sails on the Ally-Ally Oh':

Oh, my father was the captain
Of the Lusitania,
Lusitania,
Lusitania.
Oh, my father was the captain
Of the Lusitania,
On the first day of September.

(Chorus)

And the big ship sailed
On the ally, ally oh,
Ally, ally-oh,
Ally, ally-oh,
And the big ship sailed
On the ally, ally-oh,
On the first day of September.

And the big ship sank
To the bottom of the sea,
Bottom of the sea,
Bottom of the sea,
And the big ship sank
To the bottom of the sea,
On the first day of September.

(Chorus)

Thousands of miles away in the still neutral and isolationist United States, composer Charles Ives was walking through Manhattan's Hanover Square elevated railway station just as the news of the sinking broke on the news stands. In the distance, a barrel organ was playing the tune of a popular Bennett and Webster ballad 'In the Sweet By and By' when, on the station platform, someone started to sing:

There's a land that is fairer than day and
By faith we can see it afar
For the Father waits over the wave
To prepare us a dwelling place there.

Spontaneously, the whole crowd on the station took up the refrain:

In the sweet by and by
We shall meet on that beautiful shore
In the sweet by and by
We shall meet on that beautiful shore.

That communal outpouring of sorrow gradually and hauntingly evaporated like a morning mist as an arriving train soaked up the spontaneous choir, leaving only a stilled, emotively charged silence as the platform's sole, ghostly inhabitant. Ives, deeply moved by what he had witnessed in that suburban railway station, subsequently composed his 'Orchestral Set No. 2', whose final movement he titled 'From Hanover Square North, at the End of a Tragic Day, the Voice of the People Again Rose'. The upwelling of the 'Voice of the People …' would manifest itself in 1917 when the United States of America finally, after a deep search of its national conscience, entered the grotesque and bloody Great War in support of the Allies, an action of solidarity that had as part of its rallying cry that tragic spring event of 1915 that had played itself out in the calm, chill waters off Ireland's southern coast.

In Britain, the tragedy spawned further artistic outpourings, as Frank Bridge composed in one day, 14 June 1915, his poignant 'Lament' (dedicated to 'Catherine, aged 9 "Lusitania" 1915') for a small string orchestra. The dedicatee was Catherine Crompton, who was travelling with her returning parents, British businessman Paul Crompton, his wife Gladys, five siblings and their nanny, Dorothy Allen. All were lost in the tragedy.

Some responses were less artistic. In the great British naval town of Portsmouth, a vaudeville act by a German national proved to be his last appearance in the city when he challenged, perhaps correctly, the audience that they would have done the same had they been in

Schwieger's boots! In the States, Julius ('Groucho') Marx, one of the famous troupe of comedy act brothers, had to change his faux German accent after being booed off the stage.

American and Canadian towns hurriedly changed their names – e.g. German Valley, New Jersey, became Long Valley. Ship names also changed: Red Star's *Zeeland* – even though a Dutch name – became the less German sounding *Northland*. In Britain, vicious reactions included attacks on businesses with German-sounding names and even King George V changed the name of his royal house from Saxe-Coburg and Gotha to the more patriotic-sounding House of Windsor! Revenge for the sinking became a clarion call and colourful and melodramatic posters urged potential recruits to 'Avenge the *Lusitania*'.

A strongly worded American protest persuaded the Kaiser – 'The All Highest' as he liked to be called – to order a return to the 'Cruiser Rules' in submarine warfare whereby passenger liners (even if of enemy status) had to be warned of their impending destruction, allowing passengers and crew to abandon ship. This did not last for long as ramming continued and 'Q' ships (seemingly innocent merchant vessels that had cannon concealed in readiness) overrode any rules. Unrestricted submarine warfare resumed in January 1917.

Perhaps the most lethal consequence of the sinking involved Second Lieutenant W.H. Livens who, it was suggested, believed that his fiancée had been a passenger on the *Lusitania* and swore a dreadful revenge, his outrage continuing even after he found out that his belle had missed the liner's last sailing. Livens' promise to kill as many Germans as possible took on a horrific form when he devised a flame-thrower built of great lengths of piping pumping huge quantities of burning, pressurised paraffin towards the enemy trenches – a monstrous hosepipe spurting out a widening trail of blazing, liquid death.

Mainland Britain suffered a domestic disaster just over two weeks after the tragedy. At just before 7 a.m. on 22 May, 230 men were killed in what was dubbed 'the railway's *Titanic*' when their speeding troop train ploughed into a stationary local train by Quintinshill signal box, half-a-mile north of Gretna in Scotland. The majority of the victims were soldiers from the 7th Royal Scots, en route to the Dardanelles, travelling in scandalously archaic wooden gaslit carriages to join the

Aquitania at Liverpool (the liner would be replaced by another due to her grounding). To compound the death toll, as dazed survivors emerged from shattered matchwood carriages an overnight express train from London smashed into the still-suffering wreckage. In all, five locomotives were involved in the catastrophe, a nearby coal train and a train carrying naval coal supplies, both stopped in the side loops of Quintishill, becoming embroiled in the carnage. Fed by the gaslight storage cylinders, the deadly conflagration that ensued hugely exacerbated the already significant death toll. One surviving soldier commented ironically: 'I would far rather be out in Flanders – you do get a run for your money there.'

The Board of Trade held an inquiry for both the *Lusitania* and Quintinshill disasters. To divert any blame away from the Admiralty, the German Government was held to account for the loss of the *Lusitania* and Captain Turner was – unfairly – partly blamed. Much evidence is lost to history since the liner sank with the damaged starboard side downward in the Irish silt. Quintinshill was attributed to multiple breaches of regulations by two signalmen, who were subsequently briefly imprisoned. The *Lusitania* verdict was described as a 'whitewash' and some observers doubted the thoroughness of the railway enquiry as well.

Although the sinking of the *Lusitania* did not directly bring the United States into the Great War on the side of the Allies, it remained in the American consciousness until the time came to act, and when America did it would be with devastating consequences for the Triple Alliance.

11

'PLAYING THE GAME'

(Captain Arthur Henry Rostron)

After the *Lusitania* tragedy the *Mauretania*'s sailing on 29 May to New York was immediately cancelled. With an urgent imperative the liner was partially stripped of her peacetime fittings and fitted with bunks to take two regiments of 3,644 Irish troops needed for the increasingly voracious Allied landings on the Gallipoli Peninsula that extended north to south on the western side of the Dardanelles – a narrow 60-mile international waterway that led from the Mediterranean into the Black Sea – that had opened on 25 April 1915. Plans for the campaign to gain the Narrows to force access to the Black Sea dated from 2 January, when Grand Duke Nicholas of Russia appealed to Britain for assistance against the Ottomans (Turks), who were waging offensive operations in the Caucasus; it was hoped the Gallipoli action (as the campaign became known) would divert Turkish troops from that front. From 19 February naval bombardment of Turkish positions had failed miserably to dislodge the defenders, which led to the decision to take the Peninsula by force.

The big Cunard ships were idle, non-earning, and taking up berth space that could be used for vessels importing valuable cargos, and the DoT seemed delighted that Cunard were being patriotically altruistic in their terms of hire for the liners. An internal memorandum from the Director of Transport summed up the conditions of hire of the *Mauretania*, *Aquitania* and White Star's *Olympic*:

With reference to my submission yesterday [no date indicated] giving estimate of the cost of use of these 3 Liners, I have now been able to discuss the matter fully with the Cunard Company, who have made the following offer:-

They are not prepared to deal with the matter on a Commercial basis at all. No rate of hire that we will be able to pay would be a Commercial rate for vessels of this value, and cost of running.

On the other hand, the Company cannot run these vessels at present and they are at Liverpool in the way of ordinary traffic requiring Dock facilities.

Further, if these ships are not employed, the Company recognise that other vessels [i.e. smaller ships more of which would be required] which are now actually employed in ordinary business must be requisitioned and so withdrawn from Commerce.

The Company are therefore prepared in order (1st) to assist the Government, and (2nd) to prevent a further drain on the carrying power of the Country, to place the 'AQUITANIA' and 'MAURETANIA' at our service at a rate which is sufficient merely to cover their actual expenses, but given no profit nor even pays interest on the Capital involved. They therefore, are prepared to accept £10,000 a month for each of the ships. The rate payable under the Cunard agreement for these vessels would be £46,000 for the 'MAURETANIA', and £68,000 for the 'AQUITANIA.'

It is a condition of this agreement that the Government takes in addition to War Risk, the Marine Risk on the two ships, the Company giving us the benefit of their existing policies, and this we must do.

In these circumstances, the figure submitted yesterday showing an estimated cost to Government using these vessels of £28,000 the

'AQUITANIA' and £26,000 the 'MAURETANIA' per month, are a fair estimate of their cost. In addition, there will be the cost of fitting and re-instatement.

The two vessels are now being prepared for Service.

The 'OLYMPIC' will be prepared for Service if required to meet the War Office demands for Transports and an endeavour will be made to get the same terms as for the 'AQUITANIA.'

Director of Transports.

Plans for 'the event of the ship [Mauretania] being requisitioned by His Majesty's Government a further bonus of £1 for the 1st month or 15% will be paid to the crew with the exception of Officers and Engineers' (as part of the RNVR they would receive naval pay) were being dusted off a week after the sinking of the *Lusitania*. The *Mauretania*'s status changed from 'Royal Mail Steamer' (RMS) to 'His Majesty's Transport Ship' (HMTS). Her task, along with other troopships as part of the Gallipoli campaign, was to secretly convey soldiers from Britain to the Allied base at Mudros Bay on the island of Lemnos in the north-east Aegean Sea as quickly as possible and, in doing so, avenge the sinking of her sister six weeks earlier. The *Mauretania* and *Aquitania* 'entered into pay' as Military Transports on 11 May at a recalculated rate of hire of 15/- (15 shillings) per gross ton per month on the ships' respective tonnages of 30,704 and 45,647. Renegotiated rates would be agreed on 26 June and again on 23 August to 10 shillings per gross ton, well below the agreement and 'Blue Book' rates. Cunard patriotically accepted a reduction but the company was making a fair profit from their ordnance and aircraft factories. They would also bear the cost of the crew. Insurance was another problem as the *Mauretania* would be venturing beyond her proscribed limits and 'may be required to proceed to Portsmouth and to transverse routes which were not contemplated when the Company's Sea Risk Policies were taken out'. Cunard complained that they would not be able to afford an increase in insurance but said that, if the Admiralty would pay the extra charges of the marine risk to up the vessel's book value of £1,220,427, the company would reduce the rate of hire by 2/6d (2 shillings and 6 pence) per ton. Two days

later, after being called up, the larger *Aquitania* went aground on a rock ledge adjacent to the Sandon Dock, damaging her hull to such an extent that her No. 3 Hold was flooded; she had only just completed lengthy repairs after colliding in thick fog with the Leyland liner *Canadian* on 22 August 1914. The Admiralty changed its mind about using her as an AMC (as they had with the *Lusitania* and *Mauretania*) and considered putting her back on to the Atlantic service.

The first captain of HMTS *Mauretania* was J.C. Barr (010030), the Captain-hero of the *Carmania-vs-Cap Trafalgar* battle; Robert Johnstone would be his Staff Captain; and J.G. Saunders Chief Officer. Strangely, Captain Johnstone was not able to produce his 'Discharge 'A' Book' and was dismissed from the ship while still at Liverpool, rejoining soon after. After signing the Crew Agreement (itself recycled from the lost *Lusitania* as that ship's stamped name was crossed out and that of the *Mauretania* inserted) on the 19 May and before the voyage commenced on 21 May a numerically massive fifty-eight men, mostly Irish or Liverpool-Irish Firemen, failed to join the ship in spite of being offered a £1 bonus in the 'event of the ship being requisitioned by His Majesty's Government'. Terms of agreement included that the crew would serve for a period 'not exceeding one year duration' to any port 'within the limits of 15 degrees North and 60 degrees [sic] South latitude'. To replace the non-joiners, the Admiralty 'lent' replacements the following day from other AMCs in their service: thirty-nine Firemen, Trimmers and Greasers were transferred from HMS *Andes* (Royal Mail Steam Packet Company); HMS *Cedric* (White Star Line) provided four Firemen; and eight more came from HMS *Virginian* (Allan Line). Even at this pivotal moment three men deserted and eleven others failed to join just before leaving Liverpool in the early hours of 21 May, two weeks after the loss of the 'Lucy'. Perhaps that hour was too soon after the closing of the local pubs! The liner, still a merchant ship under Cunard's control and flying the Blue Ensign, was accompanied out of Liverpool by a shield of anti-submarine destroyers that had trouble keeping up with the *Mauretania* in the choppy sea. Once at sea the grey-painted Cunarder zig-zagged at speed as per Admiralty instructions to confuse any lurking submarine, but this defensive tactic resulted in steaming extra miles that quickly consumed her valuable coal. This first voyage to the Mediterranean was not without tragedy as, one day out, Seaman R.J. Longworth, who had been hospitalised with stomach cramp the day before sailing, died of 'Heart rupture'. His body was committed to the deep on the 22nd. At 9.20 a.m., shortly after Longworth's oceanic burial, another tragedy occurred when 31-year-old Sergeant J. Ashton of the 1st/4th Royal Scots Fusiliers jumped overboard. The ship was immediately turned about in a futile rescue attempt, but had she stopped to lower a boat, she could have put herself in danger – the ghosts of the *Aboukir*, *Hogue* and *Cressy* still lingered.

At 4.48 on the morning of 29 May the *Mauretania* arrived at anchor at Lemnos (occupied by the Allies since early March) in the large natural but now crowded harbour of Mudros Bay. The troops disembarked to transit encampments on the island to await transfer to smaller ships that would ship them onward to the battle zones; the big liners were too valuable to risk so close to the theatre of war. Also unloaded were welcomed stores and mails. She stayed at the anchorage for a few days before sailing at 7.19 p.m. on 10 June, three hours after taking on two naval prisoners, who were 'put on board this day for conveyance to England to be handed over to the Police Authorities'. The limited supply of coal and fresh water taken on put a heavy strain on local supplies. On the return trip back to Britain ('Blighty') the Transport *Mauretania* called into an anchorage on the east coast of Malta on 12 June, intending to top up her bunkers for the voyage home. This supply was insufficient so she sailed at 7.10 the next morning for Naples, arriving there on the 14th, thus creating a pattern that would be repeated in the months to come. Another early morning departure (4.24) on the 16th ensured that she arrived back at Liverpool six days later. It was also on the 16th that the Admiral Superintendent, Malta, tried to communicate with the *Mauretania* in 'M.V.' Code but he only received 'evasive answers' from the ship's captain, the latter believing that some unauthorised person – or even enemy – was trying to ascertain the ship's position, course and speed!

With what now seems to be a total lack of understanding that the *Mauretania* was now carrying troops on a fast service rather than Royal Mails – and considering the loss of the *Lusitania* – Mr A.M. Ogilvie of the General Post Office in London sent a strongly worded 'jobsworth'-type letter to the Admiralty on 18 June:

I am directed by the Post Master General to acquaint you, for the Lord Commissioners of the Admiralty, that on certain occasions since the outbreak of War the Cunard Steamship Company have failed to provide a mail ship to sail on Saturday from Liverpool for New York as required in Section 14 of their Agreement dated the 30th July 1903 with the Admiralty, the Board of Trade and the Post master General, and have pleaded the action of the Admiralty in requisitioning certain of their ships as a cause beyond [the] control of the Company which should exempt them from a deduction, under the terms of Section 27, from the subsidy payable under Part II of the Agreement …

… It is presumed that the requisitions have not been made under the provisions of Part I of the Agreement referred to above, but under separate powers conferred on the Admiralty.

It was pointed out that the presumptions in the PMG's letter were correct and that 'Special arrangements [had been made] with the owners', i.e. a procedure not proscribed in the 'Blue Book' regulations.

The Secretary of State, Lord Horatio Herbert Kitchener, expressed eagerness to have the '3 Big Ships' (*Mauretania*, *Aquitania* and *Olympic*) made available to transport three divisions to the Dardanelles as they could accommodate large numbers of troops, between 5,000 and 6,000 men, for an offensive on Suvla Bay. But they would only be used if the current emergency demanded as they were at risk of loss from submarine attack. Consequently, on 18 June the *Aquitania* was again taken up and five weeks later the giant ship was ready with an extra 800 extra berths with a total carrying capacity for 521 officers and 4,872 men. It seemed ironic that both the Cunard and White Star Lines had planned trios of large liners with which to operate a weekly service across the North Atlantic. Now in wartime, and after both companies had each incurred a large loss, both lines had been made to co-operate in a three-ship weekly service – but of an entirely different nature than originally intended. On 22 June, the Admiralty wrote to Alfred Booth, Chairman of Cunard:

First of all, the Cabinet has just decided that they will not use the 'Aquitania' and the 'Mauretania' for the work that we had in view. I will not express any opinion on this decision.

They have further asked me for an estimate on the cost of running these liners out to the Mediterranean and back …

That same day it was proposed to transport the required three Irish divisions to the eastern Mediterranean by other ships.

Detailed questions were asked about coal consumption, additional costs of running at high speeds, costs of conversions and, for eventual reference, times and costs of reconditioning. The *Mauretania's* speed on Government service was also questioned as, in order to qualify for an annual contracted subsidy, the ship had to be run at 24½ knots and it was suggested that the Captain 'make up' a shortfall in speed on the next voyage. But as she had already proven that she was capable of the speeds required, the Admiralty felt that the speed requirement could be waived, especially as the Government was paying the subsidy considering that, as she could not maintain 24 knots, the 21 knots she was making while in their hands was sufficient. Another opined that coal consumption was more important than the subsidy and might interfere with the service that she was on. In the event of either the *Mauretania* or *Aquitania* being lost on Government service the Director of Transport, E.J. Foley, assured Cunard that:

> … the Admiralty will make good to the Company, up to the book value of the vessel, the whole of such loss, less such sum shall be recovered by the Company in respect of such loss under the Company's existing Marine Risk Policies.

It seemed that almost anything that could float and carry troops was being requisitioned, although in July 1915 the Liverpool-based tenders, Cunard's *Skirmisher* and White Star's *Magnetic*, were declared exempt from call-up as it was deemed that they were the 'only vessels from which we can obtain water for HMSs' while continuing in their roles of transferring passengers (troops) between shore and ship. Also on the Mersey towards the end of June, the *Mauretania* was taking on coal from Rea's barges *Shad* and *Cedric*. Both were ranging about in the rough waters of the Mersey and, inevitably, they collided with the liner. In anticipation of this occurrence, Rea's had written in August 1914 that damage to barges could occur in any adverse weather so the

company was now seeking indemnification from the Government for damages caused while working alongside transports. The Divisional Naval Transport Officer (DNTO), Liverpool, responded that the company should not coal troopships at a risk of damage and that the Government 'would accept responsibility for any loss or damage that might be incurred'.

For the *Mauretania's* second voyage to the Mediterranean (nature of which: 'Trooping') the log was opened on 2 July 1915. Captain D. Dow was listed as Master (Captain J. Barr was strangely listed as Commander, probably RNVR), J. Carruthers was Chief Engineer and James Bisset joined the ship as First Officer. Bisset had been Second Officer on the *Carpathia* during the gallant rescue of the survivors of the sunken *Titanic*. The voyage began at 6.10 p.m. on the 9th but not before a large shovelful of Firemen and Trimmers (forty-five) missed the ship. Their replacements were found to be inept and nine were disrated from Fireman to Trimmer. Amongst this latter group was one J. Hurley who, four days out on the 13th, collapsed from heat stroke after completing three-and-a-half hours of his four-hour shift on the 12-to-4 a.m. watch in No. 4 Forward Stokehold, where the temperature had risen to 100°F. The night had been hot and very humid and, as the wind was following from astern, the ventilation cowls on the upper deck may not have efficiently caught the cooling breezes. Hurley was taken to the ship's Hospital at 4.15 a.m., where he was not only looked after by the ship's Surgeon but also very adequately by three military medical officers (RAMC) and then by sisters of Queen Alexandra's Imperial Military Nursing Service (QAIMNS). All this attention proved to be of no avail as Hurley passed away after failing to regain consciousness. He was buried at sea that same day at 37°12'N (Latitude), 5°24'E (Longitude), the Roman Catholic service being conducted by no lesser a personage than Lord Granard, 8th Earl of Granard and Master of the [King's] Horse!

For this voyage the *Mauretania's* wireless telegraphy (W/T) call sign was changed from her pre-war civilian 'HLTQ' to a special secret call sign 'YKN', with the intention of changing this call sign for each trip. It was urged on the ship's Captain that:

The master of a transport is responsible that the use of W/T is to be restricted to messages of the UTMOST IMPORTANCE and URGENCY, and that under no circumstances is W/T to be employed if it is practicable to make the communication by Visual means [e.g. Aldis lamp].

The great troopship arrived at Lemnos on 16 July and remained there, anchored half-a-mile offshore, for a week disembarking troops, essential stores, and mail. Obligingly, the Captain opened the ship's bars and dining rooms to provide some relief to those arriving from shore. When she sailed at 7.09 p.m. on the 23rd bound for Malta carrying but a few dozen naval and army personnel, Fireman Henry Smith – who had been absenting himself from the Stokehold and continuously refusing to do his duty for eleven days – was placed in cells by order of the Senior Naval Officer in Mudros. On the ship's return to England, he was taken ashore to face the penalty of the law. The troopship left the harbour escorted by two British and two French destroyers that were left behind as she gradually increased speed. As usual, during the passage to Malta, extra lookouts were kept for torpedoes while the ship followed a pre-ordained zig-zag. The next evening at six a shout was heard from the Crow's Nest that a periscope had been sighted. Captain Dow responded extremely quickly and ordered 'Hard a-port!' on the wheel, turning the blacked-out ship to starboard. The U-boat, 60° off the starboard bow and half-a-mile away, fired two torpedoes. The *Mauretania* quickly answered her helm and in doing so presented a smaller, end-on target, ensuring that one torpedo missed her by 30ft while the other passed to within 5 breath-stopping feet under her counter! Yet adventure and excitement were not over for the ship for that momentous day.

That very same evening as the ship steamed between the islands of Andros and Euboea the helm refused to respond to a slight change of course, putting the *Mauretania* in danger of grounding on nearby rocks. Again, the Captain's quick thinking saved the ship as he ordered the port engines to be stopped while the starboard reverse turbine was brought into action, luckily still in deep water. The ship turned when only half-a-mile from the hungry rocks. The cause of the lack of response to the helm was soon ascertained when a Junior Engineer abashedly confessed that he had removed an essential pin from the steering gear to adjust the machinery just when the order came from the Bridge for a change of course, leaving the steering gear completely unconnected. The Junior Engineer was demoted safely out of harm's way.

But the excitement of the day was *still* not over. The big troopship was heading on a southerly course when Officer of the Watch, Senior First Officer Bisset, saw a green light ahead. Bisset ordered the *Mauretania* to turn hard to port in an attempt to swing the big ship around the other vessel's stern but, to his consternation, the other ship (a small cargo vessel) then showed a red light followed by a white that meant that it was coming straight for the Cunarder! At 2.52 in the morning of 24 July the inevitable collision occurred when the smaller ship struck the liner on her starboard side just below the aft funnel. The liner was immediately swung round, coming to rest to within half-a-mile of the colliding vessel. On exchanging signals it was found that the other ship was the small cargo vessel *Cardiff Hall* (1912, 3,994 tons, 350ft in length). She had sustained considerable damage to her bow and, although taking on water, was not in danger of foundering. As two men on the *Cardiff Hall* had been injured (J. Petrie was suffering from a scalp wound and abrasions to his face, while J. Kakoulas had sustained a fracture of his right elbow) the *Mauretania*'s emergency sea boat in the charge of First Officer Bisset was lowered to get them quickly on board for treatment as Captain Dow did not want dawn – and possibly a submarine – to find his ship at a standstill. Bisset, eager to ascertain the cause of the collision, had found out from the cargo vessel's captain that the deadly confusion with the *Cardiff Hall*'s lights had arisen when her aged watch-keeper had suddenly become aware of the darkened *Mauretania*'s presence. As fast as his elderly legs could carry him, he had first uncovered the green starboard light (blacked out by sacking) before moving over to port to uncover the red!

These three closely occurring potentially fatal events happened within a short twelve-hour period – excluding the excitement created when a gunner fired a very loud round off at what he thought was a submarine; luckily in the darkness he missed as it was a French destroyer! Fifty soldiers were now seconded as anti-submarine lookouts. Armed only with rifles, their effectiveness would have been debatable had a U-boat been seen. But orders were orders!

When the troopship arrived at Malta on 25 July temporary repairs were made to her collision damage (lead was hammered between her sprung plates) and she took on coal, while the two injured crewmen from the *Cardiff Hall* were sent ashore to the charge of the Naval Authorities. Sailing at 5.55 p.m. the following day, after a slow loading of an inadequate supply of bunkers, the liner arrived at Naples on the 27th, where she took on 6,000 tons in two days. While assisting in mooring the ship an AB suffered cuts to the back of his shoulders but stoically carried on with his work. For some unknown reason the British Consul ordered that: 'no member of the crew was to be allowed ashore'. But, seamen being seamen, a few had a try, with the result that eleven were logged and fined the standard 5 shillings.

The ship returned to Liverpool on 3 August, where she was dry-docked for repairs. Other work was undertaken and Cunard invoiced the DNTO for:

Estimated cost of re-instating not including ordinary wear and tear but including 10 lifeboats commandeered by the Admiralty – £3,384.8.6 [£3,384 8s 6d].

The Mauretania was described on 18 August as being an 'unarmed hired vessel in His Majesty's service' and the Crew Agreement had 'Commissioned charter ship' deleted and 'Admiralty Transport Service' substituted.

As many of the ship's senior officers had been granted naval commissions, ship's Purser Humphreys asked to be 'placed on the same footing'. A curt official response, presumably to the Captain, imperiously answered: 'Presume you will tell this gentleman that he cannot be granted a commission.' This disappointing outcome was substantiated by departmental policy:

The question of the grant of Commissions, RNR, to Officers of Transports on Military Service has been considered frequently, but the decision not to grant such commissions has always been maintained.

The third and final sailing of the *Mauretania* as a troop transport (less eight crew members who didn't reappear after signing on) commenced from Liverpool at 11.28 a.m. on 25 August and it appears that she sailed empty. In the crew, of the 398 Firemen and Trimmers who had signed on on the 23rd, twenty had failed to join, and a similar number deserted. As usual the ship was accompanied down through the North Channel, the Irish Sea and St George's Channel by a shield of warships, again with difficulty in keeping pace with the great liner. Unusually, on the next day, the *Mauretania* called into the busy southern port of Southampton, where she must have created quite a stir. She was the third-largest ship to have used the port after the White Star Line had moved its express service there in 1907 before introducing its *Olympic* and *Titanic* in 1911/12. The use of Southampton with its double tides and deep-water berths must have reawakened already held ideas in Cunard that the Hampshire port would serve their requirements admirably once the war ended, being nearer to London and having access to Continental ports just a few short hours steaming away.

Perhaps a reason for the call might have been to investigate the use of the port in an anticipated change of role from that of troopship to hospital ship. The Gallipoli Campaign had become a total and utter failure and Southampton was advantageously a day's less steaming from the Mediterranean than was Liverpool. The huge military Royal Victoria Hospital at Netley (the largest of the military hospitals with a length of a-quarter-of-a-mile and three stories high, housed 138 wards containing about 1,000 beds) hugged the wooded shores of Southampton Water in full view of passing shipping. Many of those who went out as fresh-faced troops would be returning as casualties or as, more than likely, victims of dysentery. To some of these unfortunates a day less at sea could mean the difference between life and death.

On this final trooping voyage the *Mauretania* took on 260 officers and 3,347 troops, bringing the total for her trooping duties to 10,391 officers and men. She left Southampton at three in the afternoon of 28 August, arriving at Mudros on 3 September, after which the ship was readied to sail for Naples for coaling at 6.30 p.m. on the 9th. En route a signal was received that, due to labour unrest, the port was to be bypassed and the ship diverted to Spezia in the Gulf of Genoa. When she arrived there on 12 September it was found that the port's facilities were inadequate, and the liner took on only 2,500 tons of the black fuel in a long period of five days (the ship burnt about 150 tons a day just standing still!), so she left at 5.25 in the afternoon of the 17th. Because of reported submarine activity, the ship was advised to head for the French port of Toulon, arriving there the next day after a few hours steaming.

With her anchors keeping her head steady, the *Mauretania*'s stern was made fast to the breakwater. The ship's 'tremendous requirements of coal' caused a sensation among the inhabitants and authorities, culminating in a flurry of signals between France and Britain for clarifying instructions. Days passed and supplies of fuel, water and stores ran low, so the Captain requested that the Chief Engineer draw the furnace fires to conserve what coal reserves remained. After eleven achingly slow days a welcome signal came through on 29 September: 'Proceed to Gibraltar for coal.' Fortunately there were just enough carefully husbanded coals left in the bunkers for the ship to make two days' cautious steaming at 15 knots. After thirty-six hours of coaling (enough to get her back to Liverpool) the *Mauretania* left 'Gib', the narrow waters of which she and other transports attempted to pass in the dark, just after 5 on the morning of 2 October and arrived safely in Liverpool three days later. By this time, following an 'urgent request' by the medical authorities in the Mediterranean, HMTS *Mauretania* had a new role planned for her.

Captain Dow disembarked and formally handed his charge over to his successor, Captain Arthur Rostron who, being given charge of the much larger *Mauretania*, achieved a pinnacle in his career. He was more than amused when, as he would later recall in his memoirs, *Home from the Sea*, his predecessor indicated in the direction of the big ship and pointedly remarked, 'There she is; take her!' Rostron was hugely proud of his opportunity to do so. Captain Dow's seeming eagerness to hand the ship over may have stemmed from unascertained reasons that led to sixty-eight (presumably disgruntled) men, from the Third Engineer down to Firemen and Trimmers, being discharged through 'mutual consent' on 6 October.

Captain Rostron now began what would be a long and happy association with the ship. James Bisset would later describe the Captain as being of wiry build with piercing blue eyes; softly spoken with a Lancashire accent; temperate in habits and language; and both modest and kindly – and he wore his Cunard uniform with dash! As captain of the *Carpathia* he had been greatly lauded after his extraordinary organisation in rescuing the survivors from the *Titanic*; he was perhaps the best-known skipper on both sides of the Atlantic.

Work commenced on 12 October in converting the *Mauretania* into a hospital ship at an estimated cost of £68,000 (*Aquitania* had been similarly converted for £63,000, entering service on 4 September; White Star's *Olympic* would be retained as a troop transport). The higher cost for the smaller of the two ships included preparation for the dual roles of hospital *and* trooping duties. The latter duty, if actually intended, was worryingly in contravention of both the Geneva and Hague Conventions, but when Captain Rostron closely inspected her she had been superbly fitted solely as a hospital ship. The conversion of His Majesty's newly appointed Hospital Ship *Mauretania* was superintended by Medical Commanding Officer Lieutenant Colonel Frank Brown, and Commander Currie RN. These two officers authorised changes such as rearrangement of bulkheads and ensuring the provision of sufficient lavatory accommodation. The two men indented for the 'Red X Stores' (the humanitarian Red Cross organisation) and Lieutenant Colonel Brown was additionally tasked with keeping an officially issued 'Confidential War Dairy' for the time that the ship would spend under the organisation's flag of a red cross on a white ground – a 'negative' of the national flag of Switzerland where the organisation had originated.

To cater for 2,500 patients the ship's public rooms were converted into wards and operating theatres as, being on the upper decks, fresh sea air would aid patients' recovery. Separate wards were provided to segregate men from officers. Even the Promenade Deck had 200 cots fitted along its length, its open aspect to the sea being enclosed with temporary shutters pierced by smaller windows. The walking wounded and sick were berthed in the lower decks, where overcrowding would sometimes overpower the available ventilation.

During the conversion, stores began to arrive and continued to be shipped until 21 October, Trafalgar Day, when RAMC staff members of No. 27 General Hospital arrived along with a military medical detachment. *Mauretania* now carried forty medical officers; seventy-two QAIMNS (Queen Alexandra's Imperial Military Nursing Service) nursing sisters; 120 orderlies (later increased to 150) who did much of the fetching and carrying; accommodation for 2,500 patients; and 850 crew. Also carried were VADs – Voluntary Aid Detachment nurses colloquially known as 'Victim Always Dies' – usually made up of groups of twenty-three women jointly trained and managed by the Red Cross, St John's Ambulance Association and St Andrew's Ambulance Corps, with those of the former organisation wearing a conspicuous red cross on their pinafores. They were there to assist the professionals.

On 18 October, under the terms of the Geneva Convention, the British Government informed the Germans, through a neutral agent, of the *Mauretania's* new role as a hospital carrier. When this employment eventually ceased ta diplomatic note would inform the United States Embassy, who would then notify the German Government. German responses came through diplomatic channels in the neutral Netherlands. Now that the *Mauretania* was a hospital ship her appearance had conspicuously been changed. Gone was the grey and black of her transport livery, gone was the blackout paint from hundreds of portholes – she was completely painted in white except for a 3ft-deep green band along her sheer line broken in three places for red-painted crosses, smaller crosses fore-and-aft (below Bridge and Quarter Deck) and a larger one amidships. The broad green lines tapered off towards the stern, giving her quite a racy appearance and, with funnels painted a light buff the *Mauretania* looked very smart – reminiscent of the graceful, privately owned steam yachts that had graced sporting regattas before the war. At night she would be ablaze with lights, her markings illuminated with green and red electric lights to mark her out as a carrier of mercy and, hopefully, immune from attack.

The ship's conversion into a ship of mercy must have taken on an added imperative as, on the day that work began, the Allied nations were appalled by the 'murder' of a British nurse: Edith Cavell, whose Belgian clinic had been taken over by the Red Cross, chose to remain to bravely aid the wounded of both belligerent sides. But, because she was found to be assisting allied troops to escape, she was arrested, accused of treason, sentenced to death and executed by firing squad. The reputation of the German nation (colloquially known as 'The Hun') plumbed new depths of barbaric awfulness in the eyes of the world.

Captain Rostron called the crew together (as was required when a ship was newly commissioned) to ensure that they knew the seriousness of the work on which they were about to embark before signing on the 'T.124 [Crew Agreement] Articles'. The Captain then read the 'Articles of War', the law practised on every commissioned ship. The first crime to involve the death penalty was that of disobeying a lawful order. As the Captain emphasised the word 'Death', a cook fainted! It might have been because of the Captain's pronouncements that forty deck crew left the ship, discharged by mutual consent just before sailing (22 October) and another twenty-six deserted, perhaps having re-thought their agreeing to serve on any commissioned vessel.

Before departure the liner lay in the River Mersey until 7 p.m., when she sailed for Mudros on her first mission as HMHS *Mauretania*. The weather was thick as she entered the North Channel but cleared by the time the Isles of Scilly were abeam to port at noon the following day. Two days later she was off Lisbon and, on 25 October, passed the Rock and great naval base at Gibraltar. Bridge Messenger, Ordinary Seaman John Breeze (an apt name!) managed to inadvertently drop the 'Number 1 Set' (Deck copy) of the log overboard. The loss could have proved a windfall to any U-boat finding it. Breeze was amongst twenty – including Chief Officer J. Stone – who would leave the ship by mutual consent when it next sailed from Southampton on 7 January. First Officer Bisset took his place.

After a voyage equal to a transatlantic crossing in peacetime, the liner anchored in the Bay of Naples (28 October), taking on coal overnight to get her to the deep, sheltered natural harbour of Mudros, where she arrived on 31 October. She spent the next day topping up her coals from the limited stocks available. Casualties from the Dardanelles began to arrive on 2 November, being brought to Mudros in the small 'feeder' hospital ships *Galeka* (a requisitioned Union Castle steamer) and P&O's *Delta* (painted black and known as 'Black Carriers', these vessels were later painted in Red Cross livery) prior to transhipping the men onto the huge Cunarder. From 3 to 4 November sick and wounded arrived on board, being ferried in brass-funnelled naval pinnaces and motor barges. Stretcher cases were lifted on board in an open box attached to wire stays that, when hoisted by a deck crane, ascended at a speed that astonished the box's occupants. She departed the anchorage at 4 p.m. on

4 November with 2,312 patients but not before suffering the first death aboard when Private T. Calderbank of the 1/5 Manchester Regiment succumbed to his wounds. A member of the 3rd Field Ambulance of the Royal Navy Division (a naval division trained to fight ashore), Private F. Parker, died the following day and, sewn into a canvas shroud with an iron fire-bar at his feet, was buried at sea. Lieutenant Colonel Brown's War Diary for 7 November noted that, when still at sea, Private Lee of the 9th West Yorkshire Regiment succumbed to 'Enteric with perforation'. A post-mortem showed that he had also suffered from gangrene of the bowel. Another Private, Marchant of the 5th Fusiliers, died of dysentery, a common non-combat cause of hundreds of deaths during the ill-fated campaign. Both were committed to the deep.

The homeward-bound cot patients received the very best of medical care, food and comfort in clean surroundings. By 7.35 on the morning of 8 November the *Mauretania* was off Gibraltar where, just before the wireless apparatus broke down, a message ('Signal' in naval parlance) was received asking for accommodation for convalescents consisting of nineteen officers and eighty-one 'Other Ranks'. Wounded soldiers and sailors were not the only ones to suffer: Fireman Bowen succumbed to dysentery and pneumonia while the ship was still anchored off 'Gib'.

On 10 November 1915 the *Mauretania*, with 2,021 patients on board, sailed through the busy sea lanes and anchorages of The Solent for the second time, docking at 1.45 p.m. in the Hampshire port of Southampton, now of great military importance as a base for troopships and hospital ships. Referred to as 'Military Embarkation Port Number One', the port would become her terminus for the next few months. The carefully disembarked stretcher cases were taken to the imposing nearby hospital at Netley, which the ship had passed as she steamed up Southampton Water, and to hospitals throughout Britain. The now khaki-uniformed walking cases paraded on the quayside and marched away. Two days later the liner was put into a ten-day refit to fine-tune her hospital arrangements and make various alterations and additions including:

(1) Gutting E Deck and erection of Double Tier Berths. (2) Gutting C & D [Decks] Aft, Double Tier Berths. (3) Officers dining saloon [relocated] to C1 and old dining saloon converted into a ward for 51 swing cots. (4) Altering aseptic theatre. (5) Altering mens dining room and fitting of [an] antiseptic tank and washstands. (6) Various sanitary improvements. (7) Additions to disinfector and increase of laundry machinery. (8) Erection of Sisters [nurses] Duty Rooms.

On that first day in dock fifty Firemen and Trimmers were discharged, twenty-nine deserted and four failed to join.

Once refitted, His Majesty's Hospital Ship (HMHS) *Mauretania* sailed for Lemnos on 23 November with RAMC details and nurses on board that totalled 748 medical staff. The wards were now able to cater for around 2,000 sick and wounded and it was felt that the sea air and, hopefully, sunshine on the return trip to Britain would greatly benefit the embarked patients. On the day before sailing, Captain Rostron, concerned about the sometimes lax discipline among his crew, which probably led to the earlier mass discharges, requested that a guard of Royal Marines be embarked to enforce order. The Captain informed the Director of Transports (DoT):

With a crew of over 600 we naturally have a certain amount of trouble with the men, having an armed guard on board would to a great extent prevent indiscipline …

He strengthened his argument by adding:

There was an instance a few days ago when the 2nd Officer went down to arrest a man [and] several members of the crew assisted the man to resist arrest. The prisoner was most abusive and insulting to the officer and he was quite powerless until assistance arrived from shore.

The Captain's concerns were based on experience gained from trouble that had occurred on the *Aquitania* back in August when a large number of her crew demanded a week's advance pay, three days' leave and free railway passes to and from their homes – much in line with practices within the Royal Navy. It was considered that these conditions were impossible to grant as the liner was urgently needed as a hospital ship in the Mediterranean. In protest the ship's entire complement of Firemen downed tools and were, with difficulty, persuaded to return to their duties.

The Captain's request was declined, the DoT informing him that he should request such assistance from shore each time the ship returned to Southampton. The Captain took matters into his own hands and informed the PNTO (Principal Naval Transport Officer) at the ATO (Admiralty Transport Office) in Southampton that he intended to have a notice posted in various parts of the crew's quarters, as he felt confident that his men could be 'taught reason … a proper sense of discipline and the obligations that they owe to their country'. He wrote:

As it is my duty to maintain a strict discipline on board, so I also consider it my equal duty to do my utmost for the comfort and fair treatment of every member of the Ship's Company …

… Every man must understand that discipline will be rigorously maintained; but, I hope with a full sense of justice and fairness – without favour to any man …

… I must insist on strict discipline … carrying out all orders, and work in an efficient and orderly manner, and obeying rules and regulations as issued from time to time …

… The wages are good, also the Naval Discipline Act – gives many benefits not obtainable otherwise. Discipline is only a term for 'PLAYING THE GAME' so let us all 'PLAY THE GAME.'

By 8 December the DoT acquiesced and, in the hope of 'avoiding discontent amongst the [*Mauretania*'s] crew', suggested that the men be granted what had been asked for: 'leave on full pay … [and] a free railway ticket [i.e. a warrant issued twice a year]'. These measures would bring the ship into line with the Navy and solve the four-month-old problem. Two weeks later Cunard concurred with the arrangement but requested a trial period before complete acceptance.

November also saw a third giant ship being requisitioned while at the Belfast yard of Harland & Wolff. This was the superb *Britannic*, sister ship to *Olympic* and the lamented *Titanic*. Heavily engineered to incorporate lessons learnt from the loss of the *Titanic*, *Britannic* had been laid down to the order of the White Star Line and launched on 26 February 1914. Her completion was delayed but she was requisitioned as a hospital ship on 13 November 1915, her conversion

costing a staggering £90,000. Her luxury fittings were put into storage without being installed. As with the *Mauretania* and *Aquitania*, her status as a hospital ship would be transmitted to Berlin through a diplomatic note forwarded by the United States Embassy on 6 December 1915.

The *Mauretania* anchored in the Bay of Naples on 28 November after four days at sea, under the volcanic shadow of Vesuvius and alongside the *Aquitania* and an Italian hospital ship the *Regina d'Italia*. Previous to her arrival the German Government had been sending objections to Great Britain, via diplomatic notes passed through neutral embassies, that hospital ships were being used to transport troops, munitions and other military equipment (the basis of these complaints will be seen later). To obviate these objections the Captain opened the big Cunarder for diplomatic inspection and, after a thorough tour of the liner, a certificate was issued by the inspecting officials from three neutral countries:

We, the undersigned, hereby certify that at the request of the Commanding Officers of the ship we have this day visited and inspected His Majesty's hospital ship 'Mauretania' and are satisfied that there are no combatant troops or warlike stores in her, and that the rules of the Geneva Convention are being observed in every way.

Signed on board His Majesty's hospital ship 'Mauretania' this 29th day of November, 1915.

(Signed) S.G. MEURICOFFRE – Swiss Consul-General
JAY WHITE – American Consul
M. VON ORELLI – Danish Consul
H.C. BIAR – American Vice-Consul

Naples, November 29, 1915.

A Dutch informant (probably on the Dutch steamer *Kawi* of Royal Rotterdam Lloyd, also in harbour) later told the Legation at The Hague that the *Aquitania* was 'chock-full of British soldiers, none of whom were wounded' even as the consuls were conducting their inspection! The suspicion of carrying armaments on board a hospital ship had, a few months earlier, brought into question the habit of officers hanging up their pistols and swords by their cots. To prevent infringement, it was suggested that these articles should be stored in a place of safety.

German allegations stemmed from generally low-quality intelligence coming from untrained informants, including German prisoners of war interned on steamers such as the *Ascania* moored in The Solent who swore affidavits that hospital ships would leave Portsmouth for the Continent deeply laden and return riding higher in the water due to war materiel being shipped to the war zone. The British rebuffed the allegations and said it was due to coal being carried for both legs of the voyage that kept the ships down to their marks. The khaki-uniformed men that were reported on board Red Cross vessels were either members of the RAMC or the walking wounded and sick who in some instances still wore their uniforms. Although not fit for military service, these men had generally been laid low by malaria, enteric, frostbite and the endemic dysentery caused by swarms of flies that fed off the putrefaction of unburied bodies and the insanitary conditions of the Peninsula. Cot patients wore 'hospital undress' (a blue uniform with brown piping, and a red tie) while a supply of khaki uniforms was carried on board for non-cot cases to wear when disembarking at Southampton in accordance with the 'Standing Orders and Instructions to Officers Commanding Hospital Ships':

> When on the Mediterranean service … obtain from Ordnance Stores sufficient home-pattern khaki serge clothing, shirts, underclothing, &c., to fit out, on the homeward voyage, the maximum number of sick and wounded the ships are equipped to carry. Hospital clothing will be used for all cot cases.

On the day of sailing from Naples (30 November) an Engineers' Mess Steward, David Cohen, was diagnosed as insane after triple attempts at suicide; he was 'placed in a padded room with attendants on watch' and handed over to the relevant authorities on the ship's return to Southampton, probably being taken to the large psychiatric compound behind the Netley Hospital. HMHS *Mauretania* reached Mudros on 2 December, being guided through the protective anti-submarine netting and anchored, sometimes in company with the *Aquitania*, dwarfing the myriad of vessels of all nations and all sizes moored in lines around her, from barges, trawlers and tugs to large warships from Britain, France and Russia. She quickly embarked both cot and walking patients from the 'Black Carriers' *Delta*, *Devanha*, *Soudan* (requisitioned P&O liners) and *Nevasa* (British India), and evacuees from the shore hospital, brought there from floating dressing stations anchored off the Suvla, Hellas and ANZAC beaches, and from Malta and Alexandria.

An hour after the *Mauretania* sailed for home on 4 December Private H. Poole (No. 10369, 8th Cheshire Regiment) became yet another victim of dysentery and was buried at sea. His passing was added to three similar deaths from that same disease that was claiming so many lives, especially ashore. Even non-combatant medical staff were not immune as sufferer QAIMNS Staff Nurse Miss Stanley was transferred to Netley, where she later succumbed to that dreaded affliction.

After three days at sea, fuelling for the homeward journey was undertaken by scores of Neapolitans carrying coal in baskets to the ship's bunkering ports; she sailed from the Bay of Naples the next morning (8 December) at 7.33. Accompanied by the Sanitary Officer and the Medical Director of the Cunard Line, Lieutenant Colonel Brown led an inspection of the ship's sanitary facilities, noting several improvements for action on the ship's return to England. *Mauretania* paused in the Bay of Gibraltar for a couple of hours on the 10th, where she was boarded by naval officers seeking confirmation of the numbers of sick on board. The liner was under way by 10 p.m., rolling into a north-west wind. Two hours after arriving in Southampton at 7 a.m. on 14 December her evacuated invalids were disembarked, the walking sick in their khaki lining up on the quayside as before while the cot cases were carefully stretchered to waiting ambulance trains. Fifty-two Firemen and Trimmers were discharged before a Board of Trade superintendent in Southampton on 15 December and many more similarly left the ship or deserted between 23 December and 4 January 1916, thirty-one alone leaving the ship on 4 January! Deserters, when found, were arrested in homes, pubs and dosshouses and punished according to the law.

Meanwhile, the recently completed HMHS *Britannic* sailed from Liverpool on 23 December 1915 on her unexpected maiden voyage to the Mediterranean theatre; her subsequent sailings would be from

Southampton. References made to the '3 Big Ships' now included the new ship as *Olympic* never became a hospital ship and transferred her troop-transporting duties across the North Atlantic to Canada.

The year 1916 had not begun well. Battlefield casualties mounted distressingly and, even though Lord Kitchener's exhortation 'Your Country Needs You' had encouraged over a million volunteers to enlist in the 'New Army', more men were needed to feed the trenches' dreadful and insatiable hunger. So in March Parliament passed the 'Military Service Act' that compulsorily conscripted single men (with designated exceptions) to join the fight. But even this was not sufficient and, on 16 May, conscription was extended to include married men. The *Lusitania* tragedy of the previous year was milked for propaganda purposes and recruitment campaigns. Posters exhorted 'Irishmen, Avenge the *Lusitania!*' but this campaign was soon dropped, although thousands of Irishmen still volunteered as British problems had spread into home territory when the Irish Rising began in Dublin on Easter Monday (24 April). This was an an event that would undoubtedly have also affected the loyalties of many of the *Mauretania's* crew, especially in the Stokehold that counted many Irish and Liverpool-Irish amongst its number. Loyalties must have been hard-pressed. Ironically, the architect of the 'New Army', Field Marshal Horatio Kitchener, 1st Earl Kitchener, lost his own life in June when HMS *Hampshire,* on which he was travelling on a diplomatic mission to Russia, struck a mine in foul weather and sank.

HMHS *Mauretania* had been berthed at the White Star Dock at Southampton for two weeks before sailing on her third deployment to the Mediterranean at noon on 7 January. By now the Gallipoli Campaign had been strategically abandoned as a total failure and Allied troops were secretly evacuated from the Peninsula, much to the Turks' delighted surprise. While passing Ushant the next day the *Mauretania* passed the brand-new *Britannic*, homeward bound with her first embarkation of patients. The Cunarder made a call in at Naples on 12 January, followed by arrival in a crowded Mudros Bay at 4.45 p.m. two days later – but there were no ships at hand to start transferring patients to the *Mauretania*. A breeze from the south-east grew from 'fresh' to 'strong', causing the ship's Navigators to shift the liner to a new anchorage at 8 o'clock the next morning.

Embarkation of patients began on the 16th from the smaller 'feeder' hospital (or ambulance) ships *Morea* (P&O), *Panama* (Pacific Steam Navigation Company), *Gloucester Castle* (Union Castle) and *Essequibo* (Royal Mail Steam Packet Company) and continued into the next day. It was on this day that the *Mauretania*, *Aquitania* and *Britannic*, along with several other hospital ships and carriers, received signals that they were no longer required as the War Office had decided that there were too many such vessels employed in the service. Now that the Gallipoli Campaign had been brought to an end (its failure had extorted a high human cost: 56,000 Allied soldiers and other military personnel had lost their lives and over 123,000 men were either wounded or invalided out of the battle with disease) only thirty-four ships out of the current forty-two with a carrying capacity of around 28,700 evacuees (of which the '3 Big Ships' could carry 9,090 patients) were considered necessary. It was considered advantageous that smaller ships could now transport patients directly home rather than tranship them to the larger liners.

In contrast, a Department of Transport official opined that there was no real disadvantage in transhipping patients brought from Malta, Alexandria and Salonika to the larger hospital ships and these latter vessels should be retained because of their high speed and favourable rates of hire service and, instead, some of the smaller ships should be discharged, as these could better be employed elsewhere. It was calculated that the '3 Big [hospital] Ships' could carry 27,000 patients over three trips each in two months at a cost of £318,000, which represented a cost of around £11/15s (£11.75) per man – or 0.94d (penny) per man per mile (each leg of the voyage being about 3,800 miles), whereas the smaller, slower ships had costs of 2d per man per mile. *Mauretania* had carried 6,298 sick and wounded men attended by 2,307 medical personnel during her three voyages as a hospital ship. Another message sent to the War Office on 15 January proposed that it was intended 'to give up Aquitania, Mauretania and Britannic and 7 additional hospital ships', but arguments were still maintained that, in spite of approval being given for the ships' releases on the 17th, a Mr Graham Greene at the War Office opined that the three liners should be retained and the seven smaller ships be released.

On HMHS *Mauretania's* third and final return trip in her current guise and with 1,974 patients on board, many with frostbitten feet, Naples was reached at 4.30 p.m. on 19 January 1916, where she coaled and watered before sailing for Southampton two days later. At noon the next day the Chief Steward, Robert Davies, developed delirium tremens and was placed off-duty. Confined to his quarters under guard, he was sent to St Mary's Hospital on arrival back in Southampton four days later. Ten Firemen and Trimmers were taken off the ship on 8 February and sent to the Naval Detention Quarters at Portsmouth but later discharged. The liner remained alongside her berth until 9 February when she cast off, sailed slowly down Southampton Water, and moored in the busy naval anchorage off Ryde, Isle of Wight, by The Motherbank south of Spithead. At 4 p.m. that afternoon tenders came alongside and took off the nursing sisters and medical detachments.

Berlin was notified that the liner was no longer on the list of hospital ships so, presumably, was reinstated as a legitimate target and it could be assumed that, while at anchor, the vessel's hospital ship livery was painted over with grey camouflage paint to substantiate her non-medical role. Great concern was raised while anchored off Ryde's Cottage Hospital when Fireman Robert Tesman was taken ashore to Ryde on 13 February after developing symptoms of paratyphoid sometimes caused by poor sanitation. The condition could have been carried on board by a patient from Mudros or by crowded conditions in poorly ventilated Fireman's quarters. As the tides ebbed and flowed, the *Mauretania* swung at her anchor for several days until a decision was made to dispense with the ship's services altogether.

The next day the British were notified that the Italian Naval Authorities had raised objections to the use of Naples for the transfer of patients from small vessels to the larger ships due to 'the danger of infection at that port'. The Italians suggested that the larger ships should still coal there from Admiralty stock and then proceed to Augusta (subject to approval by the Navigation Department at the Admiralty) on the east coast of Sicily and embark patients there. The Master of the *Britannic* expressed his agreement but there was neither coal, water nor useful jetties at that alternative port and difficulty was experienced in transferring patients from ship to ship. A month later the proposed new arrangements were rescinded.

Answering questions about the now laid-up ships, T. Ashley Sparks, Resident Director of the Cunard Line in New York, said that despite articles published before the war there were no plans to convert the big Cunarders into freight (wheat) carriers. It had been costing the Admiralty £45,000 a month to run the *Mauretania* (£57,000 each for the *Aquitania* and *Britannic*) – £15,352 for the hire of the ship; £6,500 for fitting; insurance was £1,200; miscellaneous items were £5,000; but the heftiest expense was coal, the bill running to a massive £17,000! The two Cunarders were eventually joined, on 21 February, by the *Britannic* and the three giant liners lay idle in The Solent in the same waters where, a few short years' earlier, kings and princes had raced their yachts and reviewed great fleets of battleships, and where ironically the Kaiser had been weighed down with British honours. The '3 Big Ships' were soon to be obscured from view by heavy snowstorms and, without adequate heating, the liners made for very cold accommodation.

Some confusion arose about the ships' futures. As there was no other work on which they could be employed, the War Office telegrammed that they could be released but at the same time confusingly recommended that they be kept and to release seven smaller ships instead. After much on-board activity, the *Mauretania* was once again readied for sea, this time destined for Liverpool. She left The Solent at 9.52 on the morning of 24 February. A coastal voyage up through British waters saw her arriving in the River Mersey the next day. Four days later on, 29 February (1916 being a leap year), she was discharged from Government service as a hospital ship and Lieutenant Colonel Frank Brown RAMC, Officer Commanding (OC) Troops, wrote his last entry into the Confidential War Diary simply stating:

Ship being no longer required I handed over charge.

His Official War Diary would later be handed over to the Committee for the Medical History of the War to join thousands of others. Cunard was paid the previously estimated £60,000 'to cover the cost of reconditioning and hire during reconditioning'. Another recorded date for the liner's discharge was 1 March, so the probability was that she was struck from the register at midnight. After a period of being on half-hire with her hospital fitting intact, the *Aquitania* was discharged on 8 March and her reconditioning, costing a hefty £90,000, for a return to the Atlantic service was brought into effect on 10 April.

A few weeks later the Royal Navy faced its greatest test since the Battle of Trafalgar. Intelligence received from Room 40 on 31 May indicated that the German *Hochseeflotte* (High Seas Fleet) had sailed from Wilhelmshaven in Lower Saxony in an attempt to lure the Grand Fleet into a U-boat trap in the hope of reducing British naval superiority. The Royal Navy responded and 250 ships and 10,000 men of two navies raced towards each other over the waters of the North Sea. Although the German fleet was outgunned and outnumbered, the spectre of Britain losing the battle loomed large as defeat would not only destroy the effective blockade of Germany but Britain would be cut off from vital supplies and open the country to invasion. Churchill said of Admiral of the Fleet, John Jellicoe, that he was the 'the only man on either side who could lose the war in an afternoon'.

The German ruse to draw the British into a trap did not go to plan and in the late afternoon a sea battle off the Jutland peninsula ensued (the Battle of Jutland) that lasted for thirty-four hours. The Germans, in order to preserve some of its fleet and maintain 'A Fleet in being', headed for home. The British, fearing the strategically fleeing Germans were leading them into a submarine and mine trap, did not pursue. Although both sides claimed victory (the Royal Navy lost more ships, fourteen, along with 6,097 lives against German losses of eleven ships and 2,551 men), ultimate victory would be claimed by the British as the German fleet never again ventured out into the 'German Sea'. However, as a result of this inactivity U-boat development and numbers increased to such an extent that they threatened the very survival of the British Isles with a blockade of their own. The immobile *Hochseeflotte* remained in harbour, where inactivity bred discontent amongst the *matrose* until mutiny afloat and revolution ashore erupted. After Jutland there were no fast surface raiders capable of catching the *Mauretania* and submarines were too slow, especially when submerged.

After some disagreement between the War Office and the Transport Division on whether to retain the *Britannic* on half-hire for three or four months in case of an emergency arising (the latter department advised the Army Council that it would be wise to do so), the War Office insisted that she be discharged on 21 May (the crew was paid off on that day), but *Britannic* was not officially released from Government service until 6 June. Although £76,000 was paid for her reconditioning, only a little of the work was undertaken because of other essential war work. The ship would remain in lay-up, complete with fittings, until 28 August.

12

'HUSH THE SOUNDS OF WAR ...'

(William Gaskell)

On the Western Front the bloodletting continued when, at 7.30 on 1 July 1916, a joint push by the French and British began. After a week's heavy shelling over a 15-mile front, a series of shrill, monotone whistles sounded and the first waves of British troops left their trenches to 'Go over the top'. Advancing at a walking pace towards the enemy's lines, German machine guns had easy pickings and at the awful day's end 19,240 British lives had been lost, with double that number being either wounded, captured or missing. It was, by far, the worst day in British military history. Twelve days later, back in Britain desperate messages, ostensibly from General Haig, were circulated asking for a postponement of general holidays in Britain in order to help the war effort. By the time that the Battle of the Somme ground to an inglorious and bloody end after 141 days of slaughter there was an unbelievable tally of one million casualties in the British, French and their allies' ranks as well as on the German side. The horrendous land conflict in Europe had deteriorated into a war of attrition as both sides faced each other from networks of trenches, quite often with only a few yards between them, each belligerent pounding the other with industrial might. These trenches were hungry for men and to help feed that hunger on the Allied side troops had to be brought from all over the British Empire and Dominions. The next role of the *Mauretania* would help sate that deadly hunger.

Meanwhile, the *Britannic* was reactivated on 28 August when she was called to serve in the Mediterranean after hostilities erupted in the Balkans. A relatively small campaign in Salonika against the Bulgarians had escalated and an attempt was being made to divert German troops from the Western Front. Two other British offensives against the Turks in Palestine and Mesopotamia ensured that the hospital stations at Mudros were once again operational with patients arriving from Africa and India.

As Allied troops were needed urgently, it was proposed on 2 September that both *Aquitania* and *Mauretania* be entered into pay as Military Transports to convey thousands of badly needed Canadian troops, apparently all well-behaved and eager to 'finish the job'. The *Mauretania* would be 'eminently suitable' for this task and it was intended that she should be taken up and run along the same lines as the *Olympic*, which had started her service on the Canadian shuttle from Liverpool on 23 March. In response to a request for an estimate for how long it would take to prepare the *Mauretania* for service, Cunard responded that the ship had already been reconditioned and could be readied for service in about ten days to accommodate 3,200 troops. However, should the ship's carrying capacity be required to be increased for up to 5,000 then the time needed for conversion would be four weeks. From experience with the *Olympic* it was thought that it would be better to accept her with her currently available capacity, so she was accordingly requisitioned as a troopship on 29 September 'for use on urgent Government Service under the condition of Pro Forma Charter Party T.99c'. As an incentive the crew were to receive an increased bonus of £2 per month, paid to all ratings except Ordinary Seamen and boys, the latter two categories only getting £1.

This scheme was to remain in place for the continuance of the war. A week later, on 7 October, the *Mauretania* was again 'On His Majesty's Service' with Captain James Charles in command. He would remain in post for two months, other than for a short spell when Captain Rostron took over. F. Manley was Chief Officer and A. Allan the Chief Engineer.

Leaving Liverpool after dark at 9.27 on 12 October, HMTS *Mauretania* sailed for Halifax, Nova Scotia, but tragedy struck early in the voyage. Private Dougal MacDonald raised the alarm after 23-year-old Trimmer W. Downey was seen to jump overboard. The ship was immediately stopped but the crew of the hastily lowered emergency boat could find no trace of the assumed suicide.

After a crossing of six days, the big troopship arrived at her Canadian destination at 1.53 p.m. on the 18th. After seven days in port spent coaling, painting and embarking troops, she sailed on the 25th shortly after midnight. On the second day out a stowaway was found, Signal Boy J. Cameron from HMS *Niobe*, who would be handed over to the Naval Authorities following the ship's arrival home early in the morning (4.13) on 31 October. The crossing to Liverpool met with a tremendous gale, one of the worst experienced, even for that part of the world, which blew, almost without interruption, for several days. So heavy were the seas that HMSs *Brisk* and *Archer* of the Second Destroyer Flotilla, sent out from Queenstown to escort the *Mauretania* through the danger zone of the Western Approaches, had to run for shelter in Berehaven Harbour in Bantry Bay. It might have been the ferocity of the gale that caused unrest amongst the crew as, on the day after berthing, fifty-three crew members were discharged before a Board of Trade superintendent and thirty-four failed to join. Before her second departure for Halifax at 9.19 a.m. on 12 November another forty-six Firemen and Trimmers deserted. As before, the ship carried civilian passengers travelling on war business.

During the crossing the ship rolled slightly in a moderate sea and fresh breeze. While making his evening inspection rounds, the Staff Chief Engineer, Andrew Cockburn (who had been Senior Second Engineer on the *Lusitania*'s final voyage), noticed water seeping from under a bunker door. Leaving instructions to be called if the situation worsened, he was later awoken by Chief Engineer A. Allan telling him that it had and to request the Captain to stop the ship. But before waking the Captain the Staff Chief Engineer thought it best to see the flooding for himself and what he saw was disturbing. By this time the ingress of water had increased to such an extent that the lower furnaces of the boilers had been extinguished and the Stokehold crew were fighting to clear ash-blocked pumps as they attempted to clear the trespassing Atlantic as it rose and fell with the movement of the ship. There was so much dangerous free surface (a large area of water that has nothing to break its movement to either side) that the ship had taken on a worrying list, putting the *Mauretania*'s stability at risk. Captain Charles, now wide awake, ordered the ship to be put about so that the breeze came on the other side, helping to alleviate the list and give the men, struggling up to their necks in water, a chance to unblock the pumps.

This nightmare situation had been caused through the lack of the essential application – either accidentally or even deliberately – of water-tight caulking (candlewick soaked in white lead) woven round the fastening bolts of the coal ports in the ship's side before the bolts were securely tightened, even though this had been reported as being done back in Liverpool after coaling. Now, as the waters gradually receded as the husbanded pumps took effect, men clambered into the bunkers to repack the coal chute doors to prevent a reoccurrence of the flooding.

After this near disaster the *Mauretania* made a 5.50 a.m. arrival into Halifax where, over the next few days, she took on coal and stores prior to embarking her next contingent of Canadian soldiers who were to play a vital, but costly, part in the war. She eventually sailed at 4.45 p.m. on 24 November, arriving in Liverpool at 11.25 on the night of the 29th, when the last Canadian troops that she would carry were disembarked. The ship, being both too valuable and expensive to run, was laid up. Captain Charles left his command just twelve days before Christmas.

Meanwhile, the *Britannic* had made five successful sailings to the Mediterranean but, on the outward leg of her sixth voyage, carrying medical staff only, she was passing through the Kea Channel between the islands of Kea and Makronisos when, at 8.12 on the morning of 21 November, she struck a mine that had been laid by the *U-73* five weeks previously. The initial impression that a mine was involved was neglected by press reports that suggested a torpedo attack, a mis-assessment eagerly grabbed by Whitehall propagandists. She started to sink quickly and an attempt was made to beach her on Kea, but the giant liner's fate was sealed. As she sank, two lifeboats were drawn into the still-rotating propellers; thirty lives were lost and a further forty injured. Within fifty-five minutes of the explosion *Britannic* was at the bottom of the Aegean in 400ft of water, the largest merchant vessel to be lost in the Great War. One of the survivors of that horrible experience was Nurses' Stewardess Violet Jessop; she had been on board *Olympic* when the liner was rammed by HMS *Hawke* in 1911 and had also survived the sinking of the *Titanic* seven months later.

David Lloyd George succeeded Herbert Henry Asquith as Prime Minister after a short bout of political manoeuvring and, building on his successes in tax and social reforms, extended his radical ideas into government. Out went the old style of government by 'gentlemen's agreements' and in came methodical government by specialised committees, including the running of the 'War to End All Wars'. And so 1916 ended as it had begun with Britain still in a critical state but at least munitions factories, some run by Cunard, had begun to make up critical shortages on the Front.

Even after Jutland and the corralling of the High Seas Fleet the German Navy still thought that it had a fighting chance with its newer long-range submarines. On 9 January 1917, Germany announced its intention to recommence unrestricted submarine warfare and this resolution came into effect on 1 February. Although this measure had the full support of the Kaiser, the deadly decision was made against the advice of many high-placed Germans who considered that, although Americans were bringing war supplies to the Allies and were now targets, it would increase the risk of pulling the still-neutral United States into the war. One hundred and five U-boats were ready to sink – without warning - a planned monthly target of 600,000 tons of shipping, roughly twelve ships a day, which would outpace Britain's ability to replace them. Known as 'The Killing Time', this target would be exceeded in May when 230 valuable Allied ships, totalling 464,599 tons, were sent to the ocean floor, 50 per cent more than the previous month's total. Added to that appalling figure a further 300 ships were tied up in British ports unwilling to take their chances at sea. The Admiralty stubbornly refused to adopt a convoy system, still considering the scheme would put too many ships at risk at one time. Losses soared. Germany continued to

accuse the British of illegally using hospital ships to transport troops and war materials, and these allegations reached an impasse. As a result, on 28 January a specified area around Britain was declared a War Zone. This area, extending from Land's End to Ushant on the western side and Flamborough Head to Terschelling on the eastern, was one in which hospital ships became legitimate targets. The Mediterranean was similarly declared an exclusion area.

Troopship *Mauretania*, again unemployed, languished in safe lay-up for two months on the Cunard Buoy on the Sloyne. Around 23 January 1917, she received instructions to sail for the River Clyde. As she weighed anchor to leave the Mersey at 7 p.m. a south-easterly gale was blowing and, combined with a strong tide, the port cable parted. The starboard anchor could not be let go until the ship was facing downstream but it, too, parted. A tug tender (presumably Cunard's own *Skirmisher*) took the liner's sturdy manila hawser but that, too, broke. The ship was now unmanageable and drifted, luckily avoiding collision with other vessels, until coming gently to rest on a sandbank. Eventually she was pulled free, whereupon Captain Rostron took her out to sea for safety and waited for daylight when, it still being too rough to use the Cunard Buoy, he took his ship into the Gladstone Dock on the 25th to await the recovery of the missing anchors. Finally, on 29 January 1917, and engaged under 'Home Trade Only' articles, she left Liverpool, albeit in thick fog, bound for the Clyde – those very waters that had given her sister *Lusitania* her first feel of the sea. If her ratings were on a monthly rate of £11 or less they were paid £4 for the coastal journey. She had on board eighty additional Firemen (making a total of 147) along with seventy-nine Trimmers, sixty-six Electricians, Greasers, Donkeymen, Plumbers and Storemen and, for the comfort and sustenance of those on board, thirty-four Butchers, Chefs, Bedroom Stewards, Bakers and Waiters who were engaged for the 'Liverpool to Glasgow' run. On arrival, the men were paid 7 shillings Detention Money per day while she remained at anchor off Greenock.

While at anchor at the Tail o'the Bank dissatisfaction arose when, on 16 April, a group including sixteen Greasers, a Donkeyman, seven Leading Firemen, eight Trimmers and a Storeman were accused of contravening Regulation 39A of the Defence of the Realm Regulations by 'causing disaffection amongst persons engaged … in His Majesty's Service'. Their contravention of an Act of Parliament that had been rushed through to 'strictly command and enjoin our subjects to obey and conform to all instructions and regulations which may be issued by us or our admiralty or army council' was caused by refusing to obey a 'lawful command of the Chief Engineer A. Allan re-the firing of the Donkey Boiler on April 16 at 2.45 p.m. and are therefore prosecuted'. All the accused protested, saying that 'there was no refusal of duty and that it was a trumped-up charge'.

Mauretania returned to Liverpool in May, where 60-year-old Captain William 'Bowler Bill' Turner (late of the *Lusitania*) took charge of her in the Gladstone Dock on the 9th. The Captain had been given command of some of Cunard's smaller ships since the *Lusitania* had been torpedoed and recently, on New Year's Day 1917, the transport *Ivernia,* carrying 2,800 troops from Salonika to Alexandria, had been torpedoed from under him by *UB-47*, 58 miles off Cape Matapan. Now employed in a standby 'caretaker' capacity having reached retirement age, he was returning the *Mauretania* to Scottish waters, where she again anchored in lay-up off Greenock.

Three thousand miles away, the President of the United States, Woodrow Wilson, had finally lost patience with Germany's strategy of unrestricted submarine warfare, and appeared before Congress on 3 February to officially announce a break in relations with the German Empire. Two months later on 6 April the United States, even though it had only a small standing army, declared war on Germany. There was now an urgent need to enlist and train 2.8 million volunteers before transporting them overseas. The new troops would not be fully ready before late spring 1917. As the popular song promised:

Over there, over there,

Send the word, send the word over there

That the Yanks are coming, the Yanks are coming

The drums rum-tumming everywhere.

So prepare, say a prayer,

Send the word, send the word to beware –

We'll be over, we're coming over,

And we won't come back till it's over, over there …

… and somehow 'The Yanks' had to get to Europe.

Captain Turner had been charged to remain by the *Mauretania* until the end of the current half-year, i.e. 30 June, but if he or Cunard decided to terminate his agreement then two days' notice on either side was required or two days' pay forfeited. Turner was in command of the Cunarder when she made a third visit to Liverpool's Gladstone Dock on 16 July before returning to the Clyde, where she arrived four days later, the Captain having again been charged 'to remain by the ship until the end of the half year viz 31st December 1917'. Among those leaving the ship while anchored off Greenock was one man sent ashore to the Greenock Royal Infirmary, and an Able-Bodied seaman, G. MacAlpine, assessed as being insane, was committed to Greenock's Smithston Asylum and Workhouse. There were four deserters. Just after Christmas, preparations were made to return to Liverpool and, in the event of any delay, the crew was promised 7/6d detention money for any delay after twelve hours should the tide at the Mersey Bar be missed, plus 1/6d an hour (2/- at weekends) overtime in the event of the men 'being called upon to perform any extra services outside their ordinary duties'. Captain Rostron seems to have arrived on board the ship on 9 January 1918 to bring her down to Liverpool, where she arrived the following day.

The ship was yet again On His Majesty's Service. Captain Charles again took over the ship on 24 January 1918 and remained in command until 4 March, when he left to take over the *Aquitania* as her own captain, Smith, was ill. Arthur Rostron took over the *Mauretania* on the 5th and noted that she was fully gunned as an 'Armed Merchant Cruiser', although she was technically an armed troopship. Details of the ship's movements for this period were not readily available at the time of writing as a log was not kept, an oversight for which the Captain would later be censured by the Mercantile Marine Office.

Protection of a ship against attack was always a primary concern and, from 1914 to 1915, attempts were made to blend a ship with prevailing weather. Zoologist Dr John Graham Kerr advocated the use of broad areas of pastel colours such as blue or pink to camouflage vessels but, by the summer of 1915, these early schemes had been found to be ineffective and abandoned. Smoke and constantly changing conditions at sea were always indications of a ship's presence! Concerned about

Two schemes of dazzle were applied to the *Mauretania*, each having a different pattern on each side. This shows the first scheme, which employed sweeping, almost organic, curves. (Courtesy of Eric Sauder)

the ineffectiveness of nature-based schemes to camouflage, hide or disguise a ship and, after observing ships painted in uniform tones of greys, noted maritime artist Norman Wilkinson (now a Lieutenant RNVR) submitted a radical proposal in early 1917 that would render a vessel's identity, course and speed difficult to ascertain. He advocated bold disjointed blocks and stripes of colour with opposing rhythmic patterns of movement. Wilkinson wrote to the Admiralty on 27 April 1917, outlining his proposal:

> ... paint a ship with large patches of strong colour in a carefully thought out pattern and colour scheme, which will so distort the form of the vessel that the chances of successful aim [i.e. difficulty in ascertaining heading] by attacking Submarines will be greatly decreased.

The canny Lieutenant emphasised that, if adopted, his ideas would involve the use of readily available paints so that designs could be cheaply, easily and quickly implemented. About nine colours, largely pastel shades ranging from mauve to yellow, as well as greys, black and white, were suggested. The Admiralty was reasonably quick to adopt

the extraordinary proposal and by 16 June the first ship, HMS *Industry*, had been experimentally painted. The new scheme became known as 'Dazzle'. The Americans, too, were quick in adopting the idea (under Wilkinson's guidance), eventually adorning the massive USS *Leviathan* (ex-*Vaterland*) with her own distinctive dazzle in November 1917.

By October the British Admiralty issued instructions that the British Mercantile Marine in its entirety should be dazzle painted as well as warships involved in escorting the by now vital convoys.

> It has been decided to paint all merchant vessels and armed merchant ships, and certain of HM Ships, with the 'dazzle' scheme of painting.
>
> This scheme is based on the principle that invisibility at sea being unattainable, some protection may be afforded by painting ships in such a way as to confuse an enemy submarine, and by causing doubts as to the course, speed and distance, thus delay the discharge of the torpedo and cause uncertainty of aim.
>
> A number of designs are in preparation which will enable a suitable plan to be selected for any particular ship that may come in hand for refit or painting.

Officers are being selected who will represent the Director of Naval Equipment at all the principal shipping ports, and who will be furnished with plans prepared by the Admiralty.

Wilkinson was instructed to design a unique dazzle scheme for the mighty *Mauretania* incorporating a pattern of 'organic' shapes that included sweeping curves, undulating and diagonal lines (static 'targetable' vertical lines were to be avoided), with greys, olive and blue-grey as well as black and white being used, the colours toned where needed to lighter shades. A different pattern was used port and starboard. Wilkinson's scheme initially proposed for the *Mauretania* ('Type 19 Design A') was, however, given to the *Olympic* as she was already in service as a transport. The ex-*Mauretania* scheme included the painting of a faux blue shadow on the *Olympic's* starboard side under her Bridge, suggesting the presence of an overhead 'blimp', a tethered non-rigid airship of the type used for anti-submarine observation. On other vessels, faux shadows of guns would hopefully discourage any lurking submarine commander.

The first of two schemes for *Mauretania* was designated 'Type 19 Design BX', and retained some of the rhythmic shapes of earlier Wilkinson patterns. The design was transferred to the ship (possibly in February 1918) in readiness for her role in transporting thousands of US troops to Europe. To accommodate the arc of cannon fire, the bulwarks on her foredeck were shortened and obstructing railings removed, as were the wooden covers that concealed the reinforced mounting pads onto which four forward 6in guns and two aft on the Poop Deck were bolted. Perhaps, while not performing her expensively designed role as an actual Armed Merchant Cruiser, she would still be able to make a good account of herself if attacked.

Additional equipment included searchlights mounted on the after Docking Bridge, and a large lamp attached to the foremast just below the cross-tree. At the after-end of the ship, boat booms, three on each side, were stowed at an upward outward angle with their heels hinged to the ship's side below the plated-in Second Class Smoke Room promenade and these could be lowered by steel wires worked by a winch until they projected horizontally from the ship. In an emergency, men could evacuate the ship by holding on to a lifeline while edging their way outboard before clambering down a Jacob's ladder into one of the many disembarked life rafts that added to the lifesaving capacity of the ship.

From late 1917, and in anticipation of a build-up of American military assistance to the allied side, the Germans planned an offensive and built up a massive army augmented by troops released from the Eastern Front after the second (October) Revolution had taken Russia out of the war. As a result, the Germans broke through Allied lines in the spring offensive that became variously known as the *Kaiserschlacht* (Kaiser's Battle) or the 'Ludendorff Offensive'; the major attack was the 'Michael Offensive' of 21 March 1918. A million shells were fired on the first day and great losses occurred in the confused enemy lines. However, initial spectacular gains proved unsustainable and the German initiative ultimately failed.

To support the massive East-bound movement of US military manpower to Europe, the *Mauretania* played her part, her first contingent comprising the Ninth and Twelfth Regiments of Railway Engineers. Their arrival in Britain was supposed to have been secret but a plethora of Stars and Stripes flags flying in Liverpool put paid to that plan! A few days after the German offensive began a US army chaplain, Frederick Morse Cutler, left American shores on HMTS *Mauretania* with his unit to join the quarter-of-a-million of their fellow citizens already on British and European soil. On board were about 4,000 'Doughboys' mainly from the Chaplain's 55th Artillery (C.A.C.) – one of six new Coastal Artillery Regiments detailed to join the American Expeditionary Force – as well as the 65th Artillery (C.A.C.); Base Hospital Unit 116; and Medical Department Unit L. Two hundred Red Cross nurses sailed with the medical staff. The men had been embarked twenty-four hours prior to departure and spent time assessing 'the conditions under which they were going to race with the submarines'.

Chaplain Cutler later penned his experiences in *The 55th Artillery [C.A.C.] in the American Expeditionary Forces, France*, in which he recalls a typical crossing in the mighty troopship that left New York on 'Mch [March] 25, 1918':

Mahogany furnishings had been removed, so that twenty soldiers could be comfortable in a cabin where one fussy globe-trotter formerly lived in state; but it did seem peculiar to see upper berths, made of rough pine boards, nailed to the exquisite fancy woodwork of the first class cabins, where there had been only lower berths originally. The sick-bays were larger and also more workmanlike; the palatial dining-saloons were now plain mess-rooms ... In fact the giant engines down below were all that reminded one of the old 'Mauretania.'

Capt. Rostron was able to best describe his own methods of war-time navigation. 'We always make the trip alone, with an escort only at each end of the journey. We cannot travel in a convoy ...

The protective convoy system had only been brought into being on 24 May in 1917 as a result of unsustainable losses to U-boats; the Royal Navy had previously been stubbornly reluctant to commit valuable warships to convoy – in any case, the *Mauretania* was too fast and valuable to be hindered by the slow speed of a convoy, as Captain Rostron told the Chaplain ...

The others [merchant ships and escorts] cannot keep up with us. Our average speed in 22 to 23 knots, and our fastest clip is 25 knots. Our motto is to get there and not look for trouble.

The Chaplain recalled that before sailing security around the ship's berth heightened as 'divers were dragging the ship's bottom to forestall any possible danger from enemy mines'. At the time of sailing (5.47 p.m.) the *Mauretania*'s 'siren shrieked the signal to start; all men in uniform were ordered to conceal themselves indoors so as to camouflage the presence of troops on board' – rather surprising as the *Mauretania*'s purpose was well known; this order might have been to prevent a rush of men to the starboard side hoping to view the Statue of Liberty, thereby imperilling the ship's stability.

[T]he 'Mauretania' backed her huge bulk out into the Hudson River, slowly pointed her prow towards the open sea and majestically made her way past the statue which symbolized the object of our crusade, thru [sic] the Narrows and on, on, into the deepening night; the 'great adventure' had begun for the 55th ...

Feeding the troops was undertaken in two or three forty-five-minute sittings and was achieved by the construction of eighteen cafeteria-style serving counters where the queuing men were quickly served. Mealtimes were so busy that a careful watch ensured that an occasional hungry soldier did not rejoin a queue for seconds! Meals were often taken up on deck, which obviated mess below. A Steward remarked about the difference between transporting Canadian troops as against American in the danger zone: the former would sit around glumly, reading prayer books, etc., but their American counterparts who were drawing Foreign Service Pay would be singing, playing 'craps', or asking noisily when the next meal would appear!

Captain Rostron insisted on random 'Abandon Ship' exercises being held and completed in his specified time. These drills that commenced from the time that the ship left America kept the 'boys' on their toes and took place:

twice a day, when, at the bugle call, all moved promptly to assigned positions and stood in readiness to jump into life-boats. Confusion marked the first drill or two, but the discipline of the two regiments soon asserted its sway, and the nearly four thousand Americans acquired the ability to move from all parts of the vessel, absolutely emptying all the cabins, and to form line, six deep, around the outer edge of the lower decks – and to do it all within five minutes ...

The time taken to muster all the troops was originally not to Captain Rostron's satisfaction and under his assertive blue-eyed gaze the time taken to muster the troops on the Boat Deck was reduced from thirty minutes to the time that he demanded – three-and-a-half minutes – and the fastest time for an exercise was achieved by springing a surprise 'Boat stations' after dinner! But it was good exercise, maintained morale and kept the men busy. A strict blackout was vigorously enforced, with lights sheltered from outside observation and a ban placed on smoking on deck after nightfall. It was realised that in a real emergency there would be confusion at any time of the day:

There were not enough life-boats to provide one for each group of forty men, and some groups would have to depend upon life rafts which were carried on the hurricane deck; officers in charge of groups sometimes wondered who should go first if it really became necessary to abandon ship. The majors in command of the decks refused to determine questions of precedence, and so the captains and lieutenants tried to thresh it out for themselves. All officers attended these drills armed in case of possible panic, and even the Chaplain [the writer] came with a loaded automatic, hanging from his belt.

On Easter Day a bugler sounded 'Abandon Ship' in error and it was thought that a genuine emergency had arisen, but a lesson had been learnt and from then on no one was allowed to undress either during the day or at night, especially when:

> … we entered the submarine zone, the section of ocean over which hung the kaiser's threat, our voyage proceeded under increased tension; the ship's course became a series of irregular and sharp zig-zags at high speed, so that one would be thrown off one's feet when the vessel changed direction. The prohibition of lights became more stringent than ever, and the ship's officers dreaded to see the moon rise [dazzle was not so effective at night]. It was now a race for life against the lurking U-boat.

The ship rolled as she zig-zagged, belching volumes of black smoke. The nervous tension on board was palpable, especially when the ship was plunged into darkness during the Easter Service. Some disaffected men in the Stokehold chose this moment to down shovels:

> At the critical moment a mutiny occurred among the ship's stokers [the naval term for Firemen]; but by engaging thirty artillerymen at $1.75 per day, the captain managed to keep his fires burning and to maintain the speed.

Among the Firemen who had signed Articles on 7 March 1918 was 22-year-old George Garrett, who would later write of his time on board the *Mauretania* in one of his many short stories, 'The "Maurie"'. Garrett was quite a radical intellectual and, on leaving the sea, fired by the poverty that surrounded his life, would be deeply involved in the Liverpool Hunger Marches of 1921. He continued his writing after leaving the

sea and eventually became an acquaintance of renowned author George Orwell. Garrett recalled that as much coal as could be loaded was taken on, even to the extent of piling larger pieces in the Boiler Rooms. These heaps, initially impeding movement in the Stokehold, were soon diminished by being manually thrown into the furnaces. On the last day of March, 30-year-old Trimmer David Cane developed pneumonia and was sent ashore on arrival at Liverpool, where he succumbed to the disease. Within six days of his diagnosis two more men, a Fireman and a Greaser, were also sent ashore and later died from bronco-pneumonia.

As the coast of Ireland hove into view warships, sent out to escort the ship, first appeared to those watchers on the troopship as:

> faint wisps of smoke ahead of the ship, on the horizon … 'There come your American destroyers.'… it was a beautiful sight. Admiral Sims had established a reputation for 'getting' the submarine every time he went after it, and his four vessels, the hounds of the sea, gave a sense of reassurance to all on board …

There was a great excitement as the ship steamed towards Liverpool:

> Everyone was up early the next morning; the ship had passed the south of Ireland during the night and was now going from St. George's Channel into the Irish Sea with Holyhead and other Welsh hills rising on the starboard side. High in the air a dirigible watching for submarines, while occasional sea-planes would swoop about the ship; with band playing and wireless snapping we bade farewell to our destroyers, when they patiently turned again seaward on the never ending task of convoying troop-ships. As we approached the harbour of Liverpool, about noon, we were given a rousing welcome; for rumor had been abroad the day previous that the 'Mauretania' was torpedoed and lost. Harbor craft blew their whistles, and dense masses of people lined the shore on both the Birkenhead and Liverpool sides; the 55th Band responded by playing the three national anthems, American, French and British. It was 3 p.m. when we entered the dock …

On arrival the troops were marched to Lime Street Station, where they were entrained to a Rest Camp at Woodley near Romsey in Hampshire, and later to Southampton, where a steamer took them to

France. There many would take part in major actions at Saint-Mihiel, Meuse-Argonne and Lorraine.

On May Day 1918, Captain Rostron received a letter from the Mercantile Marine Office in Liverpool admonishing him, as mentioned, for not keeping an official log book for March:

> ... the question was put before the Board of Trade as to the status of this [the Mauretania] and other vessels ('Aquitania and 'Olympic') which are flying the White Ensign. The Board [Superintendent Thomas Sargent] instruct me that the crews of these vessels are to be dealt with in the same sway as those of other vessels chartered by the Shipping Controller, except in so far as they are subject to Naval Discipline.
>
> Will you be good enough to see that an Official Log Book is started at once.

The BoT Superintendent who wrote the letter was concerned that there would be no record of deaths on board the ship should any occur and requisite Certificates of Deaths not issued. Captain Rostron, a Commander in the RNVR and always a stickler for discipline, responded to the sharp letter with an innocence:

> The ship being commissioned under the White Ensign, hitherto the King's Regulations and Admiralty Instructions have been observed, and this Log Book was not supplied and was therefore not kept ...

... but undertook that in future a log book would be maintained 'in compliance with the Merchant Shipping Act'.

The Mauretania left the Mersey on 14 May at 11.22, a late sailing probably due to the fifty-six men who deserted the ship, leaving Rostron to hurriedly engage replacements. To encourage the Stokehold crew to stay with the ship, Firemen's monthly wages were increased to £12 (Leading Fireman had an extra £1) while Trimmers received £11 10s. While under hire the ship was costing £1,300 per day! In spite of all that the Atlantic could throw at her and a lack of dry-docking for maintenance she still managed 25 knots for much of her voyaging.

The big British transports brought troops over to Europe in increasingly large numbers until the flow of men was so great that several German liners – some of the old Blue Riband holders amongst them – that had been laid up in American ports since 1914 were commandeered as US troopships. Hamburg-America Line's huge Vaterland (54,000gt; 1914,) was taken over by the US Navy on America's entry into the war and transported up to 14,000 troops per voyage, well in excess of the Mauretania, which, at her best, could carry nearly 6,000. The ex-German liner had been renamed USS Leviathan in June 1917.

Carrying members of a British Mission and around 150 non-commissioned warrant army officers (on 'loan' to the United States for 'instructional purposes'), the Mauretania sailed round the north of Ireland (where she dropped her destroyer escort), for New York via Halifax, arriving at the latter harbour on 20 May 1918, after a difficult passage buffeted by westerly gales and heavy seas. Halifax still bore tragic evidence of the devastating explosion that had occurred the previous December, destroying much of the town and several thousand lives, after the Norwegian Relief ship Imo had collided with a French munitions ship, the Mont-Blanc, with 2,700 tons of explosives on board. The fire that had broken out on the French ship eventually reached its deadly cargo as hundreds of sightseers on shore had gathered to watch, blowing up in an explosion that was more powerful than any previously experienced and claiming many of the spectators ashore. Sailing from the still-recovering Nova Scotian port at 7.56 p.m. on the 21st, the liner arrived in New York two days later at 9.20 p.m. with just sufficient coal left in her bunkers. A record voyage of slowness.

On her departure for Liverpool at 9.20 in the evening of 1 June she was carrying 3,662 officers and troops, along with the Canadian Prime Minister, Sir Robert Borden. She arrived at her berth on the Mersey seven days later having made slow progress across the Atlantic, her speed reduced to 19 knots instead of 25 because of inferior coal loaded in New York. The embarked troops would join the thousands of soldiers already in Europe, the Mauretania carrying almost 11,000 men during June alone.

Before one sailing from Liverpool a packet was delivered to Captain Rostron by special messenger. The Captain initially refused it as it was addressed to the Commanding Officer of a ship of which he was unaware – HMS Tuber Rose. It turned out that this somewhat incongruous and innocuous name (perhaps *Tudor Rose* would have been more English) had been given to the mighty *Mauretania* but nobody had deemed it necessary to inform the Captain! Luckily the use of that name faded into obscurity but the secretive way in which it had been imposed had greatly annoyed the Captain.

A 7.30 evening departure direct to New York followed on 18 June, the voyage taking another seven days. Leaving the Hudson on 30 June, the transport, loaded with troops and thirty mostly Asian DBS (Distressed British Seamen), returned to the Mersey after a lengthy voyage on 7 July. Ten idle days at anchor passed before the next sailing on 17 July (these departures were never regular in order to avoid giving the enemy a routine). Before sailing, and in spite of good wages, *seventy* Firemen and Trimmers decided to desert the ship! This might have been because, as the commissioned ship was flying the White Ensign of the Royal Navy, it was said that the transport had 'all the disadvantages of both the Navy and merchant services and the advantages of neither'. As a consequence, shore leave was denied – except for the Captain – the crew having to remain by the ship, except for brief periods during the day. Despite the strict enforcement of this regulation, the Chief Steward, Mr Dickenson, requested urgent leave to visit his sick daughter. This was denied. His daughter died during the night.

Embarked for this crossing were 2,700 women and children returning to Canada, the latter presumably very excited at being on board not only one of the biggest but the world's fastest ship. Perhaps this group had been refugees from the disaster that had devastated Halifax the previous December. Also returning on his preferred ship was the Canadian Prime Minister, Sir Robert Borden. One day, just after lunch, Purser Charles Spedding was talking to the Canadian Premier outside the Dining Saloon when the six heavy guns mounted on the upper decks suddenly erupted into action. The explosions created abject terror among groups of children playing near to the two conversing men and the children's infectious panic soon spread; women and children poured up from below 'like a mad, rushing stream'. Had the gunfire vividly brought back memories of the *Mont Blanc* explosion? Both Premier and Purser did their best to calm the panic and, as their assurances took effect, explained that the firing was the result of gun practice. The Canadian parties disembarked in Halifax

on 23 July. Her arrival in New York at twenty minutes past midnight on the 30th was marked by sixteen desertions prior to a seven-day return to Liverpool. The mighty *Mauretania* – although still the undisputed Queen of the Ocean – was becoming increasingly tired. Perhaps it was fortunate that the war-long censorship imposed on the newspapers ensured that there was no public awareness of her plight.

By early August, Allied assaults along the Western Front had begun to make significant inroads in enemy lines. After the Battle of Amiens, the start of which General Erich Ludendorff called 'The black day for the German army', the High Command realised they were witnessing 'the beginning of the end' of the war.

After the *Mauretania*'s return to the Mersey, the second and certainly most bizarre of the dazzle schemes was applied to her hull ('Type 19 Design CX') and incorporated the so-called 'Harlequin' design made up of severe geometric patterns of diamonds and diagonal stripes painted mostly in contrasting tones of blues, dark greys and white. This combination was considered more effective than the previous curvilinear 'organic' design and fully exploited the attempt to obfuscate the transport's heading. It was this coating (again, each side of the ship had a different pattern) that the ship continued to wear until after the Armistice, with the pattern even extending up the foremast to the Crow's Nest. As originally intended, four cannon were mounted on the foredeck. Fifty men deserted before the bedazzled ship sailed from the Mersey on the next voyage that lasted from 17 August to 3 September (Liverpool to Liverpool, again omitting Halifax). A further twenty jumped ship in New York and two stowaways were found and sent ashore on the 24th, the day after arrival. The *Mauretania* left the Hudson on 27 August with another large contingent of fresh troops on board. Two days into this crossing a 25-year-old US Army Private, Harry Heavy from Jersey City, committed suicide by shooting himself in the head, the reason for his despair only guessed. His body was buried at sea the next day. Arriving back in Liverpool, a massive 182 men were discharged through 'mutual consent' in the presence of a Board of Trade official. Discontent in the Stokehold must have been at breaking point!

All the vagaries of North Atlantic weather (its reputation as the roughest ocean in the world was well deserved) were experienced during these trooping voyages just as they were during peacetime and varied from calm to fog to full-blown Atlantic storms. The discomfort of the troops living in close quarters can only be imagined. The Captain later recalled that the four forward guns were momentarily submerged when the bows plunged into a heavy head sea. A U-boat was sighted on one occasion 2 miles from the ship but fog, for once merciful, intervened before the cannon could be brought into action – but not before the submarine had reportedly fired two ineffective torpedoes. The late summer in Liverpool saw the transport swinging at her buoy for six long tedious weeks (3 September to 27 October). As a result of both enforced inaction and events happening on shore (as will be seen in the next chapter), another seventy-one men deserted (many, like other deserters before them, being arrested) and a further eleven were discharged.

During August a deadly and particularly virulent strain of influenza spread through American Army training camps, characterised by 'intense congestion and haemorrhage' of the lungs following a high temperature. It was thought that the 'flu had emerged on 27 August when 'when three cases of influenza were committed to the sick list' at the Commonwealth Pier in Boston. Within ten days it was widespread, infecting thousands of troops and attendant medical staff. In many cases death occurred within three days. A staggering 26 per cent of the Army became infected, with 30,000 fatally succumbing to the epidemic even before they could leave American shores for Europe. Not realising that they were carrying the infection, soldiers boarded transport ships and soon the deadly scourge of what became known as 'Spanish flu' spread like wildfire in Europe, eventually taking the lives of over 20 million people worldwide (some estimates were as high as 50 million), the immune systems of many victims reduced by the ravages of a war that itself had consumed 17 million lives.

In October alone 100 men succumbed to the pandemic in just one eastward crossing of *Mauretania*'s fleet-mate, *Caronia*. Captain Rostron recalled in his memoirs that those sailing on the *Mauretania* somehow managed to stay free from the deadly infection but at least one person was sent ashore in New York on 9 November, one day before sailing, with 'acute pneumonia'. It was not known whether the patient was suffering from Spanish flu as other pneumonia sufferers had previously been sent ashore at New York in April, May and July – well before the current virulent strain had developed.

But, as the needs of the war could not be stopped by the pandemic, another round voyage to New York left Liverpool on 27 October, the crossing taking a slow nine days. On 5 November, two days after arriving in New York, the city went wild when officially unconfirmed news of an Armistice was announced. The war – the Great War – 'The War to End All Wars' – was, it was said, about to end; New York was in a party mood and at noon, in the harbour, scores of ships sounded their whistles in a premature celebration. This 'false' armistice eventually grew into fact and the real Armistice came into effect at the 'Eleventh Hour of the Eleventh Day of the (current) Eleventh Month'. When the official announcement was wirelessed to the *Mauretania* she was at sea, having left her pier at 2.30 p.m. the day before with yet another contingent of troops eager to get 'over there'. The embarked men reacted quite restrainedly to the news as they were now going to 'miss the show', too late to join the battle. But at least the soldiers were still going to get overseas as the Captain had not received orders to return to New York. During that last eastward crossing *Mauretania* overtook a homeward-bound U-boat motoring on the surface, which signalled to the armed speeding troopship: 'I have no hostile intentions.'

The years of almost senseless slaughter had finally come to a sudden halt and an 'uncanny silence' fell over the battle grounds as guns ceased their barrage, the killing stopped, and the world order changed forever. The Armistice did not mean the defeat of Germany, and its soldiers returned to heroes' welcomes; the Kaiser – the 'All-highest' – abdicated to make way for a republic and fled to The Netherlands. In the years that followed the country would suffer internal strife and what many, even their old enemies, felt to be unfair demands for reparations.

On 5 January 1919, a new German political party was formed with a very small membership. It became known as the *Nationalsozialistsche Deutsche Arbeiterpartei* (National Socialist German Workers' Party) and would grow to threaten not only the Weimar Republic but the world itself. Its members would be called Nazis and, in an ironic twist, its party flag – featuring a crooked swastika – was in red, white and black – the very colours of Cunard!

After Germany's reluctant signing of the Peace Treaty on 28 June 1919, French Marshal Ferdinand Foch presciently said: 'This is not a Peace. It is an Armistice for twenty years.' He would be proved right.

One of the *Mauretania*'s forward cannons being unshipped at Brest after the Armistice. (US Signal Corps)

13

'STAR OF THE SEA MOST RADIANT!'

(Motet from 'Salisbury Vespers')

Sailing in war but arriving home in peace, the dazzle-painted *Mauretania* entered the River Mersey with her last contingent of eastbound American troops on 16 November 1918, after a relatively fast six-day crossing. The disembarking troops were taken to a camp at Knotty Ash – and given a medal! Over the next few days the transport was coaled and stored for her first peacetime westward crossing since 1914. After re-embarking the same soldiers that she had just brought over, the troopship started her next crossing with 'Standby Engines' at eight minutes to four on the afternoon of the 23rd but less ninety-seven deserters (seventy alone on one day), mostly Firemen and Trimmers. Some of the remaining Firemen were disrated to Trimmers by their own request.

Two days before sailing, seventy ships of the *Hochtseeflotte* – the German High Seas Fleet on which so much national treasure had been expended – had been led to internment at Scapa Flow. The German sailors had mutinied just before the war's end, preventing the fleet from sallying on one last desperate engagement. After internment, ships and men stagnated at anchor.

The *Mauretania* arrived in New York Harbor on 2 December to a tumultuous welcome. The bemused troops on the ship were generally silent as they crowded her upperworks, but they did give a rousing cheer as the ship passed the Statue of Liberty, a cheer that was taken up by sightseers on be-flagged excursion boats, other ships in the harbour, and crowds ashore, as handkerchiefs waved and rivers of ticker-tape flowed from office windows. The spectators were under the impression that the returning 4,467 American troops (mostly consisting of aero squadrons and other units) were the first American combatants to return since the Armistice – but the returnees were mostly the troops that the *Mauretania* had just delivered to Liverpool (other than 107 wounded who were helped on to deck to witness the welcome) and had not seen action! One of the 'non-combatant' troops, a Private Wilson of the 329th Aviation Squadron, had been technically wounded by the Germans – but in London. He had been visiting the capital when an enemy aircraft dropped a bomb, its shrapnel breaking his knee. As the harbour went crazy the troopship progressed to her berth, with Mayor John F. Hyland and his party having previously boarded from the Customs' steamer *Patrol* (on which a band played 'Home Sweet Home') to greet the troops while she had lain at anchor overnight at Gravesend Bay, illuminated by searchlights. As the men were landed (the wounded were ferried away on small steamers to the disembarkation hospital on Ellis Island) they were met by Red Cross workers who offered them coffee, doughnuts and sandwiches, which were gratefully devoured. Further along the pier another Red Cross contingent was doing the same, so a second helping was eagerly accepted!

A few days later, the ship left New York's Berth 54 late at night (11.38). On board were returning British officers who had been posted to America to assist in the US Army training programme, and the Russian Ambassador to Washington, who was going to Paris to prepare for the Versailles Peace Conference. Although the ship took six days to make the crossing, her course was not set for Liverpool but for Southampton,

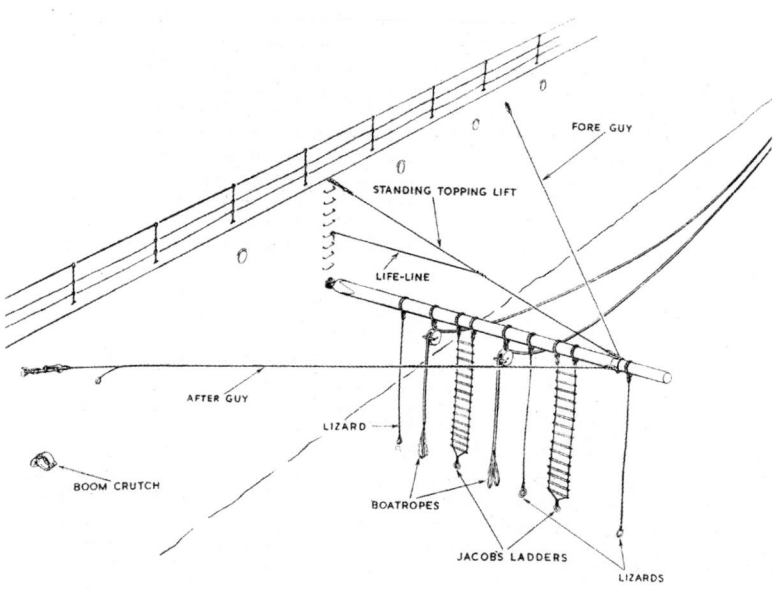

Fig. 198.—A lower boom

Mauretania's decks were crowded with men as the ship arrived in New York. The three booms (placed port and starboard) can clearly be seen. These would aid in evacuating the ship should an emergency arise. (*Admiralty Manual of Seamanship*)

The troopship's White Ensign flies proudly from her mainmast as she stems into New York Harbor. (Private Collection)

where she arrived on 11 December. The English Channel was no longer under threat and the location of the port with its double tides was to the ship's advantage. Twelve days later she cast off her lines at 2.30 in the afternoon but sailed, not for New York, but for Brest in France, only a few hours steaming away, where she anchored while her cannon were unshipped and lowered into barges snuggled alongside. But by 4.15 on the afternoon of Christmas Eve the great ship embarked jubilant 'doughboys' – 3,000 men from the 347th Infantry of the 87th Division – eager to get home and leave the now silent industrialised killing fields behind them. For these men Christmas had truly come early!

Disembarking her charges after another ecstatic welcome in New York on 30 December, she stayed in port for just over five days before sailing shortly after midnight on 4 January 1919. By this time the far-reaching nationwide prohibition on alcoholic beverages had begun its reign, coming into effect on 1 January, a Thursday – although a great many in the USA might have called it a 'Thirst-day'. The returning soldiers were denied the celebration that they had eagerly anticipated.

Since the end of the war Cunard had been in talks with the London and South-Western Railway Company, who owned Southampton Docks. In late February it was announced that the southern port would become the new home port for the shipping line's largest vessels, joining the big passenger ships of the White Star, American, Royal Mail and Union Castle lines. Cunard's Chairman, Sir Alfred Booth, said:

> The Cunard Line intends to take the place of the German lines in providing a regular service of passenger steamers of the highest class between Southampton, Cherbourg, and New York. … It may be taken that the Aquitania and Mauretania will eventually be based on Southampton while the Liverpool-New York service will be equipped with steamers of greater carrying power.

Somehow a Trimmer, the second in a fortnight, managed to break his leg on 25 February (perhaps an occupational hazard caused by scrambling over the uncertain bunker coals) and was sent ashore to St Mary's hospital in Southampton; he was followed ashore by a Greaser with pneumonia. The following day, nine Firemen and nine Trimmers deserted and twelve Firemen and six Trimmers failed to join, as did one Seaman. Three more

men deserted on the 27th, the day of sailing for Brest, and forty-four men were each fined 5 shillings for being 'Absent without leave'.

She left Brest again on 28 February full of jubilant troops two days after the huge USS *Leviathan*, but she was only a few hours behind the American transport when she arrived in New York to a filmed civic reception on 6 March, bringing home between them 13,700 troops of the 27th Infantry Division (the 'Maury' carried 3,736). Once ashore the soldiers were given a heroes' welcome with a grand parade down Broadway. By sailing day, 14 March, twenty-four Firemen and ten Trimmers along with one Able-Bodied Seaman had deserted, perhaps taken by the excitement of New York and their reception. Two men were taken to appear before the British Consul.

The mass desertions, discharges, absenteeism and insubordination that had continued to plague the ship since the previous May seemed to reflect the conditions that had prevailed in Britain before and since 'The Great Unrest' of 1916. Returning home from the Front, thousands of troops faced uncertain futures as they joined unemployed industrial workers laid off from war production work. Demand for jobs, better pay and improved working conditions instigated strikes that put fear into the heart of the British Government, where a terror of revolution, as had happened in Russia and was now happening in a desperate Germany, existed.

Even before the war had ended, swathes of British troops in French camps and depots had violently mutinied in protest at bad treatment by many an arrogant officer, poor food and delays in demobilisation. The Metropolitan police went on strike in London in late August 1918, demanding better pay and union recognition, miners wanted a huge pay rise, a shorter working day and demanded co-ownership of the mines in which they toiled. Soldiers in Sussex mutinied in the New Year of 1919, their action emulated in almost fifty other mutinies involving thousands of troops both in Britain and abroad (news of which was suppressed by the press) and soldiers' unions were formed. Unrest spread to the Royal Navy, with one ship raising the Red Flag. Railway and transport workers were all involved in waves of militant strikes; engineers rebelled at their long working week; etc. General Haig favoured shooting mutineers but fortunately common sense prevailed. At the end of January, tanks, soldiers and cannon took to the streets in Glasgow after a confrontation between the 'Red Clydesiders' and police in St George's Square ('Bloody Friday'), the first and only time that this happened in the United Kingdom. Belfast also joined the 'Forty Hours' Strike' that had gripped the munitions workers of Glasgow.

The strikes came to an end when Prime Minister Lloyd George challenged the strike leaders by asking them how they would govern a state without a unified party and leader as the Bolsheviks had bloodily done. A Bolshevik revolution in Britain was narrowly avoided as the post-war dream of 'A land fit for heroes' rapidly dissolved. The strikes affected repatriations and many of the 15,000 Canadian troops encamped at Kinmel Park near Rhyl in Wales mutinied against the multiple delays as well as against enforced half-rations, a lack of coal for heating, no pay for a month and overcrowded conditions. One soldier in the Welsh camp wrote home in April: 'strikes have held us up. Otherwise we were due to leave on the Mauretania last Saturday.' Although this correspondent added that, in spite of the weather, 'This is a fairly good place,' his letter may have been censored from mentioning that five soldiers were killed in the mutiny's suppression, seventy-eight wounded, and twenty-five convicted and sentenced to various terms of penal servitude. In the six months up to June there were thirteen such disaffections but the riots at Rhyl were by far the worst.

The *Mauretania* was still listed as an 'Admiralty Transport to and from New York' under Captain Rostron. The embarked personnel on these voyages were well looked after by 169 Waiters and Stewards under Mr T. Dickinson and meals were provided by fifty staff, including one Herbert Carter who was employed as a 'Troop Cook'. Mr S. Bartram presided over the Catering Department.

The *Mauretania* arrived back in Southampton and remained there for a few weeks, during which her 'Harlequin' dazzle was overpainted with dark grey topped with black funnels. Rebellion was in the air as Trimmer G. Dunn was fined a hefty 10 shillings on that significant day for: 'Leaving stokehold without permission and stating he would get coal out when he felt like it.' Between 11 and 14 March twenty-four men were charged with being absent without leave and fined 5s each. The ship went to Liverpool on 27 March for a few days, during which her final military paint scheme of black hull and funnels was (probably) repainted in Cunard livery (actual dates and sequences of painting the ship are difficult to ascertain with any accuracy). It was at this point that

the remaining armaments on her stern were removed along with the boat booms. Work completed, she returned to Southampton, arriving there on 31 March before sailing for Brest with Admiral Sims on board.

Perhaps some of the dissatisfaction that prevailed among the crew (especially in the Stokehold) on this crossing was due to a note pasted in the Crew Agreement amending the statutory rations (perhaps reflecting the shortages ashore) for each crew member:

… it is also agreed that during the continuance of the present war [*sic*], the allowance of meat to every of the crew shall be reduced by 50% provided that every member of the crew shall be entitled to an additional allowance of 2 ozs [ounces] of bacon per day and 3 lbs [pounds] of potatoes a week.

There were now 420 in the Engine Department under Chief Engineer J. Macdonald, whose professional side of the Department included an Assistant Chief Engineer; a Senior Second Engineer; 1st Intermediate Second Engineer; 2nd Intermediate Second; 1st Junior Second; 2nd Junior Second; 3rd Junior Second; 1st Senior Third; 2nd Senior Third; 1st Junior Third; 2nd Junior Third; 3rd Junior Third; Senior Fourth; Intermediate Fourth; Junior Fourth; Senior Fifth; Intermediate Fifth; Junior Fifth; Senior Sixth; Intermediate Sixth; Senior Seventh; Junior Seventh; Deck Engineer; and finally, a Steering Engineer. A small Electrical Department was headed by a First; Second; Third; and Fourth Electrical Engineer, and the Purser's Department of four was headed by the previously mentioned Charles Spedding.

The ship returned to Southampton. On sailing day (31 March) thirty-one men failed to join the ship after signing on and going ashore in the period prior to departure, with another nine deserting. In stark contrast, Captain Rostron must have returned to the ship in an ebullient mood as, the previous Saturday, he had been awarded the Order of Commander of the British Empire by King George V at Buckingham Palace.

The US Navy's liaison officer in Britain, Admiral Sims, along with his staff, was returning to America on the ship having been feted with a civic reception at Southampton. The Admiral remarked (perhaps without tongue in cheek) that his destroyer escorts had suffered more damage in keeping up with the *Mauretania* in rough weather after meeting her off the Irish coast than they had ever encountered at the hands of the late enemy! The ship sailed for Brest to pick up returning troops, including 1,080 American officers and men travelling with 2,700 other military personnel, many of whom had served four years at the Front and were being demobilised and repatriated with twenty-eight-days' pay. The majority of these had been recruited by the British Recruiting Mission in America – British 'ex-pats' (and now American citizens), who wanted to do 'their bit' for the old country; and 700 West Indian soldiers who had been working in the American restaurant and hotel trades and had patriotically heeded the Mother Country's cry for recruits. Unfortunately segregation and the outlandish idea that 'coloreds' were not effective in combat roles had ensured that the 700 men had been put to manual work on inland water transport rather than fight. There was also a contingent of 600 Jewish-American troops who had joined the British in the disappointed hope of being with General Allenby at the capture of Jerusalem.

One hundred miles from New York on 7 April, and much to the annoyance of all on board, the *Mauretania* ran into thick fog, delaying her expected noon arrival at Pier 54 by seven hours. That wasn't the only concern. On arrival a band on the pier played 'Hail, Hail, the Gang's All Here!' and the British-recruited troops – many of whom had been decorated, some wounded – prepared to disembark. But their disembarkation was disallowed by US Immigration Bureau officials (they had not been informed of the official arrangements) until the men had been properly manifested. The men's American officers who had managed to get ashore had to return to the ship, officials representing all sides were called, and the Captain became involved. The unhappy occurrence was resolved and the men were sent to Camp Mills to be manifested in a more civil manner.

Five thousand sacks of mail were loaded for the next eastward crossing leaving New York on 13 April with 275 First-, 154 Second- and 110 Third-Class passengers but she left behind another fifteen Firemen and seven Trimmer after their desertion – and four passengers. Just as the ship was pulling away from her berth, the errant travellers came down the pier after various delays. But at least one extra person was on board and keen to get back to Britain. Stowaway Frank Kelly was discovered after sailing and admitted to not being a member of the

Repainted in a transitional scheme of grey drab but with Cunard funnels, the liner is seen off Brooklyn and still armed at stern with 6-in guns. (Courtesy of Eric Longo)

ship's crew. He was late of the SS *Glastonbury* and put forward in his defence that he was an ex-member of the British Army, having served in the Royal Garrison Artillery. He was landed in Britain and 'handed over to authorities' on the ship's arrival on the 18th.

As the ship was still under Admiralty orders and technically still at war, an added incentive came in the form of a 'War Risk Bonus' of £3 per month paid to all members of the crew excepting first-voyage Trimmers, Outside Deck Boys and other specified exceptions, who received £1 10s. Marconi operators got nothing. The ship was in Southampton when, on 2 May 1919, labour difficulties again struck the ship. Substitutes were found by the time of sailing for the seventeen Firemen and six Trimmers who failed to join the ship, while a further ten in both areas deserted before the ship sailed. Some of the substitutes who signed on marked their names with an illiterate and sometimes blotted 'X' placed between pre-written Christian and surname. The ship sailed for New York via Halifax on 3 May, arriving in New York on the 16th. *The New York Times* reported that the liner made the journey from Halifax in twenty-six hours, '12 hours better than fastest train'!

The victorious '27th' returns in March 1919. The soldier towards the front middle front is macabrely holding a skull, while behind him (back right) a bowler-hatted head mixes incongruously with the troops. (Author's Collection)

On Sunday, 4 May Cunard's steamer *Saxonia* (which, with her sister *Ivernia,* was known as a 'Ship on a Stick' because of the height of her funnel!) inaugurated a new Cunard service to the English Channel ports by calling at Plymouth with 1,300 passengers. It was planned that a regular service between New York, Plymouth, Cherbourg and Southampton would eventually be operated by the *Mauretania, Aquitania, Caronia* and *Carmania.*

The *Mauretania*'s next sailing departed Liverpool on Sunday, 1 June at 12.20 p.m. bound for New York, again via Halifax, with 4,000 Canadian troops and invalids on board, all thankful to get away from both the war and Britain with its crippling strikes. The ship carried 100 other passengers accommodated in areas of the vessel that had been restored to a pre-war standard, including a refurbished Dining Saloon complete with 'a soft carpet'. The crossing met with cloud and generally moderate winds but rough seas were experienced on the second day out. However, the weather cleared as the ship neared Halifax where, after steaming 2,635 miles, she arrived 'Finished with engines' at 5.45 a.m. on 6 June. Before disembarking the troops were given a printed résumé of the log as a souvenir of their homeward journey. Sailing onwards, the *Mauretania* berthed in New York the next day with 100 passengers.

Before the ship sailed from the Hudson on 14 June a large number of Firemen (thirty-two) jumped ship along with nine Trimmers and two Greasers, facing certain arrest should they be caught by the increasingly vigilant emigration officers. Another Fireman, P. Grant, involuntarily stayed behind in New York for three months while he served a jail sentence for theft. Among the 561 passengers on the return trip was Sir Alfred Booth, Chairman of the Cunard Line, who told the reporter from *The New York Times* that the company was engaged in a vigorous building plan and 'concentrating efforts on getting back to a pre-war basis as speedily as possible'. A large pier-side crowd, reminiscent of the pre-war sailings, saw the liner off on a crossing that took five days, seventeen hours and fifteen minutes at an average speed of 23.4 knots. The *Mauretania* was proving that she was still a force to be reckoned with!

Another occurrence of great importance took place on 14 June that, although momentous in itself, would sound the death knell of ocean travel four decades later. This threat had its origins sixteen years earlier in 1903 when, near Kitty Hawk in North Carolina, brothers Orville and Wilbur Wright achieved what man had been dreaming of for centuries – a controlled, powered flight in a heavier-than-air machine; their piloted plane covered 120ft in a flight that lasted a mere twelve seconds. However, Wilbur Wright did acknowledge that the conception of the aeroplane and, more importantly, the flight of the world's first aeroplane, albeit unpowered, had been made by British baronet Sir George Cayley near Scarborough, Yorkshire in 1853! Six years after the Wright brothers had anxiously urged their machine through the air, a Frenchman, Louis Blériot, intrepidly flew his aircraft from Les Baraques in France, across the English Channel before safely landing in Northfall Meadow, close to Dover Castle. His flight took 36½ minutes.

Now in 1919 two English wartime aviators, Captain John Alcock and Lieutenant Arthur Whitten Brown, took their specially adapted Vickers Vimy bomber to Newfoundland for their venture. Astoundingly, they flew the aircraft across the North Atlantic to make a boggy landing near Clifden in Ireland, a day after take-off. The flight had taken them just two minutes under 16½ hours. Not only did this pioneering flight carry two passengers (kittens!) and mails (300 letters) but enough fuel remained in the tanks for a further ten hours of flying, much in the same way as Brunel's *Great Western* had proved a similar point for the steamship seventy-one years previously.

The fourteenth of June was also a notable day in Southampton. The *Aquitania* inaugurated the Cunard two-ship service that would be run with the *Mauretania* to New York. The *Aquitania* carried 5,000 Canadian troops on this austerity service departure and it would be a few months before the new luxury Express service could start in earnest. Near to the Continent and filling the vacuum left by the now absent German liners, Sir Alfred repeated his statement to *The New York Times* back in February and told *The Scotsman* on his arrival in Britain on the 20th: 'The Cunard Line intends to take the place of the German lines in providing a regular service of passengers of the highest class between Southampton, Cherbourg, and New York.' *The Scotsman*'s correspondent also reported that Cunard intended to use Plymouth as a homeward port of call, 'an arrangement which will expedite the arrival of passengers in London by several hours [as did the call into Fishguard] as compared with disembarkation at Southampton'. Among the crowd on shore waiting to greet acquaintances disembarking from the liner was Nancy Cunard, a rebellious leader of the avant-garde movement and disinterested daughter of Sir Bache Cunard, the current head of the line that bore his name.

Meanwhile, at Scapa Flow the German Fleet festered in internment, its men bored with inactivity, bad food, slow postal services and prohibitions on inter-ship communication. The Treaty of Versailles that would settle Germany's fate was due to be signed on 21 June (this momentous date was changed, unbeknown to the German sailors, to the 23rd, later changed again to the 28th) and included a stipulation that the *Hochseeflotte* was to be surrendered to the Allies on that day. On receiving a pre-arranged signal, 'Paragraph 11 – Confirm', and in one final act of defiance, the ships of the old adversary were sunk by their crews in a pre-meditated mass scuttling on the 21st, causing the exiled Kaiser to reportedly remark on hearing that his beloved fleet was no longer a 'Fleet in being': 'I no longer have a navy.'

On the *Mauretania* incentives were being given to the crew. Stewards were given a new work schedule with revised rates of overtime. When the ship was in port their hours of work would be from 7 a.m. to 5 p.m. (Monday to Friday) with an hour for breakfast and dinner. Saturday's hours were shorter – 6 a.m. to 1 p.m., again with one hour for breakfast. Overtime worked between 5 p.m. and 7 the next morning and between 1 p.m. and midnight on a Saturday would attract rates of 6*d* (sixpence) an hour for boys and 1/3*d* (one shilling and thruppence [three pence]) for Assistant Waiters. Sundays, Christmas and other holidays would attract an additional sixpence an hour. Another incentive was pasted into the Crew Agreement:

> Watchkeepers in the Stokehold Department required to move ashes before the commencement and after the completion of the ordinary four hour watch to be paid overtime at the rate of 1/6d per hour weekdays, and 2/- per hour Sundays, for all extra time worked.

The ship left for Liverpool, perhaps with Sir Alfred still on board after inspecting the company's arrangements in Southampton, arriving on the Mersey on 26 June. She emerged from her quick two-day visit looking splendid, having been repainted in full Cunard livery.

Although it had been anticipated that she would have originally sailed from Liverpool for Halifax on Saturday, 28th (a day later than scheduled), she instead returned to Southampton.

As the Peace Treaty was signed in Paris on 28 June the ship's sirens were sounded at 3.45 in celebration, their sonority carrying the momentous message over the city, as she readied to sail in the early evening. The *Mauretania*, repatriating 3,500 Canadian troops and 200 officers to Halifax, Nova Scotia, was given the honour of a mayoral send-off and the troops crowded the port side of the liner. Hundreds clambered into the lifeboats as they responded to the cheers of thousands of peace revellers on the quayside. Unfortunately, as she pulled away, Seaman C. Morris broke his right leg while operating the fo'c'sle winch. Tragedy again struck the ship as at 3.15 on the morning of 2 July, when the cabin of Senior 2nd Engineer Edward McBurney, perhaps not reporting for duty, was officially accessed and found dead in bed. Surgeon Alexander MacKenzie and Assistant Surgeon Alf Johnson were summoned and it was not until the bedclothes were removed that wounds were discovered on the Engineer's throat, apparently self-inflicted. It was assessed that he had been dead for an hour and the 'Place of Death' for his Death Certificate was logged as 'Latitude 43.50°N; Longitude 42.20°W'. His remains were committed to the deep eighteen hours later.

Amongst the great throng disembarking at Halifax the next day was 17-year-old stowaway Louis Armand, whose presence had been discovered two days after sailing. Also leaving the ship was the Prime Minister of New Zealand, W.F. Massey. He had joined the liner in an unorthodox manner by boarding her off the Isle of Wight from a destroyer that brought him from Le Havre after he had taken part in the signing of the Armistice Peace Treaty. After disembarking, Mr and Mrs Massey would almost lose their lives as the special rail car in which they were travelling derailed and caught fire. The *Mauretania*'s war effort was now at an end. She had carried 70,000 troops of all nations in safety and succoured 6,000 sick and wounded men during the course of her varied military career. The ship had steamed thousands of miles with limited maintenance and sailed at various times under five flags – the Red, White and Blue Ensigns, and the flags of the Red Cross and the Admiralty. She had achieved a proud record.

She arrived in New York a few hours ahead of schedule at 5 a.m. on 5 July, uniquely flying the national flag of Abyssinia as she carried a delegation from that African country travelling to congratulate the US on the Allied victory. The mission, in full flowing white robes, was kept waiting on the pier. When berthed at New York the liner lost nineteen Firemen and nine Trimmers through desertion and many were fined for being 'Absent without leave'. Amongst those fined was one M. Doherty who, on being read the charge in front of the Captain and asked if he had anything to say, responded: 'I'll see the Union!' Peace and Independence Day perhaps proved to be too heady a combination for many and celebrated too well as a bleak chapter for many in the United States had opened three days earlier on 1 July when the War Time Prohibition Act became law for the whole of the country rather than for just a few States. From January 1920, the manufacture, import and selling of any alcoholic beverage would be prohibited. This Act would impact on the Atlantic trade and create a new era not only on land but at sea as the 'Jazz Age' was born. Unhappily, Prohibition would lead to a scourge of gangsterism that would plague America for many years to come.

Another blow was aimed at the future of transatlantic sea travel when, on 6 July, an airship – the *R34*, built for the RNAS (Royal Naval Air Service) but commissioned under a new service – the RAF (Royal Air Force) after the amalgamation of the RNAS and the Royal Flying Corps. After leaving RAF East Fortune in East Lothian, Scotland, on 2 July, *R34* landed at Mineola on Long Island after a 108-hour flight at an average speed of 38 knots. Not only did the airship carry four experienced flyers as crew (including a member of the United States Navy, Lieutenant Commander Zachary Lansdowne) under Major George Scott, it also carried a stowaway (also experienced) – and a kitten! The crossing had met with adverse conditions that left just enough petrol to complete the flight. The 'aerial liner' was given a rousing reception as she glided in to her destination, a procedure that was not without its peril. The ground crew was inexperienced in handling large rigid airships so Acting Major J.E.M. Pritchard parachuted out of the craft to assist! This daring action made him the first passenger from Europe to arrive in the United States by air. *R34* not only proved itself but made history

when it then made an eastward return crossing to complete a record round voyage of the Atlantic, landing at RNAS (RAF) Pulham in Norfolk on the 13th after a 75-hour flight. Transatlantic air travel was now considered feasible.

The *Mauretania* had returned on 15 July and had gone into a period of renovation. Her Second- and Third-Class accommodations, which still bore the signs of war use, were renovated, her machinery overhauled and her paintwork refreshed. But towards the end of the maintenance period 800 shipyard Carpenters and Joiners went on strike, a situation that Captain S.G.S. McNeil, one-time Staff Captain on the *Mauretania*, found at the end of July when he was appointed Cunard's Southampton Marine Superintendent. The ship's rearranged sailing for 6 September was cancelled (the *Aquitania* took this sailing) and it appears that the ship was hurriedly taken to Liverpool but returned in time for a new sailing date of the 20th.

A very distinguished passenger would be boarding after being feted and wished 'bon voyage' on the platform at Waterloo Station before the 10.45 a.m. departure of one of two boat trains. The person that the well-wishers – included Winston Churchill – were seeing off was Viscount Edward Grey who, as Sir Edward, had been Foreign Secretary at the outbreak of the Great War, and was now travelling to Washington to take up the post of British Ambassador. His famous remark in 1914 – 'The lamps are going out all over Europe, we shall not see them lit again in our life-time' – proved to be personally prescient as the Viscount was suffering from failing eyesight, as evidenced by the 'coloured goggles' that he now wore. Although welcomed to the southern port by the Mayor and Sheriff of Southampton, he declined to be interviewed by the press. It was a big day for both Southampton and Cunard as the company's *Royal George* also sailed at the same time, destined for Canada. The renovated liner was waiting for her 1,400 passengers, as *The Scotsman* reported:

> … spic and span, and from the restored regal suites to the glistening paintwork of her massive hull, was once again a thing of beauty, and holder of the blue riband [*sic*] of the Atlantic … the spacious lounges, smoking rooms, and dining saloons fresh from the decorator's hands seemed particularly brilliant and luxurious.

The *Hampshire Independent*, used to the ship as a somewhat drab warhorse, similarly enthused:

> During the past five years her sumptuous interior has been almost forgotten, hidden behind shrouds of canvas, lest the unthinking hands of soldiers damaged the ship.
>
> Now she has emerged from her wartime chrysalis into the full-blown glory of peacetime array. One of the most outstanding features of the decorative scheme is the wonderful panelling, using 30 different types of wood, which meets the eye everywhere.
>
> Transatlantic passengers will no doubt welcome the news of Mauretania's re-fitting, because it means to them that the reign of the military is over.

Amongst those enjoying the refreshed liner (a stowaway, Patrick Lynch, did not have that opportunity after his discovery two days after sailing) were several British aristocrats: aviator Sir Arthur Whitten Brown, knighted since his brave pioneering flight across the Atlantic back in June (he said on board that he would not have made the flight had he known what it would have been like!); Lord Queensborough; and the wealthy Polish aristocrat Prince Hieronim Mikołaj Radziwill and Princess Radziwill (née Archduchess Renata of Austria). Also boarding the Cunard boat train was a British delegation travelling to the International Labour Conference to 'try to set the world right on Labour matters' that included four Labour Members of Parliament including the Right Honourable C.W. Bowerman, Secretary of the Parliamentary Committee and soon to become the first General Secretary of the Trades Union Congress; and D.S. Marjoribanks, Managing Director of Messrs. Armstrong Whitworth & Co.). Much needed to be done to alleviate chronic unemployment, exacerbated by ex-servicemen fighting for a 'home fit for heroes', and the demeaning abject poverty that it caused. Whether the two disparate groups met on board was not recorded.

The liner arrived in New York on 26 September and, ironically, in spite of the Labour Conference being held in Washington, the *Mauretania*'s departure from New York (eleven Stewards deserted whilst there on the 29th) was delayed because of a disruptively serious strike

by 150,000 Longshoremen. The strikers eventually lost, which opened the doors to crime and union corruption. As the supply of coal had been disrupted, the liner had to call into Halifax for supplies, where ten men took advantage of the unscheduled arrival and deserted. The liner arrived belatedly in Southampton (via Cherbourg) on 10 October, after a crossing that saw unrest in the Stokehold; Trimmer J. McMulland was fined 5 shillings for refusing duty and for 'inciting men to refuse duty on October 8th'. Some others forfeited one or two days' pay for following him. The additional eight days of the voyage had cost the company dearly, *The New York Times* reporting that the comfortable passengers who had paid for a five-day crossing still had to be fed, as did a hungry and waged crew, the food alone involving:

> 40 oxen, 10 calves, 120 sheep, 60 lambs, 2,000 chickens, 90 geese, 350 ducks, 150 turkeys, 130 pigs, 200 pheasants, 400 pigeons, 250 partridges, 250 grouse, 800 quail, and 200 snipe, to say nothing of 5 turtles, 70,000 eggs, 8,600 pounds of fish, 200 boxes of melons, 80 kegs of butter, and 300 barrels of flour.

Subsequent schedules had to be rearranged; a sailing from Southampton on 11 November (the first anniversary of the Armistice) was obviated as she did not arrive in the Hampshire port until that day. At noon a Stewardess, Miss Stairmaid, was sent to a shoreside hospital under the orders of Assistant Surgeon Mort. She had been ill for several days before reporting sick on the 7th, when she was found to have pleurisy. Two days later she developed 'difuriate pneumonia'. The rescheduled sailing on 18 November by the *Mauretania* inaugurated the much-anticipated Express Service from Southampton. The larger *Aquitania* had sailed on 14 June 1919, on an 'austerity service' to New York but the 'Maury' had the honour of being the first Cunarder to use the southern port on the Express Service. The *Aquitania* would be taken out of service in December and sent to Armstrong-Whitworth's yard on the Tyne for refurbishment and conversion to oil burning before returning to service in July 1920.

Because of the rescheduling in November, the *Mauretania*'s 13 December sailing was put back to the 10th. Andrew Cockburn was now Chief Engineer – he had survived the *Lusitania*'s torpedoing in

1915 as her Second Engineer. Some 1,500 passengers and 7,000 bags of Christmas mail were loaded. After calling in at Cherbourg, the liner headed into the ocean that had the reputation of being the roughest in the world and winter on the North Atlantic was about to live up to its reputation. On the 24th, at the time when the liner had been due to be in New York, the *Mauretania* was still in the grip of a malevolent ocean. As she plunged from the high crest of one huge wave and down into its trough, the green water crashed over her bow 'with a volcanic roar, causing the giant Cunarder to shake like a leaf' twisting 10ft of the forward bulwark. In its passing the mountainous sea 'which seemed to many passengers to have stood the Mauretania on end … partially wrecked the wooden and steel fittings of the bridge', and dented the 'cabin wall behind the bridge'. This may have been the incident that led to the legend that her Bridge front had been pushed back by several inches during her career.

A postcard writer recounted:

Mauretania, Wednesday – We are about 200 miles from N. York. Due to arrive this evening although we shall not disembark until tomorrow. We are both good sailors in spite of terrific gale on Sunday last. Some damage was done. Having an interesting time on board …

The fury of the gale spent itself and soon the ship was 'floating over sun-kissed seas as placid as the Thames at mid-summer'. A Christmas Day arrival after a crossing of six days and fifty-eight minutes assured the passengers of eating their Christmas dinners safely ashore. Among those disembarking were Edward Priaulx Tennant, Lord Glenconner, and his family travelling to plan the following year's 300th anniversary of the arrival of the Pilgrim Fathers in America. An additional passenger also disembarked: little Frances Maura (presumably named after the ship) had been born on 19 December to proud Scottish emigrant parents Elsie and Harry Astley travelling in Third Class. Some $700 was raised for the baby and an automobile, generously donated by an on-board Ford manager, was raffled on Christmas Eve, raising a further $1,301. Christmas in New York must have been a special time for many of the crew and, surprisingly, only two men, Trimmers Judd and Whiting, were logged for being 'Absent without Leave' on Boxing Day (26th) and the following day. They each forfeited two days' pay. The particularly cold weather in New York delayed the *Mauretania*'s noon sailing on Tuesday, 30 December until 6.25 as coal porters had refused to work the coal in the bitter night conditions.

While the *Mauretania* was away, Southampton welcomed the *Imperator* (52,000grt); built for the Hamburg America Line, this massive liner had appeared in 1912. At the outbreak of the Great War she was laid up in Hamburg until after the Armistice, when she was taken over by the Allied Food Shipping and Finance Agreement and allocated to the United States for short-term use as a transport with her sister ship, now the USS *Leviathan*. In September she was transferred to the British Shipping Controller, who put her under Cunard management in reparations for the loss of the *Lusitania*, displacing by far the *Aquitania* as the company's largest ship.

She was readied for sea and, with 500 passengers on board, sailed for Southampton. The crossing extended into eleven days with poor weather and poor American coal being blamed. In spite of the weather it was a dry crossing for the passengers as, because of Prohibition, American authorities refused to allow her to take on alcoholic drinks. She arrived at her new home on 21 December 1919, and then proceeded to Liverpool for dry-docking prior to joining her new fleet-mates on the Atlantic service in January 1920. However, her rudder and propellers were found to be badly damaged and the docking took longer than anticipated. She did not enter service until late February. Like the *Aquitania*, she would be converted to oil burning in 1921.

14

OIL ON TROUBLED WATERS

By now the *Mauretania* was listed at precisely 30,703.53 gross tons and 12,797.13 tons net, with Captain Arthur Rostron (Discharge Book Number, as ever, 022747) still in command.

The enormous expanse of the fearsome Atlantic Ocean gave rise to huge ship-destroying waves; to hazardous fogs (especially over the Grand Banks where the Gulf Stream and Greenland Current met); and icebergs, all conspiring to make the crossing the most dangerous ocean in the world. The letters 'WNA' conspicuously painted as part of a ship's Plimsoll line then came into their own – Winter North Atlantic. In the early morning of 3 January 1920, appalling Atlantic weather scourged the eastbound *Mauretania* and claimed a victim in 34-year-old Adolph Blank, a Swiss-born, naturalised Canadian farmer, the ship's Surgeon recording the cause of death as being effected by 'heart failure accelerated by seasickness and bronchitis'. Adolph was committed to the depths of the unforgiving Atlantic that same afternoon. *Mauretania*'s first westward crossing of 1920, due to leave Southampton on 10 January, was postponed for a week and then again for two more days. Fog and heavy weather were encountered during the crossing and a wave of such violence was met on the 21st that the liner's speed was reduced to 9 knots. She had on board 1,300 passengers and 3,500 bags of mail.

Winters on the River Hudson were approached with caution as ice floes drifted downstream and the relatively still waters alongside the berths froze. Steam from puffing attendant tugs froze on the towering hulls of their charges to paint a picturesque coat of frost. Her belated arrival into the freezing harbour on the 27th caused her scheduled Friday, 30 January 1920, return departure to Britain to be delayed as

the vital 6,000 tons of coal needed for the crossing was snow-covered and frozen in its railway wagons. Labour had to be found to chip the 'black gold' free, a task for which men were not readily available but, once freed from its icy prison, it took a further continuous forty bitter hours to load the fuel by a reluctant workforce. After three cancelled sailings, the delayed departure left New York at noon on 5 February. Mails originally intended to be carried had been transferred to other ships, although additional mails arrived by the 8 a.m. deadline. The various delays cost Cunard a hefty $40,000 in wages, maintenance and additional victualling for the crew and the 1,535 passengers, now eager to be off after experiencing several days of free Cunard hospitality. But the sailing proved to be a departure of a different kind for one Third-Class passenger. Seeking out his brother, Giuseppe Susani eventually found his sibling at 6.30 a.m. dead in bed. Instead of the two brothers joyfully travelling together, Giuseppe took the sad burden of his deceased sibling ashore.

In the USA Prohibition had spawned illicit manufacture and distribution of alcohol, and the creation of 'speakeasies', gangsterism and violence. The ship's bonded liquor store was filled with a record amount of 'legal' alcoholic beverages, which could not be accessed until the *Mauretania* was outside the 3-mile limit. Once open, the bars were besieged by a queue of thirsty Americans and, it was said, by the time the liner reached Southampton on 13 February the bars had been drunk dry! This may have been the cause of First-Class passenger Samuel Reichbart being admitted to the ship's Hospital on only the second day out suffering from delusions and occasional fits of violence, while a Third-Class passenger, Joseph Johns, died in his cabin from heart failure, bronchial catarrh and dilatation, more the result of poverty than alcohol. Three days later, pneumonia claimed Masoch Albino, who died at eight in the morning, his body being committed to the deep at 4 p.m. During the next eastbound crossing, 29-year-old Roumanian Catarina Tinez also succumbed to pneumonia on 28 March. Her demise and place of death (latitude and longitude) recorded, as required by law, in the log, the 'Parish Register', her remains being sent with due ceremony into an Atlantic resting place at 3.30 the following afternoon. Her effects were taken in charge by her brother-in-law, John Weismuller.

The great *Mauretania* had, since her introduction into service, been a favourite with high-profile and newsworthy passengers – aristocracy, wealthy socialites, sportsmen and women, and others. These still used the ship but in the post-war period public attention refocused on the ascending stars of the silver screen that suited the developing hedonistic Jazz Age, an age that made the ship's pre-war secret society of oddballs, the self-styled 'Heathens', look like a Sunday-school party. The risqué days of Dr Jones' club that went against the accepted dictates of 'decent behaviour' in the Edwardian age now became accepted as the norm.

In the face of the widespread post-war unemployment and suffering, many governments felt a very real threat from Bolshevik revolution – the 'Red Peril'. Jobs were scarce and a 'billet' as a Fireman on a ship, even with its brutality and hard slog, was eagerly sought, and sometimes obtained through an on-board connection. In spite of this, forty-eight Firemen and Trimmers (their back-breaking work was still not making their ship achieve her old speeds) deserted, along with a Scullion, Greaser and a Bosun's Mate, leaving behind a hefty £74 10s 10d (£74.52) in unclaimed wages. Perhaps some of the desertions arose from the heady influence of socialist rhetoric freely dispensed by 'barrack-room lawyers' in the Firemen's Mess. Ever since the 'Maury' had been released from Government service, slower crossings of the Atlantic had become the norm, with each leg of a voyage generally taking over six days. The liner seemed tired after her exertions during the late war, her glory days of fast four- or five-day crossings now but a distant, golden memory. Her crew became despondent as their beloved ship almost lost her will to succeed; her 139 Firemen and 157 Trimmers, whose back-breaking toil seemed to go unrewarded by the unresponsive, tired old ship, blamed sub-standard coal; an out-of-action turbine also led to its inactive propeller acting as a drag. But so far there was not another ship able to challenge her.

After sailing from Southampton on 14 April 1920, the *Mauretania* made a disappointingly slow crossing, taking one hour and twelve minutes under seven days at 17.81 knots to do so, her slowest passage since her introduction into service and barely compensated by her return at just over 20 knots. These slow crossings pleased nobody and disappointed many except, perhaps, those escaping Prohibition. Every additional day at sea meant an extra day in the bar! The slow westward crossing that left Southampton in May (8th), taking six days, nineteen hours and thirty-three minutes to complete, was further marred by the death of a young Third-Class passenger, 3-year-old William Alonzo Earley, who succumbed at half-past-midnight from 'tubercular meningitis' when the liner was off Fire Island. His little body was taken ashore for burial when the liner arrived in New York.

Twenty-year old Bertie Curtis joined the *Mauretania* as a Fireman in August 1919 for one voyage. He returned to her as a Trimmer the following April. (Courtesy of Robert Curtis)

The seven voyages of 1920 were marked by ploddingly slow passages, with only two trips taking under what had become a six-day norm. Although by now the *Mauretania* was not the largest steamer in the world, her magnificent, unbroken speed record still remained unchallenged and, in spite of her being unable to currently support her standing record, she still managed to command faithful loyalty from her regular passengers. In proof of that, she sailed from Southampton on 19 June fully booked in all classes. On the day after departing Southampton for Cherbourg at 12.10 p.m. on 21 August a young, anonymous stowaway was discovered and, in First Class, a 62-year-old American manufacturer, Joseph Jackson, suffered a fatal heart failure following Bright's disease and diabetes. His embalmed remains landed in New York on the 28th. The liner returned to Southampton via Cherbourg on 9 September, having left fifty deserters in New York (it may have been during this turnaround that AB Henry Puddy suffered a fatal accident on board. He was buried in the company's plot in New York).

Her last voyage of 1920 left Southampton, fully booked, on 16 October with General William Booth, the founder of The Salvation Army, and famed Italian soprano Madame Terazzini among the 1,700 passengers. Leaving New York at noon on the 28th, she carried boxer Ted 'Kid' Lewis on his way to fight the aptly named Johnny Basham for the European Middleweight title. On her return with 1,000 passengers she was put under a long period of lay-up before being dry-docked in No. 6 Graving Dock (the 'Trafalgar') for restoration to her pre-war glory. During the work Cunard decided 'for reasons of economy' that one section of six double-ended boilers should be temporarily decommissioned. Surveyors were requested not to look at 'No. 3 Section' (No. 3 Boiler Room) on their next inspection. After its shutdown, the associated main and auxiliary steam pipes were blanked off and their condition tested; drilled samples indicated internal corrosion that allowed for no further wastage. Similarly, inspection of cast steel regulating valves in the Engine Room showed such 'considerable internal local corrosion' that these valves would require replacement by valves of larger scantlings (sizes). Dry-docking was always a dangerous undertaking, as exampled when a young shipyard worker, Alfred Woodman, slipped and fell 30ft. Lucky to survive the ordeal, he got away with abrasions and a hip injury.

Yet another shipyard Joiners' strike caused her to make the short voyage to Cherbourg on 5 March 1921 to complete her refit, being one of many liners sent abroad for shipyard work in spite of 2 million unemployed in Britain. She carried a reduced Stokehold of seventy-one 'Greasers' [*sic* – probably Trimmers] and ninety-four Firemen. She arrived in the French port at midnight. On the 14th the liner returned to the Hampshire port and readied for her sailing on the 26th, by which time mails and parcels for the crossing had been received by Southampton's Head Post Office by the stipulated 9 p.m. three days beforehand; that same day the *Imperator* was rechristened *Berengaria*. The redecorated and repainted *Mauretania* met with great approval on both sides of the Atlantic and when she arrived in New York on 2 April with 1,476 passengers, *The New York Times* reporting that she went through Quarantine with a 'clean bill of health' without a single person being refused entry. Among the 335 First-Class passengers was Sir Ernest Shackleton, the great polar explorer.

The anticipated coal miners' strike began in April but their union's hope that the strike would spread were dashed after the infamous 'Black Friday' announcement (15 April) when, in defiance of a pre-war 'Triple Alliance' agreement, the leaders of transport and rail unions decided not to support the miners in these times of post-war unemployment. The three-month strike resulted in an acute fuel shortage, only ending when the miners were starved back to work with a massive 30 per cent wage cut. Two hundred and sixteen colliers laid up on the River Tyne alone (Newcastle being Britain's largest coaling port). The *Mauretania* would have to look elsewhere for supplies. British shipyard workers were also on strike after being told that a wage cut similar to the miners and longer hours would come into effect on 1 May. The Merchant Navy narrowly avoided a strike when the National Sailors' and Firemen's Union voted against action by a slender majority. But, in spite of the vote, on 7 May (the day that the Transport Workers' Federation called its members out on strike) wage reductions were imposed on merchant seamen, leading to a month-long general strike in the docks. Strikes were also threatened in the United States with a similar 20–30 per cent cut in wages along with radical changes in working rules being proposed by the American Steamship Owners' Association.

After leaving New York on 12 May, the *Mauretania* made her only crossing of less than six days for 1921 – five days, twenty hours and five minutes at an average speed of 21.77 knots, perhaps to conserve coal. She then made another short, cross-Channel excursion to France, this time to Brest, leaving Southampton at four in the afternoon of 25 May to fuel. The passengerless liner carried a much-reduced crew with about half the usual number of Firemen and Trimmers in the Stokehold (ninety-four and seventy-four respectively in lieu of 166 and 146), half the number in the Cooks' department (thirty-five), an increased number of Deck crew (up from twenty-five to sixty-three) and, perhaps strangely, a high number of what would appear to be non-essential Stewards, down to 101 from 327, but they would be needed to clean after coaling had been completed. The ship had been promised a supply of mixed Welsh and German coal, but the quality of the coal that arrived in lighters left a lot to be desired, worrying Mr Cockburn (the new Chief Engineer) as it showed signs of age and was grass-sprouting and weathered. Methane-depleted, it would burn but not well and produce much ash. Even during the short return to Southampton the ship experienced trouble, with more than half of her 192 furnaces having to be cleaned and the Chief Engineer informed the Captain that there was no way that the liner could get enough steam to be take her to New York by burning the inferior coal. The New York sailing scheduled for 27 May was cancelled.

In addition to the woes caused by the logistical and mechanical problems that were besetting the ship, passenger numbers were causing concern, not only in Cunard but in other shipping lines. Ever since America had been discovered and colonised, emigrants in their tens, then hundreds, thousands and later millions had sought passage to the New World, the land of opportunity, to escape religious and political persecution, poverty and hopefully achieve personal dreams and perhaps make a fortune in the process. As numbers of refugee-adventurers increased, so methods of transporting them changed. Slow, lumbering sailing vessels that took weeks of fraught and dangerous travel gave way to a more reliable service provided by steamships, a service that became more affordable as steamship companies vied for the lucrative trade. Improving developments in ship and engine design produced faster ships that not only attracted mail contracts but could quickly return to their home ports to pick up further 'cargoes' of the breathing masses desperate to cross the Atlantic. Any increases in the size of ships provided good publicity (although often not with a commensurate increase in safety) as well as enabling greater numbers to be carried in the Steerage (later referred to as Third) class that provided much of a steamship line's profit.

But in 1921 all this changed. Miss Liberty, the 305ft-high green giantess that stood guardian over the entrance to New York Harbor – the once compassionate 'Mother of Exiles' who, in 1907 alone, had allowed 1.25 million of the often desperate diaspora into America after being 'processed' on Ellis Island – must have choked with embarrassment as she was forced to renege on her brass-plaqued invitation:

> Give me your tired, your poor,
> Your huddled masses yearning to breathe free,
> The wretched refuse of your teeming shore.
> Send these, the homeless, tempest tos't to me.
> I lift my lamp beside the golden door!

The illuminated 'Golden Door' was darkened and effectively closed for millions when, on 19 May 1921, President Harding signed the Johnson Quota Act (aka Emergency Quota Act or Immigration Act), which drastically cut the numbers of immigrants allowed into the United States to a mere 3 per cent of the total numbers from any specific country already living in the States as indicated in the 1910 Census. The intention was to reduce the American fear that too many illiterate people, Roman Catholics, Jews (there were sometimes anti-Semitic feelings on board the ship), 'Reds' (post-revolutionary Communists from Soviet Russia), desperately poor and culturally resistant immigrants were being admitted into the country, especially those from Southern and Eastern Europe as it was thought by many Americans that these 'types' would threaten both the American way of life and its national security. The Act, intended to be in effect for one year, continued until it was replaced by another stringent bill in 1924 when the 3 per cent quota of 1921 was reduced to 2 per cent as the criteria set was replaced by that of the 1890 Census. Immigration fell by almost two-thirds (between 1900 and 1914, 13 million had poured into the country) although immigration from 'advanced' countries such as Britain and Germany was still encouraged.

Late May said 'Farewell' to one of those closely linked to the ship's design when Edward W. de Rusett (late of Swan Hunter's) was buried at Bywell St Peter's in Northumberland.

Returning to Southampton on 2 June, *Mauretania* was readied for her next transatlantic sailing due to commence the next day, but this was postponed until the 4th as she desperately needed some 1,000 tons of 'Best Welsh' steaming coal (from her usual supplier the Ocean [Merthyr] Steam Coal Company's 4ft seams) to mix with the 'muck' to enable it to burn with even the slightest efficiency. So the good offices of the Admiralty were sought, approved and a supply arranged. But then the coal heavers sprang into defiant action as their union had instructed them not to get involved with imported coal. Their demand for an extra £3 premium was met but when the whistle sounded at five o'clock the heavers demanded an additional £5 premium to finish the work as overtime. The managers refused and coaling was completed the next day just as the passengers were boarding, unlike nineteen crew members who failed to join.

The *Aquitania* and the delayed *Mauretania* sailed within a quarter-of-an-hour of each other; one oil-fired, the other coal. With 4,000 passengers between them, the two ships made a fine sight in the harbour with the decks of both liners crowded with cheering passengers as the *Aquitania* passed her smaller sister at eleven, the *Mauretania's* scheduled call into Cherbourg cancelled. The crossing took a slow six days, twenty hours at a poor average speed of 18.23 knots. On the last day the co-ordinates of 30.34°N by 68.49°W (about 200 miles and less than a day's steaming from the liner's destination) marked the entry into the world of an addition to the passenger manifest when Elizabeth Sandhoffer gave birth to a baby boy. Before returning to Britain, thirteen Firemen and Trimmers deserted. After her return to Southampton the vessel made another short return trip to Brest in her quest for coal, leaving the Hampshire port on 26 June, returning on 4 July 1921. As Cunard and the Atlantic shipping world fought with the current dilemma on how to fill their ships, the *Mauretania* sailed the following day for New York on a crossing that took more than a heartbreaking seven days to complete at just over an equally heartbreaking speed of 18 knots.

On her return to Southampton, the *Mauretania* docked, as usual, port side to Berth 46 in the White Star Dock (renamed 'Ocean Dock' the following year) on 22 July 1921. Her passengers disembarked, later followed by many of her crew, who went ashore on leave, and Captain Rostron, undoubtedly welcoming a few peaceful days, caught the train home to Liverpool. Three days the liner lay warped stern landward 25ft away from the quay to allow coaling barges access to her port-side coaling chutes. Several crew and various shoreside people, including a small army of cleaners, were on board readying the liner for her forthcoming voyage. Senior First Officer Bisset was returning from lunch ashore at 1.30 p.m. when the cry most dreaded of mariners resounded down the quayside …

'Fire!'

A conflagration had erupted 'with a sudden blaze' on E-Deck – Main Deck – in a starboard cabin in the First-Class area amidships. A westerly breeze blew through open portholes across the width of the ship until an area 80ft from the bulkhead that divided the area from the Engine Room was afire.

The source of the blaze was later attributed to a workman smoking while cleaning a carpet with petrol or acetone. As 'long red flames' shot up the stairway, the fire spread so quickly that 'some of the lifeboats were scorched'. Under the supervision of Cunard's Marine Superintendent Captain McNeil, now in charge of the ship during Captain Rostron's absence, the ship's crew wielded two hoses, port and starboard, their efforts hampered by low water pressure, a frustrating hindrance soon resolved by the Chief Engineer who, having survived the torpedoing of the *Lusitania*, did not want to lose her sister. The dock's fire brigade, immediately summoned and later augmented by the Southampton Borough Brigade, were hindered by the heat and thick smoke as they played cooling water on adjacent bulkheads, decks, woodwork and fittings to prevent the fire from spreading. Heat from the fire rose through ventilation trunks, scorching some of the famed panelling (heavily varnished and over-seasoned by age), carpets and silk hangings in the Main Lounge. Two tugs were enlisted but emergency plans to move the *Olympic*, berthed ahead of the *Mauretania,* were not actioned. A post-luncheon Bisset not only helped to fight the flames but also rescued firefighters overcome by thick smoke – these were taken dockside to be given oxygen.

Captain McNeil, anticipating a gradual list developing from the water being pumped into the ship, ordered the twenty-four coal chutes on each side of the ship to be closed to prevent them from catastrophically being submerged. Scuppers (deck drains), blocked by burnt debris, failed and deepening water flowed past men's feet. Open doors on the port side drained some of the water but starboard side doors remained firmly shut, effectively damming the mass of water. There was an immediate danger of this creating a 'free surface' (i.e. a body of water with a large surface area that has no restriction to its movement – always a naval architect's and seaman's nightmare that posed a huge threat to the ship's stability) and as the ship took on a list an enormous strain was placed on the thick forward mooring lines attached to dockside bollards. When these snapped the hoses were temporarily turned off before the *Mauretania* reached a point of capsize. Bisset, realising that should the vital after mooring lines also part the list would be exacerbated by allowing the free surface water to surge to starboard and seal the distressed liner's doom, tied lifelines around his waist and, joined by the ship's Carpenter, selflessly took turns in ducking under the debris-laden water to loosen the four large nuts that held the side doors' retaining bars. Under the weight of the water the doors opened and the threatening load escaped in an increasing cascade, which, as Captain McNeil later recalled with some amusement, gave the crew of a passing tug a bit of a fright! The liner, her metacentric height restored, safely resumed a dignified deportment. It took about four hours for the blaze to be brought under control and it was not until 1.30 in the morning that the last of the flames was extinguished. A careful watch was maintained overnight.

Asleep in his home in Park Avenue, Great Crosby, Captain Rostron was awoken by his son on Wednesday morning waving a newspaper headlining the news that the Captain's beloved *Mauretania* was on fire. Why had nobody thought of cabling him, it was wondered? Thinking the worst, the Captain rushed to the Cunard office and, along with the

Fighting the fire in July 1921. Water pours out of a side door as firefighters stand by. (*Illustrated London News*)

After the fire the liner was returned to the Tyne for repair and conversion to oil burning. Thousands watched her arrival. (Ian Rae Collection)

Marine Superintendent and alarmed directors, was soon on his way to Southampton. The conflagration made international headlines and *The New York Times* shouted: 'MAURETANIA AFIRE; INTERIOR IS RUINED', but an inspection of the ship following the blaze showed that the fire had fortunately been localised to three decks amidships from E-Deck upwards. A group of fifty cabins had been destroyed, and damage caused by intense heat rising through the ventilation shafts had caused various damages to the Smoking Room, Library, Reading Room and Lounge. The deck of the Lower Dining Saloon above the affected area had buckled in the heat, its carpeting scorched, putting that area out of commission. Valuable woodwork, scorched or water-damaged in several places, had been saved at least. A pungent smell of burnt timber and scorched wool carpeting permeated the ship as surveyors surveyed and repair costs were estimated.

A boiler room on the *Aquitania* demonstrates the conditions under which the Stokehold crew worked when the liner was coal-fired. (Richard de Kerbrech Collection)

Cunard, currently reorganising its finances, proposed that the ship should be sent on her next two scheduled voyages with the fire-damaged areas of the ship boarded up after a quick renovation of the Lower Dining Saloon. Captain Rostron protested that this would not create a good impression and, ultimately, his standpoint won the day. The company cancelled voyages scheduled for 30 July, 25 August and 17 September, refunded fares, and paid the stiff mail contract penalty. A Canadian Pacific liner, the *Empress of China* (ex-*Prinz Friedrich Wilhelm*) was hired to take the lost sailings while the *Mauretania* was repaired. The fire that could have spelt disaster to the ship proved to be the proverbial 'Blessing in disguise'.

It took several days to clear the charred debris and, because of a strike by local shipbuilders, it was decided to send the ship back to the Tyne for repair. Meanwhile, a bold decision was taken to activate a plan originated when the ship had been designed, a plan that would bring the increasingly outdated liner into line with other ships, and this was to convert her boilers from coal to oil burning. The *Mauretania* and her sister's dual-purpose boilers operated initially by burning coal, but as scarce and expensive oil became more readily available the boilers and bunkers could be converted to store and burn the more consistently efficient liquid fuel.

Other considerations that would affect the economies of operating the Boiler Rooms under oil were that fewer men, only 175, would be required in the Stokehold; the lengthy and messy logistics of coaling would be obviated with a resultant shorter turnaround in port; and the release from the threat of coal miners' strikes would enable the ship to maintain a more reliable schedule. Even mass desertions from the Stokehold, hard-worked under the rule of 'King Coal', might become a scourge of the past. Repair costs alone were estimated at a huge £50,000, but the conversion to oil would hugely increase Cunard's bill to a quarter of a million pounds. Sir George Hunter at Swan's wrote in *The Shipyard* magazine that his company, currently building another Cunarder, the cabin-class *Andania*, had made a loss-making bid for the repair to keep the yard's men employed and to stop the work going to Germany where rates were lower.

The *Mauretania* was coaled in Southampton for the very last time and, on 8 September, with a skeleton crew signed on for the coastal voyage to Newcastle, the ship sailed for the river of her birth at 2 p.m. the following day. Had the ship been delayed anywhere the men would have received 7/6d 'per tide of 12 hours or part thereof'. On arrival at Wallsend-on-Tyne two days later her Firemen drew the fires from the now redundant grates, many of the men joining the legions of the increasingly militant unemployed ashore. The crew left the ship and returned home, their railway fares being paid by the company. On 17 August, Cunard's Technical Department had advised Swan Hunter and Wigham Richardson of their Specification for the conversion work:

After conversion to burn oil the *Mauretania*'s boiler rooms were much cleaner environments in which to work. (Richard de Kerbrech Collection)

The 23 Double-ended and 2 Single-ended Boilers to have the existing coal burning furnace mountings removed, and the furnace fronts made suitable for taking oil burners, one to each furnace. The system to be worked under [Wallsend-] Howdens Forced Draught [a system used previously during her coal-burning days]. Bunker capacity to be provided for carrying not less than 5,500 tons of oil fuel [5,328 tons would eventually be carried, 750 tons being burnt daily in lieu of nearly 1,000 tons of coal]. This quantity it is estimated will provide sufficient fuel for a single trip, allowing for one days reserve and port use, and unpumpable oil. The oil to be used will generally be heavy Mexican oil fuel of about 0.96 specific gravity and a flash point of not less than 150°F [a system of steam coils would both pre-heat the oil and make it viscous].

The whole of the work is to be carried out to comply with the rules of Lloyds Register and the Board of Trade, and to the satisfaction of the surveyors of these bodies and the Owners Representatives.

Preparatory to the work the boilers were cleaned; the much-used See's Ash-ejecting gear removed; and ash chutes demolished, the freed spaces being utilised for extra cabins or even, as in the case of No. 2 Boiler Room (port) and No. 4 Boiler Room (starboard) commandeered for the overboard disposal of garbage.

Coal bunkers were subdivided into smaller oil-tight tanks and the twenty-three redundant coaling ports on each side of the ship were sealed, as was an internal Firemen's doorway. Four new oil-fuelling were installed on each side of the Main Deck, their capacity calculated to allow for a margin of 'one full day's consumption over and above what is required for a single crossing of the Atlantic'. Double-bottomed tanks were converted to store oil, each transverse space being divided into three smaller compartments comprising a central cross-storage tank and two wing tanks. Spaces were also allotted for overflow and the settling of the fuel. The resultant fifteen new bunkers port and starboard were provided with steam coils to heat the heavy oil and improve viscosity before being pumped into the rebuilt boilers. To reduce problematic galvanic action (corrosion) in the boilers' condensers, the 'Cumberland Electrolytic System' of cathodic protection was fitted in which an impressed current of

6–10 volts direct current passed through soft iron anodes. The fitting of the system proved to be a success and a later report noted that 'the fitting of the process … resulted in an improvement of [the boilers'] condition generally'.

But there was technical friction. The shipyard objected to some of Cunard's proposals and hastily responded in defence of their own suggestion to fit wash plates to reduce any 'free surface' effect from the liquid fuel. Swan Hunter protested that they:

… regret the decision about the wash plate bulkheads as with them the arrangement of tanks and piping would have been much simplified.

Cunard was insistent and, on 19 August, sent an urgent note in response:

The … scheme, including oil type bulkheads, washplates and positions of units, transfer pumps, as shown on the plan has already been approved by Lloyd's Register.

Taking into account that this is an old vessel being converted, and that therefore the arrangement cannot be made quite as satisfactory, as if we were commencing to build a new vessel, we shall be glad to have your approval of the storage tanks as proposed.

Correspondence, drawings, notes and telegrams were exchanged between Cunard and Swan's up until mid October, by which time the Board of Trade (BoT) was expressing some concern about the mighty turbine engines that had been continually performing at high speed throughout the war with minimum attention and, on 14 October, minuted:

The turbines of this vessel, especially the HP (high pressure) and astern casings, have in the past shown appreciable signs of distortion, indicating the necessity for careful periodic inspections of the [stiffening] ribbing … No further action if no cracks are evident in ribs especially at highest point of HP casing … He [the surveyor] should, however, carefully examine the circumferential flanges connecting the portions of each half of the astern turbines, which some years ago showed signs of warping, especially on the interior surface …

The BoT's North Shields Principal Officer also – noting that 'the casing [is] being constantly heated up and cooled down on service' – suggested (almost facetiously and forgetting that they were ground-breaking) that part of the problem was that turbines were probably more suited to 'vessels of the cross channel type'. It was recommended that if cracking was not evident in the ribbing – especially at the highest point of the HP casing – then no further action was needed. However, the cast-steel regulating valves that had been found, the previous year, to be corroded were replaced. After completion of all the work, a BoT surveyor duly inspected the machinery and at the end of the month reported that everything was satisfactory.

Not only had the *Mauretania*'s conversion into an oil-burning ship brought her up to a modern standard but her passenger accommodation had also received the full attention of the shipyard's skilled tradesmen in bringing many rooms up to a quality expected of modern British and American hotels. Numerous new staterooms appeared in the company's brochures and the names of the decks were changed, which would confuse many: the Lower Deck, the original E-Deck (the seat of the ironically fortuitous near-disaster that had instigated these modernising improvements) became the luxuriously rebuilt D-Deck. What had been D-Deck now became 'C'. The appellation of 'Shelter Deck' (the continuous uppermost deck above the Main Deck, in effect the 'roof' of a ship, on which the superstructure is built), which possibly evoked images where one had to shelter from inclement Atlantic weather, was renamed 'Upper C-Deck' to reflect the upper level of the two-deck Dining Saloon, the lower level of which was on C-Deck. Above 'Upper C' the Promenade Deck was redesignated 'B-Deck' and the Boat Deck became 'A'. Sun Deck retained its appealingly airy image.

First-Class cabins on the newly designated D-Deck were completely rebuilt, the original three cabins that flanked the port and starboard gangways to the First-Class Entrance being reconfigured by knocking the outboard pair of three-berth cabins into one and providing the resultant new luxurious staterooms with en-suite bathrooms, providing passengers entering the ship with tantalising glimpses of the luxury to come. Also on this level – and aft of the rebuilt First-Class cabins – a new block of Second-Class rooms was built taking the large, full-width

area previously occupied by dormitories for 192 Firemen. Further aft, areas previously designated as Engine Spaces were also utilised for brand-new passenger cabins. Restyled rooms appeared elsewhere on the ship, some fitted with baths, some with showers and some converted to en-suite; and the old communal lavatory and bath blocks were refurbished and extended into spaces once used for ash hoists. The newly styled B-Deck (the old Promenade Deck) now boasted luxurious suites port and starboard. What had been two three-berth rooms outboard abaft the second funnel hatch along with two sets of similar en-suite rooms each side of the dome over the Dining Salon were made into Parlour Suites by the addition of an adjoining door that made two adjoining cabins effectively into one. The six beds previously housed in each pair of rooms were reduced to two, with a divan provided in each sitting room. Three beds in the aftermost en-suite rooms was reduced to two.

New carpeting was laid in the Louise Seize Writing Room and Library, and, most importantly for the post-war Jazz Age, a superb, sprung wooden parquet dance floor was fitted in the Lounge, thus doing away with the crew's onerous duty of having to laboriously roll up carpeting. This splendid room was graced by two marble statues representing the Anglo-American spirits of Britannia and Columbia, presented to the ship by her proud builders. Similarly, the First-Class Dining Salon was restored, its buckled deck attended to, scorched carpeting replaced and its centre adorned with a large potted palm that would luxuriate in the light cascading from the dome two decks above. New furniture abounded while *Mauretania*'s famous woodwork was restored by reputable Newcastle firm Messrs. Robson and Son, 'cabinet makers of the highest standards' (Mr J. Robson would be a guest of the company during the ship's return to Southampton). Replaced furniture and carpets were taken ashore, much for 'recycling', a quantity of carpeting finding its way to Alfred Fleming's establishment in Southsea's Castle Road. The local *Portsmouth Evening News* carried advertisements for a 'grand selection of carpet and carpet strip' from the 'first class saloons' and 'grand music room' (including Wilton carpeting) suitable for 'hotels, kinemas, etc.'. Any size could be cut with prices starting from 5/6 (5 shillings and sixpence [27.5p]).

With coaling and subsequent cleaning over three or four days now obviated, the saved time would have an important economic impact on the vessel: she would spend less time in port during her turnarounds, so a tighter schedule could now be operated – a 'win-win' situation as modern parlance would have it. As time progressed a further use would be made of this extra time.

Freshly repainted after six months of heavy work, the rejuvenated *Mauretania* was ready to leave the River Tyne with a new lease of life, carrying as she did so the hopes of many.

By seven o'clock on the morning of 9 March the crew were on board, having signed on the day before; others had signed on in Southampton and then travelled north to Newcastle for the coastal voyage from 'Newcastle on Tyne to Southampton'. The rate for the run was to be £4 4s 6d (£4.22) plus one-thirtieth of their monthly sea pay 'per day counting from midnight to midnight from time of joining to time of discharge'. Once in Southampton, Deck Hands were to 'moor ship on arrival' and the crew were to remain on board 'until decks are cleared and engines are wiped down to the satisfaction of the Master'. The *Mauretania* was ready to sail on the high tide at 1.30 p.m. on the 11th, with 150 specially invited guests including the Chairman of the Cunard Line, Sir Thomas Royden and Sir John I. Thornycroft of the shipbuilding firm in Southampton. Several newspaper reporters, pencils sharpened, were also embarked for this special voyage, which began when three tugs, some screw propelled and some driven by paddles (which gave flexibility in manoeuvring), at her bow and three at her stern carefully pulled the liner away from her berth before her own engines assisted the efforts of the tugs.

As she had been facing upstream during her conversion, the *Mauretania* was guided stern-first for 2 miles down the Tyne. For this operation the tugs were rearranged with two on each bow quarter and two at her stern where they remained, hawsers tight, until the liner was where the river widened into a bay abreast of Jarrow Slake. To the north lay the staithe-lined Northumberland Basin, the site of many design experiments on a large model of the ship. In this broad expanse of water the liner was carefully turned 180º until she pointed downriver. Their work done, the tugs cast off and the ship's turbines increased their oil-fuelled power until, at last, the *Mauretania* started to glide

forward, almost without effort, accompanied by a myriad of pleasure craft bearing thousands of eager cheering, handkerchief-waving sightseers. A turn to port took her on a north-east bearing towards the river's mouth.

From the time that she pulled away from her berth the ship's progress was watched by an increasing multitude of enthusiastic onlookers until, on reaching the scarab-like pincers of the twin piers that guarded the mouth of the Tyne overlooked by the ruins of Tynemouth Abbey, thousands more cheered her regal progress as she sailed into the North Sea towards a reinvigorated future. It was said that she was 'as good if not better than when she came out' fifteen years earlier. Those on board remarked on the smoothness of the ship's passage.

In fine, sunny weather with a calm sea the liner steamed south, well out to sea and economically using only fifteen out of her twenty-four boilers. She passed colliers, coasters and sailing ships; the three-man crew of an open fishing boat cheered her as she passed. After reaching Dover, she turned eastwards to starboard and headed into the setting sun of 12 March. Further on, after passing the famed white cliffs, the liner passed the newly established Nab Tower that marked the eastern approaches to The Solent. With the Moon behind her, she passed the twinkling lights of Brading and Ryde to her port and Southsea to her starboard before finally coming to anchor in Cowes Roads, where she remained overnight, undoubtedly creating much interest in the small yachting town with the populace, by now accustomed to the latest in the maritime wonders of the age, strolling down to the fashionable Parade and Green to observe the rejuvenated liner with a critical eye.

Although the *Mauretania* had survived her biggest ordeal, her first captain, Captain John Pritchard, 'Crossed the Bar' after a three-month illness. On Sunday, 19 January, when the damaged liner was still under repair at Newcastle, the 76-year-old Captain died at his home, the appropriately named 'Anchorage', in Centurion Drive in Meols, Cheshire, leaving behind a widow (his one-time housekeeper Catherine – née Parry), and two young daughters, Elizabeth and Katherine (Betty and Kitty, to whom this book is dedicated) and a son from his first marriage, Captain William Pritchard. Many other skippers, including Captain Rostron, attended the funeral at the West Derby Cemetery, and obituaries on both sides of the Atlantic lauded

Captain Pritchard's career, which had started at the young age of 13. It appears that the Captain's pension died with him and eventually his widow and daughters would move to Southsea in Hampshire, bringing with them many precious reminders including two large Satsuma vases that he had probably bought in Japan and presentation silver given to him over the years by the ship's builders, passengers (including a Tiffany silver cigar box from German shipowner Albert Ballin) and some large photographs of the *Mauretania* taken during her early days in Newcastle that originally hung in the hall of their old home.

'Queen of the Ocean'

On the morning of 13 March the *Mauretania* up-anchored and, in the sea chop of a fresh breeze, went slow ahead, turned to starboard, and gingerly steamed between the submerged Thorn and Bramble sand banks. Another turn – this time to port – took her past Calshot Spit and its guardian castle before progressing up Southampton Water. She arrived at her berth at 11.24.

A gala dinner was held on board that evening. The Chairman of Cunard, Sir Thomas Royden, presented gifts to several crew members who had distinguished themselves in fighting the fire that had led to the liner's renewed prospects. He expressed his expectations that the *Mauretania* would retain the prestige that she had so significantly won in the past and, along with the oil-fired *Aquitania* and the soon-to-be-finished *Berengaria*, would form 'the finest Transatlantic passenger mail service ever conducted'. She was still, undoubtedly, the 'Queen of the Ocean' and remained the most beautiful as well as the swiftest of all Atlantic liners. Sir Thomas' fine words were keenly applauded, his hopes proving to be more than justified in the coming years.

To clean the ship's bottom before she re-entered service, Number 6 Dry Dock – the 'Trafalgar' – had been prepared with blocks laid along its centre and levelled to conform to the *Mauretania*'s trim. This 875ft-long dock, built by dock owners London and South Western Railways, had been the largest in the world at the time of construction but now, with ships larger than the *Mauretania* – Olympic, Aquitania,

Berengaria and latterly the largest liner in the world, White Star's *Majestic* (ex-*Bismarck*, 56,551gt, 956ft), the 'Trafalgar' was beginning to feel the squeeze. The dock could easily accommodate the *Mauretania* but the huge ex-German ships' lengths posed a problem. In 1913 the dock had been lengthened by 22ft and its entrance widened by 10ft but this was not sufficient for the ex-German liners, so a 13ft notch was cut in the landward end of the masonry, increasing the dock's length to 912ft to accommodate the bows of the bigger ships (the *Majestic*'s stern overhung the caisson!). Another solution had to be found but the non-availability of land posed a problem.

To put a ship in a dry dock, a Docking Plan was required, showing the profile, plan and sections of the ship within the dock; the sections showing where supporting breast shores had to be placed in way of strong points (e.g. bulkheads) and the profile drawing showing the ship sitting on the blocks.

After the liner was manoeuvred into position over the blocks and steadied by hawsers on each quarter, the caisson (*kay-sohn*, or *kah-soon* in Admiralty parlance) was returned to its position at the dock entrance and sunk into its retaining grooves. As the dock water was pumped out breast-shores, previously cut to length according to the Docking Plan and strategically placed along the dockside in readiness, were lowered by crane once the vessel had settled ('sued') onto the blocks; this was indicated when chalk or paint marks at the bow and stern waterlines began to 'rise' above the receding water level. The shores were then securely wedged between the masonry steps of the dock walls and the ship's side to steady the great liner.

While in dock the ship's bottom was scraped and scrubbed cleaned of marine growth prior to painting; anchors were checked and tested, as were chains, propellers and shafts; a lot of work was done on the machinery. Once work was completed the dock was again flooded, breast shores and caisson removed, and the ship carefully floated out with tug assistance. Storing for the next voyage ensued and the ship took on her first large consignment of oil – 5,500 tons of the sticky black stuff. The *Mauretania* was ready to assume her 'Nature of Voyage or Employment – North Atlantic Passengers and Mail', hopefully in readiness to improve on those very disappointingly slow crossings previously made.

In order to solve the problem of ship-bearing capacity and a more economical form of dry-docking (no caissons to operate and maintain), the London & South Western Railway commissioned an extendable, double-sided, self-docking type of floating dock (generally referred to as a 'sectional box type'), 960ft long and 134ft wide between its walls and with an overall width of 170ft. The largest of its kind in the world, the dock was designed by Clark & Standfield, London, and the order to build placed with Newcastle shipbuilders Armstrong Whitworth with delivery scheduled for 1924. With its associated workshops, the dock had a weight of 19,000 tons and would be capable of lifting a vessel of 60,000 tons once seawater had been pumped out of internal tanks in each of its seven sections. A simple folding walkway spanned both ends of the dock and travelling cranes along each side assisted with lifting. Two million tons of spoil had to be dredged to a depth of 65ft from alongside Berth 50, where the dock would be moored against two specially built brick dolphins.

In her pre-war heyday the mighty *Mauretania* had made her still-standing 1910 record crossing of the Atlantic in four days, ten hours and forty-one minutes at an average of 26.06 knots; after the Great War she was taking from six to seven days to complete the same journeys. Others had attempted to wrest the laurels – *Majestic* tried; *Leviathan* even claimed the record but she had sailed with the Gulf Stream behind her! But *Mauretania*'s record still stood and, now reinvigorated, she was ready to resume service and sailed from Southampton with 1,000 passengers full of expectation on Saturday, 25 March. This first crossing using oil immediately justified the conversion to the cleaner, more calorie-efficient fuel and almost made a hero of the unknown, previously vilified workman and his errant flame that had created the conditions under which the liner was now experiencing a renaissance.

Mauretania crossed from the newly recognised marker of the Cherbourg Breakwater (rather than the old marker of the Bishop's Rock lighthouse) on the Atlantic's European side to *Lightship LV-87* (the Ambrose Channel Light Vessel, the successor to the Sandy Hook vessel that had been anchored 8 miles to the west before the Ambrose Channel had been cut) on the American side. By the time each marker had been passed a Blue Riband contender had worked up

to full speed and on this crossing the *Mauretania* attained an excellent average of 23.93 knots, covering the distance between the markers in a magnificent five days, four hours and five minutes, almost two whole days better than her post-war worst and one day and one hour faster than her first post-war best. She arrived in New York at 6.30 a.m.

During the early part of this first crossing under oil power the liner experienced strong winds and rough seas. It was reported that she took the longer southern route of 3,161 miles as ice had been reported in the northern lane – but this had been the practice since the *Titanic* had fallen foul of ice in that region almost exactly ten years earlier. Of the elation that must have existed on board, the ship's Engineers must have been in an especially celebratory mood, particularly as the last 483 miles were completed at a mean speed of 25.31 knots.

Not only oil had been taken on for the voyage. To make the ship even more pleasant for her passengers, over 500 plants and many bouquets were placed in all classes. Pink, yellow and mauve predominated, with roses, tulips, hyacinths and azaleas providing both colour and scent, the blossoms giving added lustre and brightening up the already glistening panelling. French and Italian palms were also placed aboard the 'Ship of flowers'. An on-board gardener – green apron atop a steward's uniform – looked after the blooms (roses didn't last apparently) and each evening the arrangements were taken to a cool room to prolong their lives. It may have taken more than flowers to elevate the mood of one passenger as he was harbouring dark memories of the great deprivation and suffering that was plaguing the new Soviet Socialist Republic of post-revolutionary Russia, where millions had already died of starvation, conflict and repression as a result of a forcefully imposed ideology.

New York was pleased to welcome the Cunarder back to its harbour when she arrived on the last day of March after such a long absence, and the port swung into action to quickly turn the ship around in readiness for her return trip. The reduced time that would be spent at berth was greatly assisted by the speed and cleanliness of taking on oil bunkers, the eradication of past inefficiencies in time and labour taken in coaling helped to alleviate some of the additional costs of the new fuel, estimated to be about £5,000 for a round voyage. While the *Mauretania* was in port, Cunard's General Manager in New York,

Sir Ashley Sparks, hosted a ship-board dinner for 156 guests in honour of the ship's master, Captain Arthur Rostron. In his response to fulsome praise of his ship, the Captain presciently said that he had no doubt that she would soon regain her old records.

There was a huge increase in the numbers of Americans wanting to travel to Europe in the years after this devastating war; German expatriates wanting to visit their old homeland; Irish wanting to see how the Irish Free State was progressing; and thousands more with their own incentives. To cater for this new class of traveller, Third Class was renamed Tourist-Third. Among those booked to travel in First Class on the 4 April departure were opera singer Mme Clara Butt, and the wife of the British Prime Minister at the time of the outbreak of the Great War, Emma Alice Margaret Asquith, Countess of Oxford and Asquith, popularly known as 'Margot'; she seemed to represent what was becoming known as the Roaring Twenties. She was a socialite, a one-time Suffragette, and an authoress with quite an acerbic wit.

Germany was back on the Atlantic as it rebuilt its lost fleet but there was still no contender for the highly valued Blue Ribband on the horizon. The French, too, had returned to the Atlantic and their superb new liner *Paris* made the interiors of Cunard's older vessels with their beautiful woodwork and interiors emulating old English architecture look somewhat dated. New styles for a new age were becoming the vogue and the 35,000gt *Paris* satisfied these demands, her decor incorporating the old style but some areas were more excitingly and simply (although still luxuriously) decorated in art nouveau (her Grand Staircase was a textbook example) or in art deco, the latter foretelling the coming era. Not only were her interiors stunning but the French ship boasted telephones (one of the first wireless telephones was tested on the *Mauretania*) in all her First-Class cabins as well as superb French cuisine. It was said that more seagulls followed French ships than any other! Cunard's ace was still the *Mauretania*'s speed, but this depended on her engines, which were becoming increasingly tired. This was an issue that had to be addressed (and soon) by Cunard's Technical Department.

In spite of the general elation that greeted the *Mauretania*'s return to service, March was not a particularly happy month for her crew. They were told as a starter that if their issued blankets were not returned to stores, a hefty 10s (50p) charge would be made. This would be a chunky deduction from wages that, following precedents set ashore, were going to be substantially reduced anyway through an agreement with the National Maritime Board that would come into effect 'on and after 1st May', by an equal 10s a month in the case of Ordinary Seamen ('both grades') and Trimmers of less than a month's sea service, and 5s for Boys in the Catering Department. With huge unemployment and hunger marches ashore there were no protests.

Often eager to supplement reduced wages, some crew members would resort to other forms of income and occasionally illegal methods were employed. Smuggling was an easy, if risky, option and, as the crew signed the ship's Articles in September, their attention was directed to a special clause:

> The attention of the crew is called to the recently reported cases of smuggling opium into the United States, which is a contravention of the American Law and also of the British Order in Council. Warning is hereby given that any member of the crew detected in any attempt at smuggling will be severely dealt with – the penalty on conviction being [a] heavy fine and imprisonment.

To continue the on-board economies, two Deck Boys and four Bell Boys who had excitedly joined the fastest ship in the world on 21 May (their names being entered on the 'List of Young Persons under 16 years of Age Employed As members of the Crew' as required by the Employment of Women, Young Persons and Children Act of 1920) were discharged the next day; the disappointed boys, all of whom had been born in 1907, were still regarded as too young to be employed by the company (unless they had a relative working on board).

After passing the *Ambrose* light vessel at 1.50 p.m. on Tuesday, 25 April 1922, the *Mauretania* steamed 533 miles to noon the next day, then 591, 583, 572 and then 379 miles from noon Saturday to her arrival at Cherbourg with average noon-to-noon speeds of 24.98, 25.22, 25.47, 25.13, 24.87 and 25.23 knots, which must have given the gamblers on board who bet on the official daily run quite a thrill. A day out from Cherbourg, the liner achieved an astonishing 27½ knots for a short while. She arrived at the Cherbourg breakwater on May Day after a passage of five days, one hour and twenty-three minutes – an excellent passage during which she had steamed the 3,242 nautical miles over the course at an average speed of 25.14 knots, more than adequately fulfilling Sir Thomas Royden's prediction that she would again become the 'Queen of the Ocean'.

During the early June eastward crossing, a Third-Class passenger, 40-year-old US citizen Jonas Greblunas, had apparently overindulged in New York and, after a bout of delirium tremens, became violent and attacked his roommate. The Master-at-Arms was summoned, Greblunas was overpowered and a revolver and knife confiscated. By four o'clock on the morning of 8 June the assailant had been restrained in a straightjacket. By 6.30 the gentleman was dead; forty-five minutes later his body lay at rest in the deep ocean. This crossing from New York to Southampton, even with its tragedy, proved to be the fastest of any ship since the war. She averaged 25.26 knots (on her second day out steaming 603 miles at over 26 knots), taking five days and forty-nine minutes between markers; she arrived in Southampton on the 12th.

Her eastward passage in July would better that by, it was reported, a mere two minutes! Now sailing in conjunction with the *Aquitania* and *Berengaria*, Cunard could truly advertise that they could offer the 'Fastest Ocean Service in the World'. On board, amongst the 'largest number of saloon passengers in her career' for this special crossing that arrived in Southampton a day before America's Independence Day (also the eighty-second anniversary of the maiden voyage of Cunard's first ship, *Britannia*), was the British Ambassador in Washington, Sir Auckland Geddes (a regular traveller on board – he would return to the US in early August) and his wife, and American film actress Mae Marsh, who had appeared in D.W. Griffith's famous film *The Birth of a Nation* and in a more recent British production, *Flames of Passion*. Another great day's steaming was made during the crossing, when the liner made another post-war record of 610 miles between noon on Thursday, 29 June and noon the following day; this was only 4 miles less than a record eastward crossing in September 1909. In keeping with the times, Cunard was by now advertising a cruise for the winter of 1923 from New York to the Mediterranean by the mighty *Mauretania*.

The *Mauretania* left Southampton twice in August, on the 5th and 26th, returning there from New York on the 21 August and 12 September respectively. A short period of maintenance had preceded the Saturday, 5 August departure and during a routine fumigation of parts of the vessel on the previous Sunday two men, diver Albert Oake from London and local shore-gang bo'sun Walter Cox, were overcome by toxic fumes from the hydrocyanic acid that had been used to rid the ship of any possibility of 'plague and typhus' as required by the 'rigid requirements of the American authorities'. The two men died in hospital. Some 8,000 sacks of mail and 1,500 passengers were embarked for the next sailing, including two ambassadors, one of which was the British Ambassador to Washington, Sir Auckland Geddes. Also on board were three women and their children, all British citizens, who were travelling on the ship for the third time in a month. They had originally gone to America to join their husbands but, because the British quota for immigration had been reached, they had been turned back at Ellis Island and, as required by American law, returned on the same ship on which they had arrived. They were trying again.

The liner passed outward – several newspapers reported inward – through The Solent, where the royal sailing regatta of Cowes Week had come to an end the evening before with the traditional magnificent display of fireworks. However, the King and Queen were still on board the Royal Yacht *Victoria and Albert*, watched over by their guardship, the battleship HMS *Barham*. White Star's huge *Majestic* was also anchored in Cowes Roads in readiness for a royal inspection. As the *Mauretania* approached the busy roadstead – which presented a magnificent sight – at around one o'clock she came to a temporary halt. The ship's company lined her decks, her ensign dipped, and her bugler sounded 'The Attention' followed by 'The General Salute' as her officers raised white-gloved hands. The *Mauretania*'s band then struck up with the National Anthem. The Royal Yacht proceeded to Portsmouth Dockyard, where their Majesties transferred to the Royal Train for London.

The liner arrived in New York three hours ahead of schedule on 11 August with the fastest mail delivery since before the war, but the urge to keep up fast passages and turnarounds was beginning to tell on her engines. On this arrival in New York her engines were, as usual, being used for manoeuvring when an ominous sound emanated from her port inner low-pressure ahead turbine as if the rotor blades were coming into contact with the casing. The noise ceased when she was put ahead and remained quiet during the homeward crossing. (There was a similar occurrence in January 1908, as previously mentioned, but to her starboard astern turbine). The engine was prudently shut down before her homeward run until it could be expertly examined. As Cunard was very reluctant to withdraw the liner from service, they proposed to immobilise the port astern and low-pressure ahead turbines to restrict their common shaft from vibration when at sea. The power of the astern turbines, normally about 60 per cent of the ahead engines, was reduced by 50 per cent to 20,000hp (the astern turbine could be reactivated in a case of 'extreme need' by the removal of the temporary restraints) and the BoT Surveyor, Mr G. Parker, recommended that the three remaining ahead turbines be restricted to 18 or 19 knots after the ship's scheduled sailing from Southampton on 26 August. Cunard heeded the BoT: 'we consider (30 per cent) quite ample. We intend running this vessel for several voyages and will take the first opportunity of laying the ship up and opening the Turbine for repairs.' Technical and procedural plans began to be formulated until specifications could be distributed. Cammell Laird, Harland & Wolff and Thornycroft received invitations to tender for the work that would be put in hand in late 1923; materials would be supplied by Wigham Richardson, the original engine builders.

The liner next steamed across the Atlantic at an average precautionary speed of 19.66 knots, taking six days six hours and fifty-seven minutes to do so, her slowest crossing of the year. Her next westward was cautiously slower at 19.32 knots. That month it was announced that the liner would call into Plymouth for the very first time after leaving New York on 5 September on the afternoon of Sunday, 10 September. This was because from 1 September traffic would be using the northerly, or short course, across the Atlantic. It was anticipated that passengers wishing to do so could disembark in order to hasten their arrival in London by a few hours – 'From New York to London in just over five days' but no mention was made of unloading mails. The proposed arrangement, lasting until January, would enable Cherbourg-bound passengers to disembark on Monday morning instead of an inconvenient late Sunday night in Southampton. Now,

because of her engine problems, that inaugural call into Plymouth was 'deferred' until a later date.

It was unfortunate that the ship was making such slow speeds as she was full for her sailing of 16 September, carrying 1,400 passengers including thirty-seven dollar millionaires, such as Isaac Guggenheim (his predecessor had gone down with the *Titanic*) of the wealthy mining family. One reporter commented that carrying this wealth was 'a heavy burden even for the Mauretania'. Ten doctors were also amongst the number travelling in Cabin, and famed Scottish music-hall entertainer Sir Harry Lauder was also on board; he had previously been on the *Mauretania* when he made a bet with Sir Thomas Lipton – grocer millionaire and flamboyant yachtsman – in the only bet that the latter ever made. As Sir Thomas recounted in an interview to the *Liverpool Courier* in September 1922:

We were both going to America, he in the *Mauretania* and I on the *Baltic* [one of the beautiful 'Big Four' of the White Star Line] and to please Harry I staked 9d [nine pence] against his 4d that I would be in America first.

Sir Harry's professional reputation as a Scottish skinflint came in to comedic play:

Harry beat me but it gave him some terribly anxious moments. The *Mauretania* ran into thick fog for about three days and Harry got so excited that he went down into the engine-room [*sic*] to urge on the stokers [firemen] Then he discovered that he had lost a 6d piece and all the stokers stopped to help him look for the coin [giving the Black Gang a bit of free fun with a great performer who unwittingly gave them a break from their thankless toil]. Harry finally found it in his shoe. Anyway I lost and weeks afterwards I got a postcard from Honolulu asking me to let him have the 9d and the accrued interest. I wrote back to say that I had invested it for him and that he would get it and the dividends when I returned.

The *Daily Express* reported that the liner's cargo holds held 1,200 tons of fine goods from Lancashire and Nottingham, which had been loaded in a rush in an attempt to beat increased import duties of 56 per cent on non-US manufactured goods imposed under the Fordney-McCumber Tariff Act. Although the Act would effectively shut out British goods, the romance of sending the cargo by the world's fastest liner sadly failed as the slowed *Mauretania* arrived too late to beat the October deadline. The goods were returned to Britain. As usual her mail holds were stacked with sacks from as far afield as China and Japan as well as from the West Indies, and Central and South America.

On arrival back in Southampton the ship was docked for a three-week overhaul and a survey of the engines. A careful examination of the circumferential flanges connecting 'the portions of each half of the astern turbines' (several years previously these had shown signs of distortion on the interior surface) concluded that everything was satisfactory. A plaster had been put on her wounds. Hoping that all had been cured, the Cunarder re-entered service with plaudits as to her previous achievements, it being estimated that she had carried a record total of 385,000 passengers and, in doing so, had steamed another record of 850,000 miles (one million to include her war service).

Leaving Southampton on 28 October, the *Mauretania* broke two more records as if all was well. Dashing over at 24.08 knots she arrived in New York in thirteen minutes under five days. Despite the heavy fog that accompanied her 7 November departure from New York, followed by three days of heavy weather, she returned home in just under five days.

Practically unannounced in the press, the liner's first port of call involved a trial call deferred from September into the natural harbour of Plymouth where, at 9.25 on the evening of Sunday, 12 November and in a blaze of lights, she anchored. Seventy-three passengers (including the Earl of Granard, a traveller on the ship in her troopship days) and 2,168 bags of mail were landed in an incredible forty-two minutes. London-bound passengers were whisked away by express boat train, arriving at Paddington Station twelve hours ahead had they continued to Southampton. Plymouth had proved its worth and an hour later the liner was off to Cherbourg. Although mail 'per RMS Mauretania' was landed at Plymouth, it still had to go to Southampton where, bemusingly, Customs had moved their examination centre from Plymouth. This delayed the packages' delivery by a few hours.

While the *Mauretania* had been speeding westward on 4 November a happening occurred in far-off Egypt that would affect the culture and fashion of the Western world; buried steps were discovered in the fabled Valley of the Kings. After excavation, these led to a doorway. Three weeks later a hole was made in this door and, on being asked if he could see anything by the light of a flickering candle, the archaeologist-in-charge, Howard Carter, legendarily replied: 'Yes … wonderful things.'

After many years of searching the tomb of Pharaoh Tutankhamen had been found, full of gold and alabaster, and superbly crafted jewellery and furniture. The magnificently wrought heavy gold mask that covered the boy-king's head became iconic. The massive interest shown in the Egyptian discoveries led to a huge upsurge in bookings as tourists, who probably only knew of Egypt as the home of the Pyramids and aromatic cigarettes, clamoured to get to Cairo.

Memories of the Great War still lingered over the *Mauretania*. She left Southampton at the start of another crossing on 18 November – four years and one week after the Armistice of 1918. The ship was in pristine condition but, in those days before counselling and the discovery of post-traumatic stress disorders, many of her crew still carried vivid recollections of their experiences during the ghastly years of the Great War. Cunard subscribed to the National Scheme for Disabled Men undertaking to reserve 5 per cent of positions for veterans who still suffered from the effects of war. Sometimes those effects could prove to be too much of a challenge; when the liner reached Cherbourg a First-Class Waiter, William Stevens, was medically discharged suffering from violent hysteria. The poor man was still experiencing the debilitating effects of shell shock.

That November westward took five days, three hours and fifty-three minutes at a good average speed of 23.36 knots and the sufferings of Waiter Stevens in Cherbourg were somewhat offset by the birth of a baby boy, Jacque, a few hours out from New York to proud parents travelling in Third Class, Rachel Betman and her husband, Morri, a Russian-born watchmaker from Warsaw. The new child was born into a new Age – the Jazz Age, an Age of Prohibition, of Singapore Slings, bootleg liquor and dappers, unemployment and gangsterism, and the exuberant syncopated rhythms of the Charleston. The world had a new look.

Southampton took delivery of a new floating dock. This later view shows the *Mauretania* high and dry during a maintenance period and being overflown by a group of locally built aircraft. (Author's Collection)

After Cunard moved its Express Service to Southampton, the *Mauretania* became a familiar sight in The Solent. Here she is passing through the spectacle of Cowes Week with the Royal Yacht acting as a floating palace for King George. The cannon of the Royal Yacht Squadron can be seen in the foreground. (Author's Collection)

But the liner ended 1922 on a bitter note. After the records of her previous voyage, she approached New York flying a signal that told all around her the she was out of control. Initial reports said that she was having a slight difficulty with her steering gear as she passed the *Ambrose* light vessel. It transpired that her starboard low-pressure turbine was disabled. Tugs met her and ushered her into dock five hours late on 24 November, with her 930 passengers disembarking.

The liner left New York on the 28th with the disabled turbine still out of action. Even by omitting Plymouth the crossing took nearly five hours over six days. She was put into early maintenance and repair in Southampton and her scheduled sailing for 6 December was cancelled, much to the disappointment of the citizens of Plymouth, where she was expected to call on 23 December as the 'Christmas Ship'.

But the New Year held a new adventure for the liner.

15

MAURETANIA THE MAGNIFICENT!

The *Mauretania's* extended six weeks of maintenance saw the problem with her engines remedied – or so it was thought. Just as well, as her next voyage would see a departure from the norm – she was, for the very first time, going cruising! Before the Great War, cruising had been an uncommon occurrence, with just a few older ships being used. The shipping companies realised that winter was an unpopular time for travelling on the wild North Atlantic and, if berths were to be profitably occupied, fewer ships were needed on the route. And what better way to fill berths in the winter than to send otherwise unprofitable ships off on cruises aimed at the more affluent sector? Cunard was at the forefront of innovation when, in January 1923, they sent their year-old *Laconia* (19,695grt and built by Swan Hunter & Wigham Richardson) off on the very first around-the-world cruise. The ship called in at twenty-two ports in 130 days.

On Friday, 12 January 1923, Southampton's Ocean Dock was crowded by four ships of the same company. Cunard's three liners that made up its express service – *Mauretania* (awaiting dry-docking), *Aquitania* and *Berengaria* – along with the smaller *Antonia*, represented 145,000 tons of ships and sixteen tall, red funnels presented a magnificent sight. For the *Mauretania's* cruise two 30ft motorboats had been borrowed from the *Aquitania* for use as tenders. Captain Rostron, who was still living at '3, Park View, Morr [*sic* – Moor] Lane, Crosby', 7 miles north-west of Liverpool, was in command for this inaugural sailing and his senior officers consisted of A. Brown as his Staff Captain, G.R. Dolphin as Chief Officer and C.G. Illingworth as Senior First Officer. Experienced Chief Engineer A. Cockburn, still in charge of the Engine and oil-fired Boiler Rooms, now worked with a reduced complement of nineteen

Greasers, forty-eight Firemen and forty-one Trimmers, whose role now seemed rather incongruous. The *Mauretania* sailed from Southampton just after 11.30 on the morning of 27 January, making her way to New York, where a bevy of 550 very rich or just plain wealthy cruise passengers – the travellers were worth, it was said, a total of 200 million dollars – awaited her, as well as cargo and mail.

This first cruise, nicknamed 'The Millionaires' Special', was a charter by the Travel Department of the American Express Company and promised to take her well-heeled passengers 'Swiftly, sumptuously across the Atlantic to the blue waters [of the Mediterranean], sunny skies and glamoured shores of history, romance and story'. One gentleman, Judge Elbert Henry Gary (one-time head of the giant United States Steel Corporation – 'the biggest job in America next to the Presidency'), shelled out $25,000 (£5,500) for his six-week stay in a suite, although fares started at a more modest $930. During the cruise, her cosseted passengers' ('Guests' as they are called in modern cruising parlance) general comfort was to be looked after by 192 Stewards in First Class and 106 in Second and Third Class. There were also 136 Cooks, Stewardesses and, always out of sight and well below decks, a large and unlauded laundry staff who ensured that tablecloths were white and crisp, napkins pristine, bed linen fresh and passengers' personal laundry needs met. Under the supervision of the Head Laundress, this latter department comprised Hand Ironers; Press Operators; Shakers and Folders; and Calendar Hands. To enable Stewards to do their work well in quickly serving meals and in keeping tables and cabins supplied with fresh linen, proportions of tips given to them would permeate through the system to ensure an efficient delivery of services. A lack of sharing would result in poor cabin service and delayed plates in the Dining Room.

Sailing into the promised sunshine and azure waters after leaving the greyness of the northern waters, the *Mauretania* first called into Porta Delgado on the verdant island of São Miguel in the Azores. Then onto Madeira with its profusion of unfamiliar flowers, where European passengers joined her; then Cadiz and Gibraltar. The sights and sounds and risqué reputation of Algiers proved a curious attraction (although the heat did not) its 'wicked reputation … everyone wanted to see', individual excursionists perhaps escorted by a willing – and generously tipped, no doubt – favoured Steward. Excursions at various ports of call lasted anything from a few hours to several days. Then on to Monaco with its attractive casinos, where large amounts were traditionally lost; Naples (Italy had been experiencing political turmoil and was in the hands of its youngest prime minister to date, Benito Mussolini of the black-shirted Fascist party); bustling Constantinople; Phaleron Bay (for Athens and the Acropolis); and Haifa, for many the main purpose of the cruise as excursions, organised by the Society for the Promotion of Travel in the Holy Land, took parties to Jerusalem and other holy sites.

Her cruise turnaround was Alexandria in Egypt. One must-do excursion was to Cairo to view the Pyramids and be photographed grinning awkwardly sitting astride a dusty camel. There was an exciting visit to the Valley of the Kings or, for those not yet sated with ships, a trip down the Nile on Thomas Cook's luxurious steamer the *Arabia*, described as 'the Mauretania of the Nile'. There was talk of deepening the British-controlled Suez Canal to allow passage for large vessels such as the *Mauretania* (although her non-air-conditioned comfort in the Red Sea would be a matter of doubt!). But for Assistant Third-Class Chief Steward 28-year-old Charles Smith the ship's first adventure to Egypt proved less than happy. Five days after reporting sick, he was taken ashore on 15 March suffering from a perforated gastric ulcer. He did not survive the operating table.

The *Mauretania*'s homeward journey took her to her old wartime coaling station of Naples (nearby ancient Pompeii, frozen in time, was a great draw), Ajaccio, the Corsican birthplace of Napoleon, then on to the final port of call, Lisbon. She arrived back in Southampton on 2 April but not before she had brushed the pilot cutter that

was awaiting her in the Channel, damaging its bowsprit, its three occupants being rescued by a boat from a nearby destroyer. The liner was unscathed. On arrival in Southampton 400 American travellers continued their adventure and boarded a special train to London for a few days' sightseeing. Two hundred returned to the ship while others extended their excursion to the Continent, returning to New York on the *Mauretania*'s next sailing. Her lengthy cruise had been a great success (it was said that £10,000 of liquor had been consumed by the Prohibition refugees!) and set the pattern for future years for similar winter escapes. The liner made two sailings from Southampton in April (7th and 28th) with some travellers using the ship as a cross-Channel ferry as a start to their Continental holidays. Her arrival in Southampton on the 23rd brought a large influx of visitors for the royal wedding of Lady Elizabeth Bowes-Lyons and Prince Albert, the Duke of York, on 26 April (the royal couple would reluctantly be propelled into monarchy in the following decade). Two days after the wedding, the liner sailed fully booked.

As was routine by now, on sailing days lifeboat drills were held with the crew, wearing lifejackets, being mustered and instructed, boats swung out, and all lifesaving appliances inspected 'and [hopefully] found in good order'. Watertight doors were inspected and tested; life-jacketed passengers were mustered and instructed at their boat stations on the first day out. By now, with shorter turnarounds, the *Mauretania* was making two sailings a month. During her second April westward crossing a cotton merchant from Ivybridge in Devon, William Crump, suffered an epileptic fit that proved so severe that he succumbed to a following heart attack.

There was still some discontent amongst the crew as, on the liner's arrival in New York on 8 May twenty-two deserted. It may have been the lure of the bright lights that drew them but desertions were a problem for many shipping lines; Cunard lost 600 men in four months, White Star 500 – some of the men were arrested and prosecuted; some joined the mighty, better-paid *Leviathan* (ex-*Vaterland*) of the United States Lines when she appeared in July. A lot of technical ingenuity went into her renovation after being given to America as War Reparations and, with her gross tonnage remeasured to 59,000 (US measurement), it was claimed that she was not only the largest liner in the world (White Star protested, claiming that accolade for their own reparation, *Majestic*, ex-*Bismarck*) but also the fastest; speed trials had given her an amazing average of 27.48 knots, but that was steaming with the aid of the Gulf Stream up the Eastern Seaboard from Jupiter Light, Florida, to Cape Henry, Virginia.

Brushing aside the impudence, Cunard still claimed the fastest transatlantic record for their *Mauretania*. But the big, brash, newly Americanised ship with her three red, white and blue funnels proved to be an attractive alternative not only for British seamen but to patriotic American travellers, who ensured that she sailed with good capacities despite being 'dry' after she had made her maiden voyage from New York on, appropriately, 4 July 1923.

Arrivals and departures of important passengers such as diplomats, nobility, the wealthy, the sporty and the literati still made column inches of copy in newspapers and the sailing from New York on 8 May was particularly well covered by *The New York Times*. They noted in the long, alphabetically arranged list of prominent passengers a Mrs William B. Leeds, pointing out she had been previously and exotically known as the 'former Princess Xenia of Greece'. The next arrival of the ship brought 501 passengers, of whom 322 were United States citizens with twenty-two other nations being represented in the passenger list. Among the reduced numbers of emigrants travelling on the ship were women in the later stages of pregnancy hoping that their offspring would be born in the United States and thus become citizens of that Land of Promise. Many of these hopes were realised but in their excitement some women could not wait and gave birth on the ship. Such was the case of Austrian Third-Class passenger Maria Tvionis who, on 5 August, was 'delivered of twin female children' a day out from New York. As the births were registered on a British ship the twins were given British citizenship. As two new lives entered America in one direction, so an older one attempted to leave in the other when J. Kennedy tried to avoid paying for his passage and stowed away on the ship. Although discovered and detained, he managed to abscond when the ship reached Southampton. Some parents-to-be were not as lucky as the twice-blessed Tvionis family. Four days after sailing on the first crossing of September, little Johan Sikresch was born prematurely to his Yugoslavian parents. Complications ensured that his short life

did not extend to a third day. On that same well-booked crossing was multimillionaire W.K. Vanderbilt II, whose antecedent, Alfred Gwynne Vanderbilt, had perished on the liner's sister ship, the *Lusitania*, in 1915.

Leaving Southampton on 29 September at 1 p.m. the liner carried 1,681 passengers – including war-time Prime Minister David Lloyd George (he had recently been forced to resign in a 'Cash for Honours' scandal) – 6,500 sacks of mail, and sixty-eight boxes of gold. A reasonably smooth passage was made because Captain Rostron navigated his ship between 'the tail end of … hurricane and the commencement of the equinoctial storms'. She arrived in New York on 5 October.

Recalling the contraband aircraft that she had transported as cargo in the Great War, she carried on her after deck on her last arrival in Southampton for 1923, on 5 November, a crated 600lb, 20ft wingspan aeroplane belonging to passenger Lawrence Sperry for use during his business trips around Britain. The *Mauretania* had not made a recent crossing of less than five days, although her Engineers had done their best to nurse and monitor the ship's ailing engines. Cunard's Technical Department's plans instigated a year earlier for a major maintenance programme were soon to be put into action and, on her last arrival, she was taken out of service 'at once'.

Mauretania was taken in hand by Thornycroft's in Southampton 'where unemployment is very serious'; work was assured for 1,100 men, of whom 500 were tasked with the turbines. The material for the repairs was supplied and machined by the Wallsend Slipway and Engineering Company of Newcastle before being shipped south, with further machining and fitting undertaken by John I. Thornycroft's skilled tradesmen.

Unusually, she did not go into dry dock but was fitted 'with a [work] shop'. Although the planned maintenance work was principally to attend to her ailing turbines, her boilers and all auxiliary machinery also had to be thoroughly overhauled, five furnaces replaced, and the ship's furnishings renovated or replaced. The work on the *Mauretania* was expected to take four weeks, provide work for 650, and cost a massive £250,000. The *Mauretania* was briefly joined in lay-up by the *Aquitania* and *Berengaria*, bringing more welcome work to 'Thornys' Ship-repair Division. Additional men were taken on, assuring a prosperous Christmas for many families. The services of these two Cunarders and those of White Star's *Majestic* had been combined after the two companies had agreed to operate a sensible joint weekly service over the winter period between November and March.

Amongst the improvements carried out, a 'new-fangled' wireless direction finder was fitted to aid the ship's Navigators in cloudy or misty conditions in determining the ship's exact position by contacting dedicated radio stations on shore. Passenger comfort was also being enhanced with the forward part of B-Deck forward, port and starboard being enclosed with glazing where the Promenade and Boat Decks extended out from the line of the hull aft of the First-Class accommodation, giving a bay-window view over the ocean. This feature had allowed the wind to blow along the Promenade, thus reducing its use. The glazed improvement, it was said, would bring the old ship into line with the company's newer post-war ships and make it more accessible for passengers and for social functions; the glass had to be thick and strong enough to keep out any Atlantic wave that might attempt to inundate the ship:

> The glass is of ½ in. thick polished plate and slides in a channel, which is fitted with felt to ensure easy sliding movement, and is draught-proof.

The waist-high weather- and rattle-proof windows were supplied by Beckett, Laycock & Watkinson Ltd of Harlesden (manufacturers of the 'noiseless "Beclawat" silent window channel') and could be easily operated, as the *Shipbuilding & Shipping Record* described:

> The fitting works with a gear and screw, the screw being 1¼ in. diameter, with a double lead square thread of bronze. At its base is a ball-bearing thrust block, the gears being encased in a box filled with grease. The bottom channel which houses the glass is of brass angle, rubber lined. The gear fittings at waist rail are housed in a steel channel, and means are provided in the channel for lubricating the gears without removing the fittings.

Easily raised and lowered, two adjacent windows with fan lights above were placed in the openings between the pillars that supported the Boat Deck. Each pane weighed 'about 70 lb'.

In the Engine Room the seals between the lower and the massively heavy top turbine casings were broken and the tops carefully lifted using the ship's built-in lifting arrangements. Four guide posts on each

engine corner kept the casing tops rigidly supported to avoid contact with the rotor blading. What the inspectors discovered was disturbing and the amount of repair work required was ominously described as 'considerable' and would result in a lengthier lay-up than planned. It was found that 132,000 out of 385,700 blades needed replacement. The blade tips were connected together for mutual stiffness by distance pieces ('wedges') silver-soldered between each blade; soldered lacing wires (wound round the wedges and taken around the opposite edge of each blade) were found to have fractured through vibration, resonance, expansion, or galvanic (bi-metallic) corrosion. This left the blades susceptible to movement and rendered them liable to damage by contact with the fixed blading that lined the outer casings.

The worst of the wire breaks were in the first, fifth and sixth expansions in the low-pressure turbines, and in the fifth expansion of the rotor in the port high-pressure turbine ('expansions' were required to allow steam, after being admitted to the turbine from the boilers, to expand as it lost pressure down through the length of the turbine). To counter this loss each series of blading was increased in diameter to restore and even out the pressure losses, each series consisting of about seven rings (each made of up to twelve segments) in the first expansion with about three dozen rings in the last. Blades in the high-pressure turbines were shorter than those in the low-pressure turbines and had one set of distance wedges compared to three in the latter. During a normal major maintenance the bladed rotors would have been lifted out through dedicated port and starboard shipping hatches and taken ashore to a workshop for repair before being turned in a huge lathe to ensure blade tips were precisely the same diameter in each expansion. After being dynamically balanced to obviate whip or vibration the rotors would then be returned to the ship for reinstallation. But this ideal situation was not to be as, according to the *Shipbuilding and Shipping Record* the work was 'probably one of the most extensive turbine reconditioning jobs ever attempted *in situ* (author's emphasis) and,' perhaps understating the huge technical and physical efforts that were involved, 'some very intricate and particular work was required'.

Corrosion, always a major problem, was found in some of the steam valves in the forward ends of the high-pressure turbines, in rotors, casings and in the 'dummies':

To counteract the (axial) thrust in reaction turbines a rotating piston (which is part of the turbine rotor) at the high pressure end of the turbine is called a 'dummy'. The pressure on the dummy being in the opposite direction to the thrust. To prevent leakage of steam past the dummy, grooves are turned in its periphery and brass strip is caulked into grooves in the turbine case in the way of the dummy. This strip projects slightly into the grooves in the dummy, and almost touches the ridges between the grooves. This type of seal is known as 'labyrinth packing'.

The corroded rotors required attention and a new section, 12in long and 7ft 11½in diameter, was fitted to each rotor, while the corrosion in the casings was cut out and replaced by 1in-thick steel sleeves fitted in two halves. *S&SR* observed with professional interest that the 'boring out of the casings for the steel sleeves and cutting grooves in the casing and rotors for the blading called for the exercise of much ingenuity'. Thornycroft's skilled tradesmen provided that ingenuity as they worked to the specifications that included:

PORT HP ROTOR – Forward end of rotor cut off and new filled. All blading in 5th and 6th expansion renewed.

Rotor dummy turned up and strips renewed. During packing altered to Labyrinth Radial Type.

CASING [i.e. for Port HP Rotor] – Casing bored out and liners fitted to length of 1st expansion All blading renewed in 1st expansion. New casing dummy supplied and fitted. Forward gland labyrinth packaging renewed in casing.

STARBOARD HP – Identical to Port HP with exception that 5th expansion of rotor not renewed.

… and the inner turbine that had created noise and concern when the ship was being manoeuvred astern out of dock in New York in late August:

PORT LP ROTOR – Rotor dummy turned up and strips renewed. Dummy packaging altered to Labyrinth radial type.

Forward gland labyrinth packaging renewed in rotor.

Rotor in way of 1st expansion turned up and grooves deepened.

Blading renewed [in] 1st, 5th, and 6th expansions.

CASING – Dummy renewed. Blading [in] 1st and 5th expansions renewed.

STARBOARD LP ROTOR – Same as for port.

CASING – Same as for port LP, additionally 1 row of blading in 6th expansion renewed.

PORT ASTERN – Repairs to blading carried out where necessary.

STARBOARD ASTERN – Grooves in rotor 6th expansion turned out, and 6th expansion blading renewed in Rotor casing.

The work was almost complete when the shipyard's tradesmen went on unofficial strike (the men were after a rise of 17/6d a week instead of the 10/- negotiated with their union) and all work came to a halt. The men were locked out and the dispute spread countrywide with 100,000 other shipyard workers walking out in sympathy. Not only was the *Mauretania* affected at Thornycroft's but so too were White Star's *Majestic* and *Ohio* of Royal Mail.

There was one piece of good news during this time of uncertainty when, on 2 February 1924, Captain Rostron CBE, RD, RNR received the highest honour that could be given to a member of the Merchant Navy; he was appointed Royal Naval Reserve Aide de Camp to King George V.

The ship lay idle in the water for two months with casings elevated above the delicate rotors; her scheduled sailing of 29 March was cancelled. Finally, a decision was made to send the liner elsewhere to have the work completed: Cherbourg, having had previous experience with maintaining the liner, was chosen. British shipyard labour was still required and those on strike did their level best to prevent 'scab' labour from joining the ship. A group of workers travelled daily from the Isle of Wight to work at 'Thorny's' but fifty strikers picketed the paddle steamer ferry as it arrived from Cowes. To prevent picketers from forcibly removing non-union men from the liner, it was arranged that she should sail earlier than scheduled. Cunard boarded their own superintendents, who were joined by supervisory staff from Thornycroft's.

Assisted out of the port by a tug tender of the Alexander Towing Company, the ship was then taken in tow by five Dutch tugs of L. Smit & Co.'s International Tug Company of Rotterdam, which had been quietly employed to take the powerless liner to France, leaving Southampton at nine in the morning of 11 April with a reduced crew to stand by the ship while at Cherbourg. Within a few hours the slow convoy was in trouble as a nor'-westerly gale blew up and buffeted the powerless ship and her escort of hard-pushed Dutchmen. The wind later veered to sou'-west and then back to the nor'-west as the tugs struggled to maintain just 1½ knots of steerage against wind and tide.

Cunard sent out tugs from France in a failed effort to assist the ship and even considered sending colliers to replenish the Dutchmen. Passengers in passing vessels reported seeing the *Mauretania* fighting against the heavy weather. By late Saturday afternoon the tugs' hawsers had parted and Captain Rostron's helpless ship was drifting with the tide to the south-east, about 15 miles from Barfleur. A danger arose that her tugs would run out of coal and abandon the liner completely to whatever fate had in store for her. The storm lasted for twenty-four hours before abating and the *Mauretania* finally arrived at Cherbourg at 7 p.m. on Sunday, after a journey that had taken fifty-six exhausting hours, and docked two days later. The work that remained to be done took several weeks and the final closing of the turbines was like a surgical operation with a careful check being kept on the number of tools being used as any unaccounted for could result in catastrophe. Senior staff kept other workers away from the turbines during these critical last moments but when the last casing was about to be lowered onto its lower companion a distinct 'ping' was heard, a sound that must have stopped many a heart. Humfrey Jordan described the scene in his book *Mauretania – Landfalls and Departures of Twenty-Five Years*:

> None of the engineers had seen anything, they had only heard; but they agreed as to the spot from which the sound had come. The top casing was raised again. Very slowly the rotor was turned [such was its delicate balance] in the hope that whatever had dropped on it might be discovered. Nothing appeared; so, since it was clear that something was there which should not be there, the turbine was [again] dismantled. The rotor, weighing one

hundred and twenty tons, had to be lifted out; not a quick or easy job. While it was going on a very careful watch was kept on all the workers.

It turned out that the potential destroyer of the rotor and the cause of a huge amount of extra effort had been caused not by accident but by:

> a brass trouser button, of French manufacture … A French workman … who did not like to see the finish of a lucrative job approaching, had flicked it from the rear rank …

Jordan related that the well-aimed, ill-placed button later came into the possession of Sir John I. Thornycroft, who had it mounted on a silver cup that he later presented to the ship's Chief Engineer!

While following the *Mauretania*'s progress, the naval architect who had been at the forefront in designing the *Mauretania* and *Lusitania*, suddenly collapsed and died at his home, 'Craigmin' in Warren Road, Blundellsands, Lancashire, on 7 March 1924. Aged 66 he had been suffering from stomach problems but his demise was reportedly caused by a chill contracted during a visit to London. Although beyond retirement age, he had been retained by Cunard and had recently been appointed to a new position.

According to his many obituaries, Leonard Adolphus Peskett had joined the Cunard Technical Department forty years previously as a draughtsman. Born in Kent in 1861, Peskett had served an apprenticeship at a shipyard in Rye, Sussex, which built vessels for the Admiralty, but his ambitions eventually took him to the Royal Dockyard in Chatham. From there, in 1884, he went on to join Cunard's Technical Department, run by its then General Superintendent, Captain Watson. Eventually rising to the top through sheer ability, he became widely consulted on many aspects of liner design as well as serving on various technical committees and producing learned papers; his 'The Design of Steamships from the Owner's Point of View' had been well received in 1914. Following Cunard's debilitating losses incurred during the Great War, Peskett had been at the forefront in designing a new fleet. His endeavours were recognised on 4 June 1918 when, in the King's Birthday Honours List, he was awarded the Order of the British Empire (OBE) for his work.

But the 'acme of his achievement' was undoubtedly the design and building of the *Lusitania* and *Mauretania*. He was described as an autocrat who demanded the best standards from those under him. Nonetheless, he was greatly respected and personally liked by many, be they company directors, shipyard managers, foremen, draughtsmen, shipwrights, riveters, and many others concerned with the business of ship-owning and the arts of shipbuilding.

His funeral service at the Eshe Road Congregational Church, Blundellsands, was well attended. The many mourners included his widow (Mary), three daughters and two sons, along with Sir Thomas Royden, Cunard's Chairman; several directors and departmental managers; experienced captains; representatives of shipbuilders and shipping companies; and other notables from the maritime world. Peskett was buried at St Luke's Church, Great Crosby.

In an appreciation, Professor T.B. Abell eulogised:

Mr. Peskett was one of the few men whose characteristics were realised directly one came into his presence. His qualities seemed to radiate from him as if they were visible, tangible things tabbed and labelled. His frankness, his kindliness, his sincerity, his ability were obvious. With more intimate association his well-balanced mind, his sense and appreciation of value in regard to his own work obtruded themselves, and no one can say that he was anything but a great naval architect …

Below: Following a shipyard strike in Southampton, the *Mauretania* was towed to Cherbourg by tugs of the L. Smit & Co.'s International Tug Company of Rotterdam for completion of the work. (Author's Collection)

Although Peskett was now unable to witness the outcome of the renovative work that had been expended on his beloved ship, the time had now arrived for the *Mauretania* to be put through her paces. Extra hands were taken on (11 April) for her trials, many of whom were shipyard men signed on as 'Mechanics' at a *monthly* rate 1 shilling (5 pence)! The shipyard men had to be on board the *Mauretania* 'at once'; and among their number was 21-year-old Etonian and Oxford-educated Londoner Roger Thornycroft, a young scion of the influential shipbuilding family. Thirty more men signed the Articles on 13 April.

She left her Cherbourg dry dock under her own steam in readiness to be put through her paces in the English Channel and the excitement of the ship's potential must have been tangible, not least to Chief Engineer Cockburn. A planned course had been

set for her trials so that the ship would make a series of passes, steaming back and forth with and against the tide, incrementally building up her speed. She performed like a thoroughbred, albeit a rather elderly 16-year-old thoroughbred, averaging 26.49 knots in a twenty-eight-hour period – fourteen hours with the tide and fourteen against. Over one pass of 14 miles, albeit with the tide, it was reported that the old racehorse had remarkably clocked up an incredible 31 knots! The ship returned to Cherbourg after each day's trials and, when all the figures and measurements were accrued and assessed, it was realised that the old *Mauretania* had not let anybody down and all the hopes placed in her had been more than justified. With the wind under her tail the *Mauretania* was ready to leave for Southampton on Thursday, 22 May 1924.

She had proved herself to be still magnificent!

Following the enclosure of part of her Promenade Deck with sash-operated windows the *Mauretania* steams through The Solent. (Courtesy of Ambrose Greenway)

16

'WE GOT IT!'

With well-deserved elation among those on board, the *Mauretania* returned to Southampton on 22 May 1924 to go through the routines of preparing for her first transatlantic voyage after a six-month absence; a news hungry public had been kept well informed of her re-entry into service. Even in furthest Cornwall, the *Cornubian and Redruth Times* observed:

> Everything is perfect in her public rooms, from the carpeted floors and tapestried walls to the spacious wardrobes, dressing tables and running water supply in her luxurious staterooms.

The *Mauretania* sailed 'in good style' at 11.30 on the morning of Saturday, 31 May. Quickly gathering pace, she wasted no time and made the short passage to Cherbourg in three hours and fifty minutes, far better than the usual passage. There was a renewed pride in the ship. Even in the Purser's office that pride extended to the presentation of the Crew Agreements, with each name being written in beautiful copperplate. A sense of self-satisfaction extended a little too far with some as the First Officer was fined firstly 5 shillings and then a hefty 10 shillings for a second offence of 'using or frequenting passenger toilets', strictly forbidden in the ship's regulations!

This crossing (her 305th) marked a very special, literal milestone in her career when the *Mauretania* achieved her millionth mile of steaming. An incredible record and those on board anticipated a celebratory crossing. During the twenty-four hours from noon on Monday, 2 June she sailed at an average of 26.5 knots over a fifteen-hour period before several hours of fog were encountered. The next day (although he did not mention

the date, 3rd, in his book *Home From the Sea*) Captain Rostron was in the Lounge taking tea with a group of passengers when the ship was 'well out in the Atlantic' making over 25 knots heading into a westerly breeze with a slight swell coming from straight ahead. The first indication that something was amiss came when the Captain sensed a slight breeze coming through a door on the starboard side of the foyer, indicating that the ship had made a sudden change in course. Remaining seated with his guests, he waited for the information that he knew would be on its way. As a Bridge officer hurried into the foyer, the Captain put up his hand 'to warn him to keep silence' before discreetly excusing himself.

Accustomed to the small vibrations from his engines, Chief Engineer Cockburn noticed a slight change and excused himself from a game of bridge. Rushing to his Engine Room, the Chief found that a centrifugal governor had performed admirably in cutting off the supply of steam to a low-pressure turbine, saving it from severe damage. Measuring and regulating the speed of the engines, the recently overhauled governors had been adjusted to activate should the engines reach 250rpm. Gliding to a halt, the ship remained stationary for a quarter-of-an-hour before regaining way. It was thought that the ship had struck submerged wreckage and lost her starboard wing (inner) propeller, causing her to veer off course. As that was one of the propellers used to manoeuvre the ship when docking the rudder had to be used to compensate for its loss. Fate had not yet finished with her as, on the Tuesday evening at 8 o'clock, the westerly breeze gave way to an 80-knot south-westerly gale. This increased to hurricane force, necessitating a reduction in speed to 12 knots. From ten o'clock the high winds began to abate and by midnight the ship had regained full speed.

Arriving in New York at 2 a.m. on 6 June after a disappointing crossing of five days twelve hours and thirty-five minutes at an average speed of 22.67 knots, Captain Rostron told *The New York Times* that it had been the worst trip that he had experienced 'in eleven years'. Experiencing the traumas of this crossing first-hand was Cunard's New York Director Sir Thomas Ashley Sparks. On arrival he predicted to *The New York Times* that, although several ships were on order for the company, larger, more luxurious ships would be built in the future. His prediction was by then a certainty as plans for a 1,000ft liner were already well advanced, its proposed length theoretically allowing the ship to span the crests of two long waves. The keel of this new 'supership' would be laid down at the end of the decade at the Clydebank shipyard of John Brown and would be known by her Yard Number – '534' – until the very minute of her launching. Sir Ashley also commented on the recently revised Immigration Act that reduced immigration quotas even more stringently. Sir Ashley said that, although the shipping company had been hard hit by the reductions, the losses had been offset by various efficiencies within Cunard.

Even though the return crossing was completed on three screws, the ship still managed an excellent average of 24.25 knots, taking five days, five hours and fifty minutes between the *Ambrose* lightvessel and Cherbourg's breakwater. An inspection showed that the shaft had sheered just forward of the propeller cone so a new propeller and shaft were prepared for installation on her next return. She made another similar voyage, departing Southampton on 21 June. For this trip Lord Eric Geddes (the brother of the British Ambassador to Washington; ex-Minister of Munitions, ex-First Lord of the Admiralty, and now Chairman of the Dunlop Rubber Company) was on board. He later became Minister of Transport and as such was notorious for wielding the 'Geddes Axe', severely cutting public expenditure. Six days after her departure the new floating dock was delivered to the port and readied for an official opening by HRH the Prince of Wales. After inspecting the dock he operated a valve that lowered the facility into the river. After lunching on board the *Aquitania*, the Prince boarded an Isle of Wight ferry, the paddle steamer *Duchess of Fife*, and sailed through the submerged dock, thereby officially opening it. He reboarded the dock to watch Union Castle's *Arundel Castle* become the first vessel to be docked.

There were fewer crew members on the *Mauretania*'s return departure from New York on 2 July, eleven having deserted. Also not completing the journey was US citizen 32-year-old Alice Marsh travelling in Third Class. Alice must have been excited at the prospect of going to Europe but it might have been too much for her as the day before arrival her heart disease put a fatal end to her anticipation. Her remains were landed at Cherbourg. After arrival back in Southampton (Howard Carter, the Egyptologist who had discovered the tomb of Tutankhamen, was on board) on 8 July, *Mauretania* was dry-docked for inspection and for the fitting of a new shaft and propeller. A careful examination revealed no trace of damage either to the turbine or to the shaft's supporting A-bracket. In a similar incident in 1908 a bracket had been seriously damaged, resulting in its complete replacement. The BoT surveyor reported that had damage been found, even slight, then the Passenger Certificate would be withdrawn and returned on completion of remedial work; but if the damage had been serious, as it had been sixteen years earlier, then the Certificate would be cancelled. Luckily, none was found. After the work had been completed the ship, straining at her reins and held under control by the Captain and Chief Engineer, was again chomping at her bit. Then on 9 August, again carrying with her the expectations of the nation, she was off!

Steaming quickly through The Solent, she rounded the Nab Tower and headed south to Cherbourg. Then, heading west, she passed the breakwater at 6.45 p.m. and leapt ahead at an average speed of 25.58 knots to complete the 3,057-mile crossing (642 miles being logged on one day) to the *Ambrose* lightvessel (passing this at 5.05 on the evening of Thursday, 14 August) in four days, twenty hours and two minutes. If there was still a Stokehold band, it would have been playing itself hoarse! At the end of the crossing all were jubilant, not least the Captain who, on the liner's breathless arrival at her New York berth at six minutes past nine, told *The New York Times*: 'We knew that the Mauretania had it in her and we started this passage hoping for the best.' Elatedly he added: 'We got it!'

The Captain said that the crossing could have been made in four hours under the actual time had the ship been on the shorter northerly route and away from the opposing influence of the Gulf Stream. The reconditioned engines, originally rated at 72,000hp, had on this record trip given 78,000hp.

From then on there would be no stopping the *Mauretania*, by now not the youngest ship on the North Atlantic but certainly still the fastest. Before the start of the return crossing, which left New York on 20 August direct for Cherbourg, Captain Rostron had determined that, to match the record just completed, it would also be a record eastward trip and made his intentions known to Mr Cockburn. A slight fog bade caution at the beginning of the crossing but the haze lifted and 'fine weather, light breezes and a smooth sea' blessed the liner's progress.

The first two days were records, as was the third, and some of the more experienced passengers soon realised what was happening and news of the Captain's intent spread about the ship. Reports of daily mileages were eagerly awaited, especially by those who had a bet on the ship's 'Pool'. On being asked if he was out for the record the Captain would respond: 'Oh no; just out to do our best, that's all.' Radio messages received ashore kept an excited public abreast of what was happening daily at sea as the great liner cleaved her way through a compliant North Atlantic. The *Berengaria* was passed on the 25th and the *Mauretania* signalled: 'Best wishes from all on board for [a] pleasant voyage for [the] Prince of Wales.' The distinguished traveller 'cordially reciprocated'.

Sailing outward bound from New York, the great liner approaches the Statue of Liberty. (Author's Collection)

After a trip of four days and nineteen hours was made between markers (the full journey between New York and Southampton took an hour over five days) at an average speed of 26.25 knots, which included a record day's (twenty-three hours, nine minutes on the 'eastward day') run from noon on Thursday, 21 August of 626 miles at an amazing 27.04 knots, she broke her record of 1911. On the ship's arrival in Southampton a beaming Captain Rostron (sharply dressed as always) was met and congratulated by Mr Cotterell, Cunard's bowler-hatted Port Manager. Fast crossings of less than five days (other than thirty minutes over that time on her westward early November trip) provided her passengers with excitement for the rest of the year.

Meanwhile, dredging operations were underway in Plymouth Sound, in order to make it suitable for big ships. As a result there was a minimum of 36ft in the deep-water anchorage at low-water spring tides – the Mauretania drew 32ft. Ideas were mooted to build a quay and make Plymouth the British terminus, as French and Dutch liners had regularly been calling into Plymouth for some time. Cunard decided to trial Plymouth as a new port, as it would save a precious twelve hours in the mails' (and passengers') arrival in the metropolis, an arrangement that would be commercially advantageous to British businesses, as well as hurried travellers.

At three o'clock the liner completed the 3,026-mile crossing to the Eddystone Lighthouse that lay 13 miles south-west of Plymouth after her record passage. Dotting the waters in Plymouth Sound, a small flotilla of pleasure craft, undeterred by the greyness and a prevailing stiff breeze, sailed or motored out to greet the liner when, on 15 September, she made a triumphant call into the Devon port. Spectators lined the cliffs of Cawsand (once the haunt of smugglers) to the west of the Sound and Bovis and to the east, and on the grassy slopes of Plymouth Hoe, and the first glimpse that the expectant crowd had of the most famous liner in the world was smoke rising above the distant horizon, soon followed by the red of her impressive funnels. As soon as the entire ship was in view two tenders, one for the passengers and the other for the mails, cast off from Millbay Docks and made their way to Cawsand Bay, where the ship anchored just a few minutes adrift from the Captain's estimated time of four o'clock. So, after another record-breaking crossing of four days, eighteen hours and twenty minutes at 25.69 knots (during which a jubilant Captain Rostron had been congratulated on his twenty-fifth wedding anniversary) she was afforded a special civic reception. By 4.15 gangways had been slung between tenders and ship and a welcoming party, comprising the Mayor of Plymouth (Mr Solomon Stephens, resplendent in his chain of office) and members of the town's Chamber of Commerce and Mercantile Association, boarded the liner. As they did so the first of 1,200 bags of mail were offloaded onto the other tender to be taken ashore several hours earlier than if they been taken to Southampton.

The mayoral party was taken to Captain Rostron's cabin, a 'businesslike apartment with a pleasing admixture of comfort', where brief speeches of welcome were made with the Mayor, who had been endeavouring for some time to get Cunard to bring the *Mauretania* to Plymouth, saying:

> As a Corporation we are ready and anxious to do all we can to get this great line of steamships to come here. Now you have broken the ice and come here again, to the benefit of the trade of this country, we are deeply grateful … here at the mouth of the Channel you can land your passengers in London to-day, and it will be great advantage to them.

The *Western Morning News* reported Captain Rostron's response, telling the party that his passengers appreciated that Plymouth enabled them to get to London that same evening. He added: 'The Company have tried many times to make the Plymouth call fit in, but, unfortunately, during the last few years it has not been convenient.' Mayor Stephens expressed the hope that the line would do so in the future. Captain Rostron hinted at the possibility of success in the Mayor's efforts: 'I think now there is every prospect of our calling here more often than previously, and I am quite sure the whole of your municipality will do all they can to help us.' In a cautionary tone, he added:

> Under the conditions under which we are steaming although I have no official instructions, I think you may look forward – I'm sure we shall do our utmost to fulfil all expectations of what the Mauretania ought

to do – and I think she will do her best to arrive here to get the people to London. I thank you very much indeed on behalf of the Cunard Company and of the ship's company for welcoming us here today.

Mr W.T. Leaman, the local Cunard agent, was asked by the Plymouth paper's local reporter whether he could say officially if the call would become a permanent one. Mr Leaman declined to commit himself but said the *Mauretania* 'would make two or three more calls … and probably would do so until the end of the year'. She would continue to do so into 1925.

Captain Rostron gave the Mayor and his party a brief tour of the spectacular rooms of the ship, specially pointing out the handsome Lounge and Smoking Room, in which 'a real log fire smouldered cheerily', and the cleverly screened open-air palm garden aft where 'not the slightest chilly breeze penetrates its snug seclusion'. Tea was served in the Lounge, while the formalities of inspecting disembarking passengers' passports and transhipping baggage and mails continued elsewhere. Before the official party disembarked, Captain Rostron obliged by having his photograph taken with the group on the Bridge for the *Western Morning News*. Sharing the Mayor's tender on the return to Millbay Docks were sixty-five bars of specie worth a quarter-of-a-million pounds. The mayor joked about purloining one of the gold bars and struggled in his attempts to lift one (another photo opportunity). A total of 1,203 sacks of mail from America, the West Indies and many other countries piled the decks of the mail tender like sacs of pollen on a bee's legs, while the 103 passengers (she had a relatively low list of 475) disembarked onto the passenger tender. The Great Western's 'Ocean Liner Express' was waiting to take many of them 227 miles non-stop to London's Paddington Station (at 80mph), arriving there at 10.28 p.m.

Another visitor returning to the shore was Captain William Turner, the former Captain of the *Mauretania* and ex-Commodore of the Cunard fleet. Now almost a recluse (he had been badly affected by Churchill's attacks on him following the *Lusitania* tragedy), he lived locally at Yelverton with his housekeeper and his beehives. The old Captain had been delighted to visit his old ship and to meet many of his former shipmates. 'Bowler Bill' later moved back to Lancashire to the

quiet suburb of Great Crosby, so this visit to his old ship would probably have been his last opportunity to see the *Mauretania* for some time.

The *Mauretania*'s speedy achievements ensured that she remained the favourite of the famous and wealthy. On her next departure from Southampton on 20 September were railway and business barons; the Maurice de Rothschilds; the ex-Governor of New York, Nathan Miller; and star of the silver screen Lionel Barrymore and his wife, Irene.

The old ship – she was now 17 years old – made several subsequent record eastward crossings during the summer of 1924, their timings being to within an hour or so of each other, which famously allowed Sir Arthur to get ashore and catch the same train home to Liverpool! The crew must have been in a well-disciplined state during these record trips as none were logged for misdemeanours – either that or else the Captain had developed a more lenient frame of mind – or perhaps the prospects of alternative employment ashore were still far from assured! Her early August outward journey of four days, twenty hours and two minutes was only bettered in October by a mere – but importantly to the speed watchers – six minutes.

But not everyone was entirely happy with the flyer's outstanding performances. Over several speedy arrivals and departures her dash earned her the dubious reputation of being *the* ship that went a little too fast as she passed inward to Southampton through The Solent and Spithead; her speed and the shallow waters of the roadsteads were not a good combination. Other larger liners passing through The Solent did not create such a wash as the *Mauretania* did, causing 'the waves [to] make towards the pebbled shore' (Shakespeare), each time she sailed. Following her departures from Southampton, she would steam purposefully down Southampton Water to Calshot Reach where, after passing the Henrician castle on Calshot Spit, a turn to starboard took her through the narrow, reverse S-bend Thorn Channel between the Spit and the Thorn and Bramble sandbanks, *Calshot* lightvessel to starboard, before another turn (to port) took her through Cowes Roads.

A reverse of this S-shaped course marked her more speedy arrivals. With no depth under her keel, the displaced water curled away in combers that fanned out from her bows before roiling onto the beaches and mud berths that lined The Solent a few minutes after her passing. These delayed series of mini-tsunamis – 'the Surge's Angry

Shock' – (perhaps seven or eight of them scouring the shore before losing strength) often drenched the shoes of many an unwary observer standing at the water's edge. Some of these inundations could be quite severe and were especially exacerbated by high tides. A little later, similar but weakened waves would roll on to the distant beaches of the mainland to the north.

After a trip that had been gale-driven for two days and calling into Plymouth on 27 October to drop off 140 passengers and 3,000 bags of mail, she made her call into Cherbourg before eagerly commencing the 90-mile leg to Southampton, her British passengers eager to participate in the General Election that would be held two days later. With the tide 'exceptionally high' and in a Force 3 WSW wind and intermittent drizzle the Cunarder, full of dash and bravado, passed through The Solent like a triumphant thoroughbred entering the winner's enclosure at the end of a race. As she did so she created a particularly heavy wash likened to 'a tidal wave'. Boatyards in Cowes suffered and small boats beached up to 15ft from the water's edge were dragged into the tide by the suction of the backwash as the white-spumed water progressed along the shoreline before funnelling up slipways leading into Cowes' High Street, flooding that narrow thoroughfare, and inundating many of its shops and public houses. The wave still advanced along the town's waterside perimeter before hitting the Parade that led to the Royal Yacht Squadron, gushed through balustrades fronting the Esplanade, then stormed onto the beach that protected the sloping swath of the immaculately manicured Green, leaving shingle on the paving between beach and grass, much to the Longman's chagrin.

The proprietors of dampened premises were not impressed, neither were the Cowes Harbour Commissioners. At their December meeting that august body resolved to write official letters of complaint to the Admiralty, who in turn advised them to write to the Board of Trade. Strangely, a standard report was published in many provincial papers stating that the incident had occurred during an *outward* trip. This seems unlikely as the ship would not have built up enough speed when turning to port off Cowes having carefully navigated the channels after exiting Southampton Water. Her manoeuvres indicated an inward passage. Portsmouth's *Evening News* seems to have got it right when they reported that the apology received from Trinity House, which

censured the Pilot, stated that the speed of the *Mauretania* had been reduced to 18 knots at the Nab Tower as she approached the eastern Solent; 12 knots at the *Warner* lightvessel; an increase of 4 to 5 knots when Stokes Bay was abeam; and by the time that the 'West [Ryde] Middle Buoy' had been reached speed had been reduced to 9 to 10 knots, which should have slowed her down as she approached the Calshot channels. However, at high water there was an ebbing westerly current of nearly 4 knots off Cowes (local knowledge said that the tidal rush could be much more off Egypt Point towards the west of the inward turn) and this would have added to the ship's estimated speed as she passed the sleepy Island town in its out-of-season hibernation.

Harbour Commissioner Alderman Fellows announced at the end of December that several letters had been received that assured the Commission that the *Mauretania* would, on her future arrivals and departures, behave herself with a decorum befitting the 'Queen of the Ocean'. Cunard said that their 'captains and pilots had instructions to exercise every care' when in The Solent. There were no further complaints … yet.

As the admonished ship lay safely berthed in Southampton's Ocean Dock after that controversial inward rush, the *Olympic* arrived on the last day of October carrying the Prince of Wales on his return from a two-month holiday in America. As the White Star liner rounded the 'knuckle' into the Dock the *Mauretania* joined in the gala reception by hoisting the signal 'Welcome'. In reply the *Olympic* raised a response from the Prince: 'Thank you'. Captain Bruce Bairnsfather and his wife were among the passengers boarding the *Mauretania* from the London boat train when the liner sailed on her last transatlantic of the year on 22 November. The Captain had been instrumental in raising the morale of the nation during the Great War through his creation of 'Old Bill', a hard-done-by cartoon character who found black humour and irony in the trenches. The Captain was off to New York to direct his new play 'Ullo'. Also boarding the ship from London for a four-month tour of America and Canada were noted golfers Abe Mitchell and George Duncan, who had been afforded a popular send-off from the capital.

Returning, dense fog encountered in the entrance to the Channel on 8 December delayed the liner's return arrival in Plymouth by half-an-hour, otherwise she would have made the fastest of a fast series of crossings each of over 25 knots. $1.25 million in gold was landed and safely ensconced in the vaults of the Bank of England by the next morning. Among the incoming passengers, famed French actress Madame Simone had been rehearsing on board during the crossing and she extolled the virtues of the *Mauretania*'s ability to get to Europe in a day less than her rivals. Madame Simone would eventually create her own kind of record when, in 1985, she passed away at the age of 108! To maintain the sensation of speed even the GWR Ocean Special created a record run from Plymouth, arriving at Paddington Station seventeen minutes early. Shortly after arrival in Southampton, the next day the *Mauretania* went into her annual lay-up for maintenance that took the liner out of operation for a month until her first sailing of 1925 on 8 January. Exiting the dry dock on the 5th was delayed because of high winds, but once alongside her berth in the Ocean Dock she was in magnificent company as her companions were the world's largest liners: *Majestic, Berengaria, Olympic* and *Homeric*, this mighty quintet later being joined by the *Aquitania*.

In January, in order to encourage those with limited funds, Cunard introduced Tourist Third Class, which enabled holidaymakers to visit Canada and the United States and return on any of the big ships from New York. To encourage reluctant British tourists – the new-style class had been embraced by the Americans for several years – the company extolled that Third Class in 1925 was as good as Second Class a few years previously as furnishings, accommodation and facilities had been greatly improved and that a well-stocked library, an orchestra, good concerts, indoor and outdoor dancing, deck games and sports were all available to the prospective lower-income traveller.

The liner arrived in New York at 7 a.m. on Wednesday, 14 January 1925, after leaving Southampton on the 8th, sailing again on the 17th. Because of gales, the *Mauretania* bypassed Plymouth on 22 January, where 6,000 bags of mail, and 200 passengers and a 'large quantity of specie' were due to be unloaded. If she had arrived there at a late 5 p.m., the Captain would have been reluctant to unload the precious cargo in the dark. The gold was not the only glitter on board; the great British actress Gertrude Lawrence was travelling, as was Prince Louis de Bourbon, oft-regarded as the rightful claimant to the French crown.

The *Mauretania*, her magnificent reputation still intact, was proving to be fuel-hungry in maintaining her record-breaking high speeds. The Cunard Board decided that her oil storage capacity should be increased to give her a better range of operation as her existing fuel storage tanks only gave her a full day's consumption over and above what was required for a single crossing of the Atlantic; expensive bunkering during cruises would also be reduced. Cunard's proposal for the additional capacity followed so soon after her recent lay-up that the BoT's Southampton office in Canute Road considered it to be 'conceived in haste'. The modification work was to be completed 'as speedily as possible' during an additional ten-day lay-up following her arrival in Southampton on 22 January. The company based its reasoning on the fact that the liner had formerly sailed with her ballast tanks empty on the westward voyage and these were gradually filled with compensating water as oil fuel was expended. The same happened in reverse when sailing from New York. The intention now was 'to fill the [ballast] tanks with oil before leaving New York … where it was cheaper' and then to 'transfer it [from the double bottom tanks] to the side bunkers just prior to arriving at Southampton' to compensate for the expenditure of fuel. In way of the tanks, a preliminary survey showed that: 'With the exception of local pitting which was electrically welded, the whole of the inner bottom plating was found to be in good condition.' The 226ft-long, 36in deep, triangular-sectioned, wood-filled bilge keel was also thoroughly inspected.

Plans were for the conversion of numbers 10 to 15 double-bottomed ballast tanks between Frames 152 and 197 to carry a large volume of oil, while still being retained for use as ballast tanks, and this called for some additional structural work. To obviate the inclusion of cofferdams, which involved extra work, the planned alterations were subsequently changed to affect numbers 8 to 13 double-bottomed tanks. In addition, 'number 16 to 22 double bottom compartments and the After peak tank, all of which are usually dry, can be used for water ballast', were also adapted, should the Captain and Chief Engineer think it necessary to use them. Tanks forward and aft of the new oil fuel tanks were used for the storage of domestic (i.e. non-potable) water 'being quite independent of the fresh water service [potable water, showers, baths, etc.], it is impossible for the former to be used for drinking purposes' to prevent contamination, the plans adding 'the working of the oil fuel, ballast etc. is left to the discretion of the captain'.

Once the work was completed, the new tanks were tested for oil tightness and newly fitted pre-heating coils were tested under a hydraulic pressure of 400psi, and new oil line suction and filling pipes were similarly tested but to the lesser pressure of 100psi. Although it was considered that the ship's stability would be 'practically unaltered', it was recommended that the surveyor should be satisfied that she would have sufficient stability in her arrival condition to permit the proposed transfer of oil from the double-bottomed tanks to the side bunkers. To this end the owners, once all technical work had been completed satisfactorily, carried out an Inclining Experiment to confirm the surveyor's expectations. This standard shipyard procedure showed that there was little or no change to the ship's metacentric height, confirming her stability when in service, especially in an 'arrival condition'.

To undertake an Inclining Experiment the ship had to be in a pre-ordained condition with certain stores on board:

Weight of ship (estimated)	31,300 tons
Stores	220 tons
Baggage in holds	210 tons
Mails	40 tons
Passengers' baggage in rooms	210 tons
Fresh Water in tanks	200 tons
Cargo in No 1 Hold	200 tons
Cargo in No 2 Hold	300 tons
Oil Fuel	5,328 tons
Reserve Feed Water in Tanks Under Engine Room	506 tons
Potable water for Passenger Use (Baths, Washing, etc)	2,147 tons

A known weight would be moved from one side of the ship to the other on the upper deck and the induced angles of heel noted. From the experiments a Metacentric Height above Base was obtained of 34.68ft and an actual Metacentric Height was calculated at 4.32ft. It was also noted that if certain tanks were bilged (flooded) and the ship took on a list of 8°, then the countermeasures taken would be to flood the double-bottomed tanks on either side; empty boilers of feed water on the flooded side; and open cross-connections for levelling purposes.

Leaving Southampton on 7 February 1925, the second cruise began from New York ten days later after taking on bunkers and stores. What was becoming a familiar itinerary for these cruises took her well-cosseted passengers to Madeira (where, again, European tourists joined her), Gibraltar, Algiers, Monaco, Naples, Athens, Haifa (again organised by the Society for the Promotion of Travel in the Holy Land for passengers wishing to visit Palestine) and Alexandria 'at the very height of the season'. In conjunction with the Orient Line, arrangements had been made for tourists using the latter company's *Oronsay* and *Ormuz* to join the *Mauretania* at Naples for the return journey home, where she arrived on 18 March. The *Mauretania* recommenced her Atlantic ferry work on the 21st.

Perhaps spurred on by the publicity resulting from the *Mauretania*'s money-laden cruise – and perhaps thinking that taxpayers' money was being used to subsidise a rich man's holiday – a Member of Parliament (retired naval Commander Carlyon Bellairs) asked in the House of Commons:

> whether the First Lord of the Admiralty was aware that, owing to her size, oil consumption, and crew required, the Mauretania was of no use as a naval vessel in war; and whether the Treasury would have the subsidy expense of £90,000 per annum transferred to the Post Office for the speedy carriage of the mails.

The Secretary to the Admiralty replied that the original agreement would expire in November 1927 and did not 'see sufficient ground for making any alteration for the short remaining period'.

The liner returned to Britain on 7 April, arriving at Plymouth at 5 a.m., where she unloaded passengers and 6,000 bags of mail. Then onto Cherbourg (making her third arrival there within five minutes of each other) and finally Southampton, making three ports in one day, which delighted the Captain. Thick fog prevailed as the *Mauretania* sailed from Southampton on 11 April and again as she neared the *Ambrose* lightvessel seven days later. The fog not only hindered the giant Cunarder but proved an obstacle to smaller craft using the same waterway, an area where the sea funnelled into the channel that had become known during Prohibition as 'Rum Row' as the narrowing sea lane was frequented by smugglers bringing illegal liquor into the United States. Earlier that morning officers on the liner's Bridge had heard the sound of gunfire, apparently coming from an unseen Coastguard vessel pursuing an illicit rum-runner.

At 4.25 a.m., just as the *Mauretania* was losing way to 'drop the hook' to ride out the murk, she was hit by a motorboat that had been travelling at an estimated 30 knots, smashing its bows and cabin against the huge ship. Those on the liner's Bridge were unaware of the accident until cries for help were heard rising up from the sea. The Captain was called and, as the ship came to anchor, an emergency boat was lowered. Three men were rescued from the sea, two being treated for injuries by the ship's Surgeon, the appropriately named Doctor Mort. The lucky men described themselves as 'simple fishermen' but, considering the reputation of the area and the speed at which the motorboat had been travelling, the Captain preferred to describe the rescued men as 'Bottle fishermen'.

After an extremely turbulent return crossing, during which she sped in bouts of 26 knots to compensate for three occasions when speed was reduced, the *Mauretania* arrived at Plymouth at 8 on the morning of 28 April, only two hours behind schedule. The work of unloading mails was rushed and 3,600 bags were unshipped in the record time of fifty-eight minutes. One hundred and ninety-two passengers of the 715 on board were also whisked ashore and their train of eight coaches, pulled by the Great Western's locomotive *Shooting Star*, got them to London Paddington, 227 miles away, in four hours and three minutes – seven minutes ahead of schedule and just in time for lunch! The next arrival at Plymouth (19th) amplified the benefits of calling into the West Country harbour when nearly half the First-Class (Saloon) passengers disembarked, along with 3,000 bags of mail. The passengers were in London for lunch. By May, 50 per cent of the First-Class passengers were disembarking at Plymouth to take advantage of the arrangements to get them to London twelve hours early. A few steaming hours from Plymouth other passengers disembarked at Cherbourg, many of whom were heading for Paris where a World's Fair – the *Exposition Internationale des Arts Décoratifs et Industriels Modernes* (the International Exhibition of Modern Decorative and Industrial Arts) – had opened that month. This grand exhibition brought a new style into the world, the *Style Moderne*, better known as art deco, which would have an enormous influence on design in all aspects of life – including shipping. 'Tut-mani' was out and curvilinear was in. Architecture, interior design, furniture, fashion and jewellery took on an entirely new look incorporating simple straight lines and curves, and the style would be reflected in the interior design of a ship that revolutionised expectations of travel at sea. The year 1927 would see the debut of this pioneering liner.

Prohibition claimed another victim when on 24 May, a day out from Southampton, a tragic accident occurred that could have been avoided. Acute alcoholic poisoning, resulting from the consumption of a glass of neat rum, fatally affected the victim's brain and respiratory system. The deceased, Hungarian-born Antalova Gorgely, was only 6 years old. His distraught mother, with whom he had been travelling in Third Class, had left the glass of spirit in her cabin. The child was buried at sea twenty-four hours later.

Early June's New York heatwave affected a Longshoreman helping to load the *Mauretania* so much that he stabbed himself several times. During the crossing that followed with over 1,000 passengers on board a wreath was cast into the sea to commemorate US servicemen from the city of St Joseph who had been lost in the Great War. Another 5.30 a.m. arrival in Plymouth meant an early start for the disembarking passengers. Arrival in New York on 19 June was marred when she rammed the pier. No one was hurt, although Relief Captain Diggle just avoided serious injury. Women on deck were alarmed and excitement reigned among those on the pier. The liner's Bridge was slightly damaged.

A busy season on the Atlantic meant that for her 24 June eastward passage there were around 200 more applicants for her First-Class accommodation than she could carry. The ship was full, it was reported, of 'interesting women, prominent Society folk, and American millionaires', and that a Spanish diplomat and his wife even accepted a cabin normally used by servants! After slicing through the Atlantic at over 25 knots in fine weather that blessed the entire crossing, she anchored in Cawsand Bay on 30 June at 5.45. Here 371 passengers and 3,444 bags of mail were disembarked. Sir Alfred Booth, the former Chairman of the Cunard Line, was among those disembarking but passenger William Ayres missed the train as he was arrested for smuggling tobacco. The ship was cleared by eight o'clock and 579 passengers went on to Cherbourg and 333 to Southampton.

July was a busy month for both mails and passengers and the 4 July westward sailing marked not only American Independence Day but also the eighty-fifth anniversary of the first sailing of a Cunard vessel, the paddler *Britannia*, in 1840, which took fourteen-and-a-half days at 8½ knots to make the transatlantic crossing. On board the *Mauretania* a celebratory dinner was held, toasts were proposed to the President of the United States, and a response made by the oldest Cunard passenger, Mr Francis Hyde. Assistant Cook, William Thomson, fell ill on the outward journey so ship's Surgeons Mackenzie and Roberts successfully operated to remove his appendix, assisted by a passenger, Dr D. Geilt. Their patient, taken ashore in New York, rejoined the ship for her next return sailing.

After her next return crossing in fine weather at just over 25.5 knots, she arrived at 6 a.m. at Plymouth with a glittering passenger list on Tuesday, 18 August. The express train that met the ship continued the speed of the journey, even setting its own record with the GWR locomotive *Dartmouth Castle* pulling the 'Ocean Special' to London on a non-stop journey that arrived at Paddington eight minutes ahead of the scheduled time of ten-past-four. Visitors and sightseers flocked to see the ship either in dock or elevated above the water in the floating dock and 280 visitors from Bristol arrived on Wednesday in a fleet of ten charabancs fitted with 'grand pneumatics' to enjoy a tour of the ship. Perhaps not a few souvenirs left the ship with them! August downpours not only drenched the decks of the *Mauretania* as she lay at her berth ready for her sailing on the 22nd but they also flooded Southampton's cricket ground, bringing sporadic halts to the Hampshire game against Yorkshire. To fill some of their time, many of the Yorkshire cricket team accepted an invitation to look over the Cunarder. During their tour a call came that play would soon be resuming. A hurried return to the ground found that play had already recommenced with only five Yorkshiremen in the team backed up by four men from Hampshire!

By the time that the *Mauretania* sailed from Southampton on 12 September an Empire-wide seamen's strike was under way; this had been brought about, bizarrely, by the seamen's union itself, its chief official having suggested to the shipping companies that a wartime allowance should be scrapped, effectively a hefty pay cut of 1 pound. Although 1,500 men were on strike in Southampton, Cunard insisted that the *Mauretania* was not affected, and would sail on time with a full, regular crew. A denial that additional crew were being brought down to Southampton from Liverpool, where poverty-making unemployment was endemic, was only partly true – 250 men (carefully described not as 'seamen' but as 'seagoing types') did arrive – not in Southampton but in nearby Portsmouth. The men were tendered to the ship in Cowes Roads by two Portsmouth-to-Gosport ferries, the *Viceroy* and *Varus*, with late arrivals transferring on the tender *Flying Kestrel*. The 'seagoing types' were accompanied by representatives of the Shipping Federation and, when on board the Cunarder, were signed on by BoT officials. There was no record in the Crew Agreements. By this time there were practically no entries being made in the log for crew misdemeanours. This was either down to the Captain being less of a disciplinarian (unlikely); the men, aware that jobs were scarce ashore, were behaving themselves; or that a real fear of the 'Red Peril' of Communism and the threat of sudden strikes were creating greater leniency. Desertions or the failure to join the ship after signing on were also remarkable by their absence.

At 7.45 on the third evening out on this trip, 50-year-old passenger Augustyn Morris left the Smoke Room saying that he was feeling unwell and would retire to bed. An hour-and-a-half later his room companion, John Skritulskis, found his body, his death due to a heart problem that he had earlier described.

Three Distressed British Seamen were carried on the return trip. Ironically the president of the National Sailors' and Firemen's Union, Havelock Wilson, who had suggested the wage cuts that caused the prevailing strike was also returning to Britain after a trip to Canada to thank those countrymen for their contribution of £500,000 towards the relief of seamen during the war. Often described as a 'bosses' man', he gave an interview to the *Western Morning News* in which he railed against the threat of Communism and, somewhat deflecting responsibility from himself, blamed the seamen's strike on the Communists, saying 'the Red peril is a real one, and it must be confronted and fought'. It was not mentioned during his performance in which class he and his companions had travelled. 'The Ocean Special' non-stop express train again outdid itself by arriving at Paddington fifteen minutes ahead of schedule, having completed a record run of one mile per minute.

Leaving Southampton on the 3 October sailing was the celebrated explorer of the poles, Captain Roald Amundsen, en route for a lengthy lecture tour. During the trip a set of autographed Norwegian Arctic stamps commemorating his exploration was put up for auction. The resultant £90 went to seamen's charities. Also on board was famed Irish tenor John McCormack and family. The return call into Plymouth on the 19th meant a busy time for the Cunard agent as the *Mauretania* (with rubber baron H.S. Firestone on board on his way to start a million-acre plantation in Liberia) became the second Cunarder to be cleared within a few hours – the first being the *Ascania* the night before – and was soon followed by *Andania*. The next voyage began on the 24th with not only glitter in the passenger list but also in the holds. The first consignment of the Leverhulme collection of art treasures was on board, off to be sold in the US and valued at between £25,000 and £70,000 – a small sum compared to the £2 million in gold (reduced from the originally expected £6m); contained in 200 boxes it was stowed in the strong room in the after hold, the largest ever such shipment and probably worth more than the ship herself.

For the last three eastward crossings of 1925 the weather played its part and calls into Plymouth for 9 November and 1 and 22 December were struck through in the log. For the first of these crossings there had been mountainous waves all the way over on 'one of the worst crossings of her career'. Even so she still managed 25 knots. On the Saturday the ship's Surgeon gave medical advice via wireless to a ship whose captain had been injured on his storm-damaged ship, the American tanker *W.D. Anderson*.

The ship emerged from her winter overhaul for the opening of the 1926 season in readiness to sail on Wednesday, 3 February. Two hopeful passengers arrived at Berth 47 only to see that the ship was already in the stream of the River Test and turning in the swinging grounds (where the ship had once struck a moored yacht) prior to heading down Southampton Water. Seeing their plight, a Cunard official summoned a tug skipper to take them out to the ship. After taking on the errant two, the ship's staff requested that the tug take four visitors ashore who had missed the 'All ashore' gong. Heading back to the dock, the tug skipper's patience was pushed to the limit when the tug was requested to return and take off an unearthed stowaway. Arriving in New York on the 9th, the *Mauretania* prepared for her second cruise. While the ship lay at her berth, Assistant Cook Dominica Beltsame of London was taken ashore to St Vincent's Hospital suffering from pneumonia, which unhappily, a few days later, proved to be the instrument of his demise. Cunard took care of Beltsame's remains as they were 'on the 13th inst. buried in the Company's plot No 36 Grave No 7, Section Q, South New York Bay Cemetery, Jersey City, the service being held at the Church of the Holy Rosary, 6th St., Jersey City. Rev Tortizo officiating'.

The liner's second excursion as a cruise ship left New York on 17 February carrying her wealthy 'cargo', including Colonel House, the powerful American politician who had been an adviser to President Wilson during the Great War, to Funchal in Madeira, Gibraltar, Algiers and Villefranche. Her call into the Bay of Naples was her first visit to a recently united Italy now under the grip of dictator Mussolini, which may have appealed to some of the more excitable modernist travellers. This visit was followed by Athens, and Haifa (again for the important excursions to Jerusalem), and then on to Alexandria, arriving at the Egyptian port at 5.33 on the morning of 8 March. She remained here for a lengthy six days, giving her passengers time to discover the colour and ancient history of that country and to absorb the excitement that followed the discovery of Pharaoh Tutankhamen's treasure-laden tomb.

The *Mauretania* sailed from Alexandria on her return run in the late afternoon of the 14th, heading for Naples, where she stayed overnight. Villefranche followed (another overnighter) before turning her nose westward and home to Southampton, arriving there at 1.30 on the afternoon of 23 March. Some of her cruising passengers left the ship to tour Europe while others stayed with her to return to New York when she sailed on Saturday, 27 March. By noon on the 28th she wirelessed, as was customary, that she was 271 miles west of Bishop's Rock and at noon the following day 902 and making good speed.

On the day that the *Mauretania* left Alexandria with her souvenir-laden tourists, an event occurred across the English Channel that would change the face of liner travel for ever when another French 'revolution' began, its manifesto a lavish brochure issued by The *Compagnie Générale Transatlantique* (CGT) that illustrated the interiors of their proposed 43,153gt liner. The gastromically famed French Line was saying '*Non*' to the traditional style of the past and '*Oui*' to the future. Although of an evolutionary exterior design, the ship's interior was unlike that of any other. Gone were the past influences of palace, castle and stately home; in their place were large, airy rooms decorated simply in the new art deco style, a style that itself would be adopted ashore – the Ocean Liner style – and used in many notable buildings both private and public (e.g. Odeon cinemas). The decor of the First-Class Dining Room was another French Line temple paying homage to French cuisine, but this one was the largest afloat rising through three decks. Stunningly, it boasted a sweeping grand stairway, down which the fashionably dressed entered in theatrically flamboyant style. At the end of each evening passengers retired to cabins, all of which boasted beds instead of bunks. The new 791ft liner would be launched on 14 March 1926, as the *Île de France*. Her radically modernist yet stylish interiors became an important influence on future ship design. Naval architects and interior designers of other companies would travel in the three-funnelled French ship to seek inspiration.

At a stroke the *Mauretania*, and many like her, suddenly became old-fashioned.

Sailing from Southampton and Cherbourg on 27 March, the *Mauretania*, with just over 680 passengers on board, headed into weather already cold with squalls of snow and hail that would deteriorate further; by 2.20 p.m. on the 30th the ship's forepeak was plunging into a heavy swell coming from ahead and, prudently, engine revolutions were reduced from 180 to 160rpm. In rough seas the *Mauretania* had the reputation of being a good sea boat, remaining a dry ship forward when going at 14 to 15 knots, but today she was taking spray over her bows as she pitched into the seas. Because of the region that the ship was in, Captain Rostron ordered additional lookouts to watch for ice. At 11.40 p.m. the liner took a wave over her bow, causing damage on the foredeck. It was three hours before repairs could be effected, the ship's speed being reduced to 100rpm. Over the next few hours the liner's speed was altered according to the strength

of the 'moderate gale', now blowing from the west-nor'-west, sending spray over the ship as she pitched into the waves. To the passengers the gale must have seemed like a hurricane and many a chair in the dining rooms would be unoccupied that evening! If the wind, freezing squalls and the possibility of ice weren't enough to contend with, Humfrey Jordan recorded in his book *Mauretania*, a series of entries were made in the log in mid-afternoon:

3.25. S O S from s.s. Laleham in Lat. 39° 06' N. Long. 55° 18' W.

3.30. Proceeded full speed to assistance of Laleham.

4.00. Strong breeze. Very rough sea and swell. Cloudy and clear.

4.24. Received amended position of s.s. Laleham - Lat. 39° 06' N. Long. 56° 16' W.

In a reversal of the race to the assistance of the *Titanic* twelve years previously, it was now a case of the larger ship going to the rescue of the smaller. As with the *Carpathia*, Captain Rostron ordered the *Mauretania*'s on-board services and facilities be put into rescue mode as the liner built up to maximum speed as she headed towards the distressed vessel 180 miles away.

The drama had started on 29 March 600 miles south-west of Halifax, Nova Scotia, when the small, hapless 4,068gt *Laleham* (built on the Tyne, as was the *Mauretania*) fell afoul of the violent nor'-westerly gale, hail squalls and mountainous seas that would soon be hindering the *Mauretania*. The *Laleham* was carrying a crew of thirty-seven hands and a cargo of barley from Chile to Ipswich for her owners, Watts, Watts & Co. Ltd of London. Two days later, conditions worsened and it became obvious that the ship would not survive. Captain Stocker-Johnson ordered an SOS to be sent to say that the distressed vessel was on her beam ends with her starboard rail under water, her bunkers and stokehold flooded, and her lifeboats and engine room skylights smashed. Due to a failed electrical supply, emergency batteries came into action, reducing the range of her radio to 30 miles. Tar barrels were set on fire to indicate her position should darkness fall before assistance arrived.

The first ship to reach her just after 5 p.m. was the British tanker *Shirvan* of the Baltic Trading Co. Ltd, en route from New Orleans to Rouen. With volatile benzene in her tanks, the *Shirvan* kept well away from the sparks emanating from the burning barrels while six eager seamen under the charge of Chief Officer Strowger volunteered to man a lifeboat lowered into the heaving ocean at six o'clock. As it was too dangerous for the rescuers to approach the *Laleham*, a line, attached to a lifebuoy, was thrown for the crew to grasp and they were then pulled, one by one, towards the lifeboat. Two trips were made, firstly rescuing nineteen, then eighteen men, who were transferred to the tanker in a similar way, the rescue being completed by 10.30 by the light of the burning barrels. The boat's crew were later awarded bronze medals for Gallantry in Saving Life at Sea, one recipient receiving his from the hands of the King. (Coincidentally, a previous *Laleham*, also built on the Tyne, had also been wrecked in 1900). At 8.35, after a five-hour dash (during which the *Mauretania* reached an amazing 29 knots for an hour), Captain Rostron received confirmation that all the *Laleham*'s men had been rescued; three minutes later the liner resumed her original course. Before receiving the call for assistance, Captain Rostron had, in spite of delays caused by the weather, sent the New York office an estimated time of arrival. Even though the liner had been diverted in her rescue attempt, she still arrived in the harbour two minutes before that estimated time!

Her return trip was far less adventurous in fine weather. Her first call into Plymouth for 1926 was on 13 April, the colours of the surrounding countryside drawing comments of admiration as she anchored in Cawsand Bay at 6 a.m., while those watchers on shore admired her tall, impressive funnels that caught the sun in the early morning light. After landing about 200 passengers (she was carrying just over 480 – 216 in First; 114 in Second; and 151 in Third) and mails the liner was cleared by the Cunard agent at 7.45 and headed for Cherbourg.

Like their counterparts in Plymouth, spectators along the shorelines of The Solent observed the comings and goings of the great liners with interest. Excited holidaymakers and jaded workers alike, especially on the paddle steamers belonging to the Southampton, Isle of Wight and South of England Royal Mail Steam Packet Company Limited (still the longest name of any shipping company) as they splashed their business-like way between Southampton and Cowes, were constantly thrilled by the sight of large liners, each one individually identified by their build and livery. Sometimes the observers created a list on their much smaller craft by crowding to one side as they were treated to the spectacle of a liner at its berth in 'The Gateway to the World' or sailing or arriving to and from all parts of the British Empire. To see the *Mauretania* on one of these occasions was a special treat and those being ferried would rush to wave to those peering down at them from the rails of the ship that towered above as it passed.

After being in port for four days, the signal flag for the letter 'P' – the 'Blue Peter' – was hoisted at the foretruck informing onlookers that the ship was about to sail; the French tricolour that fluttered from her foremast top indicated her next port of call, Cherbourg. The watches in the various departments began to take their turns as each four-hour period approached, each watch roused by appointed callers who reminded groups or individuals that their 'trick' was about to start.

At 11.30 on the evening after calling into Cherbourg on 17 April the ship was well under way westward when Engineers' Storekeeper William McAlear went to call 38-year-old Second Senior Third Engineer James Copeland (from Dumfries, Scotland – a country that produced many a fine marine engineer) in readiness for the latter's midnight watch (probably in the Turbo-Generator Room that befell his rank). There was no response to the Storekeeper's knock who, imagining that the Engineer was elsewhere, abandoned his mission. He did not think it necessary to report the matter. At the appointed hour the Third did not appear for duty. A search was made but the missing officer could not be found, although Mr Pattison, Senior Second Engineer, reported seeing Copeland at the door of the Engineers' Wash House at around eleven. The two men did not speak. That seems to have been the last that anyone saw of poor James Copeland, who had been with the company for fifteen years. No note was found to explain his mysterious disappearance.

On a foggy arrival at Quarantine on 23 April the liner anchored while she was inspected and, after obtaining *Pratique* (clearance with a clean bill of health) and flying the yellow 'Q' flag that requested permission to enter New York Harbor, she weighed anchor. But as her 'hook' was being lifted it was seen that a cable was caught in the connecting shackles of her anchor chain. Weighing anchor ceased immediately. After an unsuccessful manoeuvre to free the cable – an important submerged government communications line connecting Brooklyn's Fort Hamilton and Fort Wadsworth on Staten Island – a crew member was lowered over the side but his attempt to attach a wire to the fouled cable in order to lift it free proved equally unsuccessful as the latter broke. It was an hour-and-a-half before the ship could proceed to Pier 54. On the day after arrival, and during the course of these preparations, an accident occurred with a tragic result. Able Seaman (AB) Reginald Fry had been tasked with washing down lifeboat davits but, just before 5 p.m., while he was working on those of Number 9 lifeboat (odd numbered boats were on the starboard side) he slipped and fell overboard. Another AB, R. Maunders, immediately threw a lifebuoy into the water and, as he surfaced 2 yards away from the lifebuoy, Fry started to swim towards it. Maunders called out to the swimming man to ask if he was alright. Fry looked up and answered 'Yes'. Maunders and A. West, another AB, ran down to C-Deck to throw a lifeline to Fry, but when they reached that deck there was worryingly no trace of the swimming man.

A lifeboat, already in the water for exercises and laying alongside the liner, was immediately manned under the charge of Junior Second Officer E.R. Taylor. A thorough search was made of the area where Fry had last been seen but there was no sign of him. Equipment was assembled and the waters of the dock were grappled, again to no avail; the operation was called off at eight o'clock as the Sun set. As often happens in such cases, Fry's body came to the surface two days later. Recovered by the New York police, it was taken to the NYPD's hard-pressed Fifth Precinct Station House in Manhattan's Elizabeth Street. His Britannic Majesty's Consul in New York held an official enquiry into the deaths of both Copeland and Fry, the former being recorded as missing and the latter drowned. That same day (28 April) was sailing day and among those embarking were six DBS – Distressed British Seamen – who, had for some legitimate reason, lost their ship. Under the Merchant Shipping Acts, British captains of other ships were obliged to repatriate these men.

Coal mine owners, eager to maintain their profits in spite of a falling market and a lack of investment, planned to reduce miners' wages, already down to almost half since the end of the Great War, by 13 per cent and to increase working hours. One million miners went on strike and their catchy slogan 'Not a penny off the pay, not a minute on the day!' caught on with sympathetic workers in other industries. At one minute to midnight on 3 May, the great General Strike began with docks, transport, utilities, heavy industry, etc. grinding to a halt. Units of previously organised soldiers and civilian white-collar workers were mobilised to take control of transport and some industry. Clashes between police and strikers broke out in various cities already badly affected by unemployment. The National Sailors' and Firemen's Union declined to join in the Strike, even though many of their members had been put out of work when their coal-burning vessels were converted to oil. The Strike lasted for ten, sometimes violent, days and affected the whole country before being called off by the unions. The miners were left to struggle on alone, their cause now lost.

The *Mauretania* was approaching home when the Strike began and after lunch that same day passengers were advised that 'Owing to the Labour Crisis in Great Britain' the scheduled call into Plymouth would be cancelled. This cancellation seems to have been rescinded and the ship may still have called into Plymouth as a log entry – 'Did not call' – for the following day was struck through. In Southampton the Strike ensured that there were no dock labourers to handle the *Mauretania*, so Cunard office staff rolled up their sleeves and did the work themselves, from handling mooring lines to unloading 3,500 bags of mail and several hundred pieces of luggage. In lieu of strike-bound trains, motor-coaches took passengers to their destinations in the metropolis. The *Mauretania* sailed at 2.30 on the afternoon of 8 May with a good passenger list and a full crew.

Mauretania passed the Plymouth Breakwater lighthouse exactly on time as the tender *Sir Richard Grenville* steamed out to meet her as she arrived on 26 May after a fast but rainy crossing. An early disembarkation was American John Goldstrom, who was attempting to break a record of just under thirty-six days in circumnavigating the globe. Taken off the ship by a fast motorboat, he was rushed to a nearby airfield but fog threw his finely tuned arrangements into disarray and prevented his aircraft from taking off. He returned to Millbay, where he joined the other passengers and caught the boat-train express, later catching a plane from Croydon Aerodrome to continue his race against time.

The 'Paul Jones' was still gaily danced as usual in First Class by passengers, either unaffected or annoyed by the Strike, on the second night out as an ice-breaker; but not all on board the ship were happy. For some unstated reason (it might have been due to ill feelings arising from the recent strike) twelve engineers were reverted to the ranks in Southampton on sailing day, 29 May, with subsequent reductions in salaries. These unfortunate men had to break the news to their families when the ship arrived back in England on 15 June. The liner called into Cherbourg, where an ailing 75-year-old American, Charles Chamberlain, boarded the liner anxious to be getting home by the fastest means possible. Terminally ill, he was taken straight to the ship's Hospital. He did not survive to see his homeland: he passed away as the liner passed the Statue of Liberty.

But not all was gloom. A month later in the early hours of Saturday, 3 July, the Captain, who was just finishing a long stint on the Bridge as the fog that had closed in two days after leaving New York was finally lifting, became aware of the Wireless Operator attempting to locate him in the darkness. 'Sparks' asked for a quiet word in the Chart Room. Here he gave the news that Captain Rostron had been created a KBE – a Knight of the British Empire – and was now 'Sir Arthur'. Because this news had arrived at the end of a foggy night, Sir Arthur was wittily dubbed, as many other captains were similarly nicknamed, 'The Foggy Knight'! The ship made one more voyage under the command of Captain Sir Arthur Rostron. Concurrent with his knighthood, he had also been given the Freedom of the City of New York for his 'splendid services to humanity and the City of New York and the people of the United States over many years'.

At the end of Sir Arthur's lengthy period in command, his ship seemed reluctant to lose him; in an attempt to delay the final farewell she dropped a propeller on Saturday, 24 July en route to Plymouth during rough weather that claimed and disabled other craft in its high seas. The ship lost 60 miles a day as a result of her mishap. After disembarking her passengers in Southampton, she was dry-docked to assess the extent of any sustained damage. The Mauretania was not the only one to lose something that made the news. Actress Gertrude Lawrence was very much in vogue when she arrived in England bare-legged without stockings! On the conclusion of his 240th crossing in his beloved Mauretania, Captain Sir Arthur Rostron made his final farewells to his ship and crew as he had been put in command of the much larger Berengaria; since 1922 this huge ship had been the Mauretania's successor as flagship. Captain Edgar Britten (Cdr Ret'd RNR; Discharge Book No. 031493, Extra Master's Certificate) briefly had command of the ship during a four-day lay-up during her dry-docking to replace the lost propeller, but Sir Arthur's successor would be Captain E. Diggle. For Sir Arthur, a new ship meant a new house as he moved home from Liverpool to the village of West End near Southampton.

Her next – delayed – crossing, commencing on 11 August, with Captain Diggle in command and Captain Eaken as Staff Captain, ended at 10 a.m. at her berth at the foot of West 14th Street in New York on Tuesday, 17th. There may have been some confusion about having two R. Chisholms on the ship's books – one working as the Chief Officer and the other as a Chief Steward. Discipline was maintained as Trimmer W. Bartlett was fined 5 shillings for insolence to Senior Third Officer A. MacKeller and, even though there was a great prestige associated with working on the 'Maury', there were still desertions (four) in New York. The ship was turned around in a remarkable thirty-one hours after 5,000 tons of cheaper American oil had been taken on and 75,000 items of linen taken ashore, laundered and returned to the ship in time for her sailing at 5 p.m. the next day. By the time that she reached Plymouth at 6 a.m. on the 24th on her return trip she was back on schedule to the minute! The round voyage had taken twelve-and-a-half days, almost as impressive as her hard-won, coal-fired Christmas dash of 1911. It would have taken a lesser vessel perhaps five days longer. The Mauretania's new captain had quickly made his mark and would be in charge of the old ship as she entered yet another phase of renewal.

17

'WAVES LIKE A ROLLING TRENCH ...'

(John Donne)

Following her remarkable twelve-and-a-half-day round voyage in August, the *Mauretania* made five further voyages during the remainder of 1926, continuing to astound with record crossings. Her departure from Southampton on 28 August was delayed to await a last-minute passenger, eminent neurologist Sir James Purves-Stewart, senior physician of Westminster Hospital, who had been given an hour's notice to join the ship in order to attend a patient in Montreal. The absence of a passport was countered by arrangements made on board.

The ship's surgeon, Dr B. Sydney Jones, had by now been transferred to the *Aquitania* and his almost anti-Establishment 'Ancient Order of Heathens' was replaced by the more altruistic 'Ancient Order of Tramps', founded on the *Berengaria*. the purpose of which was to foster 'a brotherly spirit among all nations' at a time when the effects of the Great War were still being felt. The 'Lodge' on board *Mauretania* was one of half-a-dozen afloat, its membership including several millionaires, businessmen, professionals and even baronets, one of whom was Sir Joseph Isherwood, the prominent Naval Architect and Marine Engineer who had developed the increasingly important 'Isherwood System' of longitudinal framing in the construction of ships.

After a return crossing in fine weather at an average above 24 knots, the liner arrived at Plymouth on the morning of 13 September at ten minutes to ten. Fifteen minutes later the tenders were snugly alongside and 133 passengers were taken off – including local boxer Ted Moore, who had been on a forty-match tour of the United States – along with 2,788 bags of mail; all were got away in record time, the tenders casting

off for Millbay Docks at 10.57. The ship was cleared for sailing with the remaining 250 passengers three minutes later.

The crew, too, seemed to be happier as some started their own on-board magazine, the *Blue Riband* (*sic*), the proceeds from which went to the ship's Sports and Athletics Club. Captain Diggle contributed to its pages, which satirised members of the crew and kept him updated on the mood and morale of his ship's company.

The mails taken off at Plymouth on 4 October came as usual from the United States, Canada, Japan, Shanghai and North China, Bermuda, Bahamas, Jamaica, Mexico and Central America, and the Leeward and Windward Islands. Also leaving the *Mauretania* that day was Cunard's senior doctor, A.W. Mackenzie; he was retiring after twenty-seven years' service with the company. A mid-October arrival at Quarantine (15th) attracted headlines that the *Mauretania* had arrived within 121 minutes of breaking her own record. Her list of titled, wealthy, eminent and famous passengers still attracted comment in column inches of newspaper copy on both sides of the Atlantic. Even in the West Country's *Cornishman* notable arrivals at Plymouth, especially those of local interest, were recorded in the regular, sometimes anti-Semitic, reports in 'Mr Sid Blake's Cornish Letter'.

With the experience gained during the winter of 1924/25 refit, the Cunard Board decided that the *Mauretania*'s current oil storage capacity could be profitably increased but the modifications involved would require another lengthy period out of service. Accordingly, Cunard's Technical Department drew up specifications and shipyards were invited to tender. Sir George Hunter was fairly confident that his yard, Swan Hunter & Wigham Richardson, would get the £25,000 contract that included improving her passenger accommodation but conceded that Thornycroft's in Southampton was better located to do the work. In the end all were surprised when it was revealed that the work would be going to Cammell Laird's of Birkenhead, the welcomed placement going to the company's Repair Department in Liverpool Docks. Thornycroft's would still have the *Berengaria* and *Aquitania* (the latter had been expected on the Tyne) for their winter overhauls.

Towards the end October storms were plaguing the Channel and the *Mauretania* arrived in Cherbourg (25th) after unloading 2,933 bags of mail at Plymouth and 114 passengers who were probably glad to get off the ship. After encountering very rough seas during the final part of the eastward trip, a thunderstorm broke over the French port. Cunard denied passenger reports that the ship was struck either by lightning or a small waterspout as she entered the harbour to discharge 208 passengers by tender. Seventy-nine storm-tossed passengers remained on board for the final leg of the crossing to Southampton.

By this time Staff Captain Eaken had been replaced by Captain W.T. Hughes, a step up from his last command, the company's much smaller *Vandulia*. Mr Cockburn, still ensconced as Chief Engineer, had under his supervision a staff greatly reduced from the ship's coal-burning days comprising thirty-three Engineers; five Electricians; two Boilermen; two Plumbers; three Electrical Attendants; five Refrigerating Attendants; two Store Keepers; two Donkeymen; twenty Greasers; fifty-three Firemen; and thirty-five Trimmers.

Armistice Day 1926 fell a day out from New York and a solemn service of Remembrance was held with all passengers (including General Giuseppe Garibaldi, grandson of the 'Liberator of Italy') and off-duty members of the crew attending the 'moving and impressive' ceremony. At the Eleventh Hour of the Eleventh Day the flag was lowered as the 'Last Post' sounded to mark the start of a two-minute silence. Men, standing in sombre mood with bare heads bowed under a grey sky, were perhaps lost in personal, traumatic reflections of the Somme, Passchendaele, Gallipoli, Mesopotamia, Jutland and many more hard-fought battles with only the sounds of the sea roiling around the ship. The silence was broken by the notes of 'Reveille'

marking the end of the observances when, suitably and poignantly, a survivor from the *Mauretania*'s torpedoed sister ship, the *Lusitania*, cast a wreath into the ocean.

At the conclusion of a very stormy crossing, which had claimed several small vessels around the Atlantic coasts (*Mauretania*'s captain said that the 'mountainous' seas were the worst that he had seen in twenty-five years), she arrived in Plymouth, where a number of craft were sheltering from the westerly gales then raging in the Channel. Anchoring in the harbour at 10 a.m. on Monday, 15 November after a crossing of five days, two hours and thirty minutes, she was a day late. One hundred and thirteen passengers and nearly 3,000 bags of mail were taken off in the Devon port, while a further 235 disembarked at Cherbourg along with another 1,000 bags of mail. Only sixty-five passengers had opted to stay with the ship until she reached Southampton and the *Grantham Journal* reported in its lengthy society gossip columns that Baroness Ravensdale had contracted a chill during the 'exceedingly rough voyage' and, on the advice of her doctor, would not be able to go hunting as planned. What some people had to suffer!

Heavy rain and floods continued to plague Britain and a particularly strong gale and heavy seas awaited the *Mauretania* off the south-west coast of Ireland on 21 November as she steamed westwards. Meanwhile, the liner's smaller fleet-mate *Andania* was standing by a distressed cargo steamer, the *Aldworth* of Sunderland, 1,000 miles further into the Atlantic. Comfortingly, advertisements publicising the *Mauretania*'s next Mediterranean cruise departing from New York on 21 February must have appealed to many, including the ship's hard-pressed crew, as they experienced the worst that the North Atlantic could throw at the ship.

Cunard's arch rival, the White Star Line, had announced in early August that it intended to build a giant liner for the Atlantic ferry and P.A.S. Franklin, President of the IMM, confirmed the announcement in Southampton when he arrived on 13 November. At a cost of £2,500,000, this proposed liner would, after a series of increases in plans, be a massive 62,000gt and, at 1,000ft, become the largest liner in the world, putting the *Mauretania* in seventh place in the largest liner league. The huge ship would be built at the Belfast shipyard of Harland & Wolff. Both Cunard and the French Line were put on their mettle.

On 7 December, at the conclusion of her final eastward crossing of 1926, the *Mauretania* was prepared for a short passage to Liverpool for a pre-docking survey. A reduced crew was signed on for the short coastal voyage to her registered home port, where a great deal of excitement and activity had been generated in anticipation of her first appearance on the Mersey for seven years. Cammell Laird's shipyard had been busy preparing for the *Mauretania*'s arrival. Twelve hundred dock blocks had been laid along the centre of the Canada Dry Dock's bottom and arranged to suit the line of the liner's keel at a trim previously determined by the yard's Drawing Office. Two hundred men and six tugs made ready for her arrival and a new four-bladed, eighteen-ton propeller, manufactured by Messrs Stone, was ready to replace the spare screw that had been fitted in Southampton in July.

There was much work to be done. In order to attempt to bring the liner up to date and to meet the expectations of the modern traveller many cabins were to be refurbished by having bunks replaced by beds (á la *Île de France*); her beautiful panelling restored; and a myriad of other improvements made to give the old lady a facelift. Letters were exchanged between technical departments as the work progressed to ensure that everything went to plan, to budget, and was completed on time; the ship was scheduled to be in dry dock for fourteen days and it was stressed that this limited time was 'on no account [to] be exceeded'. Specifications called for the conversion of an existing cross bunker into three oil fuel tanks that extended from the 'forward bulkhead of the forward Boiler room [at Frame] No. 233 to the after bulkhead of No. 2 Hold [at Frame] No. 245'. However, the tanks would still be capable of holding ballast water. Blueprints prepared by the shipyard were sent to Cunard, to the BoT's Canning Street office in Liverpool, and also to Lloyd's surveyors for consideration and technical approval. These drawings showed oil fuel suction systems; filling, overflow, ballast and separating tanks; heating coils; piping and air pipes that were to be installed in the new storage tanks. If any alterations and additions to the plans were found to be necessary during the course of the work each 'A&A' (alteration and addition) had to be officially approved. The Admiralty was not consulted as the liner was no longer of military interest.

The *Mauretania* arrived at the mouth of the River Mersey at noon on 7 December. The misty, drizzly weather that prevailed did not auger

well as, when she attempted to moor in mid-stream, an anchor was lost so she was manoeuvred alongside the Prince's Landing Stage. It was hoped to get the ship over the sill of the Sandon Dock entrance on the crucial high tide but, because of the delay, the opportunity was missed and when she was only a few hundred yards away the gates were frustratingly closed. She had to wait for the next floodtide, when a bevy of attendant tugs helped her though the gates; a mere 10½in separating the sides of her hull and the masonry of the dock entrance. Once in Canada No. 2 Dry Dock the gates were closed, the water pumped out and, as the water level decreased, timber shores were lowered to support the ship against the dock's walls. Gangs of men in small rowing boats scraped the hull clean of speed-inhibiting marine growth as the water level lowered, the odoriferousness of the discarded barnacles and weed on the dock bottom assailing the senses as it dried.

To commence the work in cramped conditions, a quantity of ballast had to be removed; this necessitated a riveted plate covering an old watertight door in the bulkhead at the forward end of the cross bunker at Frame No. 245 being cut away using pneumatically driven cold chisels, the sound being amplified in the confined spaces. The lower plating of No. 2 Bulkhead at Frame 233 was also removed. Inspection of the bulkheads requiring modification revealed corrosion of lower strakes of plating and these, too, had to be replaced with rivets drilled out and strips of plating on adjacent strakes that held lines of now empty rivet holes removed. Double-riveted butt straps were fitted to join the new plates to the old, with rivet spacing reduced to five rivet diameters apart; 5/8in rivets being used, to create an oil-tight joint. The inner bottom was found to be in generally good condition, with localised pitting being filled by electric welding.

A new Tank Deck stretching across the width of the ship was fitted between bulkheads at Frames 233 and 245, the existing centreline bulkhead – reduced in height to the level of the new deck – being slotted to take supporting channel beams. The new 'deck', fitted 3ft 6in below the existing Orlop Deck, was pierced by access manholes and carefully smithed intercostal angles connected the tank top to the ship's shell. To subdivide the newly created space, two new fore-and-aft bulkheads, sited 9ft from the centreline, were also introduced. With limited temporary lighting and basic ventilation that supplied fresh and extracted hot, foul air, the ubiquitous tobacco smoke from prohibited 'ciggies' and rust dust disturbed by the vibrations of the work created a claustrophobic working environment for a skilled workforce labouring in shirt sleeves and flat caps well before hard hats and Health and Safety regulations were even thought of. The final caulking of the new butt straps created an increasing staccato shriller than riveting and not an ear defender in sight! The men accepted these conditions as part of hard-to-come-by jobs that had to be done. The whole of the existing steelwork inside the new tank had to be cleaned of rust and scale and given two coats of red lead paint for protection, as was all new steelwork and any original steel that had been disturbed. The modified bulkheads at each end of the tank were painted white. A new 8in filling pipe and 2in steam pre-heating coils drawn from solid mild steel were fitted. As removal of the ship's old coaling arrangements would have made the current job too complex and expensive, they were retained and maintained:

> The coaling shoots [sic] are to be cleaned, scaled and given 2 coats of red lead paint, shell doors [coaling ports] to be opened, studs made 1/8 inch larger [threaded for sealing nuts to be attached] and on completion door seals were rejointed and closed.

Boilers were inspected and were generally found to be 'in a healthy condition. All parts affected by former corrosion were carefully examined; the corrosive action appears to be quite "dead".' This improvement was due to the fitting of the 'Cumberland' system for preventing corrosion when the liner had been initially converted to oil burning. However, it was noted that there was some 'slight grooving on some of the furnace throats'. The ash-ejecting gear, once hard-worked but long-since redundant, was removed.

The rejuvenated port high-pressure and low-pressure turbines were also opened up and examined. The first three rows of blades in the former were found to be in a very dirty condition 'with scale deposit … brought in from the steam belt and on after side of strainer'. The scale was removed and the cleaned areas coated with steam- and corrosion-resistant 'Apexior' paint. Although a large number of fractured binding wires, especially in the initial stages in the low-pressure turbine, were repaired, this turbine was generally in excellent condition. A new propeller shaft was also safely installed.

The entire work was carried out to 'comply with the rules of Lloyd's Register and the Board of Trade, and to the satisfaction of the Surveyors of these bodies and the Owners' Representatives'. At the end of January, Albert Haslett, *Mauretania*'s old BoT guardian since 1908, recommended that the tanks used to separate oil from water should be tested 'if possible'. A certificate was issued by the BoT's Liverpool office on 9 February 1927:

> The new oil storage tanks and connections have now been completed. The heater coils and pipes were satisfactorily tested to three times working pressure (viz. 585 lbs) and the OF [oil fuel] suction pipes and connections to 75 lbs per square inch. All joints and connections were found to be perfectly tight. I inspected the separating tank on completion and when full. As the cover on the top of the tank is only of light material it was not possible to test with any head pressure. A declaration has now been issued to cover a period up to 18th November 1927 …
>
> … signed GH Haller, E&S Surv, 9.2.27., The Principal Officer, Liverpool.

To complete the modernisation, the two motorboats that had previously been borrowed from the *Aquitania* for the *Mauretania*'s first cruise were retained, having been converted to motor-lifeboats by their original builders, Messrs. Thornycroft Launch Works at Hampton on the River Thames. Because these craft were also to be used as lifeboats, the original Thornycroft M/4 Standard Type engines (built at the company's Basingstoke works) raised an official eyebrow as they had not been 'built under the Board's [BoT] survey, nor are any tests of the material available'. The alterations and additions made to these Honduras mahogany, carvel-built, double-skinned boats were many: their American elm keels were stiffened by the addition of 8in by 3¼in capping pieces; their two bulkheads were doubled in thickness; two collapsible bamboo masts per boat were fitted to take wireless aerials; buoyancy tank capacities were increased; six lifebuoys were added for the safety of the occupants; and 'Little Bull' signal horns gave the vessels a voice. A new cabin of varnished African mahogany crowned both.

The ship's post-refit appearance created much interest, not least in Cunard's own publicity. One brochure called her 'The 1927 *Mauretania*' and illustrated some of the enlarged and refurbished rooms with new furniture in many areas, en-suite and Regal staterooms laid with carpets of 'fuchsia-red' or 'purple with a silver design', the latter matching the rooms' colour scheme augmented with 'modern shot silk' wall coverings, sumptuous silk-covered eiderdown-quilted beds, 'a refurbished Verandah Café', potted palms reaching to the skylights of public rooms hinting of semi-tropical cruise destinations, repolished woodwork, its intricate carving glinting in reflected light, and baths supplied with hot salt water from a new heating system. In Cunard's attempts to show that the 'Queen of the Ocean' was up to the challenge of the new competition, the 1927 brochure carried a page of quotes from several nationwide newspapers whose reporters, probably well fed and watered by the company, gushingly penned their impressions. The *Bristol Times and Mirror* carried:

> The famous liner, the pride of the British Merchant Service, has been thoroughly modernised … with the result that the 'Mauretania's' accommodation remains unsurpassed …

… while the prestigious *Daily Telegraph*'s reporter seemingly missed some of the updated cabins and dwelt too much on the ship's aged but still-impressive style:

> With a record of service unchallenged by any of the great ships which cross the Atlantic, the 'Mauretania' re-enters the Cunard sailing list after an elaborate refit in her old port of Liverpool. … It is not only her speed that makes the 'Mauretania' a favourite ship among those who pass across the Atlantic. The handsome apartments, which are more like rooms in a stately home, are unchanged, and the famous panelling, which for nearly twenty years has been the envy of other shipowners, still stands unequalled [and would remain so in style as the modernist style took hold] in the decorative schemes of larger and newer ships.

'A hundred staterooms have been re-planned' countered the *Daily Chronicle* and, noting Cunard's attempt to play catch-up with the

French with some cabins on B-Deck redecorated in art deco style, observed that 'each contains a bed – not a bunk. Pullman berths have been transformed so as to give the idea of an 18th-century four-post bed with valances and curtains', 'some … fitted with painted silk reproduced from the Marie Antoinette boudoir' said *The Scotsman*, which also noted the hot and cold running water in every First-Class stateroom, their floors fitted with 'carpeting and furnishing to harmonious colour schemes'. The *Morning Post* also focused on 'The new wallpaper … a masterpiece; the … painted silk makes every man feel a millionaire, or wish he were one'.

Wood and wallcoverings attracted a lot of attention as newspapers enthused about the still-impressive quality of the old liner's internal decoration, its renovation inspiring many admiring column inches. Subtly hinting that the ship's ageing style of panelling was outdated Manchester's *Daily Dispatch* told its readers:

> Reflecting the glory of a departed craftsmanship, huge hand-carved panels of incalculable value have been so revived … that they will, this year, create a sensation among the expected record rush of Atlantic travellers …

A brochure strangely illustrated the Boat Deck at the time of her trials, and even *The Scotsman*, normally enthusiastic about the *Mauretania*'s progress, concentrated on aspects of the liner's original appearance, its review almost harking back to 1906:

> Specially pleasing in general effect is the dining-room, with its panelling and pillars in natural creamy oak, its upper gallery and its great central dome with a gilded boss to represent the sun, and a scheme of decoration which displays the signs of the zodiac round the base.
>
> The woodwork and carving of the succession of spacious rooms on the upper decks give the 'Mauretania' an aspect of handsome dignity.

But hope for the liner's future (one columnist predicated that she had another twenty years ahead of her!) shone through the reviews. The *Manchester Guardian* and the maritime professionals' paper *Lloyd's List* spoke of these hopes:

But apart from the question of speed, the 'Mauretania' will remain one of the most striking examples of a happy combination of perfection in naval architecture – for no ship of her size has more graceful and impressive lines – and of the art of the decorator working with a free hand in design and expenditure ...

Altogether the 'Mauretania' has added to her still unparalleled speed the amenities of newer ships, and looks like retaining, for a long time, the reputation of being the favourite Transatlantic liner.

While the ship was out of service, the Germans announced in the New Year that they were back in the game and were proposing to build two prestigious liners of 46,000gt for the North German Lloyd line. Previously, German shipyards had not exceeded boiler pressures of 260psi, but these new ships would be built with turbines more powerful than those of the Cunarder, worked by a pressure of 350psi. The ships would be built as contenders for the *Mauretania's* magnificent speed record.

Signing men on for the return coastal voyage south on 4 February 1927, the repainted, renewed and reinvented liner sailed at 12.35 p.m. the following day. Watched by thousands of Liverpudlians, this would probably be their last sight of the great liner that proudly bore the name of their city on her stern as she headed for Southampton, where she arrived on the 7th, joining the *Berengaria* and *Majestic* in dock. It was reported that the *Mauretania* made 26 knots for two hours during this short trial trip, a speed that equalled the best of her records!

She was readied for her sailing to New York on 9 February under the command of Captain Diggle, with P. Alexander as Staff, and S. W. Tansley as Chief Officer. Because of the increased demand for music, the liner now carried two Bandmasters leading groups of six and four musicians. To show what the liner was now capable of, she arrived in Cherbourg from Southampton in a very short three-and-a-half hours. The oft-wild North Atlantic was again seemingly jealous of the beauty of the ship and was determined to make a mockery of her restored youth. Gale force winds were encountered on this gala crossing and on the 11th a mountainous wave ripped away 40ft of foredeck railing before damaging the foremost boat davits and shifting a heavy, newly refurbished motor boat from its chocks; the radio antenna was washed away. Somewhat battered, she arrived in New York on 15 February where Glory Hole Steward, A.E. Williams, was taken ashore to St Vincent's Hospital with pneumonia. The ship stayed alongside her berth for six days while the storm damage was repaired and preparations made for her next voyage – another cruise – taking on stores and additional staff to serve the First-Saloon and Second-Class tourists who would be embarking for her sailing on the 21st. Because of her speed – she would steam at around 23–24 knots between ports – she was able reach more ports in her 10,000-mile journey in less time than other cruising vessels. Her itinerary was much the same as before: after an Atlantic crossing she made an early arrival in Madeira at 1.22 a.m. on the 26th, but during the crossing to Gibraltar a First-Class Waiter, Charles Haymer (transferred from the *Berengaria*) mysteriously disappeared. Reported missing since 5.20 on the morning of the 28th, it was 'Presumed that he has gone overboard'. Undoubtedly, an inquiry was held in Gibraltar, this being the liner's first British port of call following the incident. The liner stayed by 'The Rock' until 1 March, when she sailed for Algiers, arriving there at 6.35 the following morning.

A day's sailing brought her passengers to Villefranche on the fabulous French Riviera, from where the town of Cannes was a favourite destination having attracted the first wealthy refugees from a wintry smog-bound London years previously. Others would seek an excursion to Nice, where one could hope to bump into Rudolph Valentino or Douglas Fairbanks perhaps filming in the local studios. A Diaghilev ballet might be experienced at the Casino Theatre or a drive along the beautiful French Riviera – the exclusive Côte d'Azur – might be a prerequisite. An overnight stay in the Hôtel du Cap, gastronomic adventures in the cafes, restaurants or casinos might be sought, or even a venture on to the risqué beaches where, while sporting a suitably fashionable swimming costume (or not!), an equally fashionable suntan might be painfully obtained. The famed and luxurious Blue Train (*le Train Bleu*) whisked those so inclined to the small state of Monaco and the famed and sophisticated casino town of Monte Carlo. From France to Naples to see the emerging ruins of ancient Pompeii. From thence to Athens and the inspiring sights of the Acropolis before two days' steaming brought her to Haifa, where several passengers went ashore in Palestine and onwards to Jerusalem and the religious ambitions of their lives.

The 'Egyptian season' was in full swing and the following six-day stay in Alexandria enabled essential excursions to be made to the mighty Pyramids of Giza (more camels, more photographs) and to the Valley of the Kings, where the continuing excavation of Tutankhamen's tomb was still causing much excitement. Alexandria was the end of the outward cruise and here a group of British tourists joined the ship in the Egyptian port for the journey home. Villefranche was revisited for another extravagant overnighter. One gentleman, 70-year-old Sir Charles Walstow, had boarded here on 4 March during the liner's original call but did not make the return. Suffering from 'Angina Pectoris' (coronary heart disease), he passed away as the cruise ship entered the port. His remains were kept on the ship until she returned to Southampton. On the 27th the travelled liner passed the Nab Tower at the eastern approaches of The Solent at 10.33 a.m. and docked just after lunch. The ship had on board a 'Deck cargo [of] oil fuel in double bottoms [of] 272 tons'. This figure would be replicated on many a return. During the twenty-nine days of the sunshine cruise only one day had been marred by rain, the evenings being star- and moon-lit. Always proud of his ship, Captain Rostron said that the *Mauretania* did 'anything that you asked of her'.

The ship's tonnage was noted in the log as being raised from a precise 30,695.58 to a more rounded 30,696!

A French Revolution

Sir Thomas Royden of Cunard hinted in April that Cunard coal-burning ships that had been converted to burn oil might, as their boilers still had their firebars, revert to using coal as the solid fuel was 24 shillings (£1 4s – £1.20) a ton, whereas the Americans were charging 30 shillings per ton for their oil. The suggestion came to naught.

Taking passage on the liner on her sailing of the 23 April was Polish stage and motion picture actor and director Richard Boleslavsky. It was he who introduced and taught the Stanislavsky system of acting to the United States, the system later becoming more popularly known as 'Method acting'.

Competition on the North Atlantic was gathering momentum. The *Île de France* left le Havre on 22 June on her maiden voyage to New York, where her arrival was met with enthusiasm and a great deal of interest. Thousands of curious people crowded the dock area just to look at the new liner, while her astounding interiors remained accessible to a select few. Three funnels had superseded the previous fashion of four and the new French ship soon became popular among the youthful, the stylish and the famous – the *chic* – and her First-Class bookings set records for years to come. But in spite of the new ship's modernist appeal many travellers still preferred the reassuringly traditional, comfortable ambience of the speedier *Mauretania*, even though her splendid panelled interiors were considered passé by some.

Captain Diggle handed over command of his ship for the voyage that commenced on 16 July; Relief Captain S.G.S. McNeil formally took over and, after all chronometers, instruments and books had been formally handed over, took her out to sea – but not before several Engineers were re-rated in rank. The crossing had its drama when a Czech passenger in Third Class, 55-year-old Mrs Maria Kotulova, suffered a fatal stroke. At the end of the crossing, a First-Class Waiter deserted in New York, an event that was becoming decidedly rare.

The *Mauretania* arrived back in The Solent on Tuesday, 2 August after 750 bags of mail had been taken off at Plymouth along with 170 'express' passengers that included J. Pierpont Morgan Jr, son of the famous American financier en route for a family holiday at his English home. The liner steamed sedately through the spectacle of Cowes Week – the annual glorious yachting regatta where wealth met water – the ship providing a dramatic contrast in colour to the whiteness of the scores of racing craft that surrounded her, creating an added excitement for the crowds watching from ashore. The ship was carefully navigated, blowing her siren in warning when necessary to ensure that she did not run down any of the cloud-like yachts: the old adage of 'Steam give way to sail' was difficult to execute but, as it was the responsibility of every helmsman to avoid a collision at all times, a small craft would be foolish to argue with a huge ocean liner! The liner's ensign dipped in salute as she passed the Royal Yacht *Victoria and Albert* (King George, 'The Sailor King', loved sailing in his beloved cutter *Britannia* during 'The Week') and the powerful array of international guardships, led by the British 15in gun battleship HMS *Ramillies*, smartly rode at anchor as they watched over their various nationals racing on the waters, gravely impressing shipboard observers and shoreside promenaders.

Two days after her arrival in Southampton, the liner was lifted in the floating dock for her mid-summer overhaul. During a record seventeen hours spent high and dry, a large workforce scraped and cleaned her bottom plates prior to painting. Captain Diggle would be once more on board when the *Mauretania* steamed outwards on 6 August. This voyage would be the fastest of the year; even after encountering strong winds and rough seas she averaged 25.29 knots during the latter part of the return crossing. On board were mails 'via Southampton ... per s.s. Mauretania' destined for Europe, the USA, Canada, Newfoundland, Central and South America, Japan, China, Bahamas, Bermuda, Cuba, Mexico, Panama, Ecuador, Colombia, Jamaica, Costa Rica, Fiji and the Leeward Islands. She arrived back in Southampton on 23 August after a stay in New York between the 11th and 17th.

As she was preparing to sail on 27 August, a taxi sped up along the quay at Southampton, its driver rushing on board bearing a package containing £237 10s in cash that Third-Class passenger Rabbi Nasztyl had left under his mattress in his hotel room. Luckily the chambermaid had been an honest person, the sum of money being almost a year's wages for her. Other passengers included Sir Harold Snagge, Managing Director of aircraft manufacturers D. Napier and Son.

The liner continued her season of fast voyages, covering the 3,092 miles in less than five-and-a-half-days, reaching New York on 1 September in five days, four hours and twenty-nine minutes. The voyage that left Southampton on 17 September arrived back in Plymouth on 4 October at 10 a.m., two hours late because of thick fog encountered near the oft-treacherous Western Approaches. As soon as the mail tender was alongside, the *Mauretania*'s chutes were rigged between the tender and the ship, down which 4,000 mail sacks soughed in quick order to be manhandled into large wicker baskets by the tender's crew. The First and Second Officers were on hand to supervise this all-important task, carefully counting each sack. Among the 152 passengers disembarking at Plymouth was a Miss Luigia Vanzetti en route to Italy carrying the ashes of her brother Bartolomeo

Vanzetti and his companion Nicola Sacco, two purported 'Red' radicals who had been – many maintain wrongly – executed in the electric chair in Charlestown. The liner left for Cherbourg at 11.45.

During the month, 82-year-old Sir George Hunter announced his impending retirement as Chairman of Swan Hunter and Wigham Richardson's shipyard. During forty-eight years of shipbuilding Sir George had seen the size of ships increase from 500 to 56,000 tons and materials change from wood to iron to steel. His ubiquitous attire of reefer jacket and yachting cap would be missed in the shipping and shipbuilding worlds, although he would still retain a position on the Board.

In the post-war era women were consolidating their freedoms found during the Great War and groups of usually affluent 'bright young things' set the legend of the Roaring Twenties. Gone were the long hobble skirts and dresses, tight waist-pinching corsets and large picture hats covered with crime scenes of avian massacres or exotic specimens from a botanical garden, and in came heightened hemlines, bobbed hair and cloche hats, lashings of eyeliner and mascara and rosebud-painted lips. Parties were wild; the Cakewalk dance was out and the less-inhibited Charleston was in. Not satisfied with the thrills of travelling in the world's fastest ship or in cars that went at unheard-of speeds, some ladies turned their vamp-like gaze to the skies as the lure of quickly developing aircraft took their feminine fancy.

One such lady, American Ruth Elder, was determined to be the first woman to cross the Atlantic by air. She and a companion, Captain George W. Haldeman, along with supplies of turkey sandwiches, coffee and chocolate, had taken off on 11 October in an aircraft appropriately named *American Girl*. Although the intention was to follow the path of the North Atlantic liners (for safety), the aviators knew that they were heading into unfavourable weather. Perhaps not unexpectedly, the plane was reported missing and the *Mauretania*'s Navigators, along with those on many other ships, were tasked to keep a sharp lookout. The ill-timed adventure finally came to an end when the plane was forced to ditch a mere 300 miles from its destination. The rescued aviators subsequently planned to return home in the *Mauretania*. It seemed to be the silly season for flying across the Atlantic – two fliers were lost until they saw the *Mauretania* below them!

The *Mauretania's* arrival in New York on 13 October coincided with Cunard issuing £1,000,000 in new shares. This was to finance the design of a planned new 'super Cunarder'. Conjectured to be around 60,000 tons, details of the new ship's size, and speed (a suggested 30 knots being regarded by 'practical shipping … [as] … most improbable'), etc. were still closely guarded secrets as company officials wanted to await results from the powerful new German liners, *Bremen* and *Europa*, then being built and the new White Star liner *Oceanic* about to be laid down in Belfast. It had been decided that this latter ship would be driven by internal combustion engines, making her twice the size of the then largest motorship, the Italian *Augustus*. The American Shipping Board, not to be outdone, said it was considering a fleet of ten 'super-liners' capable of 32½ knots! The cost of the new 1,000ft Cunarder to be built on either the Tyne or the Clyde was estimated at around £5 to £6 million.

The *Mauretania's* late October arrival in Plymouth saw two unlisted passengers disembarking – one a stowaway claiming that he had been robbed in Canada, and the other an albatross that had landed on the ship in mid-Atlantic. Towards the end of the crossing a watch was kept for yet another transatlantic hopeful, aviatrix Mrs Frances Grayson – along with a pilot and navigator – in her plane *Dawn*, which disappeared after radioing distress near Nova Scotia.

The British express trains did their best to follow the *Mauretania's* speedy crossings. After a very good crossing that left New York on Wednesday, 9 November, she covered the 3,025 miles in moderately fine weather to the Eddystone light, averaging 25 knots with daily mileages of 271, 592, 571, 580, 581 and 455. She arrived at Plymouth at 7.40 a.m. on Tuesday 15th, where, after a speedy disembarkation for 155 passengers into the tenders in Cawsand Bay (254 others would go ashore at Cherbourg and the remaining eighty-eight at Southampton) along with 3,296 sacks of mail, the Great Western express train drawn by the locomotive *Bluith Castle* sped towards Paddington Station in London at the 'exceptionally fast speed' of 59mph, the 227-mile non-stop rail journey taking four hours and ten minutes. When the train arrived in London nineteen minutes ahead of schedule the travellers had reached their destination five days and eight hours after leaving New York.

The agreement between the Cunard Steam Ship Company and the Government when the *Lusitania* and *Mauretania* were originally built

expired on 15 November and the company was in discussions with the Post Office for a new mail contract to date from the 16th.

Winter was setting in on the North Atlantic and it was living up to its reputation of being the roughest ocean in the world. By the time that the *Mauretania* was abreast of the Eddystone light on Tuesday, 6 December, Captain Diggle decided that the sea was too rough, as it often was in that area during a good blow, to take the ship into Plymouth and the 7.30 a.m. call was cancelled. The 180 undoubtedly disappointed passengers and 1,650 bags of mail were perforce disembarked in Southampton at three in the afternoon at a time when most of them should have been in London had the Plymouth call been made.

Newly appointed Staff Captain Alexander's first trip on the ship met with hazardous icy conditions for the sailing at the Winter Solstice, 21 December. In their efforts to reach London's Waterloo Station to catch the 'Cunard Express', several passengers were delayed as their motor cars fell afoul of the slippery roads. On eventually reaching the station they were not unsurprised to find other passengers pacing the station forecourt in an attempt to keep warm, luggage piled on the concourse, and unsure at which platform their train, delayed by an hour and twenty-five minutes due to frozen points, would arrive. By the time the train did get into Southampton Docks it was two hours late. However, the ship's staff had been alerted that the boat train would be late and it took a mere nineteen hectic minutes to transfer passengers and baggage to the liner. For the first time the *Mauretania* was late in sailing – scheduled to leave at 11 sharp, she did not get away until 11.50.

And if any of the 800 passengers, mostly Americans travelling home for the New Year, thought that Christmas at sea would be rather dull then they were in for a surprise. The First-Class Dining Room had been particularly beautifully decorated with holly and mistletoe garlands draping from the underside of the balcony of the Upper Dining Saloon. In the centre of the lower room stood a towering 20ft Christmas tree laden with coloured lights and presents. Food and drink had been taken on in abundance for the festive season. Head Chef M. Ricoult told a reporter that 2 tons of ingredients for the Christmas puddings had been loaded along with 500 turkeys, geese and ducks, fifteen calves, fifty oxen, seventy lambs, 160 pigs and 200 sheep. Four hundred grouse, 500 partridges, 400 pheasants and 8,000 quail had selflessly sacrificed themselves to ensure that the passengers did not go hungry, and all this washed down with 5,000 bottles of wine, 3,000 of spirits, 600 of liqueurs and 15,000 bottles of beer! Four days after leaving Cherbourg at 8 p.m., Christmas Day was grandly celebrated in mid-Atlantic. Following the traditional Divine Service conducted by the Captain, Father Christmas made an appearance accompanied by Pierrots, clowns and goblins (some killjoys said that these characters were actually members of the crew dressed up!) and presents were distributed to the children. Ship's staff sang carols and, as a prelude to dinner that evening, a group of trumpeters led a procession of white-clad stewards bearing turkeys and flaming Empire Christmas puddings made to the recipe enjoyed by the King himself. The day ended with a ball and carnival.

Undoubtedly some of this bounty would be enjoyed by the crew, a far cry from their fare of the past. Renowned yacht helmsman Tom Diaper, from the village of Itchen Ferry near Southampton, recalled when working on the 'Cape boats' to South Africa as a deck boy: 'We had salt pork and peas and salt beef and potatoes every other day, biscuits [ship's] and butter for tea and breakfast, and only boiled rice and molasses for Saturday's dinner. We had no fresh meat after three days out until reaching Capetown.' Diaper remembered with dismay the crews' gastronomical hierarchy: 'The able seamen were very strict on the [deck] boys at meal times, the boys had to stand back, the men taking their share first. After them the ordinary seamen took theirs, then came the boys to help themselves to what was left. Sometimes ... they had a pretty poor share.' He bemoaned the absence of soft bread. Spurred by the Merchant Shipping Act of 1906, a seaman's rations improved over the years and Crew Agreements stipulated that each man's weekly allowance would be:

28 quarts water; 3 lb [pounds] soft bread; 4 lb biscuit; 3 lb salt beef; 2 lb salt pork; 2¼ lb preserved meat; ¾ lb fish; 6 lb potatoes; ½ lb dried or compressed vegetables; ⅔ pint spit peas; 2 pints garden peas; ⅓ pint calavances or haricot beans; 2 lb flour; ½ lb rice; 8 oz [ounces] oatmeal; 1¾ oz tea; 4 oz coffee; 1¼ lb sugar; ⅓ lb condensed milk; ½ lb butter; 1 lb marmalade or jam; ½ lb syrup or molasses; 4 oz suet; ½ pint pickles; 5 oz dried fruit; 2 oz fine salt; ¼ oz mustard; ¼ oz pepper; ¼ oz curry powder; 3 oz onions (on a Monday) ...

This was as well as lime juice – or suitable substitutes – that gave British sailors their nickname of 'Limeys'. Although passengers fared better, all had not been well on board the ship. Before the Great War, when the liner was new, an American opined that, 'The ship is intensely British ... the methods and manners of ship life were settled by the Cunard Company before you were born and will go on unchanged years after you have passed away,' and his dissatisfaction overflowed to the food served on the ship: 'the passenger, who is supposed to say little, to eat anything that is put before him, and to worship at the shrine of Brussels sprouts and plain boiled potatoes ... eat five tame and tasteless meals a day ... go quietly to bed'!

The Christmas voyage lived up to its natal origin as, on Christmas Day and attended by ship's surgeon W. Case and his assistant, Russell, twin girls were born to their parents returning in Third Class, William and Florence McAndrew, who had emigrated to America five years previously. The newborns were named Stella Maris ('Star of the Sea') and – rather less exotically – Margaret. Their mother was presented with the £70 collected on their behalf.

The ship was due to return to Britain at 11 p.m on 30 December from the foot of West 14th Street with an unusually full passenger list for that time of year (twenty-five First Class hopefuls even sailed in Second, so full was the ship) but, because of the fog, said to be the thickest in thirty years, laying over New York Harbor, her departure was delayed until four o'clock the following afternoon of New Year's Eve. It took a full six hours of careful navigation for the liner, fog whistles booming to warn other vessels, to travel the 25 miles to the *Ambrose* lightvessel. The gloom dogged the ship for two days and the mood did not lift with the fog as, on the third day of the New Year, Bedroom Steward George Muster died in the ship's Hospital from acute abdominal ulceration and pneumonia. His remains were solemnly committed to the deep.

After a slower crossing than usual but still at a commendable average of 24.36 knots (she steamed the 3,025 miles to the Eddystone Lighthouse in five days, four hours and twelve minutes, her best day's steaming being 576 miles) fog again descended and lasted for two days, delaying the liner's approach to Britain. As usual, the liner radioed her noon position as she approached the Bishop's Rock lighthouse, giving her distance to the west of the rock that in turn gave an indication of when she would be arriving at Plymouth (she similarly radioed her position when east of New York). The fog was followed by a westerly gale, strong enough to cause damage ashore, that continued as the liner entered Plymouth Sound for a delayed arrival at 8.50 a.m. on 6 January, making anchoring in the safer upper reaches of Cawsand Bay difficult. So rough were the waters in the bay that the three tenders – the *Sir Francis Drake*, *Sir Walter Raleigh* and the *Sir Neville Grenville* – had to manoeuvre alongside the sheltered lee side of the ship in order to gingerly take off 250 passengers and 5,000 bags of mail. The *Mauretania* sailed for Cherbourg at 11.10, reaching the French port three hours late on the seventh. Following her arrival in Southampton, the liner was lifted in the large floating dock for her annual winter overhaul that took all of January. Among other work, her anchors and chains were lowered to the dock floor for inspection, her bottom plates cleaned and painted, and decor and furniture further modernised. Captain Diggle handed over command of the ship to Captain McNeill on 7 February. She sailed for Cherbourg the next day and arrived at New York at 7 a.m. six days later after a slow (for her) crossing. She would not return to Southampton until the end of March. Another winter-dodging Mediterranean cruise with her elite group of travellers began from New York on the 21st.

The year 1928 had not started well for the old ship and threats to her future position were looming, not only at sea but in the air. In Britain a large rigid airship, the *R100*, was nearing completion at Cardington for the Air Ministry, the first of twenty planned to operate between Britain, Australia and the USA. Almost as long as the *Mauretania*, wider than Westminster Abbey and containing a vast 5,250,000cu.ft of gas, this type of craft had 'an immense commercial future' carrying 100 passengers and 25 tons of cargo at 76mph. The *R100* was to be ready for her first transatlantic trip two months after her trials in July. Competition would appear around the same time in the form of the German soon-to-be-famous airship LZ127, the *Graf Zeppelin*, being built by *Luftschiffbau Zeppelin GmBH* (the Zeppelin Company). The old rivalry between Germany and Great Britain was seemingly transferring from the oceans to the air.

Her first cruise call on 26 February was, as usual, Funchal, where the island's flora was enjoyed and European tourists embarked. After two days' steaming, Gibraltar was reached on the 28th, where the bargains of Main Street and the famed apes awaited the travellers. The by now regular haunts of Algiers, Villefranche for the French Riviera (the Côte d'Azur), Naples, Athens and Haifa were visited, with the cruise turnaround during a seven-day stay in Alexandria, where she arrived on 11 March. Other liners were in the same port and, as each had to exercise its crew in lifeboat handling, a 'Liners' Boat Race' against boats from other cruising ships, including the Cunard's own *Laconia*, was organised with a silver cup being presented to the winning crew. It did not go to the *Mauretania*'s team. Homeward calls were made at Naples, Villefranche and finally Southampton, where the cruise terminated at 11 a.m. on Monday, 26 March.

A new suit of four-bladed propellers, each costing £3,000, manufactured by Messrs J. Stone's at their works at Charlton on the Thames, were readied for fitting at the ship's next dry-docking, each 16ft 9in diameter, four-bladed propeller was cast from 30 tons of 'Turbiston' – a hard, special cavitation-resisting bronze. Weighing 18.5 tons after machining, polishing and balancing, the screws would be the heaviest for their size in the world. Turning at 200rpm, it was calculated that the blade tips would rotate 2 miles every minute. With the new German liners formally named *Bremen* and *Europa*, and the announcement of two new fast Italian liners, the old *Mauretania* prepared to face some serious competition and, meanwhile, with the *Berengaria* and *Aquitania*, still provided what was advertised as the 'Fastest Ocean Service in the World'.

Although the liner ran into fog after leaving New York on 11 April, a good crossing was still made in a minute under five days between markers. During the crossing the usual concert was given by volunteer or coerced passengers. The entertainment, chaired by no less a distinguished personage than Brigadier General John George Stewart-Murray, the eighth Duke of Atholl, and an Aide-de-Camp to King George V, began at 9.15 on the evening of 14 April and included renditions by noted composer and playwright Leyla George. A retiring collection was made on behalf of seamen's charities. A mere 650 bags of mail were landed at Plymouth along with 160 passengers, the British passengers arriving home in time for the Cup Final between Huddersfield Town and Blackburn Rovers.

The *Mauretania* left New York at 5 p.m. on Wednesday, 2 May with 714 passengers on board as part of the holiday rush to Europe. Individuals or groups of recent immigrants or their descendants were returning to their old home countries as tourists; others intended to make the 'power tour' of several European cities ('It's Tuesday – it must be Paris!'); some were headed to Amsterdam for the 1928 Summer Olympic Games; and, not unusually, the ship carried a prince (Prince Alfred zu Hohenlohe-Wallenberg-Schillingsfürst of the Austro-Hungarian Embassy in Washington D.C., whose estranged wife would become a confidant of a future, notorious German Chancellor), a duke and a baronet. There were also some eminent musicians on the passenger list, including composer and conductor E. Goossens. The passengers were blessed with the smooth seas of perfect spring weather before arriving at Plymouth the following Tuesday at 3.30 a.m. – half an hour before schedule for the second time that season. She sailed at 7.40 for Cherbourg and, after disembarkations there, her accommodation was almost empty as she headed for Southampton.

After leaving New York on Wednesday, 23 May, her 918 travellers also had the good fortune of fine weather. She averaged a speed of 25 knots, the best day's distance between noon sightings being 587 nautical miles. The Great Western train that awaited her on the following Tuesday had a specially reinforced, windowless coach attached to its rear. This was to carry over £1.3 million in gold weighing 7 tons 15cwt (7.9 tonnes) in 106 iron-ringed wooden casks, 18in deep and 12in in diameter. A total of 276 passengers disembarked, including the Earl and Countess of Denbigh and the Premier of Ontario, Howard. G. Ferguson. Those who boarded the Cunard boat train were unaware of the bullion's presence, also London-bound. The liner sailed at 7 a.m. for Cherbourg, where one passenger, 94-year-old Mrs Robert Hoe – a regular Cunard traveller – was going ashore with her daughter en route for Paris. An enthusiastic traveller, Mrs Hoe's first transatlantic experience had been on board Brunel's *Great Eastern*!

On arrival at Paddington Station at 1 p.m. (four hours before the *Mauretania* docked in Southampton), the boat train was met by police to oversee the unloading of the gold into three Great Western express delivery vans, the first two each pulled by a pair of heavy horses, the third motorised. It took two perspiring porters to transfer each bullion-laden barrel to a waiting van backed up to the railway coach. As soon as one van was loaded, its tailboard was secured and, with a policeman aboard, driven off to the receiving banks.

Commodore Sir James Charles (highly respected but with a reputation of a gastronomic adventurer at his table) made a voyage of farewell in the *Mauretania* that, following a similar relief voyage in the *Berengaria*, had given him command of the Cunard's 'Big Three' in the few weeks preceding his retirement. He was in command for the first of June's two Southampton departures, which left on the 2nd. Noël Coward, playwright, actor, composer, raconteur and singer, was travelling and one can only hope that his stateroom emulated his song 'A Room With a View'! Colonel William 'Wild Bill' Donovan, the dynamic and talented US Acting Attorney General – a co-founder of the American Legion and later head the of the American secret intelligence service, the OSS, and later the CIA, based on the British pattern – was among those boarding the liner, as was American film actress Blanche Sweet, whose presence added to the on-board glamour.

The liner departed New York on 13 June at 5 p.m. and, the following day, the new suit of four-bladed propellers that had been cast and painstakingly hand-finished and polished to precision left their Thames-side foundry to begin the slow journey from London to the dockside in Southampton in time for the *Mauretania*'s return. After a record crossing with 848 passengers and 1,101 bags of mail, the liner arrived in Cawsand Bay at 6.13 a.m. on the 19th and by 7.45 she was off to Cherbourg. After his penultimate return to Southampton, Captain (Commodore) Sir James Charles returned the *Mauretania* to Captain McNeill before the ship sailed on 23 June, an act formally recorded in the log:

Captain Sir James Charles KBE CB RD RNR was this day superseded by Captain S.G.S. McNeill. All chronometers, instruments and Books for the safe Navigation of the vessel were handed over.

Returning to his beloved *Aquitania*, Sir James had only three more weeks to retirement, to enjoy his ship – and to live. Junior officer Robert Thelwell later recalled in his book *I Captained the Big Ships* that, during his last crossing, Captain Charles, already ill, murmured to his Staff Captain: 'I never realized how hard the parting would be.'

Arriving at Cherbourg on 15 July, the ailing Captain insisted on docking his ship before collapsing with an internal haemorrhage. Ship's Surgeon, Dr Sydney B. Jones, attended him until the critically ill and unconscious Commodore could be transferred to Southampton's hospital, where he died a few hours later.

It was said that, in effect, Sir James had died of a broken heart.

Flags on the company's ships flew at half-mast in Southampton and Sir Arthur Rostron succeeded Sir James as Commodore of the Cunard Line.

Seafaring adrenalin had been running high in the late spring of 1928 and when it was announced that White Star's huge, motor-driven *Oceanic* was about to be laid down in Belfast it was rumoured that the *Mauretania* might be converted to motor propulsion to give her added speed. Cunard, eager to show what their ship was still capable of, planned a twelve-and-a-half-day return voyage scheduled to sail on 23 June. Joining the ship were three undergraduate engineering students from Cambridge University including 21-year-old Lord Pentland who, as a Junior Engineer on the ship, would serve a regular four-on-eight-off watch. The ship arrived at her New York pier on the 28th, followed shortly by the company's *Lancastria*. An Assistant Cook fled the ship before it sailed.

She arrived in Plymouth on Friday, 6 July after creating another record, even after a seven-hour delay due to fog going into New York, where she was turned around in thirty-two hours. She made the round voyage in the planned twelve-and-a half days with an average eastward speed of 25.3 knots, the fastest ever made by a steamship. It was recorded that she had reached 26.5 knots for several hours and had made 611 miles during her best day's steaming. She continued on to Cherbourg and Southampton before starting a week's break for her summer overhaul. But before she reached her final port she once again caused consternation in Cowes as, an hour after high water when the ebbing tide was running at its fastest of nearly 4 knots, her wash repeated the flooding of 1924 but this time to a greater effect as the summer holiday season was under way. Moored yachts that were preparing for the sailing season ranged about their buoys and concerned parents rushed to pluck their children from the water as large waves crashed onto the crowded bathing beach by the Prince's Green.

The *Mauretania* left Southampton on Saturday, 14 July in a sweltering summer heatwave while the reputedly wildest cocktail party ever to take place was held in a swimming bath in London the previous night (Friday the 13th), almost symbolising the end of the 'Roaring Twenties' and the post-war madness of extravagance, gangsterism, strikes, the poverty of unemployment, hunger marches and near revolution.

With the bit between her teeth and new propellers, the *Mauretania* broke yet another of her own records on her next westward run. She left Cherbourg at 5.09 p.m. on Saturday, 14 July and arrived at Quarantine the following Thursday (she had been scheduled to arrive the next day) after beating her own record over the route, even after being delayed by fog. Due to some confusion in the press, Cunard issued a qualifying release:

Mauretania arrived New York from Cherbourg 4.25 p.m. [Eastern Standard Time] having made the passage in five days three hours seventeen minutes, beating her previous world's record in August 1924 on this route by three minutes.

Also during this passage she twice beat her record for best day's run on this route, covering 654 miles noon Monday to noon Tuesday, and 653 miles noon Tuesday to noon Wednesday, average speed 25.16 and 25.46 [knots] respectively.

Captain McNeil told *The New York Times*: 'We thought we would still get another kick out of the old girl and that she was not through by a shot.' Even at this late stage in her already illustrious career the romance of the *Mauretania* still inspired the popular imagination. A dance band in Newcastle was named after her, as was another successful thoroughbred – a racehorse! The liner returned to Britain in hot but fine weather with smooth seas and a fair wind but, as the tenders came alongside in Plymouth, the passengers were greeted with a heavy summer deluge. However, this would be as nothing compared to the economic storm gathering over the horizon on the other side of the 'Frantic Atlantic', a storm that would inundate not only America but Europe and the rest of the world.

18

'THE SURGE'S ANGRY SHOCK'

(Samuel Johnson)

The growing threat from the air was partially taken up by the sea. Even though the epoch-making *Île de France* might not have been the fastest vessel in the world, she revolutionised the delivery of the transatlantic mails when a catapult was fitted over the ship's stern, which could launch one of two specially-built CAMS 37/10 flying boats. Even though strangely facing aft away from the forward motion of the ship (the aircraft lost the advantage of added lift), it massively speeded delivery of mail to the States by one day, the first such airborne mail reaching New York on 13 August. On the return the first eastward airmails arrived in Paris on the 23rd, six days after leaving New York. Ultimately the innovation proved too expensive a luxury, even for such an innovative ship, and the catapult was removed in 1930. The Germans, however, adopted the idea for their two imminent German superliners and on 15 August 1928 the first of these two new sleek, rounded bridge, bulbous fore-footed, streamlined, low-funnelled superliners, the 49,746grt *Europa*, was launched at the Hamburg shipyard of Blohm & Voss by the American Ambassador to Berlin, Mr Jacob Gould Schurman. The second of the sisters, the 51,656grt *Bremen*, was sent into the water the following day at the Bremen yard of Deutsche Schiff-und Machinenbau (Deschimag AG 'Weser') by Paul von Hindenburg, President of the German (Weimar) Republic. The exiled Kaiser offered his opinion that the two ships should have been named *Frederick the Great* and *William the Great*!

With turbines producing 105,000shp (a 50 per cent increase on those of the *Mauretania*), the two quadruple-screwed German ships were planned to provide a weekly service. But some felt that the interior decor was rather stark. As mentioned, the ships would be fitted with mail-speeding aircraft – seaplanes of the Heinkel He 58 type that would, in the following decade, be used to secretly train pilots of the banned Luftwaffe to navigate the air approaches to Southampton with its docks and aircraft factory.

At the end of the month, White Star officially announced the contract to build their new 60,000-ton, £6 million, 1,000ft liner at the Belfast yard of Harland & Wolff. The type of engine had still not been decided upon as progress in machinery was constantly in flux. There was even talk of atoms being used as a power source, with the process of atomic reaction being described as 'annihilation'. Suggestions that the new vessel might challenge the forthcoming German attempts to capture the *Mauretania*'s record were not taken too seriously but a French minister shocked an international conference in Geneva when he openly and presciently propounded that Germany was fast becoming a formidable 'potential antagonist'.

Fog had forced a reduction in speed before the *Mauretania*'s arrival in New York on 9 August 1928, after an otherwise fast crossing. On her return trip sailing from New York at 5 p.m. a week later, she carried 4,289 bags of mail but four fewer crew members: Charles Dear of Southampton had dived into the waters of the dock for a swim and was not seen again, while two Second Class and one Third Class Waiter deserted. When the reigning undefeated champion of the North Atlantic left the North River, she carried the retired, undefeated champion of the boxing ring. The gloves might be off for the coming fight for the Blue Ribband but famed boxer Gene Tunney arrived in England on 22 August as a 'private citizen' seeking to 'sink as far into obscurity as possible' as he told waiting reporters, emphasising his point that he was travelling without a single item of boxing equipment as he was embarking on a walking holiday with his friend, author Thornton Wilder.

Sightseeing visits to the great liners in Southampton still proved to be popular as a day excursion and coaches travelled from afar, those from Bristol charging a fare of 8*s* 6*d* (42.5p) while, from Exeter, the Southern Railway charged 6*s*, which included a visit to the floating dock. Another 2*s* would buy a trip around the docks and through The Solent by paddle steamer. A visit to the liner would be concluded by visitors running the gauntlet of a line of stewards, palms extended in the hope of a tip. The liner's 30 August westward crossing saw her arrive at the *Ambrose* after a fast passage but just fifty-five minutes short of her record crossing of two trips previously. Although she reached Quarantine at 7.30, she did not get alongside until 10 p.m. as a strong tide kept her off her pier.

During the *Mauretania's* next stay in New York one of her boats took part in the second annual Neptune Association international lifeboat race on Thursday, 3 September, competing against crews from six other liners of varying nationalities. After the boats were weighed, the race was run over a course of 1 mile between the Statue of Liberty and The Battery. Aided by a strong flood tide – and despite the rain – the Cunarder's crew (comprising four from each of the Deck and Engine Departments and coxed by Third Officer Powell-Tuck) won the event in nine minutes, four seconds, winning a large silver cup, the Todd Trophy.

The 'Queen of the Ocean' continued her remarkable series of fast voyages for the year. Her arrival at Plymouth on 11 September marked her third record in three months, making the crossing in five days and six minutes. Her time from New York to the Eddystone Light was four days, twenty-three hours and ten minutes. Mr T. Nightingale (Managing Director of Sheffield Steel Products) told waiting reporters that he had been at the liner's launch twenty-one years previously and had been one of the privileged guests to have been chauffeured through the famed tunnel formed by the liner's funnels laid end to end in the shipyard.

The dangers of the seafaring life were again exemplified when, just before the ship sailed on Saturday, 15 September, AB Thomas Kidney fell 50ft, fracturing his skull. He died in hospital. The ever-present dangers of the sea were also in force as, at the outset and during the final hours of the crossing, two north-east gale-force storms of 'unusual severity' were encountered (not even the £400,000 of gold bars could improve her ballast!) but the liner arrived in the North River on schedule on 20 September, creating a new record for the run of five days, two hours and thirty-four minutes, clipping forty-three minutes off her record – a magnificent way to celebrate her twenty-second birthday! She was still – and would remain forever – 'The Pride of the Tyne'! The liner had, it will be remembered, been launched on 20 September 1906, but for some curious reason her majority, her coming of age, was being toasted on board during her eastward crossing on 21 September 1928! The twenty-first anniversary of her taking the Blue Ribband in 1907 was not due to be celebrated until the following month. However, the press gave the event coverage and duly noted that there were still two of her original crew serving on board including Steward Robert Parkins, who had only missed two of the ship's voyages. The liner completed this crossing in five days, one hour and twenty-two minutes, and Captain McNeil was quoted as saying that 'the old girl' was still the 'fastest and best liner in the world'.

The commercial threat from the air was slowly taking form and one serious contender was the German Zeppelin *Graf Zeppelin*, which made the return flight with a huge fare of £600 ($3,000) each way. The westward flight lasted over four-and-a-half days and was an unmitigated public relations disaster, although she landed at Lakehurst late in the evening on 15 October to great celebration after overflying New York and the White House. The dirigible, buffeted in a storm during the crossing, threw passengers about 'like ninepins'. One wealthy American returned by the *Mauretania*, vowing 'never again'. He opined the aircraft to be underpowered. As far as the steamship companies were concerned, there was 'no immediate threat from the air'. In contrast, the return flight of the airship was oversubscribed and she overflew the *Mauretania* at sea heading west. Just after noon on 30 October, when 600 nautical miles east of Newfoundland and pitching, the Cunarder picked up a message from the airship and reported:

Just been in communication with Graf Zeppelin. All O.K. Think he is a bit north not more than 50 miles away. Our position 45.53 [North]. 41.40 W with moderate south-east gale.

It was not only the 'Zepp' that was being given a very rough ride; a small aircraft that had been privately chartered to collect a batch of important papers from the *Mauretania* when she arrived at Plymouth on 23 October crashed shortly after take-off on its way to London.

Whatever good publicity steamship travel made from the plight of the *Graf Zeppelin's* troubled flight was soon obviated when, two hours into her last crossing of the season that left New York at 11 p.m. on Wednesday, 7 November, the *Mauretania* ran into rough weather that lasted for three days. The ship was under the command of Captain William Prothero in the new position of a regular Relief Captain, which enabled ships' masters to rest every fourth trip, a scheme instigated after the death of Captain Charles. For several hours on Saturday she fought a ferocious gale with blows reaching an estimated 100mph. Huge green seas fell on the ship; one, described as a 'tidal wave' that 'looked higher than the … funnels', inundated her upper deck, but 'the great ship rose to meet the challenge' shaking 'herself clear … while… forging ahead', still at 25 knots! Miraculously, the liner was not damaged as she rolled and pitched in the storm. The liner rode the seas well and, as usual, her officers did not suffer from *mal de mer* as they might have done on a lesser ship. Furniture and crockery were broken in the Dining Saloon and passengers accommodated on B- and C-Decks were ordered below. One passenger was thrown out of his bunk and across his cabin in the melee and twenty – passengers and crew – suffered minor injuries. But even on the roughest days between noon positions (presumably based on propeller revolutions) she still managed 575, 585, 560 nautical miles, with 581 being achieved on the fourth, less turbulent, day. She arrived in Plymouth on 13 November at 7 a.m., only an hour behind schedule, after a credable crossing of five days and forty-five minutes at an average speed of 25.06 knots. The 1,179 bags of mail were happily unaffected by the storm that had left lesser vessels in distress, but some passengers bore signs of their torment.

Cunard announced that they would soon be placing the contract for their new, big ship that would be over 1,000ft long, fast and luxurious.

Speed without luxury would be pointless, they said, although, like the new White Star vessel, the power plant would be a problem as advances were constantly being made in marine engineering.

The *Mauretania* was taken in hand by Thornycroft's ship repair division for her winter overhaul, lifted in the floating dock, and invaded by an army of shipwrights, engineers, fitters, joiners, painters, pipeworkers, etc. Her bottom was cleaned and painted, anchors and chains inspected, new feed pumps fitted and a myriad of other essential jobs undertaken. Other work included repairs and overhauls of turbines, boilers (considered to be good until at least 1935), modifications to the oil fuel installation, new auxiliary pumps, new plates and tubes in her condensers, and fire extinguishing appliances fitted in machinery spaces. To aid with navigation a new piece of equipment – a new-fangled 'Fathometer' system, supplied by the Submarine Signal Corporation – was fitted to the hull above numbers 2 and 3 Tanks with hydrophone receivers being installed 3ft 6in from the centreline. After undocking, work was continued afloat and it was hoped that the work would prepare her for the German challenge to come. After a final clean and polish she looked as good as new, ready for whatever 1929 had in store. It was while the great liner was elevated in the floating dock that the twenty-first anniversary of her maiden voyage was marked.

The Grand Old Lady of the Atlantic

The customary annual cruise to the Mediterranean was now advertised as an opportunity to use the *Mauretania* as a ferry between ports, enabling those who had wintered in Egypt to return home by the world's fastest liner. Also advertised was a new service of Caribbean winter cruises between New York and Havana that had been inaugurated by the *Caronia* on 27 December. These weekly jaunts would be cheaper and less exclusive than the *Mauretania's* Mediterranean adventures and therefore open to a larger market.

The *Mauretania's* first post-refit crossing left Southampton on 2 January 1929, and became, as Captain McNeil told *The New York Times*, 'the worst passage he had made in thirty-three years in the North

Atlantic trade'. He had made worse crossings but the foul weather on this trip was continuous. The liner made full speed for only a mere seventeen hours, sometimes slowing down to 14 knots. On the Sunday (6th) a big sea smashed twelve plate-glass windows on the Upper Promenade Deck and another washed over the Bridge, caving in three more. Teak railing on the Bridge was damaged and a Deck Boy received injuries as he, along with some dislodged fire buckets, was carried away by the flood, only being saved by the quick action of the Bo'sun's Mate.

Although the liner arrived late in New York late – the crossing taking over six days – she made a fast return on an almost summer-like sea, leaving her New York berth on 12 January. Her passenger list included a Russian princess, a British earl and a Member of Parliament. She arrived at Plymouth, not only before her scheduled time on Thursday, 17th but also having taken a laudatory two hours and two minutes off her old eastward crossing, making the trip in four days, nineteen hours and fifty-five minutes at an average of 25.38 knots. Hopes were running high that, given the right conditions, the old ship would be able to rise and meet the forthcoming German challenge.

After her sailing on 6 February, Southampton would not see her again for several weeks, as she would be on her penultimate Mediterranean cruise. Before she sailed from England, fifteen Engineers were re-rated with a commensurate reduction in salary. Arriving at New York five days later at 8.58 p.m. with 545 passengers and 6,000 sacks of mail, she remained at her berth for five busy days while being prepared to take on her cosseted tourists. During this time Ronald Scanes, a Bell Boy, was admitted to the Willard Parker Hospital for communicable diseases located on East 16th Street suffering from the scourge of mumps. Perhaps exacerbated by the excitement of the forthcoming cruise, 62-year-old widow Fannie Rood of Portland, Oregon, died of 'long standing heart disease' before the ship sailed.

Leaving the wintry city at 12.10 p.m., the cruise ship arrived at Madeira on 21 February, where she stayed overnight and left the next day at 2.12 p.m. Arriving at Gibraltar on the 23rd for another overnighter, it was then on to Algiers (overnight 24–25 February) with all its exotic delights; Villefranche-sur-Mer on the 27th for an overnight stay to enable her passengers to gamble in Monte Carlo or discover the Côte d'Azur into the night; Naples for a visit to Pompeii; a day's stay at Athens

on the 4th, which she left at 9.17 p.m. Haifa followed for the religiously minded (or just plain curious) to travel to Jerusalem, then a short steam down to Alexandria, where a three-day stay enabled her tourists to take in all the Ancient Egyptian history that they could desire. Then, heading for home, overnight stays ensued both at Naples and Villefranche, which she left at 1 a.m. on 19 March. She arrived in Southampton three days later. The old ship resumed her North Atlantic sailings on 30 March under the continuing command of Captain McNeill.

Tragedy again struck on the first post-cruise eastward trip when, on 12 April, Bedroom Steward Frank Dawe's knock on the door of First-Class cabin D-51 elicited no response from 38-year-old James Gow, a manufacturer from Sheffield. The Steward reported his concerns to Staff Captain L.R. Carr, who in turn informed Captain McNeill. Orders were given that the cabin be forcibly entered. The Staff Captain along with Surgeon H.W. Case, Second Purser Lionel Carine and Chief Steward Biddlecombe entered the cabin and what met their eyes was far from pleasant as, hanging from a hook with a length of curtain cord around his neck, was the body of Gow. The doctor examined the late passenger and ascertained that death, 'due to strangulation', had occurred about nine hours previously. The place of Gow's unhappy demise was officially recorded at 5.55 p.m. at latitude 40°32'N, longitude 49°42'W. No one on board would know the cause of such a dreadful finality; there was no explanation and no note. Two days later, at 7.06 a.m., the businessman's body was committed to the deep, the funeral service being conducted by Staff Captain Carr.

After berthing at her pier at the foot of West 14th Street on 17 May, *The New York Times* blazoned an article header 'Liner Docks Six Hours Late'. The *Mauretania* had encountered, as Captain McNeill described it, a sunless mid-winter crossing in mid-spring with winds of up to 55 nautical miles an hour with 'steep seas' that left many passengers prostrate with seasickness. Full speed had been limited to a thirty-six-hour period and 9 knots became the limit on the Sunday.

New York was left on 12 June less one passenger, Mrs Lucy Ropers who, taken with the enthusiasm of the cheering crowds shoreside, decided to join them. After hearing the sound of the ship's whistles that signalled the gangways being lowered, Mrs Ropers realised her dilemma as the band of swirling water between ship and pier widened, leaving the stranded and distraught lady on the pier side, her luggage and passport on the accelerating ship! She did, however, miss a rough crossing as one passenger wrote home: 'Have had two stormy days at sea and I am a landlubber.' Perhaps daunted by his experience, he added: 'I'm disembarking at Plymouth to save one day less at sea and half day longer in London.'

Mauretania continued her spring voyages with good passenger lists. When she left New York on 29 June she had 410 in First Class, 288 in Second, and 446 in Third. On the last day of that crossing the liner met with a moderate gale with a quartering sea. Some 300 bags of mail, along with 284 passengers, were landed at Plymouth, where she arrived at 4 a.m. on 5 July. Unusually, she took a long time in being cleared as she did not leave the Devon port until 7.45.

Captain 'Sandy' McNeil was given a break during the eight-day summer lay-up when Relief Captain William Prothero took the ship after her 5 July 6 p.m. arrival back at Southampton following her fastest crossing for some time, averaging a magnificent 25.47 knots. The liner was again lifted in the floating dock (ironically recently vacated by the two-squat-funnelled, streamlined *Bremen*, which had used it for her final painting, her unusual bulbous forefoot being seen to great advantage), during which time she was overflown by three Supermarine Southampton flying boats at the outset of a round-Britain flight. Before the next 13 July sailing the Chief Engineer, Alexander Cockburn, failed to produce his necessary Discharge Book (No. 929883) when signing on. It seems that his place was temporarily taken by J. Bell, leaving the old Chief possibly regretting his oversight as this voyage would be a fateful one in his old ship's career as the 'Wonder Ship' was expected to 'have something up her sleeve' after her recent machinery reconditioning to counter the *Bremen*'s rumoured 31 knots.

Two days after the *Mauretania*'s sailing from Southampton, the brand-new *Bremen* (the first of the duo, *Europa*, had had her debut postponed because of damage caused by fire during her fitting out) departed Bremerhaven under the command of Commodore Leopold Ziegenbein. She arrived at her berth at Pier 4, 58th Street, Brooklyn, in New York at 4 p.m. on 22 July after a record crossing of four days, seventeen hours and forty-two minutes at an average speed of 27.83 knots. On the German liner's arrival (she was 50 per cent more

than the Cunarder in tonnage and horsepower and 150ft longer) the *Mauretania* struck her colours in honour of the new record-holder and, as a show of submission, Captain McNeil generously sent a telegram:

> Captain Ziegenbein, officers and ship's crew of the S.S. Bremen … Captain McNeil, officers and ship's company of the steamship Mauretania heartily congratulate you on your record passage and wish you every success.

After twenty-two remarkable years – in itself an unbeaten record – the westbound record was no longer in the possession of the *Mauretania*. No longer was she the undisputed reigning 'Queen of the Ocean', an appellation so richly deserved; she could only strive to attempt to regain her previous glory. In this she would ultimately fail but, in doing so, would beat her own records and thereby earn herself another noble epithet:

'The Grand Old Lady of the Atlantic'

Bremen then took the eastward record away from the *Mauretania* at just under 28 knots. The crew of the *Mauretania* must have felt despondent – even rankled – to not only lose the record but to lose it to the 'old enemy' - to 'Jerry' – against whom many of the crew had been in opposition of a different deadly sort only eleven years previously.

The *Mauretania*'s arrival alongside her New York pier prior to losing the record had elicited a sudden and informal raid by three Prohibition agents on the lookout for illicit liquor. They unearthed nine bottles of ale – three in the Engineers' quarters and six belonging to old hands in the Bedroom Stewards' department – each item receiving a 20 cent fine for its owner. Relief Chief Engineer Bell had to contend with not only losing the record but also losing his beer as he was one of those caught, having only one bottle in his possession.

The 'Grand Old Lady' did not give up her long-held laurels easily. It was rumoured on the waterfront that Captain McNeil and Chief Engineer Cockburn had something up their gold-laced sleeves and intended to make every effort to fight back. And fight back they did, although her Captain (normally 'the cheery optimist of the Atlantic') thought that, even with an unknown reserve after her recent thorough overhaul, she would not make more than 27¾ knots. His Chief Engineer, too, considered the nine-hour difference in time was too big a challenge but, with her fighting spirit still intact, the *Mauretania* put in a splendid performance, even though after her departure from Southampton on 3 August she had left Cherbourg in the face of 'a strong wind … rough seas and adverse tide'. On Monday, 5 August she magnificently beat her best-ever daily performance for the twenty-five-hour westward noon-to-noon distance by 4 nautical miles, achieving 680 nautical miles at a speed of 27.2 knots. Her previous best had been in January 1911 with 27.04 knots, which she matched up to noon on Wednesday, 7th. The following day's official noon-to-noon run achieved an even better result with 27½ knots being recorded. The ship then encountered the 'tail end of a south-west gale and … fog'. Even at speed the ship's passage was so smooth that she hardly had to slow to enable her doctors, W.H. Case and his assistant G.S. Thompson, to perform an appendectomy on American businessman M.D. Rogers.

Still in fog, the liner passed the *Ambrose* lightship at 10.52 a.m., after a 3,162 nautical miles passage of four days and twenty-three hours, beating her previous record by three hours and thirty-four minutes, at an average of 26.85 knots. The gap with the *Bremen* (she had had calm weather all the way) had been narrowed by a creditable four hours. She reached Sandy Hook at 11.15, anchored at Quarantine twenty-one minutes later and then, lowering the yellow flag of quarantine, proceeded to Pier 54. Passengers disembarked an hour after berthing.

Her return was another great effort made in fair weather, during which she again beat her own daily record in the twenty-three hours eastward noon-to-noon between Monday (19th) and Tuesday of 626 nautical miles by four miles at 27.4 knots. She arrived in Plymouth just after midnight after averaging 27.33 knots, clipping two hours off her previous best. She put on a final burst of speed en route to Cherbourg, apparently making 29.7 knots – one report had her going at a vibration-free 32! Joyous welcomes awaited the liner both at Cherbourg and Southampton as aircraft flew overhead and ships' sirens rasped out their throaty congratulations. Newsreel cameras awaited the Captain.

But it was still not enough; although defeated in speed the great liner's dignity was still intact. Her seemingly vibration-less turbines performed like 'sewing machines' during the voyage and it was said that the harder she was driven the smoother she seemed to run as if enjoying being pushed. One gentleman wrote to *The Times* in August 1930 that he had 'travelled in the Mauretania from New York … In my cabin, just abaft the second funnel, I could not tell, even at 25 knots, whether the engines were running or not.' In contrast, the speedy *Bremen* was said to suffer from vibration at high speed, which would be a mark against the new ship. She had also rolled towards the end of her maiden voyage, her depleted oil tanks not being designed to be re-ballasted with water.

The *Mauretania*'s Kelso-born Chief Engineer Andrew Cockburn – 'The Wizard of the Atlantic' – described the voyage as the most momentous occasion in his forty-year career, even though he had survived the traumatic sinking of the *Lusitania* as her Second Engineer in 1915. He opined that the *Mauretania,* being a generation of ship design away from the German liner, had the disadvantage of external resistance-creating bilge keels, whereas the *Bremen* had internal anti-rolling tanks. In support of the Chief Engineer's remarks and in championing the *Mauretania*, the highly respected and influential British Naval Architect and shipbuilder Sir Alfred Yarrow wrote a letter headed 'Mauretania v. Bremen' to the London *Times* (8 August 1929):

Sir, – As readers of The Times are not all naval architects, may I make the following remarks:-

– Length is essential to speed. It is not fair, therefore, to compare the Mauretania, which is 760ft. long, with the Bremen, which is 920ft. long.

– It is not fair to compare a vessel with water-tube boilers, which are fitted in the Bremen, with one having the old-fashioned cylindrical boilers as in the Mauretania. It is well known that water-tube boilers will give approximately a knot more speed than cylindrical boilers in a fast liner.

– It is not fair to compare a vessel over 20 years old with one newly built.

I hope the British public do not consider the engineers and shipbuilders of this country have been asleep for 20 years …

Sir Alfred's last line subtly referred to Cunard's plans that were about to reach fruition.

The tussle on the Atlantic calmed down for the old Cunarder but she still continued to impress. The Blue Ribband was kept for a while by the *Bremen* before passing it on to her sister, the *Europa*, which held it until 1933 when the Italian speedster *Rex* took it on the westward run. The *Bremen* would hold the eastward record until 1935.

The old Cunarder was still popular and received more publicity when matinee idols Douglas Fairbanks and Mary Pickford travelled in her, arriving on 10 September en route to Switzerland.

Relief Captain William Prothero again took the *Mauretania* over for the 5 and 26 October departures. On the former westward crossing the liner once again carried actor and playwright Noël Coward, who was travelling with the main leads of his show 'Bitter Sweet' scheduled to open on Broadway in November. Also travelling and returning from their honeymoon was dashing film star John Gilbert and his new wife, actress Ina Claire, as was Princess Xenia of Russia. After two days of gales and a day of fog the liner was a few hours late arriving at Quarantine, where she was met by a show of opulence. The Princess's husband, William B. Leeds Jr., heir to the fortune of his late father, 'The Tin Plate King', met the ship in his recently acquired steam yacht – the two-funnelled 25-knot *Flying Fox*. This destroyer-like yacht accompanied the liner to her berth, where the Princess transferred to be taken to their Long Island house, 'Kenwood', on Oyster Bay. The Leeds would divorce a year later!

British contenders for the Schneider Cup Trophy – 'the "Oscar" of fast flight' – were maintained at Calshot at the mouth of Southampton Water. Here, as the *Mauretania* passes the base inward-bound, a Gloster VI is prepared for launch in readiness for the 1929 race. (Collection of Chris Michell)

'5,300 MILES FOR $155 ...'

'Good for a generation'

During the 26 October 1929 outward trip from Southampton worrying news reached the liner. An early September financial crisis on Wall Street now saw a major fall in stock prices, which had risen remarkably since the end of the Great War, making fortunes for many. Three days later the crisis reached boiling point and the market crashed – 'Black Tuesday' – signifying a meltdown that would soon have global significance. Wealthy stockholders as well as small investors saw fortunes evaporate overnight and it was likely that many of those travelling on the *Mauretania* saw their entire wealth disappear as billions of dollars were lost as stocks plummeted.

With Sir Percy Bates, Deputy Chairman of the Cunard Line, on the passenger list, her 7 November sailing from New York led her into two days of fierce gales that claimed several fishing boats around the British coast. But she still managed a good passage of four days, twenty-three hours, and forty-four minutes, just five hours and fifty-five minutes above her record.

Captain McNeil was back in command for the 16 November sailing (with Captain A.C. Grieg as his Staff) on a voyage that would dramatically embrace both tragedy and danger in full measure. At 7.20 on the morning of 22 November, a few hours before the ship's arrival in New York, Trimmer Humphries went to rally the next Stokehold Watch. Trimmer John Ramsden acknowledged the call – but then failed to appear at his station. Thirty-five minutes later the 22-year-old was found dead in his bunk. At the conclusion of the crossing (made at an average speed of 21.47 knots, taking six minutes over six days to

complete) his remains were taken ashore for internment, presumably in the company's plot. Drama stayed with the ship as, after six days spent alongside Pier 54 and shortly after leaving the Upper Bay on 27 November with $6 million in gold on board bound for Paris, the liner collided with a railway car float comprising two 250ft barges, each heavily loaded with several freight cars crossing from Brooklyn to New Jersey in the extremely busy Greenville Channel. The liner sounded a single blast on her whistle to indicate that she was keeping to her side of the channel and desired to pass to port.

The towing tug, which had a float on either side that somewhat obscured its skipper's line of sight, did not respond, so the *Mauretania* again signalled. This time the towing tug replied with two, indicating that she would cross the liner's path. Captain McNeil ordered 'Full astern port' and for the helm to be put hard a-starboard. The liner's forward motion slowed to 4 knots but her bow made angular contact with the near side barge, taking it with her as the tug carried on ahead with the other. Of the seven freight cars on the float, three went overboard and sank. Luckily there were no injuries and the quickly lowered emergency lifeboat was not needed. The buckled car float – *No. 61* of the New York, Haven & Hartford Railroad – remained impaled on the now stationary liner's bow for seventeen minutes before drifting away (it was later towed back to Staten Island, assisted by the Coastguard Cutter *Manhattan* summoned by the liner. The *Mauretania* returned to Quarantine under her own power, where an external examination, carried out from a police launch, showed two stem plates had been buckled with two 4ft by 10ft holes in the port side.

At 7.30 a.m. the liner returned to her pier. Temporary repairs took fifty men (rushed to the quayside in taxis) eight hours to complete. Damaged plates were cut away using acetylene torches, replaced by a perfectly fitting plate supplied by a local shipyard, securely bolted in place, and strengthened with cement. Many passengers, unaware of the collision, awoke to find the ship at her berth and not out at sea on the wide ocean as expected. Though unfortunate the accident enabled American passengers (including fifteen agricultural advisers en route to Stalinist Russia) to enjoy their Thanksgiving dinner on American soil. When the liner finally sailed in a blizzard two days later just after midnight she grazed the wreckage of one of the sunken railway cars, causing some further consternation on board.

The liner sailed into 'mountainous seas', during which she 'never ceased heaving', which most of the passengers probably emulated! That storm claimed many ships over the Atlantic and its coasts but the *Mauretania* made her three landfalls on 4 December, landing 277 grateful passengers from the large list of 300 First, 170 Second, and 400 Third Class, and 4,000 bags of mail at Plymouth, only one day late, at 7 a.m. having taken five days and forty-six minutes. On 1 December it was announced that the contract for Cunard's new fast, luxury ship had been signed and that the keel of this mammoth liner would be laid on the 27th and, until the moment of her launching, would be known purely by her shipyard designation – *Number 534*.

Following the *Leviathan* out of Southampton on 17 December, the 'Grand Old Lady of the Atlantic' was the last ship to sail bearing Christmas mail – 6,000 sacks containing 6 million letters and parcels of imperial and foreign mail. 'The Most Beautiful Woman in the World' – socialite and one-time actress Lady Diana Duff-Cooper, Viscountess of Norwich – boarded the most beautiful ship in the world from the 'Cunard Express' from London with her husband en route to a West Indian holiday. She told the waiting press that their three-month-old baby, John Julius, had been left at home as he was too young to travel at that time of year.

The liner spent Christmas Day alongside her berth and the bright lights of New York may have been the temptation that caused Bellboy W. Fitzsimmonds to desert. On her return departure two days later, kegs containing a total of $11.25 million in gold were stowed in her Specie Room as part of the huge movement of the precious commodity away from the American slump. The old 'Maury' still remained in the public's affection and her name was used for two seasonal pantomime characters, 'The Ugly Sisters', who were called after the beautiful ship and her handsome running companion, the *Aquitania*. Babies were also named after her, as was a chrysanthemum!

Arriving in New York Harbor at 5 p.m. on 23 December in good visibility, despite a slight snowstorm, she again narrowly avoided another collision with a train ferry that shot out directly in front of her. A good lookout and prompt orders to the Engine Room were met with an equally prompt response and the *Mauretania* was brought to a halt. Sailing at 11 p.m. on Friday, 27 December, she carried a consignment of $11,250,000 in gold and arrived home on the second day of 1930. Her passenger list was just as rich and included Grand Duke Boris of Russia – a cousin of the late Czar – and his wife. Shortly after arrival in Southampton the Cunarder was put into the hands of J.I. Thornycroft's shipyard team for overhaul and survey to renew her Passenger Certificate. Raised in the floating dock, she presented a wonderful sight to all those who saw her from a distance.

However, all was not as wonderful with the ship as her survey showed that she was ageing. Time, speed, collisions and groundings had taken their toll. and it was found that caulking (during her building the edges of plates had been slightly spit and the inner part beaten – 'caulked' – into the adjacent faying plate edge to make a water-tight seal) had fractured between hull plates and the more rigid stern casting. Defective shell plates and rivets were discovered around the aft peak tank abreast the stress-inducing vibrations of the inner propellers, and loosened rivets and double nutted 1¾in bolts that attached frames and floors to the stern casting's webbing needed replacement. Because of the limited access due to the very fine form of the hull at the after cut-up, repairs were undertaken with great difficulty. However, work was completed and the ship's certificate renewed for another year. Her next sailing from 'The Gateway to the World' on 5 February 1930 meant that Southampton would not see its favourite daughter for seven weeks as Cunard needed to find profitable employment for the *Mauretania* during these increasingly austere times that resulted in over-tonnaging on the Atlantic. So, to reduce the costs of fuel, stores and crews' wages expended during each lengthy turnaround in New York it was decided to send her on short weekend cruises to the West Indies.

Hoping to dispel the popularly held view that cruising was purely for the wealthy (there now seemed to be fewer of these following 'The Crash'), the liner would now join the 'Pretty Sisters' *Carmania* and *Caronia* that made twice-weekly cruises on the 'Sunshine route'. The *Mauretania*'s speed would enable her to make longer cruises in the time available, so the first sailing of the 'The Largest and Fastest Steamer' left New York on 12 February for Havana, where the Cuban harbour had been specially dredged. America's Ward Line soon protested that Cunard was taking the cream of the Cuban traffic and welcomed recent amendments to the 1916 Shipping Act and the 1928 Revenue Act that aided American shipping in the face of British competition by taxing the profits of British companies sailing from US ports.

As would be expected, the *Mauretania* made a record run of forty-four hours and twenty-six minutes, beating the previous record to Cuba by several hours. She also carried a record number of passengers – 558 – the largest ever carried on one ship on the route. To the rhythmic music of welcoming bands, the *Mauretania* arrived flag-bedecked in Havana on 14 February, watched by thousands along the shoreline and many more watching from balconies that had even the slightest view of the harbour. The ship's officers were dined that evening by the Cuban Navy and, by a special decree, the city's shops remained open until 11 p.m. Returning from the gala weekend jaunt, the liner (the Duke of Manchester was on board after a failed attempt to get a divorce from his wife in Cuba) made 26.62 knots (aided by the slower-than-usual Gulf Stream's 1.5 knots) and, as she approached the *Scotland* Lightship on Staten Island at 5 p.m. on Monday, 17 February, the liner grazed an underwater obstruction. Thinking that the liner had grounded on a sandbank, Captain McNeil rang 'Stop engines' before putting the ship astern. The liner seemed unharmed and continued to Quarantine. The following day Lloyds' ship surveyors gave the vessel a clean bill of health.

The sixth Mediterranean cruise, on which the Earl of Lichfield travelled, began on 20 February and took in the customary ports of call. During her absence, Cunard announced in mid March that

their new superliner would go all out to recapture the Blue Ribband. Although troubled White Star's *Oceanic* had been 'deferred', it was confidently felt that Cunard would produce a worthy replacement for the *Mauretania* and regain Britain's lost laurels. As if to dispel the British confidence, the day before the Cunarder returned to Southampton on 26 March the Germans again triumphed when the fire-delayed *Europa* made her maiden voyage from Cherbourg to the *Ambrose*, clipping eighteen minutes off her sister *Bremen*'s record by taking four days, seventeen hours and six minutes. 'Germany Again!' shouted exasperated British headlines as the resurgent nation became victorious both at sea and in the air.

Captain McNeil went ashore on leave and Relief Captain Prothero once again took over command in time for a very turbulent post-cruise westward crossing that left Southampton at noon on Saturday, 29 March. The *Mauretania* took over six-and-a-half days to make the trip as Sunday's moderate gale was followed by continuously rough weather; from noon Monday to noon Tuesday she made a mere 214 nautical miles. Friday's north-east gale spiced with heavy lashing rain, sleet, snow and high seas caused further delays and she arrived a day late on 5 April. Her disembarking 654 passengers included a brilliant 27-year-old tap-dancer – 'the greatest in the world' and soon to make his mark in the movies – Fred Astaire.

Captain 'Sandy' McNeil was reunited with his ship for the 19 April sailing and the glittering First-Class passenger list for that westward crossing included a princess, a count and his countess, two titled Englishwomen, and the great Russian composer, pianist and conductor Sergei Rachmaninov and his wife. The 30 April return trip included the very popular Scottish comedian and singer, Sir Harry Lauder, after a world tour of 60,000 miles. Two stowaways, Charles Ward (21) and Edward Arnold (22), did not get far after the next Southampton sailing on 10 May. They were discovered just after sailing and put ashore at Cherbourg. Arrival in New York was accompanied by tragedy when Able Seaman Percy May was admitted to the ship's Hospital at 10.10 on the morning of the 17th suffering from a fractured skull. Twenty-five minutes later he was dead and his remains were later interred in the Evergreen Cemetery in Brooklyn. The silly season for young stowaways seemed to be well under way as, shortly after sailing from New York on 21 May, a 21-year-old Briton, Maurice Caplin, was discovered. But all was not drama as two days out from Southampton on 23 June the ship's Hospital echoed to the cries of a newborn son delivered to Third-Class Hungarian passenger Susanna Feleki, who had boarded at Cherbourg. After arrival at Pier 54 two Waiters deserted.

An announcement in early July that the *Mauretania* would make a repeat cruise to Havana the following February was the first indication that the seventh Mediterranean cruise might be shelved as numbers travelling in First and Second Class had decreased by 18–20 per cent, although those in Tourist-Third and Third had increased. Wealth, it seemed, was being conserved.

The ship was attracting chancers in increasing numbers. Three desertions before the eastward departure on 24 July were followed by the flushing out of David Love and John McWhirter, both British, at two in the morning. This was followed by the discovery of James Pollock and John Galloway at 4.15 a.m. and, four hours later, a trio comprising brothers Stanley and Edward Morley, and John Archer was unearthed. The seven men, a new and unwelcome record for the ship, were handed over to the authorities in Southampton. Taken to the Bargate Police Station, the men were later brought before a magistrate. That was not all. At 10.50, two days after the discoveries of the illicit travellers, Master-at-Arms, H. Sheen, and Saloon Steward, A. Baker, found 40-year-old Trimmer William Hughes prostrate on the deck. He had been on his way to call the next Stokehold Watch when, suddenly taken ill, he collapsed. In spite of medical assistance, he died shortly afterwards in the ship's Hospital from a burst stomach ulcer. The Trimmer's remains were buried at sea two days later, his place of death being logged as latitude 45°25′N, longitude 34°15′W.

Captain McNeil was probably glad to get ashore for the next voyage as relief Captain Prothero once again took over the ship's documents and instruments. But his tenure was not without incident. On 8 August, when still alongside in New York, an Able Seaman, Frank Smith, slipped off a wooden box while painting one of the liner's distinctive large ventilators on the Sun Deck and fractured his left foot. Five days later, on sailing day, the 56-year-old AB was discharged from the ship's Hospital with orders not to resume work and to report to the surgery each day. Two days went by and he failed to do so and the

Dispenser, W, Middleton, sent for him. The Bo'sun, Fred Grey, reported Smith missing from his quarters but, after a thorough search, no trace could be found. Last seen at 7.40 p.m. on the 14th, it was presumed that he had fallen – or jumped – overboard.

The *Mauretania* left Cherbourg on 23 August on a westward crossing, when the *Europa* slowly approached from astern. The two liners ran abeam for several miles before the sleek German liner slowly pulled ahead of the veteran speedster at 27 knots, leaving the indignant 'Grand Old Lady' in her wake.

Competition on the holiday route to Cuba increased when the rival Ward Line introduced its new air-conditioned *Morro Castle* on 27 August. At 20 knots, she took fifty-nine hours to reach Havana – the *Mauretania* had done it in forty-four. Although the new ship had been specially built for warm water cruising, the Cunarder's luxurious cabins, although lacking air-conditioning, were advertised as still being the largest available on the run.

The working environment on any vessel can be dangerous and a ship's galley was no exception. Shortly after lunch on 30 August, First Class Waiter Edward Frampton was walking through the First Class Galley just as it was being scrubbed out and, as the Second Cook threw a bucket of hot water on the deck, the Waiter suffered scalds to his right leg. He was admitted to the Hospital and kept under observation for five hours.

Following her successes in 1928 and 1929 when the *Mauretania's* entry made first and fourth places in the eagerly anticipated annual ships' lifeboat race in New York (run on a course from a point below Grant's Tomb to the finishing line off 81st Street), the crew for the 1930 entry felt that they were in with a good chance. One of the rules, probably based on experience, stipulated that 'boats' bottoms [were] not to be greased and oars not to be weighted inboard'. If won for a third time, as with the Schneider air race, the winning boat would keep the trophy. The result is not known.

Towards the end of September, Prime Minister Ramsay MacDonald's Labour Government declined to guarantee the huge insurance risks on the still-building 'New Cunarder' considering that the now 75,000-ton ship was a too-expensive advertisement for Britain and the risks too high. The building was delayed. British international air travel also suffered a major setback when, on 5 October, the year-old airship *R101*, the largest aircraft in the world, crashed in France during its inaugural overseas flight, killing forty-eight of the fifty-four people on board.

What was becoming known as 'The Great Depression' was blighting the lives of millions by the end of November. The northern industrial concentrations of Britain were devastated as demand for traditional industrial products collapsed and, affecting a fifth of the workforce, unemployment rose from 1 million to 2.5 million and the value of exports fell by 50 per cent. On the ocean, cruising rates were reduced in order to attract tourists travelling to Bermuda and the West Indies. For the *Mauretania* this meant a cut of $30 on her upcoming 11 February cruise rates to Havana, the lowest fare being reduced to $160. Shipping lines were also cutting Atlantic rates and for the *Mauretania* there was a reduction of $5 in Second Class. The fall in receipts and the increase in the numbers of Tourist Third passengers over the previous few seasons encouraged Cunard to extend its summer season from 1 July to the 15th eastbound, and from 1 August to 30 September westbound. Six British shipping lines agreed to cut wasteful competition during the slack winter months in an attempt to counter the stiff German challenge. Sailings from British ports were reduced by two-thirds (four per week), and the remaining ships in service were scheduled to avoid duplication.

The westward mid November crossing met with foul weather that caused sinkings, groundings, collisions and loss of life on both sides of the Atlantic. Captain McNeil did not like pushing his outward-bound ship in the face of such weather, so the *Mauretania*'s speed was reduced to about 22½ knots. At 2.26 a.m. on the 19th, she received an SOS distress call from a Swedish cargo vessel, the *Ovidia* (3,343 tons; 1897) belonging to the *Afrikanska Rederei A/B* of Gothenburg. Her cargo of timber had shifted, causing the vessel to develop a dangerous list. To add to her woes, sprung plating had admitted water and the freighter was in a sinking condition. Four ships answered the distress call, one being the American liner *America*, the same distance away as the *Mauretania*. The Second Officer alerted the Captain, the position of the liner was worked out (latitude 44°18'N, longitude 47°41'W), and a course set for the floundering freighter at latitude 42°30'N, longitude

50°44'W – about 400 miles south-by-south-east of Cape Race. The *Mauretania* covered the 200 miles at just over 22 knots, arriving at the scene at 1.06 p.m. The *America* arrived an hour later and stood by.

Giving up hope of being towed to safety, *Ovidia*'s Captain Carlsson decided to abandon ship, realising that the two mail ships standing by were eager to continue their voyages. Two lifeboats left the sinking vessel as passengers lined the railings of the 'Maury', watching concernedly as the small boats disappeared into the troughs of the waves and breathing sighs of relief when they reappeared on the crests. The twenty-eight that were rescued from the Swedish vessel, including the Captain's wife and the ship's cat, were cheered as they boarded the liner. By 2.06 p.m. the *Mauretania* was under way, her passengers assisting the survivors by donating clothing; actress Viola Tree gave clothing to Mrs Carlsson. The dramatic rescue had been filmed from the *Mauretania* and the clip would soon be shown in newsreel cinemas. An interview with Captain McNeil was filmed when the *Mauretania* arrived late in New York on Friday at 11 a.m. Subsequent to the rescue, the Swedish Naval Attaché, Commander Oberg, presented a commemorative gold shield on behalf of the Swedish Navy League to Captain McNeil and the ship's staff for their gallantry.

During recent voyages the Aft Peak tank had been flooding with water up the level of the tank top. To allow a survey at sea, the Engineers pumped out the flood water using a 3in hose, run at full bore, connected to the fore-end suction pipe. The emptied tank was inspected by a Surveyor, who suspected that slack rivets or broken plates were probably the cause of the leakage. On completion of the survey the manholes were replaced, the pumping stopped, and the tank allowed to re-flood. As it had been impossible to ascertain either the source of the leakage or the condition of the surrounding framing, it was decided to survey the ship thoroughly during her next dry-docking.

There were always a few who were determined to make a crossing on the North Atlantic as economically as they could and two British men, Alex McGlashan and Donald McAdam, were apprehended stowing away after the liner had left New York on 26 November. At the end of the crossing they were 'landed at Southampton and put in charge of the authorities'. The *Mauretania*'s fame may have caused her to be chosen by Dutch construction engineer Charles Michaux to stow away for her fast sailing to Southampton on 16 December, but he was discovered the next day as he nonchalantly promenaded with the passengers. This crossing also attracted four others to try their luck – London cook Georgalli Tikki, waiter George Avramides, Liverpudlian bricklayer Harry Allmark and Belfast painter John Donelly. Their luck ran out with discovery and four weeks imprisonment after the ship's arrival home.

In the second week of December, Cunard's New York General Passenger Manager, Harold Borer, unveiled a plan to further reduce the time *Mauretania* spent alongside in New York. The intention was for her to make *four* complete crossings of the Atlantic a month. This demanding new schedule would dispense with the hitherto regular sailings from Southampton every third Saturday and from New York every third Wednesday, and the changes to 'uniform sailings' would disrupt the schedules of the other two express ships. Her late December arrival in Southampton set yet another record for the 'Old Girl' when she completed the strenuous four crossings of the North Atlantic in a record thirty-two days – in spite of a thirty-hour delay – which had previously taken five-and-a-half weeks to achieve. Following instructions from the New York office, her hard-pressed crew quickly prepared the ship for her next sailing in one rather than the accustomed four to five days.

The demanding four-a-month office-enforced regime was proving to be too ambitious: the veteran speedster was capable but the batterings that she experienced pushed both her fabric and her crew to the limit. What had seemed a good idea on the shoreside office desk was proving to be unsustainable at sea. The new schedule was dropped and the company concentrated on her lucrative, less arduous weekend cruises.

The old ship would need that break in the sun although her 250th voyage that left Southampton at noon on her regular Saturday, 27 December, should have been one that continued the recent Christmas celebrations. But the time of year and Nature conspired against her as the grey murk that surrounded her sailing grew worse as she rounded the Nab Tower at the eastern end of The Solent on her way to Cherbourg. Westward-bound, the ship passed the French breakwater at 7.13 p.m. having on board a total of 399 passengers and

564 crew. Humfrey Jordan recalled in his excellent book *Mauretania* that, as she headed out into the North Atlantic, the 'barometer was falling and the thermometer rising, not good signs'. She met with increasingly bad weather and, five hours into the crossing, she passed The Lizard, where she met 'squalls of gale force'.

'[G]ales moderate, fresh and whole' remained with her for the rest of the crossing. Pitching into the seas she 'was labouring' and, as the head seas changed to a beam sea, 'lurching' (yawing). A particularly big sea broke Wheelhouse windows and her engines were frequently slowed as a precaution as the old liner experienced 'noise, wet, cold, violence of movement across three thousand miles of sea … spraying over all, shipping water fore and aft'. It was said that the ship was so covered in spray at times that only her funnels could be seen rising above it! Captain McNeil remarked that it had been the most consistently bad weather that he had ever met and, not liking to force his ship into a gale, reduced her speed further to allow an appendectomy to be performed.

That crossing took the 'old girl' almost seven days averaging, for her, a very poor 18.46 knots. Although she arrived late at her berth at 4.48 on the morning of 3 January, battered and very much behind time, she was readied by 1 p.m., the following day to sail for home. New York's hurried turnaround still resulted in a late arrival in Plymouth Sound, anchoring in the bay at ten o'clock on the evening of Friday, 9 January 1931. Ninety-seven passengers were tendered ashore along with 1,000 bags of mail that were, as usual, whisked up to the quay on a conveyor belt prior to being taken to the baggage warehouse for examination.

After all that she had been put through during a quarter-century of scrapes, groundings, the effects of continuous high-speed crossings, collisions and the not inconsiderable wrath of a defied and jealous ocean, the *Mauretania* was in need of maintenance and a thorough survey and, for over two weeks in January, shipyard staff and BoT surveyors pored over her. Lifted impressively lifted high out of the water in the floating dock, she presented a grand spectacle, especially when floodlit at night as work continued on board, attracting many sightseers and, viewed from Below Bar, she seemed to loom over the bottom of Southampton's High Street. The repairs from the previous year were inspected and, somehow, her certificate was renewed. The liner returned to service for whatever another year could throw at her.

A French challenge for the Blue Riband and to the anticipated British contender was made on 26 January when the keel of the new 'Super *Ile de France*' was laid down in St Nazaire as *T6*. This huge ship would exceed the publicity-making and long sought-after 1,000ft length with her 1,029ft of overall length, longer than *No. 534* by 11ft as the latter ship did not have *T6*'s thrusting clipper bow! However, the 965ft length between perpendiculars (almost waterline length) technically made the British ship the longer by 3ft. The lengths of the two Ships of State might have been correct but their declared tonnages would mischievously increase in competition during their building. With construction details kept secret, it was anticipated that the British liner would be ready for trials by September 1933.

On board the freshly painted *Mauretania* for the 4 February departure was American inventor Paul MacNeill, carrying with him his new 'All-weather Sextant' that claimed to enable a navigator to take a reading even when the Sun was obscured by fog or cloud. Demonstrated during the westward crossing, the instrument met with the approval of the liner's navigators and, later that year, would be taken to London for testing by the British Air Ministry. There were chances a plenty to put the instrument through its paces as the ship met with storms that delayed the New York arrival by two hours.

Boarding the *Mauretania* for the scheduled late evening return sailing of 13 February (the superstitious among the passengers successfully prevailed upon the Captain to delay his sailing until a few minutes after midnight) for his first trip to his native England for several years was film star Charlie Chaplin, creator of the highly popular comic character 'The Little Tramp'. To entertain his fellow passengers he had with him a print of his recently released – and considered his most successful movie – *City Lights*, a silent movie produced in the age of the 'talkies'. Also travelling, but at a slower speed than was his norm, was Captain Malcom Campbell, his record-breaking racing motor car *Bluebird II* having been loaded from a derrick lighter earlier that day. Champion jockey Steve Donoghue made up a star-studded triumvirate.

That traditionally unlucky Friday the 13th enhanced its reputation when Sir Charles Parsons, the inventor of the turbines that drove the record-breaking liner, passed away while on a cruise aboard the *Duchess of Richmond*. He had been predeceased by another great name in the engineering achievements of the ship: Andrew Laing, the designer and builder of the ship's engines, died at his home in Osborne Road, Newcastle upon Tyne, on 25 January. One of Laing's earlier successes had been the Fairfield-built *Alaska* – the first ship to be designated as an 'Atlantic Greyhound', an appellation that had been passed on to a succession of fast ships, not least the *Mauretania*. Also 'Crossing the Bar' on 21 January was the liner's wartime master, Captain Daniel Dow, aged 71, at his home in Elton Avenue, Blundellsands.

The liner's arrival at Plymouth at 7.25 a.m. on the 19th was greeted by a score of newspapermen who had boarded the tender at 5 a.m. eager, but probably grumpy because of the early hour, to interview the three celebrities who, under Charlie Chaplin's direction, gave the 'hacks' plenty to write about by clowning around in front of the cameras. Chaplin then disembarked with his precious reels of film and, mobbed by a happy crowd at the Great Western Docks, was whisked away to London, where he was greeted the next day with great enthusiasm. Chaplin's Japanese valet, Keno, was perhaps happier to leave the ship as he had suffered from seasickness. Officially cleared, the liner steamed off for Cherbourg at 8.30 with record-breaking speedster Malcolm Campbell remaining on board (the liner steaming at one-tenth the speed of his motor car). An official welcome awaited him in Southampton followed by a gala dinner at the prestigious South Western Hotel with the Minister of Transport, Herbert Morrison, in attendance, after which the famed driver was to broadcast to a nationwide audience eager to hear about his 246mph record dash.

At Cherbourg, Captain Campbell faced more newsmen. Nearby a passenger, Frederick Hyde, one of only *twenty* travelling in Second Class, somehow fell overboard. The dashing sportsman was the first to react and, in full view of the press, cameras and pencils conveniently at the ready, sprang to the ship's rail and threw a lifebuoy into the water for the succour of the floundering man. And the excitement of the trip was not yet over. At 5.45 p.m., as the liner was manoeuvred through the difficult dog-legged channel that led into Southampton Water, a point was reached by the West Brambles shoal where a turn to port would lead towards the busy docks, just 6 miles ahead. A fog lay over the waters and the murky conditions were exacerbated by an exceptionally low spring tide. The liner began her turn when, to the concern of all on board, a strong vibration ran throughout the ship, followed by the ringing of alarm bells and the ship came to a stop. She was aground. Her vulnerable stern had touched the sandbank – Captain McNeil said that she 'smelled the mud' – and the vibrations of the astern turbines increased in the attempt to release the hapless vessel from her shingle embrace.

Tugs were immediately summoned from Southampton along with a tender, the latter to take the passengers off the ship, the former to take the ship off the bank. Four tugs arrived; two set about pushing the *Mauretania* amidships while two pulled on steel hawsers attached to her stern bitts through the fairleads. With the manoeuvring of the tugs and a rising tide the liner was at last released, seemingly undamaged, at around 9.30. She finally reached her berth at 10.30 (at the same time as the passenger-loaded tender) and was greeted by a late evening cacophony of ship's sirens and whistles that must have startled may a sleeping Sotonian, a greeting intended for Malcolm Campbell but also appropriate for the great ship's reprieve. To the surprise of the large crowd gathered to greet him, the sportsman unexpectedly clambered up the gangway from the humble tender rather than disembarking from the great liner. Once on the quayside, the sportsman was presented with a message from the King informing him that he was now 'Sir Malcolm'. The dinner of welcome had continued in his absence; the radio broadcast delayed; the expectant nation still enthusiastic.

The formidable channel that had delayed the *Mauretania* in its clutch had also claimed the unintended attention of other expensive ships, the *Berengaria* and the Dutch *Statendam* amongst them. As a consequence the channel would soon be dredged to a width of 1,000ft and to a depth of 35ft with the removal of 2.5 million cubic yards of shingle at a cost of a quarter-of-a-million pounds.

Because of the deepening Depression, the *Mauretania*'s Mediterranean cruise for 1931, her seventh, scheduled to start on 21 February was expected to incur a serious loss. Cunard had tried tempting new customers by altruistically stating that the lowest fares for the cruise were being reduced by $200 to $640 in order to 'bring the mid-winter vacation in foreign climates within the reach of families of even moderate income'. The bait failed and the cruise was cancelled. She would not make such another. A Havana cruise was also cancelled and

the liner returned to the transatlantic service as the *Berengaria*'s annual maintenance had been extended. With the latter's turbine problems overcome, she rejoined the Express run and the 'Maury's' sailing on 28 March marked the resumption of the Big Three's 1931 season of regular Saturday sailings from Southampton.

For the travelling public, Second Class had become increasingly unpopular (it will be remembered that there were only twenty travelling in that class earlier in February) so it was redesignated 'Tourist Third Cabin', 'Third' being included because of international conference agreements. Fares were based on the old Third-Class rates. Minimum First-Class fares were also adjusted to suit the current climate, with rates from Southampton tumbling to £53. Less fortunate than erstwhile travellers and pleasure seekers was a group that included 'public enemies', not only gangsters but more vulnerable women and children whose breadwinners had either died or had deserted them. Now classed as aliens by US Immigration, they were taken to Ellis Island for deportation on various liners, including *Mauretania*.

Cunard put their three big Express liners into the weekend cruise market hoping to attract 150,000 customers from all walks of life and resources. After discharging her passengers at Pier 54 on 24 April (including scientist Sir James Jeans en route to discuss matters of time and space with Edwin Hubble in California), the *Mauretania* was immediately prepared for the first cruise by a large liner to Nassau in the Bahamas. Fares had been set from $50 to $150 but, to discourage such traffic, $90 (plus) was being charged one way. In an attempt to smooth the ruffled feathers of competitors, Cunard explained that their use of the *Mauretania* was not to compete with ships already on the short run but as 'a means of introducing an Atlantic liner to persons who may be considering a trip abroad'.

Prior to that cruise the liner left New York on 6 March for Europe with 142 passengers in First, a low 66 in Second, and 177 in Third Class and immediately encountered 60mph head winds and very rough weather with steep seas that blew unabated for 3,000 miles. On one day she made only 465 miles – 563 being her best – her average speed being 23.35 knots. The Captain anticipated a late arrival in Plymouth and consequently would miss calling at her usual three ports in one day. The severe weather abated towards the end of the crossing and the old ship managed to make up some lost time. Arriving at Plymouth on the 12th at 10.44 a.m. and not the anticipated late time of 1 p.m. on the 11th, she bore marks of her struggle with the elements with salt-stained funnels and broken ports. Mails and 115 doubtlessly thankful passengers disembarked into the Plymouth tenders to a less-than-welcoming cold, snowy south-west England.

Back in America, and with mostly New Yorkers among the 815 tourists fleeing Depression and Prohibition, the *Mauretania* sailed at 5 p.m. on Friday, 24 April on the first of many weekend cruises that would very gainfully employ Cunard's big ships during their otherwise idle turnarounds. To compensate for the additional workload, the crews looked forward to generous tips from the jubilant vacationers on these increasingly popular cruises.

Not to be outdone, Southampton sailings now offered eighteen-day holiday cruises for £41 10s return. An extra £10 would provide a stay in New York while the ship went cruising, and £16 10s would give an opportunity to visit Philadelphia and Washington. Competition was hotting up on the West Indies luxury route as the largest liner to be built on the River Tyne since the *Mauretania*, the luxuriously appointed *Monarch of Bermuda*, entered the river on 17 March. Specially built for the New York to Bermuda run for Furness-Withy & Co. Ltd, she would become hugely popular with wealthier passengers. As the new liner lay alongside her fitting-out berth, luxury and penury existed side-by-side as the workforce at Swan Hunter's yard that had built her joined the expanding queues of unemployed.

Of the three Express ships it was the *Mauretania*'s speed that enabled her to make the longest of the cruises in the four days available; the *Aquitania* and *Berengaria* would only cruise the Gulf Stream and Cunard said that many potential tourists, apparently of a different ilk, on the latter two ships' cruises showed only 'a slight interest in going ashore'. These 'Cruises to Nowhere' became popularly known as 'Booze Cruises', the ships' bars being opened when outside American waters. But this plan was eventually changed to appease the American Jones Act and calls into the British territories of Bermuda (St George) and the northerly destination of Nova Scotia (Halifax) were introduced.

Arriving in Nassau at noon, *Mauretania*'s tourists spent the afternoon ashore before rejoining the liner and returning to New York on the

28 April. Twenty-four hours later she sailed for Southampton, where her presence inspired many to take three-and-sixpenny trips by paddle steamers from Southsea and Ryde to see the liner at her berth. Included in the fare was a one-shilling tour of the great ship (the author's father recalled the outstretched palms of smiling stewards lined up at the exit after a similar visit to White Star's *Homeric*!).

May was a typically busy month for the 'Old Girl'. After a favourable crossing that reflected increasingly dry weather in America, where drought was feared, she arrived at Plymouth three hours early at 3.20 in the morning of 5 May and cleared for departure at 7.10. The second cruise from New York was hurriedly prepared (Third Class wasn't used) as the liner, delayed by bad weather on the North Atlantic, was late in docking on Wednesday, 13 May. Fuel and provisions were hastened aboard and linen laundered ashore. Meanwhile, the crew worked wonders in getting the ship away two days later, even if three hours late at 8 p.m. Cruise departures were always a gala occasion with crowds lining the apron of Pier 54 waving and calling to their departing friends. The ship's impressive speed soon made up lost time and ensured that the revellers would still spend their allotted times ashore.

When the liner's return from sunny Bermuda on 19 May was greeted by thick fog she hove-to outside the normally bustling harbour in company with the *Baltic* and *Paris*, both inbound from Europe, remaining fog-bound for nine hours. In accordance with the Eighteenth Amendment, the ship's bars were shut and sealed, leaving 711 mostly thirsty passengers with nothing to do. A protesting group threatened to break down doors and storm the bars, so Captain McNeil posted guards but later relented, opening the bars for one-and-a-half hours.

That same day, as part of troubled Germany's post-war revival, a 'pocket battleship', the *Deutschland*, was launched, the largest armoured ship that could be built under the restrictions of the Treaty of Versailles. On her eastward crossing the Cunarder carried representatives to discuss problems arising from Germany's Reparation Payments as that country struggled with near revolution. She also left behind crew member J. O'Brien with appendicitis but he fared better than 15-year-old Bell Boy Jack Elson. This was the youngster's first voyage on the *Mauretania* and, perhaps fearful of his nail-inspecting superior and wanting to make a good showing, turned up on duty while feeling ill. Two days later he collapsed at his post. Taken to the ship's Hospital, he was diagnosed with 'septic double pneumonia'. After the liner's arrival at Plymouth at 4.24 a.m. on the 26th young Elson, oxygen mask attached, was stretchered ashore on the tender *Sir John Hawkins* and taken to Plymouth's hospital. He passed away three days later with his grieving parents at his side. His death touched the heart of the nation and, through donations, a chartered railway coach carried his remains home to Port Talbot. On that same crossing was famed passenger Captain Bruce Bairnsfather, whose cartoon character 'Old Bill' had lifted morale during the Great War with his amusing comments: turning to a grumbling co-inhabitant of a bombarded shell-hole, Old Bill remarked: 'Well, if you knows of a better 'ole, go to it.' The Captain, about to be divorced from his wife Cecilia, was travelling home hoping for a reconciliation. Curiously, he left the ship at Cherbourg. The liner's arrival at Southampton on 26 May completed a 10,000-mile journey.

Public enthusiasm for *No. 534* then building was stimulated when Cunard announced that Princess Elizabeth, in company with her father, the Duke of York, might launch the giant ship, which would consequently be named in her honour. (Perhaps the Southampton paddle steamer *Princess Elizabeth* of 1927 had been similarly named to reserve the appellation.) It was also anticipated that a sister to the New Cunarder would also be built at Clydeside.

Sir Arthur Rostron of the *Berengaria* retired in early June after forty-six years at sea, all but ten being spent with Cunard that included 240 crossings of the Atlantic in his beloved *Mauretania*. He was superseded as Commodore of the Line by Captain E.G. Diggle, who would hold the post for only a few short months before his own retirement. Captain 'Sandy' McNeill would go on leave at the termination of the *Mauretania*'s next arrival in Southampton on 3 July before his retirement. This news surprised all on board – not least the Captain himself. After forty-seven years at sea, the last three of which had been in command of the *Mauretania*, the Captain had proved to be popular with both passengers and crew, the latter evidenced by fewer disciplinary entries in the log books! His place would be taken by one of her Relief Captains, currently master of the *Ausonia*, Captain Reginald Vernon Peel, who hailed from Rock Ferry on the Wirral Peninsula.

On his final arrival, Captain McNeil ('I have nothing to celebrate. I have always loved the sea. I regret to leave it,' he told *The New York Times*) was on the Bridge of his 'Old Girl' with the pilot as she arrived back in The Solent. Those waters were continuously busy with liners arriving or departing to all parts of the world, as well as sailing and steam yachts, barges, tugs, dredgers, paddle ferries and excursion boats, sailing ships, warships, coasters and cargo vessels. On this particularly poignant arrival for the Captain, the Cunarder was in the Thorn-Brambles Channel after her tight turn to starboard by the West Brambles buoy. Just having passed the site of her sojourn on the shingle in February, she approached the turn to port by the *Calshot* lightvessel into Southampton Water as a French cargo vessel approached from ahead.

The loaded freighter (of about 8,000 tons) rounded Calshot at 6 p.m. and the two closing ships exchanged a single blast on their whistles, Captain McNeil expecting the French ship to safely pass. When the two vessels were about 600 yards from each other, the French ship suddenly veered to port and headed towards the great liner; apparently she had touched the mud of Calshot Spit. The cargo ship blew three short blasts, indicating that she was manoeuvring to go full astern but still continued towards the proud black hull of the liner, whose pilot ordered 'Full astern'. However, as this would take time to take effect, the Captain countered the Pilot's order by ordering the helm hard-a-starboard, then rang 'Full ahead' on the starboard engines and 'Full astern' on the port. In effect the *Mauretania* sped up and swerved around the still approaching freighter, which passed closely astern of the old greyhound, missing her by 15ft! The whole episode had taken a breath-stopping four minutes.

The Captain's retirement would sadly be cut short. He completed his memoirs *In Great Waters* shortly after leaving the sea but he passed away on 8 May 1936 at the early age of 64. His tenure as Captain of the *Mauretania* had been a remarkable one, including record passages both west and east of 26.9 knots and 27.22 knots respectively – this when his command was twenty-two years old! Following the ship's arrival in Southampton, Captain Peel took command of the liner from Captain McNeil after going through the usual formalities.

The *Mauretania*'s first arrival in New York with Captain Peel in command was closely scrutinised by an interested passenger on board the departing *Berengaria*. Captain Rostron, now retired, watched with poignancy as his old ship made her grand entrance into the harbour. He later said: 'It was like meeting an old friend. I shall probably never see her again at sea.' Her owners reckoned that the popular old ship was 'good for a generation yet' and it was proposed to charter her for a series of high-speed winter cruises from New York to the Mediterranean. Meanwhile, her short in-between cruises continued but when the ship arrived back from a trip to Nassau, it may have been the 9 June arrival, it was discovered that a mail bag had been tampered with (as sometimes happened to registered mail) and £5,000 stolen, the felony probably occurring before departing the Bahamian port.

A week later the Bermuda and West Indies Steamship Company's three-year-old *Bermuda* (19,086grt) specially built for 'The Millionaires' Run' to Bermuda, caught fire while at Hamilton. Eventually towed back to her builder's (Workman Clark & Co.) in Belfast for repairs, she again burnt when almost complete. To complete the ignominy, she was wrecked en route to the breakers.

By the middle of 1931 the Depression had tightened its grip and it was estimated that a big luxury ship could lose £10,000 on one round voyage. Although sailings were cancelled, Cunard's 'Big Three' kept to their schedules, absorbing passengers from laid-up vessels. The 'Maury's' mid-June eastward crossing was spiced with excitement as it was expected that she would pass the converted polar exploration submarine *Nautilus*. Lady Wilkins, the wife of the submarine's commander, was on board the liner but the liaison was cancelled when it was learned that the submarine had been disabled and was being towed to Plymouth for engine repairs. The two vessels finally met on 28 July when, following her Devonport Dockyard repairs, the outward-bound submarine and her crew were cheered by passengers in the passing tender and then from the decks of the anchored *Mauretania*. Near-record temperatures of 73°F accompanied the *Mauretania* on her westward crossing at the end of June, giving her passengers a flavour of her cruising days.

Four of the liner's cruises from New York between July and September 1931 were away from the heat of the West Indies and took her on the 1,200-mile route to Halifax in Nova Scotia for just £13. At least this placated the American Neptune Society, which had

loudly protested at British liners making cruises to nowhere. During the mid-September Halifax cruise three determined men spent the entire trip in the Dining Room – just eating! Huge breakfasts, lunches and dinners – even the midnight buffet – were consumed and it was reckoned that the caviar alone covered the cost of their fares! These cruises were undertaken at almost half-speed and it took two days to get to Halifax rather than one. Captain Peel was reported as saying that he sometimes took the ship out on a longer course to enable her to attain her natural speed. She once returned to New York at full speed after having to return to the Nova Scotian port to collect six missing passengers, and after another return the passengers were treated to the unusual spectacle of three waterspouts rising into the sky.

In Britain, Ramsey MacDonald's Labour Government was taking financial measures to cope with the effects of the Depression, one of which was to increase taxes whilst reducing Government spending. This would have the effect of reducing vital unemployment benefits (the dole) by 20 per cent, thereby badly hitting an already-impoverished sector of society that had elected the Labour Party into power with so much hopeful anticipation. Even King George V protested at the additional hardship that this measure would cause his people. Cunard's Chairman, Sir Percy Bates, advocated the 'capitalisation of the dole' to encourage the emigration of many of the unemployed, especially in the hard-hit industrial north, to the colonies and dominions, perhaps (coincidentally) increasing his company's business to Canada. The Government collapsed two months later.

To encourage First-Class passengers, Cunard drastically cut its luxury rates; on the *Mauretania* what had cost £828 in 1921 for a Regal Suite (sitting room, dining room, two bedrooms, a bath and toilet) was now down to £224, and a £128 Parlour Suite (bedroom, sitting room, bath and toilet) was now £53. These rates would be reduced further following an International Shipping Conference scheduled for October. Tourist-Third was also renamed more temptingly as 'Tourist' and, in a popular move, the whole of the liner's previously poorly patronised Second Class was made available to the new class. Despite these reductions, there were still those who took the chance of a free crossing. One 20-year-old American, reportedly 'fed up' with his home country, hiked all the way from the US West Coast before classically stowing away in a ship's lifeboat. Two days later hunger drove him out onto the decks and detection.

Curtailing a visit to the US because of the political crisis at home, British politician Percy Prybus was on board for the eastward sailing of 2 September, during the course of which he received a radiogram informing him of his appointment as Minister of Transport in the new National Government. His fellow travellers may have interested him as they included Anton 'Anthony' Fokker, a Dutch-born designer and builder of many infamous German aircraft used to great effect in the Great War. Fokker predicted that there would soon be a regular transatlantic air service and, having recently sold the American branch of his firm to General Motors, he was en route to England for the Schneider Trophy air race, a great international showcase of air technology, which was to be held over The Solent on 12 September. Railways were also represented in the person of Sir Percy Girouard, a retired distinguished builder of railways and colonial governor.

With a new Staff Captain, L.R. Carr, the liner left Southampton on 12 September and, as she sailed through The Solent, passed scores of crowded vessels lining the route of the big air race, including White Star's *Homeric* being used as a luxury grandstand. Two days into the crossing, a 21-year-old American in Third Class, Mrs Julia Skirka, (probably trying to make it back home for the event), gave birth to a baby girl. For the return trip another extra passenger was carried – Cypriot-born British citizen Spiros Kole. He was landed at Southampton as a stowaway.

The final Mediterranean cruise having now been cancelled, advertised cruises for the coming winter included two ten-day trips to the West Indies (Havana, La Guaira, Curaçao, Colón) scheduled to leave New York on 19 November and 3 December, the first since the *Mauretania*'s record-breaking run to Havana in February 1930. Although day visits would be made to Bermuda and Nassau, three days and nights would be spent partying in Havana. The liner was faring better than her smaller fleet-mates *Carmania* and *Caronia*, both laid up in the Thames Estuary. If employment could not be found for the Depression-hit 'Pretty Sisters' then the shipbreakers would surely beckon.

Calling into Plymouth at 3 a.m. on 29 September after her 261st eastbound, the *Mauretania* carried 59 in First Class, 153 in Tourist and 310 in Third. The seventy-one that disembarked after breakfast must have left those remaining in First Class rattling around almost empty accommodation! The ship was cleared for Cherbourg at 7.45. After arrival in Southampton the liner was raised in the floating dock, where she remained, and at berth, in maintenance and survey for most of October. Though the liner was faster than her companions both on the Express Run and on longer-range weekend cruise itineraries, her remaining sailings for the month were unexpectedly cancelled. With her passenger certificate somehow renewed, the *Mauretania* sailed for New York with Christmas mails on Armistice Day, 11 November; traveling were the Duke of Leinster and J.P. Morgan Jr, who complained that a small, yapping dog in the adjacent suite should have been kept in the kennels.

The first cruise to the West Indies began on 19 November as scheduled and day calls into Bermuda and Nassau were followed by three hedonistic nights in Havana, where her 7 a.m. flag-bedecked arrival on Friday, 27th, her first since her record voyage of February 1930, was watched by thousands. During her approach the liner touched ground. Divers engaged by the local Lloyd's surveyor found that, although the rudder and shell plating remained unscathed, both port propellers had suffered bent tips and 40ft of bilge keel aft had been damaged. Captain Peel's comments to the Pilot are lost to history! That same day it was announced that the liner would emulate her successful cruises from New York and cruise from Britain to Gibraltar. Since Britain had left the Gold Standard in September and the pound had fallen by 25 per cent against the dollar, this would be the 'patriotic' thing to do. Five days later she returned to New York with her bleary-eyed travellers.

Her second Cuban cruise departed 3 December, with a third on the 19th with Cap-Haïtien on the north coast of Haiti, La Guaira, Colón and Panama among her destinations. At this time Cunard announced that, although it was intended that the current three ships on the Express run would eventually be replaced by two larger vessels, including *No. 534*, the *Mauretania* would remain. The next day losses of £2.25 million for 1931 were posted; with only £1.1 million in the bank, work on the 73,000-ton *No. 534* ceased though only three months from completion. Suggestions that she might be scrapped on the stocks were denied. As for the *Mauretania*, Sir Percy Bates declared reassuringly, but rather ambiguously, that she was good 'for as long as we need her'. Her future was brighter than that of British aviation, which suffered another setback when the huge and prestigious airship *R100* was sold for scrap following the previous year's disaster that befell her sister ship, *R101*.

At the end of her current cruises *Mauretania* arrived in bustling New York Harbor on 8 January 1932 along with nine other liners. Although she had been expected to be in American waters until April, she sailed for Southampton that same day, arriving in Plymouth at 11 a.m. on the 15th on a high tide and in bright sunshine. Seemingly dominating The Sound, she was the city's first Cunarder of the season. The liner battled a fierce gale and heavy seas as she returned from her last cruise of the series, docking in a typical wintry New York several hours late on 5 February. Arriving in New York on the 27th after a turbulent Atlantic crossing, the liner sported damage claimed as payment by the jealous seas as an ingress of water through a broken port had spoiled 300 packages of general cargo, including a consignment of fur pelts.

Readjustments of rates at the end of the month were meant to boost the increasingly important tourist trade, and other shipping lines followed the *Mauretania*'s innovation of converting Second Class to Tourist Third. So serious was the financial situation that First-Class Atlantic fares on the *Mauretania* were reduced again from £47 to £44 5s, still £3 5s less than her Express companions. The eastbound crossing of voyage 267, ending in Plymouth on 3 March 1932, had been plagued firstly by fog for the first two days after sailing and then, halfway over, by a strong gale; the weather improved for the last two days. Sailing westwards on the 16th, she carried Sir Ashley Sparks, Cunard's Director in New York and, on arrival in New York, he opined that Britain was beginning to see the last of the Depression.

20

'EVERYBODY SINGS WHEN THE BOAT PULLS OUT'

Leaving a miserable New York on Thursday, 24 March after a quick turnaround, the *Mauretania* sailed on a four-day Easter cruise to Nassau with 800 excited passengers on board leaving the Depression – and 300 disappointed applicants – behind. When the ship sailed from Nassau on the 26th, a local song celebrated the event:

> Everybody sings when the boat pulls out
> Everybody whistles and laughs and shouts
> Everybody sings when boat pulls out
> From Nassau

As the prosperity brought by the cruise ships was being welcomed in the West Indies, Depression-ridden Great Britain welcomed the joyous news that work on the abandoned *No. 534* was to be resumed, an event that would mark the easing of the crippling unemployment that had been besieging the country. Anticipating that the new liner would be in service by the summer of 1934, it was whispered that the old *Mauretania* would be sent for demolition when the new giant ship was online.

In financially and politically besieged Germany, Adolf Hitler of the National Socialist Party – the Nazis – narrowly missed being appointed President of Germany after an election on 10 April. On that same day, five days from the twentieth anniversary of the sinking of the *Titanic*, an unusually large number of icebergs were reported on the Western Atlantic – 350 alone being counted by the International Ice Patrol that

had been founded after the disaster that had befallen the great White Star liner. The shipping lanes were prudently diverted 10 miles south.

With too many ships chasing too few passengers the *Mauretania's* arrival in Southampton on 21 April brought her sailings to a sudden halt and her next sailing scheduled for 30 April was cancelled, her disappointed passengers being transferred to the company's *Laconia* sailing from Liverpool. Less fortunate were the elegant 'Pretty Sisters'. Victims of the Depression, *Carmania* was on her way for scrapping at Blyth while *Caronia* was already at the breakers in Japan. During this enforced lay-up the *Mauretania* was readied for her first, much-publicised, cruise to Gibraltar and she was opened for inspection to an always enthusiastic public for 1/- (1 shilling) a head. Excursion paddle steamers again brought day-trippers from Portsmouth and the Isle of Wight, and charabancs (coaches) arrived from inland. A few days before leaving, the liner became a film extra in a 'talkie' when she, along with eighty human extras, was hired by British Pictorial Productions for the shooting of a thirty-five-minute short film, *Double Bluff*, a crime story revolving around an on-board cardsharp.

During the liner's absence from New York, Pier 54 was destroyed by a fierce fire on 6 May, which even fifty fire engines and five fireboats failed to extinguish. Plans were immediately put in hand to rebuild the ravaged structure and, scheduled to be finished by the following March, the new pier was completed ahead of time and opened on 10 January 1933. During the rebuild Cunard's ships had to use other berths, often racing other vessels to obtain the best. Other Chelsea

After the big fire at Pier 54 in New York the *Mauretania* was berthed at Hoboken until the pier was rebuilt. (Collection of William H. Miller)

piers on the New Jersey side at Hoboken were utilised and, ironically, the *Berengaria* would return to Pier 4 that she had used in pre-war days as Hamburg America Line's *Imperator*.

The Depression's deadly reign was not yet over and in May another Transatlantic Steamship Conference agreed to bring fares down to pre-war levels for the lower out-of-season winter rates. For the *Mauretania* this meant First-Class rates would be massively reduced from $258 to $188. After her fortnight's lay-up, the liner left Southampton at 5.30 p.m. on Saturday, 14 May on her long-anticipated five-day 2,300-mile Whitsun cruise to Gibraltar, advertised as being for those who wanted 'the glamour of a long sea voyage on a crack ship', the first such cruise from the UK. Demand had been high and tickets, sold out for months beforehand, ranged from eight guineas (£8 8s) – or 3/4d (three farthings) a mile – a millionaire's holiday at less cost, it was said, than a third-class ticket on the railways! The 900 holidaymakers on board included 500 young people, temporarily giving the old ship the epithet of 'The Ship of Youth'. White Star had recently adopted the in-between-voyage short cruises for their ships and, sailing on the same day as the *Mauretania*, the *Olympic* departed on her first three-day cruise.

As pretty girls in their colourful beach pyjamas strolled about the decks enjoying the ocean breezes in the prevailing fine weather, the festive Cunarder was navigated to allow her passengers to view the passing coast of Portugal. A gala dinner, concerts, a ball and cabaret (under the direction of Leon Fraser and the *Mauretania* Orchestra) entertained. For the more active there was a day of sports – deck tennis, quoits, putting and swimming, plus boxing matches put on by members of the crew's Boxing Club. For the less active there was always a good book to be languidly enjoyed in a deckchair, or a visit to the cinema might while away a few hours between activities and meals.

The holiday ship reached 'The Rock' at 8 a.m. the following Tuesday and the few short hours spent ashore either shopping in Main Street or sightseeing (the Barbary Apes were a 'must') quickly passed. And then 'All aboard!' and the liner sailed at 1 p.m. The return trip to Southampton gave the old liner an opportunity to show her mettle and set another fine weather record by making the passage of 1,166 miles in twenty-two hours and one important minute at an impressive average speed of 25.33 knots. Cunard's gamble had paid off and the immense

popularity and thrills of the cruise encouraged Cunard to put other big ships on the route. By the time she returned to Southampton on 21 May, both passengers and transatlantic mails for exotic and faraway destinations – China, Fiji, Jamaica, Japan, New Zealand and Samoa – awaited her departure for New York that same day.

Six days later the *Mauretania* departed on a Bermuda cruise from New York before returning to Britain on 1 June. Her daily noon-to-noon runs of 382, 598, 595, 582 and 368 nautical miles to the Eddystone gave an average speed of just over 25 knots. Of the 179 First (including British film actor Nigel Bruce and his wife), 305 Tourist and 694 Third-Class passengers, 167 boarded the tenders in Cawsand Bay, while 2,250 bags of mail were ferried ashore in the mail boat. Southampton saw the liner berthing at 6 in the evening. Elsewhere at sea, the Cunard liner *Scythia* was experimenting with a patent hybrid fuel composed of 60 per cent oil and 40 per cent pulverised coal, devised by Cunard's own Technical Department, who altruistically intended it to be used generally in an attempt to alleviate the chronic unemployment in Britain's struggling coal industry.

The American holiday season then began in earnest in June. The liner left Southampton on 11 June, cruised from New York, and then left for Britain at 5 p.m. At the end of her next transatlantic on the 30th she was one of three Cunarders arriving in Britain that brought in 3,500 American tourists, the *Mauretania* arriving at Plymouth after averaging a good 24.91 knots with 137 in First, 378 in Tourist and a large 654 in Third. Other than the *Andania*, all Cunard ships were at sea when Cunard celebrated its ninety-second anniversary on 4 July. Ashore in Britain, rumours circulated that an amalgamation between Cunard and the ailing White Star Line might be a possibility.

Cruises began from New York on 9 July with a five-day jaunt followed by a lengthier one to the West Indies. She completed two more transatlantic voyages before sailing from Southampton at noon on 28 December 1932, not to reappear in the port until the following April after completing nine cruises of varying duration.

The old liner's glorious record receded further into the past when the Italians were the next to take the Blue Riband with their brand-new *Rex*, eventually taking the accolade on a voyage that ended in New York on 16 August 1933. Any good publicity was advantageous and the old *Mauretania* was pushed to prove herself amongst her younger rivals: after leaving her Hoboken pier at 5.11 p.m. on 14 September, she overhauled the *Île de France* that had sailed at noon and arrived at Plymouth (with a low passenger list of sixty-one – including a princess – in First, 116 in Tourist, and 132 in Tourist Third) one and a half hours ahead of the French ship. The *Bremen* sailed after the *Mauretania* and, without a Plymouth call, reached Cherbourg first.

On 24 September 1932 the liner was reported as usual from St Catherine's Point on the southern tip of the Isle of Wight as she steamed into the distance en route for Cherbourg, the visibility was good, the sea slight with a moderate wind from the south-west, the air temperature 59°F. Five days later she made an arrival in New York. Her return reflected the changing season when two days of gales and high seas hindered her passage, which took her five days, four hours and twenty-three minutes, arriving in Plymouth on 10 October after determinedly averaging 24.59 knots with the lowest passenger list of her long and illustrious career – fifty-nine in First; seventy-one in Tourist; and seventy-seven in Third – plus one stowaway who, posing as American seaman Peter Porculis, was, in fact, Liverpudlian James Grace, 35. Although arrested in Southampton, he was not prosecuted.

In Southampton she was the first of the big liners to be withdrawn from service for a two-month maintenance period. An important event in the port's history occurred on 19 October 1932 when the *Mauretania*, carefully guided by smoke-belching tugs of the Alexander Towing Company, was transferred to the New – or Western – Docks. By doing so the great liner formally opened the magnificent, recently completed £13 million, 7,000ft quay, for access to which a channel had been dredged to a low-water depth of 35ft and 600ft wide. Behind the quays were 400 acres of mudflats that, when reclaimed, would form a new industrial estate. At the far end of the quay, a huge dry dock was still under construction that would be opened by the King the following July and named, appropriately, the 'King George V Graving Dock'. This impressive structure was planned to take the 'New Cunarder' when she came into service. The following month (November 1932) marked the twenty-fifth anniversary of the 'Grand Old Lady of the North Atlantic's' departure from the Tyne, the river of her birth, on her way to ultimate fame and glory, a fine testament to the skills of those who

had designed her and the craftsmen who had built her. Appropriately, a portrait of Sir George B. Hunter by Thomas van Oss was unveiled in the Boardroom of Swan Hunter and Wigham Richardson.

During the survey and maintenance work her ballast tanks were emptied, cleaned, inspected and tested under steam pressure. The survey must have been approached with apprehension as, during her voyaging, the After Peak tank had been flooding 'as usual', the source of the leakage undetermined. An application to extend the period of dry-docking was granted and the old liner was manoeuvred into the Southern Railway's Floating Dock on 23 November.

As the dock's tanks were emptied and the dock and ship raised, it became apparent that previous remedial work had not been successful. As the underwater hull rose above the water level, water began to pour from rivet holes that connected Frames 4, 5 and 6 to the shell plating. Once high and dry, further inspection revealed that forty-five rivets on each side had been loosened by vibration and by erosion of the rivets' shanks, so much so that the fasteners could be pushed in or pulled out by hand, in some instances by ¾in! Not only were two shell rivets completely missing (one on each side) but 172 others needed replacement, as did eighty-two floor rivets and fifty-three floor bolts. A steel patch covering a 2½in diameter hole had also worked loose. Perhaps, not surprisingly, after her record of groundings, *both* pintle doors on the rudder were found to be missing! Below their crowns, wing oil bunkers F1, E2, E3 and D2 had been distorted or fractured from lightening holes to outboard. F-Deck beams, frames and web frames were buckled and, as similar damage had occurred to the *Majestic*, it was surmised that the distortions had been caused by the twisting of the hull in heavy weather.

Re-riveting the thick plating in the very fine and narrow part of the stern would require the drilling of larger holes for larger diameter rivets but as space limitations precluded a riveter's 'Holder-upper' (dolly-holder) from gaining access, it was decided to re-caulk and weld the plates onto the stern casting. Once repaired, the tank was tested by filling with water. It passed and, after all other structural work had been completed, a BoT Passenger Certificate was issued. Disappointingly, it was found that – in spite of all the work that had been done – 'the after peak tank filled as usual during the first voyage to New York'.

It was concluded that the tank 'appears incapable of standing against the conditions met with in service'. The 'Old Lady' was wearing out.

While the *Mauretania* was being carefully attended she became part of a grand spectacle in Southampton when, on 26 November 1932, seven of the world's greatest liners were in port together. She was, at 30,695grt, the smallest in a fleet that comprised *Majestic* (56,621grt); *Berengaria* (52,226); *Olympic* (46,439); *Aquitania* (45,647); Canadian Pacific's beautiful new *Empress of Britain* (42,348grt and the only non-Cunard or White Star vessel in the group); and the *Homeric* (34,356). Three days later, in St Nazaire, *T6*, the biggest ship in the world, was launched as the *Normandie*. At 1,027ft she was longer overall than the New Cunarder and, at a reported 75,000grt, would exceed *No. 534* by 2,000 tons. The British, however, had a surprise up their sleeves.

While still in the hands of the ship repairers, local shipyard workman Fred Rowe, fell 50ft from the *Mauretania* into the water and, overcome by cramp, disappeared into the depths. His workmate, Boiler Scaler Robert Cornelius, slid down a rope, dived into the freezing river, seized Rowe by the hair and pulled him to the surface. Meanwhile, a third workman, Rigger Donald Stuart, clambered down the rope to assist Cornelius in keeping Rowe afloat before all three were rescued. Rowe was taken to hospital, while his rescuers satisfied themselves with a cup of tea and a change of clothing before returning to work!

' … you did it again!'

Meanwhile, progress had been made in the negotiations between the Government and Cunard and it was hoped that work on *No. 534* would be resumed before Christmas. Shipyard workers were put on a twenty-four-hour standby – wonderful news considering that 30 per cent of Glaswegians were unemployed due to the severe decline in heavy industry. However, the prospect of a sister ship, anticipated to be built on the Tyne, receded into an indefinite future.

The *Mauretania* was readied for her scheduled departure on 28 December 1932 and would not see Southampton again for four months. At eight o'clock, four hours before the noon departure,

Captain Peel felt unwell so his command was assumed by Relief Captain, Captain J.C. Townley (Extra-Masters' Certificate No. 034482). This first crossing after her worrying survey tested the liner to the limit as for four days she fought 'whole gales, strong gales, hurricane squalls, mountainous seas, and snow flurries'. The worst weather was from noon Saturday to Sunday when winds of 90mph hit the ship. One passenger, Poet Laureate John Masefield ('I must go down to the seas again, to the lonely sea and the sky'), expressed his admiration for the old ship. The £2,000,000 in gold on board being sent to the United States as part of the war debt payment remained impassive and New Year's Day must have passed almost unnoticed! The *Mauretania* fought through those extreme trials of nature, averaging 22.69 knots and covering the distance between Cherbourg and New York in five days, sixteen hours and eighteen minutes.

Arriving at her temporary berth in Hoboken on the third day of 1933, the liner, storm-weary and making her first appearance in the North River for many weeks, was met with flags flying from ships that blew their sirens to acknowledge the *Mauretania*'s great achievement – not only was she the only ship to arrive on schedule after surviving one of the worst North Atlantic storms of recent memory but she had outpaced both the *Bremen* and *Leviathan* that came in two days late. Captain Townley received many telegrams of congratulation on behalf of the ship, including a triumphant:

Well you did it again … you showed them all.

Back in Britain on the last day of 1932, while his old ship was being storm-tossed, 61-year-old Andrew Cockburn, 'The Wizard of the Atlantic', retired. A modest man, he paid fulsome tribute to all the Engineers who had handled the *Mauretania* so well during his tenure as her Chief Engineer. Such was his faith in the ship's reliability he would often tell an enquiring passenger at what time the liner would berth in Southampton if they had a particular train to catch. He had been in charge of the 'Maury's' engines on many a record-breaking occasion, including her epic voyage of August 1929, crowned by the brilliant passage between Plymouth and Cherbourg. The old Chief even had a miniature golf course in his cabin and, known as the 'Golf Champion of the Atlantic', had beaten many professionals at their own game: 'It was the motion of the ship that upset [their] calculations … I was [only] beaten [once] when the ship was at a standstill.' Surviving the sinking of the *Lusitania*, he was awarded an OBE in June 1935. The old Chief's retirement ended with his death in the Southampton suburb of Shirley in August 1955. His place as Chief Engineer was taken by E. Barton of Roxburgh.

Great changes were taking in place in Europe that would influence world history. A sinister era was beginning in Germany where, as unemployment was reaching a peak, an ex-lance corporal from the Great War, Adolf Hitler, was elected as Chancellor in a vain attempt to keep his party, the National Socialist Party (Nazis), under control. After being appointed Chancellor on 30 January 1933, Hitler soon contrived to become one of history's most feared and loathed dictators. The party's equally loathed Swastika flag was soon hoisted from the stern jack staffs of the great NDL duo, the *Bremen* and *Europa*, as well as over the shipping company's international offices, including those in Britain. The German ships' mail-carrying seaplanes continued to fly from their on-board latticed launch platforms but the aircraft were now surreptitiously piloted by trainees in the secretly revived *Luftwaffe*. As the planes flew up Southampton Water, their pilots, using the spires of the St Michael and St Mary churches as navigational aids, landed in the River Itchen in the heart of Southampton's dockland near the Supermarine aircraft factory that would eventually produce the legendary Spitfire fighter. It left no doubt why the accurate bombing raids on both docks and works in a yet-unenvisaged war left the two prominent spires untouched.

From New York the *Mauretania* began a series of six twelve-day cruises, the first leaving at one minute to midnight on 7 January 1933. As for her subsequent sailings on 21 January, 4 and 18 February, and 4 and 18 March, the midnight hours (11 p.m. to 1 a.m.) seemed to be popular for party-laden departures. The late hour of sailing ensured that the boarding passengers, warmly wrapped against New York's biting winter chill, would, on rising for breakfast, feel the benefits of the Gulf Stream as they headed south. Plans were announced to put the *Mauretania* on two spring cruises to Bermuda and Havana before returning her to her regular North Atlantic service, and also to inaugurate a new concept in

cruising – using the ship as the world's first passport-free cruising club to undertake two cruises from Southampton to Gibraltar and Madeira leaving Southampton on 3 and 10 June.

The ship now boasted a host and hostess to look after passengers' social needs, and sports instructors to look after fitness demands. A new sports area had been arranged on the appropriately named Sun Deck with painted white lines for various deck games – a temporary wood and canvas swimming pool was even erected just forward of the Aft Docking Bridge. Boxing matches between competent members of the crew's Sports and Social Club also kept the holidaymakers entertained. A chiropodist, valet service, a manicuring and beauty parlour, and a chocolate and souvenir shop were all advertised to attract an increasingly demanding clientele, many never having even seen the ocean, and Broadway-style cabarets took to the seas in the 'Club Mauretania' that replaced the self-organised passenger benefit concerts of old, although the latter remained popular on the Atlantic run. Winter cruises would take the ship from a bitter New York to sunnier climes, while those in the summer months whisked the vacationers from a hot, sticky city to balmier destinations.

In his book *Pilot Aboard*, Pilot Captain John Radford recollected an earlier (1929) five-month world cruise in the *Franconia* that reflected a similar mood of expectancy prevailing on the *Mauretania*. After mentioning that the British Treasury eagerly welcomed American dollars as a 'much needed contribution to the Exchequer' he continued:

We left the Hudson River on a day of snow and fierce east winds, and as soon as we dropped our oilskin-clad New York pilot, steered a southerly course so as to leave the winter weather astern.

As the *Mauretania* entered the Gulf Stream:

… the sky cleared, the sun shone forth in all its glory, the grey sea changed to opalescence and then to aquamarine, finally deepening to cobalt, the fabulous, beautiful ocean blue of the tropics.

With the passengers' winter clothing put away and forgotten until the ship returned to New York, Captain Radford continued:

The effect on our passengers was instantaneous. It was as if some beneficent fairy had waved her magic wand, and changed the upper deck to a living carpet of colour; a kaleidoscope of gaily-dressed people, like a rainbow-hued tidal wave, ebbed and flowed ceaselessly around the ship, their faces turned adoringly to the sun …

A rapport between fashionably attired passengers and working crew, the latter happy to be both in the sun as well as in lucrative employment, soon developed:

We talked, laughed and gossiped, getting to know each other and having fun at the same time … Our passengers were in a holiday mood, they were eager to be amused and entertained, and frankly appreciative of anything done for their pleasure or comfort. Quite soon there developed a cordiality more joyous than I would have thought possible on board a ship. In this atmosphere of perfect weather, excellent food and faultless service, friendships ripened to something more, and romance was in the air …

… the latter, at least for the maintenance of crew discipline, for the passengers!

Steaming down to Port of Spain in Trinidad, the liner passed between the Leeward and Windward Islands, giving the vacationers a tantalising glimpse of tropical lushness. It was said that islanders could keep a time-check as the ship passed by with regularity!

After three days at sea the *Mauretania* arrived at Trinidad, the southernmost island in the Caribbean, at 10.35 p.m. on 10 January 1933, her tourists' cash welcomed after the collapse of the island's sugar and cocoa industries during the Depression. Port of Spain hosted the ship for a stay of almost twelve hours (the Angostura factory a favourite destination), then through life-rich waters to La Guaira, Venezuela's island port 30km from the city of Caracas, arriving there at 11.30 a.m. on the 11th for another twelve-hour sojourn. Sailing that night, an eleven-hour hop brought the ship ('tourist boat' as cruising ships became locally known) to Willemstad on the Dutch island of Curaçao. Six hours sufficed on that island as nineteen hours were required to get her to Cartagena, arriving there at 9.06 the following morning.

The *Mauretania* then headed for Colón near the northern entrance to the Panama Canal, where an early arrival on the 14 January ensured that her tourists had time to buy Panama hats, order bespoke linen suits, or purchase Spanish shawls and silk shirts. Havana, the main port of call for the cruise, was a day's sailing away and she berthed there just after 4 p.m. on the 16th. This was her first visit to Cuba since the exploratory call of February 1930. Cunard's brochure welcomed the tourists to the island and demurely extolled the attractions that awaited them during their twenty-eight-hour stay – the places of interest, the night life of the city, 'the Spanish Club … the Chinese Quarters … the famous Sans Souci Night Club'. But an alternative local leaflet handed to *Mauretania*'s pleasure-seekers enticingly and more hedonistically advertised the 'Tokio Cabaret' with its 'dancing until dawn' and 'Girls, Girls, Girls'!

The temptations of the ship's itineraries sometimes proved too much for a few of the crew. Unlike the intemperate among the passengers, their overindulgences ashore in ports of call where the sailors' favourite, rum, was readily and cheaply available was held to account on their return to the liner. Miscreants were logged and fined – or worse, dismissed from the ship. After leaving Havana, about 100 miles north of the island, Special Lookout S. Webb was found sound asleep in the Crow's Nest at 1.30 in the morning 'under the influence of liquor'. Hauled before the Staff Captain, he was disrated to AB and dismissed on the liner's return to New York. The disgraced Lookout was replaced by A. Gallichan but, despite being given a 10 shilling raise to £8 12s a month, he soon reverted to being an AB at his own request.

Crew member A. Saunders returned from a night ashore in Havana in such a state that he had to be carried back on board. Unable to keep his midnight watch, he was fined the customary 5 shillings, as was F. Kirkman, absent from duty twice and fined 5 shillings for each offence. On being fined for his use of threatening language and assaulting the Master-at-Arms, T. Churcher, crewman O'Connell retorted: 'You cannot fine me five shillings!' His Cuban rebellion resulted in his dismissal at the end of the cruise. As the effects of the Depression were still being felt it can be assumed that many passengers who bought cheap rum at various ports of call would have attempted to consume it by the time the ship reached American waters. Their states of health can only be imagined as they disembarked onto American soil!

Waiting in the wings of this brightly lit stage and party-filled gaiety that accompanied the departures and arrivals of these cruises, the Muse of Tragedy was ever-ready to take her cue. 'Cruise ship' *Mauretania* arrived back at New York at 7.30 on the evening of 19 January 1933, and, a day before the 21 January sailing, two crew members were discharged to Ellis Island suffering from mental illnesses: Bedroom Steward Harry Hooper had been 'observed mental' and Alick Croucher, a Third Class Waiter, became insane, the causes of both men's suffering un-noted. Shortly after the liner's berthing that terminated the next arrival in New York in mid March at 2.14 p.m., 72-year-old tourist John B. l'Ecuyere collapsed and tragically died as he disembarked.

Having recovered from a bout of painful lumbago, Captain Peel arrived on the *Aquitania* to rejoin his ship assuming command at 10 a.m. on 3 February in readiness for the ship's early departure the next day at 1 a.m. The day before sailing a crewman was sent ashore to Ellis Island. This time the demon drink was not to blame but the effects of other pleasures in the form of venereal disease. The sixth and last cruise of the successful series to the West Indies terminated in New York at 12.50 p.m. on 30 March 1933. During the final cruise Cunard announced that the *Mauretania* would be taken off the Atlantic service for a whole year to concentrate solely on cruising, either as a permanent arrangement or just for the current season. This decision would leave her regular travellers and admirers regretting her absence, finding it hard to imagine the North Atlantic without her 'speed, grace of line, her seaworthiness'. Her absence meant that the famed Express Service was now reduced to the two slower ships until the 'New Cunarder' came on line, and *Olympic* would take over her Plymouth calls. Meanwhile, the Germans introduced the *Columbus* to make a fast three-ship service with the *Bremen* and *Europa*. The *Mauretania* went on two short cruises to Bermuda and Havana, departing New York on 1 and 9 April, the latter concluding on 18 April. On sailing three days later, a Steward, 49-year-old Victor Whitehead, was taken ill with pneumonia. He passed away a day into the crossing, his buoys being kept on board until her arrival home.

She arrived in Plymouth Sound for the first time that season at 6 a.m. on Thursday, 27 April with only 103 in First Class, ninety-nine in Second and eighty-three in Third. Some 1,476 bags of mail were tendered ashore along with ninety-seven passengers, many of whom caught the 9.40 to Paddington. A special launch took a batch of photographs of Prime Minister Ramsay MacDonald's recent visit to New York and rushed them to a waiting London-bound aircraft. Eighty-one barrels containing $5 million in gold were unloaded at Cherbourg before the liner headed north, arriving in Southampton at 6.15 that evening. The liner was then taken out of service for a month-long period of maintenance.

While the old Cunarder was being cosseted, the *Bremen* arrived in the docks, the first NDL liner to do so since before the Great War, watched by a large crowd. She stayed for less than three hours to take advantage of reduced dock charges. Ominously, from her stern jack she flew the increasingly dreaded red, white and black (ironically the same colours as the Cunard livery) crooked Swastika flag of the Nazi party that now held power in Germany. In Europe tensions were growing as Adolf Hitler tightened his grip and Austria joined the group of Fascist dictatorships.

At the end of her period of maintenance and survey, the *Mauretania* emerged with a startling change in appearance – she had been painted white! It had taken 100 men, working almost elbow-to-elbow standing on suspended wooden platforms, two weeks to change her livery with 5 tons of white paint. Her boot-topping below the waterline had been changed from red to green, and pale green deck heads sent a soft reflected glow onto the whiteness of her deckhouse sides. The ship's foremast and derricks were now white, as was the lower part of the mainmast (aft), its upper half painted black to disguise the effects of oily smoke as it plumed astern. Although reducing her on-board temperature in hot climates by an anticipated 9°F, the *Mauretania*'s newly painted hull would be expensive to maintain in normal service. Now dubbed 'Britain's White Speed Queen', one local observer reportedly remarked as she passed down Southampton Water that she looked like 'a bloomin' wedding cake!'

Her April cruises were booking well but over on the other side of The Pond the Furness Withy Company's sister ships, the *Monarch of Bermuda* and *Queen of Bermuda,* were posing a threat on the luxury trade to Hamilton. On the Atlantic the *Majestic* was one of many ships sailing with reduced passenger loads, so it was well that the 'Maury' was cruising full-time. The British, like their American counterparts who novelty tortoise races and crew's boxing matches in which one pugilist, perhaps fancy-dressed as Charlie Chaplin's 'Little Tramp', would fool around – all on the agenda.

At Whitsuntide, 3 June, the first cruise left Southampton for Casablanca, Morocco, with a first-night menu that satisfied even the most demanding appetite (there were twenty hors-d'oeuvres alone, five choices of fish, fifteen meats and fowl, and twelve puddings and ice creams). The liner arrived at her exotic African destination, substituted for the more British-themed Gibraltar, in the early morning of 6 June. Her holiday-enthused passengers spent fourteen warm and wondrous hours ashore before the ship romantically steamed away at midnight, lines of brightly lit ports festooning her white hull reflecting across the bay, funnels and smoke catching the glow of her deck lights.

Returning to Southampton after steaming 2,334 nautical miles on the morning of 9 June, she was cleaned and stored for her next excursion that left Southampton the next afternoon. As her travellers arrived at the docks, their impressions of the ship were enthusiastic. To them she was, as she waited to receive over 600 passengers, 'magnificent in her summer

To reduce on-board temperatures when cruising the *Mauretania* was painted white, making her look like '*a bloomin' wedding cake!*' (Author's Collection)

were benefitting from President Franklin D. Roosevelt's 'New Deal', had caught the cruising bug and cruise ships were sailing to capacity.

Fares for the two long-anticipated cruises from Southampton were marketed from eleven guineas (£11 11s) and, with no booking fees and no licensing restrictions on board, the cruising capacity of 700–800 berths soon sold out. The cruises were definitely for entertainment rather than for education, with deck games, talkie shows (the films were shown on portable equipment supplied by GB Equipments Ltd on their 'Transportable Type S.P.60' projector), bridge tournaments, dances, midnight suppers and entertainments, balls and carnivals – even

Resplendent in cruising white and dressed overall, the *Mauretania* is ready to sail at the outset of another cruise. (Collection of Ambrose Greenway)

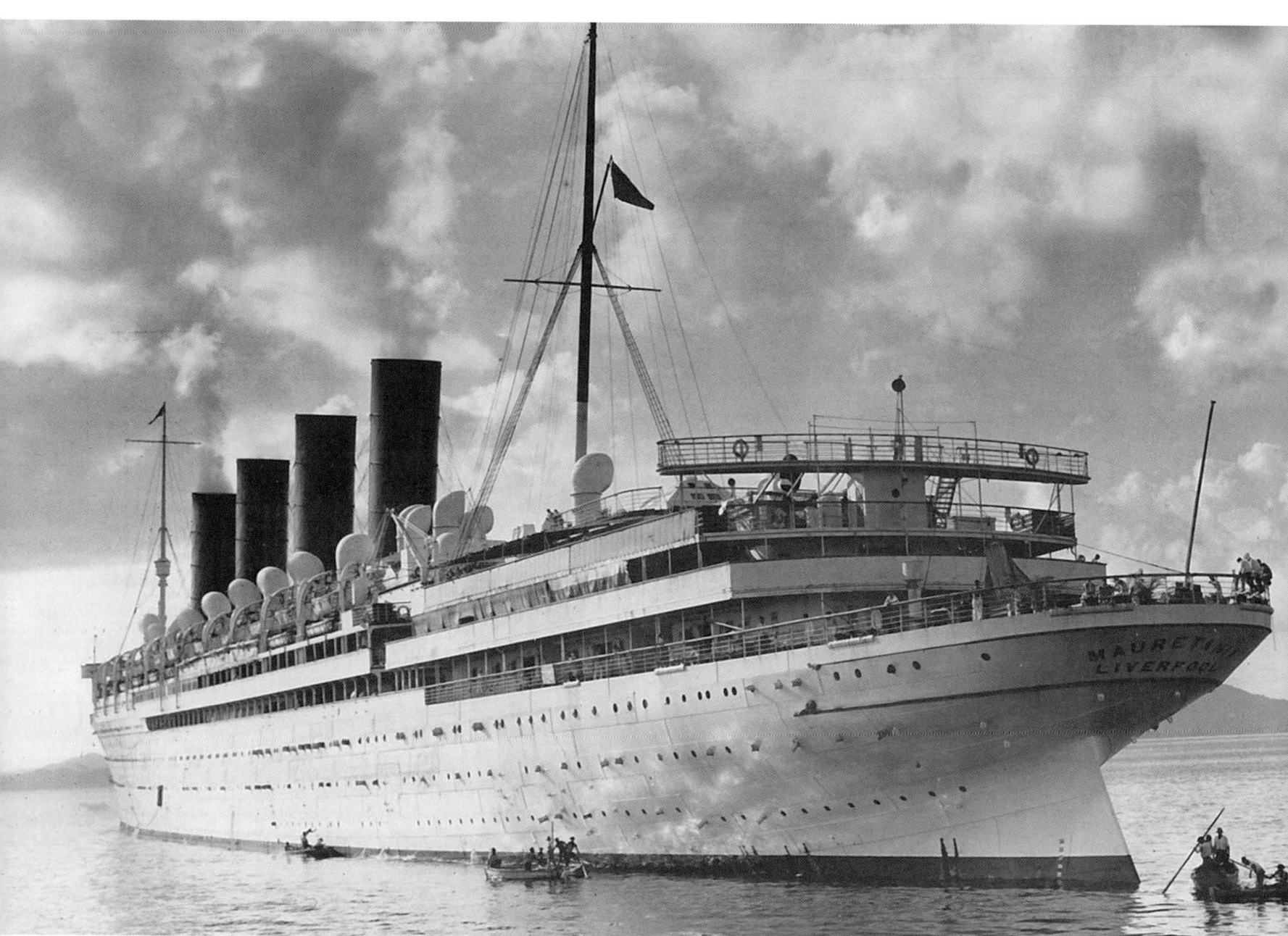

This evocative photograph shows the sparkling *Mauretania* in one of her cruising destinations. (Author's Collection)

The passengers were entertained during the time spent at sea and boxing matches put on by the crew were especially popular. (Author's Collection)

In the floating dock in 1933 for her annual maintenance, the retractable breast shores can be seen on either side of the ship. (Author's Collection)

coat of white … conscious of her beauty'. As the passengers boarded they were greeted by 'a long line of white-gloved, brass-buttoned stewards … ready to receive the voyagers'.

Arriving in Madeira's Funchal harbour, the liner anchored offshore in company with Union-Castle Line's lavender-hulled, four-funnelled *Windsor Castle*. Local boats surrounded the Cunarder as vendors showed off their wares and boys dived for coins tossed from the ship. Travellers going ashore enjoyed Madeira's flowers, palms, banana plantations, vines and quaint cobbled streets, the latter celebrated by passenger-comedian-actor Norman Long who, probably 'resting' after the release of his talkie *The New Hotel*, sat down at a piano and extemporised a ballad: 'There's a street where the cobblestones harass the feet …'. The 'White Speed Queen' weighed anchor at 1 a.m. to return to Southampton where she arrived in the early afternoon of 16 June, her travellers singing the praises of both the Cunard Company and the ship's staff for making the 2,674 nautical mile cruise 'so memorable', and vowing to cruise again.

The Royal Mail Ship (RMS) *Mauretania* was still Britain's fastest form of overseas postal delivery – a letter could be posted to the United States for three-ha'pence (1½*d*) and the usual newspaper notices called for Imperial and Foreign mails specified to be carried by the ship to be received at General Post Offices. After her British cruises the ship was again laid up for maintenance, emerging to depart for New York at 11.30 a.m. on 1 July for another series of five West Indian cruises following her arrival in New York on the 6th. Another, but sadder, departure had occurred before the liner sailed when, on 23 June, Captain William 'Bowler Bill' Turner passed away at his home in De Villiers Avenue, Great Crosby, near Liverpool. The 77-year-old skipper had captained the *Mauretania* from 1910 to 1914 and had been her 'caretaker captain' as she awaited war duties. Made Commodore of the Line in 1913, he had received the King and Queen on board during that year's River Mersey shipping review, during which His Majesty conferred him with the rank of Commander of the RNR. Later, in recognition of his war service, he received an OBE (Order of the British Empire).

En route to New York, an Admiralty notice was received announcing that Captain Peel RNR (Retired) had been promoted to the rank of Commodore Second Class in the Royal Naval Reserve, becoming only the second Cunard captain to receive that rank. On arrival in New York he sailed home on the *Aquitania* for a month's leave. His Staff Captain, Kingsley Howe, had been promoted as a Captain RNR. Another celebration during the crossing elicited a shower of fireworks and patriotic songs for both Cunard's ninety-third anniversary and American Independence Day. *Mauretania* steamed out of the North River on 8 July on the first of her five twelve-and-a-half-day West Indies cruises, the promise of adventure keeping the problems of the Depression and unemployment at bay for a few days for the lucky vacationers. The big liners were kept busy on cruising schedules, even though it was felt that business on the North Atlantic was gradually improving.

The old ship had not finished with making records and was eager to show her capabilities. The day after sailing homeward from Havana at 1.18 p.m. on 19 July the old Cunarder's engines were opened up in the favourable Gulf Stream off the eastern US coast. She covered 603 nautical miles at a very creditable 27.78 knots and, for an hour's 'test' run between the Carysfort Reef Lighthouse (about 6 nautical miles east of Key Largo, Florida) and the Jupiter Inlet Lighthouse (on the north side of the Jupiter Inlet, also in Florida), a distance of about 105 nautical miles, she reached an incredible 32 knots, the highest ever for any ship.

Subsequent sailings in the series were on 22 July, 5 and 22 of August and 9 September. The last port of call should have been Havana but the 16 August call was cancelled because of political unrest following riots and strikes that had brought down the regime of President Gerardo Machado y Morales. Two Cunarders, *Mauretania* and *Franconia*, were held up outside the harbour along with other vessels, presumably freighters, that had been there for two weeks. After a hasty rearrangement, she steamed off to Nassau. The *Mauretania's* next visit to Havana on 3 September was also cancelled. The so-called 'Cuba-Brownsville Hurricane' had hit the beleaguered island with devastating 120mph winds on 1 September, causing seventy deaths and severe damage that left tens of thousands homeless. As some vessels had been driven ashore in the area, the *Mauretania* was taken to shelter at Cape San Antonio at the western extremity of Cuba, hoping in vain to enter Havana on the 3rd. A tender managed to get alongside in the big swell to land passengers but it smashed the ship's gangway in the process. Vibration was noticeable, especially in the crew areas, which made letter writing difficult. The Cuban city was able to receive the liner on her next scheduled call on the 19th for an overnight stay. Her West Indies travels ended in New York on the 22nd.

In mid August the British Government finally agreed to the merger of the Cunard and White Star Lines as part of the deal to complete *No. 534*.

Departing for Southampton at five in the afternoon of 27 September, the crossing was only *Mauretania's* second that year on the Atlantic ferry. Fine weather accompanied her throughout the trip and she averaged a good 24.47 knots. Distances covered noon-to-noon each day were 401, 584, 576, 585, 567 and then 313 nautical miles to the Eddystone Light. She arrived in Cawsand Bay at 5.30 a.m. on 3 October to disembark sixty-six passengers and a meagre 287 bags of mail; this was the first time that Plymouth had seen her in her cruising whites. An hour-and-a-half later the gleaming ship continued on to Cherbourg, where she delivered a further thirty-nine travellers and 153 kegs of gold valued at £2.7 million. She continued to Southampton with eighty-one passengers before laying up for six weeks, the first of the big ships to be overhauled that season, in work that would cost £75,000. The year's Express Service ended with the *Aquitania's* sailing on Saturday, 21 October.

The *Mauretania* spent her twenty-sixth birthday high and dry in the floating dock where, as the night shift worked, she looked resplendent, her white paintwork floodlit to great advantage. Two-hundred men in thirty different trades worked in overhauling and testing her turbines and auxiliary machinery; checking her navigational equipment; laying 2 miles of new carpeting; and applying a mighty 2,500 gallons of paint to freshen-up the old girl's make-up. Her Passenger Certificate was reissued on 11 November, Armistice Day 1933, (previous repairs to her Aft Peak tank were found to be in a surprisingly 'very satisfactory' condition). She was ready to take on the North Atlantic.

With passengers for the sailing (including the American women's hockey team) and mails for the western hemisphere safely on board, she sailed on 15 November and arrived in New York six days later, where an unannounced visit by some very zealous customs officials searched the cabins of the Captain, Staff Captain and Ship's Surgeon for illicit liquor, an action that surprised Captain Peel as the Eighteenth Amendment was about to be repealed.

Speculation abounded that some of the 'famous old timers' might be scrapped within five years of the expected merger of Cunard and White Star's Atlantic interests. The 'Grand Old Lady', the beloved *Mauretania*, was among the suggestions along with the *Berengaria*, probably the *Olympic* and either the *Homeric* or *Majestic*, even though it seemed as if the old liner might return to the North Atlantic service as new rates for the New Year were advertised for the Express Service and included an attractive £23 15s for a round voyage in Third Class with favourable rates in First.

The first of three West Indies cruises (an eventual nine had been planned) of twelve-and-a-half days left New York on a wintry 25 November, the second on 9 December (a count and a Rockefeller were on board for this one) and the third, her Christmas cruise, left New York two days before the big day and called at Nassau in lieu of Havana. For this cruise the 'Maury' took on an early Christmas present in the form of a new anchor that had been brought over on the *Berengaria* to replace one that had been lost in Havana, perhaps during the recent hurricane.

Her return to New York from her last West Indies cruise was affected by fog, resulting in her next sailing on 6 January 1934 being postponed for fourteen hours. This was expected to delay her arrival in Plymouth, her penultimate visit there of the year (the next would be in April) until ten in the evening of the 11th. Even these revised expectations were thwarted. By early Wednesday evening the wind had increased and by nine o'clock the liner's Navigators were experiencing poor visibility in a 60mph gale and a heavy sea that developed into one of the severest full-blown gales of the year with winds of 70mph. The storm was at its worse on the morning of the 11th when in the Chops of the Channel, where a heavy sea was running. The *Mauretania* was due to disembark thirty passengers at Plymouth along with 1,500 bags of mail and a decrease in the strength of the gale gave rise to hopes of a late arrival, but these, too, were dashed as the winds again strengthened in the late afternoon. Not surprisingly, at 7 p.m., as the liner battled with a strong southerly gale, high seas, and blinding rain, the Captain decided to give Plymouth a

miss and to proceed directly to Cherbourg and Southampton, where she was expected to dock at noon on the 12th.

The appalling weather that had been battering and flooding Britain's coasts had not improved by the time she was ready for her next departure on Saturday, 17 January. Among those arriving at Southampton on the Cunard Express Special were the Athlones en route for a ten-week cruise and holiday in the Bahamas. The Earl of Athlone, a brother of the Queen and a former Governor General of South Africa, was accompanied by his wife, Princess Alice of Teck, Countess of Athlone, who would later describe the ensuing crossing as 'boisterous'. Film actor Henry Wilcoxon was off to Hollywood to take up a massive £500-per-week contract, making him the highest-paid British actor, after successfully screen-testing for Cecil B. DeMille of Paramount Studios, and more wealth was in the Specie Room – £50,000 in gold for Mexico, probably for delivery during her impending cruise call into Colón on 2 February. Experiencing continuous storms, she arrived in New York a day late on Tuesday, 23 February making the crossing one of the roughest and slowest in her brilliant career, and perhaps straining her wounded stern plates. She averaged less than 20 knots.

The new King George V ('KGV') dry dock had been opened by the King and Queen in the Royal Yacht *Victoria and Albert* and was subsequently inaugurated by the world's biggest ship, the *Majestic*, so Southern Railways decided to sell its floating dock that had been used in a publicly spectacular way. Japan and Brazil expressed interest in buying it.

Events in their homeland looked a little brighter for Americans when the Twenty-first Amendment repealed the Eighteenth Amendment (Prohibition), which had reportedly caused more problems than it had solved. However, the cruises of the *Mauretania* would not be affected: of nine scheduled cruises the first six were to be back-to-back, with sailing dates of 27 January, then two both in February (10 and 24) and March (9 and 23) and 6 April. Avoiding the bitter –14°F temperatures of New York City, the first cruise of the series took her to her customary first call of Trinidad, where her 'cargo' soon forgot about the cold and troubles at home.

Wishing you a Happy New Year *Alan*

Cunard Express Steamer "Mauretania." Launched at Wallsend-on-Tyne, Sept. 20th, 1906.
Gross Tonnage, 32,500.   Turbine Engines.   The "Mauretania" and "Lusitania"
(her sister ship) are the largest vessels in the world.   [Issued 187, Westgate

Far left: A splendid caricature of Lord Inverclyde, the Chairman of the Cunard Line, by 'Spy' (Leslie Ward) appeared in the 28 July 1904 edition of *Vanity Fair*. Lord Inverclyde's vision brought the two 'New Cunarders' into being. (Author's Collection)

Left: An early artist's impression (this one by Odin Rosenvinge) showing the *Mauretania* with a funnel configuration similar to that of the German flyers, based on a drawing of 'The Express Cunard SSs as they will appear' that appeared in the technical press. (Author's Collection)

The dimensions of the
Q. T. S. S. *Mauretania* are:
Length Overall . . . 787 ft
Between Perpendicu-
lars, ... 760 ft
Beam, ... 88 ft.
Depth, . . . 60 ft. 6 in.
Gross Tonnage, . 33,200.
Maximum Draught, 37 ft.
corresponding to a Dis-
placement of 43,000 tons.
The I. H. P. of her Turbines
being 68,000, she can travel
27 knots per hour.

FRANK.
PHOTO. GATESHEAD.
COPYRIGHT.

(QUADRUPLE TURBINE) S.S. MAURETANIA.
THE LARGEST VESSEL AFLOAT.

With her hull freshly painted in the black of the Cunard livery, the 'Pride of the Tyne' triumphantly leaves the river of her birth. (Author's Collection)

Above: To reach the Canada dry dock the liner had to pass through the Sandon Dock; in this painting by James Mann she is passing through the Sandon gate. (Collection of Charles A. Haas)

Left: An atmospheric impression by Sam Brown of the *Mauretania* in midstream on the river Mersey. Not only was she the 'Pride of the Tyne', she was also the 'Pride of the Port'. Before the First World War only two of the eventual 'Three Graces' had been built, as the Cunard Building was still under construction. (Author's Collection)

Before her maiden voyage, the *Mauretania* transferred to Liverpool's Princes Landing Stage, where she would visit for subsequent departures. (Author's Collection)

CUNARD LINE

ROYAL MAIL FOUR SCREW STEAMERS LUSITANIA & MAURETANIA
Finest, Fastest & Largest Steamers in the World.
790 Feet Long, 30,000 Tons, 43,000 Tons displacement, 75,000 Horse Power.

Norman Wilkinson, who devised the 'Dazzle' scheme during the First World War, also did a lot of artwork for Cunard. Among other works, he produced this wonderful poster to advertise the two sisters. (Author's Collection)

Left: A tinted photograph of the *Mauretania* alongside Liverpool's Landing Stage. She always proved an attraction for eager sightseers as well as for passengers. (Author's Collection)

Below: Sailing away from the Landing Stage, the *Mauretania* heads towards the open sea. (Author's Collection)

The "Mauretania" from Floating Bridge, Liverpool.

R.M.S. MAURETANIA, LANDING STAGE, LIVERPOOL.

Opposite page:

Above left: The magnificently decorated First-Class lounge with tapestries. (Author's Collection)

Above centre: The beautiful woodwork in the Library and other rooms shows how the shipbuilders managed to exceed their budget. (Author's Collection)

Above right: The Second-Class lounge was light and airy. (Author's Collection)

Below: A painting by Russel shows the liner underway at sea. (Estate of Captain Pritchard/Author's collection)

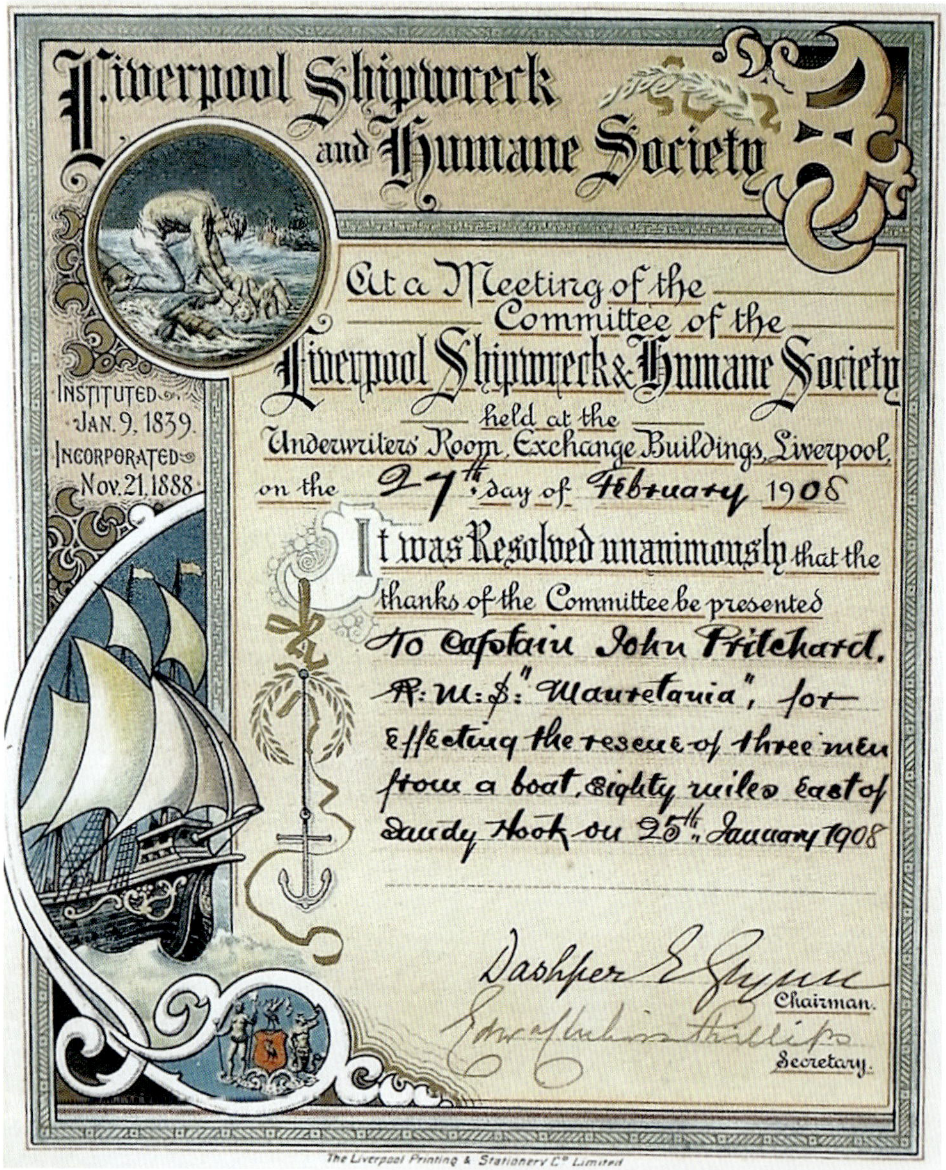

Liverpool Shipwreck and Humane Society

Instituted Jan. 9, 1839. Incorporated Nov. 21, 1888.

At a Meeting of the Committee of the Liverpool Shipwreck & Humane Society held at the Underwriters' Room, Exchange Buildings, Liverpool, on the 27th day of February 1908

It was Resolved unanimously that the thanks of the Committee be presented to Captain John Pritchard, R.M.S. "Mauretania", for effecting the rescue of three men from a boat, eighty miles east of Sandy Hook on 25th January 1908

Chairman.

Secretary.

The Liverpool Printing & Stationery Co. Limited

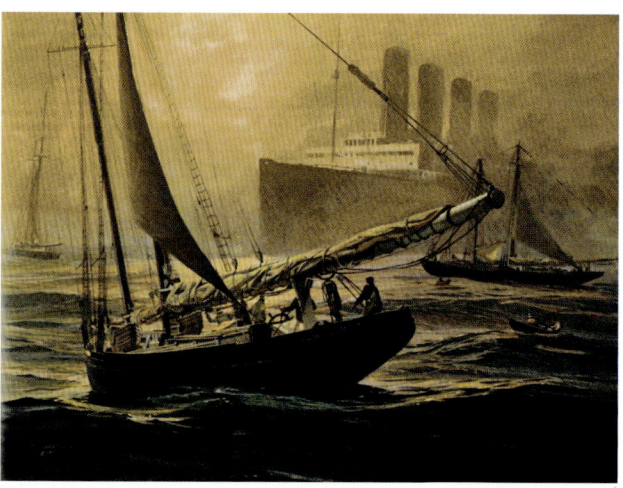

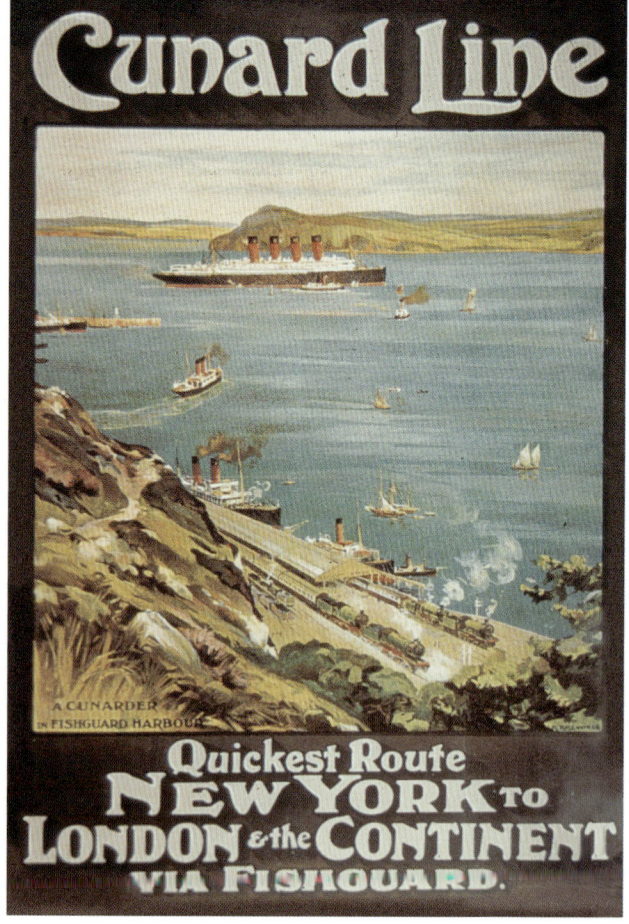

Above: Citation in recognition of Captain Pritchard's rescue of the crew from the American barge *Fall River*, 25 January 1908. (Estate of Captain Pritchard/Author's collection)

Above right: The perils of large ships travelling at speed through the Grand Banks fishing grounds are well illustrated in this painting by Thomas Hoyne. Was it a fishing boat or a wreck that caused extensive damage to the *Mauretania* in 1908? (Author's Collection)

Below right: The call into Fishguard that sped up mails and passenger disembarkation began in August 1909. (Author's Collection)

Above: The great liner inspired much music, which did a lot to keep the liner in the public's attention. (Author's Collection)

Right: Shown here without its gilded frame, this beautifully illuminated address was made and presented to Captain Pritchard by his crew. (Estate of Captain Pritchard, now lodged with Merseyside Museums)

1858

To
Captain John Pritchard
Dear Sir,
We, the members of the Steward Department of the "R.M.S. Mauretania" wish you to accept this Gold Watch and Stick as tokens of the respect we have for you, and we feel that we cannot allow you to retire from the Cunard Service without expressing the pride and pleasure we have at all times experienced in sailing under your command. Wishing you good health and long life on behalf of the above department we beg to remain respectfully yours

W.T. Brigden

Evan Hy Hughes
Wm McIntosh
Wm S. Fletcher
D.C. Handlin

DESIGNED AND EXECUTED BY
Ernest J. Dowden
1909

Albert Rudge
B.C. Nagel
John Sands
P. Biddlecombe

Above left: During his tenure, Captain Pritchard gave Captain John Pritchard this engraved Tiffany silver cigar box made by German shipowner Albert Ballin. (Estate of Captain Pritchard)

Abov right: Presentation plate 'Last Westward Passage Dec 11–16 1908'. (Estate of Captain Pritchard)

Left: Miss Elizabeth 'Kitty' Pritchard, one of two daughters from the Captain's marriage to his housekeeper, poses by the Captain's portrait and some of the presentation silver. (Author's Collection)

Opposite page:

Left: The famed 'Christmas Dash' of December 1911 is captured in this illustration of the ship in the heavy seas that she endured during the westward crossing. (Author's Collection)

Above right: Following the Royal review on the Mersey in July 1913, the King and Queen opened the new Gladstone Docks, which is described on this card as 'the largest in the world'. (Author's Collection)

Below right: A typical bill of fare for luncheon in First Class. One American complained at the standard of Cunard's cuisine. (Author's Collection)

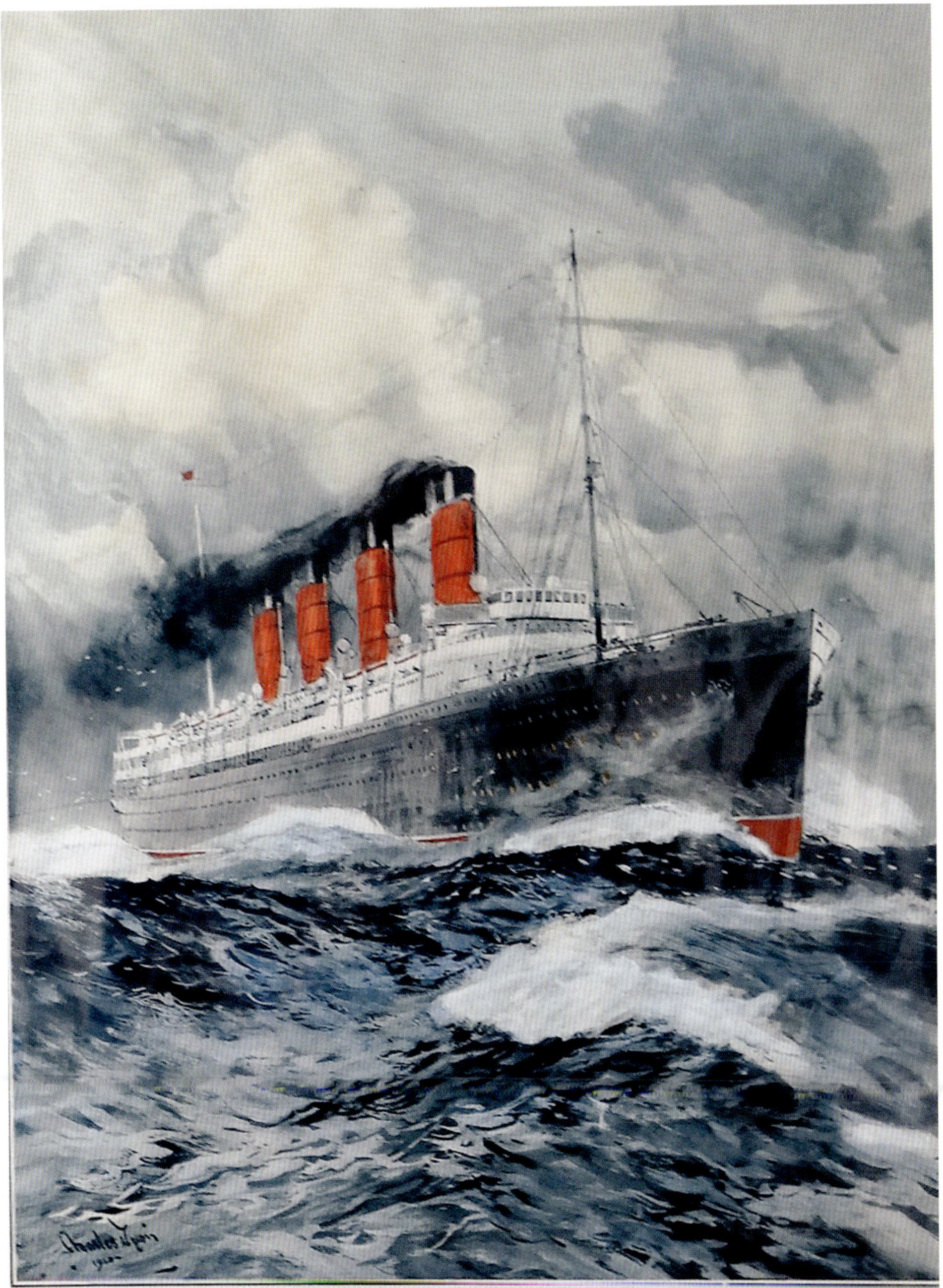

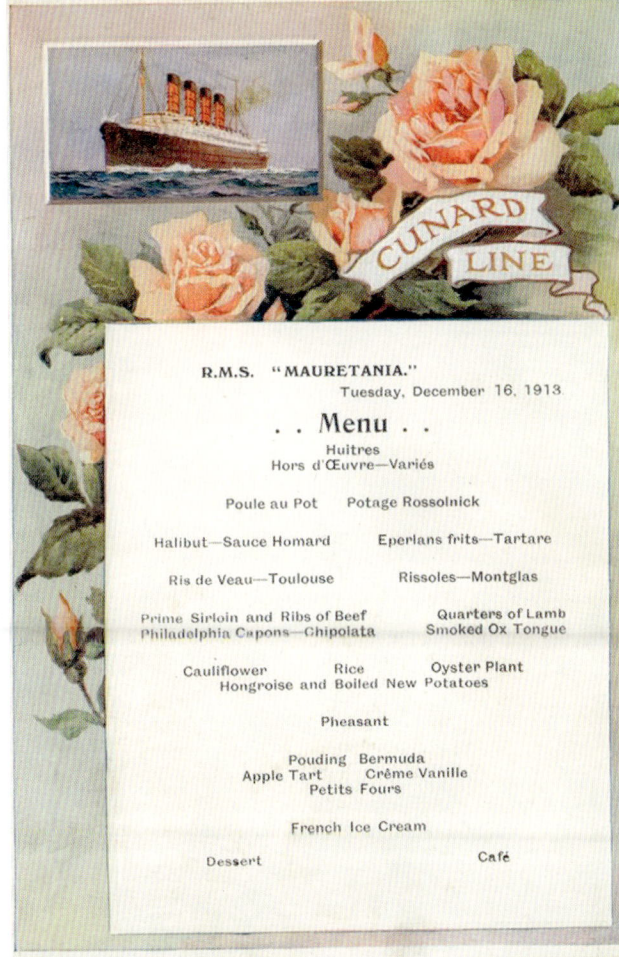

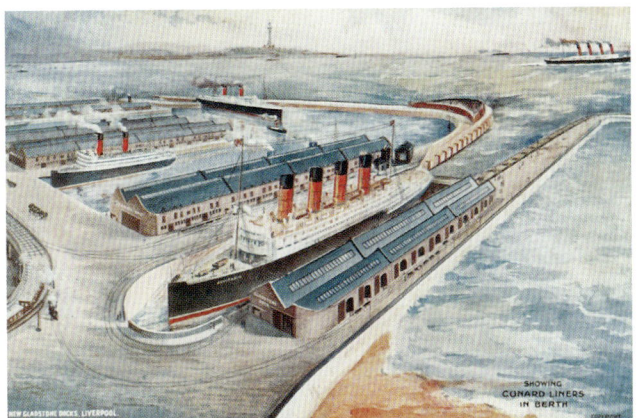

Copyrighted in the United States and Canada.

Drawn by Charles Dixon, R.I.

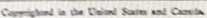

A MODERN MAYFLOWER

The amazing growth of the American nation, which had its birth in the little colony that was established by the band of Pilgrims who sailed in the Mayflower from Plymouth three hundred years ago, is made plain without crossing the Atlantic by seeing a modern monster Mayflower, like the Mauretania (shown here) returning from the other side of the Atlantic. With her gross tonnage of 30,700 tons, the great liner could swallow up about 170 vessels like the Pilgrims' little bark of 180 tons, and she reckons her passengers by the thousand, whereas the Mayflower carried but a hundred and two souls. Moreover, in the matter of speed the development has been as remarkable, for, steaming at 25 knots, the Mauretania crosses the Atlantic in a few days, whereas the voyage of the Pilgrims lasted the greater part of four months.

NEW GLADSTONE DOCKS, LIVERPOOL.
THE LARGEST IN THE WORLD.
SHOWING
CUNARD LINERS
IN BERTH
COPYRIGHT

CUNARD LINE

R.M.S. "MAURETANIA."
Tuesday, December 16, 1913.

.. Menu ..

Huitres
Hors d'Œuvre—Variés

Poule au Pot   Potage Rossolnick

Halibut—Sauce Homard   Eperlans frits—Tartare

Ris de Veau—Toulouse   Rissoles—Montglas

Prime Sirloin and Ribs of Beef   Quarters of Lamb
Philadelphia Capons—Chipolata   Smoked Ox Tongue

Cauliflower   Rice   Oyster Plant
Hongroise and Boiled New Potatoes

Pheasant

Pouding Bermuda
Apple Tart   Crême Vanille
Petits Fours

French Ice Cream

Dessert   Café

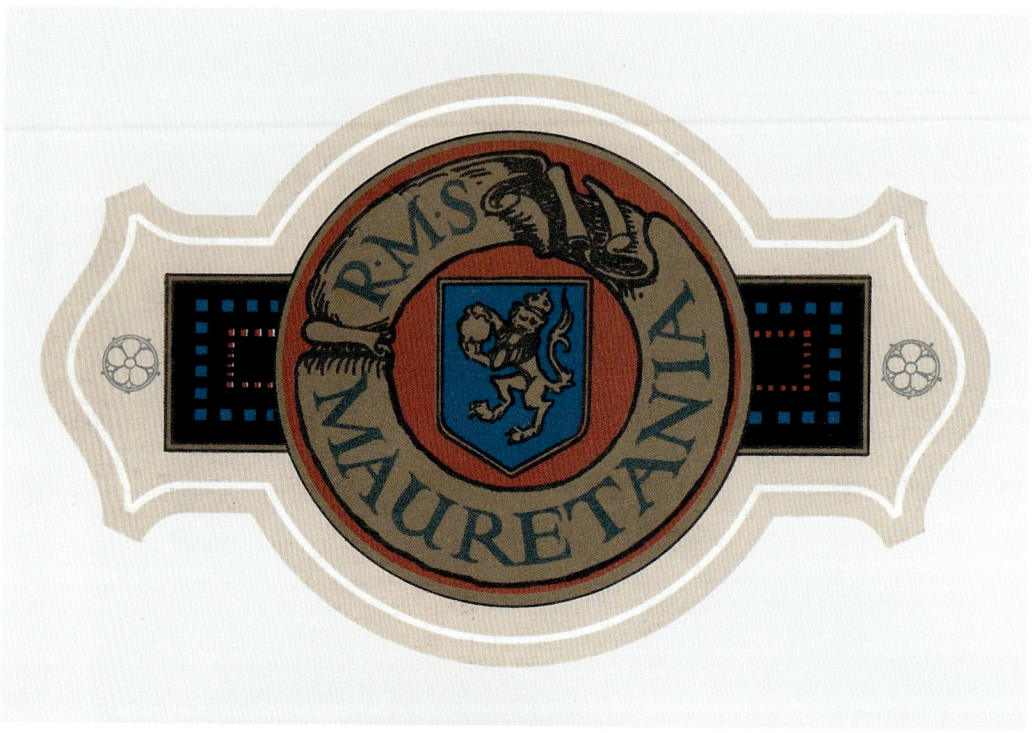

S.S. MAURETANIA.

Above left: 1919 saw the *Mauretania* return to commercial service and this small but lavish brochure attempted to attract travellers back to the ship. (Author's Collection)

Above right: A Publicity Department's embellishment for a post-war brochure indicating the lavishness of the ship. (Author's Collection)

Left: An illustration of the *Mauretania* by W. Fred Mitchell, who produced many maritime paintings. His work is much sought after among collectors. (Author's Collection)

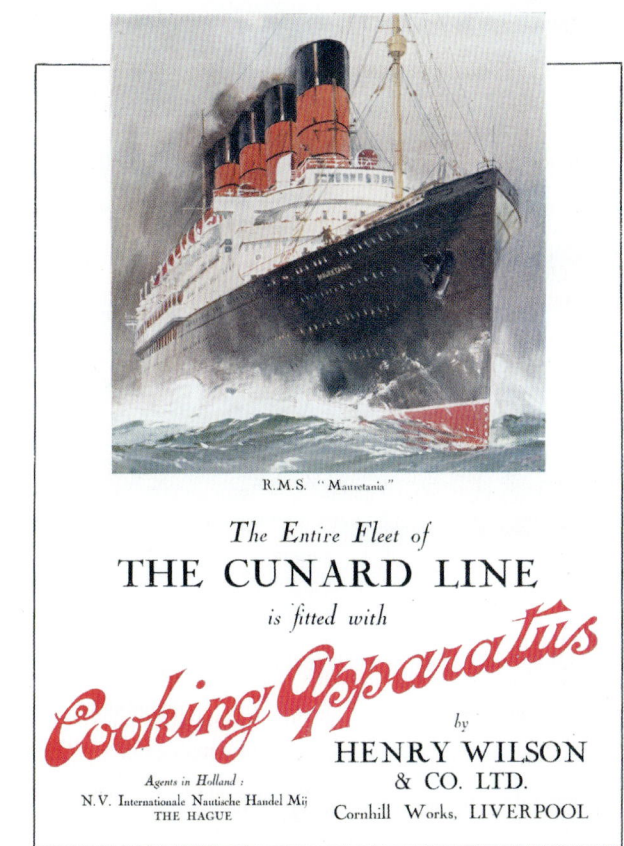

Left: This watercolour by E. Jane is a very proficient rendition of C.E. Turner's superb painting, which was used for company postcards – and for the dust-jacket of this title. (Author's Collection)

Below: C.E. Turner's evocative painting of the *Mauretania* was also used in advertising. (Author's Collection)

R.M.S. "Mauretania"

The Entire Fleet of

THE CUNARD LINE

is fitted with

Cooking Apparatus

by

HENRY WILSON & CO. LTD.

Agents in Holland:
N.V. Internationale Nautische Handel Mij
THE HAGUE

Cornhill Works, LIVERPOOL

The magnificent *Mauretania* was an excellent subject for trade cards given away with packets of cigarettes, chocolate, comics, etc. She was also immortalised on an aluminium medallion issued by the Cunard in celebration of the 700th Anniversary of the Incorporation of Liverpool in 1907, and on an Isle of Man crown (5/-) issued in 1988. (Author's Collection)

This stereo set of pictures show the *Mauretania* being moored in Southampton. (Author's Collection)

An impressive view of the *Mauretania* high-and-dry in the floating dock. (*Simon Mills Collection*)

WILLS'S CIGARETTES

Left: An evocative painting of the liner in her cruising-white at dusk, painted for a cigarette card. One wonders what happened to the original artwork. (Author's Collection)

Below: The *Mauretania* overhauling the Swedish four-masted barque *Abraham Rydberg*, April 1934. (Original watercolour by Colin M. Baxter)

Colin M. Baxter

Above: The brass letters of the ship's name once hung over the entrance to the Mauretania Hotel in Bristol. They have since been sold individually. (Author's Collection)

Right: Useful items of treen were made from decking and hand-rails. This unusual piece, with its little commemorative brass plaque, is an egg timer in the form of a traffic light. (Estate of Doris Hutchings (née Way))

This superb model was sold at auction for a record sum (£162,000). Presented by Cunard to Winchester Cathedral as a votive offering, it subsequently went the now defunct Shipping Gallery at the Science Museum in London, then placed in storage before finally being put to auction. (Courtesy of Charles Miller Ltd)

21

HER COURSE IS RUN

A Monster Burlesque

As all entries into the log books were legally bound to be factual, false statements were deemed illegal and possibly punishable. With this in mind Senior (later Chief) First Officer Stanley W. Moughton made an entry on 30 January when the cruising *Mauretania* was about a mile off the Dutch island of St Eustatius:

Sighted sea-monster, headed south-west at 1.20 p.m., clear afternoon, about a mile of the island of Saint Eustias [*sic*].

Senior Third Officer J.W. Caunce also saw the animal just as it disappeared. Too large to be a whale or dolphin, it was described as having a large head about 2ft wide lifted 6ft above the water on a long, jet-black body, of which 45ft could be seen rising in curves above the surface while another 20ft remained submerged. Captain Peel saw no reason to disbelieve his officers but, despite the logged observations of the responsible men, the entry was later rubbished as being a 'burlesque'. However, the story received the approval of none other than retired Captain Sir Arthur Rostron, that most sober and reliable mariner, who was quoted as seeing such a creature while he was Chief Officer on the old *Campania* when approaching Queenstown on 11 June 1911. A second but different creature was later seen off La Guiara on 2 February.

The holiday mood of the passengers was tempered as they headed for home as the big white ship sailed into a blinding snowstorm on 6 February. Arrival back into the cold was delayed by several hours more by fog over the entrance to New York Harbor, where winter's grip had been severe, its waterways hazarded by floes of thick ice coming from upstate New York. The danger was compounded by clouds of icy vapour, aptly named 'Arctic smoke', which rose from the freezing water. Transport within the city had been affected and there had been many deaths, especially among the Depression's destitute. The mood of the relaxed and bronzed vacationers must have tumbled as they disembarked back into harsh reality and shuffled into waiting warm Yellow Cabs, Fords and luxury motor cars.

An important day came on 9 February, when the British Government had given its blessing to the merging of the Cunard and White Star Lines' North Atlantic fleets, to be known as Cunard-White Star. The Treasury agreed to provide finance – not exceeding £3 million to complete *No. 534*, on which work had been suspended since 1931; to provide £1.5 million as working capital for the new company; and £5 million for an additional ship or ships to be built either on the Clyde, the Tyne or the Lagan. This good news meant that up to 2,000 men would be employed when work recommenced on the New Cunarder in early April to ready her for a late-autumn launching – and with 9,000–10,000 more being employed in the supply chain nationwide the decision signalled a virtual end to the Depression in Great Britain. The day after that important announcement the *Mauretania* sailed for Trinidad.

Towards the end of February the rates for the *Mauretania* were reduced by 10 per cent, in all classes making travel on her cheaper than on the *Aquitania* and *Berengaria*:

A photograph of the sailing vessel *Abraham Rydberg* taken from the *Mauretania*. This plucky Swedish barque made a brave attempt to race the giant liner! (Author's Collection)

MAURETANIA	Old Rate	New Rate
First Class Single	£44 00s	£40 00s
First Class Return	£83 10s	£76 00s
Tourist Class Single	£25 10s	£23 5s
Tourist Class Return	£45 15s	£41 15s
Third Class Single	£18 15s	£17 00s
Third class Return	£33 15s	£30 15s

After her successful cruise season, the *Mauretania* left for Southampton on 20 April. Travelling (First Class) was the celebrated ex-Captain of the Hampshire and England cricket teams Lionel, 3rd Baron Tennyson, grandson of the late, famed British Poet Laureate, Alfred, Lord Tennyson. He and his new (second) wife, American widow and heiress, Mrs Joseph Donner (formerly British socialite Carroll Elting) were on their way to spend part of their honeymoon at 'Farringford', the family home at Freshwater on the Isle of Wight.

The liner encountered a strong gale accompanied by high seas on the last two days of this, her 311th crossing. On Wednesday, 25 April she overhauled a Swedish four-masted barque, the *Abraham Rydberg* (3,250 tons), which would have stirred the late Poet Laureate's pen. As the weather had somewhat moderated, Captain Peel took the *Mauretania* to within 500 yards of the sailing ship, keeping her to port to give his passengers (and, more than likely, to recall his own time in a sail trainer) a good view of the sailer that, carrying 40,000 bags of wheat, was leading in a 108-day grain race against twenty other windjammers from Wallaroo, Australia, to The Lizard. Both ships dipped their ensigns in mutual salute as the great white liner's cosseted occupants cheered the barque, plunging and rising in the heavy swell, its crew of fifty-two hands (including forty cadets) responding led by Captain Sune Tamm, who then ordered the main top-gallant sails to be set. For a while, the barque did very well in racing the huge liner but inevitably the *Mauretania* pulled ahead.

After the rough weather the liner still came to anchor in Cawsand Bay punctually at 6 a.m. on 26 April after averaging 24.95 knots. Of 143 in First Class, 152 in Tourist, but only fifty-eight in Third she delivered ninety-four into the Plymouth-bound tender for the London-bound express train as well as 1,220 sacks of precious mail. The local Cunard agent cleared the ship and she was off to Cherbourg by 8. Arriving in Southampton that same day, the *Mauretania* went out of service for the entire month of May, during which time it was announced that HM Queen Mary had accepted an invitation to name and launch the rapidly completing *No. 534*. Possible names without Cunard's suffix of 'ia' or White Star's 'ic' were still being propounded – should it be *Magnifica*?... *Beatifica*?... *Heroica*?... *Collosica*?... or, in honour of the Queen, *Imperatricia*? ... or, more soberly (although with Cunard's 'ia'), *Britannia*, or even *Scotia* in honour of the country of her birth?

Circulating rumours in mid-June that the old 'Maury' might be withdrawn from service surprised Sir Ashley Sparks who, while conceding that event would happen eventually, gave an assurance that when that day came she would neither be sold to foreign interests and used in a run-down capacity nor be run aground at 'a wrecker's wharf, but would be sent to the shipbreaker's to be dismantled properly'. The British press still followed the Cunarder's progress with great interest and the *Nottingham Evening Post* picked up on the current mood, noting presciently that 'the Mauretania is too old for useful service.

She is 27 years of age …' and rather gloomily reflected: 'She must prepare for her last voyages.' The ship was to make five cruises in July and August and, on her return from the States, make a four-month pleasure cruise before – possibly – going to the shipbreaker's. Enquiries had already been received for the purchase of particular mementoes.

As the liner lay at her berth in Southampton on 27 June preparing for her next departure, her old captain was being feted. A new 2,700-seat cinema and restaurant, the 'Regal' (later to be renamed the 'Odeon'), had been built Above Bar (the High Street) and Sir Arthur Rostron had been invited to perform the opening honours. As he – resplendent in white tie and tails – and Lady Rostron arrived, a 'Blue Peter' flag was raised over the new theatre,signifying that it was about to proceed. A huge crowd of excited spectators had to be controlled by mounted police as it was holding up traffic.

As Sir Arthur arrived at 8 p.m. 'eight bells' was rung on board his old ship in the docks while, in the cinema, ex-Quartermasters from the *Mauretania* called 'All's well!' before the Portsmouth Band of the Royal Marines struck up with jaunty maritime melodies. Film producer Basil Dean made a speech praising the British film industry and introduced the stars of the evening's film, *Love, Life and Laughter*, Valerie Hopper and the ever-popular Gracie Fields (a *Mauretania* traveller herself), who sang three numbers including her best-known 'Sally'. At the following reception Lady Rostron sliced into a special cake and Sir Arthur proposed 'Bon voyage!' to the cinema, probably recalling anecdotes of making appointments in one port prior to sailing and getting his beloved *Mauretania* over to the next in perfect time to keep them!

June the 30th marked both the official merger day between Cunard and White Star and the departure of the *Mauretania* at 11.30 a.m. after a refit that had seen her hull and boilers successfully surveyed. Because of reduced passenger loads during cruises, four collapsible lifeboats were put ashore and five boats on each side swung out to create additional recreation space. Brass window casements, painted over during the Great War, were stripped, cleaned, and smartly polished. Arriving in New York at 5.03 a.m. on 6 July, she sailed at 7 p.m. the next day on the first of five cruises. Subsequent cruises would depart on the 21st, then on 4 and 20 August and the last on 8 September. On the evening of departure on the first cruise, First Class Waiter W. Simkin

arrived back on board after his shore leave decidedly the worse for wear, having obviously celebrated the city's now Prohibition-free bars with too much enthusiasm. He was hauled up before Staff Captain Illingworth and fined the usual 5 shillings.

The usual itinerary was involved on each cruise except that Nassau would be the final port of call rather than Havana; Cartagena was also omitted. The first cruise left New York City at 7 p.m. and arrived at Trinidad at 8.45 a.m. after four relaxing days at sea. Sailing at 5.11 p.m., she reached La Guaira at 6.36 a.m. the next day (12 August) and, after almost twelve hours in the port, left at 6 p.m. The next port of call, Curaçao, was reached at 4.55 a.m. on the morning of the 13th and the short stay ended with a 1.12 p.m. sailing. Colón, for Panama, was reached at 5.14 p.m. on 14 August and, after an overnighter, the *Mauretania* steamed away at 6 p.m. A balmy day at sea ended at Nassau, where she berthed at 5.52 p.m. on the 17th. After spending nearly twenty-five hours in the port, she sailed for New York, berthing two days later at 12.18 p.m., fourteen days after departure.

On the evening of the second sailing five of Waiter Simkin's shipmates were similarly hauled before the Staff and arraigned for being both under the influence and subsequently absent from duty. They all suffered either the 'five bob' fine or a full day's pay of 5/5d (five pence extra). Ten days later, another First Class Waiter, C. Skipp, struck his colleague W. Glossop, cutting the latter's eye. He was lucky to get away with just a fine. After leaving Nassau at the beginning of August there was an altercation between the Chief Master-at-Arms, A. Dimmer, and his subordinate, R. Craven, when the latter hit his chief in the face. The entry in the Log was subsequently cancelled and the matter referred to the Acting Vice Consul in New York City. Both were deemed to blame and Craven's fine was refunded. He was quickly transferred to the *Aquitania* with a non-blemishing 'Very Good' stamped in his Discharge Book, a seaman's 'passport' to work at sea. The bright lights of New York City were still proving an attraction to off-duty crew and several Trimmers were logged as being absent from duty; all were fined 5s and, just before sailing on 4 August, a First Class Waiter had second thoughts and deserted. Reluctant to pay the fare, US citizen Charles Mason was discovered stowing away at noon on the 6th when about 700 miles from Nassau. As the ship returned to New York, Bedroom Steward George

Searle collapsed and died following a stroke at around 6 p.m. Thirteen hours later, and about 340 nautical miles further on, his remains were committed to the deep, his effects being sent home on the *Berengaria*.

The *Mauretania's* last cruise of the season left New York City at 7 p.m. on 8 September, sailing from a berth in Hoboken as the Chelsea Piers were overtaxed. The weather was appalling and other departing steamers anchored for safety in Gravesend Bay off Brooklyn, the *Western Prince* of Furness Withy, having sailed, returned to find shelter. Ward Line's vessel *Morro Castle* had been due to arrive at the Ward Line's Pier 14 terminal at the foot of Wall St on the East River in Lower Manhattan after her cruise to Havana, leaving there on the 5th with 549 on board. (This four-year-old, 508ft, 11,520gt, turbo-electric ship had been built under a US Act that provided $250 million towards modernising the American Merchant Marine). Experiencing high winds and rough seas as she steamed northwards (this storm had deposited nearly five deadly, damaging inches of rain on New York City in twenty-four hours), she was a few hours into finishing her cruise when her captain died of a heart attack following a stomach complaint (brought on, it was thought, by poison!). A few hours later, just before 3 a.m., a fire was detected, having suspiciously started in a cupboard in the Writing Room – a room panelled with varnished, highly flammable wood panelling. It spread rapidly and the ensuing panic and badly organised firefighting and evacuation procedures caused the deaths of 137 of those on board. Well ablaze, the ship was anchored 3 miles off Sea Girt Lighthouse to enable the light to act as a beacon for the survivors. In a later salvage attempt the anchor cable was cut, but during the ensuing tow the smouldering ship broke loose and beached herself at Asbury Park in full view of the abundant tourists.

The loss of the Ward liner instigated new legislation that would, hopefully, improve the safety of ships in the future. But the construction of the old *Mauretania* had preceded the consequences of both the *Titanic* and *Morro Castle* disasters – the woods, seasoned for decades before her construction, used in her beautifully polished panelling were now tinder dry. Only one passenger cancelled following the Ward liner's destruction. Although autumn and West Indies cruises for the 1935 season had been discussed, the newly released winter schedule created concern; the *Mauretania* – the 'Grand Old Lady of the North Atlantic' – was *not* on it.

The return to New York at 11.15 on the morning of 21 September must have been sombre; the prognosis for the old Cunarder was not good. That the 'Maury', with her 'grace of line', still one of the fastest passenger ships afloat and the most admired ship in the whole international mercantile marine, could possibly be scrapped beggared the popular imagination. Rather than deteriorating, her engines had, like a vintage wine, actually improved with age. Her hull and now her extensive tinder-dry woodwork were other matters!

Far away in Scotland, as the *Mauretania* left New York at ten minutes past five on 26 September for Southampton (expectedly for dry-docking before another series of cruises), HM Queen Mary named and launched *No. 534* – 'a day of national importance' – the day drenched with rain and wind, which merited more comment in HM's diary than the launch itself! The long-speculated name of the ship that the Queen sent into the cold waters of the River Clyde caused a cheer from beneath a sea of glistening umbrellas as she christened the grey-painted liner *QUEEN MARY*. How the New Cunarder got her name has for long been debated but a letter to the current author from the late, eminent liner historian, Frank Braynard, explained:

'My father was part of a small delegation from the Cunard Line that called on King George V to ask his permission to name their new superliner after Queen Victoria …'

So began a piece of fascinating dinner conversation … The person talking was a lovely woman with sparkling eyes and a cordial manner. I jumped to attention because I knew the story she was going to tell. In fact, I had used it 40 years before in my first book 'Lives of the Liners' [1947] and ever since I had smarted at word that my story was bunkum. Cunard denied it, point blank. It was just made up. I listened with eagerness.

'You know that all Cunard ships have had names that ended with "… ia" and "Victoria" would have been a perfect choice, being well-suited for the world's largest ship then being built by the company.'

She continued, 'My father opened the conversation with His Majesty by saying something to the effect that Cunard wished to name its new ship "… after England's [*sic*] greatest queen." Queen Mary, who was with her husband on this occasion, smiled and said, "I would be delighted."'

Suddenly laid up after her last crossing in September 1934, the still-beautiful but rust-stained *Mauretania* awaits her fate at her berth in Southampton. (Author's Collection)

And so one of the greatest names of all maritime history was selected. The Queen Mary remains to this day perhaps the best known of all modern liners. And I felt most gratified because the lady telling the story was none other than the daughter of Sir Ashley Sparks [the then] Chairman of the Cunard Line in America.

Queen Mary was an excellent choice, pleasing both Cunard (... *ia*) and White Star (... *ic*) sensibilities as it favoured neither. To enable the French to keep their pride for a little longer, the new ship's tonnage was still kept at 73,000. Names for a possible sister ship to the *Queen Mary* were now being propounded and David Kirkwood, the Member of Parliament for Kirkwood whose actions did so much to get work on the abandoned *No. 534* restarted, suggested *King George* or *Princess Royal*.

As the *Mauretania* ploughed her way across the North Atlantic at a creditable 24.4 knots, there was another air of national loss on board; a group of passengers was smarting from its failure to win back the coveted sailing trophy, the America's Cup, by racing their beautiful yacht, the 'J-class' *Endeavour* (built for aircraft designer Sir Thomas 'Tommy' Sopwith), against the American yacht *Rainbow*. The yacht's designer Charles Nicholson, sailmaker J.S. Lapthorn, and yacht club officials, were returning to Britain with tales of seeming unfairness in the race's result.

The old liner steamed eastwards for the 318th time as pertly as usual and arrived on time into Plymouth's busy Sound at 5.50 a.m. on 2 September, her future now hanging in the balance. An officer mournfully told the *Western Morning Press*: 'Nobody knows what is going to happen to this fine ship. She is not scheduled to make any more trips.' Had it been announced that this might have been her final trip she would have been fully booked by those wishing to bid her 'Farewell' but, as it was, she carried a meagre list – seventy-six in First Class, seventy-five in Tourist and seventy-three in Third. Some 580 bags of mail were unloaded, along with seventy-two passengers who, other than for locals, headed for the express train to London. After clearance by the Cunard agent at 7.58 she steamed away for Cherbourg, remaining there for exactly an hour before sailing at 1.30 p.m., pointing her bow northwards to Southampton, where she arrived at ten minutes past six.

There was still no official confirmation that her active career might have just ended.

That Happy Ship

The old *Mauretania*, that 'happy ship', that 'lucky ship', went into an uncertain lay-up alongside the still-building New Docks. Other ships came and went, berthing either ahead or astern of the still elegant white liner. With no schedules to keep, no other employment in the offing, and no news of her future, it was not considered worthwhile to expensively overhaul or paint her until a decision had been made about her future. That would be for at least two months and it was costly to keep a ship idle – dock dues and wages for a skeleton crew and engineers employed on a care-and-maintenance basis were estimated to be around £4,000 a month. Even now a Cunard-White Star Line official stated that 'in all probability' the *Mauretania* would become a full-time cruise ship. When, in early October, a new list of fare rates was issued for the fleet the liner was included but for sailings that might not happen.

November arrived and Captain Peel was transferred to the smaller *Alaunia*, whose Captain H. Bond had been taken to hospital with pleurisy, where complications hastened his demise. Rumours still abounded while the old ship remained at her quay. In December a whisper said that she might become a show ship for British goods or even be used as a grandstand for the forthcoming Jubilee Review of the Fleet – or used as an emigrant ship for the mass of unemployed. Big changes were happening to the amalgamated fleet and many old White Star hands were displaced on their vessels by Cunard men. Captain Sir Edgar Britten became Commodore (later being given command of the *Queen Mary*) and Captain Peel took over command of the *Olympic* from Captain John Binks; 'The Old Reliable' was soon to be sent cruising out of New York when the motorships *Britannic* and *Georgic* transferred from Liverpool to Southampton.

The 'Maury' languished at her berth as the winter weather took its toll; rust wept from hawsepipes, mooring bitts and ports, streaking her once pristine white hull with tears of neglect. Hopes of her return to service in February were raised when it was suggested that she was the only British liner currently capable of competing against the *Bremen* and the *Europa* – and the new *Normandie* – until the new *Queen Mary* was ready to enter service. The following month even that vague hope was dashed when newspapers carried the news that the *Mauretania* was to be sold and:

'BROKEN UP'!

The devastating news was made official when Cunard-White Star confirmed that interested British and foreign firms had already inspected the liner 'with a view to the purchase of the liner for disposal', a second inspection being made two days later on 20 March; tenders were taken for either demolition or further use. If the ship was to be demolished, interest had already been shown in buying certain fittings, particularly her mahogany panelling 'considered to be without equal in any ship afloat'. Certain items, including crockery and cutlery, had already been removed, some to the *Queen Mary*.

Avoiding making an announcement on Monday, 1 April – April Fool's Day – Cunard-White Star waited until the next day before releasing the news that the *Mauretania* – 'something living' and 'without doubt the most famous liner ever launched' – had been sold. Beating offers from Italian and Japanese breakers, the successful buyer was Metal Industries Ltd of Glasgow, who planned to dismantle the liner at their facility in the Naval Dockyard at Rosyth. She would be the largest vessel to be broken there and it was estimated that it would take eight months to reduce her. The shipbreaker's men had achieved practice in their craft by previously breaking another famous vessel, Gustav Erikson's three-masted sailing ship *Grace Harwar* (1889, 1,816grt), rather a glamour ship having previously starred in the acclaimed film *Windjammer*. Currently, the White Star *Calgaric* was being demolished and the salvaged capsized wreck of the scuttled German battleship *Bayern* was due in early May. Cunard's old, graceful ocean greyhound would leave her berth in Southampton within a fortnight of the sale with a skeleton crew and a small party of specially invited guests. To avoid the final indignity of being towed, she would sail north under her own steam, unlike her old rival, the French liner *Paris*, which had recently been towed to Dunkirk for demolition.

On 12 April (coincidentally three days before the twenty-third anniversary of the demise of her sister) the *Olympic* berthed ahead of the *Mauretania*, both with their bows pointing upstream on the River Test quays. Cunard–White Star would not comment on whether 'The Old Reliable' would be put to cruising as previously proposed or, like the *Mauretania*, be broken up. The magnificent *Empress of Britain* of Canadian-Pacific momentarily became the fastest British liner and on at least one occasion berthed astern of the two veterans.

Although it was suggested that the Cunarder be opened for public inspection to enable hundreds to have one last look and to mourn her passing, the purchasers announced that an on-board auction of the liner's fittings would be held while still at her berth. Besides allowing the public a chance to own a piece of the old ship, an auction would also defray some of Metal Industries costs and dispose of fittings unnecessary for the trip. Besides hastening the stripping process, the ship would be rid of much flammable material, also easing the breaker's task and risk. Posters in red and black were pasted around Southampton proclaiming the forthcoming auction and the notice of the 'The Biggest Sale in History' read like a eulogy:

By direction of Metal Industries Limited of Glasgow
THE MAURETANIA
Appointments, Furnishings, Panelling, etc
of the World Famous Cunarder
including sets of chairs, settees, easy & arm chairs
APPOINTMENTS OF THE CABINS
In satinwood, mahogany, etc. Electric light fittings. FINE QUALITY
CARPETS, etc.
ARTISTIC PANELLING
IN THE ITALIAN RENAISSANCE & ENGLISH 18TH
CENTURY TASTE
VALUABLE WEATHERED OAK PANELLING
OF THE FIRST CLASS DINING SALOONS
EXQUISITELY CARVED IN THE FRANCOIS 1er STYLE
Equipment of ship's cuisine, bar, officer, cinemas, etc. Lifts,
NAVIGATION instruments, SHIP'S Ensigns and SIGNALLING
flags. Ship's bells and lettering. And many souvenirs of this famous ship,
together with the LIFE BOATS.
HAMPTON & SONS
Are instructed the above by AUCTION ON BOARD THE LINER,
SOUTHAMPTON DOCKS (by permission of the Southern
Railway Company) on TUESDAY, MAY 14th, 1935, and several
following days, at 11.30 a.m. each day. Private view (ADMISSION
BY CATALOGUE ONLY, price 5s each) FRIDAY, SATURDAY and
MONDAY, MAY 10th, 11th, and 13th, from 9.30 a.m. to 4.30 p.m.,
obtainable from the Auctioneers
20, ST JAMES SQUARE, LONDON, SW1, or from the
CUNARD WHITE STAR, LIMITED, SOUTHAMPTON

The 3,503 lots incorporating nearly 20,000 items were listed in the two-and-sixpenny (2/6*d*) 191-page catalogue that doubled as admission to the docks; a 5-shilling special edition was issued for those wishing to attend a private pre-auction viewing on 9 May. Three days of viewing followed on the 10th, 11th and 13th when sailors from the German liner *Europa* paid their old competitor a respectful 'auf Wiedersehen' during their ship's brief call, joining potential bidders (special trains from London were laid on) as they roamed the ship checking off items in their catalogues against tags fluttering in the breeze or hanging listlessly. With smoke lazily curling from a funnel and paintwork still glistening in spite of the hull-staining rust steaks, she seemed no longer to be a ship but a vast 'repository for thousands of lots'.

Promptly at 11.30 on the morning of Tuesday, 14 May, Messrs Hampton & Sons' auctioneer, Mr J.H. Fisk, took the podium and, before formally opening the eight-day auction, made a brief speech saying that he felt very privileged to be playing even a small part in the last days of 'this wonderful and much-loved ship, famous throughout the world, full of happy memories for a very large number of travellers'. Referring to the passing of the *Mauretania* as a very sad occasion, he looked to the coming of the *Queen* Mary as 'a mark of progress'. The auction was to be one of those rare occasions 'when sentiment and business join in hand', so much so that it was expected that many items would exceed their current commercial value. Several rooms, cabins and their fittings, although to be sold were not to be removed from the ship until she reached Rosyth as they would be needed on the northwards journey. Much of the plumbing was also retained to avoid flooding.

The opening day of the sale was attended by 200 hopeful buyers comfortably seated at long tables in the First Class Lounge, itself to be sold that day in forty-six lots in two halves. The first items to be auctioned were the contents of First-Class cabins from A-Deck, starboard side and consisted of twenty lots, the first being 'two small mahogany wardrobes with bevelled mirror doors and drawers beneath'.

The bidding soon became a keen contest between three protagonists – Mr Harold Sandrey, the Lloyd's agent from the Isles of Scilly who had seen the *Mauretania* passing the islands on many a voyage; Mr Walter Martin, a retired cigar merchant from Guernsey; and Sheffield builder Mr Charles Boot, who successfully bid for the magnificent 11ft-high panelling and fixtures from the First Class Library (sold in two lots), cabin interiors of maple and mahogany, and several chandeliers. These purchases were intended for installation in new film studios to be built near Iver Heath in Buckinghamshire. The Library would retain its use and as a staff restroom (later used as a Board Room and as a set for films) and the cabins as dressing rooms. His partner in this venture was

the scion of a wealthy flour-milling family, Mr J. Arthur Rank. The first day's auction, recorded by the BBC, realised receipts totalling £2,500 for items valued at £50,000.

The second day of the sale brought a larger attendance and workmen began carefully dismantling the woodwork previously sold on A-Deck, each piece having been photographed and marked to ensure accurate re-erection on shore in one of the new specially heated dock sheds.

Fixtures and fittings from B-Deck, Upper C-Deck and C-Deck – including the First Class Dining Saloon, cabins and suites – were auctioned in the C-Deck Dining Saloon. Keen competition ensured that good prices were fetched for the 'magnificent weathered-oak panelling and woodwork in the Francois 1er style' of the Dining Saloon, the main part being on C-Deck with its balcony on Upper C, the latter going to Mr Walter Martin of Guernsey for 290 guineas (one guinea = £1 1s) and the fittings for 279 guineas. The main Dining Saloon fetched 784 guineas. The day's sale totalled over £2,000.

The third and fourth days' sales were again held in the C-Deck Dining Saloon. B-Deck cabins and corridors came under the auctioneer's gavel on the 16th and, on the following day, other cabins, the Barber's Shop, Children's Room, and the Doctor's and Purser's cabins were offered. On Friday 17th the sale moved to the Tourist Class Smoke Room on B-Deck. On offer in thirteen lots with a starting price of £1,000 was the magnificent Grand Staircase that extended from A-Deck to D-Deck. This sold for £1,500, its purchaser, Bristol wine merchant Mr Ronald Avery, adding it to other items intended for new offices or other buildings, wanted the lots as a memento of his firm's valuable first shipment of wine to the United States on the ship following the repeal of Prohibition.

Just before the conclusion of the first half of the auction, Lot 1567 – two copper fire extinguishers that could not be removed until the ship reached Rosyth – was brought into the room when, suddenly, one of the appliances started spraying its contents over several of the bidders. The auctioneer quickly joked that it was fortunate that the accident had happened as it could be seen that the items were fully functional!

After a weekend's interval the sale resumed on Monday 20th. Harry Tate, the famed British comedian and actor, was amongst the attendees and joked that he was going to bid for two of the funnels to turn them into tie pins. Tourist facilities on B-Deck came under the hammer on Tuesday. Included were the Smoke Room, Upper C and C-Deck cabins, Dining Saloon, staircase, kitchens, etc. Wednesday's sale encompassed Tourist-Class cabins from D-Deck and Third-Class Smoke Room, D-Deck cabins, furniture and carpets.

The final day of the auction, Thursday 23rd, saw a third and final shift of venue down to the Third Class Dining Saloon on C-Deck. Tables and chairs abounded, as did the contents of officers' cabins including the Captain's, Staff Captain's and Engineers'. Desirable maritime mementoes – Navigational instruments, Bridge equipment, signalling flags and the lettering of the ship's name – were expected to fetch good prices. Lifebuoys, emblazoned with the ship's name, were keenly sought and the sale of twenty-seven fully equipped lifeboats fetched £386 4s. As anticipated, a feeling of sentiment crept in when signal flags were offered with two large Cunard house flags going for 15 guineas, and the Blue Ensign for 6 guineas, all bought by the ever-enthusiastic Scillonian. Particularly anticipated were the ship's steering wheel, the brass 20in-diameter Crow's Nest bell (this fetched a meagre 65 guineas against an anticipated £500), navigation instruments, and the fore and aft sirens that had sounded so many farewells, greetings and warnings. The foremost half-ton whistle (50 guineas) went to the magnificent resort of Lilleshall Hall in Newport, Shropshire, where the instrument was intended for use by compressed air to produce a blast that could be heard as far away as Wolverhampton! This would signal the nightly operation of a searchlight. The aft siren went for 38 guineas.

The 24in brass letters, 'those magic letters', of the ship's name on each side of the bow, were offered individually, the port-side lettering with its more desirable backward's slope fetched 150 guineas (all bought by Mr Martin) while the forward-sloping starboard letters realised 40 guineas. Mr Martin also bought the complete counter-stern lettering:

MAURETANIA
LIVERPOOL

for 60 guineas.

Lot 3503 – one of several bench seats composed of an iron frame with teak battens – brought the sale to an end. A satisfactory result of £15,000 had been realised, helping to defray Metal Industries' costs.

The final concussion of the Auctioneer's gavel sounded the death knell of the old ship. Mr Fisk made a short speech and, in a spontaneous display of emotion, bidder Harold Sandrey stood on a chair and led the assembly in a moving rendition of the National Anthem. (Author's note: for the current location of much of the surviving fittings the reader is referred to *Triumph and Resurrection* by Peter Newall.) Until she left the port, workmen removed those sold items that would not be needed for the journey north as well as 40ft of her mast tips to enable her to pass safely under the Forth Railway Bridge. The Lord Mayor of Newcastle requested the offcuts for use as flagpoles as a memorial to the great ship and made a further request that the liner call in to Newcastle as she travelled north.

At the beginning of June the beautiful French liner *Normandie* made a triumphant maiden entrance into New York Harbor after undisputedly smashing all records by achieving an average speed of over 30 knots. She did not, and never would, use Southampton Docks, anchoring instead at The Motherbank off Ryde. The new British challenger, *Mauretania*'s great successor, had yet to make her debut.

Volunteers signed on as crew for the ship's Home Trade coastal voyage to Rosyth. Captain A.T. Brown from Bromley, Kent, was on the Bridge as Master and Chief Engineer H. Bolling was in charge of her Engine Department where, to avoid risks in cleaning her bunkers once at Rosyth, only sufficient oil was taken on board to get her to her destination. Even at this late stage in her career she was still well maintained, a report stating 'particular attention is given to the cleanliness of the stokeholds'. Draughts of 29ft 10in forward and 33ft 11in aft were essentially noted. Before the old liner departed on her funereal voyage, the Mayor of Southampton and Admiral of the Port, Councillor G.A. Waller, was invited to dine on board. One hundred First-Class cabins had been kept intact and sixty-five passengers boarded for the short coastal voyage, including guests invited by Cunard-White Star and Metal Industries Ltd. Representatives from various trades that had helped to build the ship and veterans from different departments who had served on her over the years were sailing on this last journey. These included Jim Thompson, a Shipwright from Wallsend-on-Tyne who had been an assistant at her launch; R.J. Hubbard, Chief Electrician; A. Robertson, Fireman; T. Hale, Trimmer; J. Powell, Bedroom Steward; and Mrs H. Edwards, Chief Stewardess. Harry Allport had been on the *Mauretania*'s lost sister ship, the *Lusitania*, when she had been torpedoed and sunk.

Mr Walter Martin, one of the major successful bidders, was also travelling and during the trip became incensed enough to send a radiogram to Sir George Hunter: 'For the grand old lady of the sea to have been allowed to pass along to the knackers yard is to my mind a national disgrace.' He opined that the ship should have been kept for the Mercantile Marine in much the same way as Nelson's revered *Victory* had been preserved as a testament to the Royal Navy. Saddened though he was at her passing, Sir George recognised with the professional eye of a naval architect that the maintenance of an old vessel was expensive and with continuing improvements in ship design she had to 'give way to newer ships' – 'she has done her work … done her work well'. As his creation had latterly been popularly called 'The (Grand) Old Lady of the Atlantic', so Sir George had been dubbed 'The Grand Old Man of Tyne and Wear'. As a memento of his 'child', Cunard-White Star returned to him the statue of Columbia from the *Mauretania*'s Lounge; he in turn gave it to the Sunderland museum. Sir Arthur Rostron had been invited to make this final sailing but he declined, preferring to keep her as a 'beautiful memory'. Refusing to board the partially stripped ship for a last look, he watched the final departure from the quayside, remembering her 'as she was at the height of her glory and fame'. He returned with his memories to his home at Chalk Hill, in Southampton's West End.

At nine o'clock, as the daylight of 1 July dimmed, thousands within the docks watched as the *Mauretania*, flying only the Cunard house flag, was pulled away from the berth that had been her home for many weeks. As she did so the guests on board linked arms and sang to the strains of a band on the quayside as it played 'Auld Lang Syne'. The dirge of ships' sirens bewailed her passing. As the Blue Peter was lowered a 20ft blue banner proclaiming the ship's unbeaten record '1907–1929' was raised and saluted by the attending officers before they walked away talking in subdued tones. This banner was soon to be misidentified as being the actual Blue Riband! With a few deck

lights glowing and escorted by smaller vessels, she steamed down Southampton Water for the last time. She passed other craft, including a pleasure steamer whose dancing occupants paused in their pursuit to cheer the gallant old liner; other vessels lowered their flags to a respectful half-mast. Steaming into the English Channel at just above 12 knots, she was bid a fitting farewell as Nature saluted her old adversary with vivid flashes of lightning, rolling peels of thunder and an absolution of heavy rain.

The next day her slow, sad progress up the east coast was followed by thousands flocking to the coastline from towns and villages to watch the still proud liner as she steamed by as close in as possible. In the busy waters of the North Sea craft of all sizes signalled their farewells. In an effort to take his work home, Captain Brown slowed the ship as she approached his birthplace of Scarborough, arriving off the fashionable spa town at 10 p.m. Met by a small flotilla in the gathering gloom, she fired three rockets. As she sailed away she was accompanied by two heavily loaded paddle steamers.

The on-board auction of the ship's fittings is under way. The microphone at the end of the table indicates that this was taken during the BBC broadcast of the event. (*Shipbuilding and Shipping Record*)

Steaming overnight, the liner was 3 miles from the shore off Souter Point, Marsden, by 8.15 the next morning on a calm, sunlit sea as she approached Newcastle upon Tyne, the city of her creation where the Lord Mayor, Councillor R.S. Dalgliesh, had requested that the liner call as she made her way to Rosyth; it was still not certain that she would do so but thousands crowded every vantage point from South Shields to beyond Whitley Bay to watch the liner as she passed. In spite of her ultimate destination she looked splendid as the sun caught her white paint … her great red funnels … the blue banner …

To the Lord Mayor and Lady Mayoress and all Tyneside folk, Newcastle-on-Tyne.

Thank you for your greeting. For twenty-eight years have I striven to be a credit to you and now my day is done. Though I pass on, may Tyneside ever reach out to further and greater triumphs.

With pride and affection I greet you.

Farewell
Mauretania

With a few lights aglow, the *Mauretania* heads down Southampton Water towards her ultimate destiny. (Author's Collection)

When the *Mauretania* was abreast of the Tyne she made an unexpected turn to port and, at 3 to 4 knots, moved carefully shorewards. Not only was the Mayor's request for the liner to steam near to the Tyne being granted but, in a surprise move, the liner was being stopped outside the river for half an hour in honour of the town and those that had built her so long ago, firing rockets from her Bridge as she did so. Small aircraft swooped overhead as she came to a halt off the North Pier and hundreds lining the rails of be-flagged ferries, pleasure craft, tugs, trawlers and the Shields Pilot Cutter cheered and cheered, and sirens sounded for a full ten minutes.

Arriving alongside on the bobbing tug *Plover*, the Lord Mayor of Newcastle boarded the huge, steady liner via an open port and a civic welcome was held on the Bridge both for him and the Mayor of South Shields (Alderman J.W. Watson), who had arrived on a separate launch. Touring the ship, it was noted that bulkheads, already stripped

Sailing up the east coast, the liner slowed when off Scarborough at 10 p.m. on 2 July (sunset was at 9.30). (Collection of Charles A. Haas)

The 'Pride of the Tyne' made an unexpected but hoped-for stop when off Newcastle to bid an emotive-laden farewell to the town that had built her. (Collection of Ian Rae)

of panelling, showed chalked names and messages written by the men who had so proudly built her so many years before. On disembarking, the civic leaders and their parties lined their improvised civic yachts, stood to attention, and sang 'Auld Land Syne', their respectful refrain being taken up by the throng that surrounded them and by those on board the *Mauretania*. It was a grand, grand farewell.

There had been so much emotion on Tyneside that day – from the surviving proud men (those still of working age perhaps now amongst the mass of unemployed) who had built her, from the families who had been told with pride all about her, and from those who had followed her every move with patriotic pride. Some wept openly. She was, in every sense, the 'Pride of the Tyne', a pride that still exists decades later.

That half hour was all too short and, after sounding her siren and firing more rockets, the *Mauretania* continued on her slow progress north to meet her Nemesis, passing Whitley Bay in full view of those who crowded the clifftops who watched her until she disappeared from view. Steaming onwards, she passed many a crowded viewing point on the beautiful rugged coast, including the small isle of Coquet and the little coaling port of Amble at the mouth of the River Coquet. The town's council sent a message calling her 'still the finest ship on the seas', to which the *Mauretania* replied: 'To the last and kindliest port in England, greetings and thanks', an epithet that remains the town's motto to this day. She steamed out of English into Scottish waters, her journey almost done as she took a turn to the north-east towards Largs Bay and the northern shore of the Firth of Forth. From Leven and Methil to Burntisland Roads, crowds waited to see perhaps the greatest ship ever built. Between these vantage points the view of the liner's now south-westerly course was briefly obscured by mist even though she was steaming close in. On reaching Kirkcaldy, the *Dundee Courier* reported, a school sports day was interrupted when 'the cry got up "The *Mauretania* is passing!"' when the tops of her funnels appeared above the chimneys. An excellent view was had of the ship from Kinghorn and Burntisland as she sailed between the latter and the rocky outcrop of Inchkeith Island. Waiting for the tide, she anchored for the night with her darkened hull lit every fifteen seconds by the intermittent flash from the island's brownstone lighthouse.

Earlier than scheduled at three o'clock on the morning of 4 July, the *Mauretania* began one of the shortest – but most final – journeys of her long and illustrious career. The thirty-hour voyage from Southampton that had cost an estimated £3,000 was reaching its final irreversible conclusion. Slowly coming in, she briefly anchored in Inverkeithing Bay before continuing onwards assisted by the Leith tugs *Herwit* and *Oxcar* that had awaited her arrival like mourners at a lychgate. With the rising sun that caught her stained white hull from aft, she presented a magnificent sight as she passed under the equally impressive spans and arches of the Forth Rail Bridge, her shortened masts appearing to those on board to just miss the structure above them. The impressive scene inspired artist Charles Pears to create a painting that would hang in the new *Queen Mary*, in much the same way as HM Queen Elizabeth would wear a miniature of her late, beloved father, King George VI, on her lapel.

With the scene being filmed from aircraft that buzzed in the skies above and with the lush green hills of the Lothians on the opposite shore contrasting with her white hull and red funnels, the liner took a slight turn to starboard into the Main Channel that led to the entrance lock of the dockyard's Main Basin, arriving there at 5.20 a.m. The basin was occupied by several warships of the Reserve Fleet, the dockyard having been under a care-and-maintenance basis since the Great War. As she prepared to leave the sea for the last time, a strong sou'-westerly half-gale blew the smoke horizontally as it wispily issued from her funnels. Her poignant approach to the lock entrance was accentuated by a solitary piper, Adam MacGillivray, who played a lament from the quayside, the liner towering above him. An urgency arose as a sudden gust caught her massive hull, veered her to starboard, and caused spectators on the lock wall to scatter! She made a soft contact with the wood piles that lined the lock and gently rubbed along them until the surprised tugs could regain control. The piper hurriedly crossed the liner's bow via a caisson (lock gate) and played again from the opposite wall.

By the time she was in the basin two more tugs, the paddle tug *Elie* from Grangemouth and the Admiralty tug *Buckieburn*, waited to assist in placing the *Mauretania* in Graving Dock No. 1, but as the wind was too strong to attempt the manoeuvre she was temporarily moored. By now the procedure was an hour behind schedule – a rare event for the 'Maury'! Her final voyage now ended, Captain Brown rang 'Finished with Engines' and the beautiful turbines ceased their hum. Renowned maritime author John Maxton Graham recalled being told that, as the turbines stopped, they gave a sigh as if the old ship had finally accepted her fate and given herself up to her destiny.

Accompanied by their various thoughts and feelings, Captain Brown and the 110 crew left the *Mauretania* for the last time, leaving the 'old girl' alone and looking derelict, safely moored until the wind subsided.

Fuel for the coastal voyage had been carefully calculated to get her to Rosyth, but, probably because of her manoeuvres off the Tyne, there was not enough remaining for her to manoeuvre into the graving dock under her own steam. In the early hours of 7 July, with Pilot William Prince on the Bridge, the liner, held by tugs and with hawsers attached to bollards ashore, was guided into the graving dock, narrowly missing a collision with the aircraft carrier *Argus* as she did so. The delicate manoeuvre took three hours with engineers, dockyard workers and office staff assisting in the process as, concerned about working conditions, the breaker's workforce was still on a strike called by the Transport and General Workers' Union.

The first work in breaking the *Mauretania* was not due to start for another two weeks, so it was decided to allow the public on board to inspect the ship. On the first day a queue one-third of a mile long gathered at the dockyard gate. Admission was 1 shilling for adults and sixpence for children (a lot of money for those on the dole). Boarding started at 10 a.m. and the ship remained open until four o'clock (9 p.m. on other days). As the ship was in a Royal Dockyard, visitors were subject to the Official Secrets Act and Admiralty Police diligently confiscated hundreds of cameras that could later be reclaimed

That first day was hot and sunny and as the crowds reached the gangway the three-deep queue started to become disorderly, growing to seven deep. Crowding occurred as queue jumpers exacerbated the situation and the resultant scramble deterred several hundred visitors from boarding the ship, contenting themselves with a dockside view. The crowd's poor behaviour continued on board. 'No Smoking' signs were ignored, which resulted in several alarms being raised and, whether through disappointment that the ship had been shorn of much of her glory or whether it was caused by a sense of social inequality exacerbated by unemployment or just plain vandalism (the causes were

Still flying her pennant, the liner approaches the dock gates. (Author's Collection)

never ascertained), a considerable amount of damage was perpetrated during that first open day. Auctioned panelling was scratched, valuable carvings broken, doors forced open and windows broken to gain entry into locked rooms; the Captain's cabin was attacked with penknives and 'souvenirs' disappeared at an alarming rate. Appalled at the nature and extent of the wanton damage, Metal Industries took drastic action to protect their investment and, in an attempt to confine future visitors to the Main Deck, displayed a notice:

Owing to the damage and depredations of the public, the directors of Metal Industries, Ltd, regret that the privileges of entering accommodation have been cancelled. Visitors are requested to keep to route laid down.

A restricted, miserable trek along gloomy decks guided by chalked arrows, barricaded doors and roped off areas now indicated the permitted route. Glimpses of the once beautiful rooms, now with shorn walls and hanging wires where gorgeous light fittings once hung, could only be obtained through dusty windows. Many opined that the final farewell should have been at Southampton.

The workforce broke its strike on 9 July and returned to work by lifting decking from the Sun Deck. This not only started the demolition process but also prevented public access as the work in progress created serious hazards for the daily visitors, numbered in their thousands, many arriving by coach or special trains. The viewing period ended with only 500 touring the ship on Sunday, 14 July. Reports of attendances varied but it was reported that 10,000 had toured the ship on the first day alone, 2,000 on the 10th, and thousands – perhaps 5,000 – had arrived from Newcastle on their annual outing in a hundred coaches, perhaps leaving disappointed in their last view of 'their' ship.

A Mighty Crash

Much of the decking from the *Mauretania* found a second life and was bought by the load. Their bid for the entire ship being rejected, Hughes Blocklow Shipbreaking Co., of Blyth bought a mass of teak and carefully turned it into treen, advertised under the slogan 'A Happy Ending for the Timbers of the Majestic Vessel Which Was the Pride of All England', each piece affixed with a small brass plate testifying that it had been:

MADE FROM TEAKWOOD TAKEN FROM
R.M.S. MAURETANIA
BY THE HUGHES BOLCKOW SHIPBREAKING Co. Ltd
BLYTH, NORTHUMBERLAND

and another …

FROM THE DECKING OF THE
MAURETANIA
THE OLD LADY OF THE ATLANTIC

Souvenirs varied in size and use; smokers were well catered for with cigarette boxes (6/6d), ash trays (2/6d), and small barrels that could be used for matches or toothpicks. The home, too, was well supplied with everything from book holders to lamp standards to rocker blotters

Blowing a half-gale on the early morning of 4 July, solitary kilted piper Adam MacGillivray pipes the *Mauretania* through the main lock entrance. (Collection of Eric Longo)

(2/-), perpetual calendars (4/-), candlesticks and even egg timers with a plastic traffic light with sand-filled glass timer. Garden furniture was also offered: chaises longue could be had for five guineas and teak garden seats (with the ship's name and profile carved into the back lathes) was an expensive £6 15s 0d.

Dunfermline Athletic Football Club at East End Park took 20 tons of decking, which would continue its underfoot use as terracing. A local sawmill purchased a quantity of well-seasoned timber to sell as bundles of kindling to warm many a home on a cold night. Cold nights were also made more comfortable at a children's camp in Echt, Aberdeenshire, where thirty of the remaining beds were purchased by the 'Willing Shilling Fund'. Furniture and other items, unsold in Southampton, were offered at bargain prices.

Breaking the liner would be undertaken afloat and the first of 300 men began preparing the ship on 16 July by ridding her of all remaining combustibles: accrued rubbish, remaining panelling and furniture, residual oil (after her delivery voyage only about 15 tons remained), etc. The decks were to be 'swept' (demolished) downwards one by one and, as over the previous two decades oxyacetylene burning had replaced wrecking balls and hammers and chisels, it was anticipated that (hopefully) 1,000 tons of scrap would be taken from the hull each week, and that within four months the ship would be cut down to her waterline and, in nine be no more.

Meanwhile in Hampshire, the passing of the *Mauretania* was being honoured in Winchester's magnificent and ancient cathedral in an uncommon tribute. At the annual Shipping Festival, held on 23 July to celebrate Britain's indispensable Mercantile Marine, a superb 2-ton, 15ft model of the old ship, presented by Cunard-White Star, was offered in a revival of the old custom of placing a votive ship model in a church – thought to be the first model of a steamship to be offered in such a way – and placed in the Mariners' Chapel in the North Transept 'for all time'. With members of the old ship's crew in company with captains Sir Arthur Rostron, 'Sandy' McNeil and Robert Peel, officials from the shipping line and the mayors of Southampton and Winchester in the congregation, the model was unveiled by the Lord Lieutenant of Hampshire, Lord Mottistone, to the poignant sound of bugles playing 'Sunset'. The dedication by Bishop Arthur Karney, Bishop of

Southampton, was followed by a march through the city's streets with flags flying and bands playing. In later years the superb model, along with others in the collection, was transferred to the Shipping Gallery in London's Science Museum. When that gallery was closed, the model was sent to the museum's National Collections Centre at Wroughton (formerly RAF Wroughton) for storage.

An unsuccessful bidder for the ship, Sir John Jervis (retired High Sheriff of Surrey), acting on behalf of the county's altruistic scheme to ease joblessness in Jarrow, (the Tyneside town still suffering chronic, impoverishing unemployment) had wanted to buy the ship for demolition at the recently closed Palmer's shipyard. Having already given the town a Greek steamer to break, unemployment was still rife and, a year later, 200 desperate, rain-bedraggled men marched to London in the famous 'Jarrow Crusade' to petition the Labour Government. Sir John was undeterred by the loss of the *Mauretania* (he had offered £40,000; her final selling price was undisclosed) and became determined to bid for the much larger *Olympic*. His bid of £97,500 was successful. From 26 August 'The Old Reliable' was opened for public inspection before the auction of her fittings began on 5 October. Six days later she quietly sailed for Jarrow under the command of Captain P.R. Vaughan. Without profit, Sir John then resold the ship to Thos. W. Ward Ltd on condition that she would be broken to her sheer line at Jarrow before being towed to the Inverkeithing breakers.

With demolition of the *Mauretania* now under way the large, prominent ventilator cowls that distinguished the ship's appearance were among the first items to be cut down, but while the ship still had her four funnels in place she was still outwardly the *Mauretania*. But on 11 September this changed when, with a crash that could be heard all over Rosyth, her fourth, aftermost, funnel came tumbling down, falling aft onto the centreline with a technique and accuracy that would have made a lumberjack glow with pride. A close inspection of the ¾in-thick paint revealed a stratification of colours that reflected her history throughout both war and peace. Soon afterwards, her third funnel and then the second came crashing down, imploding as they did so, leaving her with her forward stack solitarily and defiantly struggling to maintain her dignity above the wrecked and levelled deckhouses stretching behind it.

In *Heart of Darkness* Joseph Conrad wrote of ships whose 'names are like jewels flashing in the night of time'. The *Mauretania* had been one of those ships and the Cunard–White Star Line decided to reserve her name for a future build. Accordingly, in mid-September, the company approached the Southampton, Isle of Wight and South of England Royal Mail Steam Packet Company Limited (the ferry company now known as Red Funnel), who obligingly renamed their two-funnelled excursion paddle steamer *Queen* (345gt; 1902) with the illustrious appellation the following April. During her travels the diminutive 'new' *Mauretania*, loaded with happy holidaymakers, splashed her way from Southampton to Bournemouth Pier, where Pier Keeper A.J. Moss kept the memory of the old *Mauretania* alive – he had been a Senior First Officer on the great liner.

On 15 March 1941, Metal Industries Ltd Manager Max Wilkinson (as a small boy he had seen the liner pass down the Tyne to the sea) read a paper, 'The Demolition of the *Mauretania*', before the Manchester Association of Engineers, giving an insightful stage-by-stage account of her final months. Mr Wilkinson detailed the breakers' bid for the ship had been expertly estimated on the liner's light displacement tonnage of 30,800 tons. After making various calculations that included the deduction of weights of oil fuel, boiler water, combustibles (much of which was profitably sold), and other items weighed as they were taken off the ship, the offer made was on an 'out-turn' (the amount of profitable scrap) of 26,000 tons but this included a 'ball park' estimate of the useless weight of years of accumulated paint, unsalable material and rubbish.

Before steel cutting could commence, both sides of the line of cut had to be chipped clear of paint as toxic fumes posed a health hazard, especially from the primer coat of red lead. Contemporary face masks provided insufficient protection so the health of the men was medically monitored, milky cocoa being recommended as a precautionary measure against lead poisoning. Sparks from the cutting operation posed a risk and fire parties kept vigil. To assist in obviating the risk, scrap asbestos, stripped from the Engine Room, was dampened, stuffed into sacks and used to plug deep trunks.

As the ship was reduced and floated higher in the water, Mr Wilkinson admired the beautifully designed curves of her fine lines:

Demolition became more evident when the funnels felled with a crash that could be heard all over Rosyth. As the funnels fell they collapsed in on themselves. (Author's Collection)

The last piece is hoisted from the beach. ('The Demolition of the "Mauretania"', Michael Moss/Author's Collection)

The changing seasons brought with them the bitterness and mournfulness of a Scottish winter. The hull was reduced along 100ft lengths from forward and aft, leaving a higher midships section to give strength to the hull, giving a stepped appearance to the ship's diminishing profile. Scrap was sorted into consignments depending on its type and value and broken down into 10-ton sections that could be safely craned ashore and cut into 6ft by 4ft pieces. With projections from surrounding frames etc. not exceeding 8in, the pieces had the appearance of bizarre racks of lamb. Steels of ¼in or less were compressed into bales. Some 500 tons of scrap was produced each week (not the 1,000 tons anticipated earlier), with the whole breaking process eventually taking thirteen months.

The *Mauretania*, built using the best of materials, now yielded quantities of high-quality scrap that could be recycled – literally in the case of the water-tubes from the boilers as these could be redrawn for bicycle-frame manufacture and even for washing-line posts. Anchors and cables were reconditioned, retested and reused, while propeller shafts and other round-sectioned steels were re-forged. The high-quality heavy plating that formed the casing of the boilers was in such good condition that, after removal of lines of rivet holes and laps, it was sent for re-rolling. Of special interest were the 3 tons of aluminium from the lift grilles, and 20 tons of skylight plate glass and the sliding windows fitted in 1923.

The most valuable of the scrap were the non-ferrous metals that had been used prolifically, especially in the tightly packed machinery spaces. Brass was in abundance, as were various grades of copper, sometimes of a thicker gauge than expected. The expansion piece in the Main Steam Line that ran between Boiler and Engine Rooms was a massive 75in in diameter and bends in piping demonstrated the skill of the Coppersmiths. Gunmetal condenser plates and tubes, lead, spelter, white metal … all produced valuable scrap, as did thousands of turbine blades. Some brass fittings such as portholes were cut away with remnants of steel still attached that had to be painstakingly removed by hand with hammer and chisel. To give access to the stern, the bow was flooded and, once the stern had risen, the upper half of the 63-ton balanced rudder was cut away. The 30-ton crane then lifted the lower half, allowing access to the substantial 1–2ft thicknesses of the stern casting. With the stern now riding high out of the water the highly prized propellers were removed.

When the ship had been cut down to the main deck, she was lying against a dead straight granite quay. By this time she was riding high out of the water and her under-water portion was exposed. It was most remarkable to find that in the 760 feet of length she only touched the quay for a matter of 6 feet. Her lines showed the reason for holding the record for 22 years.

Constant vigilance ensured that the remains of the hull did not hog (bend upwards amidships) during the removal of heavy weights, and when it became necessary to move the hulk from the graving dock to the tidal basin the remains had to be lightened as much as possible to reduce further stresses amidships as the structure showed signs of bending.

As cracking appeared at some squared corners, a policy was adopted of cutting these corners either diagonally or rounded to distribute stresses. To check for movement, an improvised gauge was made by fixing two 40ft battens along the structure with freely moving ends overlapping by 12in; a pencil mark across these two ends would indicate any movement.

To reserve the old liner's illustrious name Cunard approached the Southampton to Cowes ferry company to temporarily rename one of their steamers. The paddle steamer Queen was chosen for the honour. (Author's Collection)

The 'new' *Mauretania* was visited by Captain Rostron, being greeted here by the small vessel's appropriately named Captain Seaman. (Red Funnel Group)

What remained of the once-proud *Mauretania* was taken out of the graving dock and moored alongside a jetty. The forward bulkhead spaces were again flooded, the stern raised and the outboard propeller shafts drawn into the ship for removal. Stern tubes were cut off and sealed. In order to complete the final acts of demolition it was necessary to beach the floating but leaking platform outside the lock by gradually pulling the delicate carcase stern-first up onto a beach. What remained of the devastated hull had draughts of 14ft forward and 10ft aft and, with a local tidal range of 18ft, this was accomplished without too much difficulty. As 10-ton sections were lifted ashore, the diminishing remains were gradually coaxed landwards on high tides to await the cutters' torches as she took the ground on the low.

Oil residue was absorbed with quantities of ash before digging it out or simply by burning it. The double-bottomed oil bunkers had been lined with cement, into which channels were now chipped to allow burning torches to do their work. Cement residue on removed scrap was either chipped off by hand or using a cast-iron ball dropped onto it from a height. Chipping, burning, cutting and lifting continued through all weathers until only one section was left on the mud.

When this last piece was craned away it marked the end of perhaps the greatest liner ever to have sailed the North Atlantic and one of the greatest liners of all time. No longer would her slender, graceful lines, the slight rake of her familiar four funnels be seen as she ploughed – sometimes battled – her seemingly effortless way across the ocean. She had been a credit to her builders and to her owners; she had been the wonder of her age; she had the reputation of always being a lucky ship; she had held the Blue Ribband against all competition and for a record, unbroken length of time; she had served her country well in times of war as well as in peace; she had earned the respect – and the love – of many of those who had sailed on her as crew or as passengers; she had epitomised the term 'Ocean Greyhound'.

She had been …

… the Mauretania.

BIBLIOGRAPHY

Ihave gleaned much information in the production of this book from a host of publications; contemporary newspapers (the British Newspaper Archive was an absolutely invaluable mine of information: as Philip Graham of *The Washington Post* once said, 'Journalism is the first draft of history'); technical reports; official records; and many other sources. Any omissions and errors in interpretation, analysis and opinion remain entirely mine, as are any 'probables' that are made on 'best guesses'. Any corrections would be welcomed via the publisher. Where extracts are used in short quotes no copyright infringement is intended and my sincerest apologies if any has been.

In this account of the ship's career I have decided to omit references and footnotes that only seem to detract from the flow of a book's narrative and take up too much narrative space. I apologise to those who might find these omissions an inconvenience.

Of special value are the facsimile reprints (reproduced and edited by Mark Warren) of the special editions of *The Engineer* and *The Shipbuilder*, which made fine 'working copies' of the originals in my collection. For those who might desire further information on aspects of both the building and technical operation of the magnificent *Mauretania* these publications provide technical details in abundance. I am also very mindful of my debt to Professor Ian Buxton for his detailed paper '*Mauretania* and Her Builders' that appeared in the *Mariner's Mirror* Volume 82 No. 1 (February 1996).

My thanks are also extended to the late Peter Newall who, while preparing his own excellent book (MAURETANIA – *Triumph and Resurrection*) a few years back, had the courtesy to inform and reassure me that our books would not compete but happily complement each other. I would be honoured to think that they do so! I recommend his book for the current location of much of the ship's surviving fittings.

Books

Anderson, Roy, *White Star* (T. Stephenson & Sons Ltd, 1964)

Bisset, Sir James (Commodore), *Commodore: War, Peace and Big Ships* (Angus and Robertson, 1961)

Bonsor, N.R.P., *North Atlantic Seaway: An Illustrated History of the Passenger Services Linking the Old World with the New in Four Volumes, Volume 3* (David & Charles, 1975)

Braynard, Frank O. (ed. Robert H. Burgess), *The Big Ship: The Story of the SS United States* (The Mariners' Museum, Newport News, VA 1981)

Brittain, Vera (ed. Alan Bishop), *Chronicle of Youth: Great War Diary 1913–1917* (Phoenix Press, 2000)

Brook-Shepherd, Gordon, *Uncle of Europe: The Social and Diplomatic Life of Edward VII* (Collins, 1975)

Brown, David K. (RCNC), *The Way of the Ship in the Midst of the Sea: The Life and Work of William Froude* (Periscope Publishing, 2006)

Burgess, Douglas R., *Seize the Trident: The Race for Superliner Supremacy and How it Altered the Great War* (International Marine/McGraw-Hill, 2005)

Carmichael, A.W., *Practical Ship Production:* (McGraw-Hill Book Company, Inc., 1941)

Chernow, Ron, *The House of Morgan: An American Banking Dynasty* (Touchstone, 1990)

Chirnside, Mark, *RMS Olympic: Titanic's Sister* (The History Press, 2015)

Coleman, Terry, *The Liners: A History of the North Atlantic Crossing* (Penguin Books Ltd, 1976)

Cressy, Edward, *All About Engines* (Cassell & Co., *c.* 1925)

Clements, Eric L., *Captain of the* Carpathia: *The Seafaring Life of* Titanic *Hero Sir Arthur Henry Rostron* (Bloomsbury Publishing, 2016)

Cutler, Frederick Morse, *The 55th (C.A.C.) in the American Expeditionary Forces, France 1918* (Commonwealth Press, 1920)

Dickens, Charles, *American Notes* (Chapman and Hall, 1850)

Dixon, June, *Uffa Fox: a Personal Biography* (Angus & Robertson, 1978)

Farquharson-Roberts, Mike, *A History of the Royal Navy: World War I* (I.B. Taurus & Co. Ltd, 2014)

Fox, Stephen, *Transatlantic: Samuel Cunard, Isambard Brunel, and the Great Atlantic Steamships* (HarperCollins, 2003)

Garrett, George, *The Collected George Garrett: The Maurie* (Trent Editions, 1999)

Haldane, J.W.C., *Steamships and Their Machinery: From First to Last* (E & FN Spon, 1893)

Hampshire, A. Cecil, *The Blockaders* (William Kimber, 1980)

HM Stationery Office, *The Efficient Use of Fuel* (HMSO, 1944)

Hutchings, David F., *Caronia: Legacy of a 'Pretty Sister'* (Shipping Books Press, 2000)

Hutchings, David F., *Pride of the North Atlantic* (amended) (Waterfront/Kingfisher Productions, 2003)

Jones, B.S. (Dr) (ed. Kenneth Shaw), *Archives of the Heathens: Tales of a Secret Society on the RMS Mauretania 1908–1914* (Xlibris, 2016)

Jordan, Humfreym, *Mauretania: Landfalls and Departures of Twenty-Five Years* (Hodder and Stoughton, 1936)

Keble, Chatterton, E., *Danger Zone: The Story of the Queenstown Command* (Rich & Cowan, 1934)

Kerbrech, Richard de, *Ships of the White Star Line* (Ian Allan, 2009)

Kerbrech, Richard de, *Down Amongst the Black Gang: The World and Workplace of RMS Titanic's Stokers* (The History Press, 2014)

Hyde, Francis E., *Cunard and the North Atlantic 1840–1973* (The Macmillan Press Ltd, 1975)

Kemp, Peter, *History of Ships* (Macdonald & Co., 1988)

Kludas, Arnold, *Great Passenger Ships of the World: Volume 1 1858–1912* (Patrick Stephens Ltd, 1978)

Kludas, Arnold, *Great Passenger Ships of the World: Volume 2 1913–1923* (Patrick Stephens Ltd, 1976)

Kludas, Arnold, *Record Breakers of the North Atlantic: Blue Riband Liners 1838–1952* (Chatham Publishing, 1999)

Layton, J. Kent, *The Edwardian Superliners: A Trio of Trios* (Amberley Publishing, 2011)

Lloyd's Register, *Annals of Lloyd's Register: Centenary Edition* (Lloyds, 1934)

Mackay, James, *The Man Who Invented Himself: A Life of Sir Thomas Lipton* (Mainstream Publishing Company Ltd, 1998)

Mackrow, Clement and Woollard, Lloyd, *The Naval Architect's and Shipbuilder's Pocket-Book* (The Technical Press Ltd, 1931)

McNeil, S.G.S. (Captain), *In Great Waters: Memoirs of a Master Mariner* (Faber & Faber Ltd, 1932)

Miller, Charles, *Battle For the Bundu: The First World War in East Africa* (Purnell Book Services Ltd, 1974)

Mills, Simon, *Hostage to Fortune: The Dramatic Story of the Last Olympian, HMHS Britannic* (Wordsmith Publications, 2002)

Milne, Graeme, *North-East England 1850–1914: The Dynamics of a Maritime-Industrial Region* (The Boydell Press, 2006)

Mumford, Michael Robert, *Caernarfon Tre'r Mileniwm (The Millennium Town Caernarfon)* (Historical Book & Print Publisher, 2000)

Newall, Peter, Mauretania: *Triumph and Resurrection* (Ships in Focus Publications, 2006)

Newall, Peter, *Cunard Line: A Fleet History* (Ships in Focus Publications, 2012)

Newman, Brian, *Plate and Section Working Machinery in British Shipbuilding 1850–1945* (Centre for Business History in Scotland, Research Papers in the History of British Shipbuilding, 1993)

Newton, R.N. (RCNC), *Practical Construction of Warships* (Longmans, Green and Co. Ltd, 1964)

Oldham, Wilton J., *The Ismay Line* (The Journal of Commerce, 1961)

Palmer, Alan, *The Kaiser: Warlord of the Second Reich* (Weidenfeld & Nicolson, 1978)

Peeke, Mitch and Walsh-Johnson, Kevin, *Lusitania and Beyond: The Life of Commodore William Thomas Turner* (Avid Publications, 2001)

Public Record Office (now National Archives), *Formal Investigation into the Loss of the S.S.* Titanic (PRO Publications, 1912)

Radford, John, *Pilot Aboard* (William Blackwood & Sons Ltd, 1966)

Rae, Ian & Smith, Ken, *Swan Hunter: The Pride and the Tears* (Tyne Bridge Publishing, 2001)

Smith, Ken, *The Story of Charles Parsons and His Ocean Greyhound* (Newcastle Libraries &Information Services Department and Tyne & Wear Museums, 1996)

Smith, Ken, Mauretania: *Pride of the Tyne* (Newcastle Libraries &Information Services Department and Tyne & Wear Museums, 1997)

Stodola, Dr A. (Trans. Loewenstein. Dr Louis C.), *Steam and Gas Turbines* (McGraw-Hill Book Company, Inc., 1927)

Warren, Mark D. (ed.) *The Cunard Turbine-Driven Quadrable-Screw Atlantic Liner 'Mauretania'; Authentically Reproduced From a Rare 1907 Commemorative Edition of 'Engineering* (Wellingborough: Patrick Stephens, 1987)

Warren, Mark D., *The Royal Mail Twin-Screw Steamers* Campania and Lucania (Patrick Stephens Limited, 1993)

Warren, Mark (ed.), *The Shipbuilder: Distinguished Liners 1906–1914* (Blue Riband Pubns Inc., 1995)

Wilkinson, Norman, *A Brush With Life* (Seeley Service & Co., 1969)

Winchester, Simon, *Atlantic: A Vast Ocean of a Million Stories* (HarperPress, 2010)

Williams, David L. and de Kerbrech, Richard P., *Glory Days: Swan Hunter* (Ian Allan Publishing, 2008)

Articles and Papers

Anon., 'Further Model Experiments in connection with the "Mauretania" and "Lusitania' Propellers", *Our Headlights*, pp. 79–80

Anon., 'Mauretania', *The Shipbuilder* (Vol. 2, Special Number, 1907)

Anon., 'Our Retired Chairman – Sir GB Hunter, K.B.E. D.Sc. J.P.', *The Shipyard*, (Vol. 10, No. 104, May–June 1928) p. 53

Anon., 'The Names of the New Cunarders', *The Mid-Tyne Link* (Vol. 2, No. 8) pp. 220–1

Anon., 'The Use of High-Tensile Steel in the Construction of the "Mauretania"' *The Shipbuilder* (Vol. 1, 1906–7) p. 15

Brown, D.K. and Wells, Captain J.G., 'HMS *Warrior* – The Design Aspects', *RINA Transactions and Annual Report 1987.*

Buxton, Ian, '*Mauretania* and her builders', *The Mariner's Mirror* (vol. 82, no. 1, 1996) pp. 55–73

Hood, A., 'The Building of an Atlantic Express Steamship', *The Mid-Tyne Link* (Vol. 2, No. 7) pp. 171–85

Hood, A., 'The New Cunard Flyers', *The Mid-Tyne Link* (Vol. 1, No. 1) pp. 29–34

Luke, W.J., 'On Some Points of Interest in Connection With the Design, Building and Launching of the "Lusitania"', *Transactions of the Institution of Naval Architects*, 1907

Maughan, P., 'The Maiden Voyage of R.M.S. Carpathia', *The Mid-Tyne Link* (Vol. 1, No. 1) pp. 41–8

Miscellaneous. No. 16 (1917), *Correspondence with the German Government regarding the Alleged Misuse of British Hospital Ships* (XXXVIII 1917) p. 391.

Peskett, L., 'The Design of Steamships from the Owner's Point of View', *Transactions of the Institution of Naval Architects*, 1914

Ramsey, et al., 'The Erosion of High-Speed Bronze Propellers', *Engineering* (January 1912) pp. 3–47

Silberrad, O., 'On the Erosion of Bronze Propellers', *The Marine Engineer and Naval Architect* (February 1910) pp. 256–61

Sims, P., 'Comparative Naval Architecture of Passenger Ships', *SNAME 2003 Transactions*, Volume 111.

Sontag, Raymond J. 'The Cowes Interview and the Kruger Telegram', *Political Science Quarterly* (vol. 40, no. 2, 1925) pp. 217–47.

The Cunard Steamship Company, Limited, *Copy of an Agreement between the Admiralty, the Board of Trade, and Postmaster General and the Cunard Steamship Company, Limited (dated 30th July 1903), with Treasury Minute Thereon (dated 30th July 1903); with Together with Copies of Memorandum and Articles of Association of the Cunard Steamship Company, Limited, and Draft Trust Deed for Securing Debenture Stock* (XXXVI, 1903) p. 157.

Wilkinson, M., The Demolition of the 'Mauretania', *Manchester Association of Engineers*, read on 15 March 1940 (Session 1939–40 [6]).

Document Sources

All materials from the National Archives (Public Records Office) used are available under the Open Government Licence v3.0.

Periodicals

New York Times, The
New York Times, The
Scotsman, The
Ships Monthly
Times, The

Websites

archive.scotsman.com
www.bl.uk/world-war-one/articles/origins-and-outbreak
www.britishnewspaperarchive.co.uk
www.georgegarrettarchive.co.uk
www.seangrabb.co.uk
www.thetimes.co.uk/tto/archive
www.mersey-gateway.org (Portcities Liverpool)
www.missilesofkeywest.com/65thHISTORY
www.nytimes.com/ref/membercenter/nytarchive